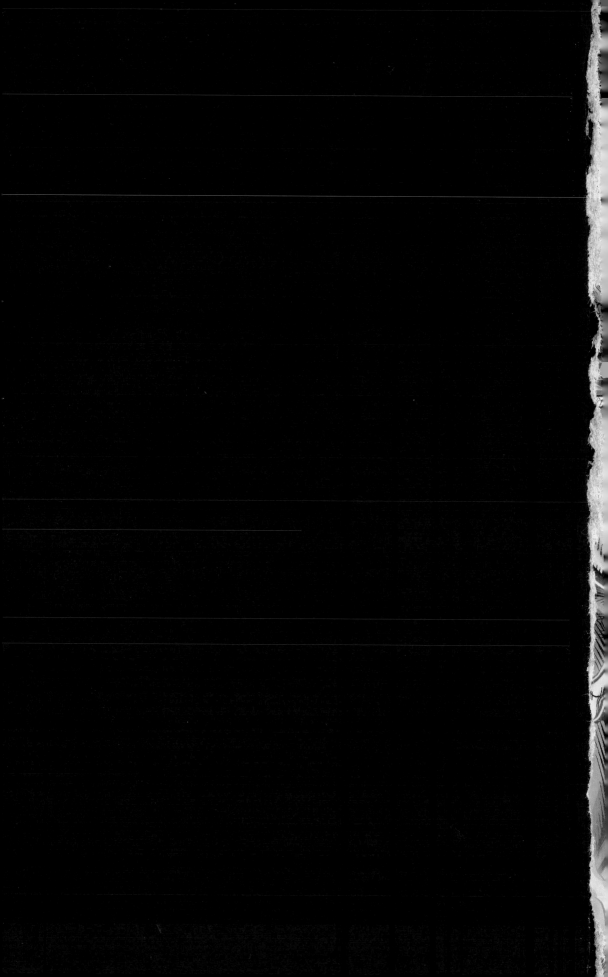

BLACKEST NIGHT
GREEN LANTERN

JIM LEE
WILLIAMS
SINC

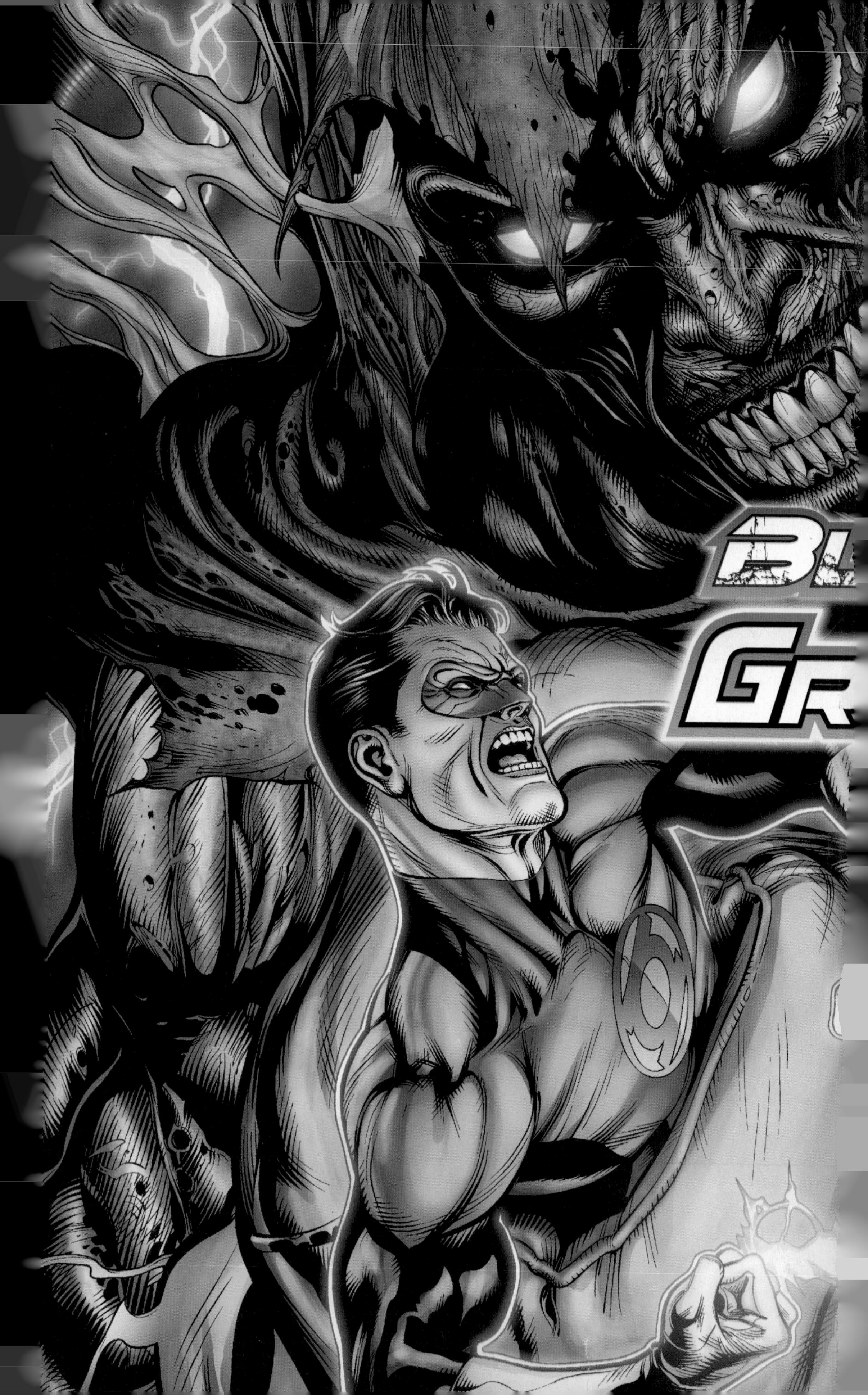

GEOFF JOHNS
WRITER

DOUG MAHNKE
PENCILLER

ED BENES
MARCOS MARZ
ADDITIONAL PENCILS

ACKEST NIGHT
EEN LANTERN

CHRISTIAN ALAMY
DOUG MAHNKE
TOM NGUYEN
RODNEY RAMOS
MARK IRWIN
ED BENES
LUCIANA DEL NEGRO
REBECCA BUCHMAN
KEITH CHAMPAGNE
INKERS

RANDY MAYOR
GABE ELTAEB
HI-FI
CARRIE STRACHAN
COLORISTS

ROB LEIGH
LETTERER

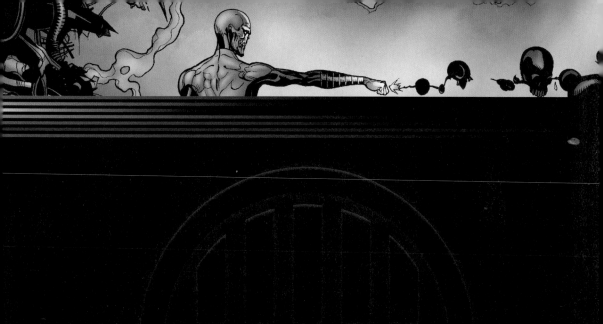

Eddie Berganza *Editor-original series* / Adam Schlagman *Associate Editor-original series*
Bob Harras *Group Editor-Collected Editions* / Sean Mackiewicz *Editor*
Robbin Brosterman *Design Director-Books* / Curtis King Jr. *Senior Art Director*

DC COMICS / Diane Nelson *President* / Dan DiDio and Jim Lee *Co-Publishers*
Geoff Johns *Chief Creative Officer* / Patrick Caldon *EVP–Finance and Administration*
John Rood *EVP–Sales, Marketing and Business Development* / Amy Genkins *SVP–Business and Legal Affairs*
Steve Rotterdam *SVP–Sales and Marketing* / John Cunningham *VP–Marketing*
Terri Cunningham *VP–Managing Editor* / Alison Gill *VP–Manufacturing* / David Hyde *VP–Publicity*
Sue Pohja *VP–Book Trade Sales* / Alysse Soll *VP–Advertising and Custom Publishing*
Bob Wayne *VP–Sales* / Mark Chiarello *Art Director*

Cover by Ivan Reis and Rodolfo Migliari

BLACKEST NIGHT: GREEN LANTERN Published by DC Comics.

DC COMICS 1700 Broadway, New York, NY 10019 A Warner Bros. Entertainment Company

Printed by RR Donnelley, Salem, VA, USA. 6/9/10. First printing.

HC ISBN: 978-1-4012-2786-9
SC ISBN: 978-1-4012-2952-8

SUSTAINABLE FORESTRY INITIATIVE
Certified Chain of Custody
Promoting Sustainable Forest Management
www.sfiprogram.org

Fiber used in this product line meets the sourcing requirements of the SFI program. www.sfiprogram.org NFS-SPICOC-C0001801

THE STORY SO FAR...

Billions of years ago, the self-appointed Guardians of the Universe recruited thousands of sentient beings from across the cosmos to join their intergalactic police force: the Green Lantern Corps.

Chosen because they are able to overcome great fear, the Green Lanterns patrol their respective space sectors armed with power rings capable of wielding the emerald energy of willpower into whatever constructs they can imagine.

Hal Jordan is the greatest of them all.

When the dying Green Lantern Abin Sur crashed on Earth, he chose Hal Jordan to be his successor, for his indomitable will and ability to overcome great fear. As the protector of Sector 2814, Hal has saved Earth from destruction, even died in its service and been reborn.

Thaal Sinestro of Korugar was once considered the greatest Green Lantern of them all.

As Abin Sur's friend, Sinestro became Jordan's mentor in the Corps. But after being sentenced to the Anti-Matter Universe for abusing his power, Sinestro learned of the yellow light of fear being mined on Qward. Wielding a new golden power ring fueled by terror, Sinestro drafted thousands of the most horrific, psychotic and sadistic beings in the universe, and with their doctrine of fear, burned all who opposed them.

When the Green Lantern Corps battled their former ally during the Sinestro Corps War, the skies burned with green and gold as Earth erupted into an epic battle between good and evil. Though the Green Lanterns won, their brotherhood was broken and the peace they achieved was short-lived. In its aftermath, the Guardians rewrote the Book of Oa, the very laws by which their corps abides, and dissent grew within their members.

Now Hal Jordan will face his greatest challenge yet, as the prophecy foretold by Abin Sur in his dying moments finally comes to pass.

The emotional spectrum has splintered into seven factions. Seven corps were born.

The Green Lanterns. The Sinestro Corps. Atrocitus and the enraged Red Lanterns. Larfleeze, the avaricious keeper of the Orange Light. Former Guardians Ganthet and Sayd's small but hopeful Blue Lantern Corps. The Zamarons and their army of fierce and loving Star Sapphires. And the mysterious Indigo Tribe.

As the War of Light ignited between these Lantern bearers, the skies on every world darkened. In Sector 666, on the planet Ryut, a black lantern grew around the Anti-Monitor's corpse, using his vast energies to empower it.

The first of the Black Lanterns, the Black Hand, has risen from the dead, heralding a greater power that will extinguish all of the light—and life—in the universe.

Now across thousands of worlds, the dead have risen, and Hal Jordan and all of Earth's greatest heroes must bear witness to Blackest Night, which will descend upon them all, without prejudice, mercy or reason.

GREEN LANTERN 43
Cover by Doug Mahnke and Christian Alamy with Alex Sinclair

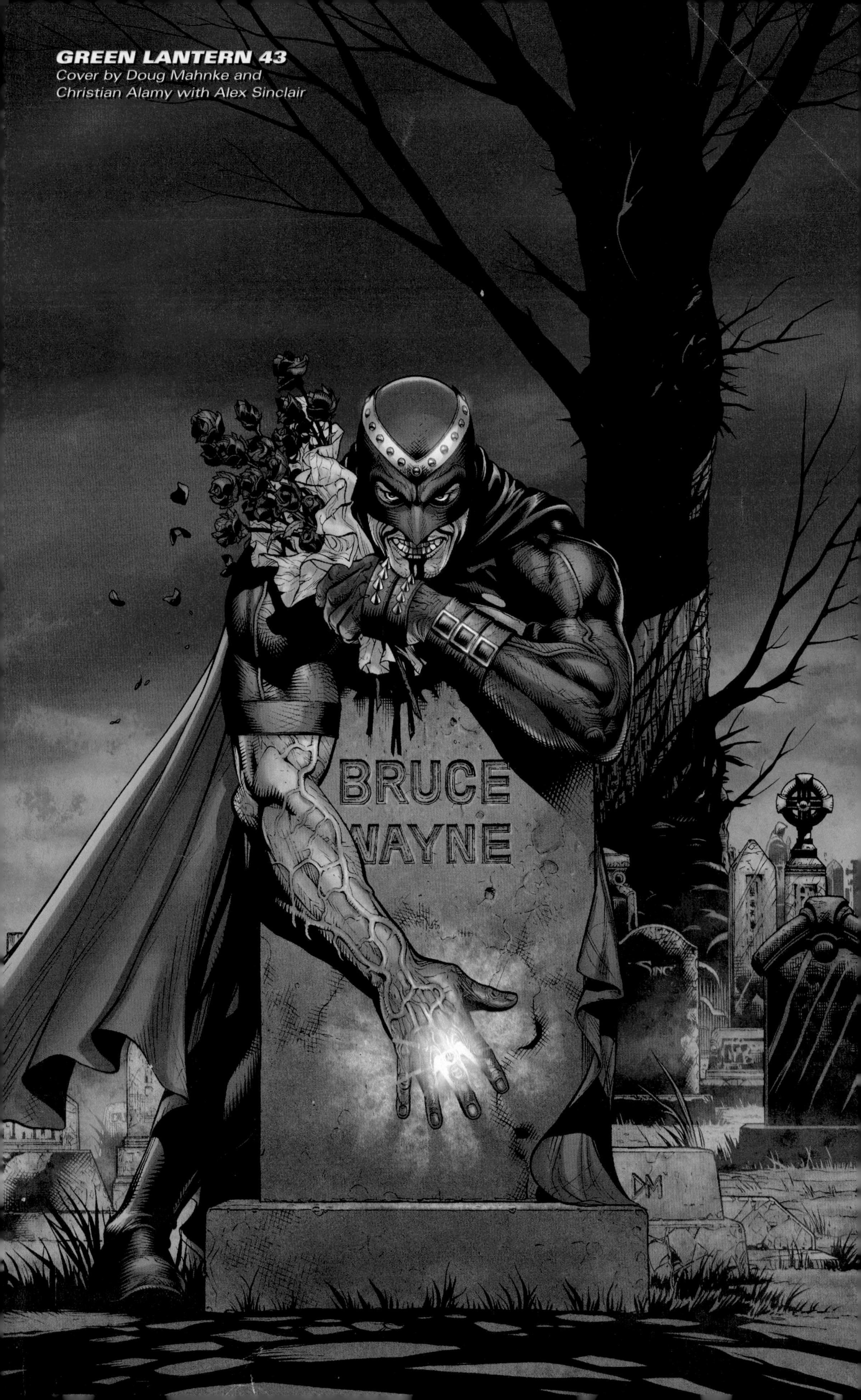
BRUCE

TALE OF THE BLACK LANTERN

DOUG MAHNKE
PENCILS

CHRISTIAN ALAMY
INKS

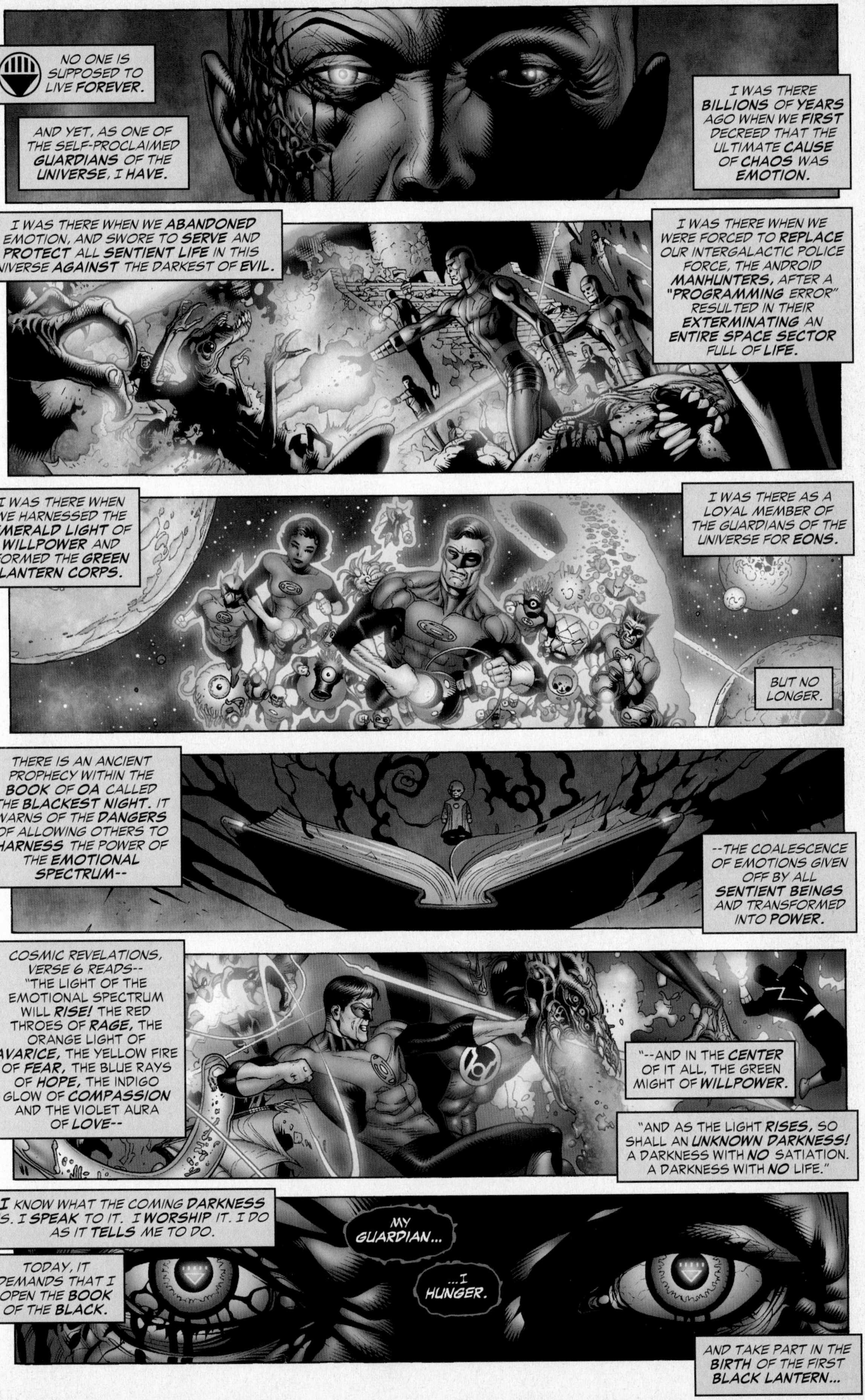
NO ONE IS SUPPOSED TO LIVE FOREVER.
AND YET, AS ONE OF THE SELF-PROCLAIMED GUARDIANS OF THE UNIVERSE, I HAVE.
I WAS THERE BILLIONS OF YEARS AGO WHEN WE FIRST DECREED THAT THE ULTIMATE CAUSE OF CHAOS WAS EMOTION.
I WAS THERE WHEN WE ABANDONED EMOTION, AND SWORE TO SERVE AND PROTECT ALL SENTIENT LIFE IN THIS UNIVERSE AGAINST THE DARKEST OF EVIL.
I WAS THERE WHEN WE WERE FORCED TO REPLACE OUR INTERGALACTIC POLICE FORCE, THE ANDROID MANHUNTERS, AFTER A "PROGRAMMING ERROR" RESULTED IN THEIR EXTERMINATING AN ENTIRE SPACE SECTOR FULL OF LIFE.
I WAS THERE WHEN WE HARNESSED THE EMERALD LIGHT OF WILLPOWER AND FORMED THE GREEN LANTERN CORPS.
I WAS THERE AS A LOYAL MEMBER OF THE GUARDIANS OF THE UNIVERSE FOR EONS.
BUT NO LONGER.
THERE IS AN ANCIENT PROPHECY WITHIN THE BOOK OF OA CALLED THE BLACKEST NIGHT. IT WARNS OF THE DANGERS OF ALLOWING OTHERS TO HARNESS THE POWER OF THE EMOTIONAL SPECTRUM--
--THE COALESCENCE OF EMOTIONS GIVEN OFF BY ALL SENTIENT BEINGS AND TRANSFORMED INTO POWER.
COSMIC REVELATIONS, VERSE 6 READS-- "THE LIGHT OF THE EMOTIONAL SPECTRUM WILL RISE! THE RED THROES OF RAGE, THE ORANGE LIGHT OF AVARICE, THE YELLOW FIRE OF FEAR, THE BLUE RAYS OF HOPE, THE INDIGO GLOW OF COMPASSION AND THE VIOLET AURA OF LOVE--
"--AND IN THE CENTER OF IT ALL, THE GREEN MIGHT OF WILLPOWER.
"AND AS THE LIGHT RISES, SO SHALL AN UNKNOWN DARKNESS! A DARKNESS WITH NO SATIATION. A DARKNESS WITH NO LIFE."
I KNOW WHAT THE COMING DARKNESS IS. I SPEAK TO IT. I WORSHIP IT. I DO AS IT TELLS ME TO DO.
MY GUARDIAN...
TODAY, IT DEMANDS THAT I OPEN THE BOOK OF THE BLACK.
...I HUNGER.
AND TAKE PART IN THE BIRTH OF THE FIRST BLACK LANTERN...

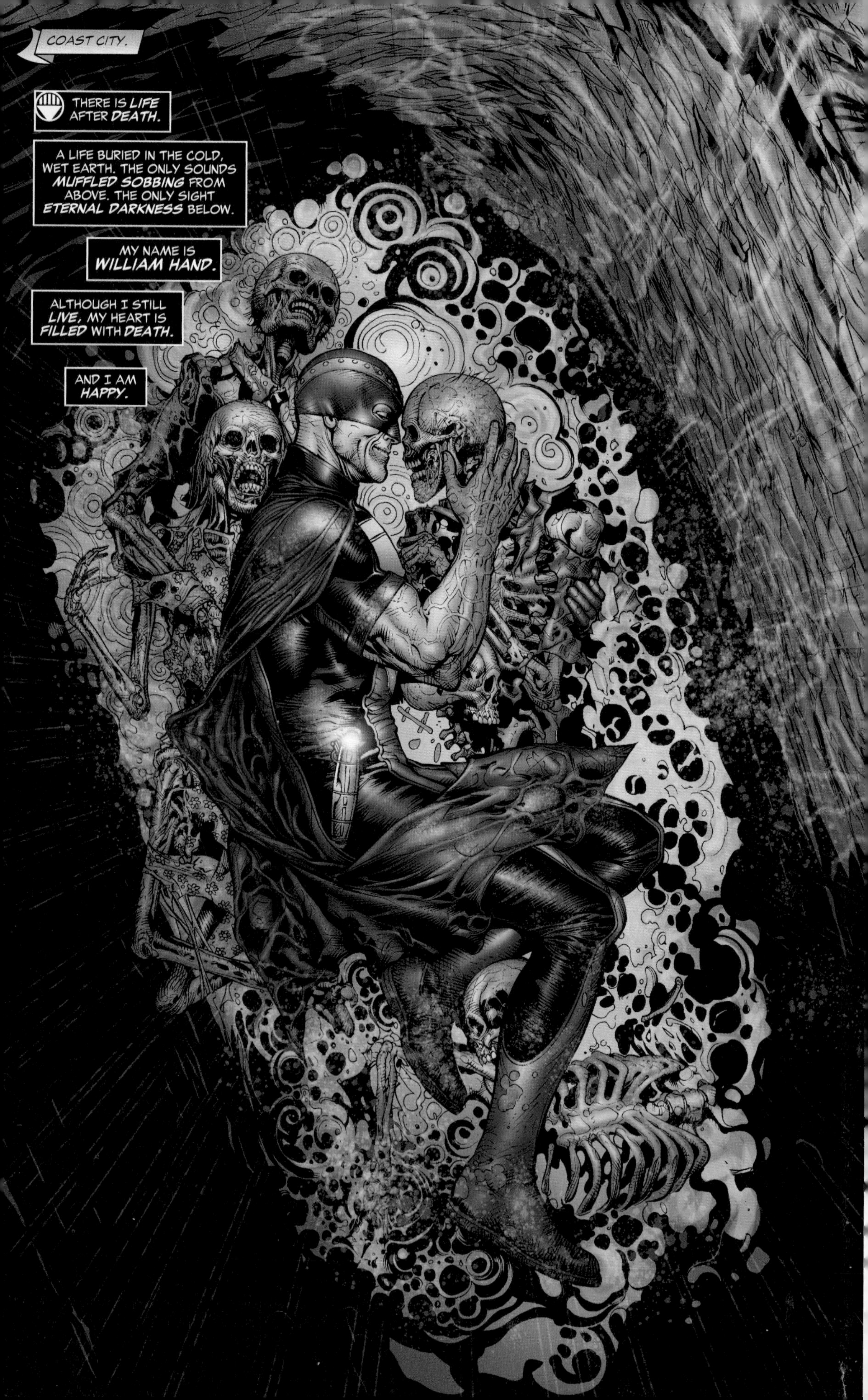
COAST CITY.
THERE IS LIFE AFTER DEATH.
A LIFE BURIED IN THE COLD, WET EARTH. THE ONLY SOUNDS MUFFLED SOBBING FROM ABOVE. THE ONLY SIGHT ETERNAL DARKNESS BELOW.
MY NAME IS WILLIAM HAND.
ALTHOUGH I STILL LIVE, MY HEART IS FILLED WITH DEATH.
AND I AM HAPPY.

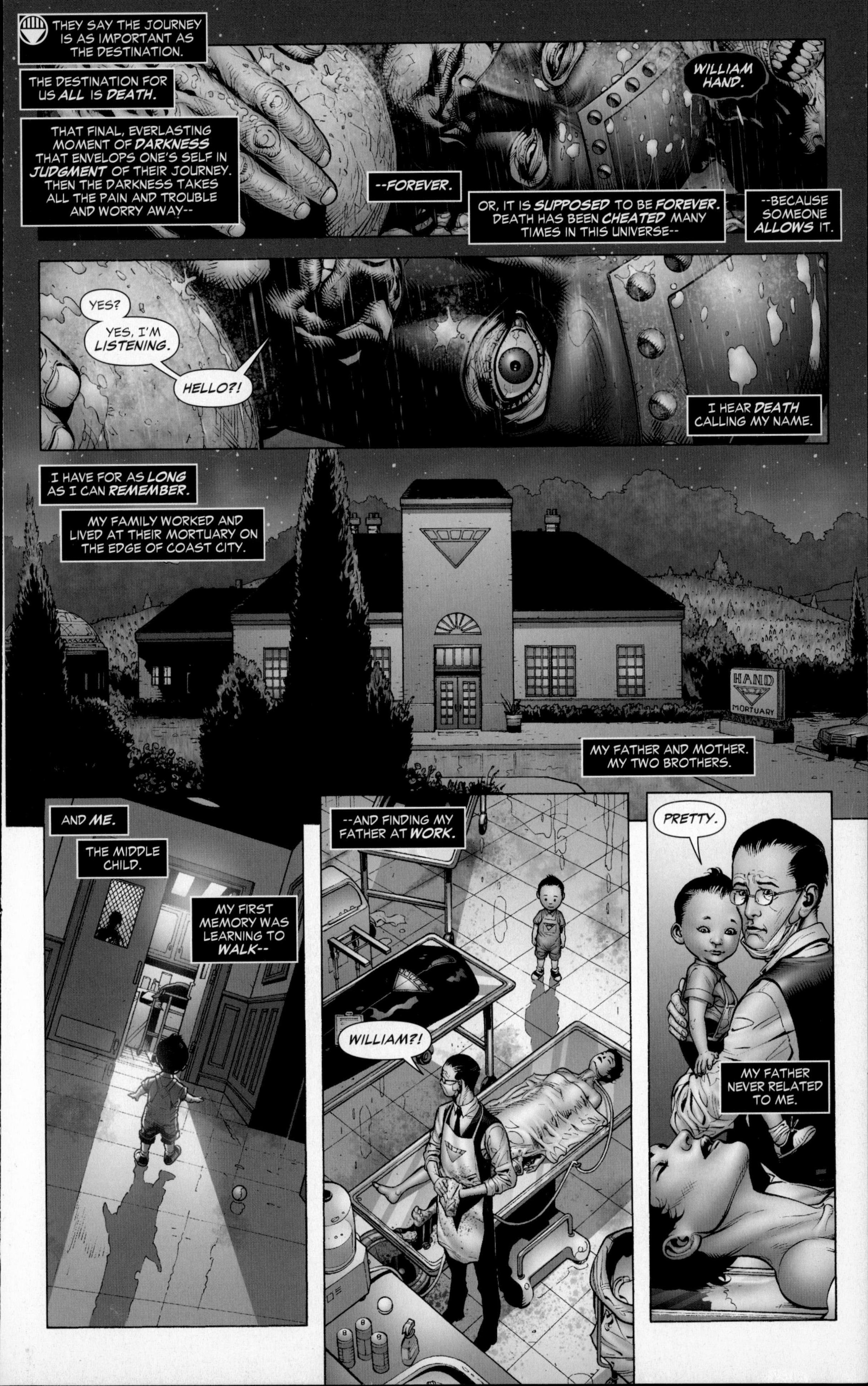
THEY SAY THE JOURNEY IS AS IMPORTANT AS THE DESTINATION.
THE DESTINATION FOR US ALL IS DEATH.
THAT FINAL, EVERLASTING MOMENT OF DARKNESS THAT ENVELOPS ONE'S SELF IN JUDGMENT OF THEIR JOURNEY. THEN THE DARKNESS TAKES ALL THE PAIN AND TROUBLE AND WORRY AWAY--
--FOREVER.
WILLIAM HAND.
OR, IT IS SUPPOSED TO BE FOREVER. DEATH HAS BEEN CHEATED MANY TIMES IN THIS UNIVERSE--
--BECAUSE SOMEONE ALLOWS IT.
YES?
YES, I'M LISTENING.
HELLO?!
I HEAR DEATH CALLING MY NAME.
I HAVE FOR AS LONG AS I CAN REMEMBER.
MY FAMILY WORKED AND LIVED AT THEIR MORTUARY ON THE EDGE OF COAST CITY.
HAND MORTUARY
MY FATHER AND MOTHER. MY TWO BROTHERS.
AND ME.
THE MIDDLE CHILD.
MY FIRST MEMORY WAS LEARNING TO WALK--
--AND FINDING MY FATHER AT WORK.
WILLIAM?!
PRETTY.
MY FATHER NEVER RELATED TO ME.

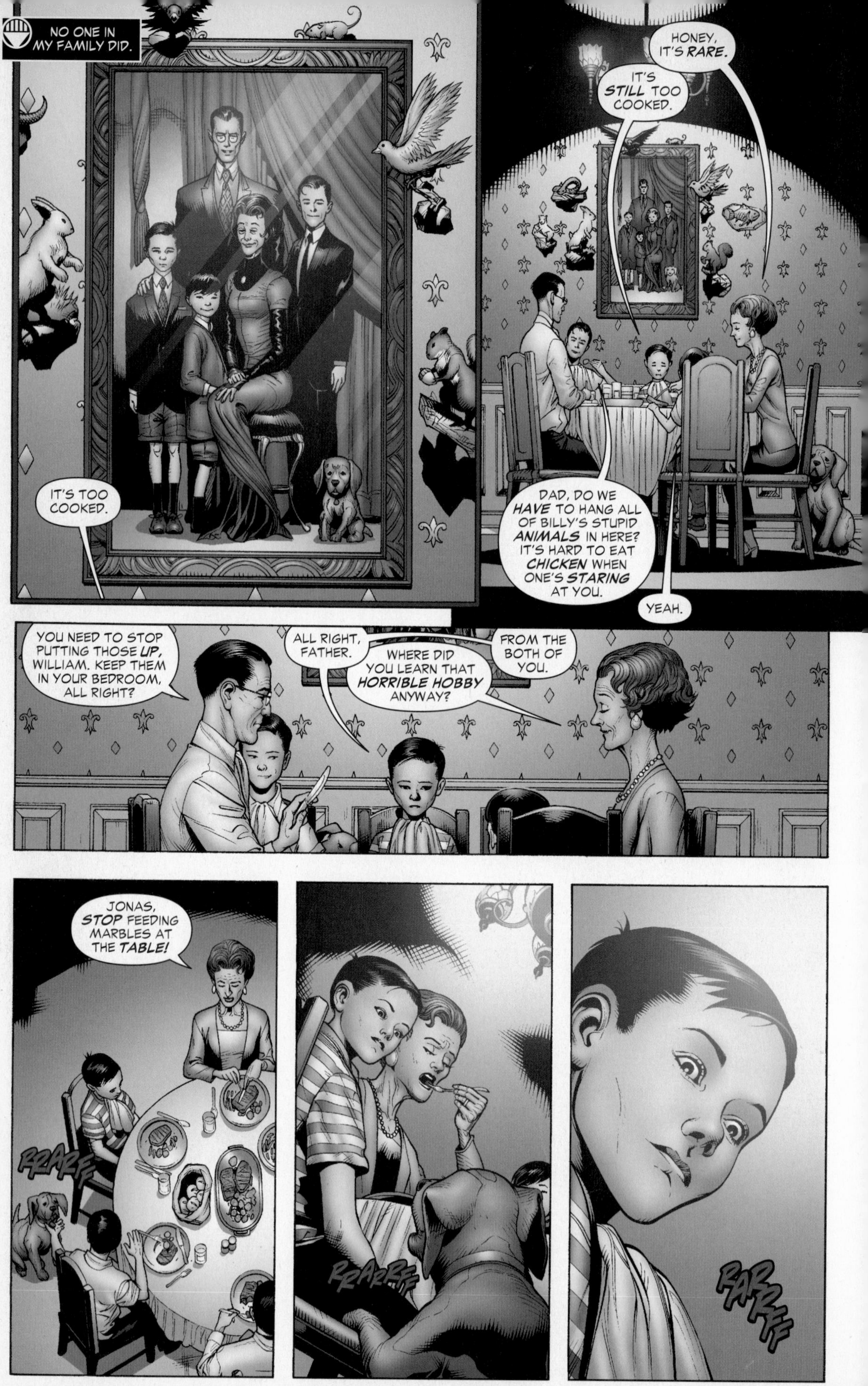
NO ONE IN MY FAMILY DID.
IT'S TOO COOKED.
HONEY, IT'S RARE.
IT'S STILL TOO COOKED.
DAD, DO WE HAVE TO HANG ALL OF BILLY'S STUPID ANIMALS IN HERE? IT'S HARD TO EAT CHICKEN WHEN ONE'S STARING AT YOU.
YEAH.
YOU NEED TO STOP PUTTING THOSE UP, WILLIAM. KEEP THEM IN YOUR BEDROOM, ALL RIGHT?
ALL RIGHT, FATHER.
WHERE DID YOU LEARN THAT HORRIBLE HOBBY ANYWAY?
FROM THE BOTH OF YOU.
JONAS, STOP FEEDING MARBLES AT THE TABLE!
RRARFF
RRARRFF
RARRFF

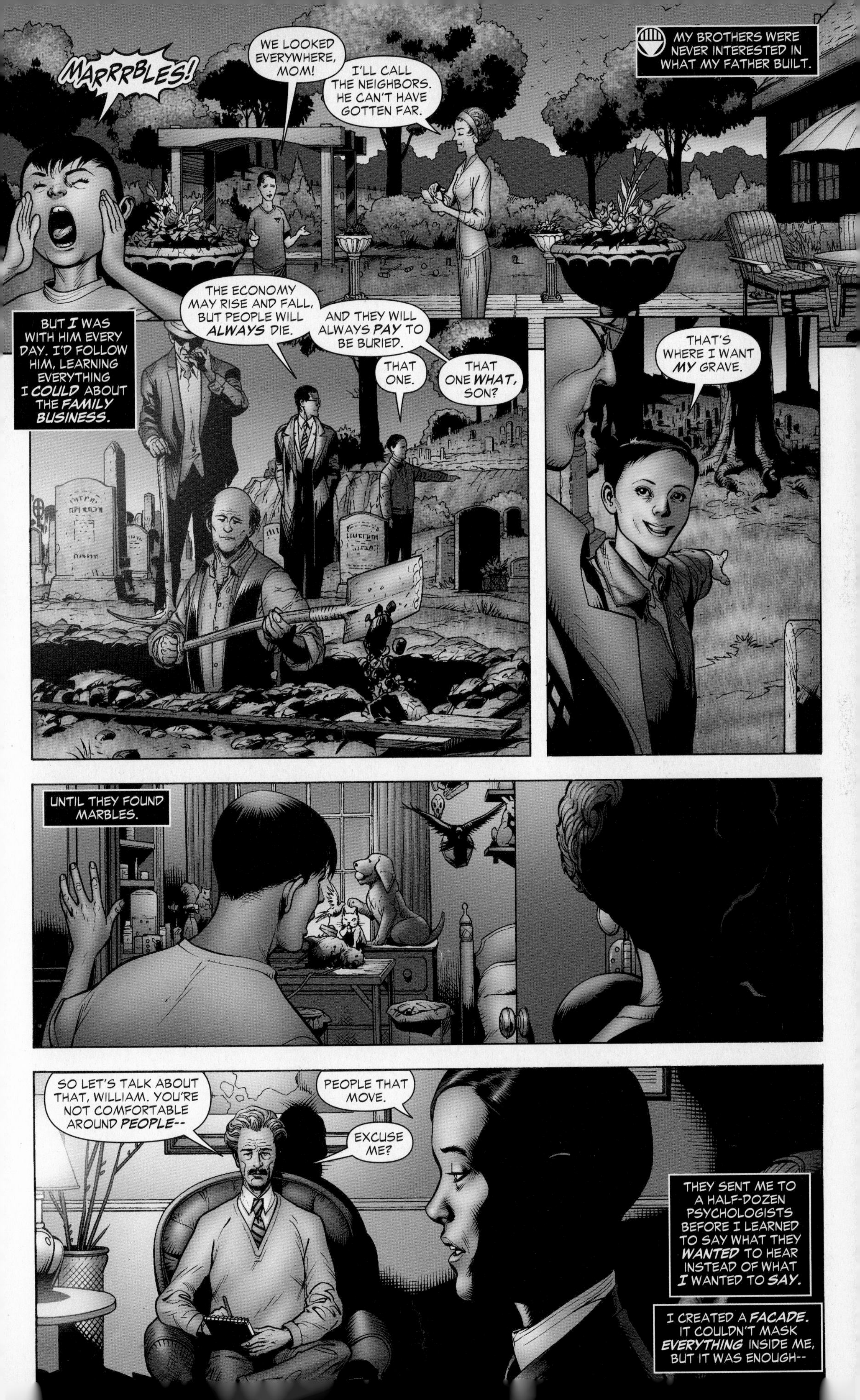
MY BROTHERS WERE NEVER INTERESTED IN WHAT MY FATHER BUILT.
MARRRBLES!
WE LOOKED EVERYWHERE, MOM!
I'LL CALL THE NEIGHBORS. HE CAN'T HAVE GOTTEN FAR.
BUT I WAS WITH HIM EVERY DAY. I'D FOLLOW HIM, LEARNING EVERYTHING I COULD ABOUT THE FAMILY BUSINESS.
THE ECONOMY MAY RISE AND FALL, BUT PEOPLE WILL ALWAYS DIE.
AND THEY WILL ALWAYS PAY TO BE BURIED.
THAT ONE.
THAT ONE WHAT, SON?
THAT'S WHERE I WANT MY GRAVE.
UNTIL THEY FOUND MARBLES.
SO LET'S TALK ABOUT THAT, WILLIAM. YOU'RE NOT COMFORTABLE AROUND PEOPLE--
PEOPLE THAT MOVE.
EXCUSE ME?
THEY SENT ME TO A HALF-DOZEN PSYCHOLOGISTS BEFORE I LEARNED TO SAY WHAT THEY WANTED TO HEAR INSTEAD OF WHAT I WANTED TO SAY.
I CREATED A FACADE. IT COULDN'T MASK EVERYTHING INSIDE ME, BUT IT WAS ENOUGH--

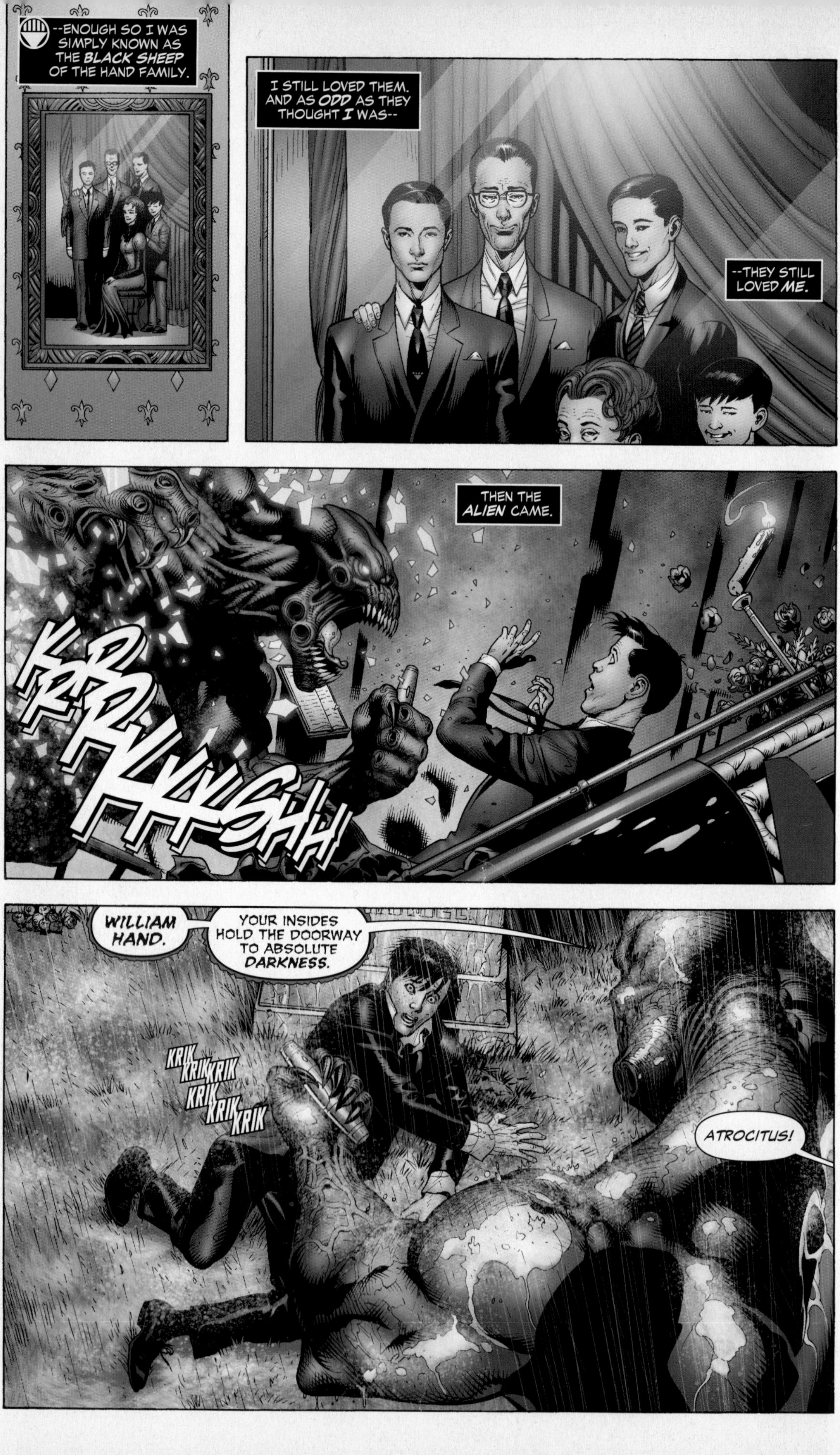
--ENOUGH SO I WAS SIMPLY KNOWN AS THE BLACK SHEEP OF THE HAND FAMILY.
I STILL LOVED THEM. AND AS ODD AS THEY THOUGHT I WAS--
--THEY STILL LOVED ME.
THEN THE ALIEN CAME.
KRRKKKSHH
WILLIAM HAND.
YOUR INSIDES HOLD THE DOORWAY TO ABSOLUTE DARKNESS.
KRIK KRIK KRIK KRIK KRIK KRIK KRIK
ATROCITUS!

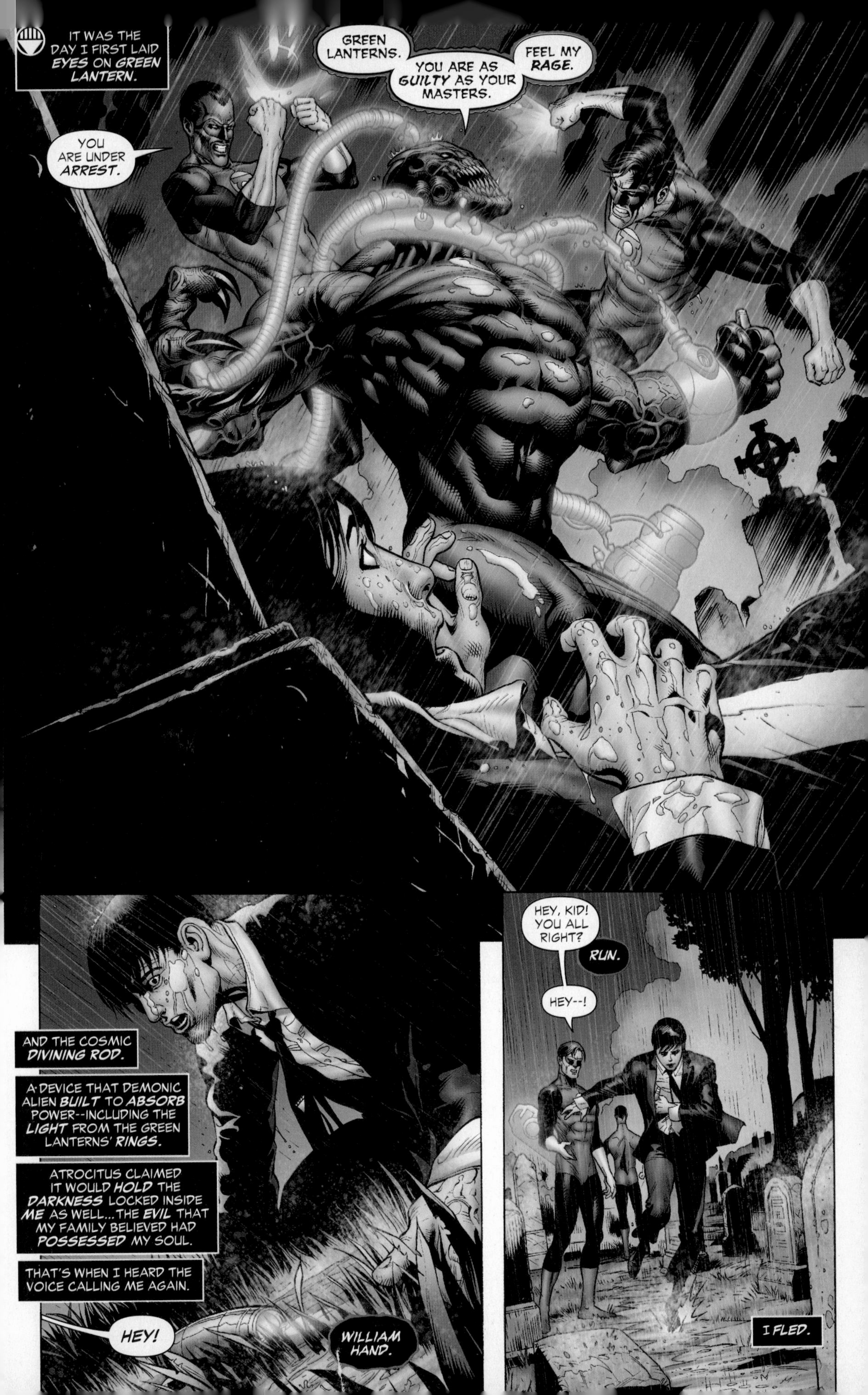
IT WAS THE DAY I FIRST LAID EYES ON GREEN LANTERN.
GREEN LANTERNS.
YOU ARE AS GUILTY AS YOUR MASTERS.
FEEL MY RAGE.
YOU ARE UNDER ARREST.
AND THE COSMIC DIVINING ROD.
A DEVICE THAT DEMONIC ALIEN BUILT TO ABSORB POWER--INCLUDING THE LIGHT FROM THE GREEN LANTERNS' RINGS.
ATROCITUS CLAIMED IT WOULD HOLD THE DARKNESS LOCKED INSIDE ME AS WELL...THE EVIL THAT MY FAMILY BELIEVED HAD POSSESSED MY SOUL.
THAT'S WHEN I HEARD THE VOICE CALLING ME AGAIN.
HEY!
WILLIAM HAND.
HEY, KID! YOU ALL RIGHT?
RUN.
HEY--!
I FLED.

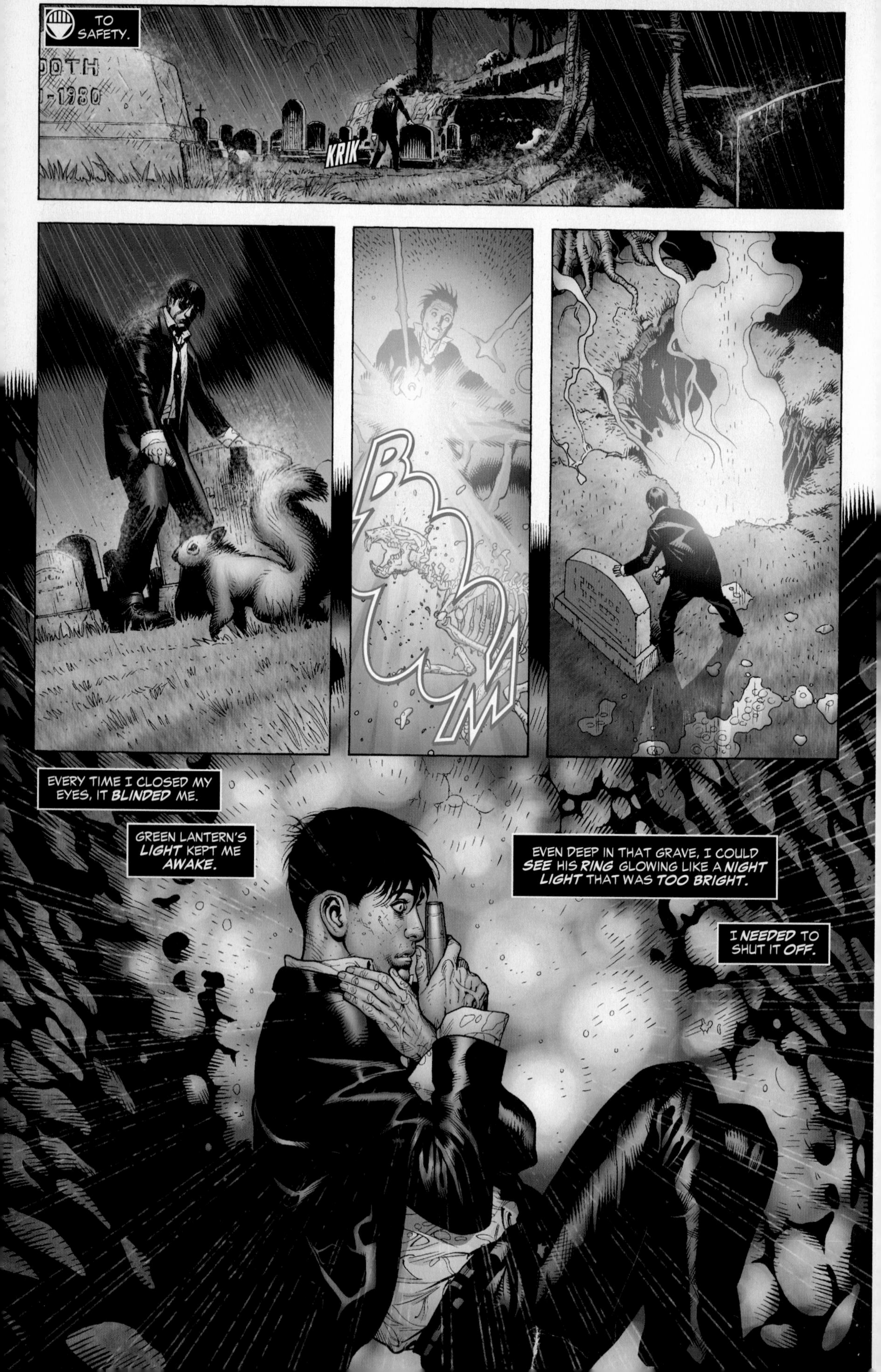
TO SAFETY.
OOTH
-1980
KRIK
BOOM
EVERY TIME I CLOSED MY EYES, IT BLINDED ME.
GREEN LANTERN'S LIGHT KEPT ME AWAKE.
EVEN DEEP IN THAT GRAVE, I COULD SEE HIS RING GLOWING LIKE A NIGHT LIGHT THAT WAS TOO BRIGHT.
I NEEDED TO SHUT IT OFF.

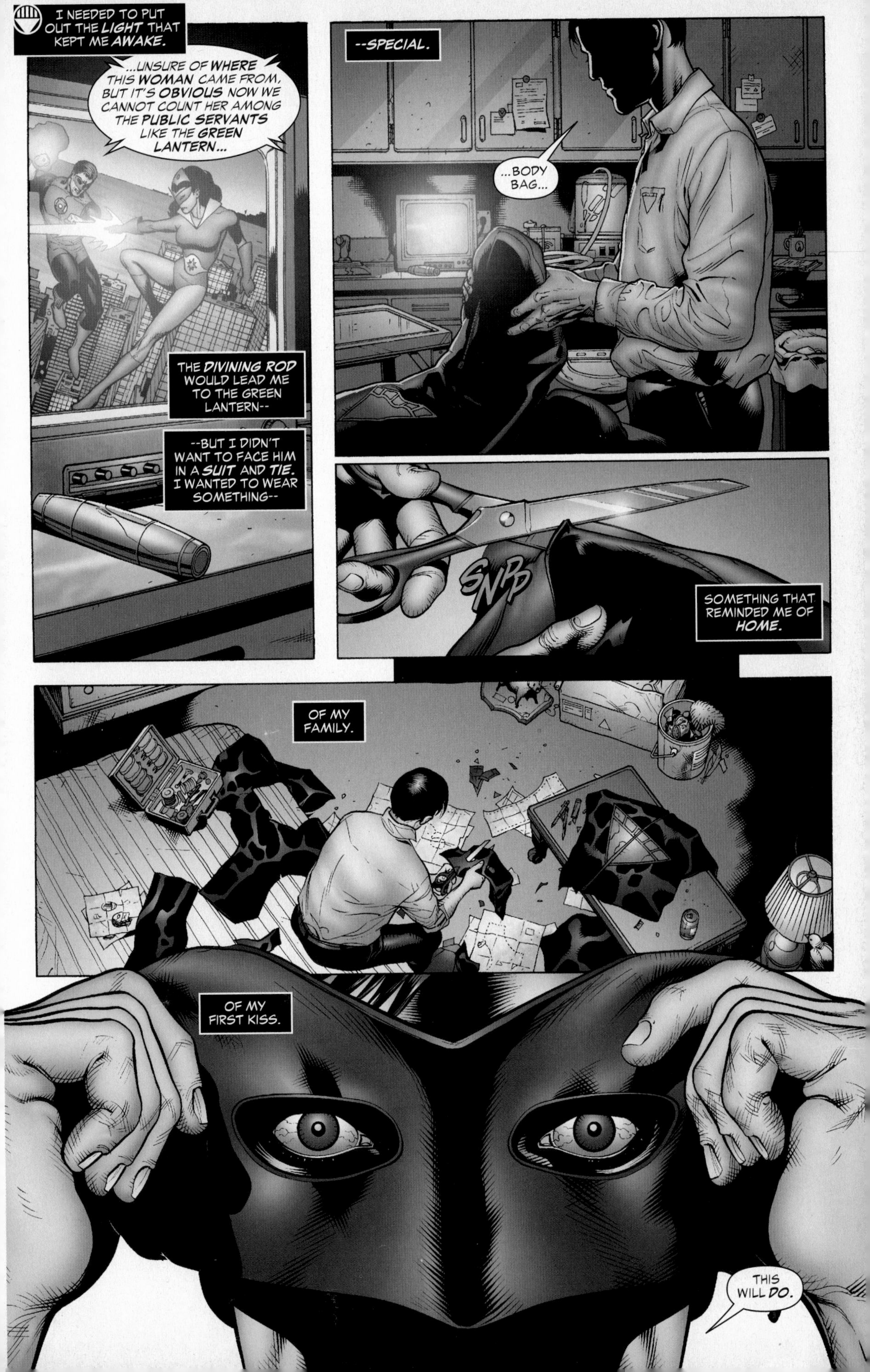
I NEEDED TO PUT OUT THE LIGHT THAT KEPT ME AWAKE.
...UNSURE OF WHERE THIS WOMAN CAME FROM, BUT IT'S OBVIOUS NOW WE CANNOT COUNT HER AMONG THE PUBLIC SERVANTS LIKE THE GREEN LANTERN...
THE DIVINING ROD WOULD LEAD ME TO THE GREEN LANTERN--
--BUT I DIDN'T WANT TO FACE HIM IN A SUIT AND TIE. I WANTED TO WEAR SOMETHING--
--SPECIAL.
...BODY BAG...
SNPP
SOMETHING THAT REMINDED ME OF HOME.
OF MY FAMILY.
OF MY FIRST KISS.
THIS WILL DO.

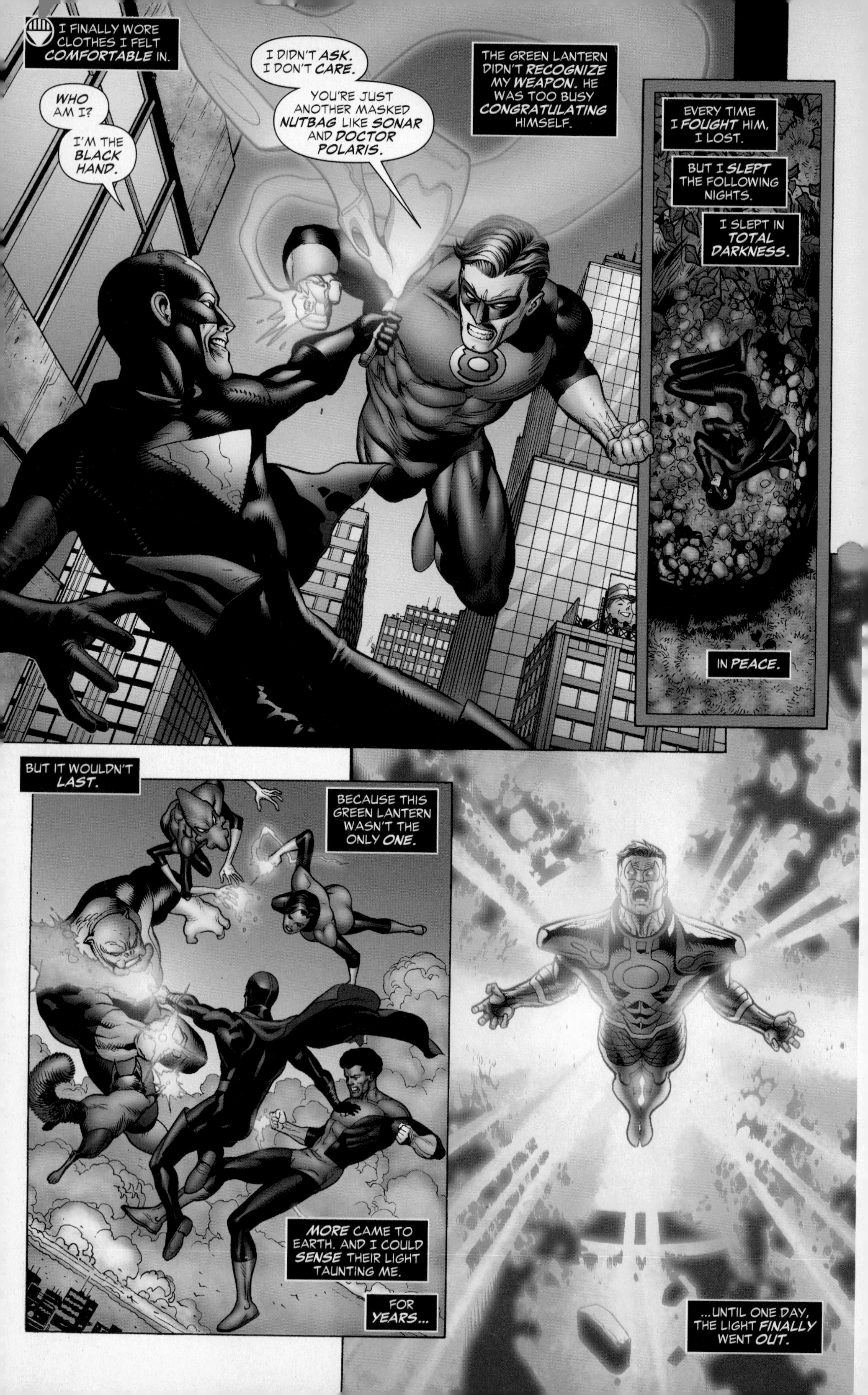

I FINALLY WORE CLOTHES I FELT COMFORTABLE IN.
WHO AM I?
I'M THE BLACK HAND.
I DIDN'T ASK. I DON'T CARE.
YOU'RE JUST ANOTHER MASKED NUTBAG LIKE SONAR AND DOCTOR POLARIS.
THE GREEN LANTERN DIDN'T RECOGNIZE MY WEAPON. HE WAS TOO BUSY CONGRATULATING HIMSELF.
EVERY TIME I FOUGHT HIM, I LOST.
BUT I SLEPT THE FOLLOWING NIGHTS.
I SLEPT IN TOTAL DARKNESS.
IN PEACE.
BUT IT WOULDN'T LAST.
BECAUSE THIS GREEN LANTERN WASN'T THE ONLY ONE.
MORE CAME TO EARTH. AND I COULD SENSE THEIR LIGHT TAUNTING ME.
FOR YEARS...
...UNTIL ONE DAY, THE LIGHT FINALLY WENT OUT.

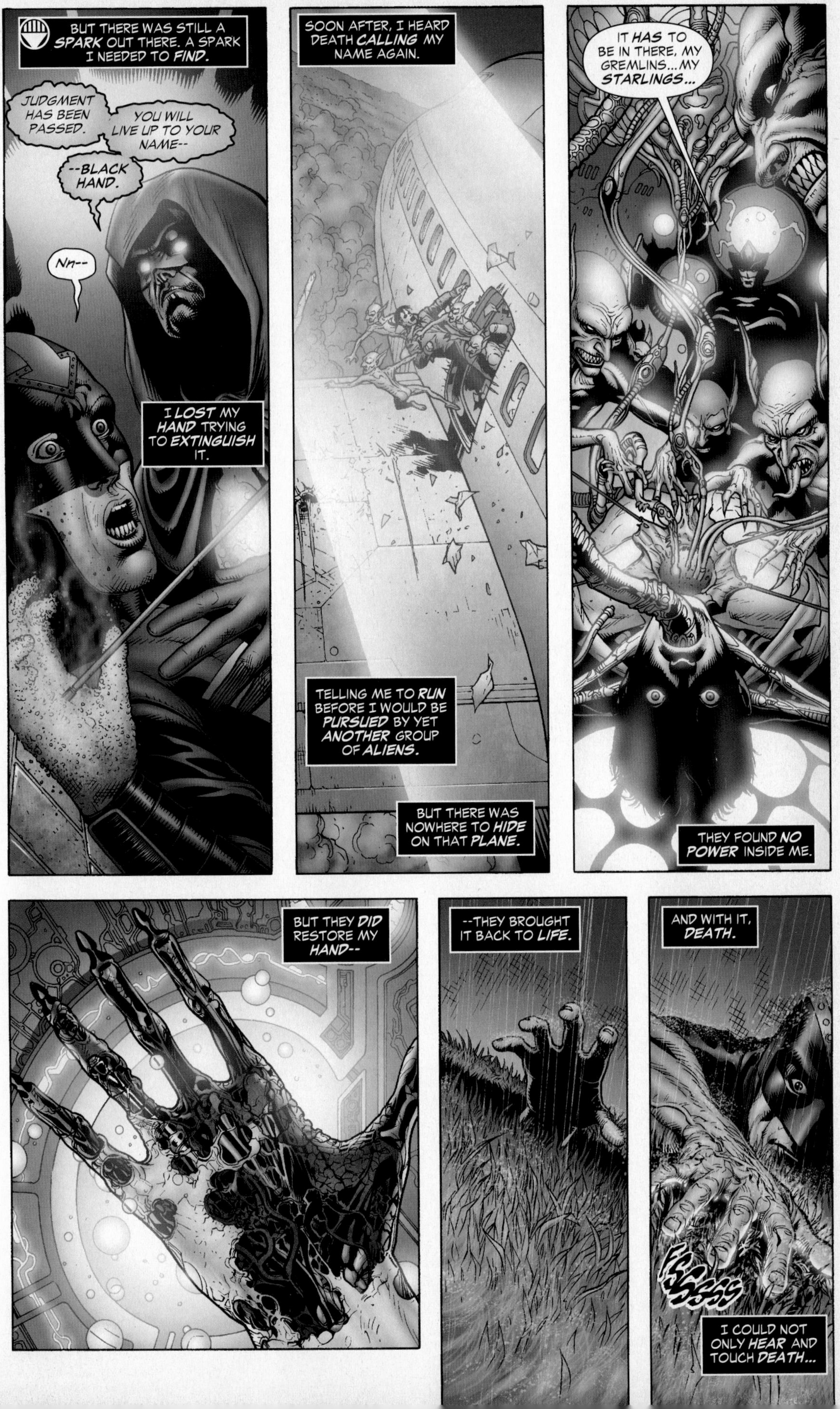
BUT THERE WAS STILL A SPARK OUT THERE. A SPARK I NEEDED TO FIND.
JUDGMENT HAS BEEN PASSED.
YOU WILL LIVE UP TO YOUR NAME--
--BLACK HAND.
Nn--
I LOST MY HAND TRYING TO EXTINGUISH IT.
SOON AFTER, I HEARD DEATH CALLING MY NAME AGAIN.
TELLING ME TO RUN BEFORE I WOULD BE PURSUED BY YET ANOTHER GROUP OF ALIENS.
BUT THERE WAS NOWHERE TO HIDE ON THAT PLANE.
IT HAS TO BE IN THERE, MY GREMLINS... MY STARLINGS...
THEY FOUND NO POWER INSIDE ME.
BUT THEY DID RESTORE MY HAND--
--THEY BROUGHT IT BACK TO LIFE.
AND WITH IT, DEATH.
FSSSSS
I COULD NOT ONLY HEAR AND TOUCH DEATH...

NOW I COULD SEE IT.

I COULD SEE IT ALL AROUND ME.

TULA.

AL PRATT.

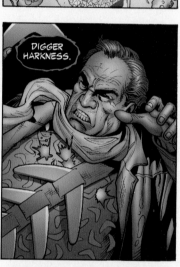

DIGGER HARKNESS.

TED KORD.

DEE TYLER.

ROY LINCOLN.

RALPH DIBNY.

JEAN LORING.

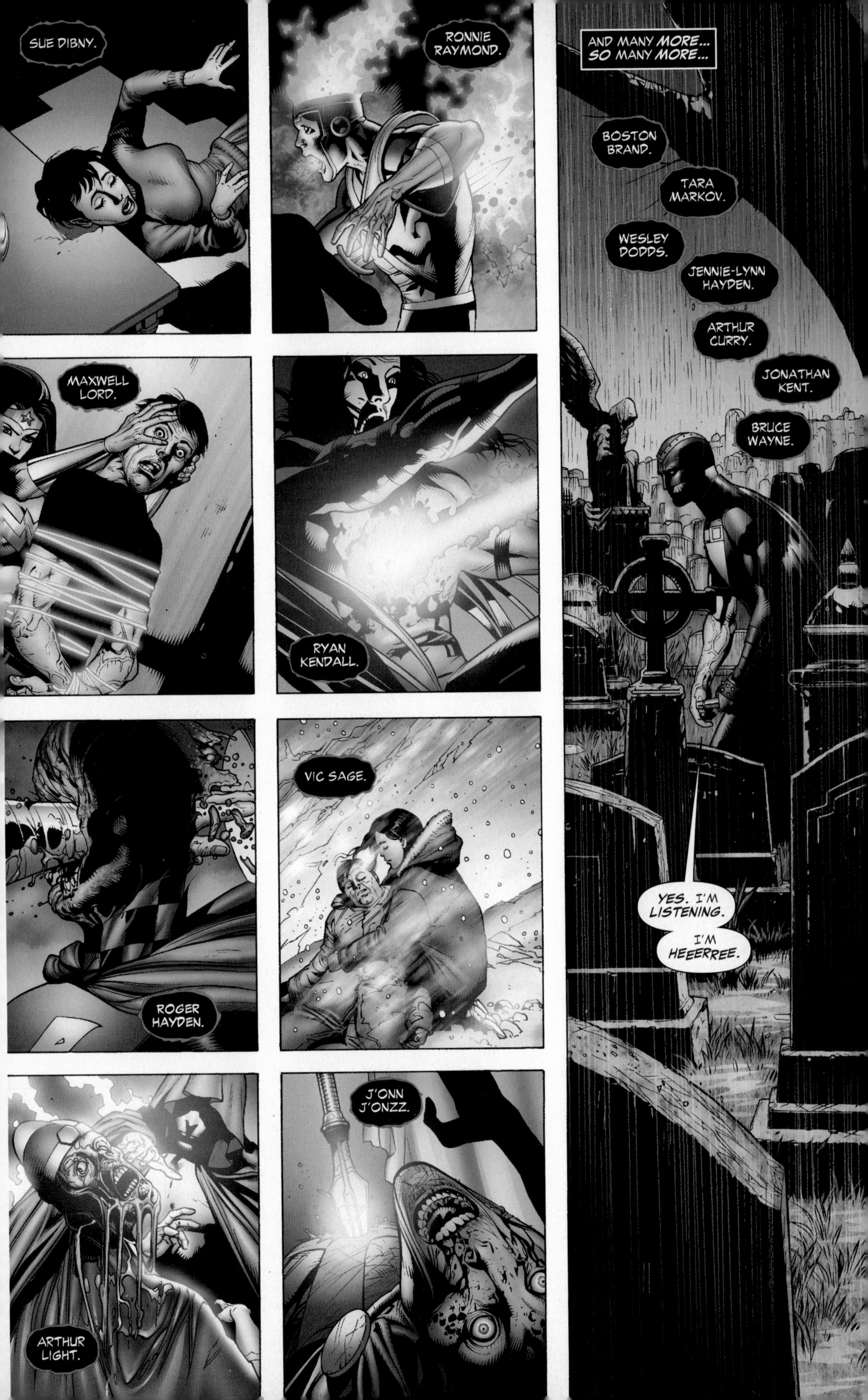
SUE DIBNY.
RONNIE RAYMOND.
MAXWELL LORD.
RYAN KENDALL.
ROGER HAYDEN.
VIC SAGE.
ARTHUR LIGHT.
J'ONN J'ONZZ.
AND MANY MORE... SO MANY MORE...
BOSTON BRAND.
TARA MARKOV.
WESLEY DODDS.
JENNIE-LYNN HAYDEN.
ARTHUR CURRY.
JONATHAN KENT.
BRUCE WAYNE.
YES. I'M LISTENING.
I'M HEEERREE.

YES, I SEE THEM *ALL*...

...AND I SEE THOSE THAT HAVE *ESCAPED* DEATH.

THOSE THAT HAVE *DIED* AND YET BEEN *RESURRECTED*.

CLARK KENT.

DIANA PRINCE.

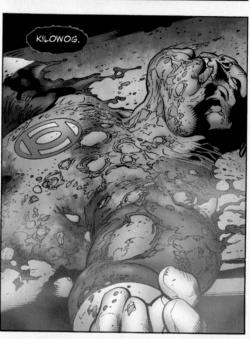

KILOWOG.

HAL JORDAN.

CONNER KENT.

BART ALLEN.

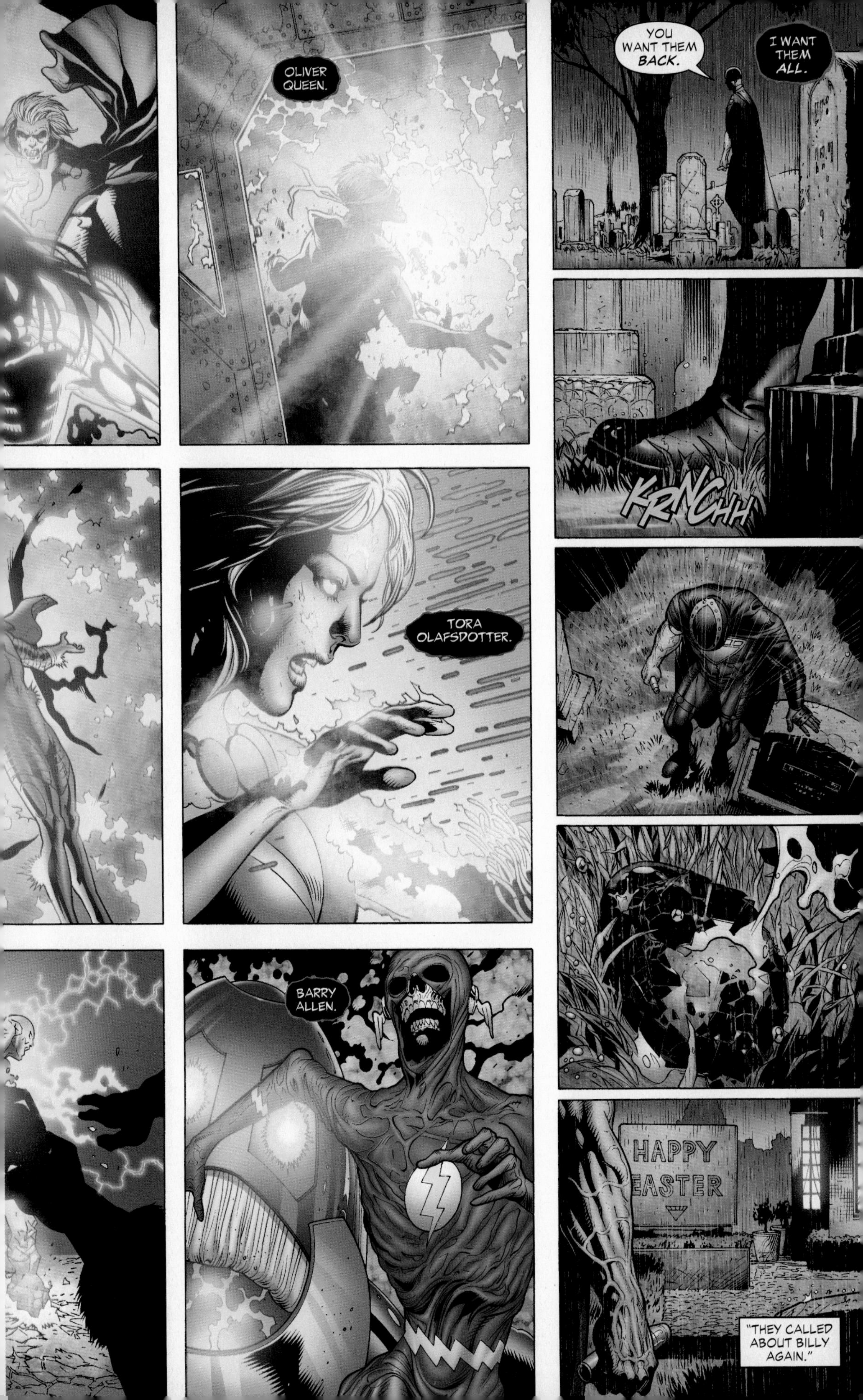
OLIVER QUEEN.
TORA OLAFSDOTTER.
BARRY ALLEN.
YOU WANT THEM BACK.
I WANT THEM ALL.
KRNCHH
HAPPY EASTER
"THEY CALLED ABOUT BILLY AGAIN."

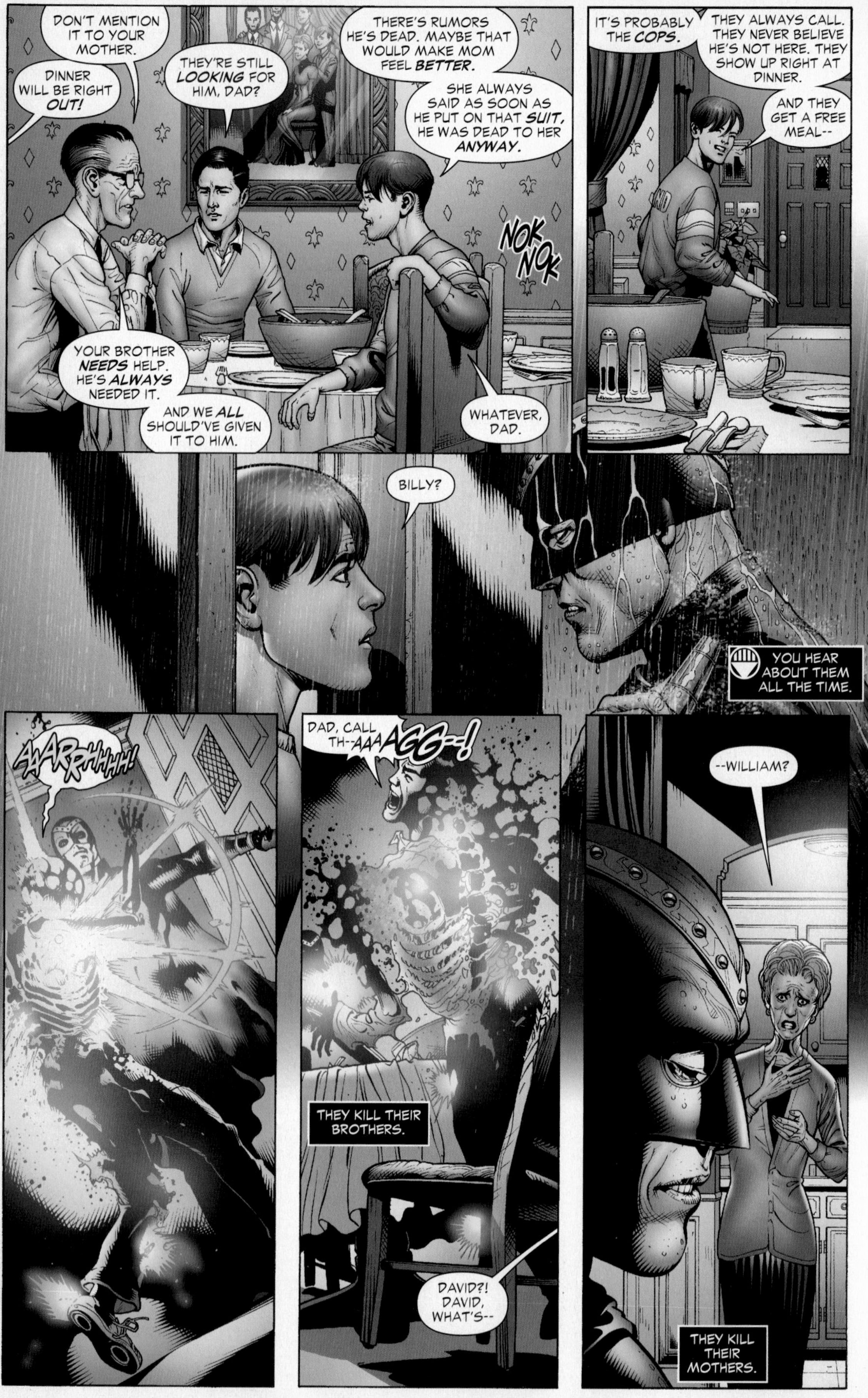
DON'T MENTION IT TO YOUR MOTHER.
DINNER WILL BE RIGHT OUT!
THEY'RE STILL LOOKING FOR HIM, DAD?
THERE'S RUMORS HE'S DEAD. MAYBE THAT WOULD MAKE MOM FEEL BETTER.
SHE ALWAYS SAID AS SOON AS HE PUT ON THAT SUIT, HE WAS DEAD TO HER ANYWAY.
YOUR BROTHER NEEDS HELP. HE'S ALWAYS NEEDED IT.
AND WE ALL SHOULD'VE GIVEN IT TO HIM.
WHATEVER, DAD.
NOK NOK
IT'S PROBABLY THE COPS.
THEY ALWAYS CALL. THEY NEVER BELIEVE HE'S NOT HERE. THEY SHOW UP RIGHT AT DINNER.
AND THEY GET A FREE MEAL--
BILLY?
YOU HEAR ABOUT THEM ALL THE TIME.
AAARRHHHH!
DAD, CALL TH--AAAAGG--!
THEY KILL THEIR BROTHERS.
DAVID?! DAVID, WHAT'S--
--WILLIAM?
THEY KILL THEIR MOTHERS.

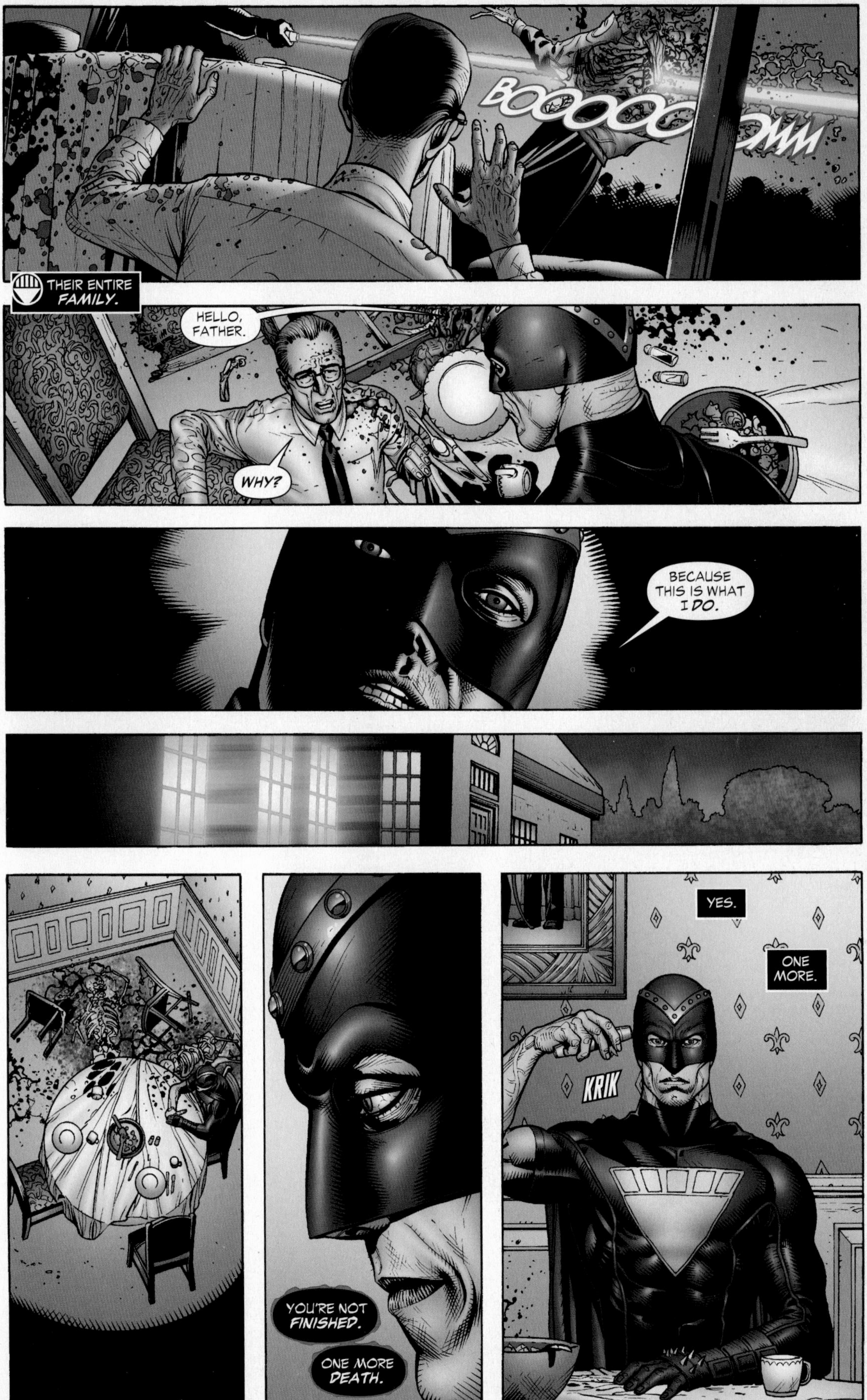
BOOOOOOOMM
THEIR ENTIRE FAMILY.
HELLO, FATHER.
WHY?
BECAUSE THIS IS WHAT I DO.
YOU'RE NOT FINISHED.
ONE MORE DEATH.
YES.
ONE MORE.
KRIK

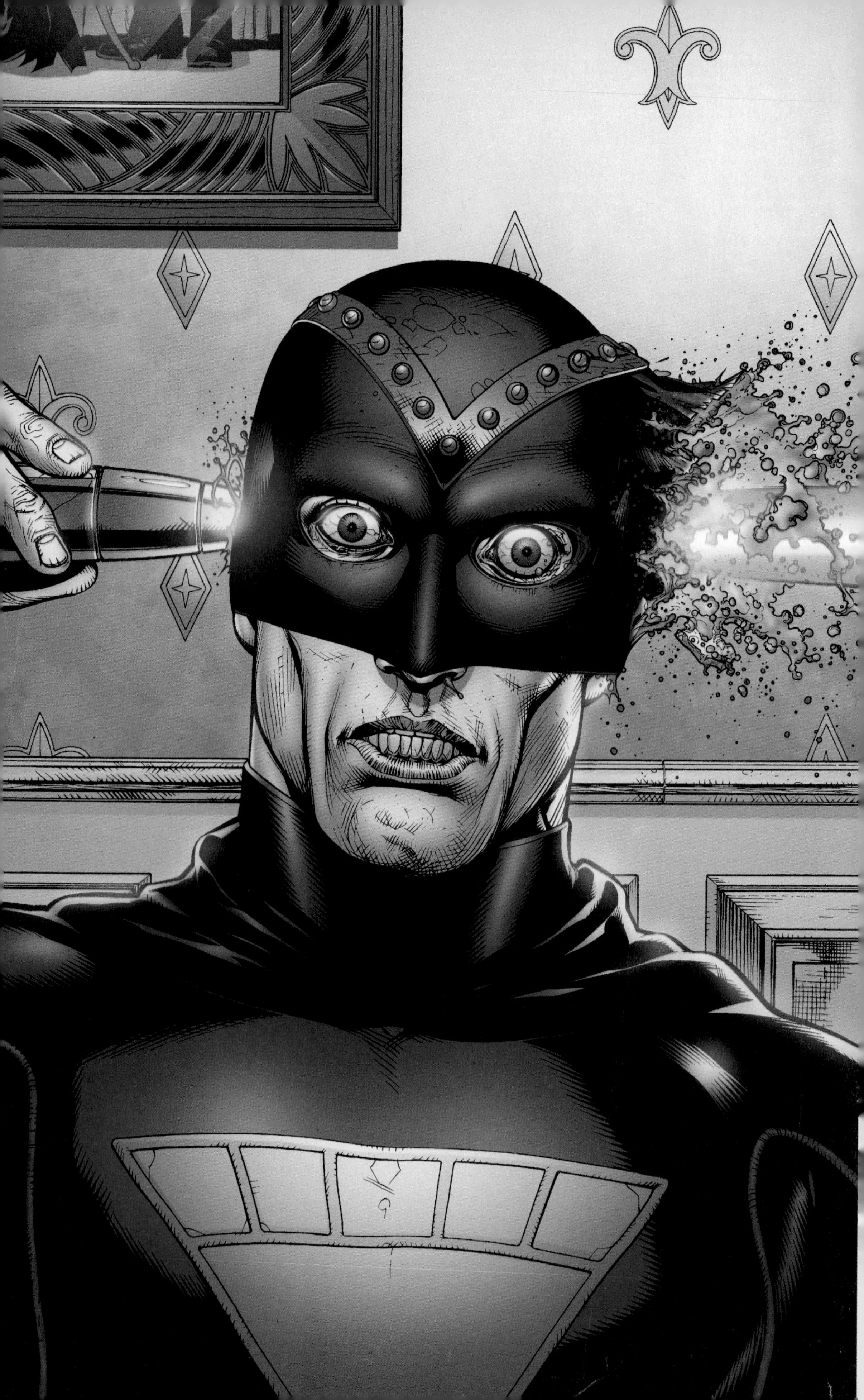

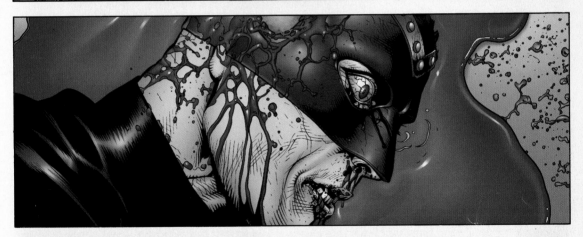

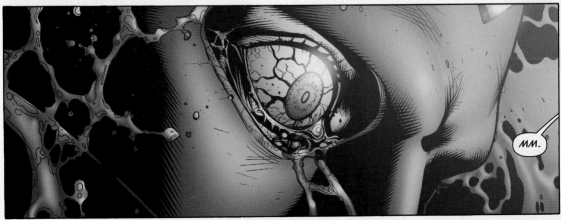

MM.

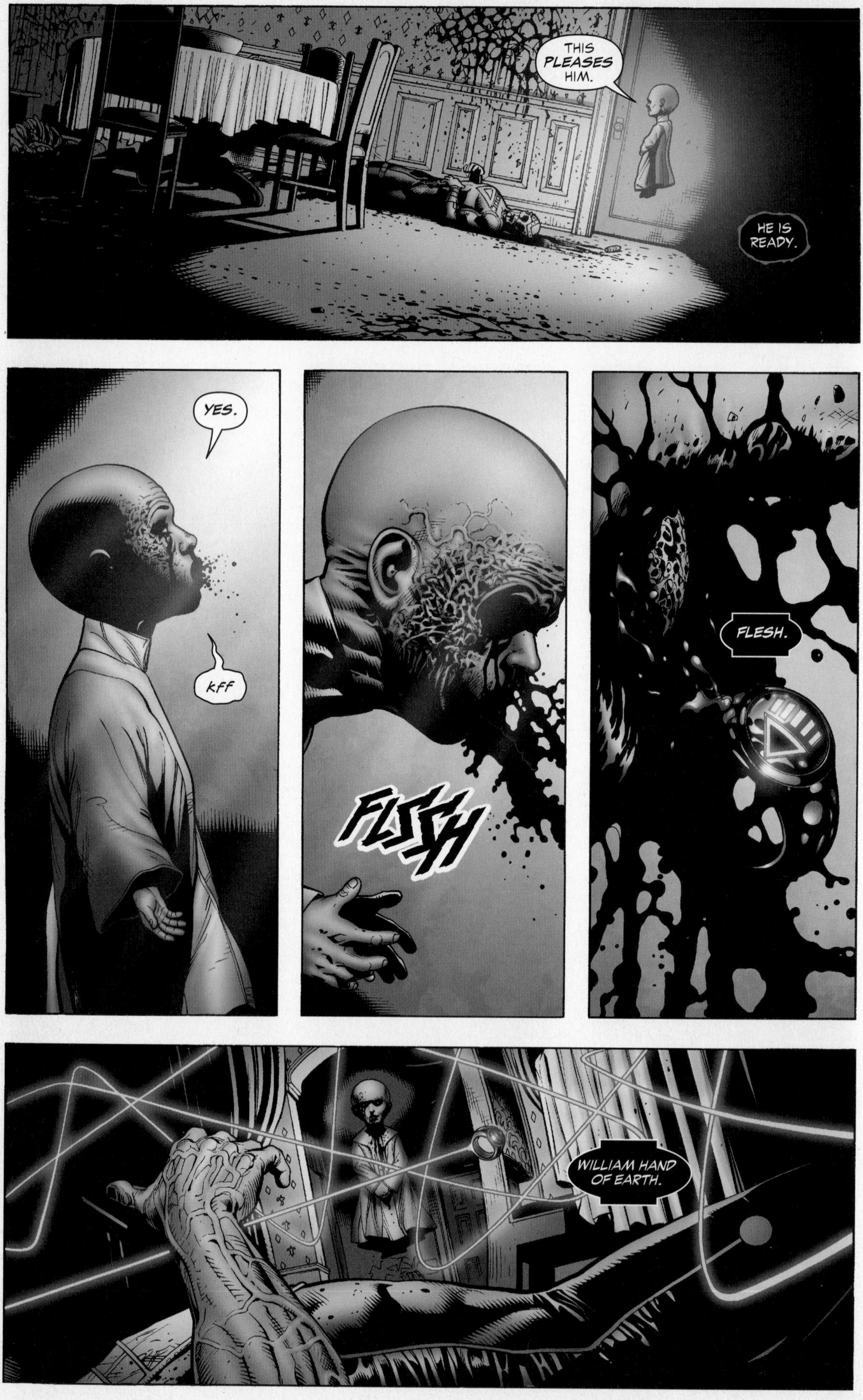
THIS PLEASES HIM.
HE IS READY.
YES.
kff
FLSSH
FLESH.
WILLIAM HAND OF EARTH.

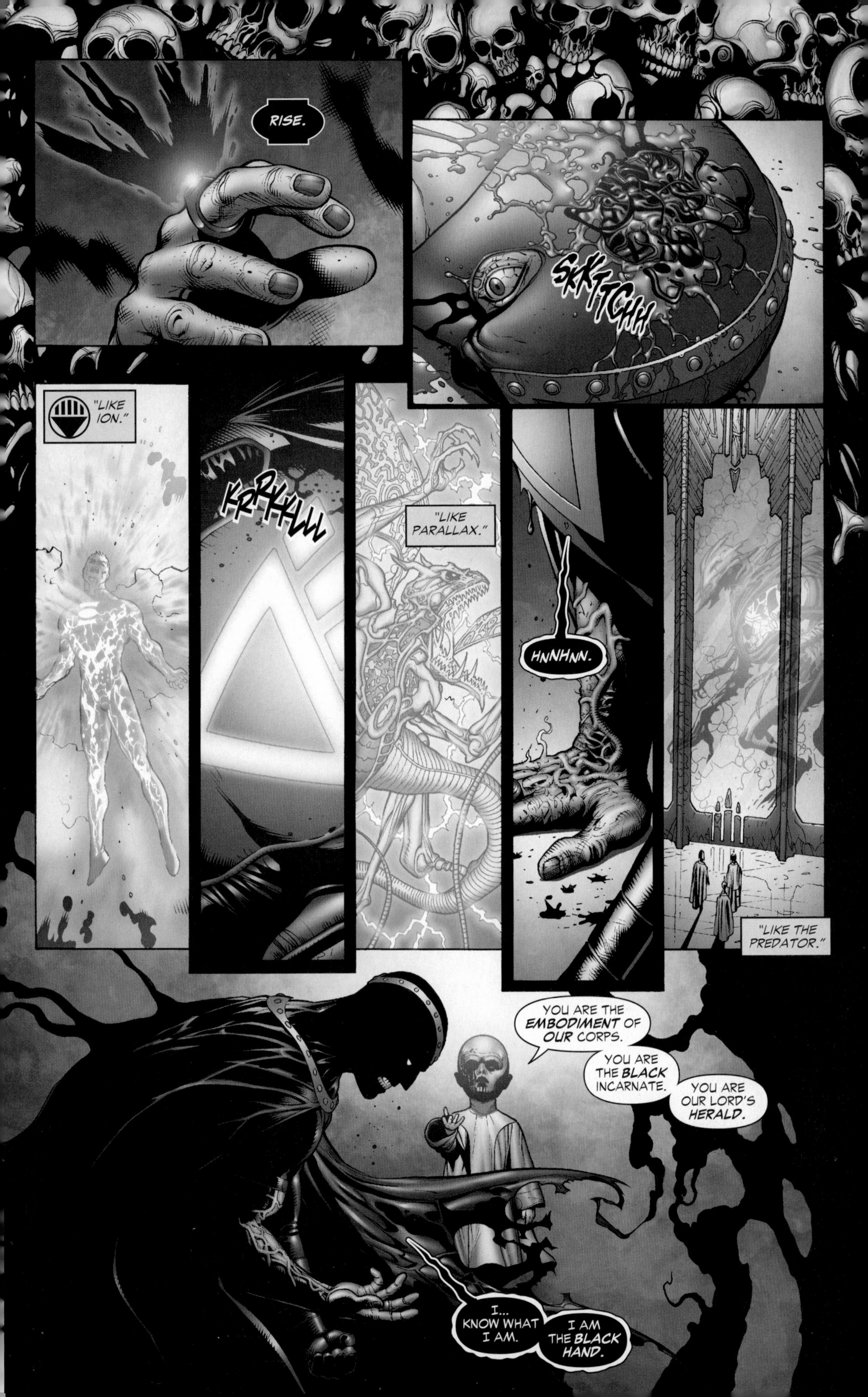
RISE.
SKKTCHH
"LIKE ION."
KRRKKLLL
"LIKE PARALLAX."
HNNHNN.
"LIKE THE PREDATOR."
YOU ARE THE EMBODIMENT OF OUR CORPS.
YOU ARE THE BLACK INCARNATE.
YOU ARE OUR LORD'S HERALD.
I... KNOW WHAT I AM.
I AM THE BLACK HAND.

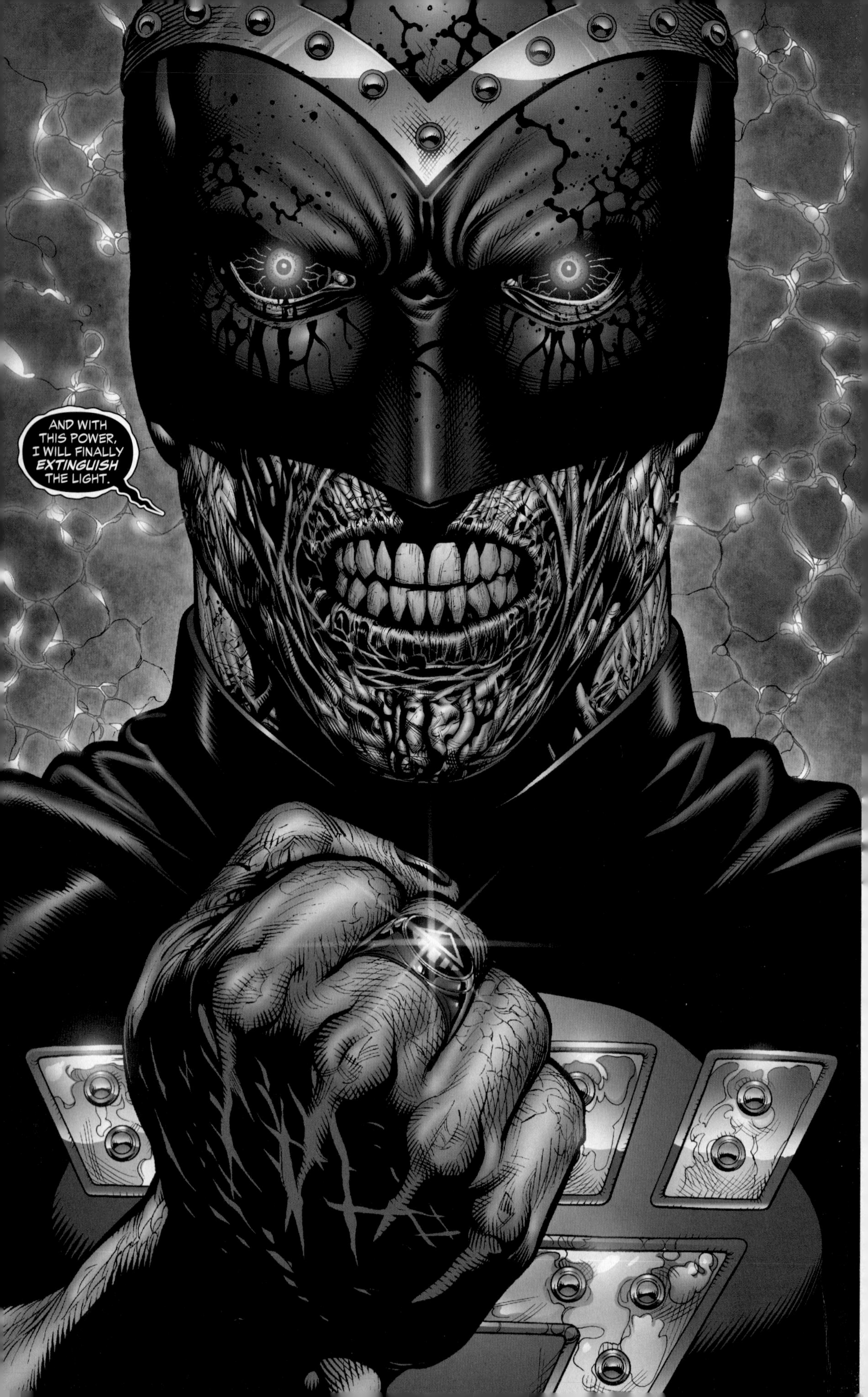
AND WITH THIS POWER, I WILL FINALLY *EXTINGUISH* THE LIGHT.

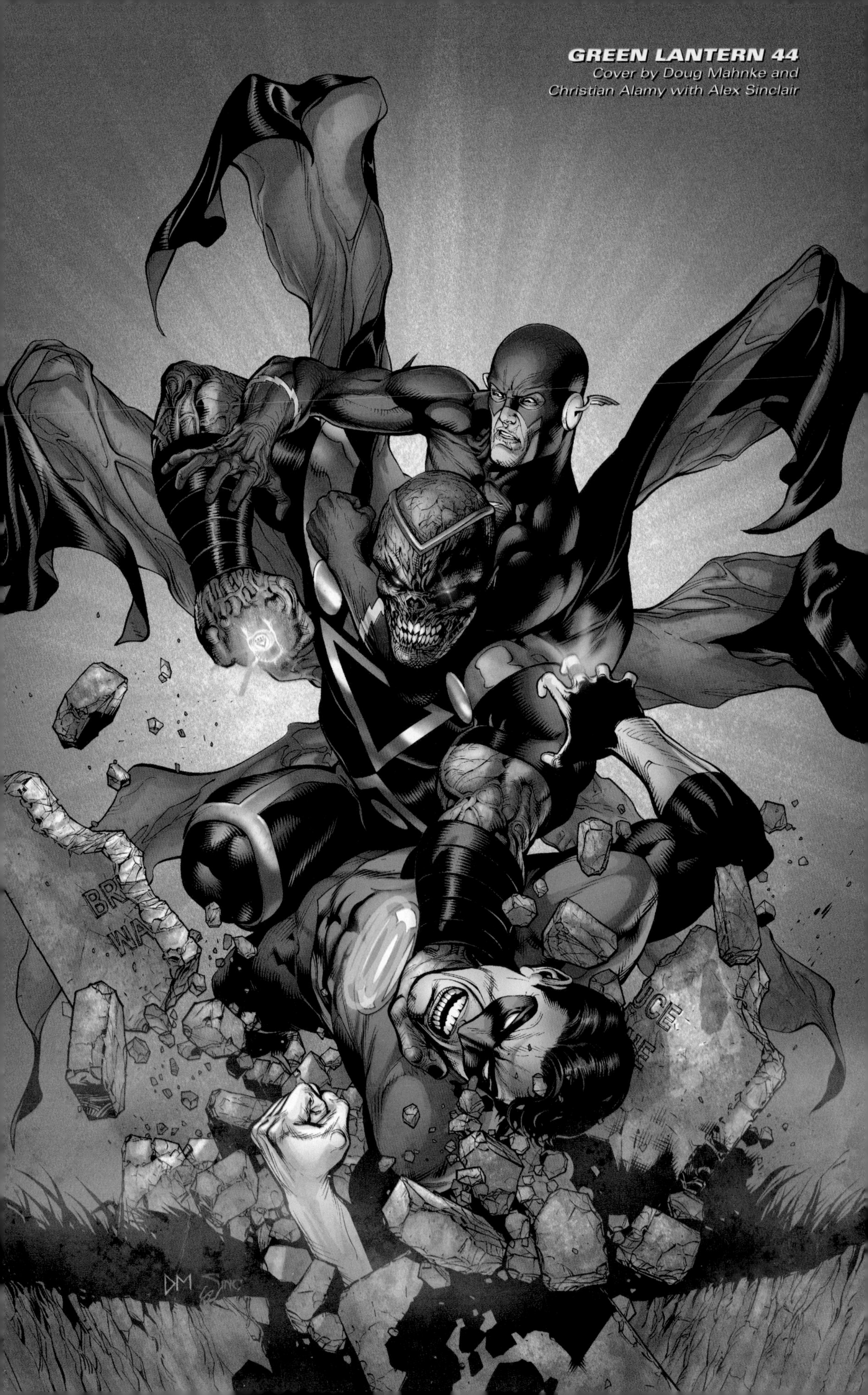

GREEN LANTERN 44
Cover by Doug Mahnke and Christian Alamy with Alex Sinclair

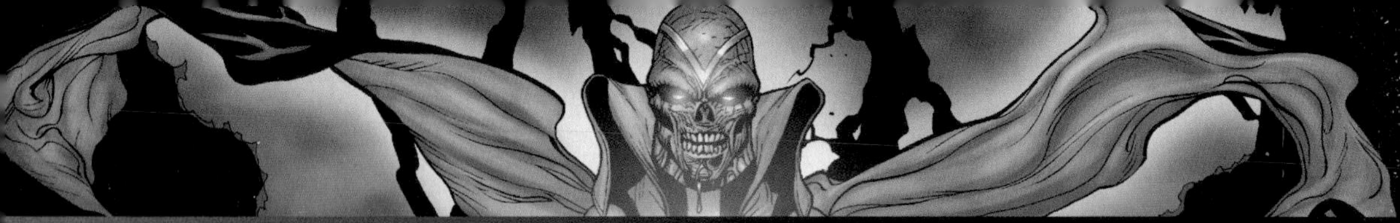

Now empowered to extinguish the light of the universe, Black Hand digs up Bruce Wayne's skull under his unseen master's orders.

Meanwhile, across the universe in Sector 666, a black power battery emerges, spewing a horde of black rings. When these rings attach themselves to the dead, the deceased become unliving Black Lanterns with seemingly all the characteristics of their former selves—except for any mercy.

Earth is the focus of their main attack. Heroes like Hawkman and Hawkgirl have already been killed at the hands of former allies. They are just the first to fall victim...

ONLY THE GOOD DIE YOUNG

DOUG MAHNKE
PENCILS

CHRISTIAN ALAMY
DOUG MAHNKE
TOM NGUYEN
RODNEY RAMOS
INKS

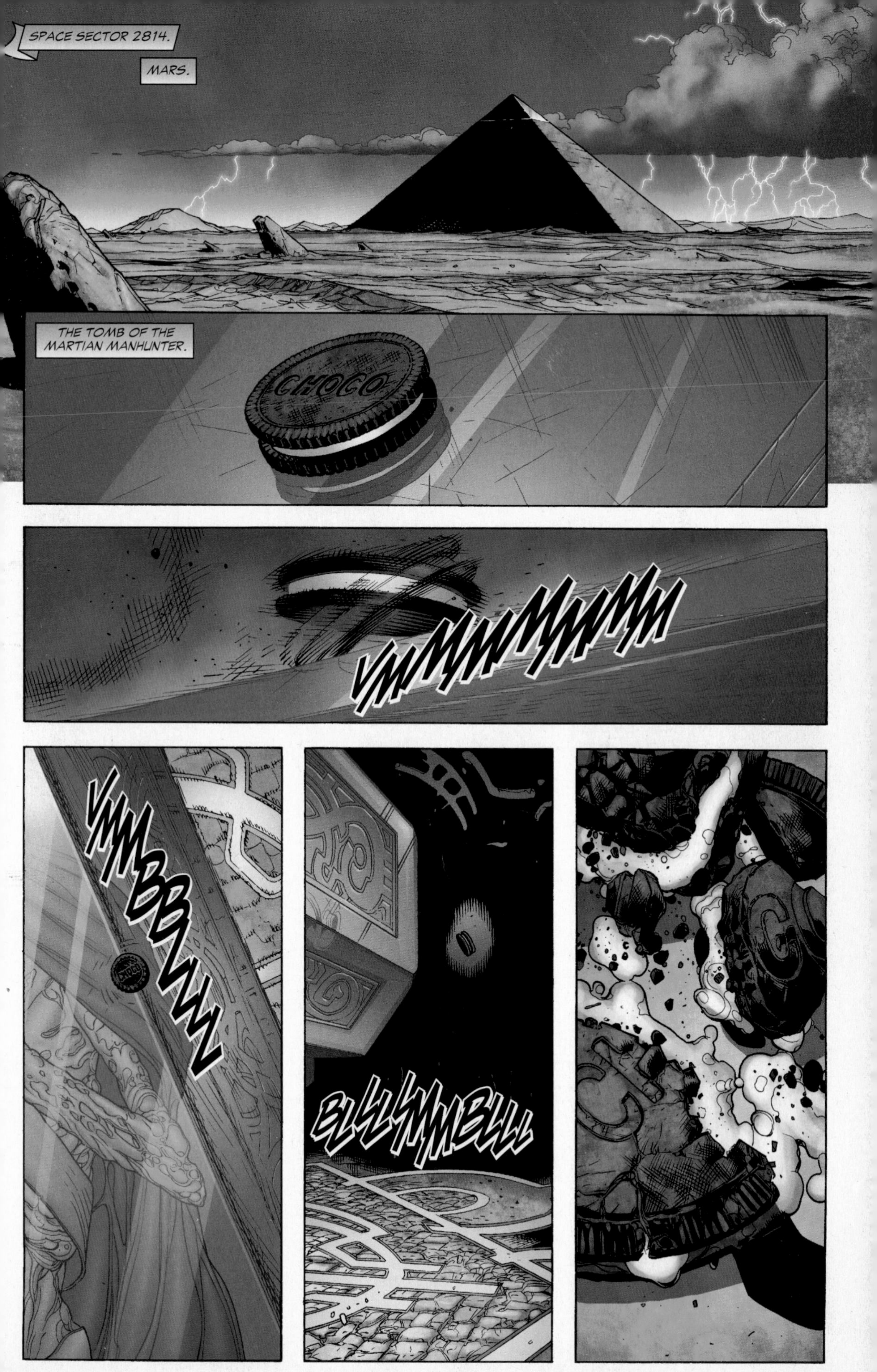
SPACE SECTOR 2814.
MARS.
THE TOMB OF THE MARTIAN MANHUNTER.
CHOCO
VMMMMMMMMMM
VMMBBZZZZ
BLLLMMBLLL

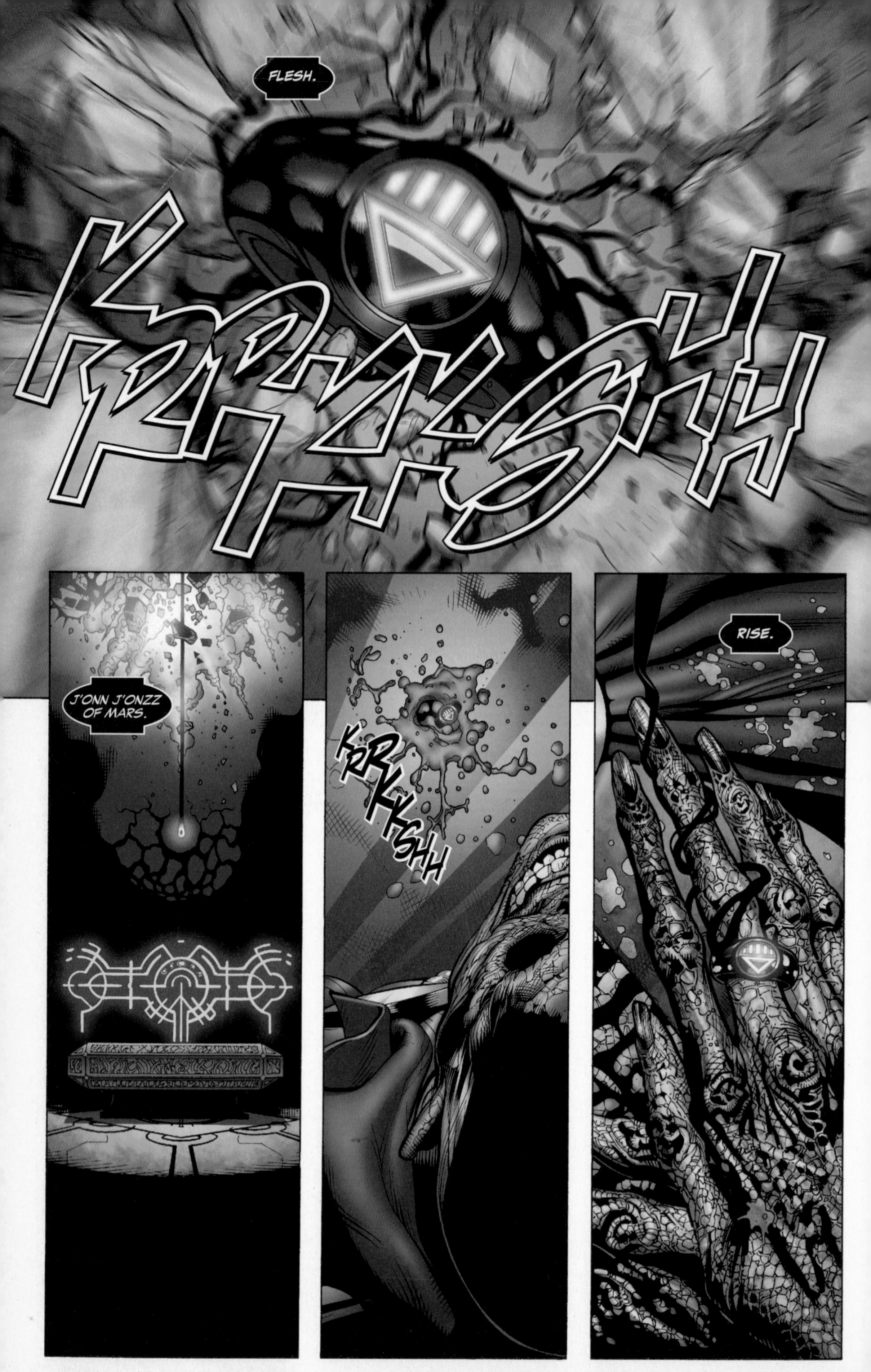
FLESH.
KRAKASHH
J'ONN J'ONZZ OF MARS.
KRRKKSHH
RISE.

FWP
FWP FWP
FWP
FWP
HFFF.
SKTCH
FWAASH

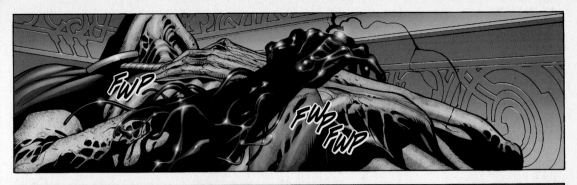

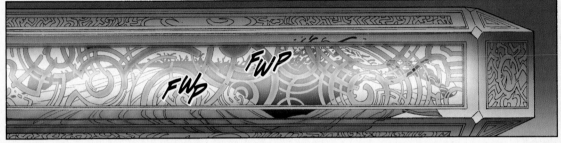

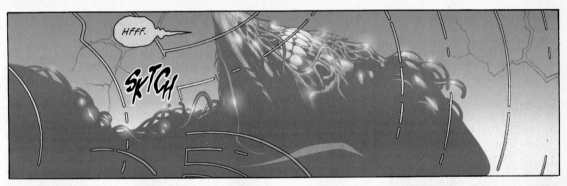

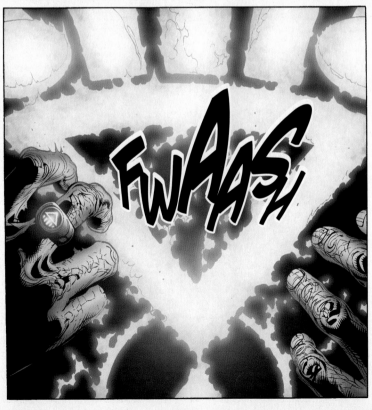

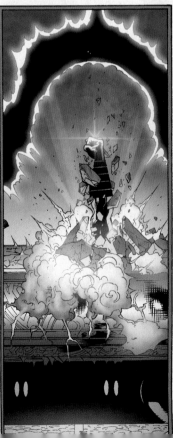

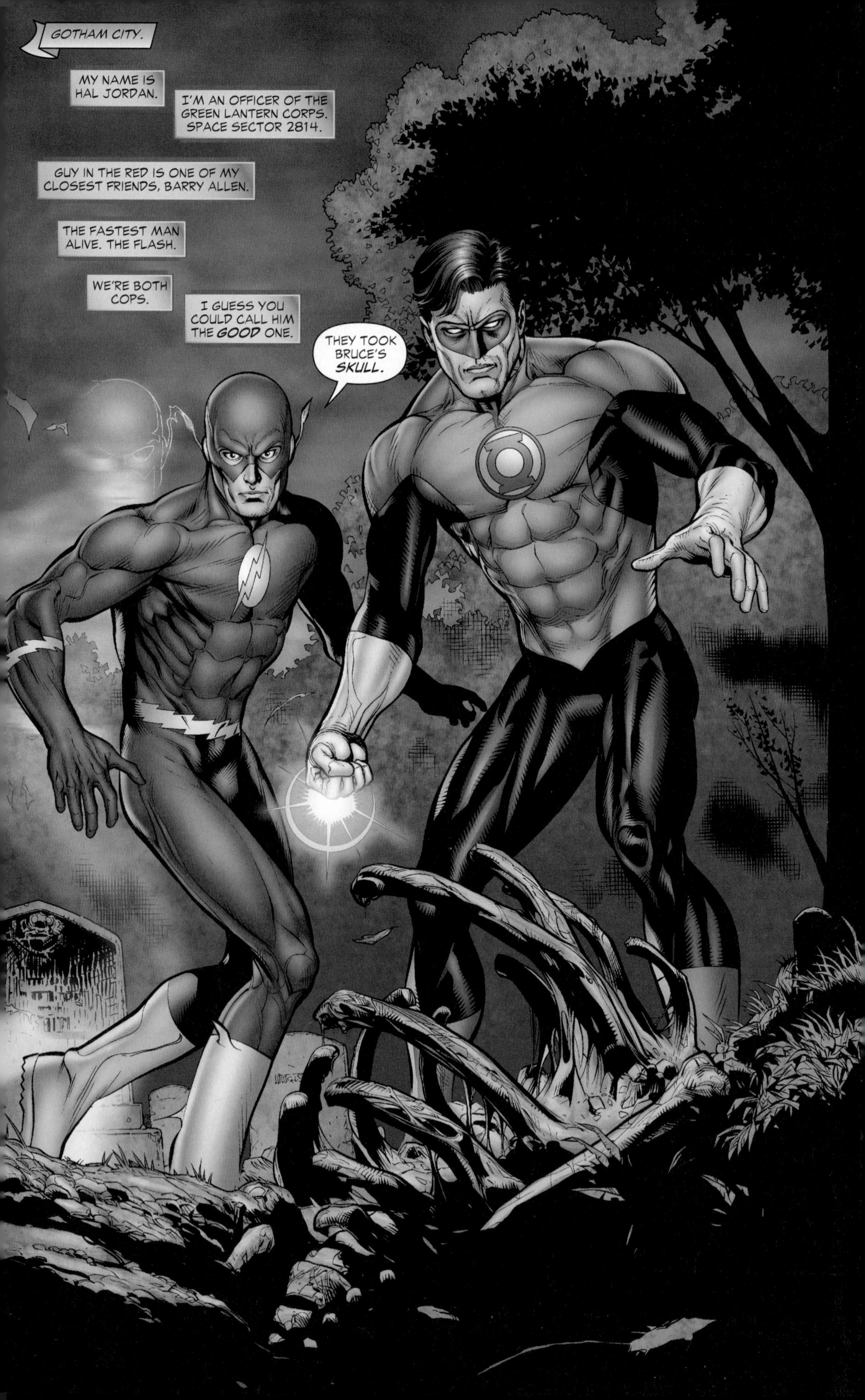
GOTHAM CITY.
MY NAME IS HAL JORDAN.
I'M AN OFFICER OF THE GREEN LANTERN CORPS. SPACE SECTOR 2814.
GUY IN THE RED IS ONE OF MY CLOSEST FRIENDS, BARRY ALLEN.
THE FASTEST MAN ALIVE. THE FLASH.
WE'RE BOTH COPS.
I GUESS YOU COULD CALL HIM THE GOOD ONE.
THEY TOOK BRUCE'S SKULL.

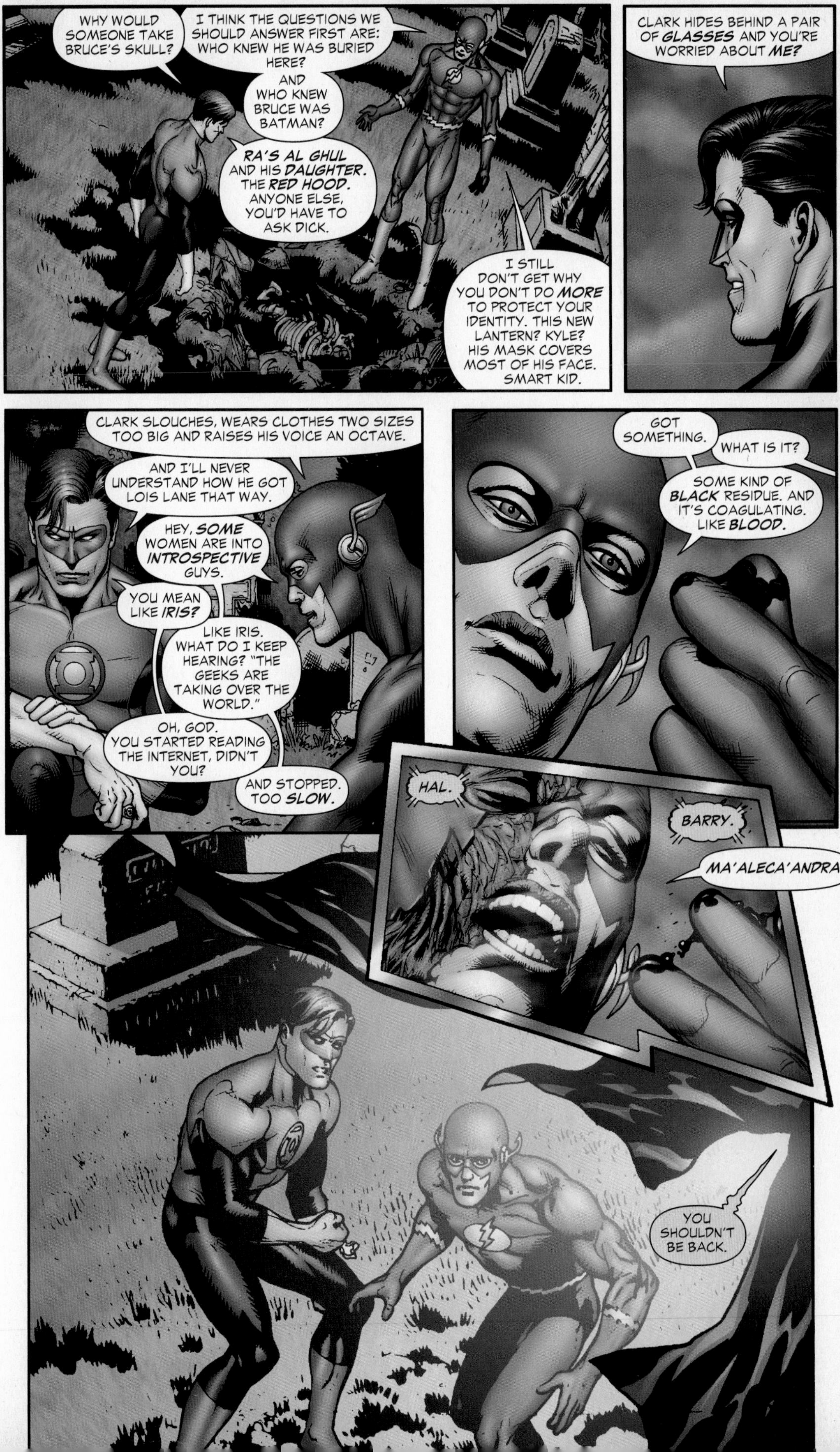
WHY WOULD SOMEONE TAKE BRUCE'S SKULL?
I THINK THE QUESTIONS WE SHOULD ANSWER FIRST ARE: WHO KNEW HE WAS BURIED HERE?
AND WHO KNEW BRUCE WAS BATMAN?
RA'S AL GHUL AND HIS DAUGHTER. THE RED HOOD. ANYONE ELSE, YOU'D HAVE TO ASK DICK.
I STILL DON'T GET WHY YOU DON'T DO MORE TO PROTECT YOUR IDENTITY. THIS NEW LANTERN? KYLE? HIS MASK COVERS MOST OF HIS FACE. SMART KID.
CLARK HIDES BEHIND A PAIR OF GLASSES AND YOU'RE WORRIED ABOUT ME?
CLARK SLOUCHES, WEARS CLOTHES TWO SIZES TOO BIG AND RAISES HIS VOICE AN OCTAVE.
AND I'LL NEVER UNDERSTAND HOW HE GOT LOIS LANE THAT WAY.
HEY, SOME WOMEN ARE INTO INTROSPECTIVE GUYS.
YOU MEAN LIKE IRIS?
LIKE IRIS. WHAT DO I KEEP HEARING? "THE GEEKS ARE TAKING OVER THE WORLD."
OH, GOD. YOU STARTED READING THE INTERNET, DIDN'T YOU?
AND STOPPED. TOO SLOW.
GOT SOMETHING.
WHAT IS IT?
SOME KIND OF BLACK RESIDUE. AND IT'S COAGULATING. LIKE BLOOD.
HAL.
BARRY.
MA'ALECA'ANDRA.
YOU SHOULDN'T BE BACK.

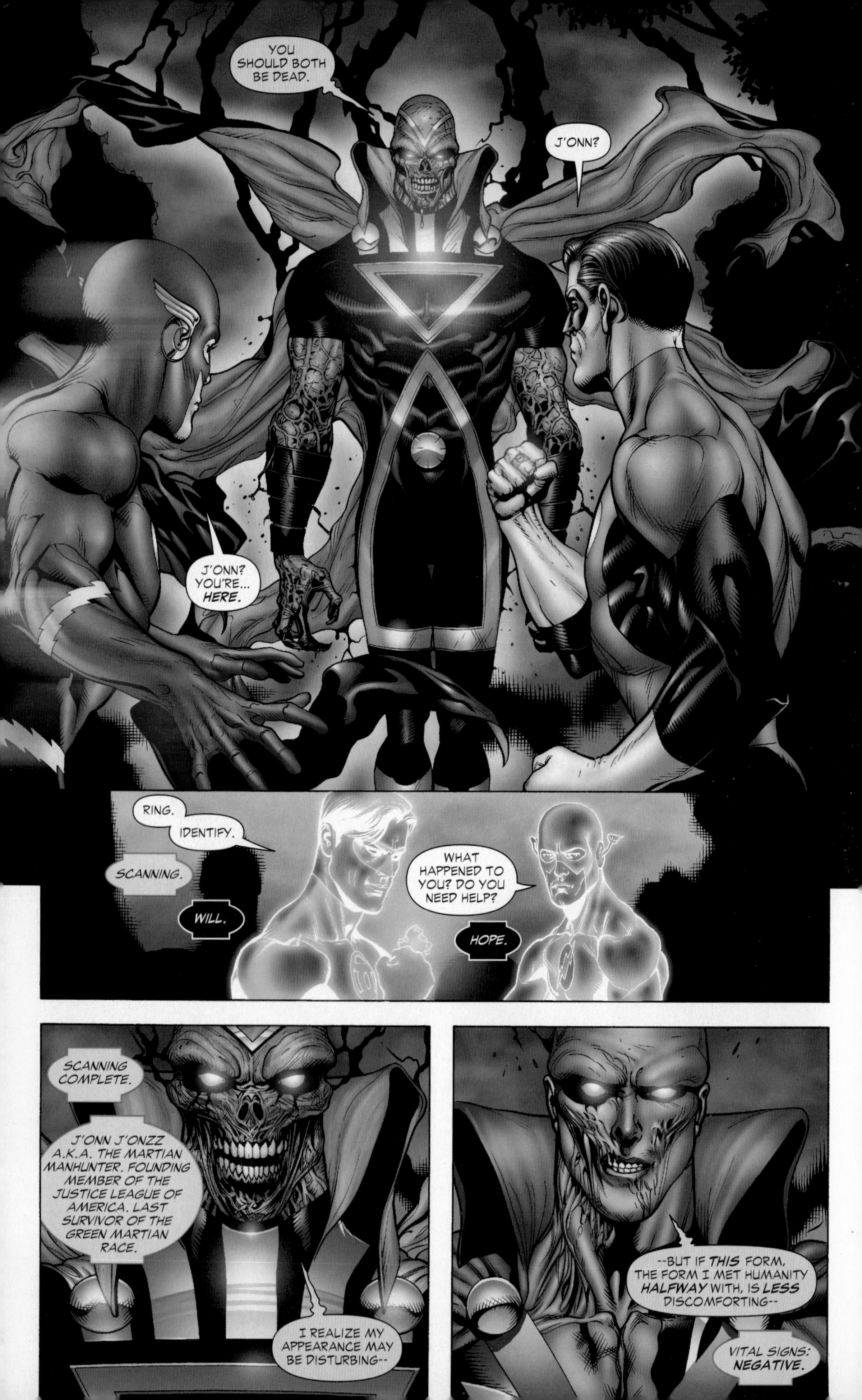
YOU SHOULD BOTH BE DEAD.
J'ONN?
J'ONN? YOU'RE... HERE.
RING.
IDENTIFY.
SCANNING.
WILL.
WHAT HAPPENED TO YOU? DO YOU NEED HELP?
HOPE.
SCANNING COMPLETE.
J'ONN J'ONZZ A.K.A. THE MARTIAN MANHUNTER. FOUNDING MEMBER OF THE JUSTICE LEAGUE OF AMERICA. LAST SURVIVOR OF THE GREEN MARTIAN RACE.
I REALIZE MY APPEARANCE MAY BE DISTURBING--
--BUT IF THIS FORM, THE FORM I MET HUMANITY HALFWAY WITH, IS LESS DISCOMFORTING--
VITAL SIGNS: NEGATIVE.

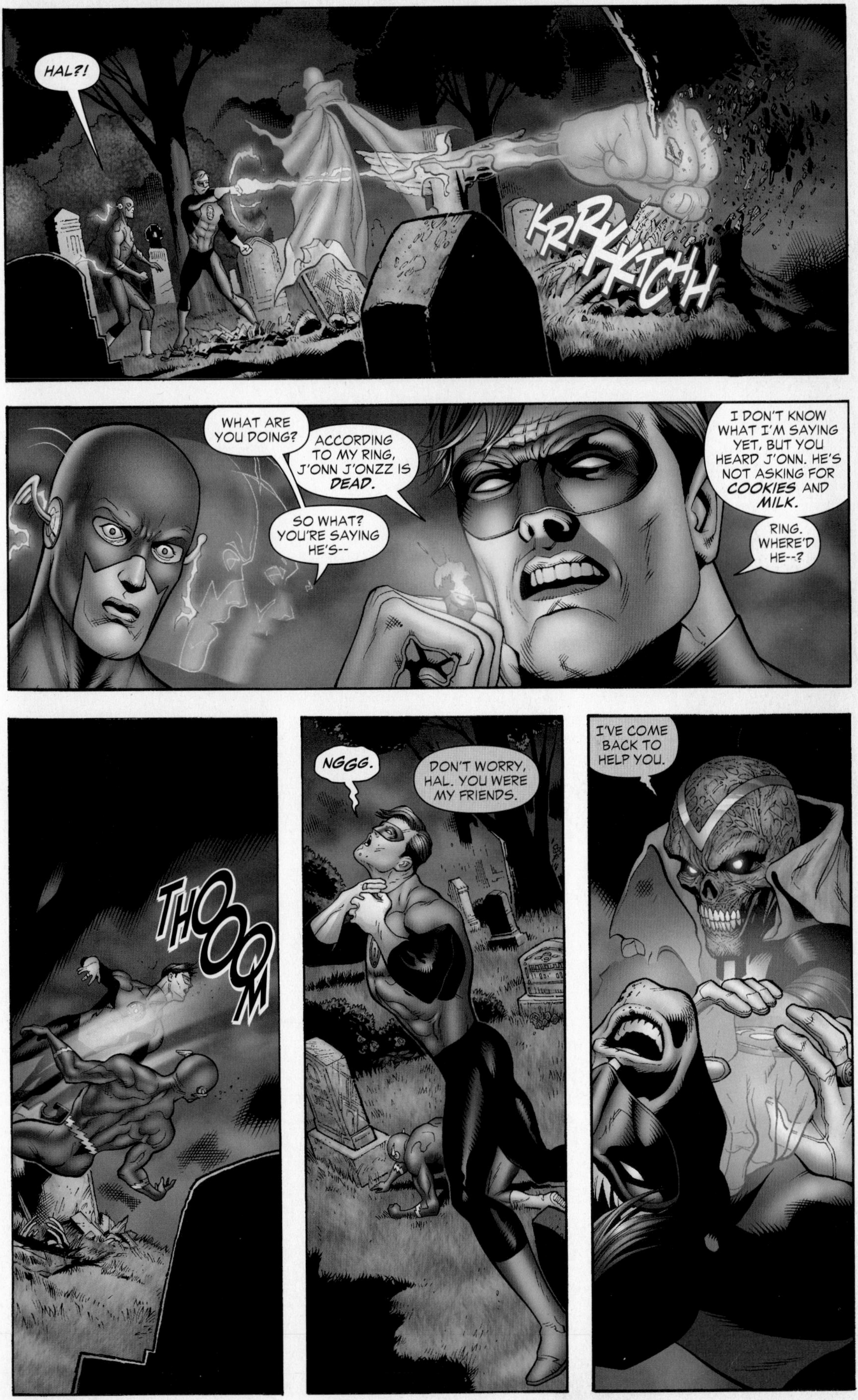
HAL?!
KRRKKTCHH
WHAT ARE YOU DOING?
ACCORDING TO MY RING, J'ONN J'ONZZ IS DEAD.
SO WHAT? YOU'RE SAYING HE'S--
I DON'T KNOW WHAT I'M SAYING YET, BUT YOU HEARD J'ONN. HE'S NOT ASKING FOR COOKIES AND MILK.
RING. WHERE'D HE--?
THOOOM
NGGG.
DON'T WORRY, HAL. YOU WERE MY FRIENDS.
I'VE COME BACK TO HELP YOU.

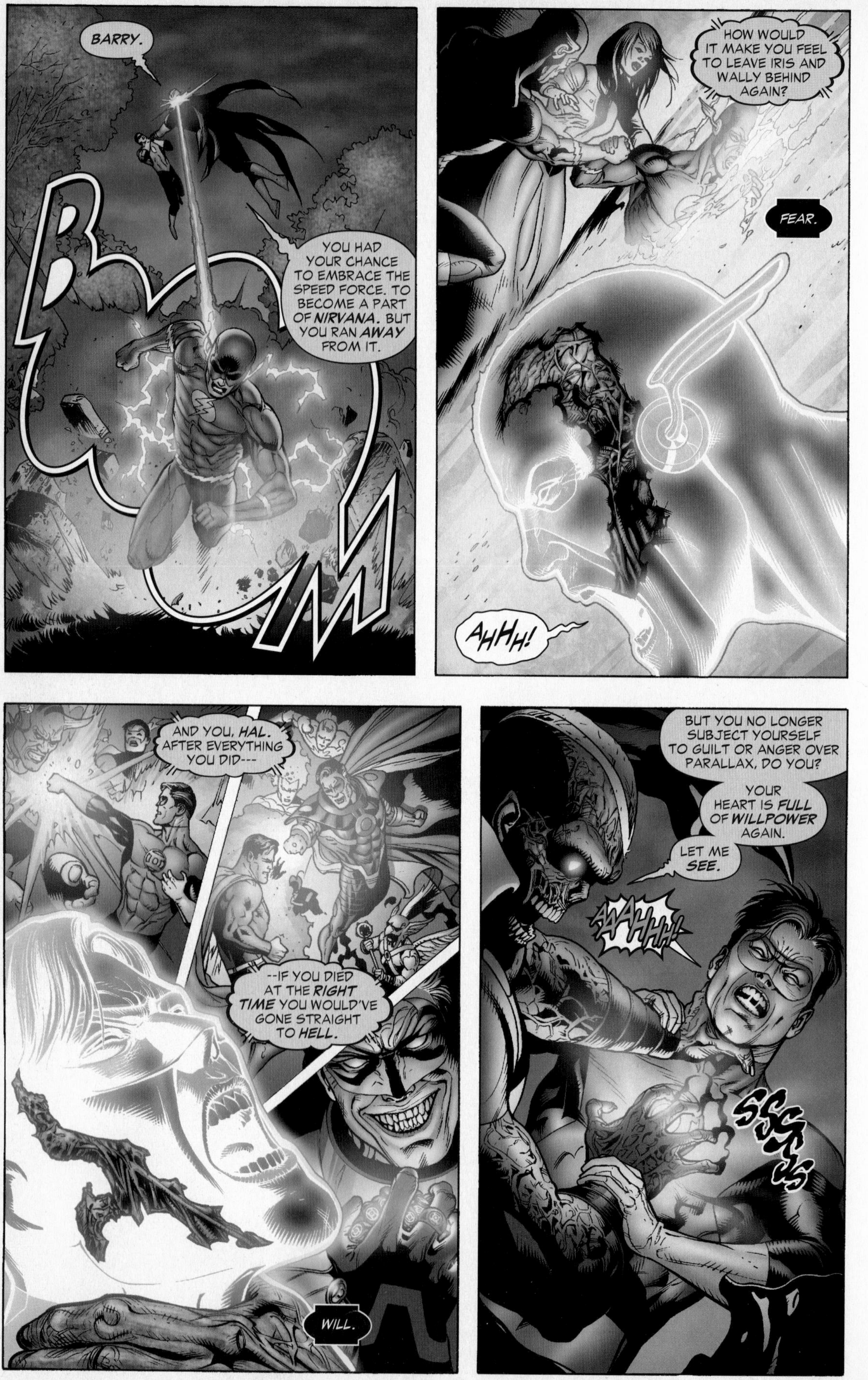
BARRY.
BOOM
YOU HAD YOUR CHANCE TO EMBRACE THE SPEED FORCE. TO BECOME A PART OF NIRVANA. BUT YOU RAN AWAY FROM IT.
HOW WOULD IT MAKE YOU FEEL TO LEAVE IRIS AND WALLY BEHIND AGAIN?
FEAR.
AHHH!
AND YOU, HAL. AFTER EVERYTHING YOU DID---
--IF YOU DIED AT THE RIGHT TIME YOU WOULD'VE GONE STRAIGHT TO HELL.
WILL.
BUT YOU NO LONGER SUBJECT YOURSELF TO GUILT OR ANGER OVER PARALLAX, DO YOU?
YOUR HEART IS FULL OF WILLPOWER AGAIN.
LET ME SEE.
AAAHHH!
SSSSS

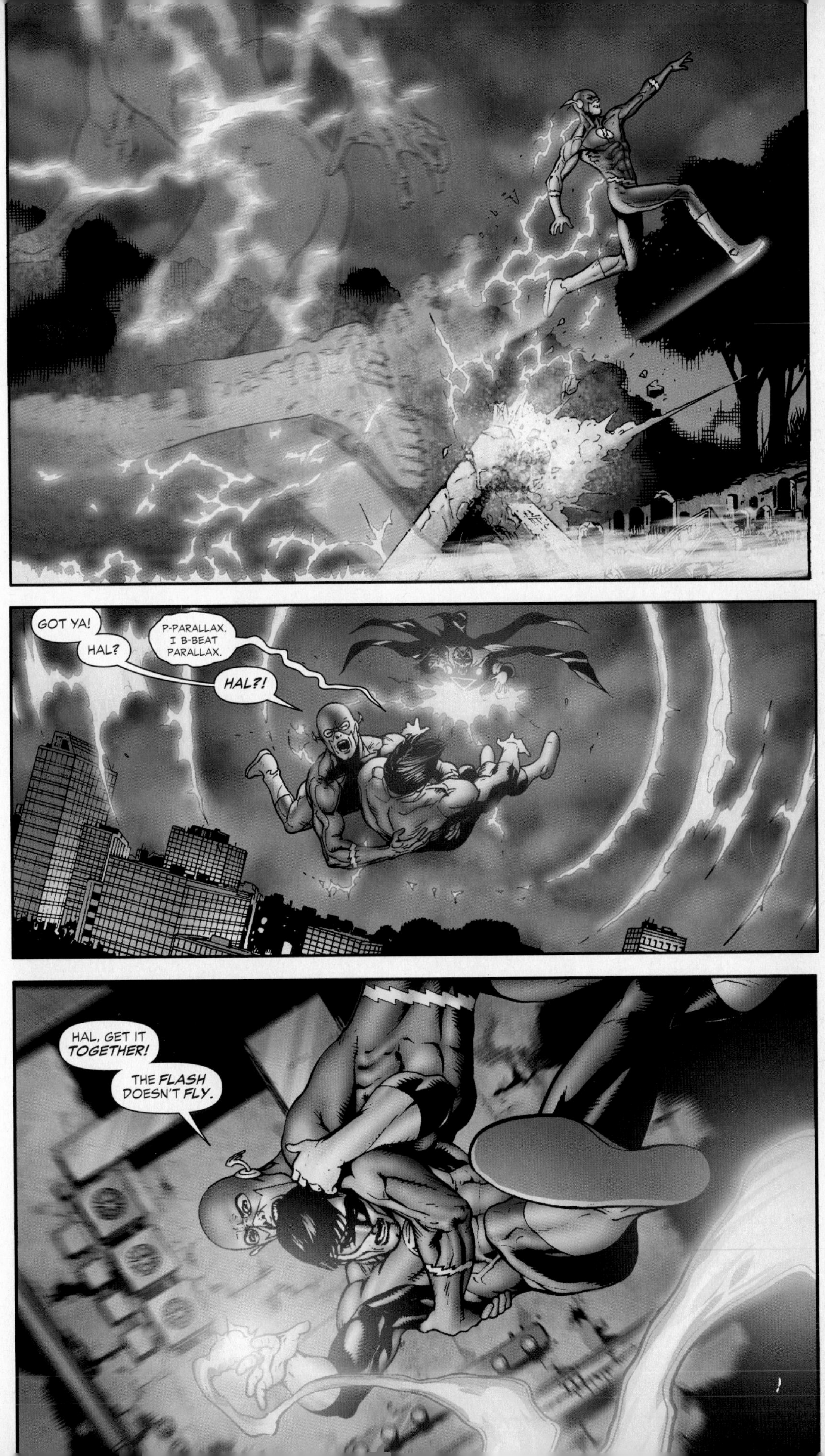
GOT YA!
HAL?
P-PARALLAX. I B-BEAT PARALLAX.
HAL?!
HAL, GET IT TOGETHER!
THE FLASH DOESN'T FLY.

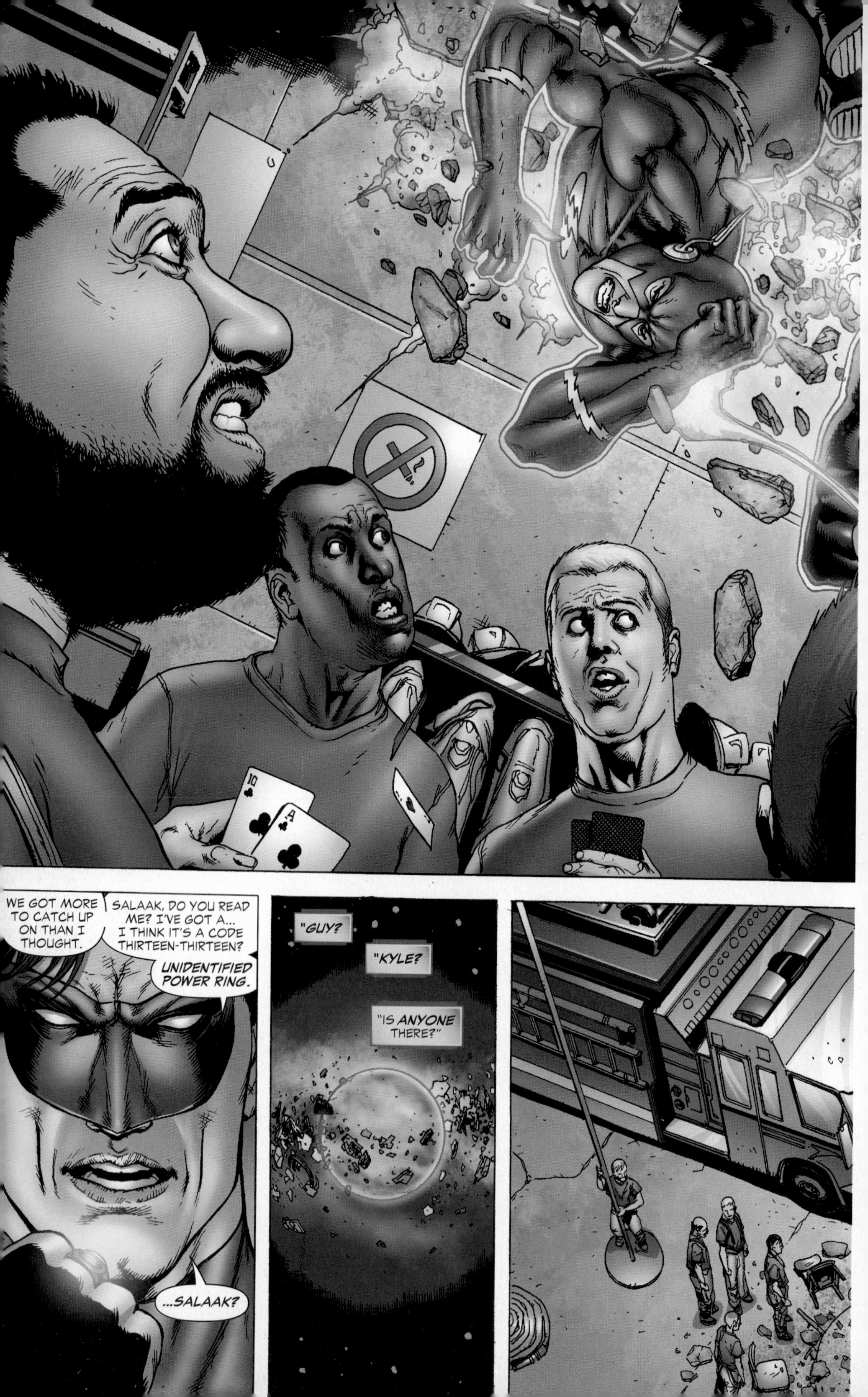
WE GOT MORE TO CATCH UP ON THAN I THOUGHT.
SALAAK, DO YOU READ ME? I'VE GOT A... I THINK IT'S A CODE THIRTEEN-THIRTEEN?
UNIDENTIFIED POWER RING.
...SALAAK?
"GUY?
"KYLE?
"IS ANYONE THERE?"

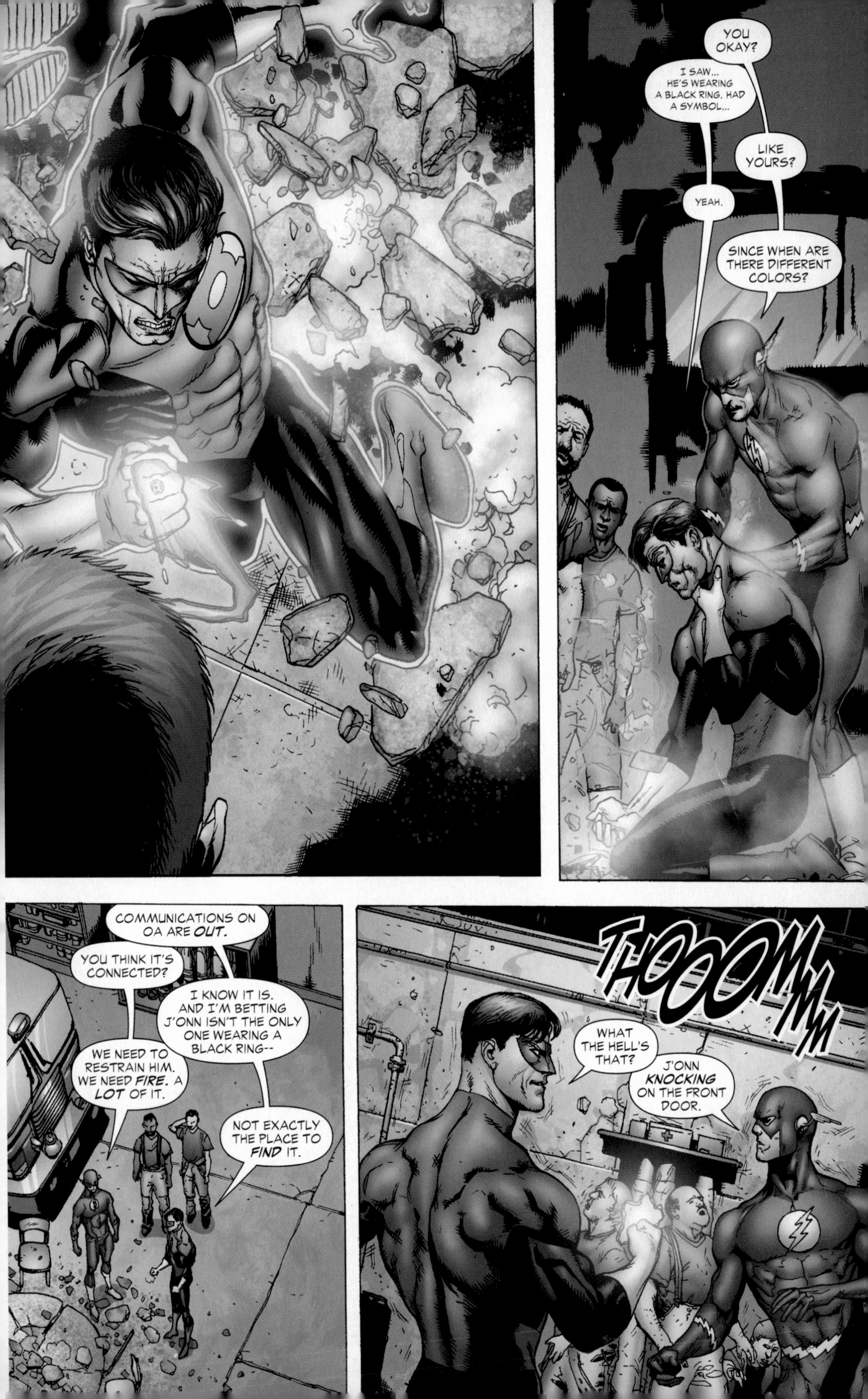
YOU OKAY?
I SAW... HE'S WEARING A BLACK RING. HAD A SYMBOL...
LIKE YOURS?
YEAH.
SINCE WHEN ARE THERE DIFFERENT COLORS?
COMMUNICATIONS ON OA ARE OUT.
YOU THINK IT'S CONNECTED?
I KNOW IT IS. AND I'M BETTING J'ONN ISN'T THE ONLY ONE WEARING A BLACK RING--
WE NEED TO RESTRAIN HIM. WE NEED FIRE. A LOT OF IT.
NOT EXACTLY THE PLACE TO FIND IT.
THOOOMMM
WHAT THE HELL'S THAT?
J'ONN KNOCKING ON THE FRONT DOOR.

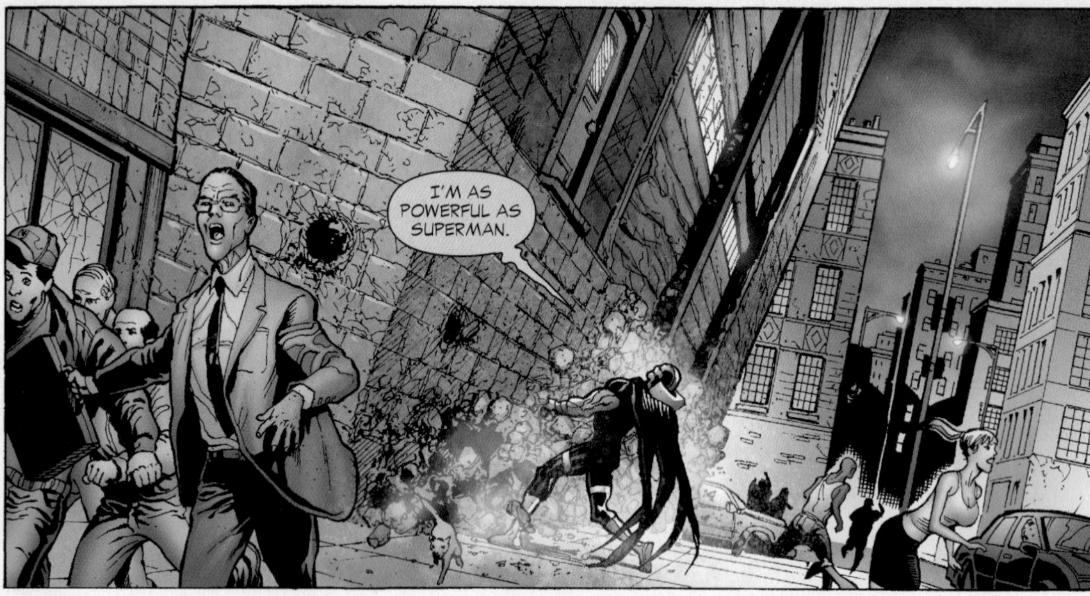
I'M AS POWERFUL AS SUPERMAN.

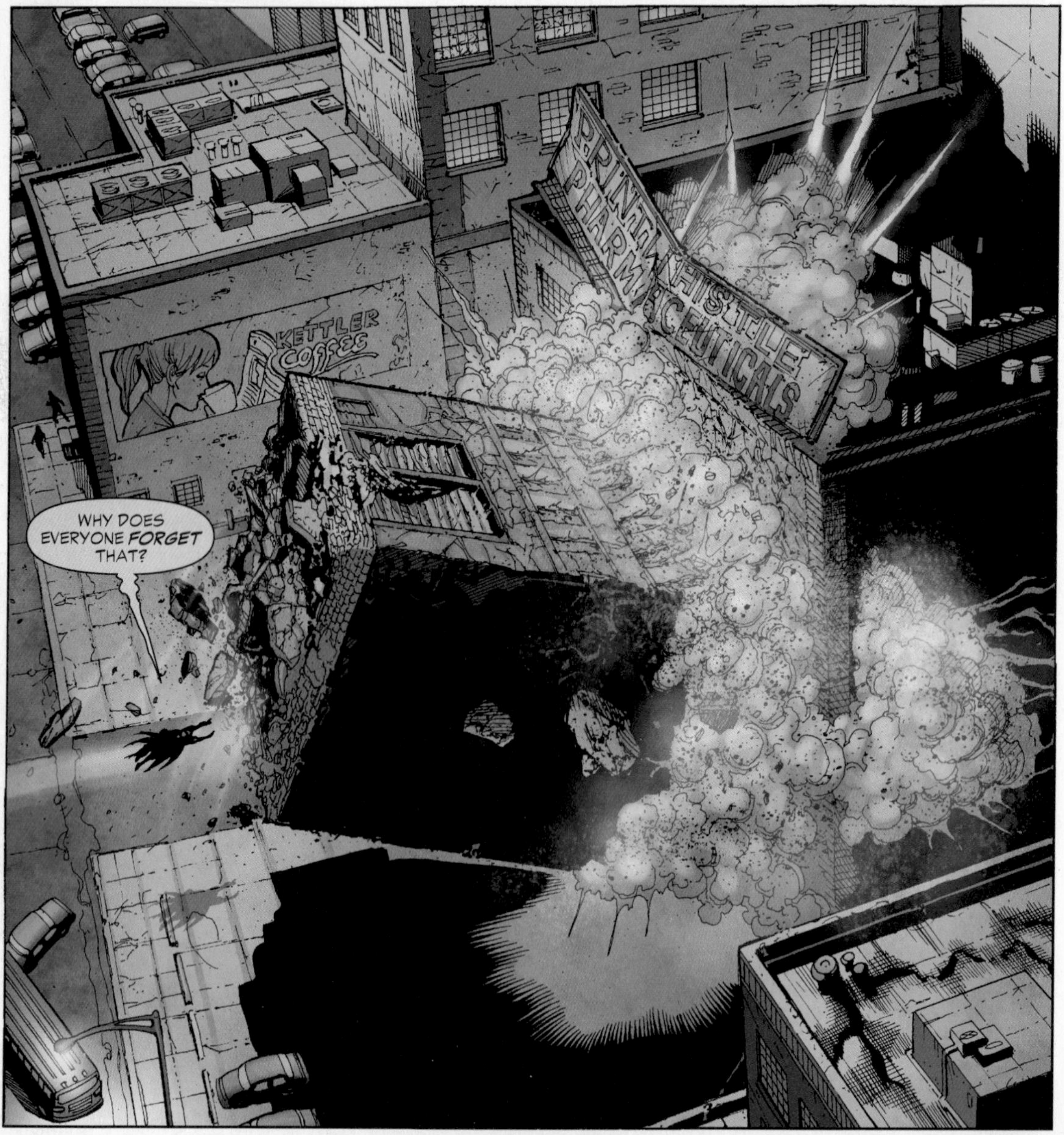
WHY DOES EVERYONE *FORGET* THAT?

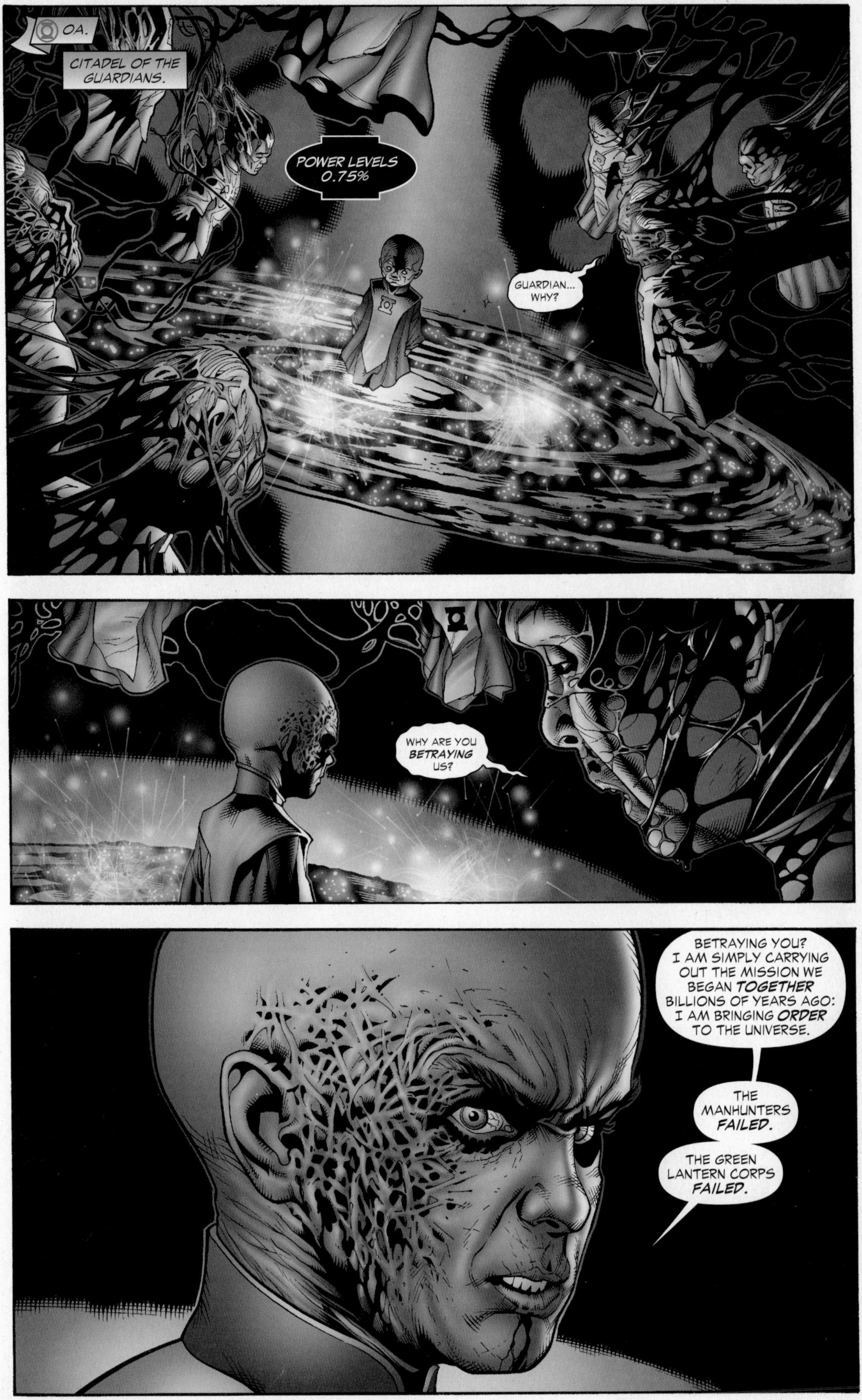
OA.
CITADEL OF THE GUARDIANS.
POWER LEVELS 0.75%
GUARDIAN... WHY?
WHY ARE YOU BETRAYING US?
BETRAYING YOU? I AM SIMPLY CARRYING OUT THE MISSION WE BEGAN TOGETHER BILLIONS OF YEARS AGO: I AM BRINGING ORDER TO THE UNIVERSE.
THE MANHUNTERS FAILED.
THE GREEN LANTERN CORPS FAILED.

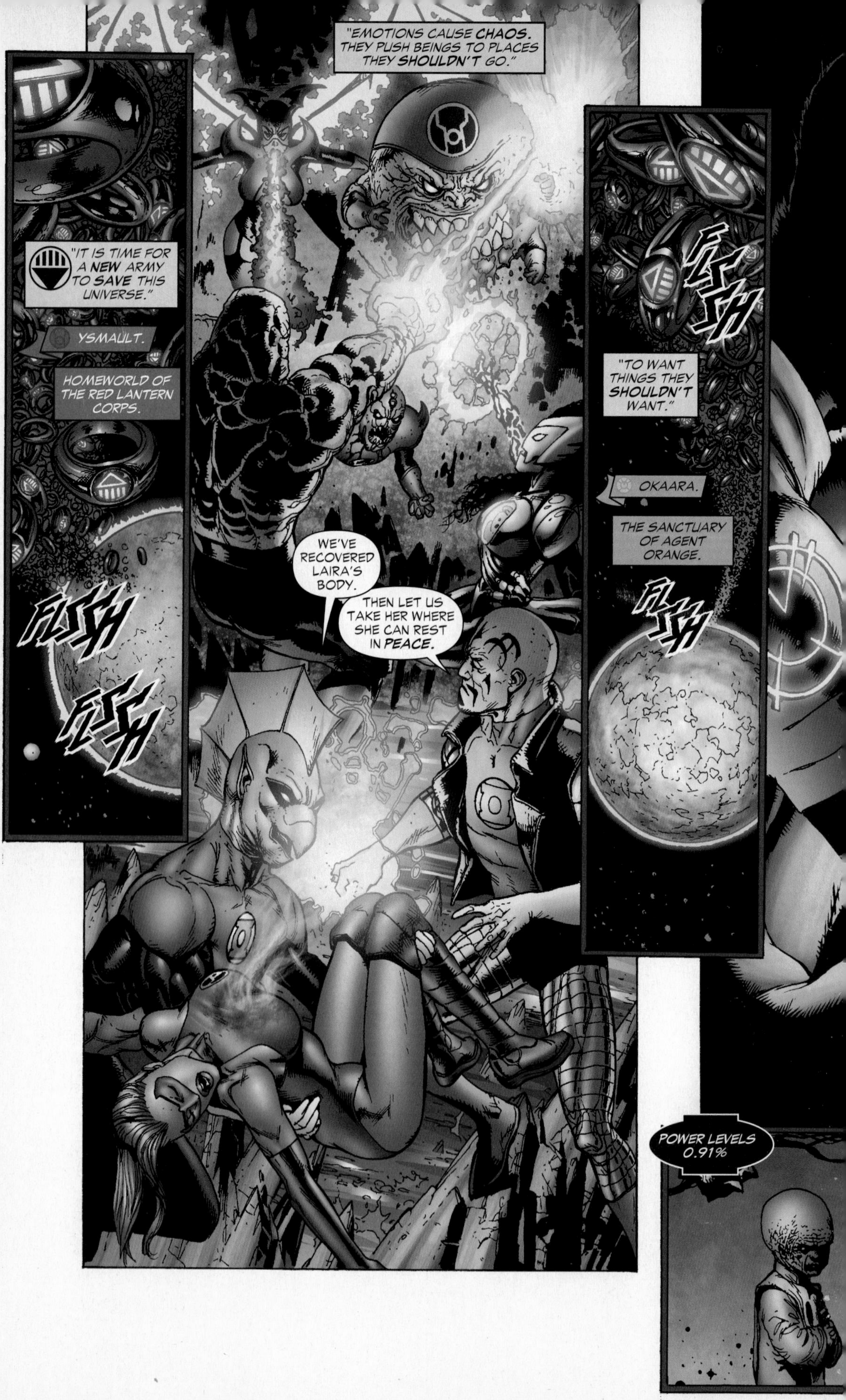
"EMOTIONS CAUSE CHAOS. THEY PUSH BEINGS TO PLACES THEY SHOULDN'T GO."
"IT IS TIME FOR A NEW ARMY TO SAVE THIS UNIVERSE."
YSMAULT.
HOMEWORLD OF THE RED LANTERN CORPS.
FLSSH
FLSSH
WE'VE RECOVERED LAIRA'S BODY.
THEN LET US TAKE HER WHERE SHE CAN REST IN PEACE.
FLSSH
"TO WANT THINGS THEY SHOULDN'T WANT."
OKAARA.
THE SANCTUARY OF AGENT ORANGE.
FLSSH
POWER LEVELS 0.91%

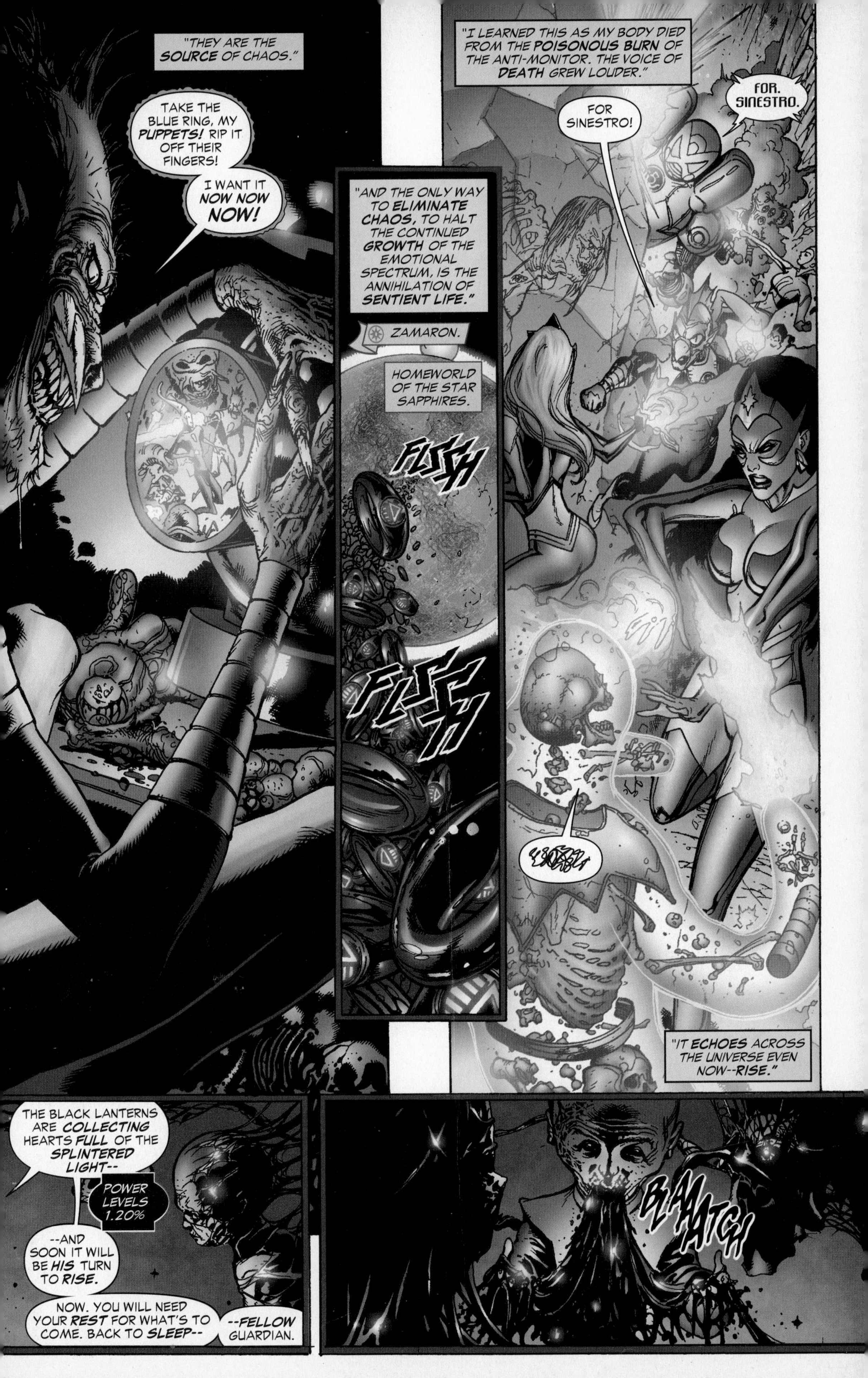
"THEY ARE THE SOURCE OF CHAOS."
TAKE THE BLUE RING, MY PUPPETS! RIP IT OFF THEIR FINGERS!
I WANT IT NOW NOW NOW!
"AND THE ONLY WAY TO ELIMINATE CHAOS, TO HALT THE CONTINUED GROWTH OF THE EMOTIONAL SPECTRUM, IS THE ANNIHILATION OF SENTIENT LIFE."
ZAMARON.
HOMEWORLD OF THE STAR SAPPHIRES.
FLSSH
FLSSH
"I LEARNED THIS AS MY BODY DIED FROM THE POISONOUS BURN OF THE ANTI-MONITOR. THE VOICE OF DEATH GREW LOUDER."
FOR SINESTRO!
FOR. SINESTRO.
"IT ECHOES ACROSS THE UNIVERSE EVEN NOW--RISE."
THE BLACK LANTERNS ARE COLLECTING HEARTS FULL OF THE SPLINTERED LIGHT--
POWER LEVELS 1.20%
--AND SOON IT WILL BE HIS TURN TO RISE.
NOW. YOU WILL NEED YOUR REST FOR WHAT'S TO COME. BACK TO SLEEP--
--FELLOW GUARDIAN.
BLAAATCH

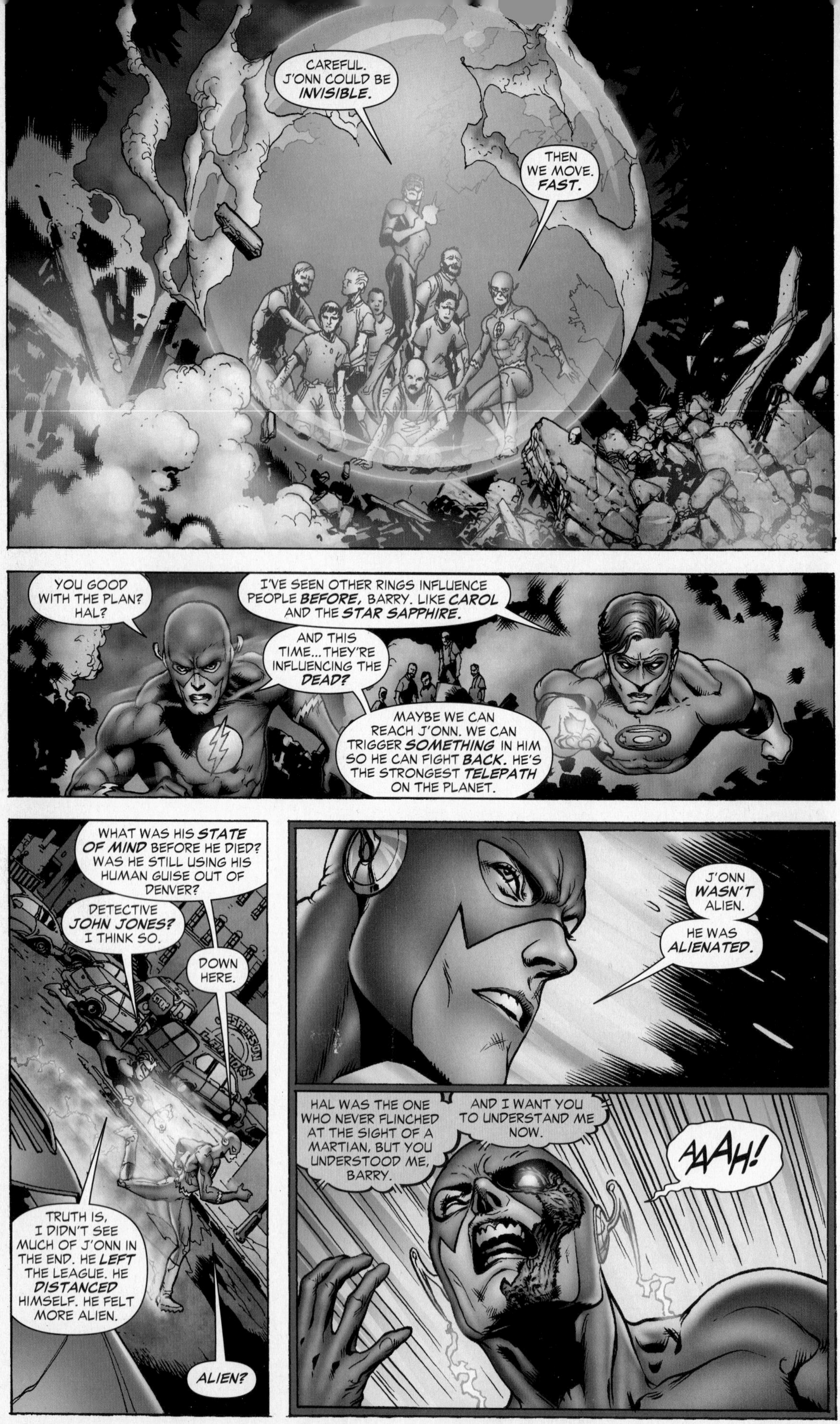

CAREFUL. J'ONN COULD BE INVISIBLE.
THEN WE MOVE. FAST.
YOU GOOD WITH THE PLAN? HAL?
I'VE SEEN OTHER RINGS INFLUENCE PEOPLE BEFORE, BARRY. LIKE CAROL AND THE STAR SAPPHIRE.
AND THIS TIME...THEY'RE INFLUENCING THE DEAD?
MAYBE WE CAN REACH J'ONN. WE CAN TRIGGER SOMETHING IN HIM SO HE CAN FIGHT BACK. HE'S THE STRONGEST TELEPATH ON THE PLANET.
WHAT WAS HIS STATE OF MIND BEFORE HE DIED? WAS HE STILL USING HIS HUMAN GUISE OUT OF DENVER?
DETECTIVE JOHN JONES? I THINK SO.
DOWN HERE.
TRUTH IS, I DIDN'T SEE MUCH OF J'ONN IN THE END. HE LEFT THE LEAGUE. HE DISTANCED HIMSELF. HE FELT MORE ALIEN.
ALIEN?
J'ONN WASN'T ALIEN.
HE WAS ALIENATED.
HAL WAS THE ONE WHO NEVER FLINCHED AT THE SIGHT OF A MARTIAN, BUT YOU UNDERSTOOD ME, BARRY.
AND I WANT YOU TO UNDERSTAND ME NOW.
AAAH!

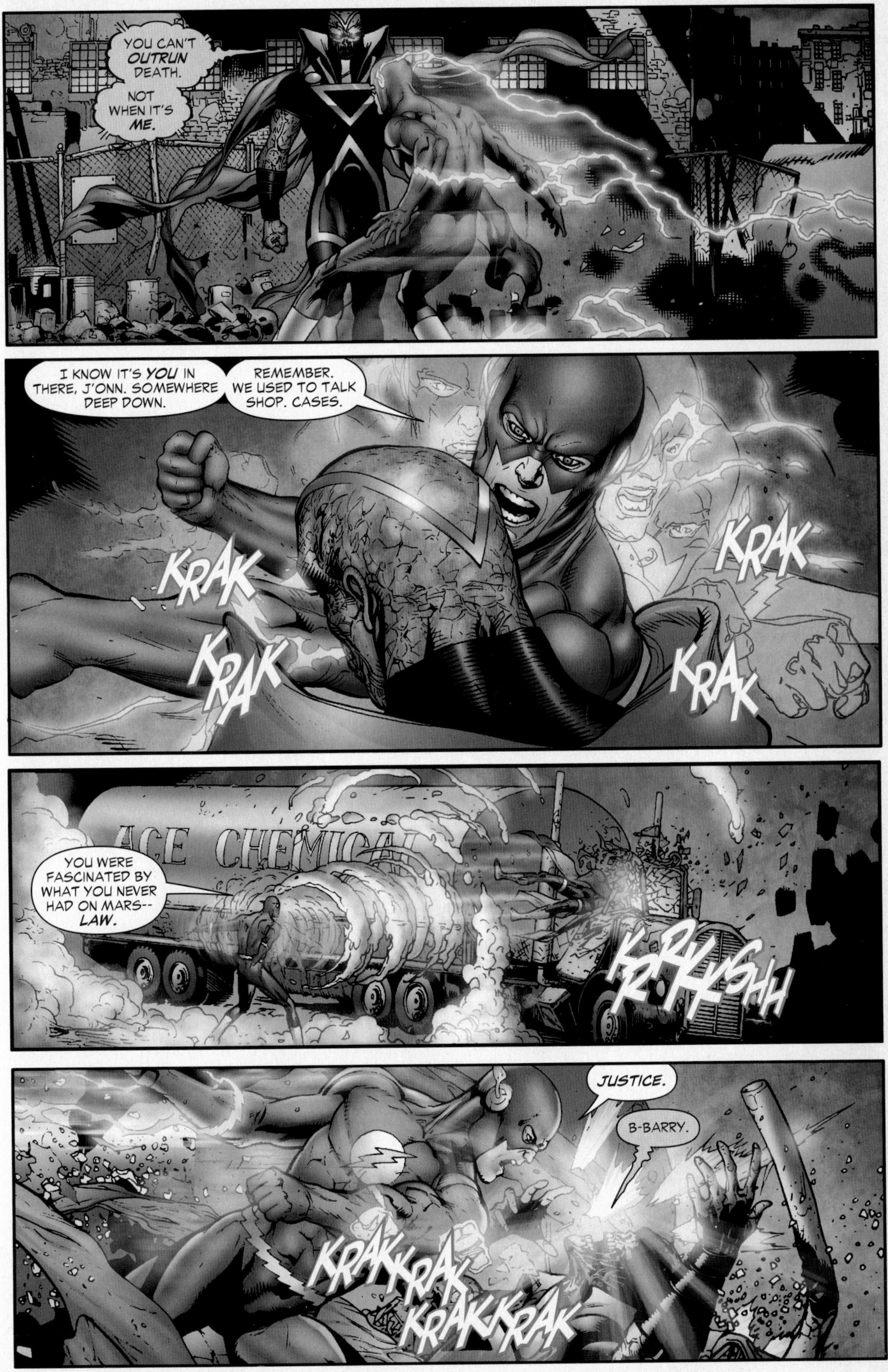
YOU CAN'T OUTRUN DEATH.
NOT WHEN IT'S ME.
I KNOW IT'S YOU IN THERE, J'ONN. SOMEWHERE DEEP DOWN.
REMEMBER. WE USED TO TALK SHOP. CASES.
KRAK
KRAK
KRAK
KRAK
ACE CHEMICAL
YOU WERE FASCINATED BY WHAT YOU NEVER HAD ON MARS-- LAW.
KRRKKSHH
JUSTICE.
B-BARRY.
KRAKKRAK
KRAKKRAK

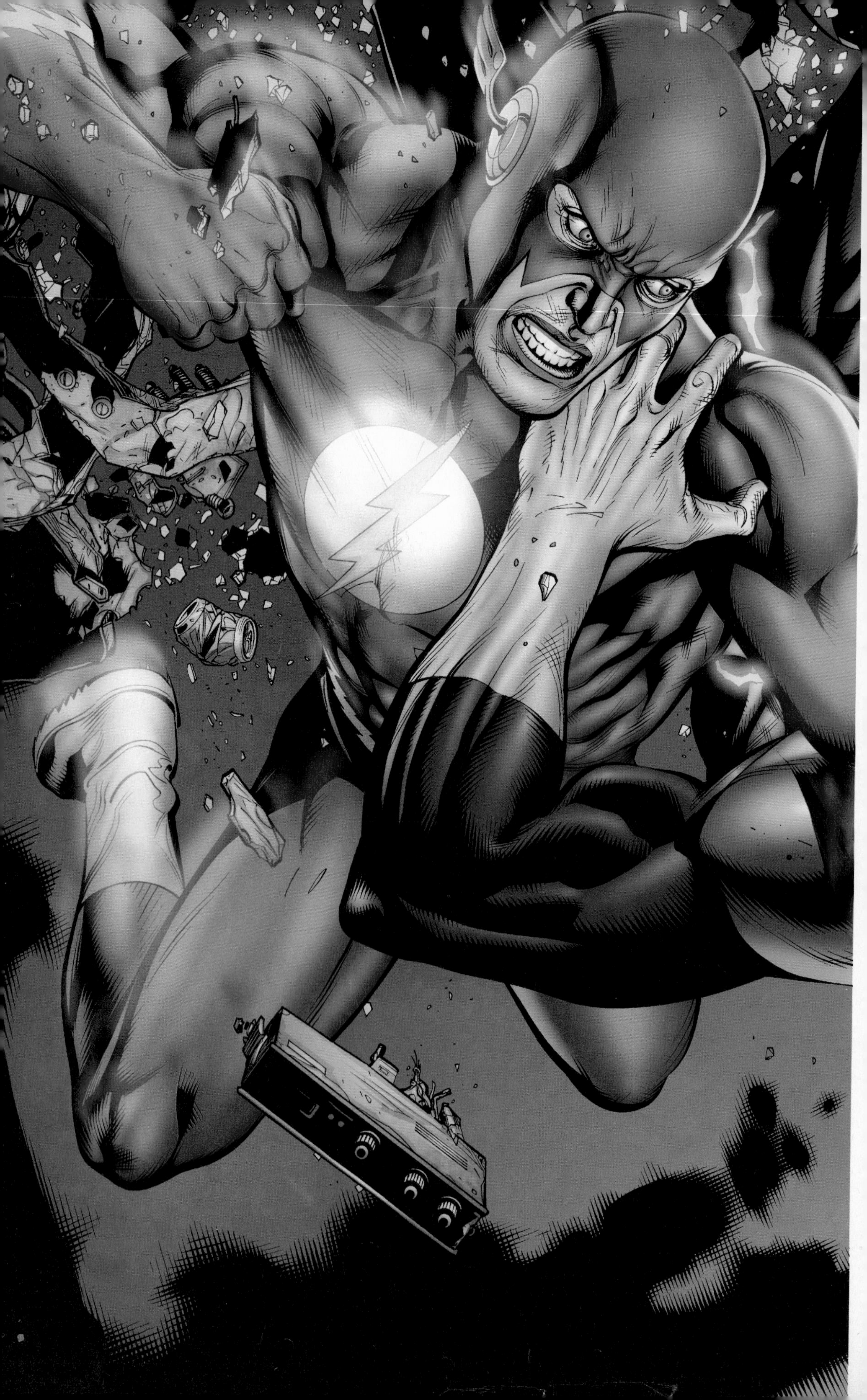

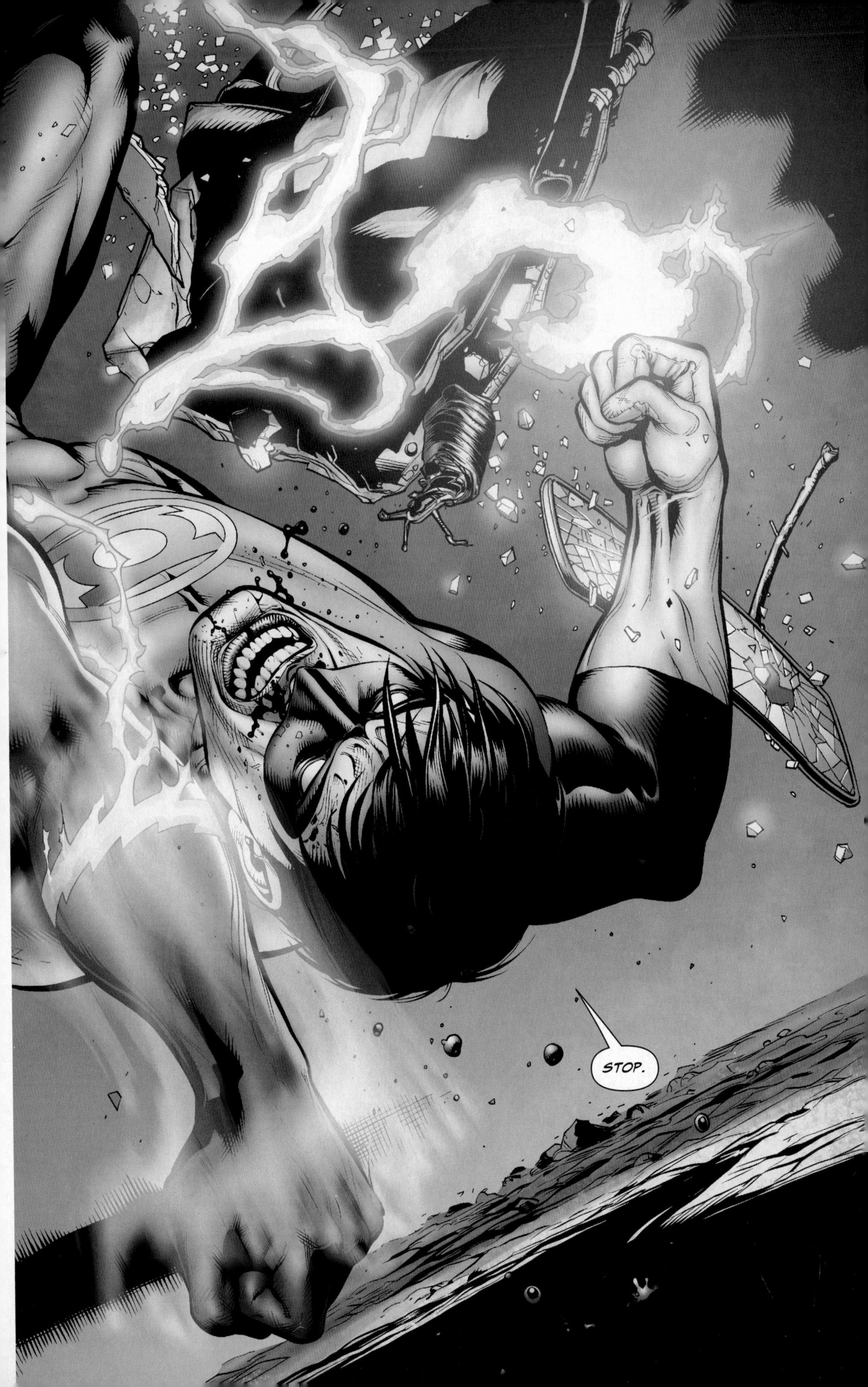
STOP.

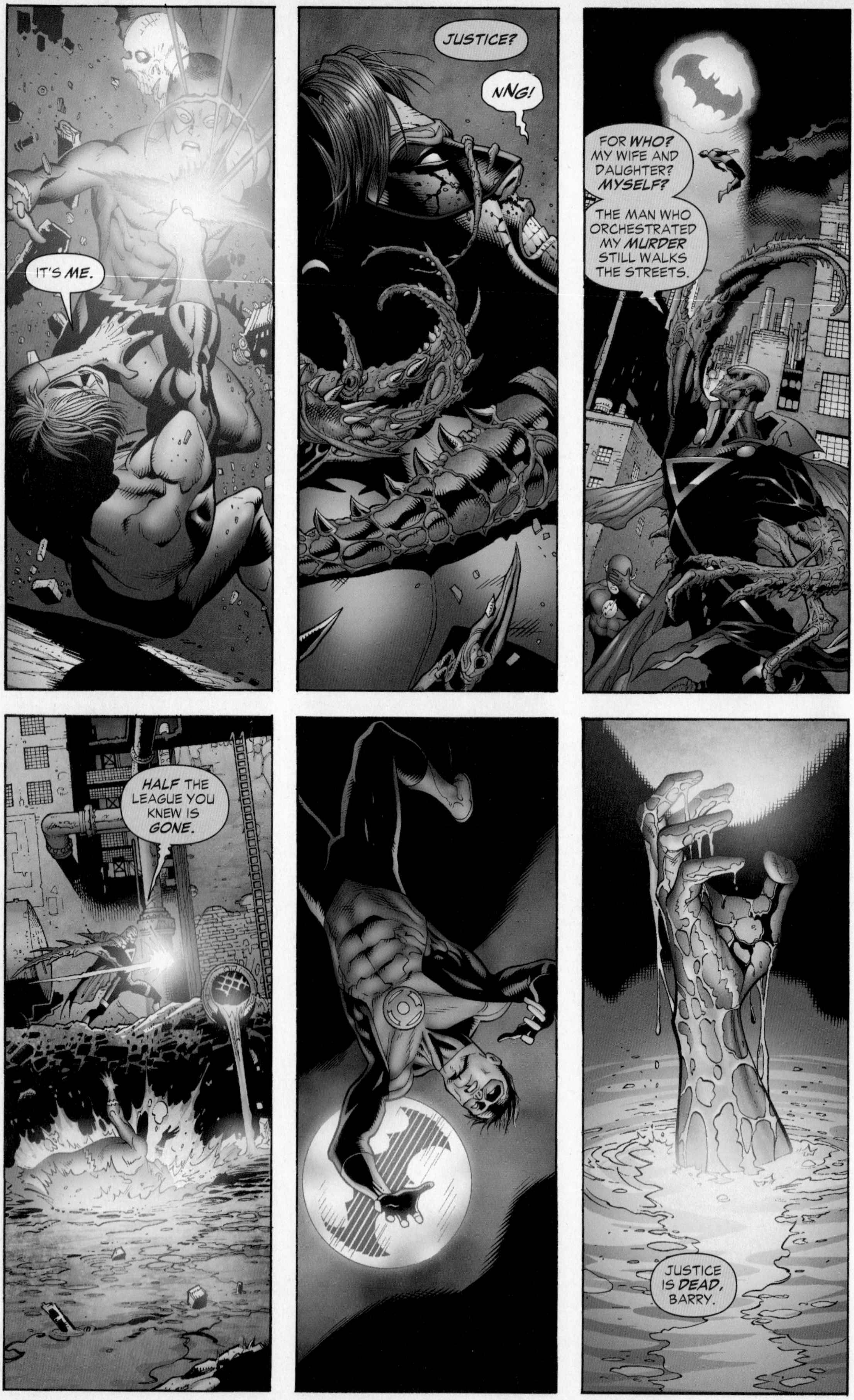
IT'S ME.
JUSTICE?
NNG!
FOR WHO? MY WIFE AND DAUGHTER? MYSELF?
THE MAN WHO ORCHESTRATED MY MURDER STILL WALKS THE STREETS.
HALF THE LEAGUE YOU KNEW IS GONE.
JUSTICE IS DEAD, BARRY.

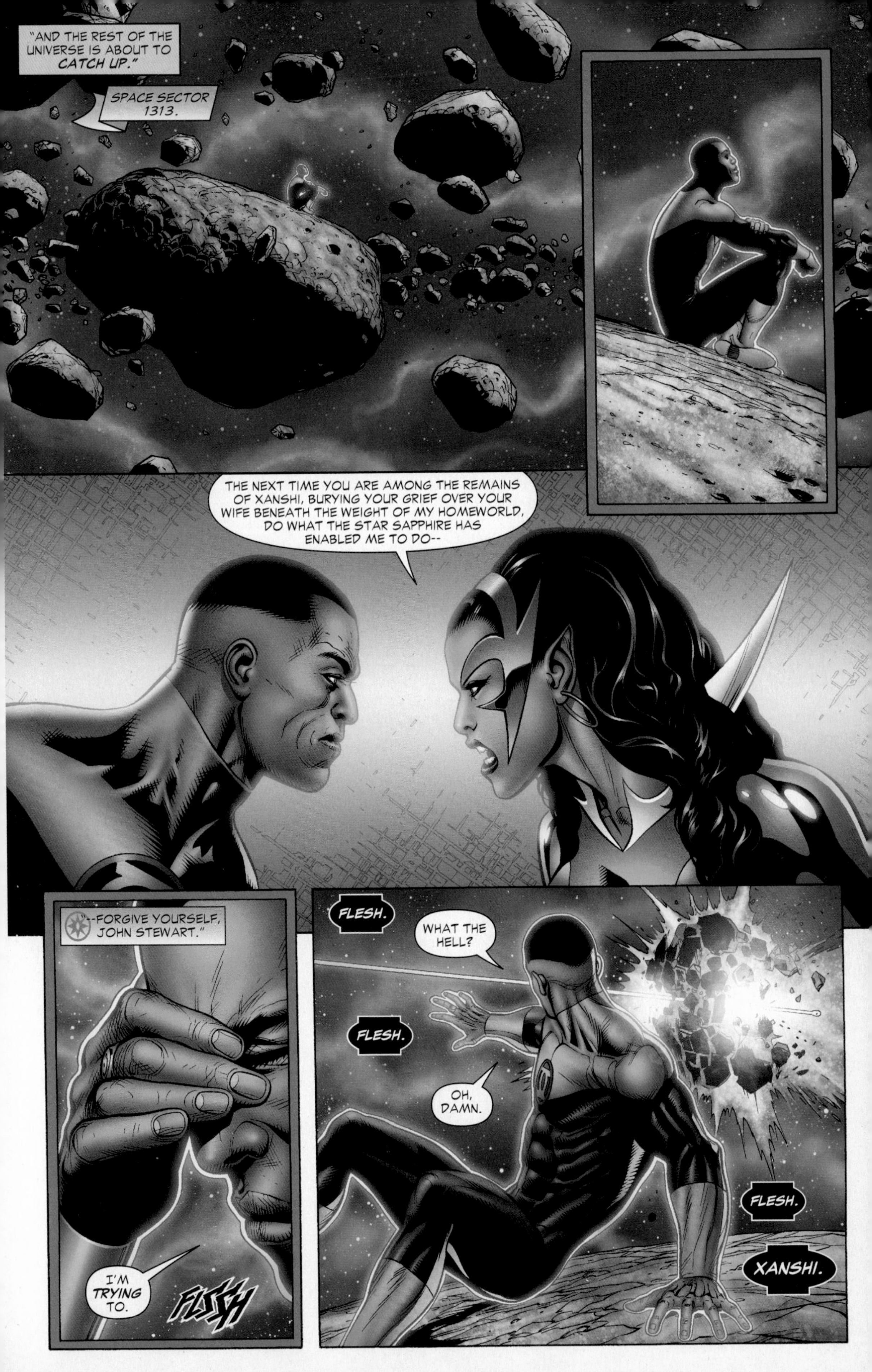
"AND THE REST OF THE UNIVERSE IS ABOUT TO CATCH UP."
SPACE SECTOR 1313.
THE NEXT TIME YOU ARE AMONG THE REMAINS OF XANSHI, BURYING YOUR GRIEF OVER YOUR WIFE BENEATH THE WEIGHT OF MY HOMEWORLD, DO WHAT THE STAR SAPPHIRE HAS ENABLED ME TO DO--
"--FORGIVE YOURSELF, JOHN STEWART."
I'M TRYING TO.
FLSSH
FLESH.
WHAT THE HELL?
FLESH.
OH, DAMN.
FLESH.
XANSHI.

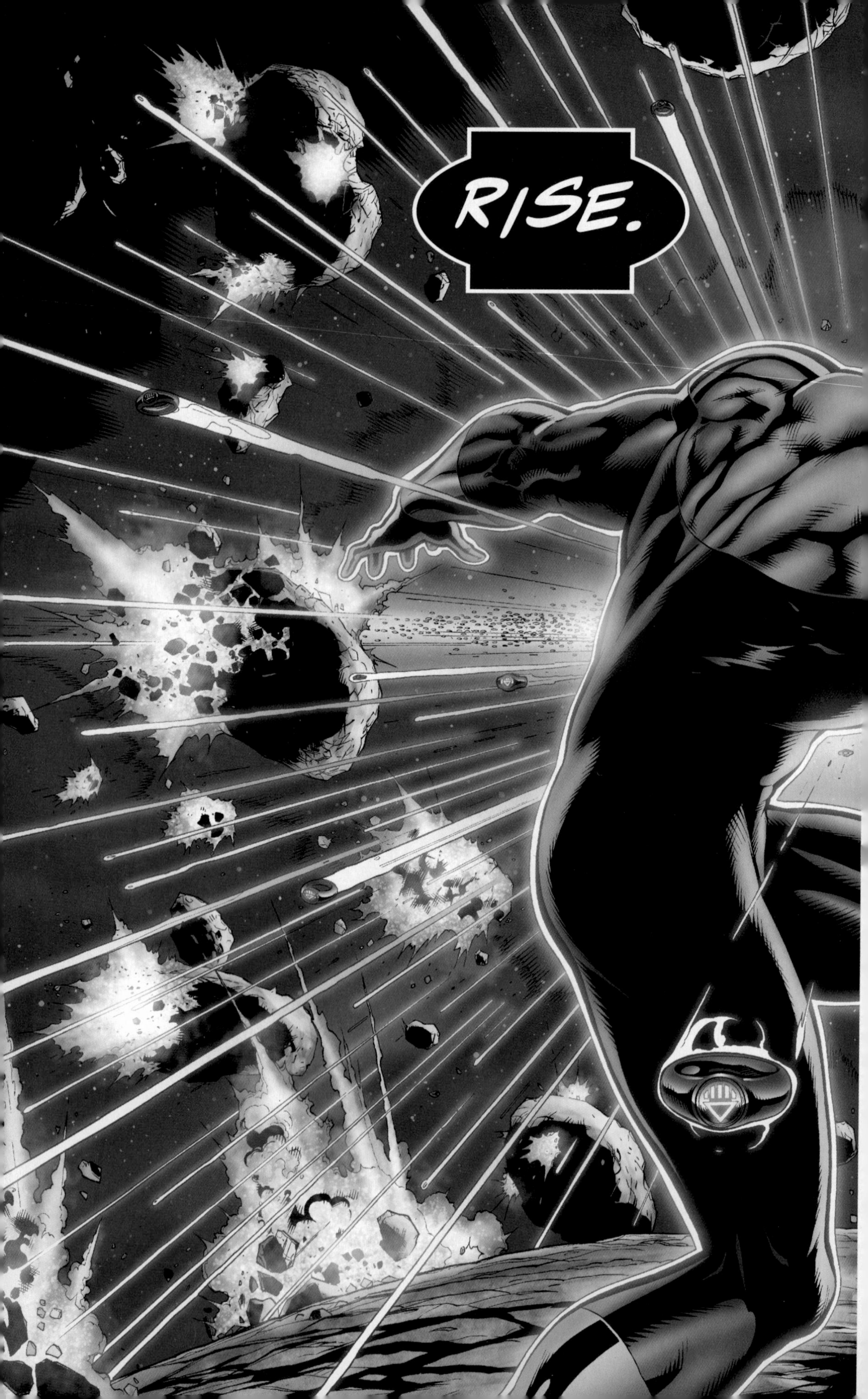
RISE.

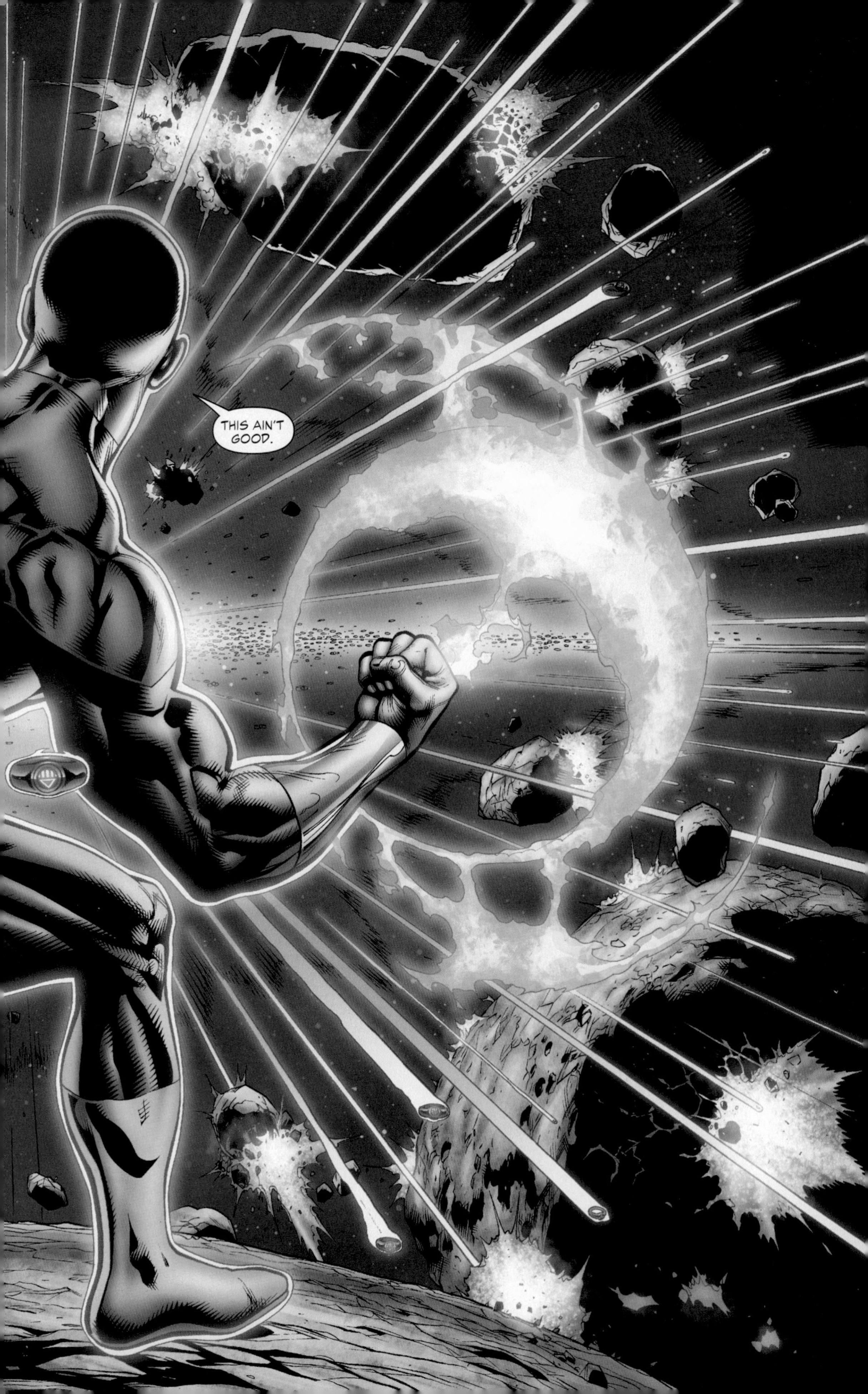
THIS AIN'T GOOD.

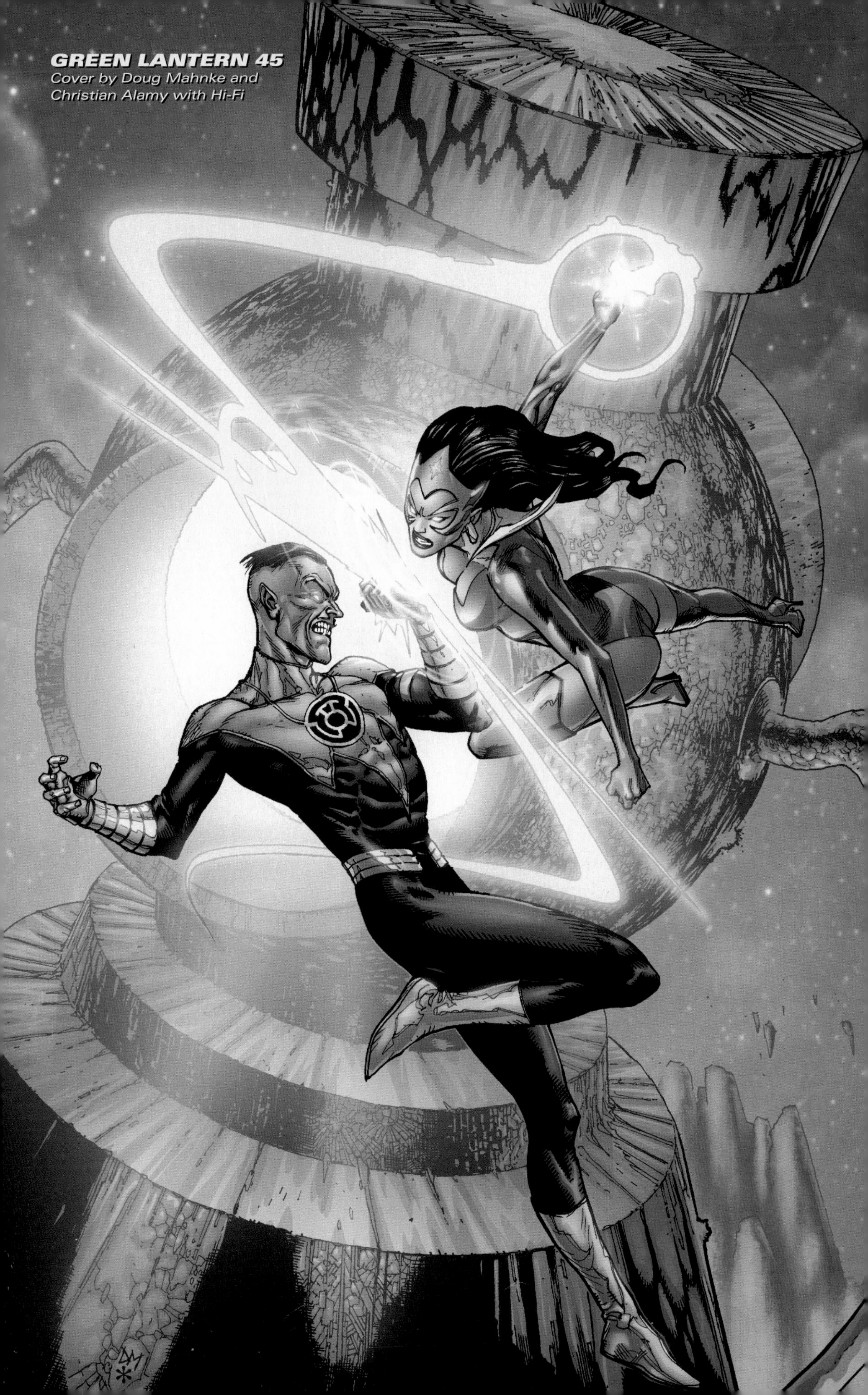

GREEN LANTERN 45
Cover by Doug Mahnke and Christian Alamy with Hi-Fi

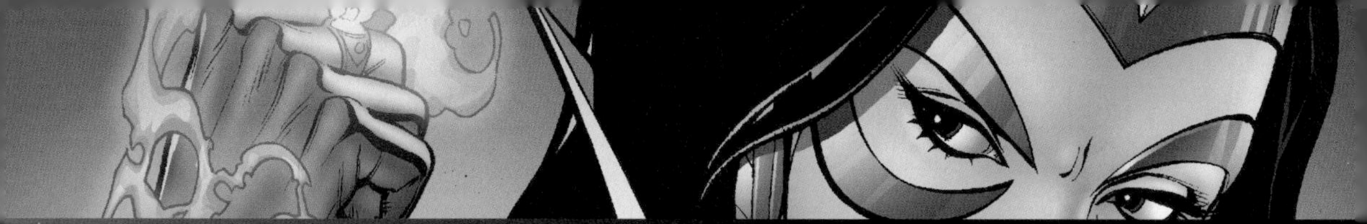

The prophecy from the great Book of Oa foretold the coming of various colored Lanterns beyond the will-driven Green Lantern Corps.

It told of their feuds and what would befall them all.

But no one heeded the warnings and now they all stand on the precipice of extinction...

LOVE HURTS

DOUG MAHNKE
PENCILS

CHRISTIAN ALAMY
DOUG MAHNKE
TOM NGUYEN
INKS

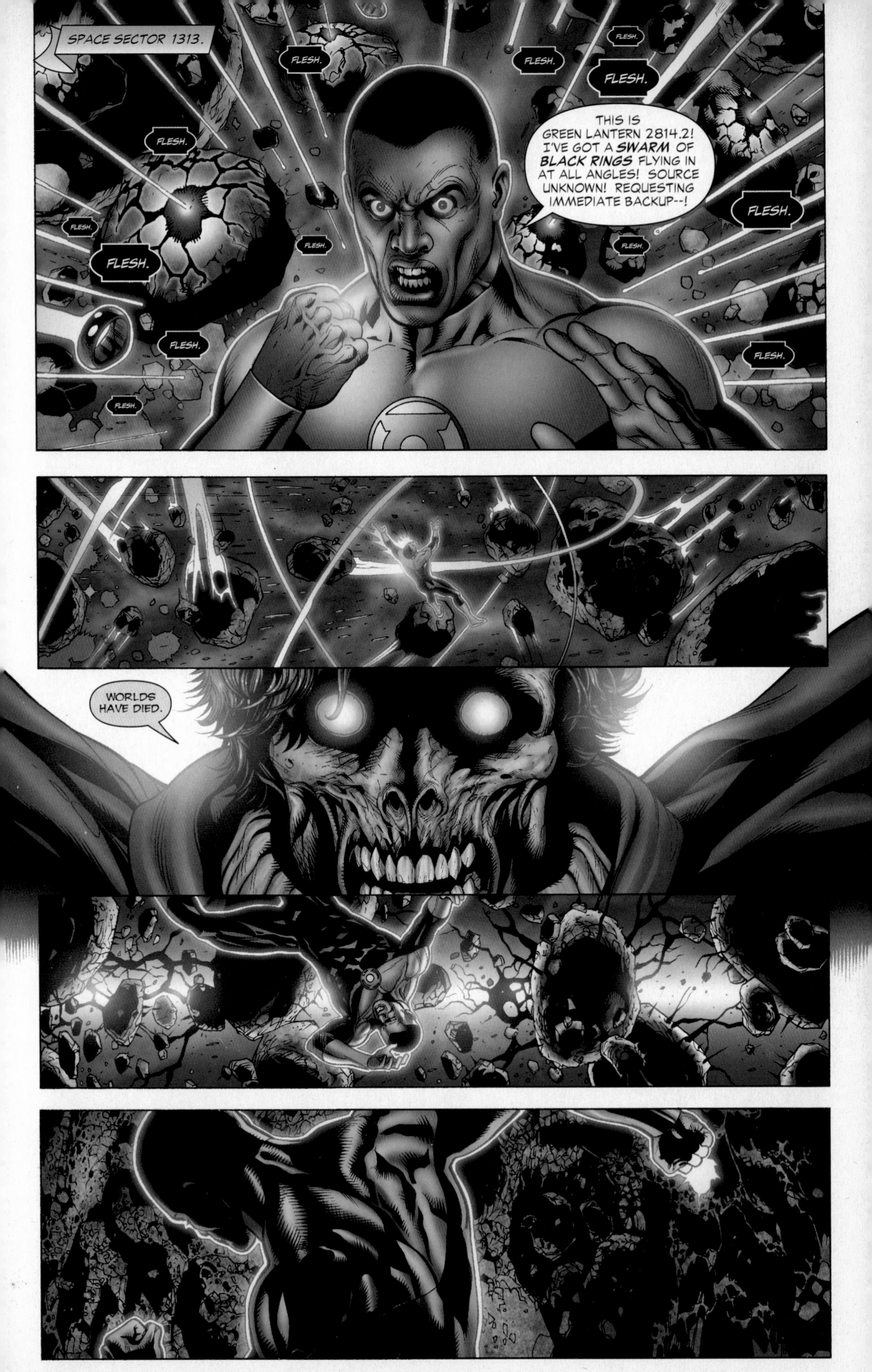
SPACE SECTOR 1313.
FLESH.
FLESH.
FLESH.
FLESH.
THIS IS GREEN LANTERN 2814.2! I'VE GOT A SWARM OF BLACK RINGS FLYING IN AT ALL ANGLES! SOURCE UNKNOWN! REQUESTING IMMEDIATE BACKUP--!
FLESH.
FLESH.
FLESH.
FLESH.
FLESH.
FLESH.
FLESH.
FLESH.
FLESH.
WORLDS HAVE DIED.

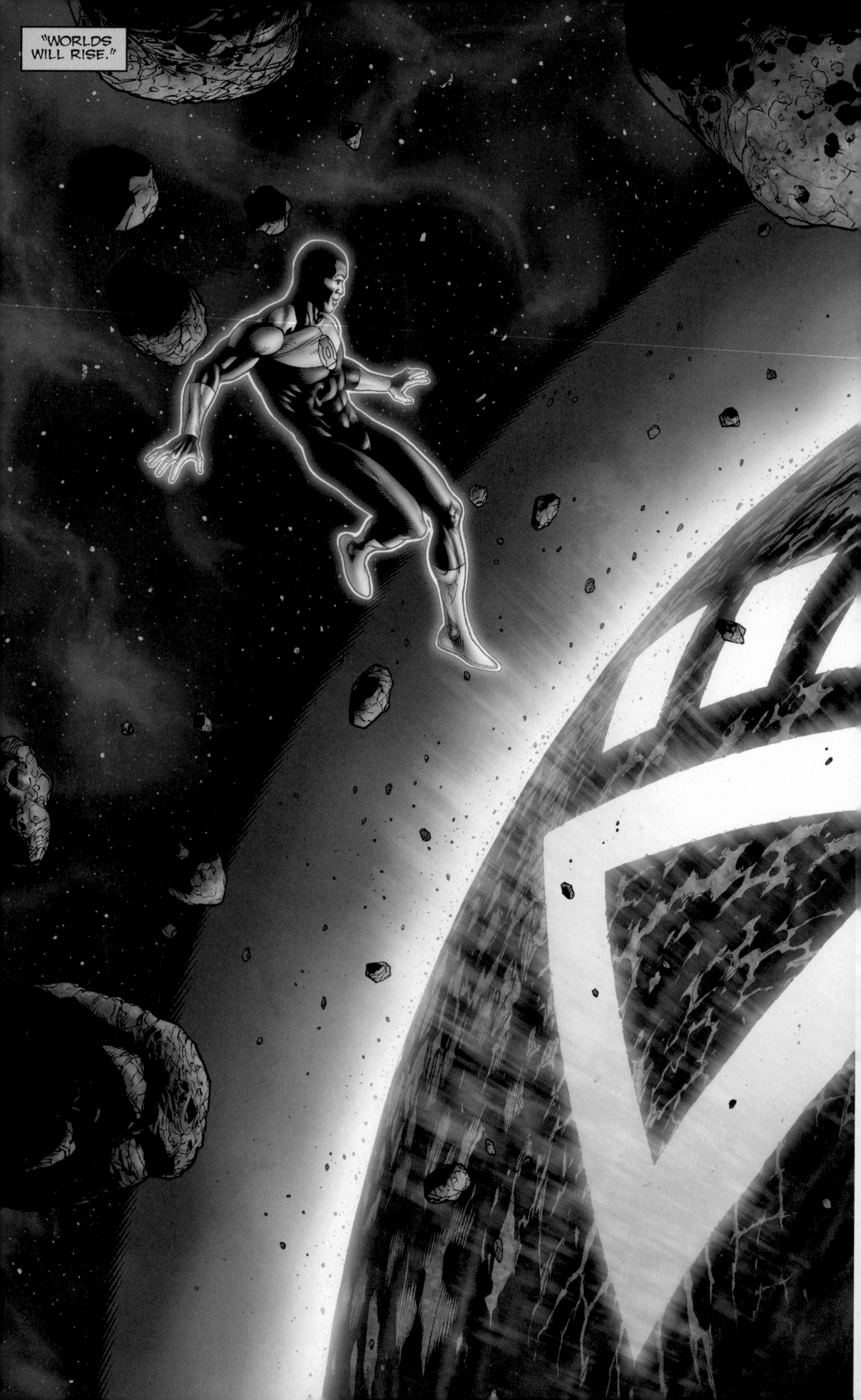
"WORLDS WILL RISE."

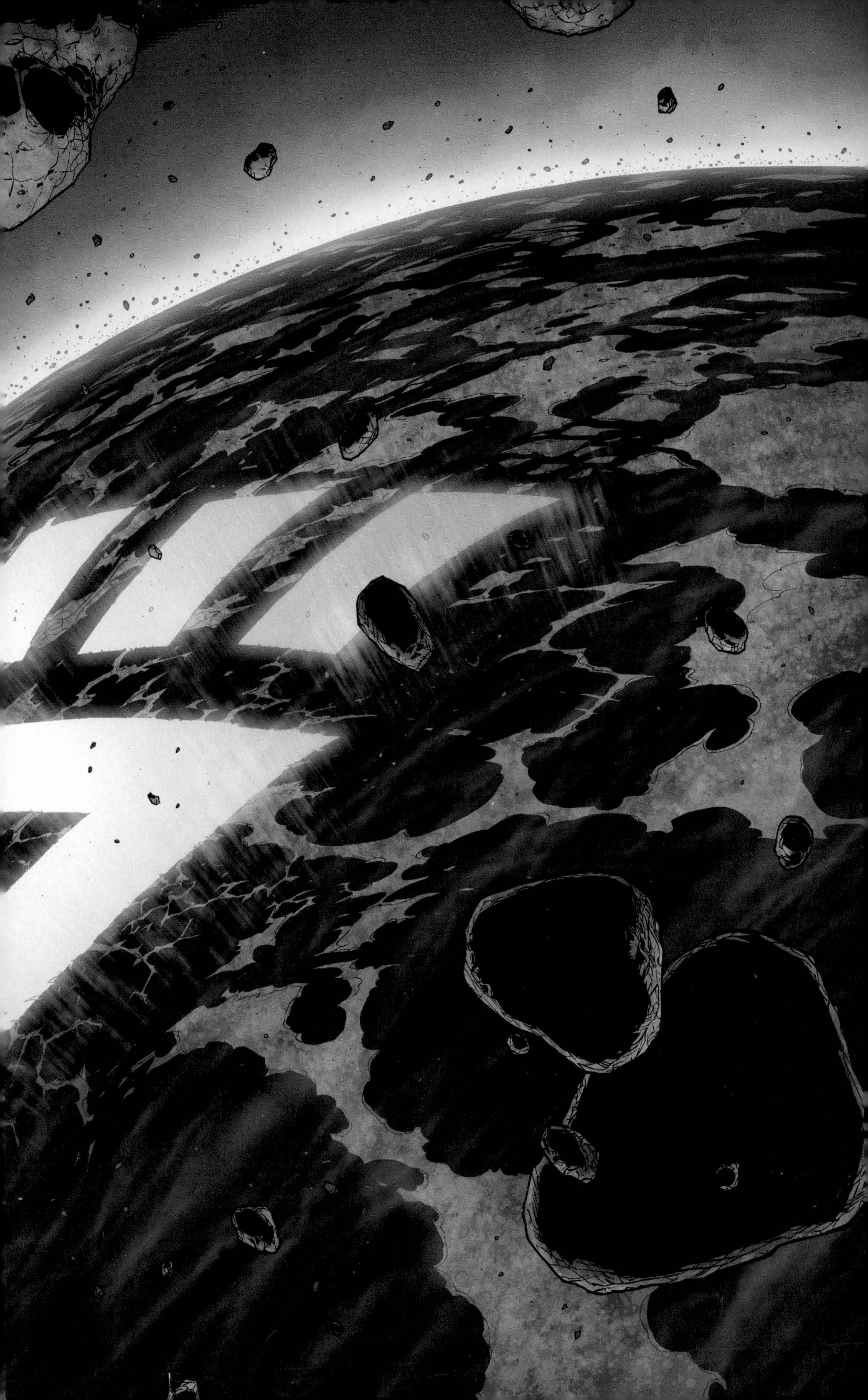

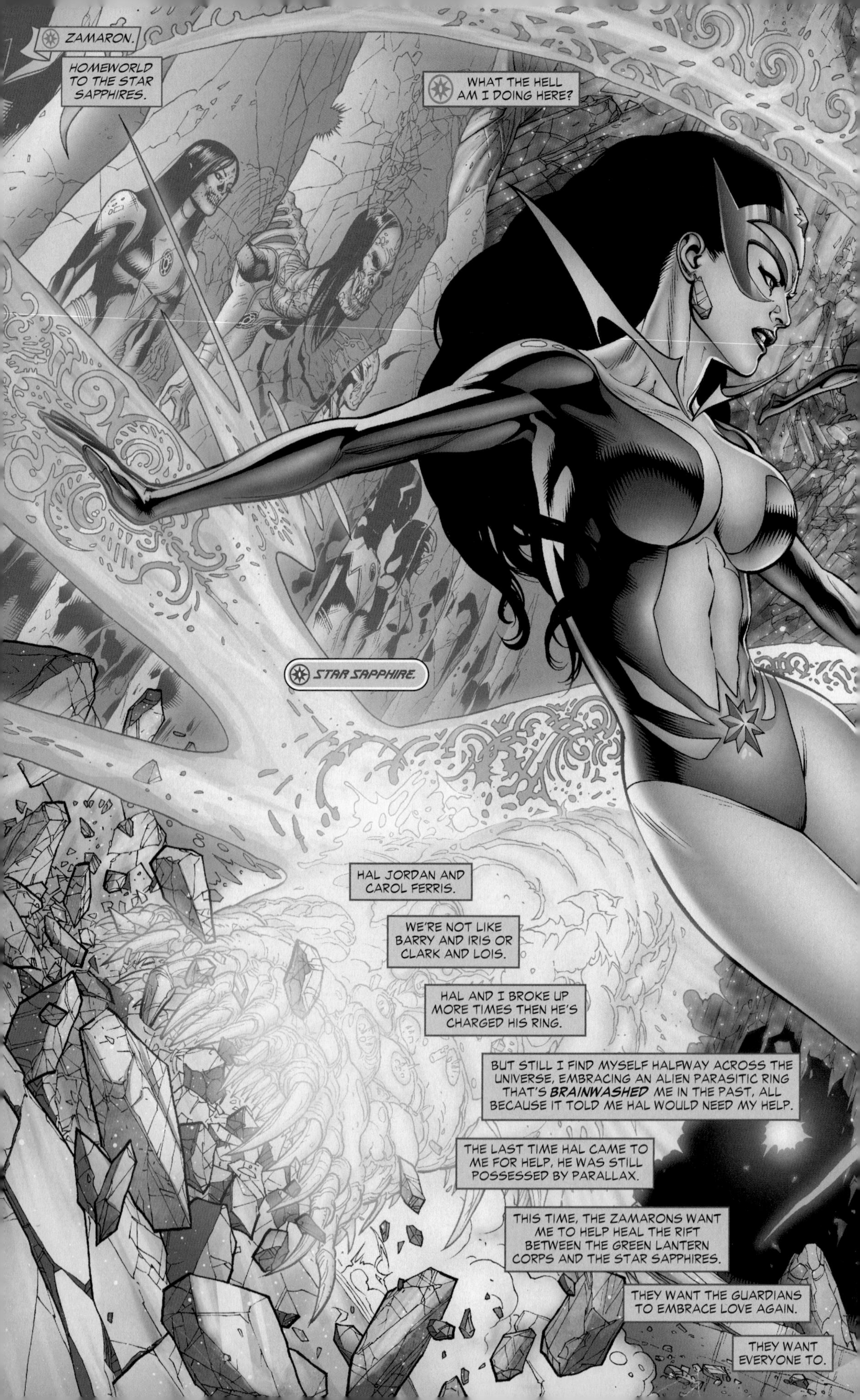
ZAMARON.
HOMEWORLD TO THE STAR SAPPHIRES.
WHAT THE HELL AM I DOING HERE?
STAR SAPPHIRE.
HAL JORDAN AND CAROL FERRIS.
WE'RE NOT LIKE BARRY AND IRIS OR CLARK AND LOIS.
HAL AND I BROKE UP MORE TIMES THEN HE'S CHARGED HIS RING.
BUT STILL I FIND MYSELF HALFWAY ACROSS THE UNIVERSE, EMBRACING AN ALIEN PARASITIC RING THAT'S BRAINWASHED ME IN THE PAST, ALL BECAUSE IT TOLD ME HAL WOULD NEED MY HELP.
THE LAST TIME HAL CAME TO ME FOR HELP, HE WAS STILL POSSESSED BY PARALLAX.
THIS TIME, THE ZAMARONS WANT ME TO HELP HEAL THE RIFT BETWEEN THE GREEN LANTERN CORPS AND THE STAR SAPPHIRES.
THEY WANT THE GUARDIANS TO EMBRACE LOVE AGAIN.
THEY WANT EVERYONE TO.

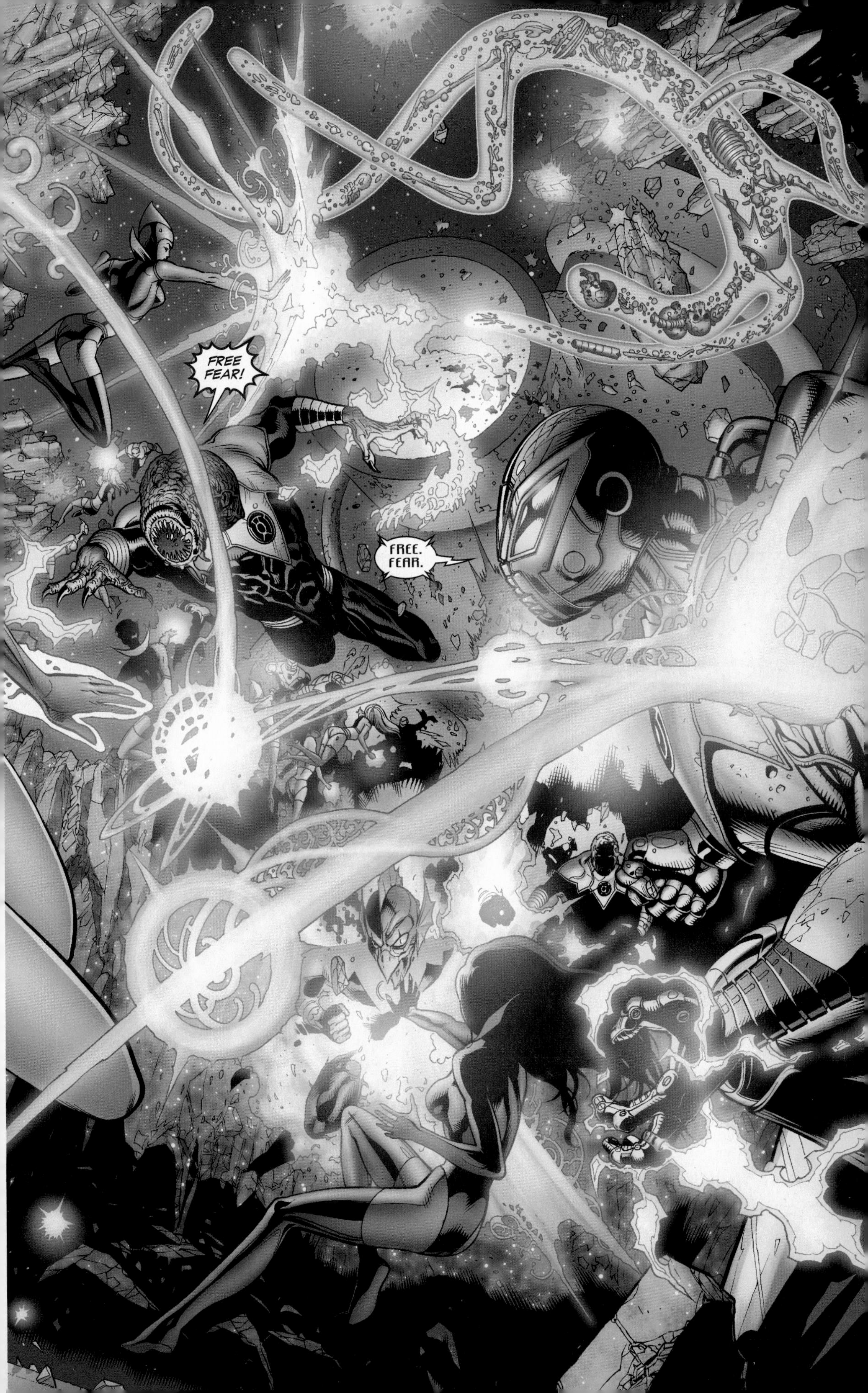
FREE FEAR!
FREE. FEAR.

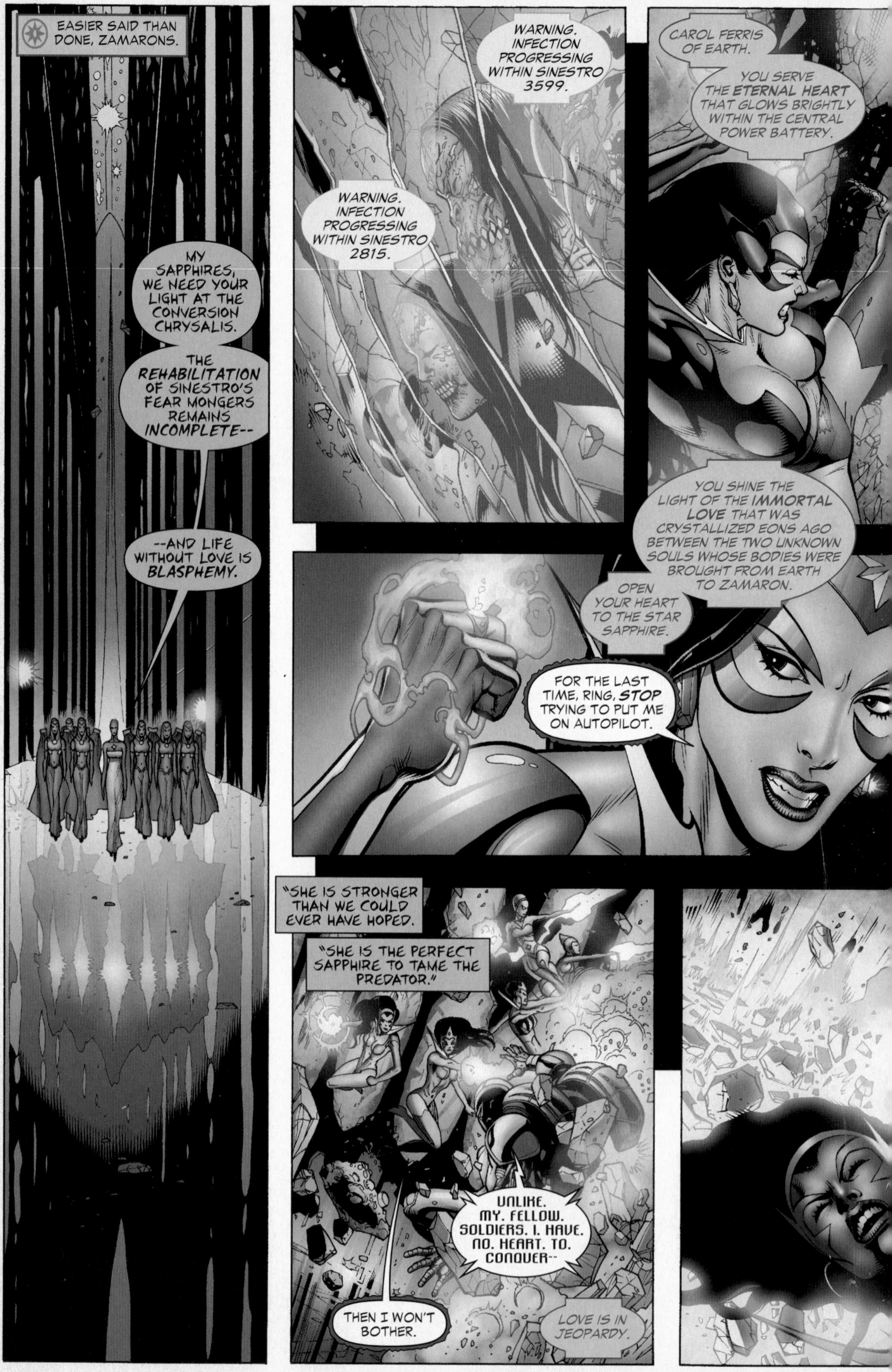
EASIER SAID THAN DONE, ZAMARONS.
MY SAPPHIRES, WE NEED YOUR LIGHT AT THE CONVERSION CHRYSALIS.
THE REHABILITATION OF SINESTRO'S FEAR MONGERS REMAINS INCOMPLETE--
--AND LIFE WITHOUT LOVE IS BLASPHEMY.
WARNING. INFECTION PROGRESSING WITHIN SINESTRO 3599.
WARNING. INFECTION PROGRESSING WITHIN SINESTRO 2815.
CAROL FERRIS OF EARTH.
YOU SERVE THE ETERNAL HEART THAT GLOWS BRIGHTLY WITHIN THE CENTRAL POWER BATTERY.
YOU SHINE THE LIGHT OF THE IMMORTAL LOVE THAT WAS CRYSTALLIZED EONS AGO BETWEEN THE TWO UNKNOWN SOULS WHOSE BODIES WERE BROUGHT FROM EARTH TO ZAMARON.
OPEN YOUR HEART TO THE STAR SAPPHIRE.
FOR THE LAST TIME, RING, STOP TRYING TO PUT ME ON AUTOPILOT.
"SHE IS STRONGER THAN WE COULD EVER HAVE HOPED.
"SHE IS THE PERFECT SAPPHIRE TO TAME THE PREDATOR."
UNLIKE. MY. FELLOW. SOLDIERS. I. HAVE. NO. HEART. TO. CONQUER--
THEN I WON'T BOTHER.
LOVE IS IN JEOPARDY.

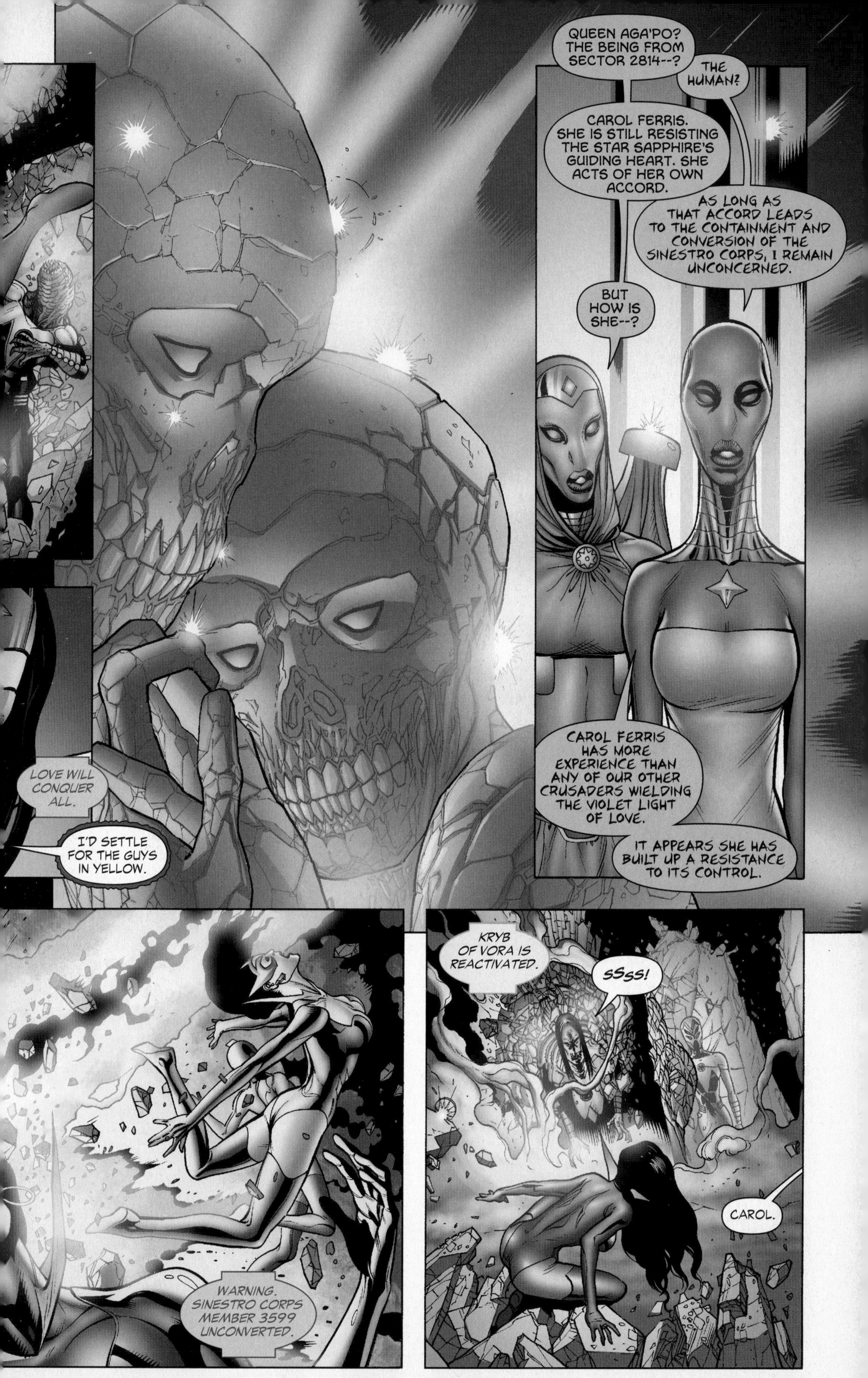
QUEEN AGA'PO? THE BEING FROM SECTOR 2814--?
THE HUMAN?
CAROL FERRIS. SHE IS STILL RESISTING THE STAR SAPPHIRE'S GUIDING HEART. SHE ACTS OF HER OWN ACCORD.
AS LONG AS THAT ACCORD LEADS TO THE CONTAINMENT AND CONVERSION OF THE SINESTRO CORPS, I REMAIN UNCONCERNED.
BUT HOW IS SHE--?
CAROL FERRIS HAS MORE EXPERIENCE THAN ANY OF OUR OTHER CRUSADERS WIELDING THE VIOLET LIGHT OF LOVE.
IT APPEARS SHE HAS BUILT UP A RESISTANCE TO ITS CONTROL.
LOVE WILL CONQUER ALL.
I'D SETTLE FOR THE GUYS IN YELLOW.
WARNING. SINESTRO CORPS MEMBER 3599 UNCONVERTED.
KRYB OF VORA IS REACTIVATED.
SSSS!
CAROL.

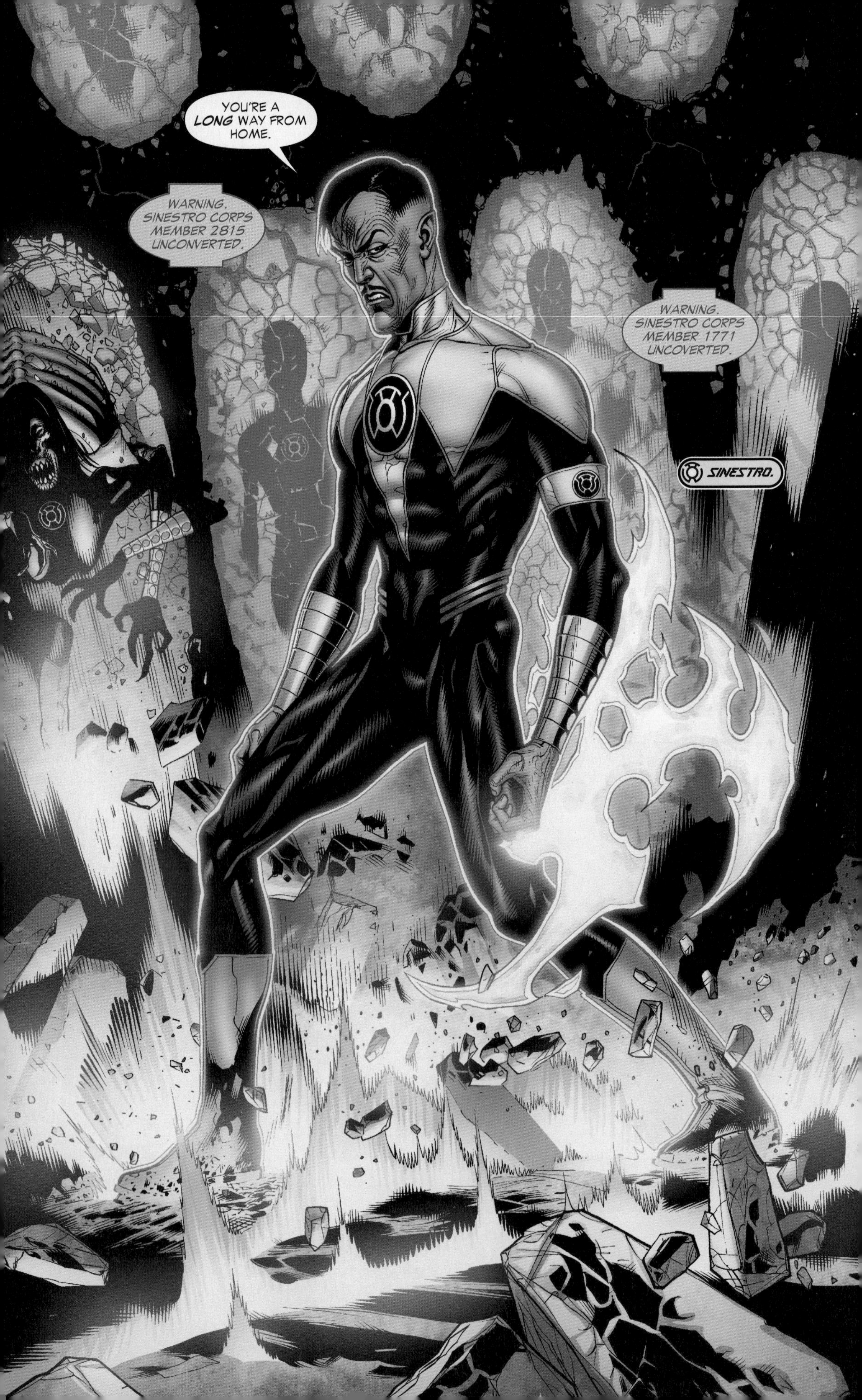
YOU'RE A LONG WAY FROM HOME.
WARNING. SINESTRO CORPS MEMBER 2815 UNCONVERTED.
WARNING. SINESTRO CORPS MEMBER 1771 UNCOVERTED.
SINESTRO.

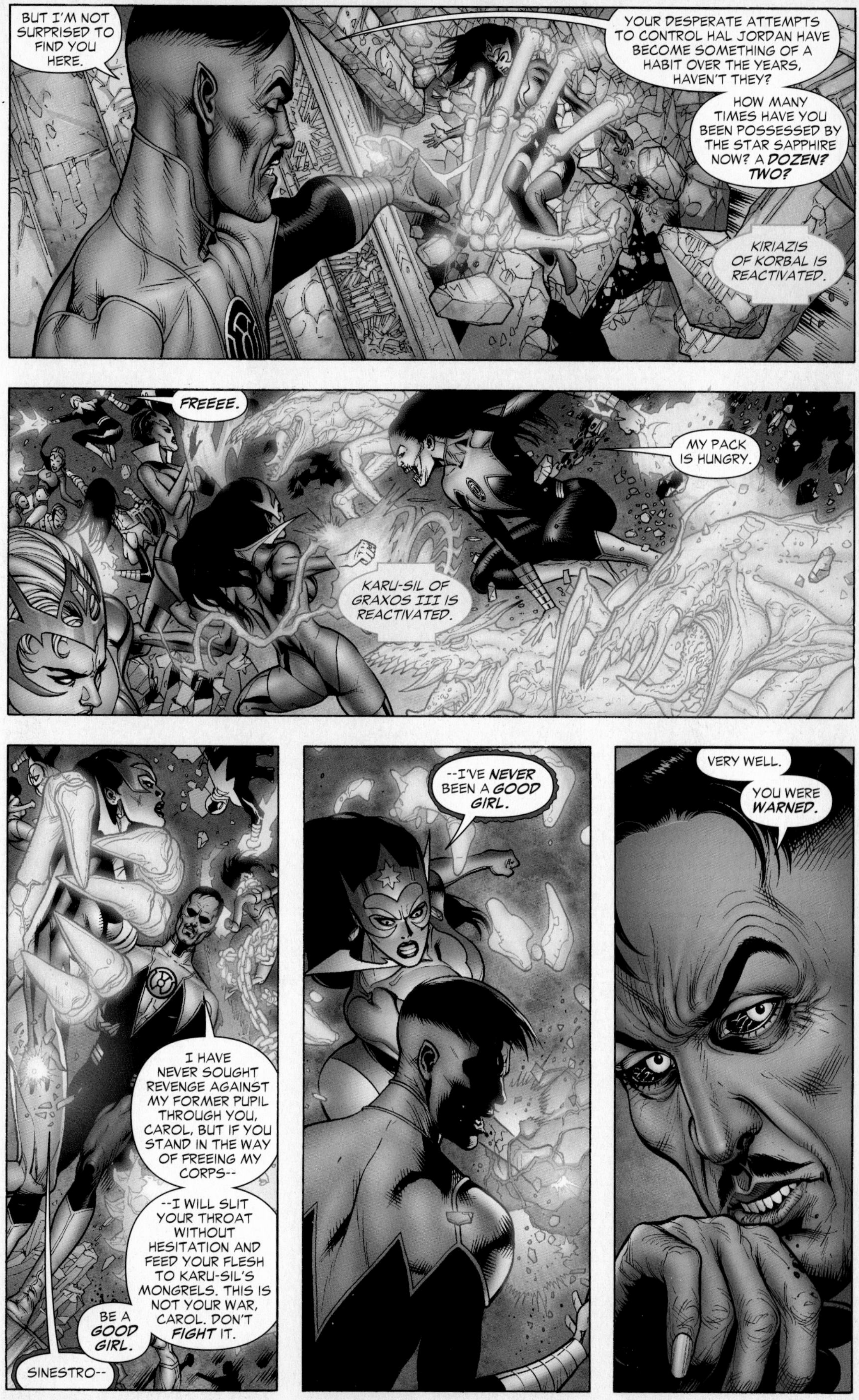
BUT I'M NOT SURPRISED TO FIND YOU HERE.
YOUR DESPERATE ATTEMPTS TO CONTROL HAL JORDAN HAVE BECOME SOMETHING OF A HABIT OVER THE YEARS, HAVEN'T THEY?
HOW MANY TIMES HAVE YOU BEEN POSSESSED BY THE STAR SAPPHIRE NOW? A DOZEN? TWO?
KIRIAZIS OF KORBAL IS REACTIVATED.
FREEEE.
MY PACK IS HUNGRY.
KARU-SIL OF GRAXOS III IS REACTIVATED.
I HAVE NEVER SOUGHT REVENGE AGAINST MY FORMER PUPIL THROUGH YOU, CAROL, BUT IF YOU STAND IN THE WAY OF FREEING MY CORPS--
--I WILL SLIT YOUR THROAT WITHOUT HESITATION AND FEED YOUR FLESH TO KARU-SIL'S MONGRELS. THIS IS NOT YOUR WAR, CAROL. DON'T FIGHT IT.
BE A GOOD GIRL.
SINESTRO--
--I'VE NEVER BEEN A GOOD GIRL.
VERY WELL.
YOU WERE WARNED.

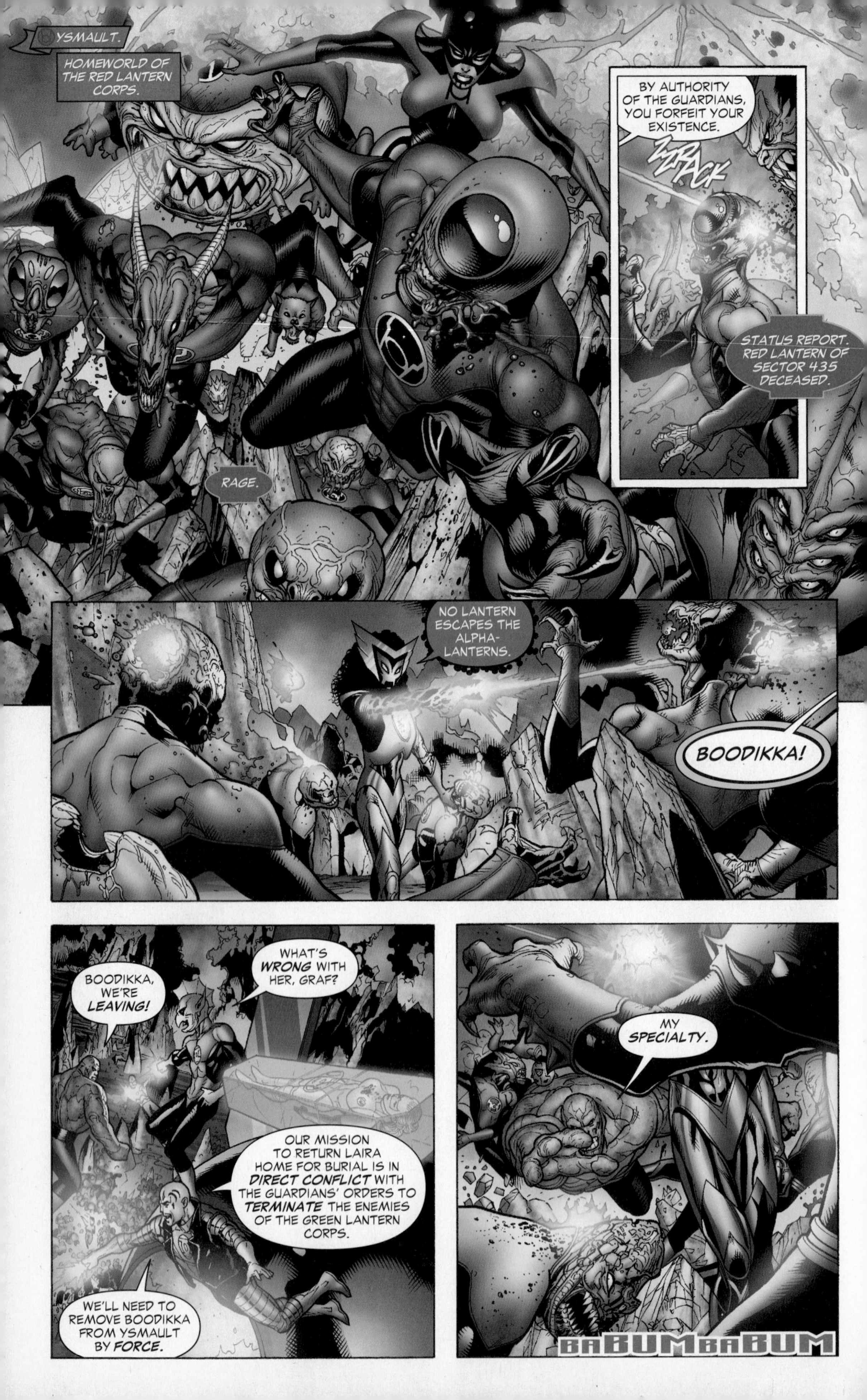
YSMAULT.
HOMEWORLD OF THE RED LANTERN CORPS.
BY AUTHORITY OF THE GUARDIANS, YOU FORFEIT YOUR EXISTENCE.
ZZRACK
STATUS REPORT. RED LANTERN OF SECTOR 435 DECEASED.
RAGE.
NO LANTERN ESCAPES THE ALPHA-LANTERNS.
BOODIKKA!
BOODIKKA, WE'RE LEAVING!
WHAT'S WRONG WITH HER, GRAF?
OUR MISSION TO RETURN LAIRA HOME FOR BURIAL IS IN DIRECT CONFLICT WITH THE GUARDIANS' ORDERS TO TERMINATE THE ENEMIES OF THE GREEN LANTERN CORPS.
WE'LL NEED TO REMOVE BOODIKKA FROM YSMAULT BY FORCE.
MY SPECIALTY.
BABUMBABUM

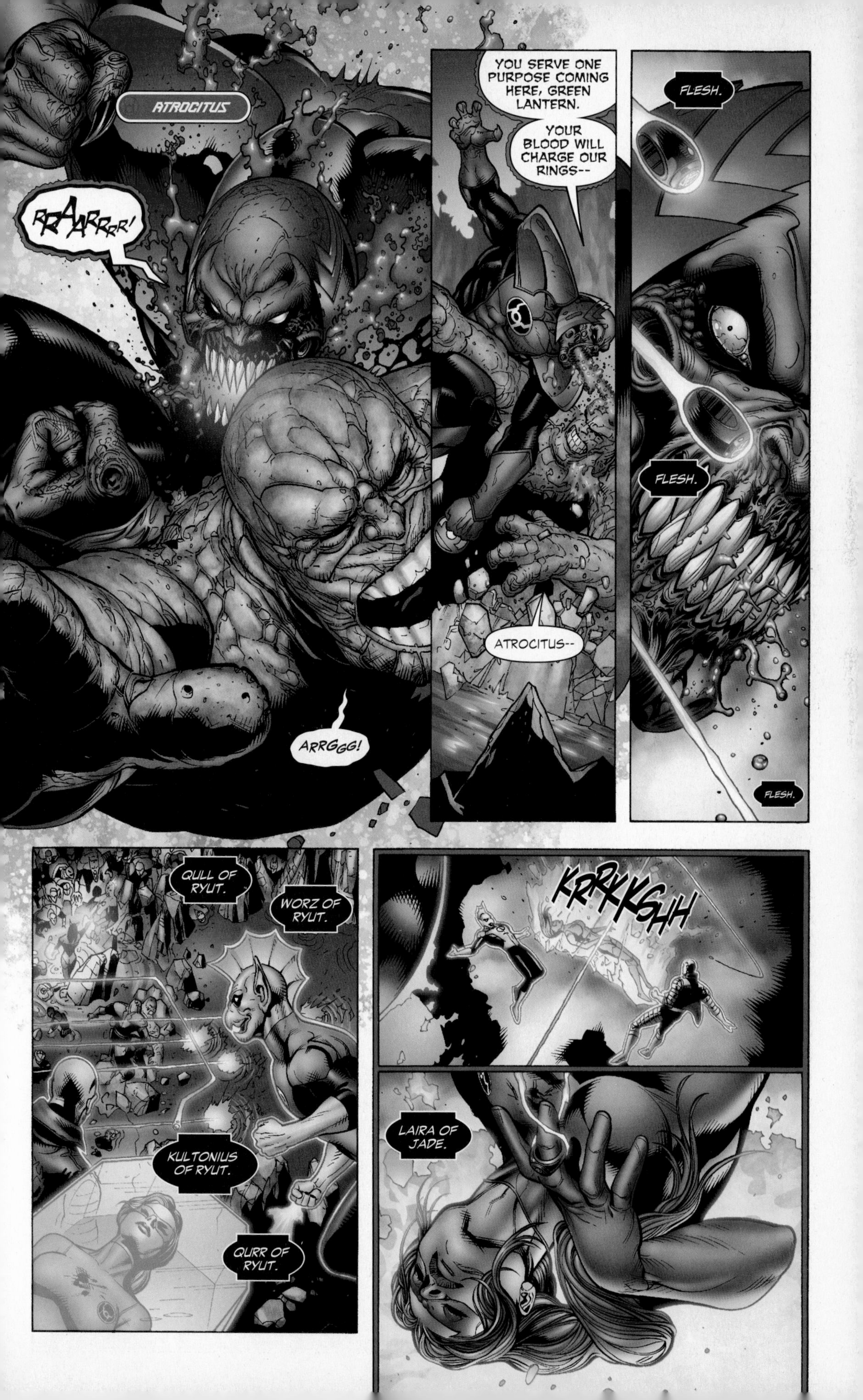
ATROCITUS
RRAARRRR!
ARRGGG!
YOU SERVE ONE PURPOSE COMING HERE, GREEN LANTERN.
YOUR BLOOD WILL CHARGE OUR RINGS--
ATROCITUS--
FLESH.
FLESH.
FLESH.
QULL OF RYUT.
WORZ OF RYUT.
KULTONIUS OF RYUT.
QURR OF RYUT.
KRRKKSHH
LAIRA OF JADE.

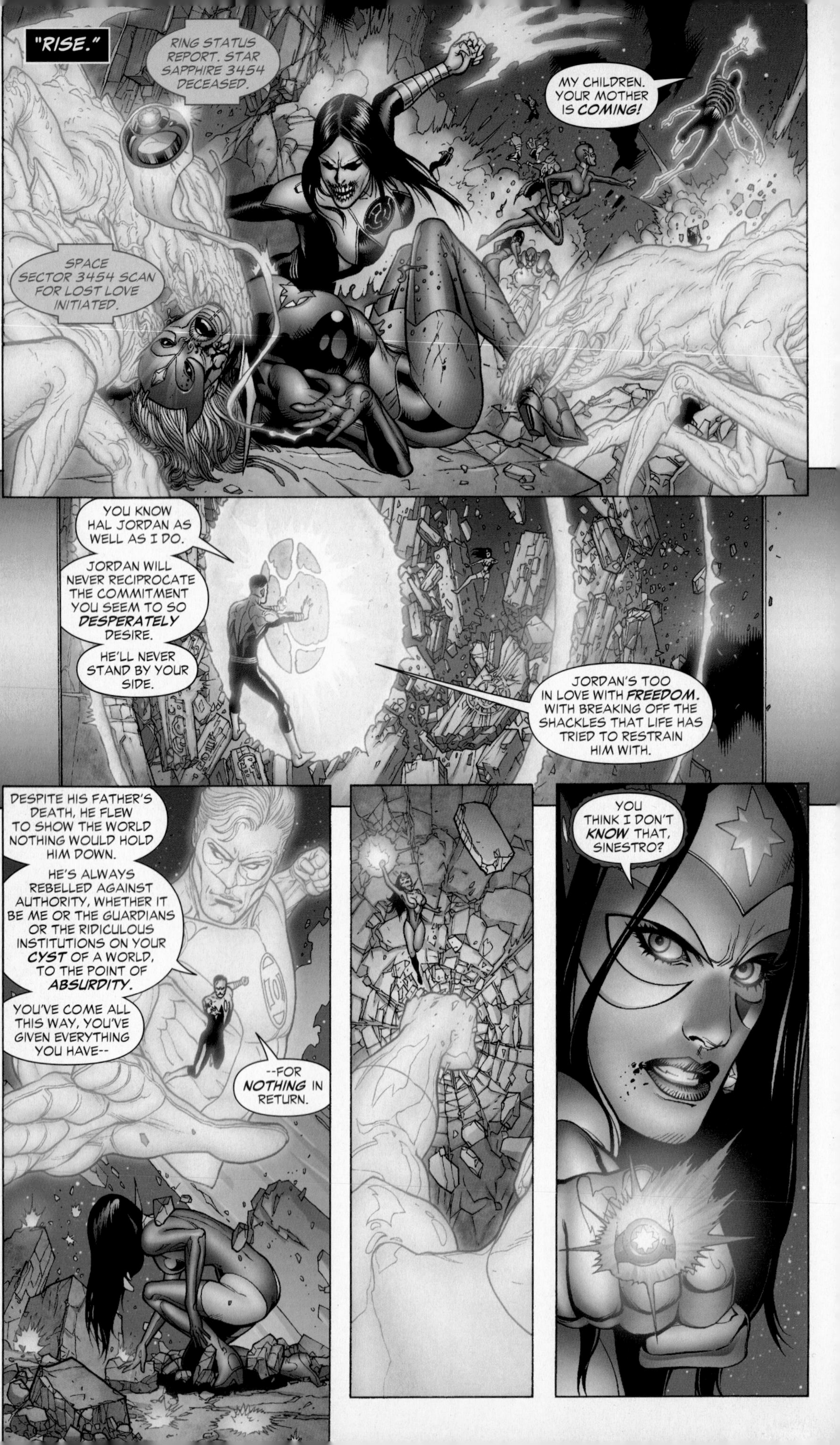

"RISE."
RING STATUS REPORT. STAR SAPPHIRE 3454 DECEASED.
MY CHILDREN. YOUR MOTHER IS COMING!
SPACE SECTOR 3454 SCAN FOR LOST LOVE INITIATED.
YOU KNOW HAL JORDAN AS WELL AS I DO.
JORDAN WILL NEVER RECIPROCATE THE COMMITMENT YOU SEEM TO SO DESPERATELY DESIRE.
HE'LL NEVER STAND BY YOUR SIDE.
JORDAN'S TOO IN LOVE WITH FREEDOM. WITH BREAKING OFF THE SHACKLES THAT LIFE HAS TRIED TO RESTRAIN HIM WITH.
DESPITE HIS FATHER'S DEATH, HE FLEW TO SHOW THE WORLD NOTHING WOULD HOLD HIM DOWN.
HE'S ALWAYS REBELLED AGAINST AUTHORITY, WHETHER IT BE ME OR THE GUARDIANS OR THE RIDICULOUS INSTITUTIONS ON YOUR CYST OF A WORLD, TO THE POINT OF ABSURDITY.
YOU'VE COME ALL THIS WAY, YOU'VE GIVEN EVERYTHING YOU HAVE--
--FOR NOTHING IN RETURN.
YOU THINK I DON'T KNOW THAT, SINESTRO?

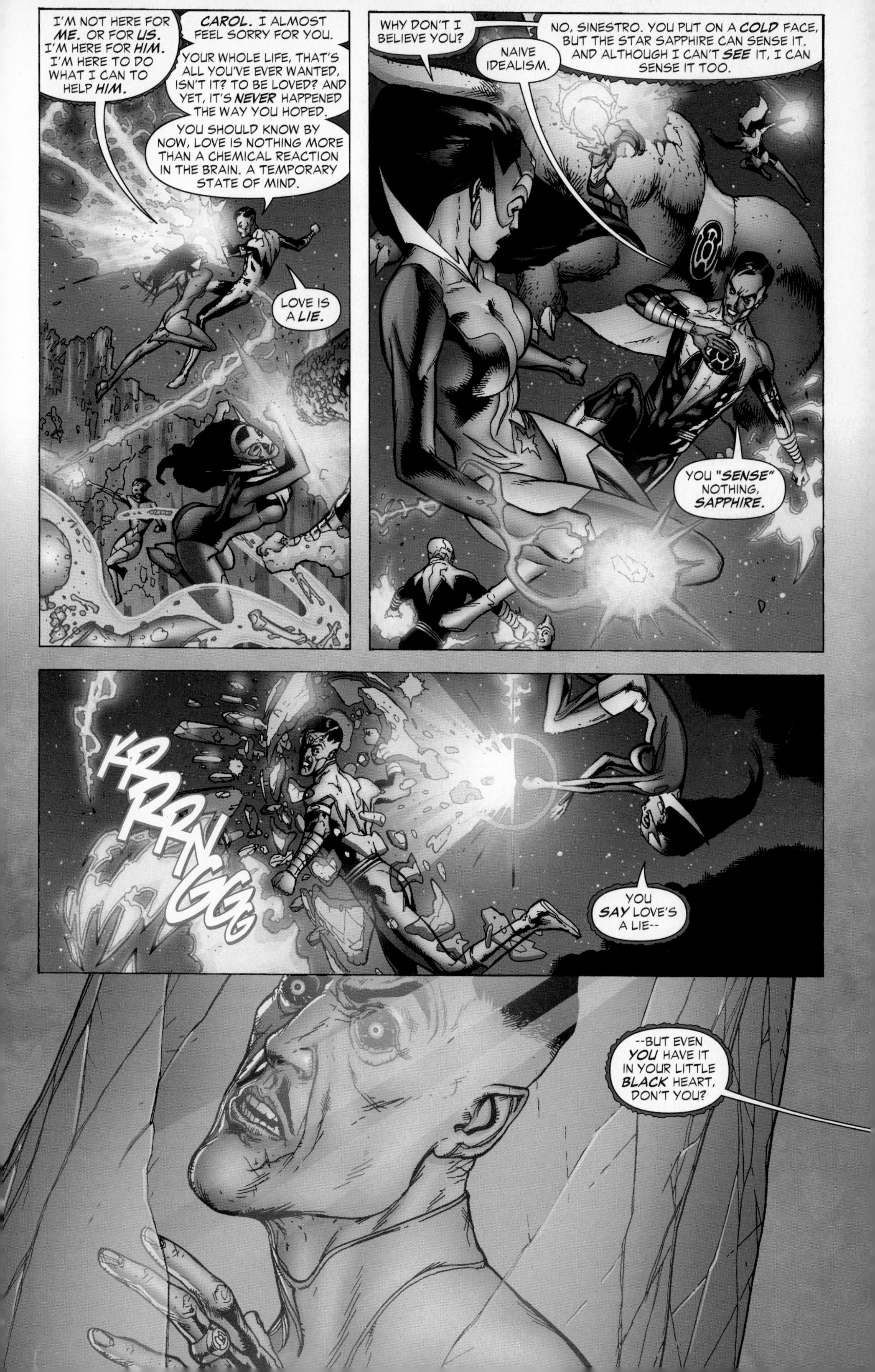
I'M NOT HERE FOR ME. OR FOR US. I'M HERE FOR HIM. I'M HERE TO DO WHAT I CAN TO HELP HIM.
CAROL. I ALMOST FEEL SORRY FOR YOU.
YOUR WHOLE LIFE, THAT'S ALL YOU'VE EVER WANTED, ISN'T IT? TO BE LOVED? AND YET, IT'S NEVER HAPPENED THE WAY YOU HOPED.
YOU SHOULD KNOW BY NOW, LOVE IS NOTHING MORE THAN A CHEMICAL REACTION IN THE BRAIN. A TEMPORARY STATE OF MIND.
LOVE IS A LIE.
WHY DON'T I BELIEVE YOU?
NAIVE IDEALISM.
NO, SINESTRO. YOU PUT ON A COLD FACE, BUT THE STAR SAPPHIRE CAN SENSE IT. AND ALTHOUGH I CAN'T SEE IT, I CAN SENSE IT TOO.
YOU "SENSE" NOTHING, SAPPHIRE.
KRRRNGGG
YOU SAY LOVE'S A LIE--
--BUT EVEN YOU HAVE IT IN YOUR LITTLE BLACK HEART, DON'T YOU?

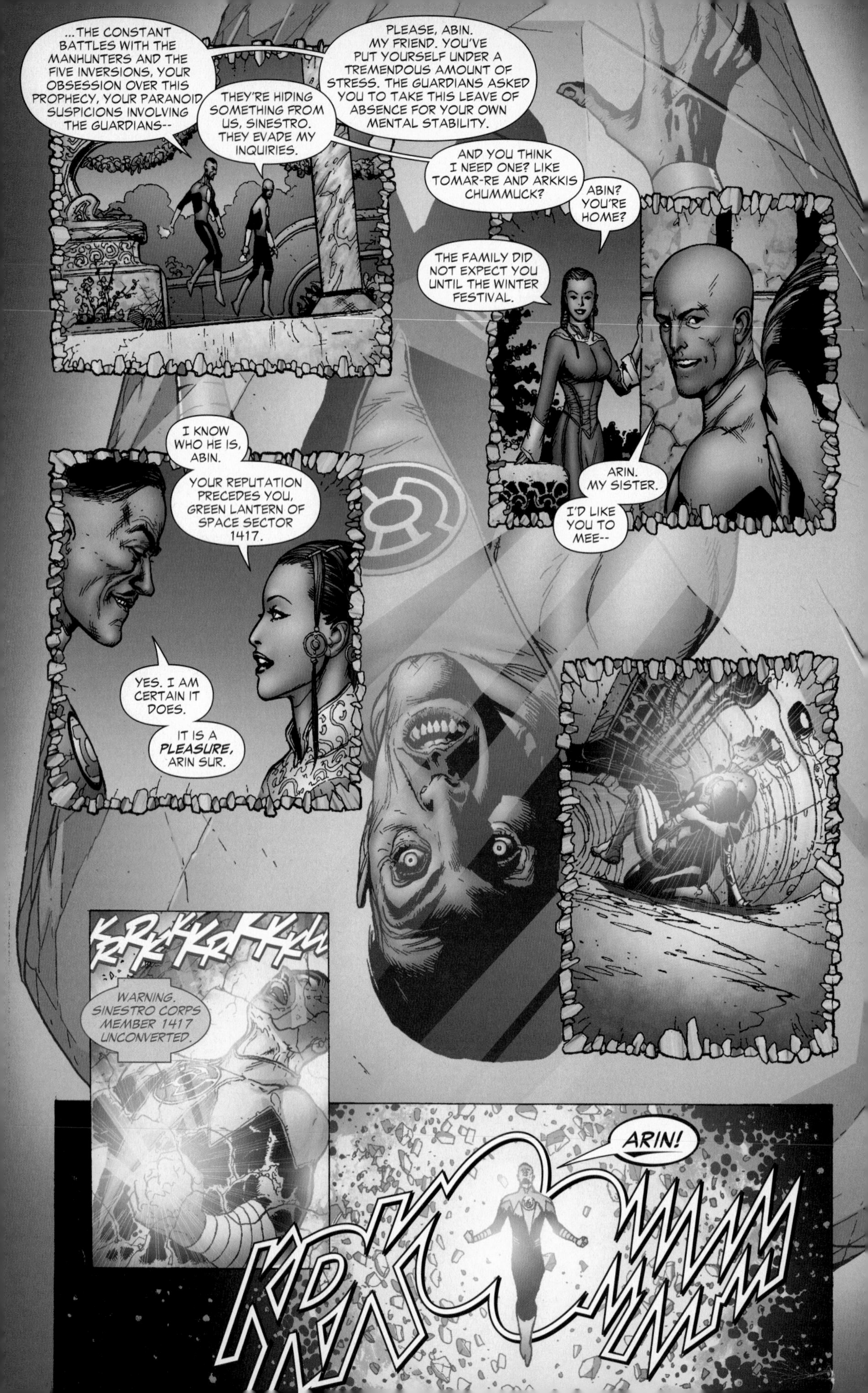
...THE CONSTANT BATTLES WITH THE MANHUNTERS AND THE FIVE INVERSIONS, YOUR OBSESSION OVER THIS PROPHECY, YOUR PARANOID SUSPICIONS INVOLVING THE GUARDIANS--
THEY'RE HIDING SOMETHING FROM US, SINESTRO. THEY EVADE MY INQUIRIES.
PLEASE, ABIN. MY FRIEND. YOU'VE PUT YOURSELF UNDER A TREMENDOUS AMOUNT OF STRESS. THE GUARDIANS ASKED YOU TO TAKE THIS LEAVE OF ABSENCE FOR YOUR OWN MENTAL STABILITY.
AND YOU THINK I NEED ONE? LIKE TOMAR-RE AND ARKKIS CHUMMUCK?
ABIN? YOU'RE HOME?
THE FAMILY DID NOT EXPECT YOU UNTIL THE WINTER FESTIVAL.
ARIN. MY SISTER.
I'D LIKE YOU TO MEE--
I KNOW WHO HE IS, ABIN.
YOUR REPUTATION PRECEDES YOU, GREEN LANTERN OF SPACE SECTOR 1417.
YES. I AM CERTAIN IT DOES.
IT IS A *PLEASURE,* ARIN SUR.
KRRKKKRKKKK
WARNING. SINESTRO CORPS MEMBER 1417 UNCONVERTED.
ARIN!
KRASCHOOMMMM

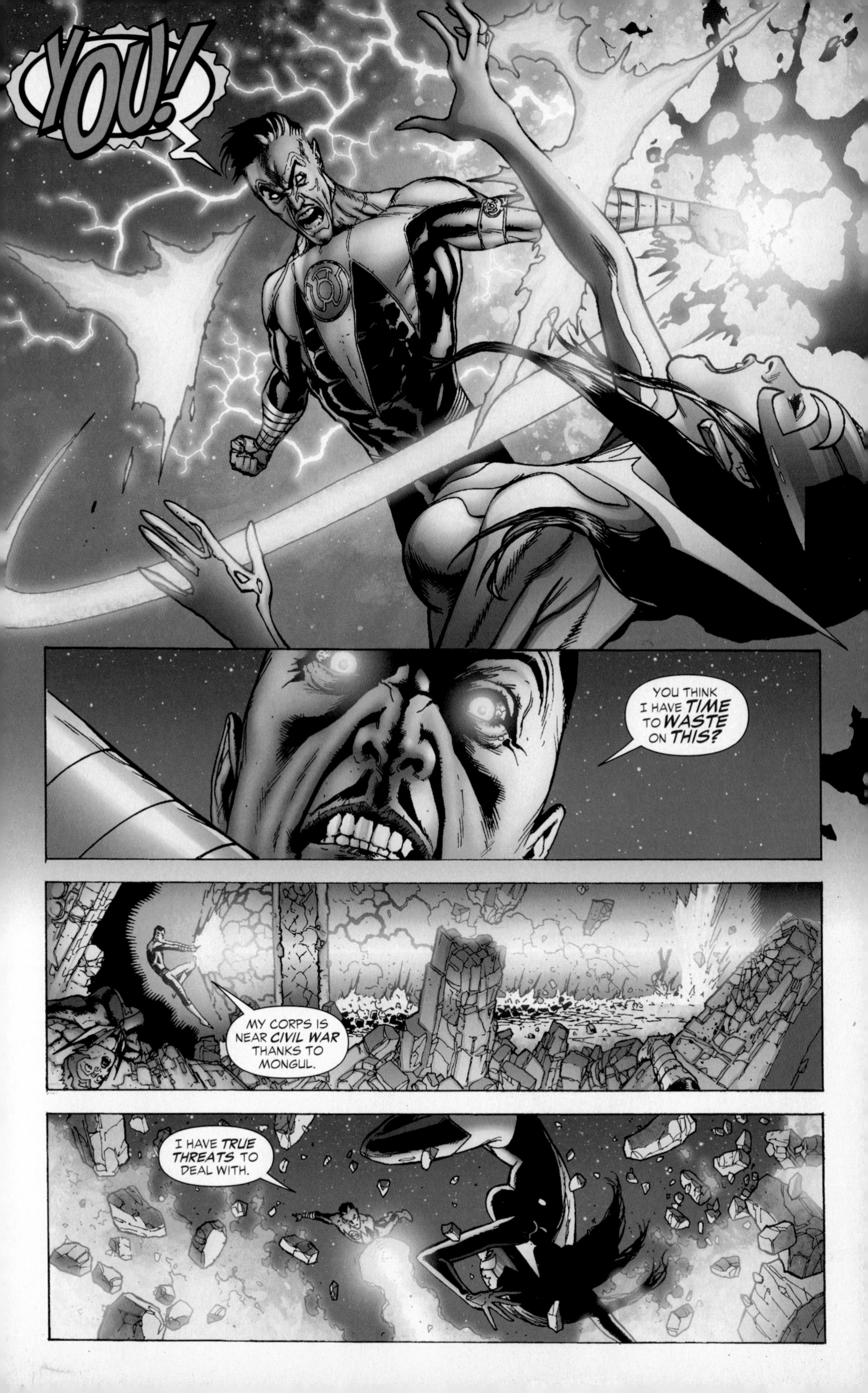
YOU!
YOU THINK I HAVE TIME TO WASTE ON THIS?
MY CORPS IS NEAR CIVIL WAR THANKS TO MONGUL.
I HAVE TRUE THREATS TO DEAL WITH.

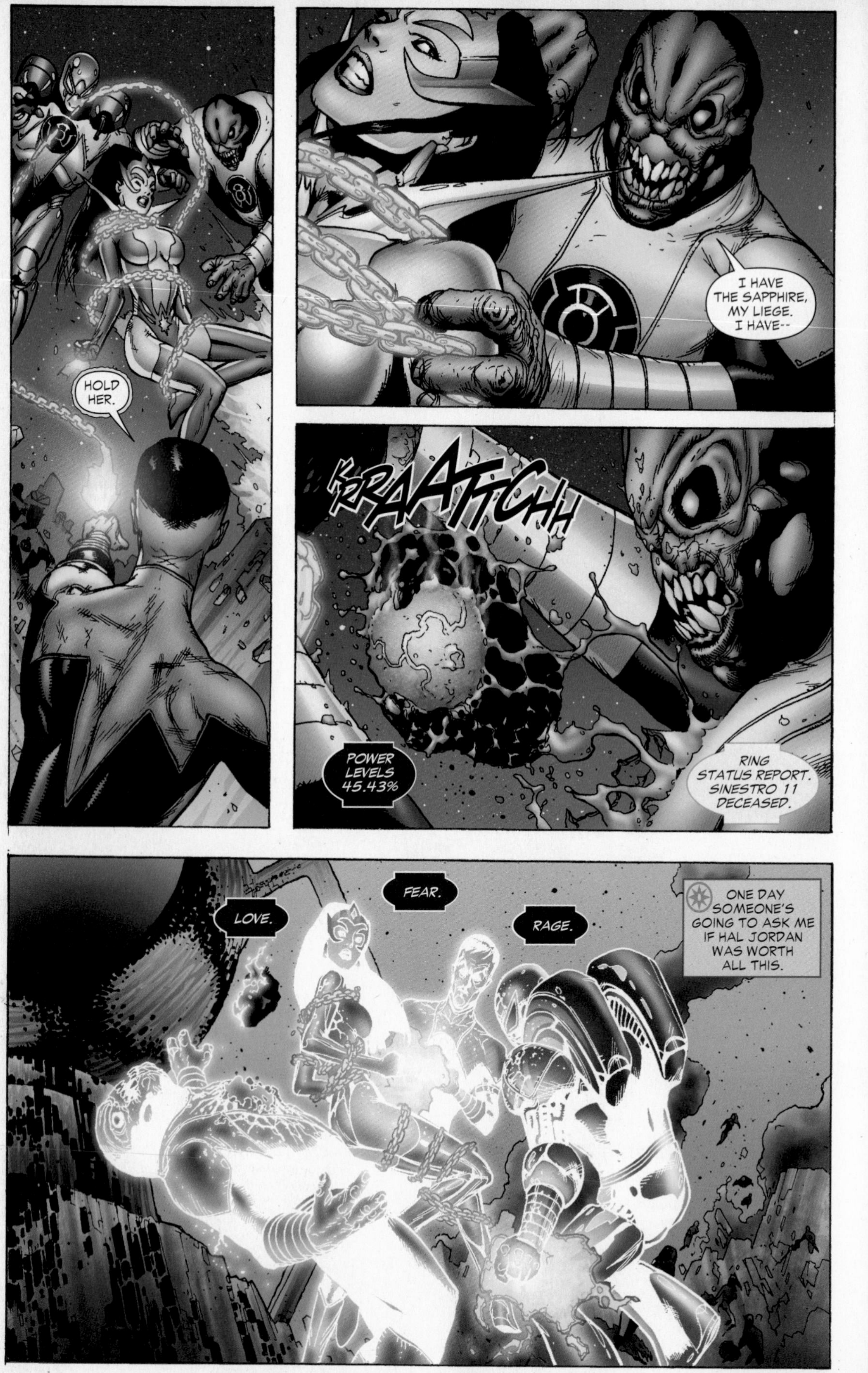
HOLD HER.
I HAVE THE SAPPHIRE, MY LIEGE. I HAVE--
KRAATTCHH
POWER LEVELS 45.43%
RING STATUS REPORT. SINESTRO 11 DECEASED.
LOVE.
FEAR.
RAGE.
ONE DAY SOMEONE'S GOING TO ASK ME IF HAL JORDAN WAS WORTH ALL THIS.

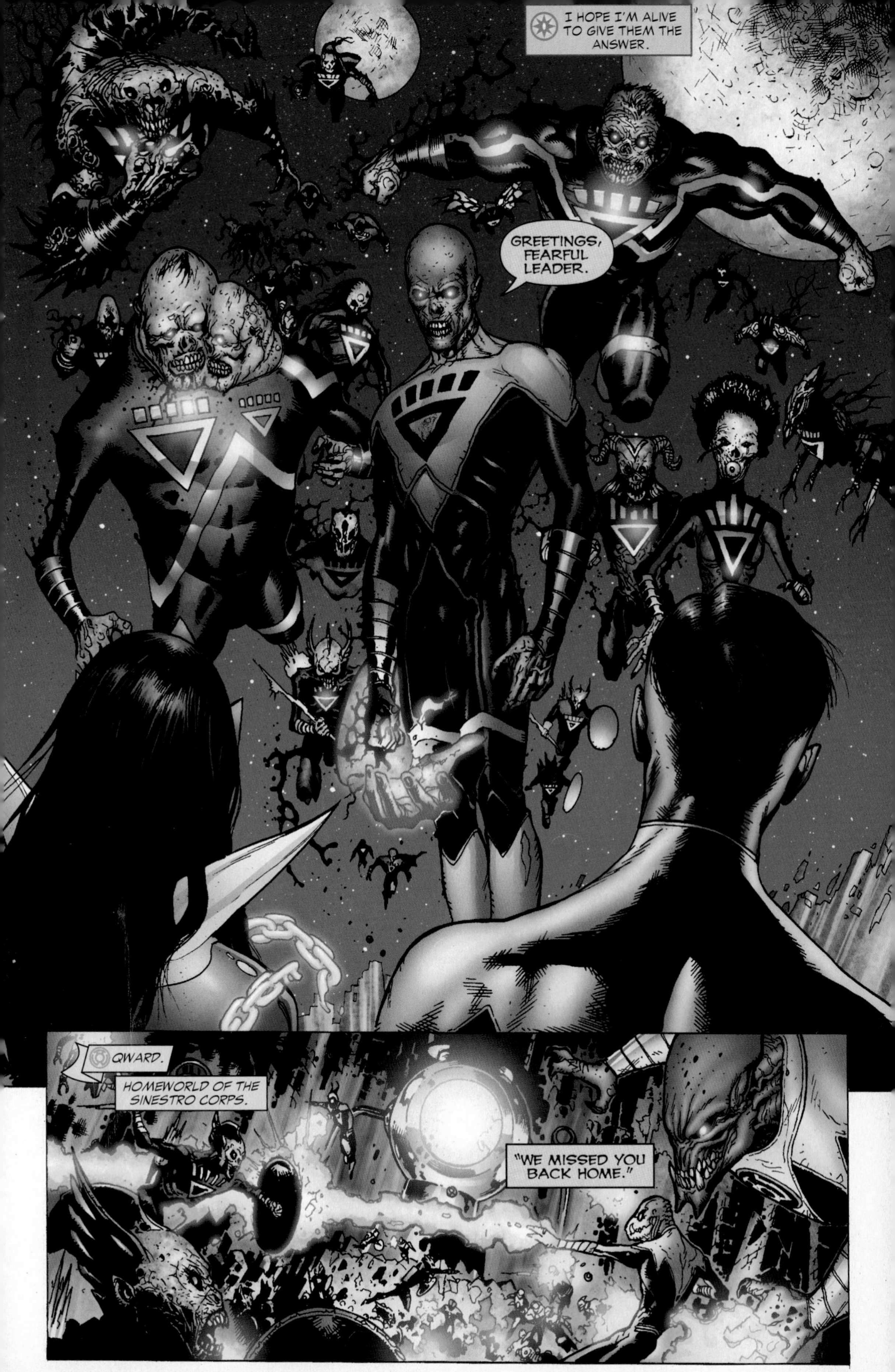
I HOPE I'M ALIVE TO GIVE THEM THE ANSWER.
GREETINGS, FEARFUL LEADER.
QWARD.
HOMEWORLD OF THE SINESTRO CORPS.
"WE MISSED YOU BACK HOME."

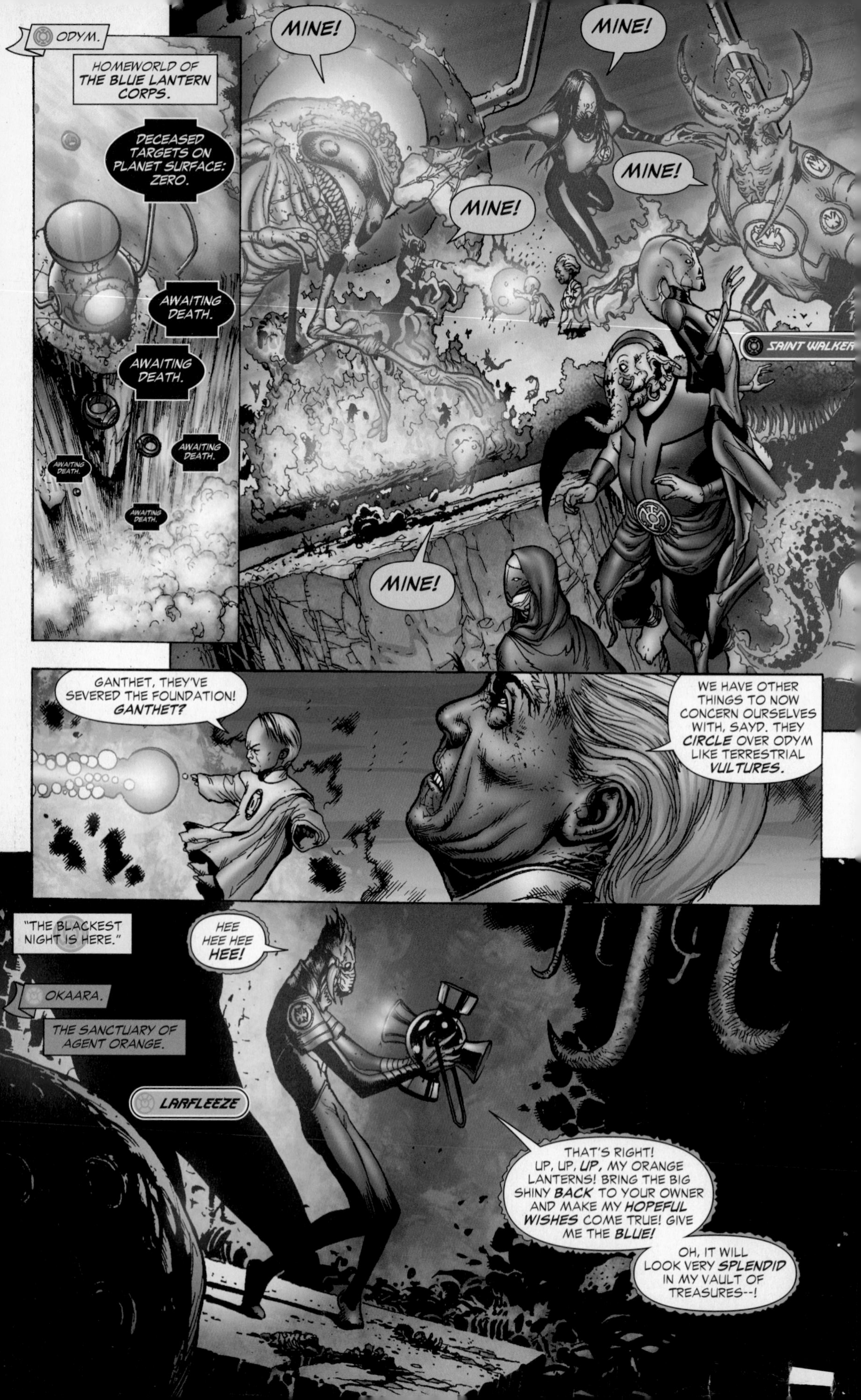
ODYM.
HOMEWORLD OF THE BLUE LANTERN CORPS.
MINE!
MINE!
DECEASED TARGETS ON PLANET SURFACE: ZERO.
MINE!
MINE!
AWAITING DEATH.
AWAITING DEATH.
SAINT WALKER
AWAITING DEATH.
AWAITING DEATH.
AWAITING DEATH.
MINE!
GANTHET, THEY'VE SEVERED THE FOUNDATION! GANTHET?
WE HAVE OTHER THINGS TO NOW CONCERN OURSELVES WITH, SAYD. THEY CIRCLE OVER ODYM LIKE TERRESTRIAL VULTURES.
"THE BLACKEST NIGHT IS HERE."
HEE HEE HEE HEE!
OKAARA.
THE SANCTUARY OF AGENT ORANGE.
LARFLEEZE
THAT'S RIGHT! UP, UP, UP, MY ORANGE LANTERNS! BRING THE BIG SHINY BACK TO YOUR OWNER AND MAKE MY HOPEFUL WISHES COME TRUE! GIVE ME THE BLUE!
OH, IT WILL LOOK VERY SPLENDID IN MY VAULT OF TREASURES--!

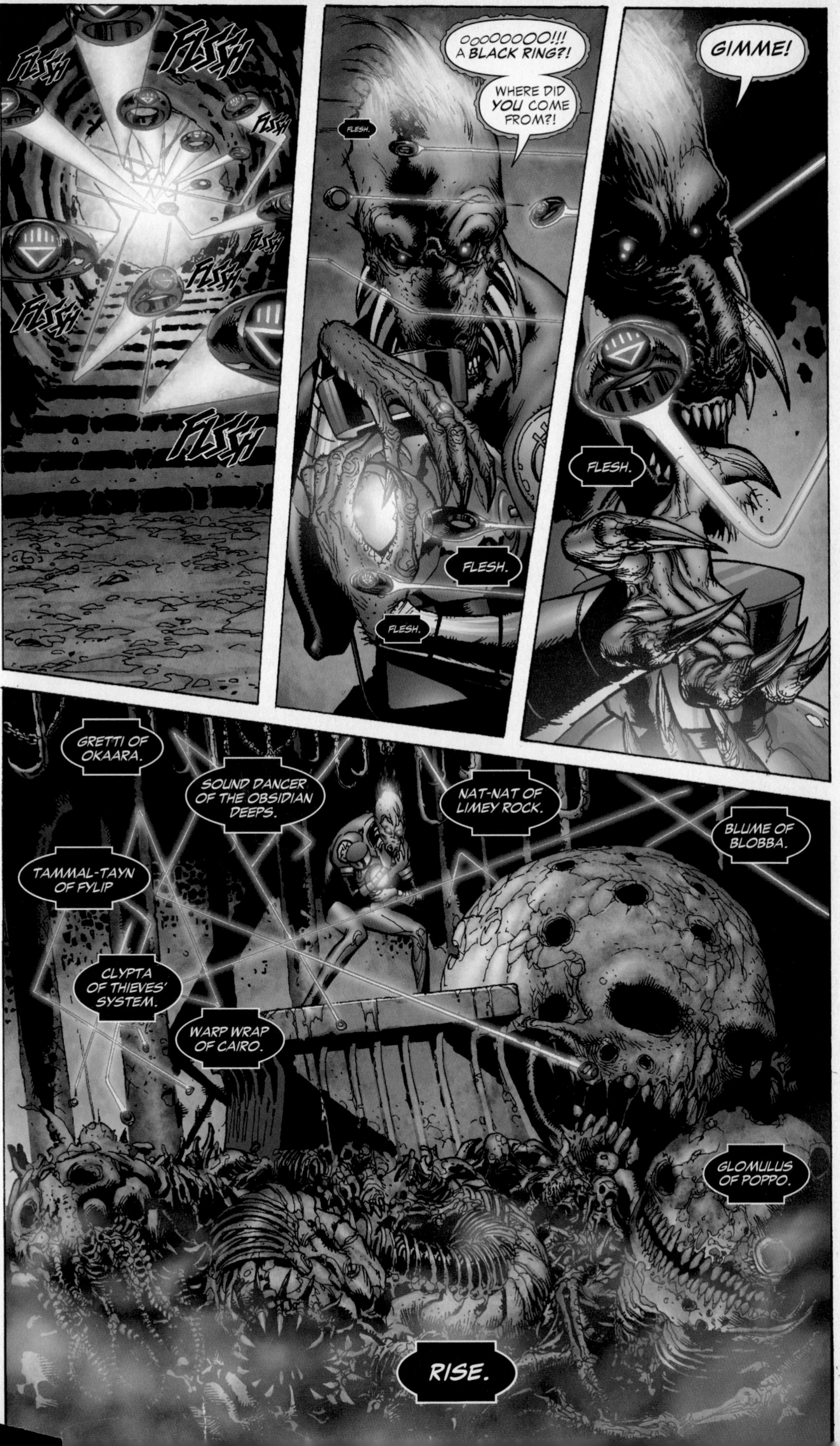
FLSSH
FLSSH
FLSSH
FLSSH
FLSSH
FLSSH
FLSSH
OOOOOOOO!!! A BLACK RING?!
WHERE DID YOU COME FROM?!
FLESH.
FLESH.
FLESH.
GIMME!
FLESH.
GRETTI OF OKAARA.
SOUND DANCER OF THE OBSIDIAN DEEPS.
NAT-NAT OF LIMEY ROCK.
BLUME OF BLOBBA.
TAMMAL-TAYN OF FYLIP
CLYPTA OF THIEVES' SYSTEM.
WARP WRAP OF CAIRO.
GLOMULUS OF POPPO.
RISE.

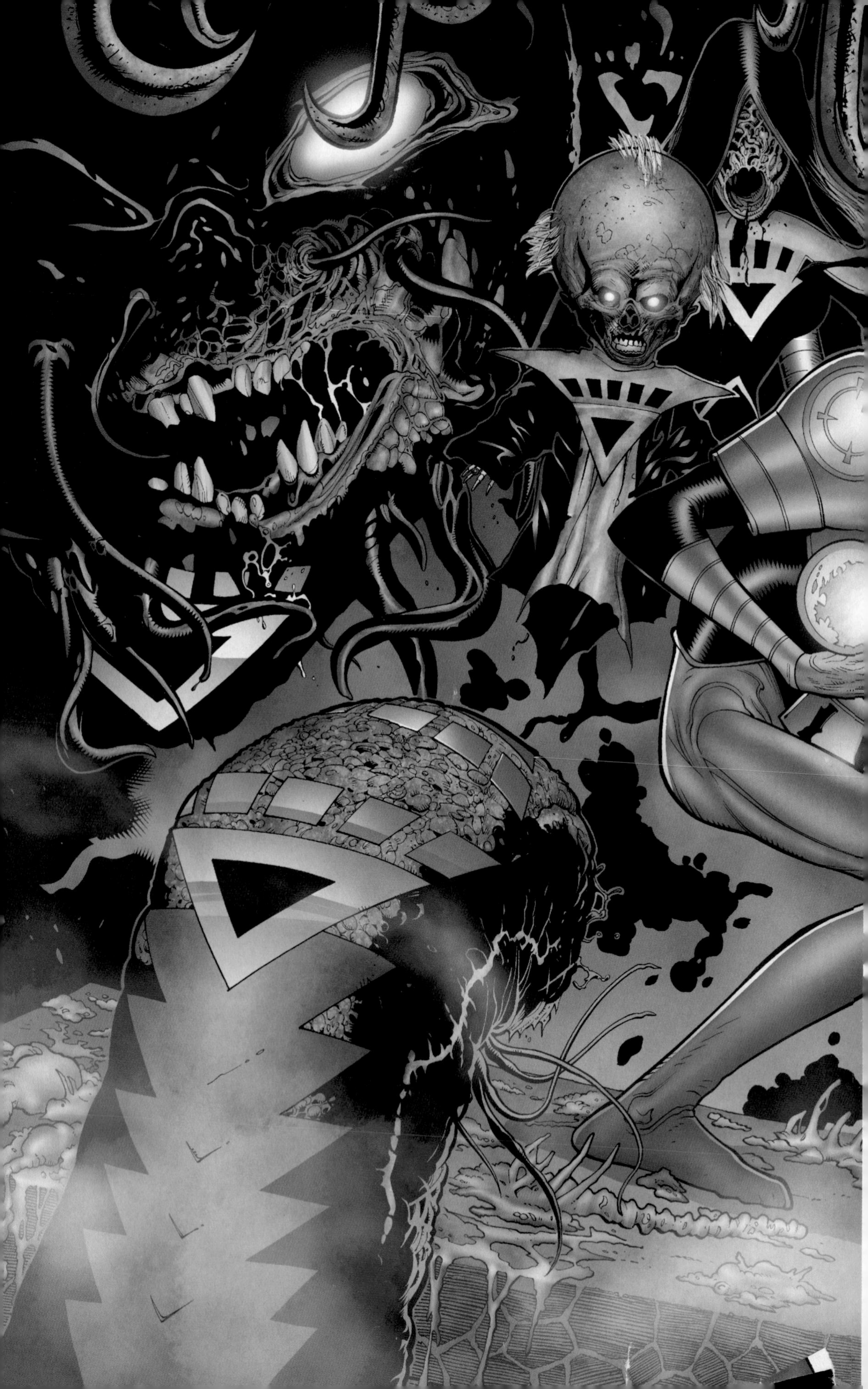

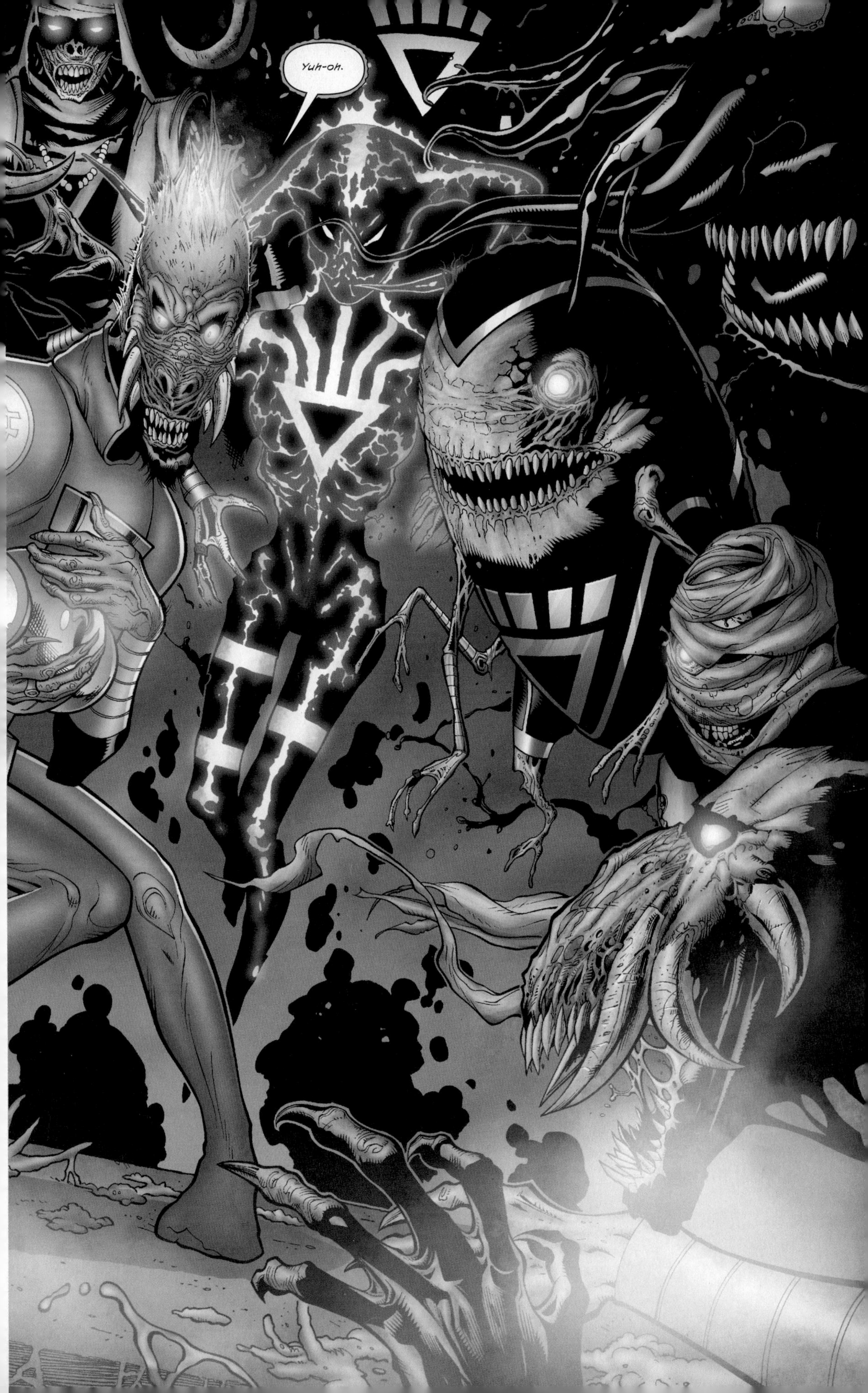
Yuh-oh.

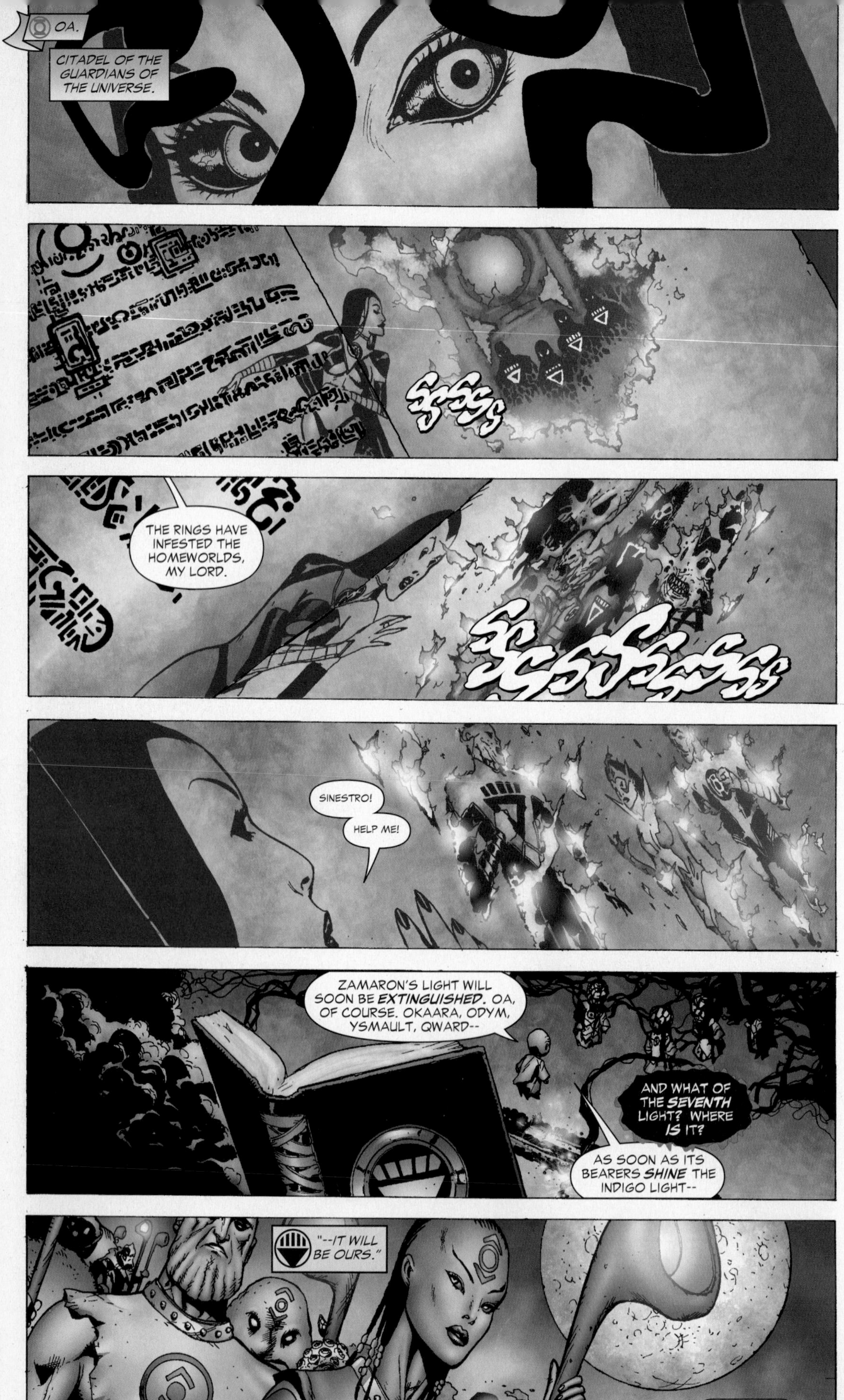
OA.
CITADEL OF THE GUARDIANS OF THE UNIVERSE.
SSSSS
THE RINGS HAVE INFESTED THE HOMEWORLDS, MY LORD.
SSSSSSSSSSS
SINESTRO!
HELP ME!
ZAMARON'S LIGHT WILL SOON BE EXTINGUISHED. OA, OF COURSE. OKAARA, ODYM, YSMAULT, QWARD--
AND WHAT OF THE SEVENTH LIGHT? WHERE IS IT?
AS SOON AS ITS BEARERS SHINE THE INDIGO LIGHT--
"--IT WILL BE OURS."
INDIGO-1.

GREEN LANTERN 46
Cover by Doug Mahnke and Christian Alamy with Hi-Fi

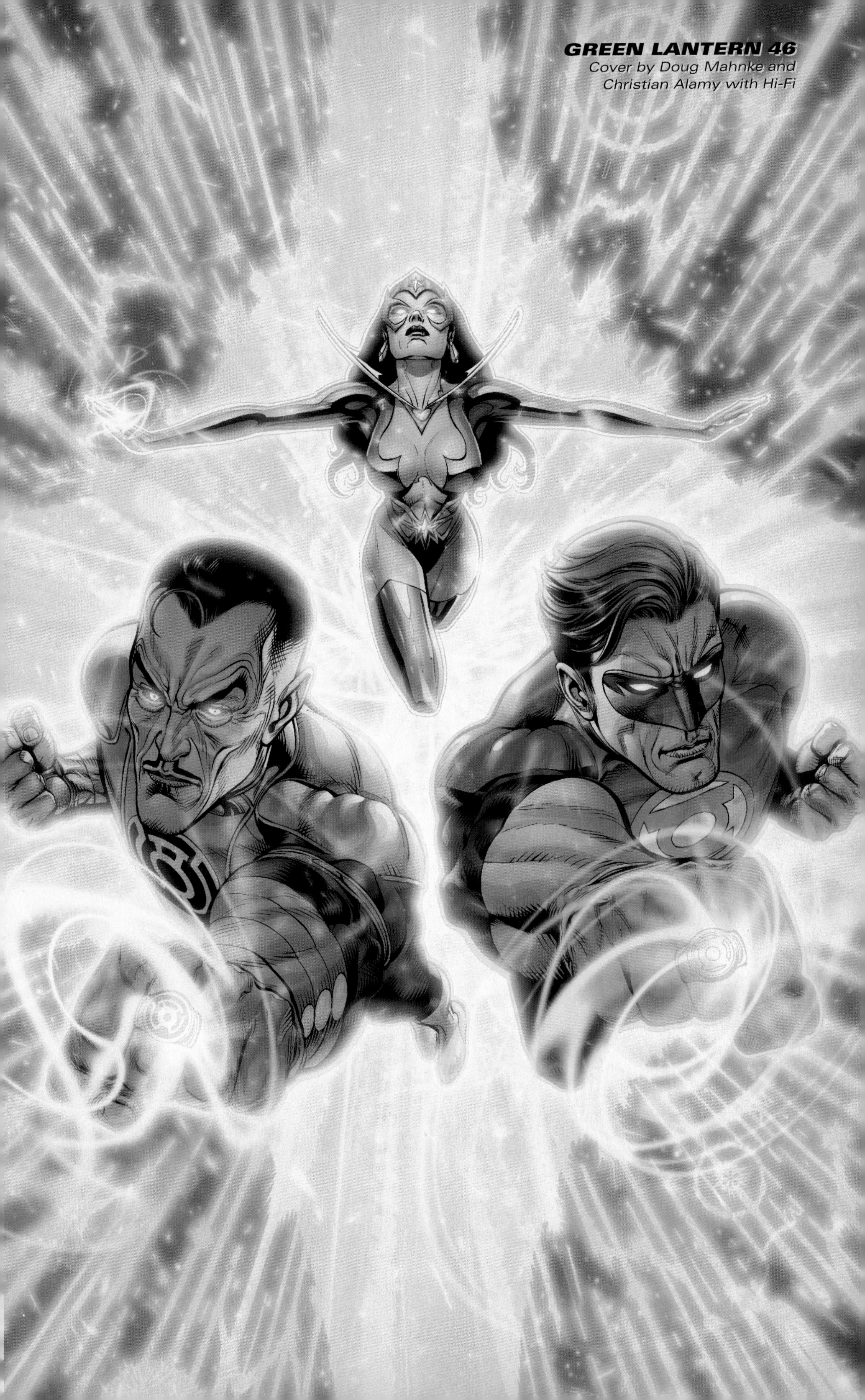

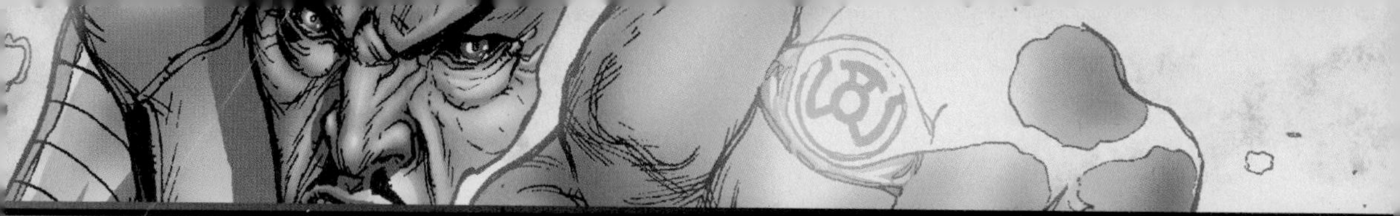

As Black Lanterns overwhelm Hal Jordan and his allies, salvation comes in the form of the seventh light: the Indigo Tribe. Their leader, Indigo-1, shows them that the combined powers of a Green Lantern and Lantern of another spectrum can destroy a Black Lantern, and together they stave off the assault.

Reluctantly teleported off Earth, Jordan's new mission is to unite the separate Corps before they kill each other. But his biggest challenge is making peace with his most hated enemy, Sinestro, whose personal war to reclaim leadership of his own Corps is about to ignite...

FEARED

DOUG MAHNKE
PENCILS

CHRISTIAN ALAMY
TOM NGUYEN
DOUG MAHNKE
INKS

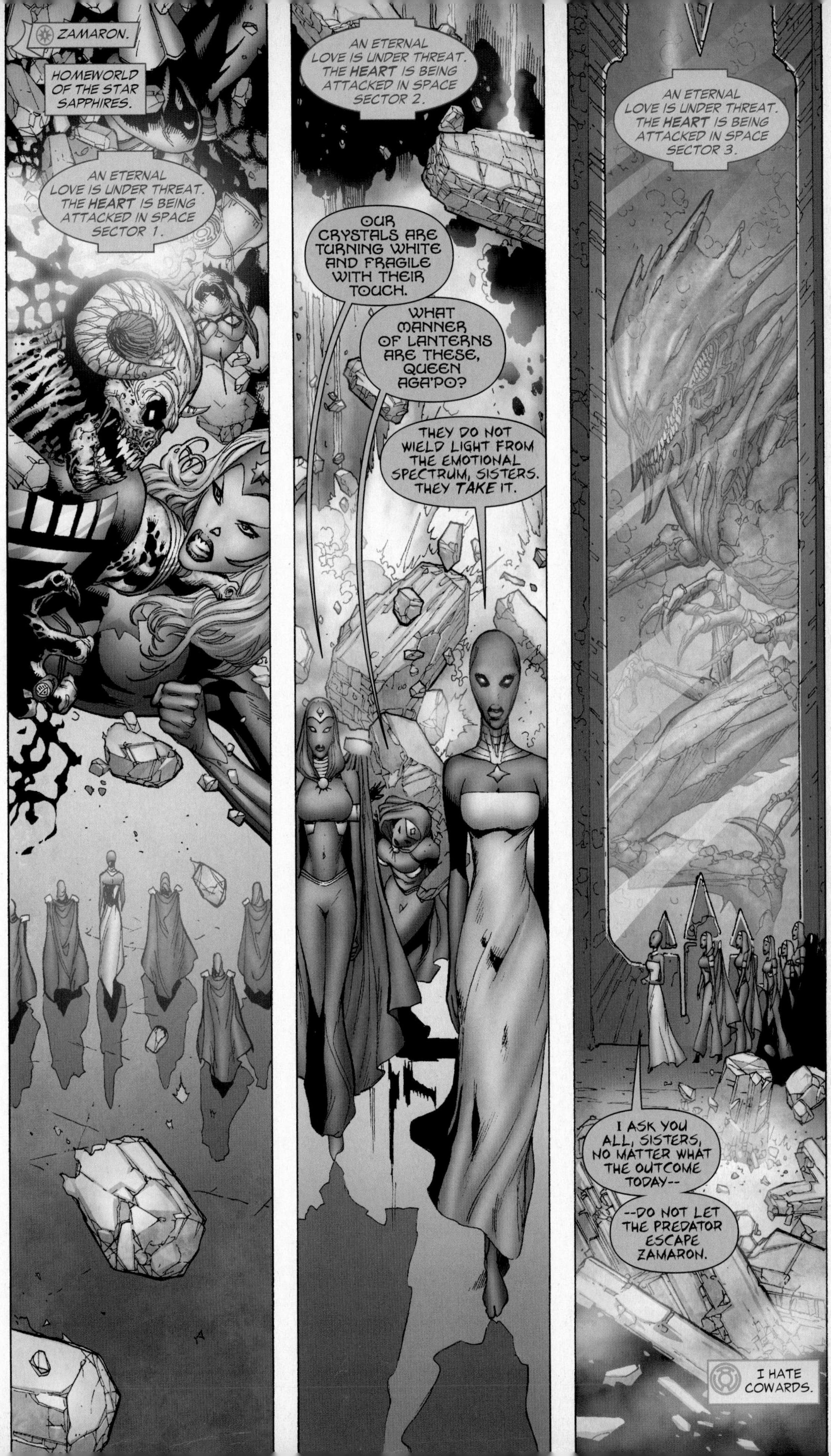
ZAMARON.
HOMEWORLD OF THE STAR SAPPHIRES.
AN ETERNAL LOVE IS UNDER THREAT. THE HEART IS BEING ATTACKED IN SPACE SECTOR 1.
AN ETERNAL LOVE IS UNDER THREAT. THE HEART IS BEING ATTACKED IN SPACE SECTOR 2.
OUR CRYSTALS ARE TURNING WHITE AND FRAGILE WITH THEIR TOUCH.
WHAT MANNER OF LANTERNS ARE THESE, QUEEN AGA'PO?
THEY DO NOT WIELD LIGHT FROM THE EMOTIONAL SPECTRUM, SISTERS. THEY TAKE IT.
AN ETERNAL LOVE IS UNDER THREAT. THE HEART IS BEING ATTACKED IN SPACE SECTOR 3.
I ASK YOU ALL, SISTERS, NO MATTER WHAT THE OUTCOME TODAY--
--DO NOT LET THE PREDATOR ESCAPE ZAMARON.
I HATE COWARDS.

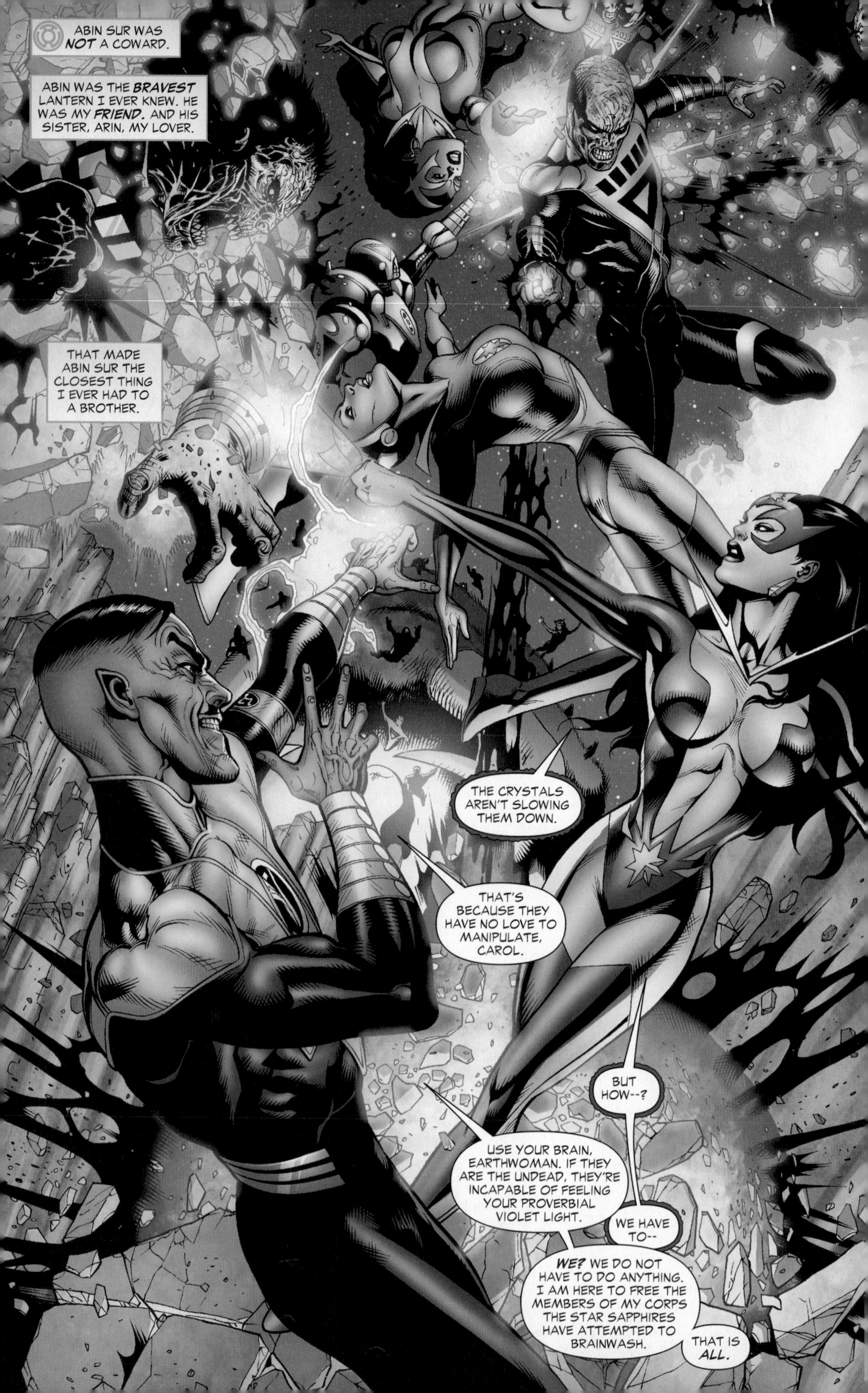

ABIN SUR WAS NOT A COWARD.
ABIN WAS THE BRAVEST LANTERN I EVER KNEW. HE WAS MY FRIEND. AND HIS SISTER, ARIN, MY LOVER.
THAT MADE ABIN SUR THE CLOSEST THING I EVER HAD TO A BROTHER.
THE CRYSTALS AREN'T SLOWING THEM DOWN.
THAT'S BECAUSE THEY HAVE NO LOVE TO MANIPULATE, CAROL.
BUT HOW--?
USE YOUR BRAIN, EARTHWOMAN. IF THEY ARE THE UNDEAD, THEY'RE INCAPABLE OF FEELING YOUR PROVERBIAL VIOLET LIGHT.
WE HAVE TO--
WE? WE DO NOT HAVE TO DO ANYTHING. I AM HERE TO FREE THE MEMBERS OF MY CORPS THE STAR SAPPHIRES HAVE ATTEMPTED TO BRAINWASH.
THAT IS ALL.

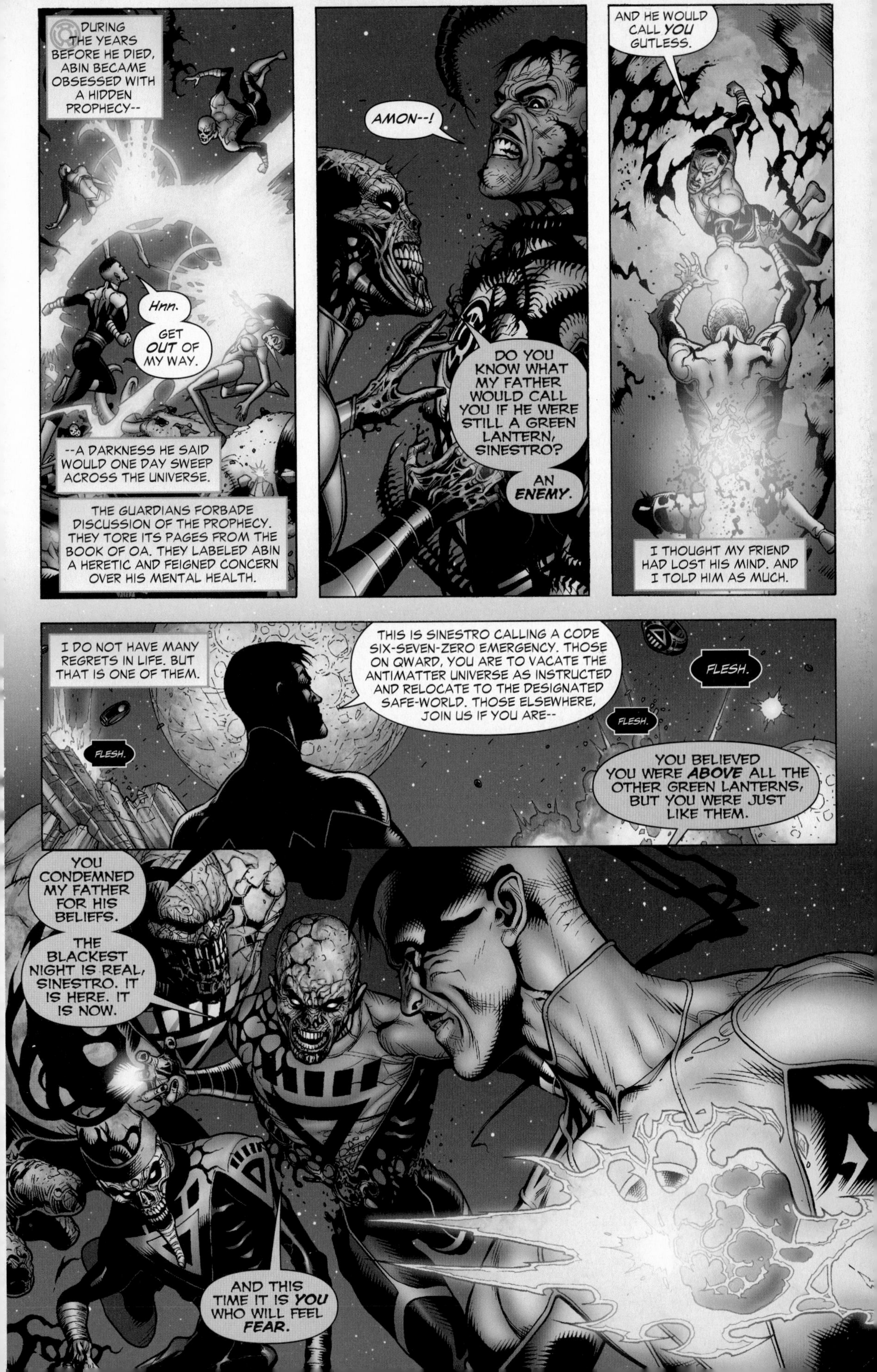
DURING THE YEARS BEFORE HE DIED, ABIN BECAME OBSESSED WITH A HIDDEN PROPHECY--
Hnn.
GET OUT OF MY WAY.
--A DARKNESS HE SAID WOULD ONE DAY SWEEP ACROSS THE UNIVERSE.
THE GUARDIANS FORBADE DISCUSSION OF THE PROPHECY. THEY TORE ITS PAGES FROM THE BOOK OF OA. THEY LABELED ABIN A HERETIC AND FEIGNED CONCERN OVER HIS MENTAL HEALTH.
AMON--!
DO YOU KNOW WHAT MY FATHER WOULD CALL YOU IF HE WERE STILL A GREEN LANTERN, SINESTRO?
AN ENEMY.
AND HE WOULD CALL YOU GUTLESS.
I THOUGHT MY FRIEND HAD LOST HIS MIND. AND I TOLD HIM AS MUCH.
I DO NOT HAVE MANY REGRETS IN LIFE. BUT THAT IS ONE OF THEM.
THIS IS SINESTRO CALLING A CODE SIX-SEVEN-ZERO EMERGENCY. THOSE ON QWARD, YOU ARE TO VACATE THE ANTIMATTER UNIVERSE AS INSTRUCTED AND RELOCATE TO THE DESIGNATED SAFE-WORLD. THOSE ELSEWHERE, JOIN US IF YOU ARE--
FLESH.
FLESH.
FLESH.
YOU BELIEVED YOU WERE ABOVE ALL THE OTHER GREEN LANTERNS, BUT YOU WERE JUST LIKE THEM.
YOU CONDEMNED MY FATHER FOR HIS BELIEFS.
THE BLACKEST NIGHT IS REAL, SINESTRO. IT IS HERE. IT IS NOW.
AND THIS TIME IT IS YOU WHO WILL FEEL FEAR.

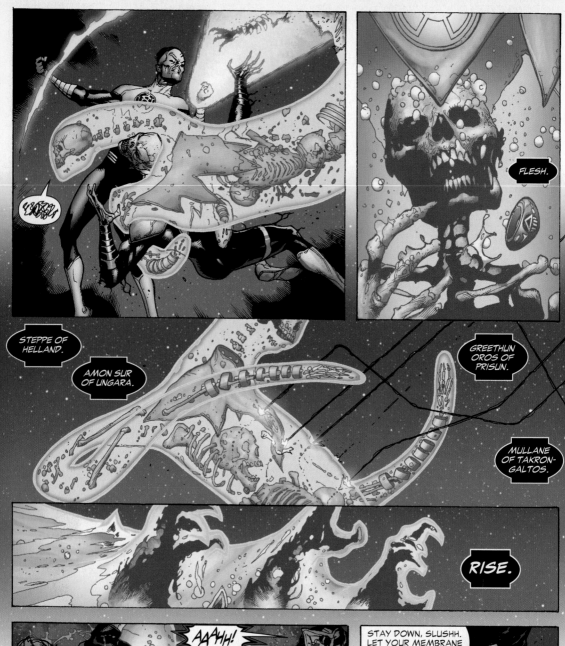

FLESH.

STEPPE OF HELLAND.

AMON SUR OF UNGARA.

GREETHUN OROS OF PRISUN.

MULLANE OF TAKRON-GALTOS.

RISE.

AAAHH!

STAY DOWN, SLUSHH. LET YOUR MEMBRANE HEAL. WE WILL DEAL WITH THE BLACK LANTERNS--

WARNING. EMOTIONAL SPECTRUM DETONATION IMMINENT.

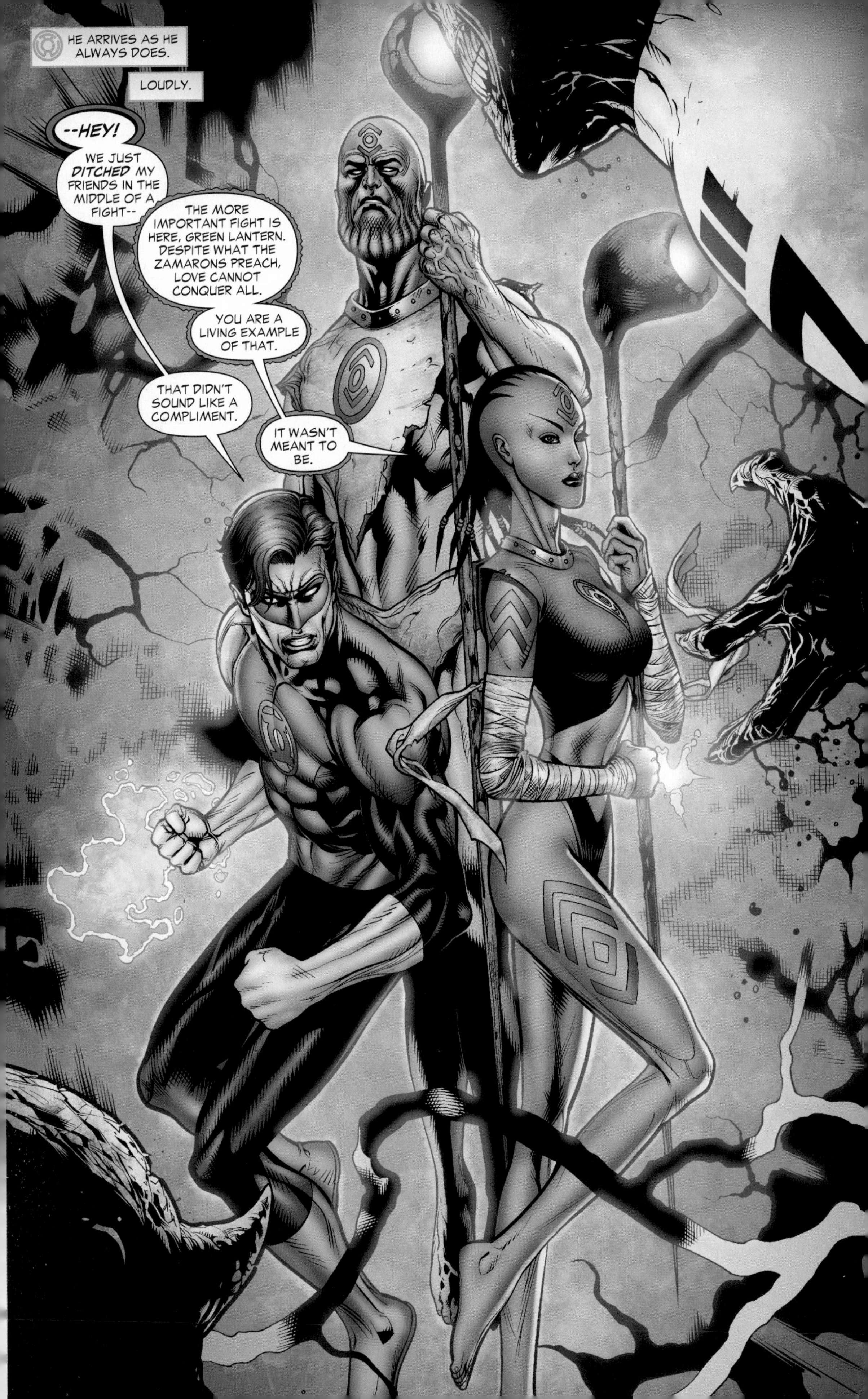

HE ARRIVES AS HE ALWAYS DOES.
LOUDLY.
--HEY!
WE JUST DITCHED MY FRIENDS IN THE MIDDLE OF A FIGHT--
THE MORE IMPORTANT FIGHT IS HERE, GREEN LANTERN. DESPITE WHAT THE ZAMARONS PREACH, LOVE CANNOT CONQUER ALL.
YOU ARE A LIVING EXAMPLE OF THAT.
THAT DIDN'T SOUND LIKE A COMPLIMENT.
IT WASN'T MEANT TO BE.

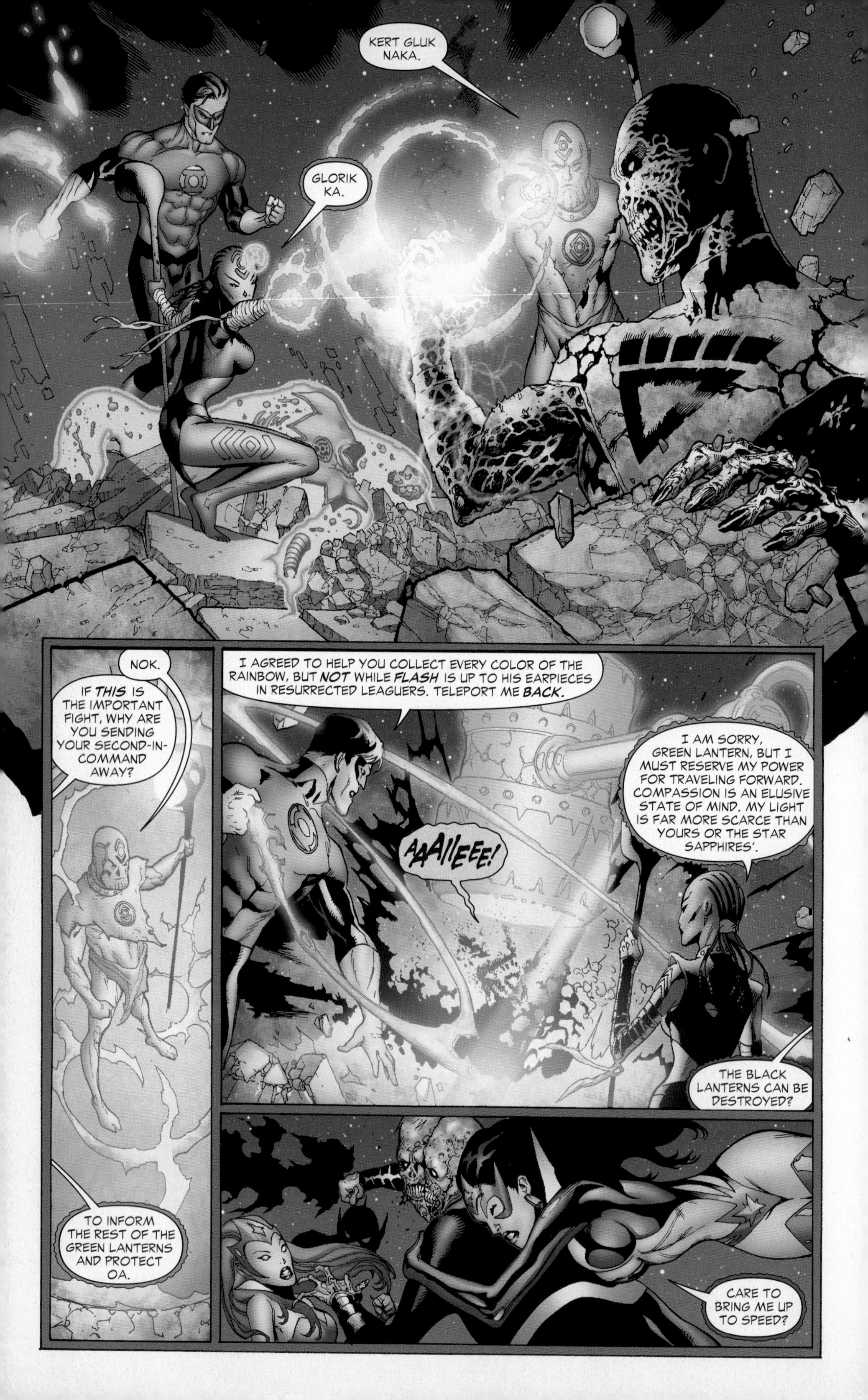
KERT GLUK NAKA.
GLORIK KA.
NOK.
IF THIS IS THE IMPORTANT FIGHT, WHY ARE YOU SENDING YOUR SECOND-IN-COMMAND AWAY?
I AGREED TO HELP YOU COLLECT EVERY COLOR OF THE RAINBOW, BUT NOT WHILE FLASH IS UP TO HIS EARPIECES IN RESURRECTED LEAGUERS. TELEPORT ME BACK.
I AM SORRY, GREEN LANTERN, BUT I MUST RESERVE MY POWER FOR TRAVELING FORWARD. COMPASSION IS AN ELUSIVE STATE OF MIND. MY LIGHT IS FAR MORE SCARCE THAN YOURS OR THE STAR SAPPHIRES'.
AAAIIEEE!
THE BLACK LANTERNS CAN BE DESTROYED?
TO INFORM THE REST OF THE GREEN LANTERNS AND PROTECT OA.
CARE TO BRING ME UP TO SPEED?

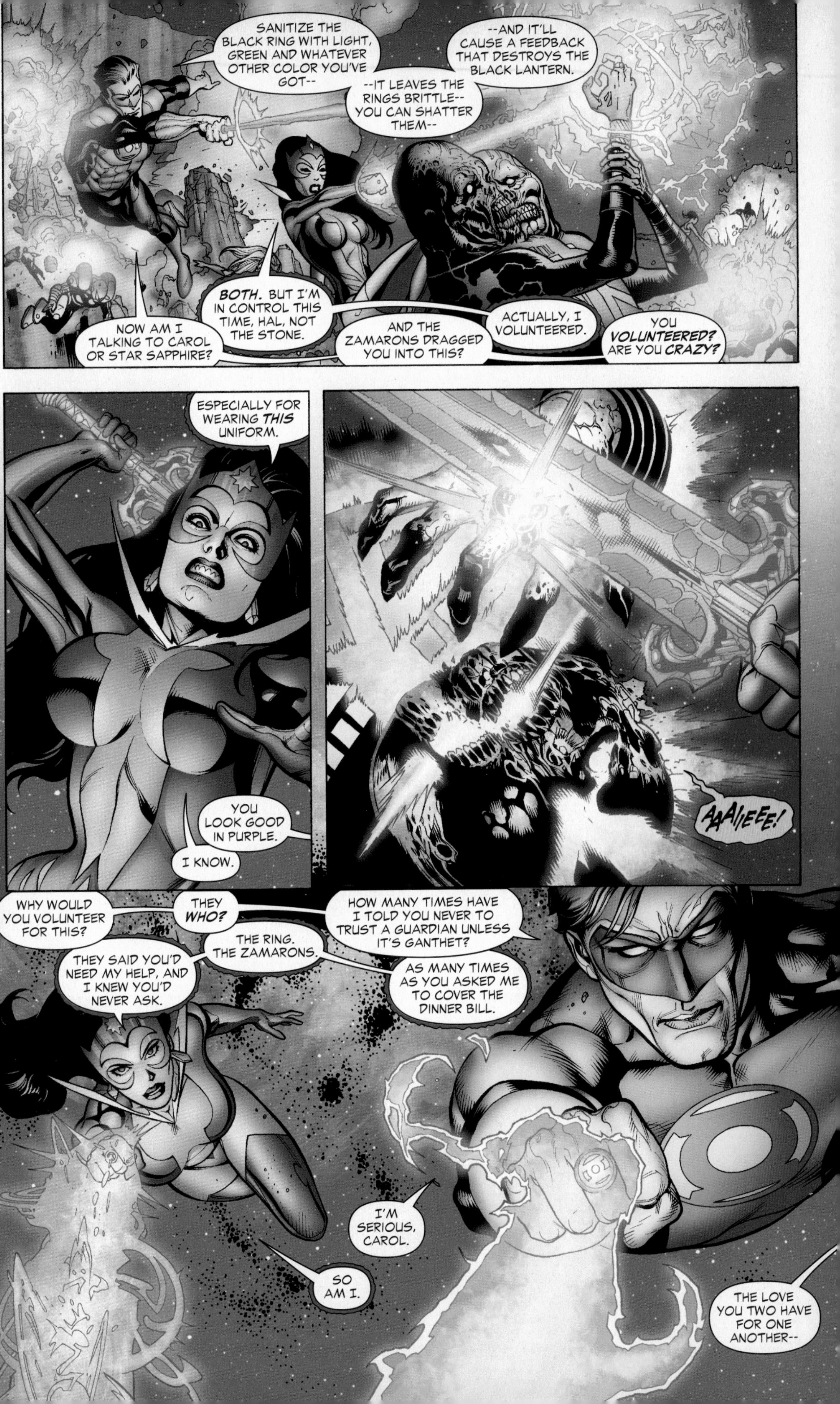

SANITIZE THE BLACK RING WITH LIGHT, GREEN AND WHATEVER OTHER COLOR YOU'VE GOT--
--IT LEAVES THE RINGS BRITTLE-- YOU CAN SHATTER THEM--
--AND IT'LL CAUSE A FEEDBACK THAT DESTROYS THE BLACK LANTERN.
NOW AM I TALKING TO CAROL OR STAR SAPPHIRE?
BOTH. BUT I'M IN CONTROL THIS TIME, HAL, NOT THE STONE.
AND THE ZAMARONS DRAGGED YOU INTO THIS?
ACTUALLY, I VOLUNTEERED.
YOU VOLUNTEERED? ARE YOU CRAZY?
ESPECIALLY FOR WEARING THIS UNIFORM.
YOU LOOK GOOD IN PURPLE.
I KNOW.
AAAIIEEE!
WHY WOULD YOU VOLUNTEER FOR THIS?
THEY SAID YOU'D NEED MY HELP, AND I KNEW YOU'D NEVER ASK.
THEY WHO?
THE RING. THE ZAMARONS.
HOW MANY TIMES HAVE I TOLD YOU NEVER TO TRUST A GUARDIAN UNLESS IT'S GANTHET?
AS MANY TIMES AS YOU ASKED ME TO COVER THE DINNER BILL.
I'M SERIOUS, CAROL.
SO AM I.
THE LOVE YOU TWO HAVE FOR ONE ANOTHER--

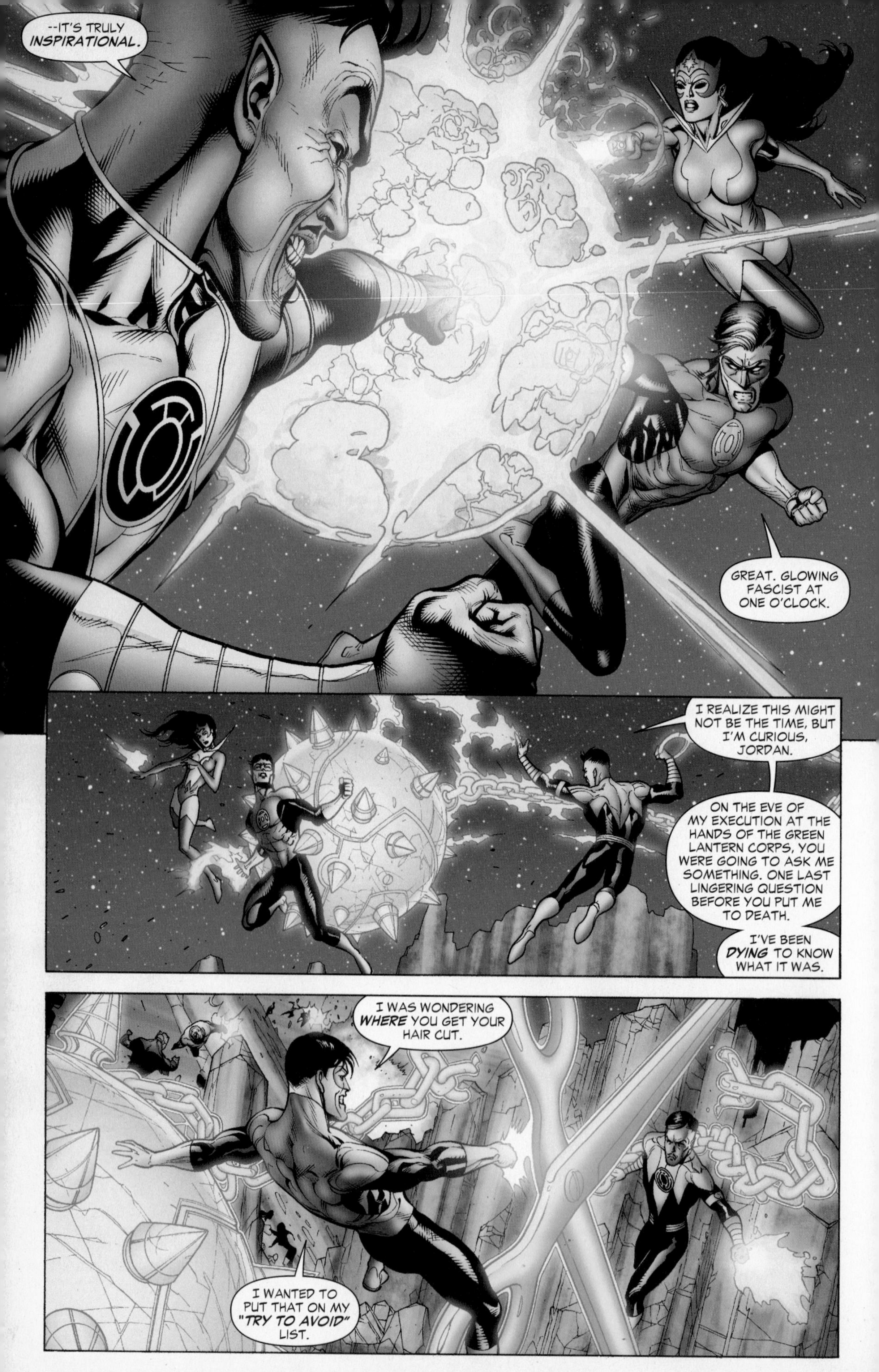
--IT'S TRULY *INSPIRATIONAL.*
GREAT. GLOWING FASCIST AT ONE O'CLOCK.
I REALIZE THIS MIGHT NOT BE THE TIME, BUT I'M CURIOUS, JORDAN.
ON THE EVE OF MY EXECUTION AT THE HANDS OF THE GREEN LANTERN CORPS, YOU WERE GOING TO ASK ME SOMETHING. ONE LAST LINGERING QUESTION BEFORE YOU PUT ME TO DEATH.
I'VE BEEN *DYING* TO KNOW WHAT IT WAS.
I WAS WONDERING *WHERE* YOU GET YOUR HAIR CUT.
I WANTED TO PUT THAT ON MY *"TRY TO AVOID"* LIST.

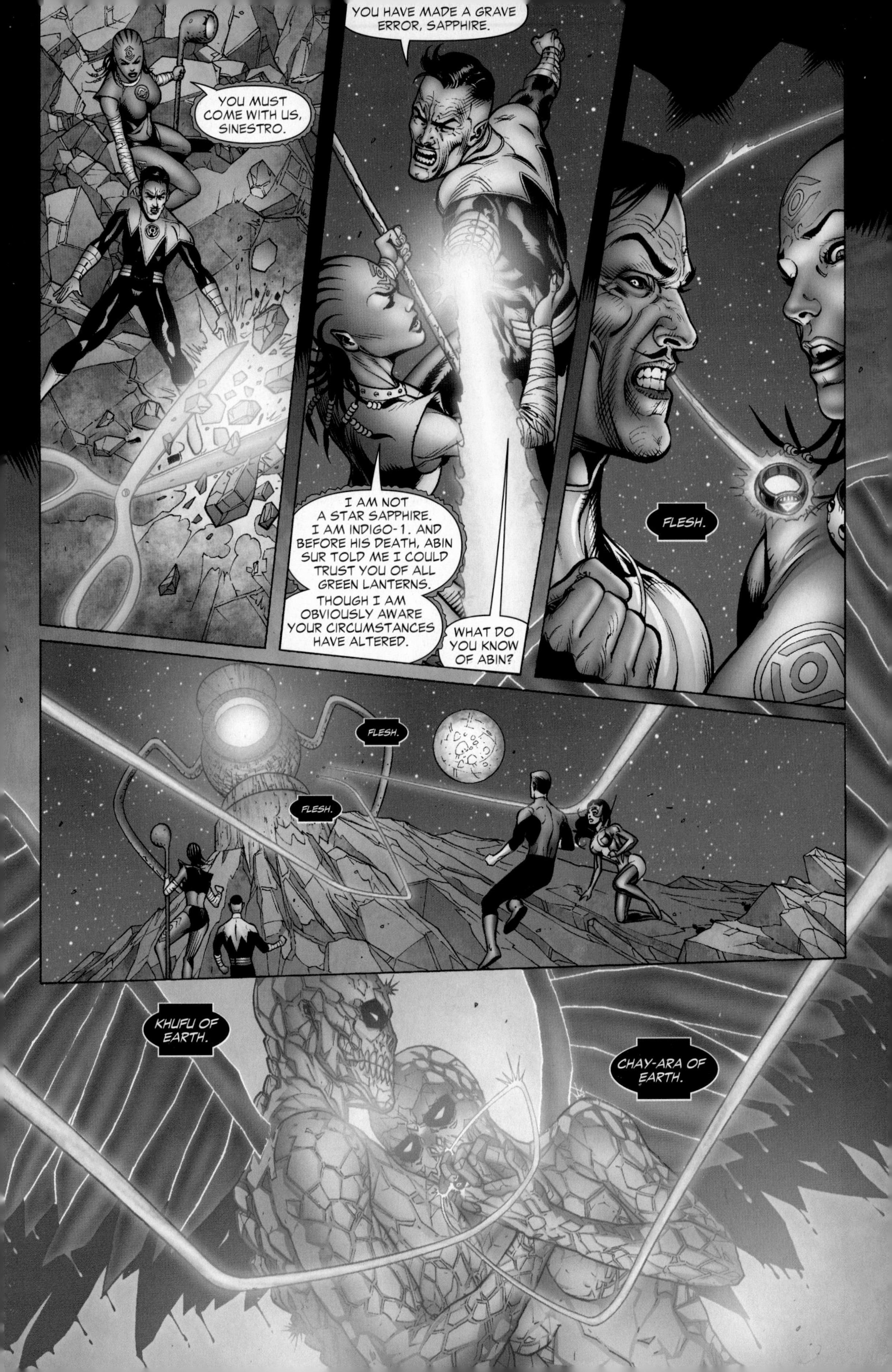
YOU MUST COME WITH US, SINESTRO.
YOU HAVE MADE A GRAVE ERROR, SAPPHIRE.
I AM NOT A STAR SAPPHIRE. I AM INDIGO-1. AND BEFORE HIS DEATH, ABIN SUR TOLD ME I COULD TRUST YOU OF ALL GREEN LANTERNS.
THOUGH I AM OBVIOUSLY AWARE YOUR CIRCUMSTANCES HAVE ALTERED.
WHAT DO YOU KNOW OF ABIN?
FLESH.
FLESH.
FLESH.
KHUFU OF EARTH.
CHAY-ARA OF EARTH.

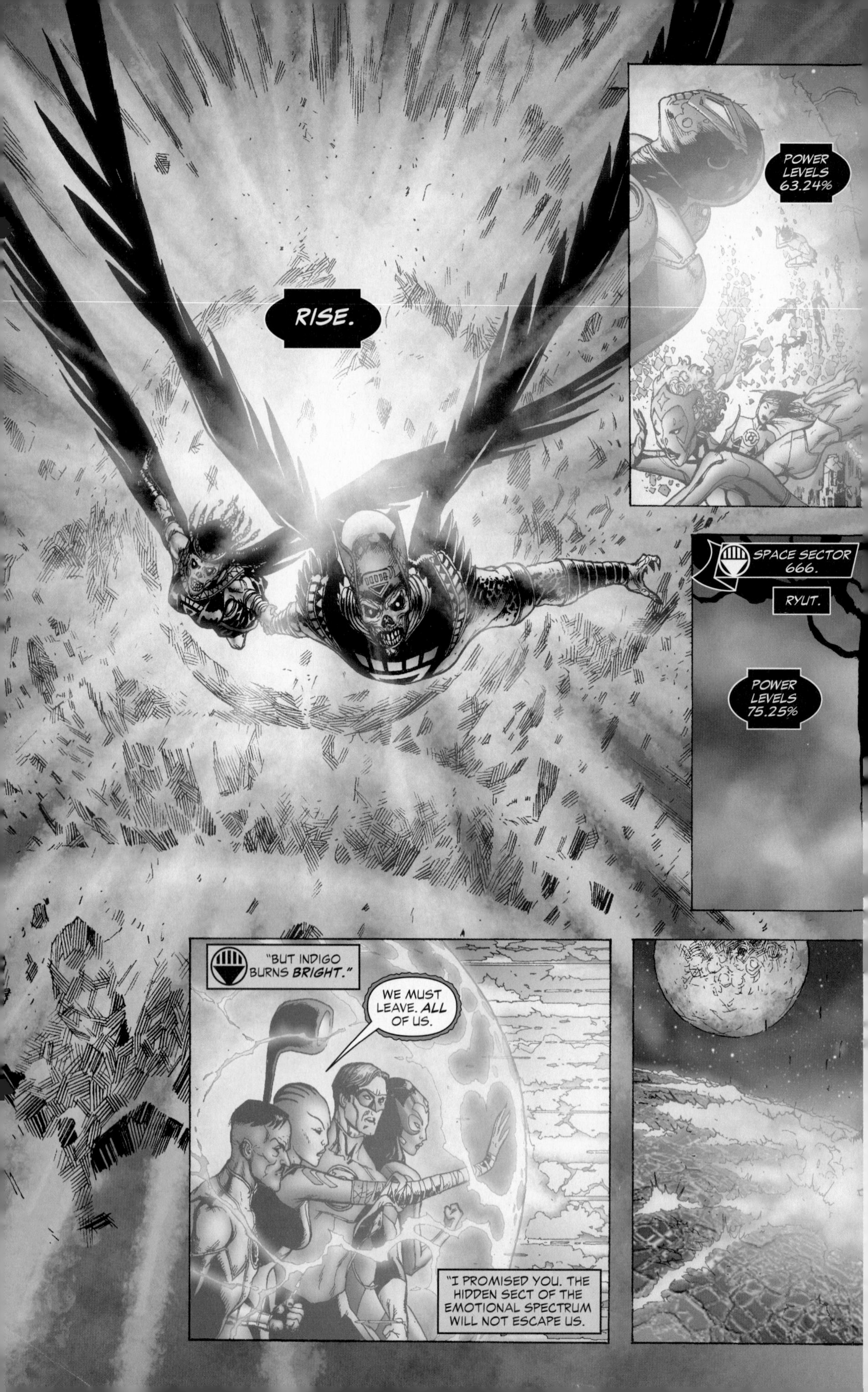
RISE.
POWER LEVELS 63.24%
SPACE SECTOR 666.
RYUT.
POWER LEVELS 75.25%
"BUT INDIGO BURNS BRIGHT."
WE MUST LEAVE. ALL OF US.
"I PROMISED YOU. THE HIDDEN SECT OF THE EMOTIONAL SPECTRUM WILL NOT ESCAPE US.

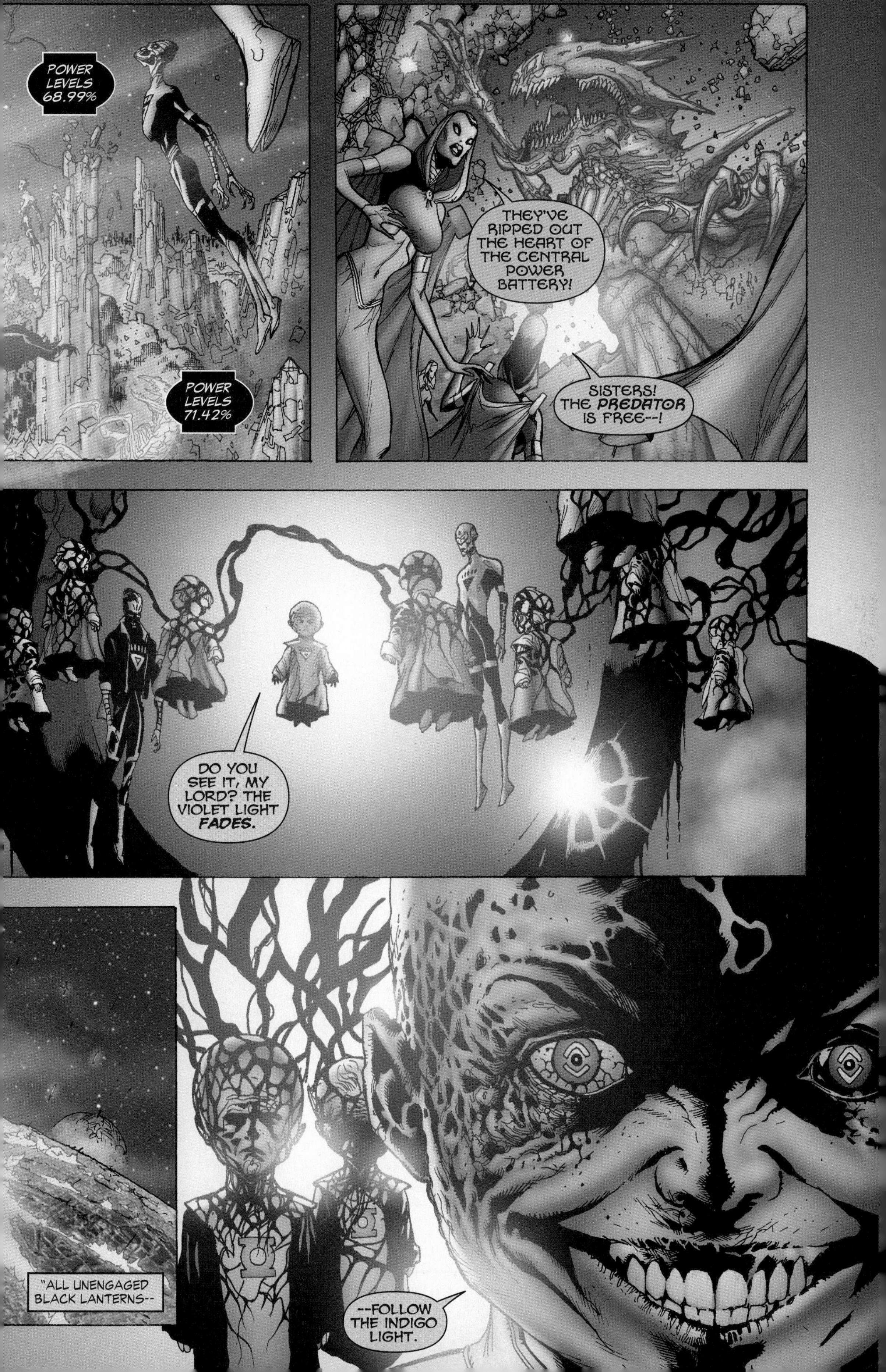
POWER LEVELS 68.99%
POWER LEVELS 71.42%
THEY'VE RIPPED OUT THE HEART OF THE CENTRAL POWER BATTERY!
SISTERS! THE PREDATOR IS FREE--!
DO YOU SEE IT, MY LORD? THE VIOLET LIGHT FADES.
"ALL UNENGAGED BLACK LANTERNS--
--FOLLOW THE INDIGO LIGHT.

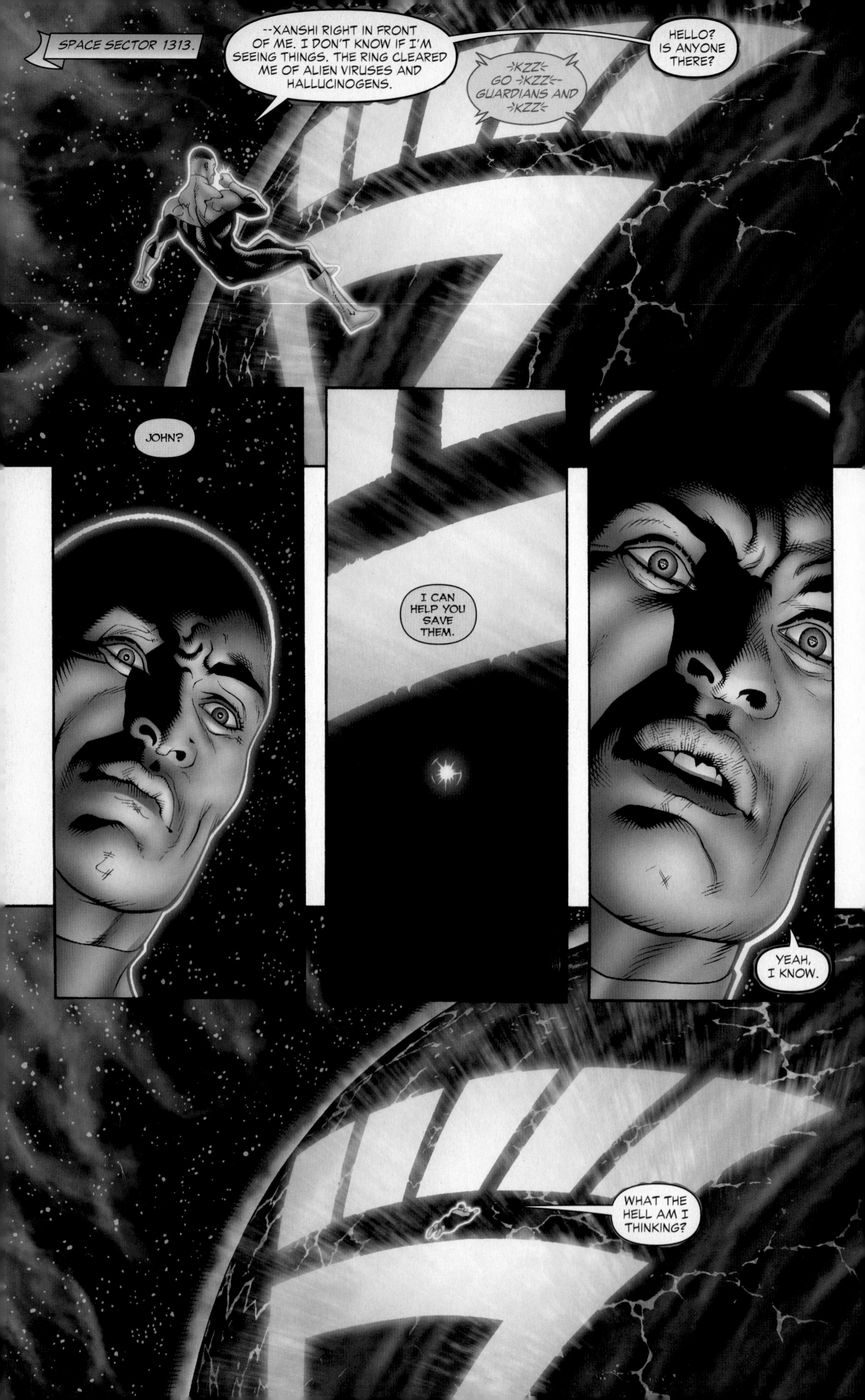
SPACE SECTOR 1313.
--XANSHI RIGHT IN FRONT OF ME. I DON'T KNOW IF I'M SEEING THINGS. THE RING CLEARED ME OF ALIEN VIRUSES AND HALLUCINOGENS.
-KZZ- GO -KZZ- GUARDIANS AND -KZZ-
HELLO? IS ANYONE THERE?
JOHN?
I CAN HELP YOU SAVE THEM.
YEAH, I KNOW.
WHAT THE HELL AM I THINKING?

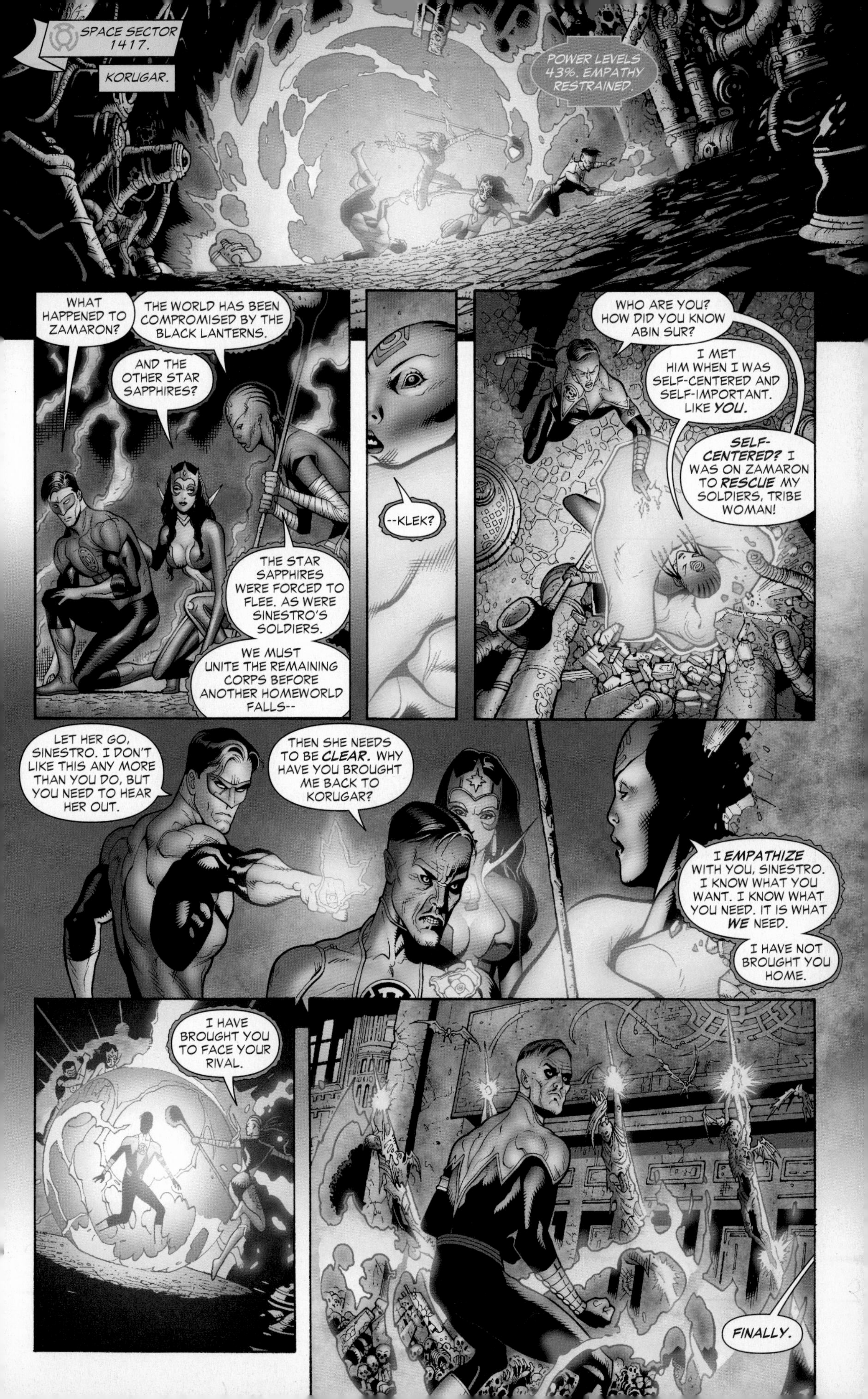
SPACE SECTOR 1417.
KORUGAR.
POWER LEVELS 43%. EMPATHY RESTRAINED.
WHAT HAPPENED TO ZAMARON?
THE WORLD HAS BEEN COMPROMISED BY THE BLACK LANTERNS.
AND THE OTHER STAR SAPPHIRES?
THE STAR SAPPHIRES WERE FORCED TO FLEE. AS WERE SINESTRO'S SOLDIERS.
WE MUST UNITE THE REMAINING CORPS BEFORE ANOTHER HOMEWORLD FALLS--
--KLEK?
WHO ARE YOU? HOW DID YOU KNOW ABIN SUR?
I MET HIM WHEN I WAS SELF-CENTERED AND SELF-IMPORTANT. LIKE YOU.
SELF-CENTERED? I WAS ON ZAMARON TO RESCUE MY SOLDIERS, TRIBE WOMAN!
LET HER GO, SINESTRO. I DON'T LIKE THIS ANY MORE THAN YOU DO, BUT YOU NEED TO HEAR HER OUT.
THEN SHE NEEDS TO BE CLEAR. WHY HAVE YOU BROUGHT ME BACK TO KORUGAR?
I EMPATHIZE WITH YOU, SINESTRO. I KNOW WHAT YOU WANT. I KNOW WHAT YOU NEED. IT IS WHAT WE NEED.
I HAVE NOT BROUGHT YOU HOME.
I HAVE BROUGHT YOU TO FACE YOUR RIVAL.
FINALLY.

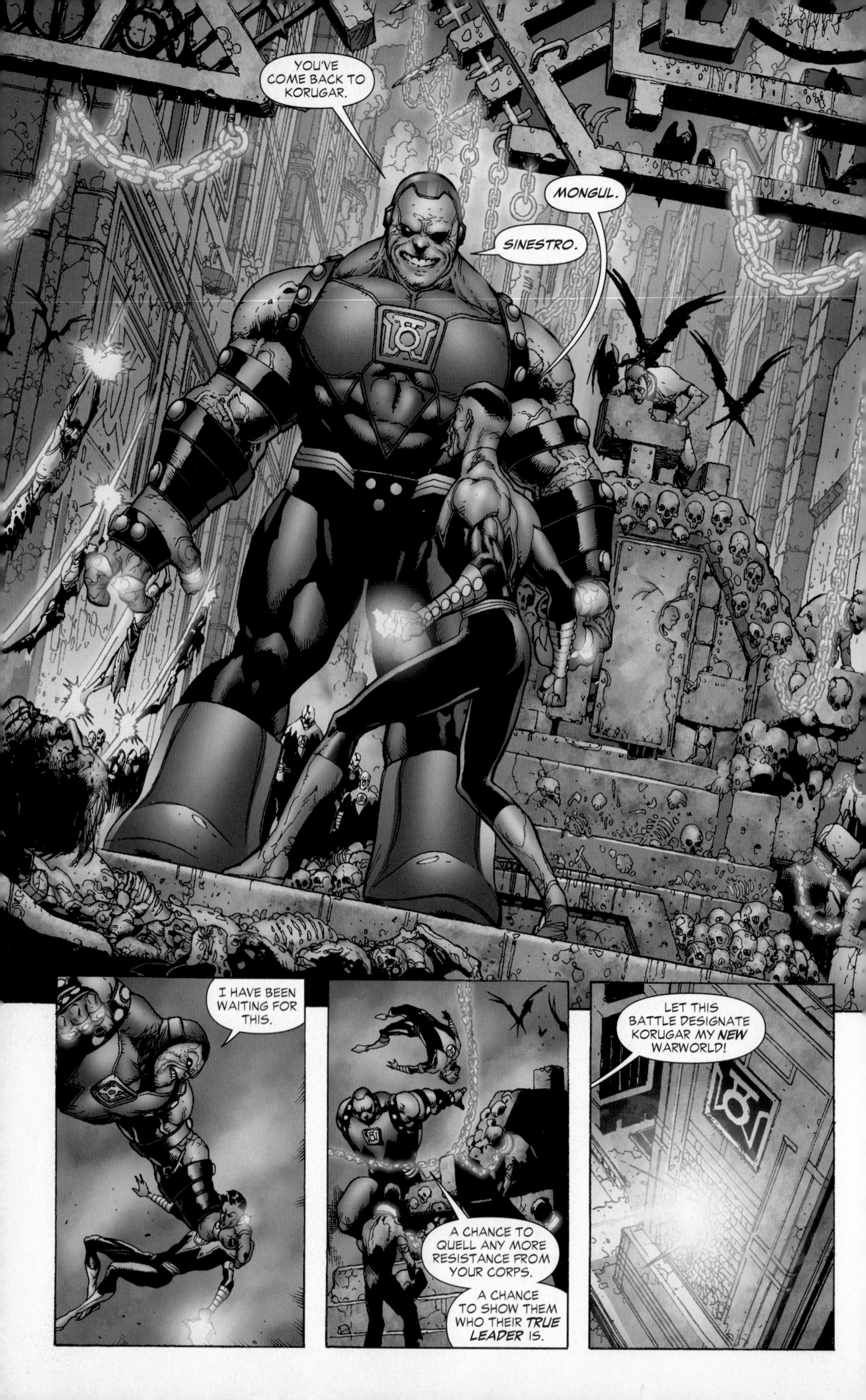
YOU'VE COME BACK TO KORUGAR.
MONGUL.
SINESTRO.
I HAVE BEEN WAITING FOR THIS.
A CHANCE TO QUELL ANY MORE RESISTANCE FROM YOUR CORPS.
A CHANCE TO SHOW THEM WHO THEIR TRUE LEADER IS.
LET THIS BATTLE DESIGNATE KORUGAR MY NEW WARWORLD!

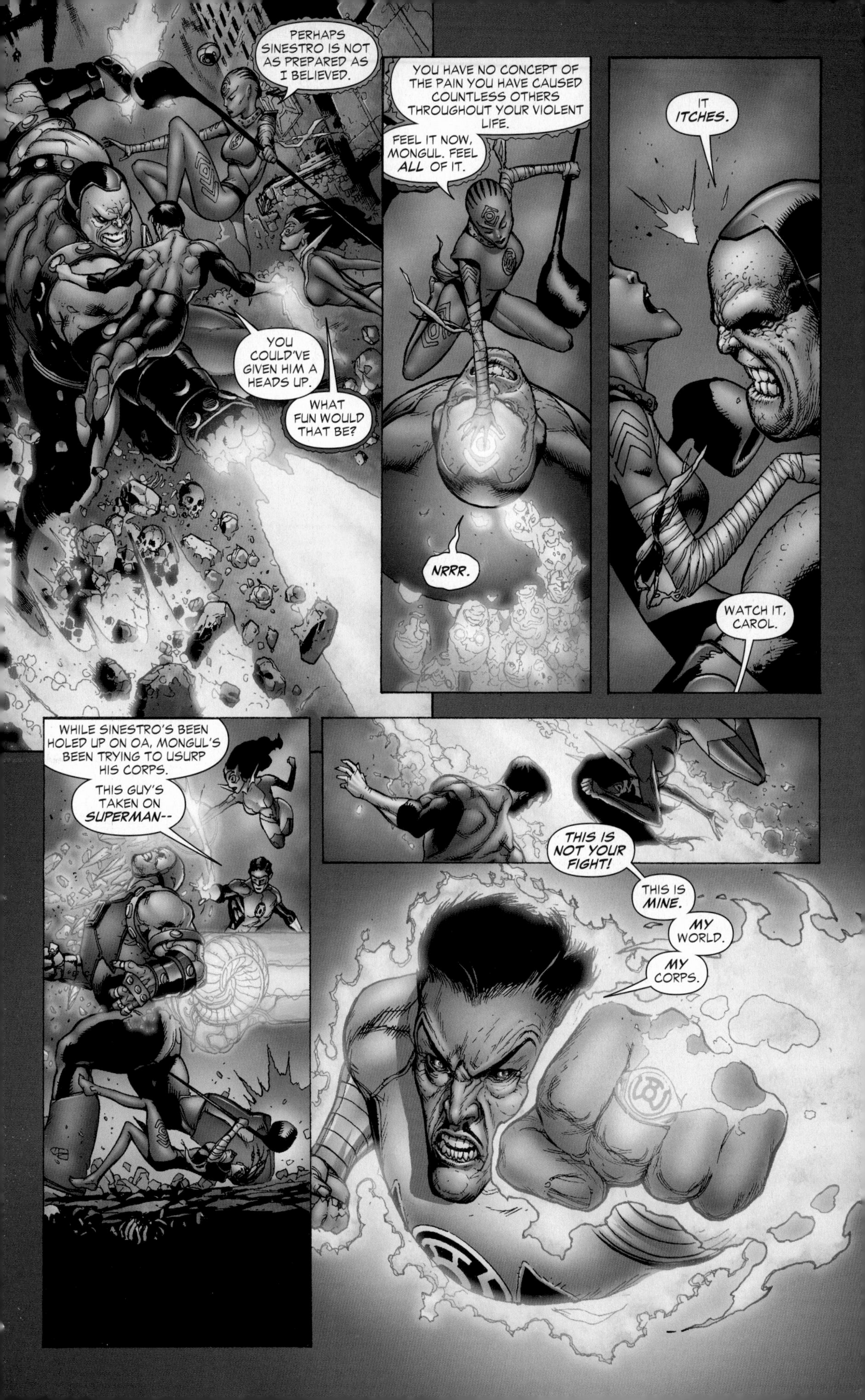
PERHAPS SINESTRO IS NOT AS PREPARED AS I BELIEVED.
YOU COULD'VE GIVEN HIM A HEADS UP.
WHAT FUN WOULD THAT BE?
YOU HAVE NO CONCEPT OF THE PAIN YOU HAVE CAUSED COUNTLESS OTHERS THROUGHOUT YOUR VIOLENT LIFE.
FEEL IT NOW, MONGUL. FEEL ALL OF IT.
NRRR.
IT ITCHES.
WATCH IT, CAROL.
WHILE SINESTRO'S BEEN HOLED UP ON OA, MONGUL'S BEEN TRYING TO USURP HIS CORPS.
THIS GUY'S TAKEN ON SUPERMAN--
THIS IS NOT YOUR FIGHT!
THIS IS MINE.
MY WORLD.
MY CORPS.

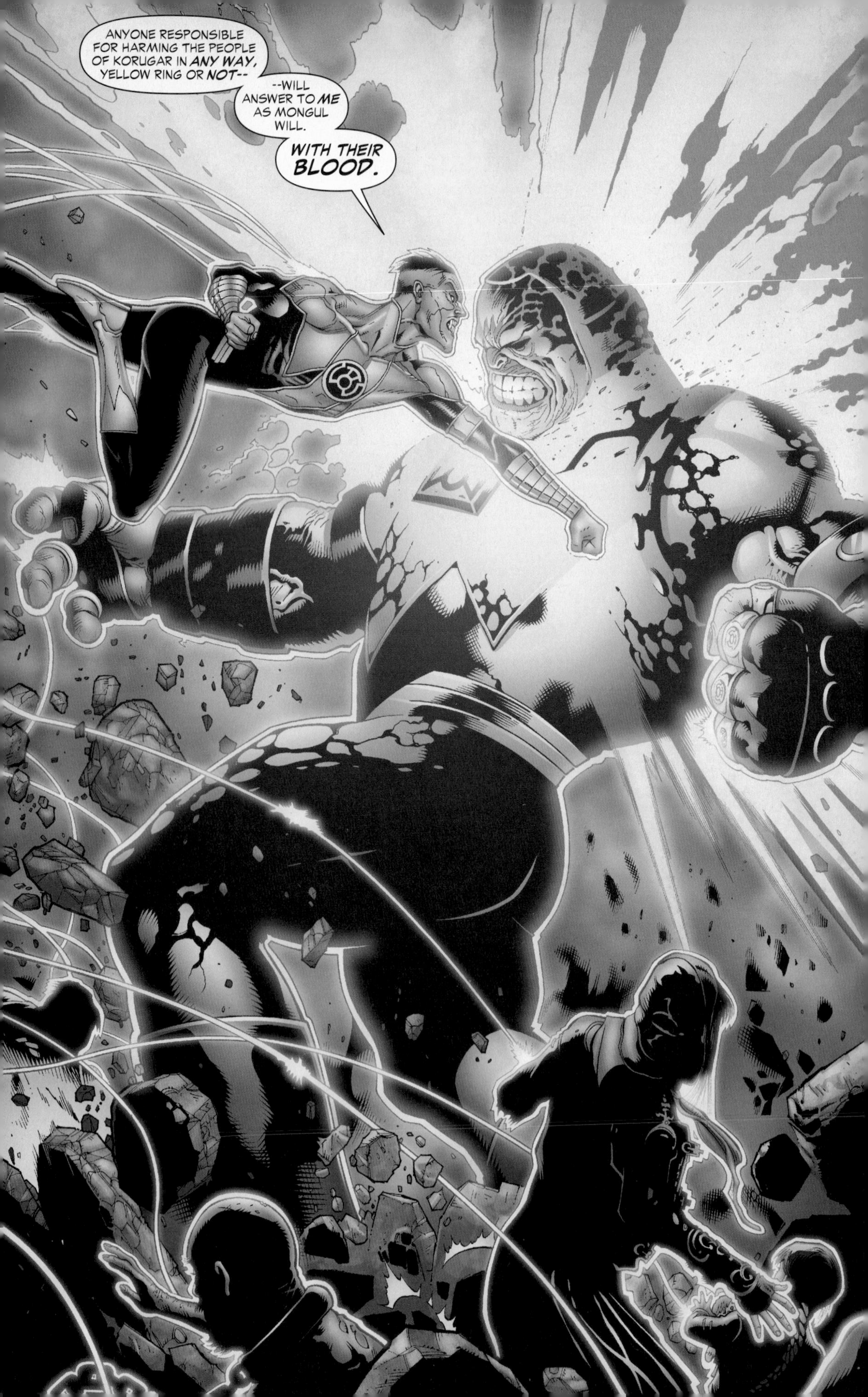
ANYONE RESPONSIBLE FOR HARMING THE PEOPLE OF KORUGAR IN ANY WAY, YELLOW RING OR NOT--
--WILL ANSWER TO ME AS MONGUL WILL.
WITH THEIR BLOOD.

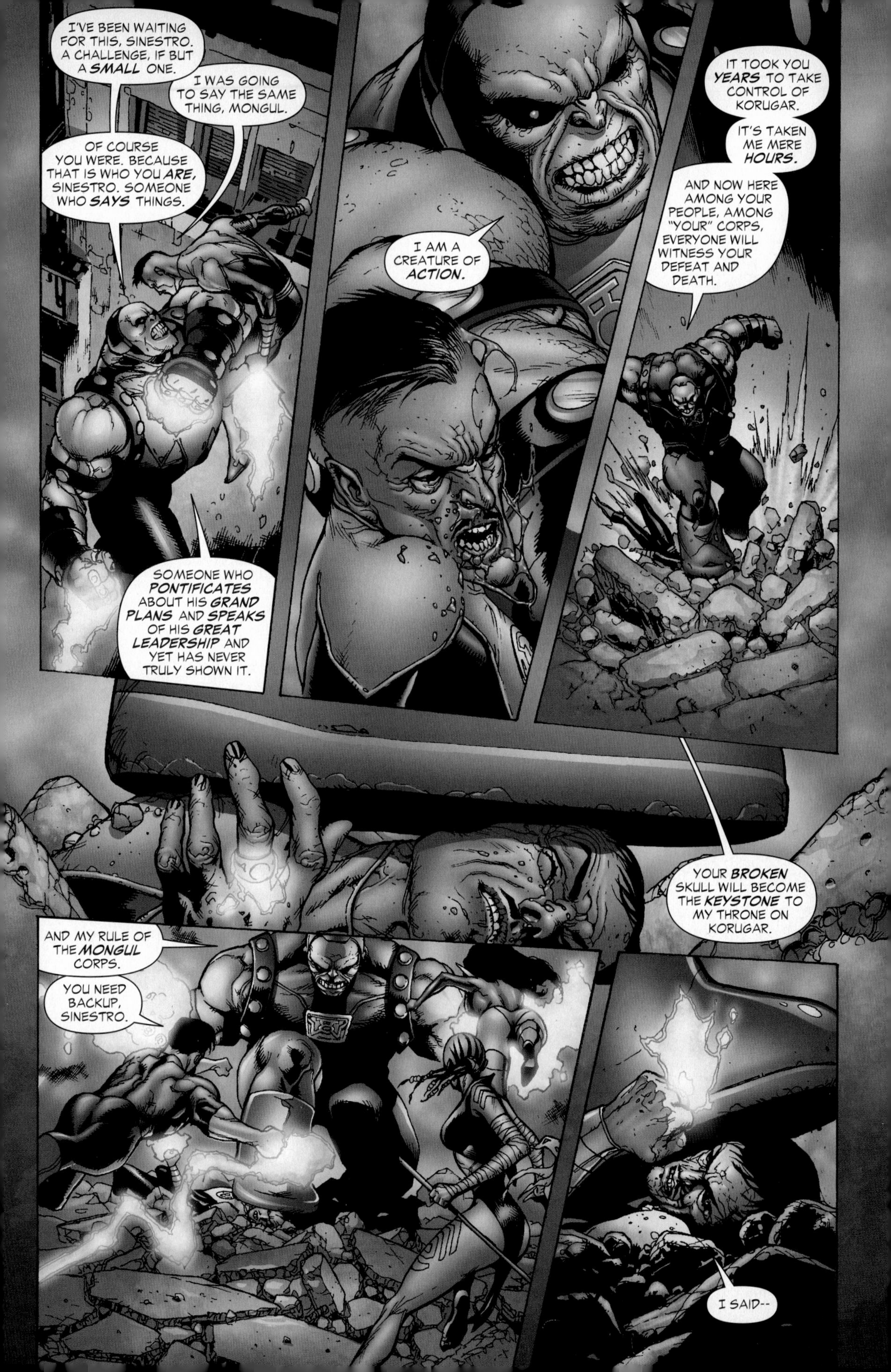
I'VE BEEN WAITING FOR THIS, SINESTRO. A CHALLENGE, IF BUT A SMALL ONE.
I WAS GOING TO SAY THE SAME THING, MONGUL.
OF COURSE YOU WERE. BECAUSE THAT IS WHO YOU ARE, SINESTRO. SOMEONE WHO SAYS THINGS.
SOMEONE WHO PONTIFICATES ABOUT HIS GRAND PLANS AND SPEAKS OF HIS GREAT LEADERSHIP AND YET HAS NEVER TRULY SHOWN IT.
I AM A CREATURE OF ACTION.
IT TOOK YOU YEARS TO TAKE CONTROL OF KORUGAR.
IT'S TAKEN ME MERE HOURS.
AND NOW HERE AMONG YOUR PEOPLE, AMONG "YOUR" CORPS, EVERYONE WILL WITNESS YOUR DEFEAT AND DEATH.
YOUR BROKEN SKULL WILL BECOME THE KEYSTONE TO MY THRONE ON KORUGAR.
AND MY RULE OF THE MONGUL CORPS.
YOU NEED BACKUP, SINESTRO.
I SAID--

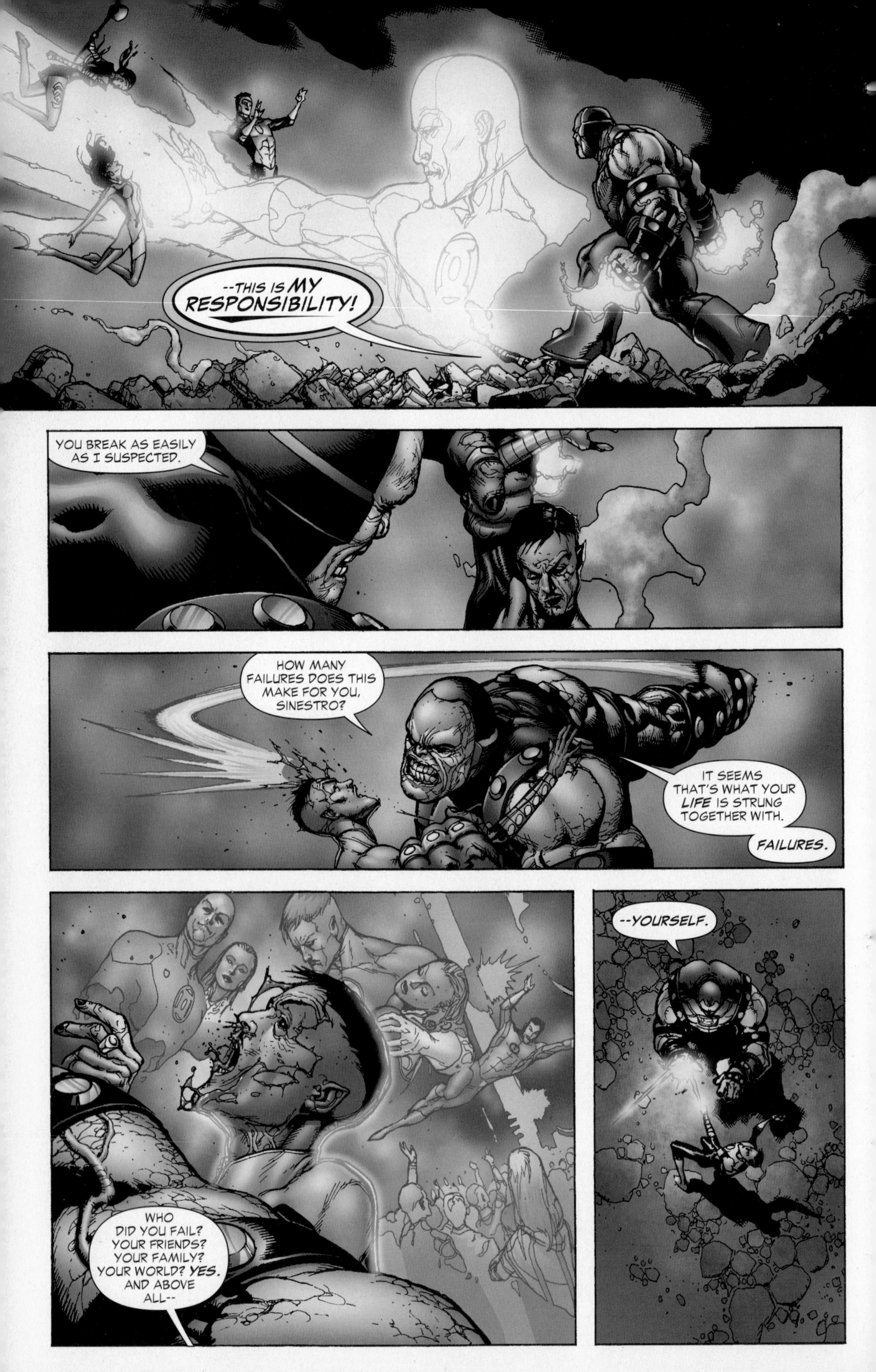
--THIS IS MY RESPONSIBILITY!
YOU BREAK AS EASILY AS I SUSPECTED.
HOW MANY FAILURES DOES THIS MAKE FOR YOU, SINESTRO?
IT SEEMS THAT'S WHAT YOUR LIFE IS STRUNG TOGETHER WITH.
FAILURES.
WHO DID YOU FAIL? YOUR FRIENDS? YOUR FAMILY? YOUR WORLD? YES. AND ABOVE ALL--
--YOURSELF.

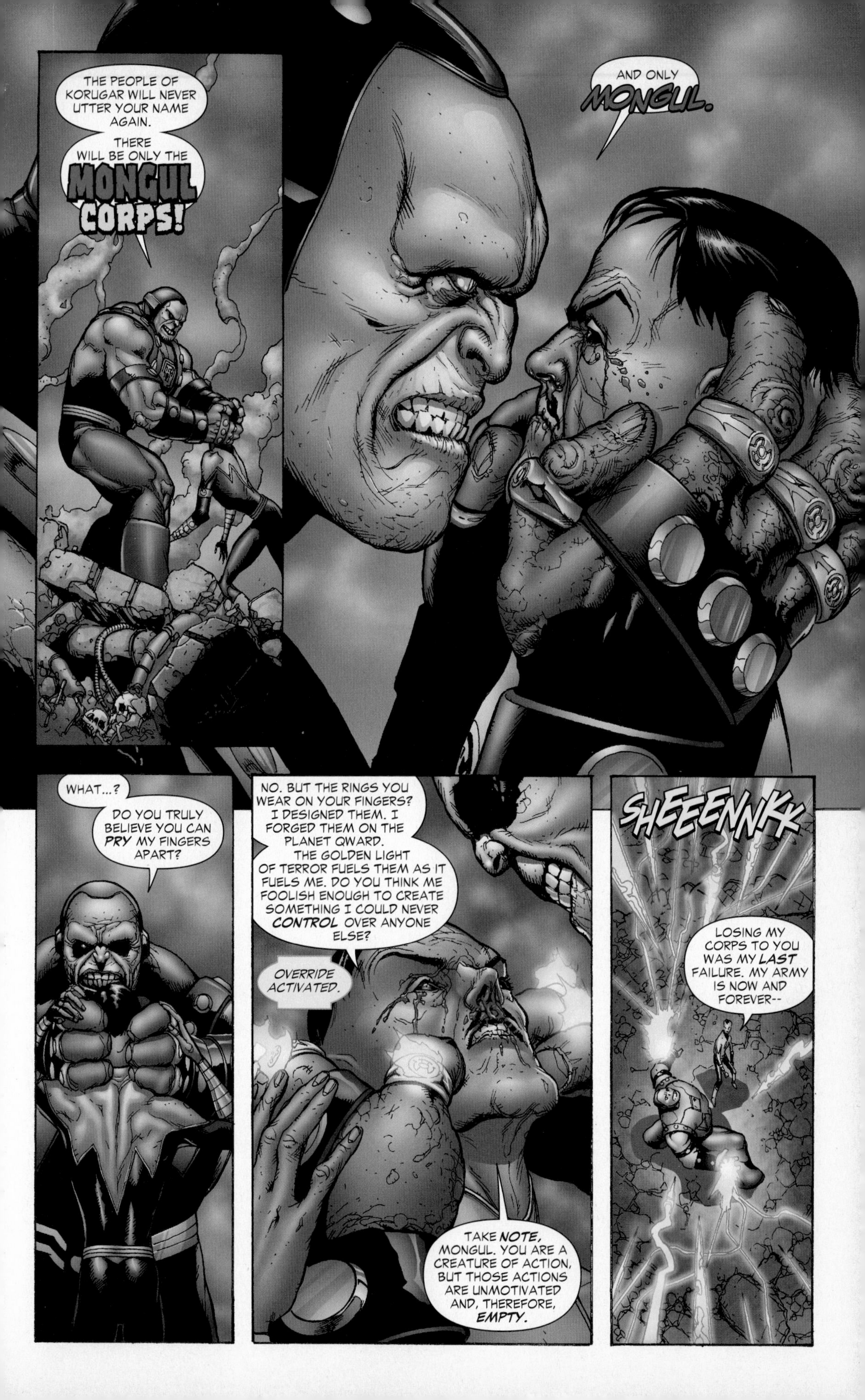
THE PEOPLE OF KORUGAR WILL NEVER UTTER YOUR NAME AGAIN.
THERE WILL BE ONLY THE MONGUL CORPS!
AND ONLY MONGUL.
WHAT...?
DO YOU TRULY BELIEVE YOU CAN PRY MY FINGERS APART?
NO. BUT THE RINGS YOU WEAR ON YOUR FINGERS? I DESIGNED THEM. I FORGED THEM ON THE PLANET QWARD.
THE GOLDEN LIGHT OF TERROR FUELS THEM AS IT FUELS ME. DO YOU THINK ME FOOLISH ENOUGH TO CREATE SOMETHING I COULD NEVER CONTROL OVER ANYONE ELSE?
OVERRIDE ACTIVATED.
TAKE NOTE, MONGUL. YOU ARE A CREATURE OF ACTION, BUT THOSE ACTIONS ARE UNMOTIVATED AND, THEREFORE, EMPTY.
SHEEENNKK
LOSING MY CORPS TO YOU WAS MY LAST FAILURE. MY ARMY IS NOW AND FOREVER--

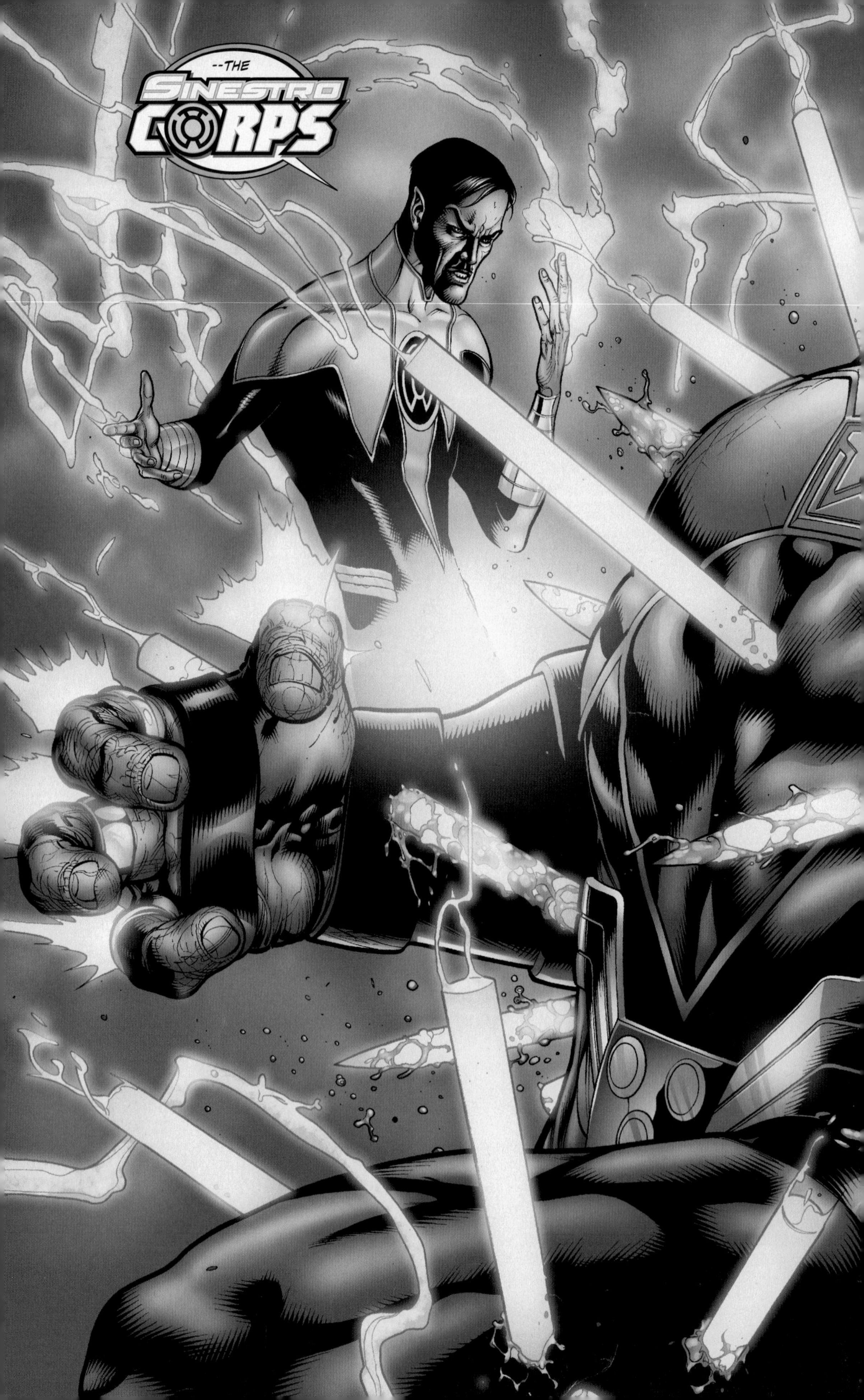
--THE SINESTRO CORPS

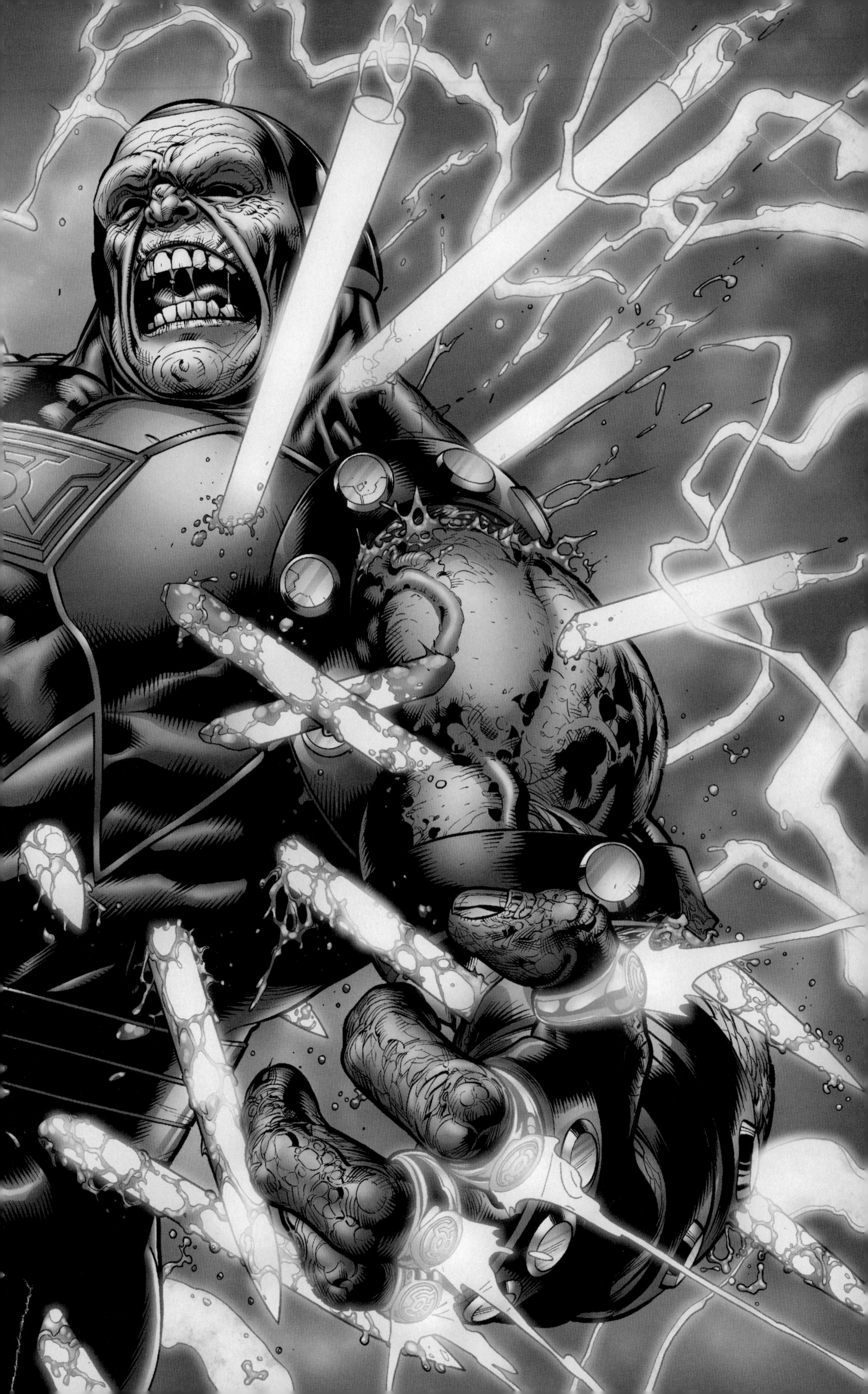

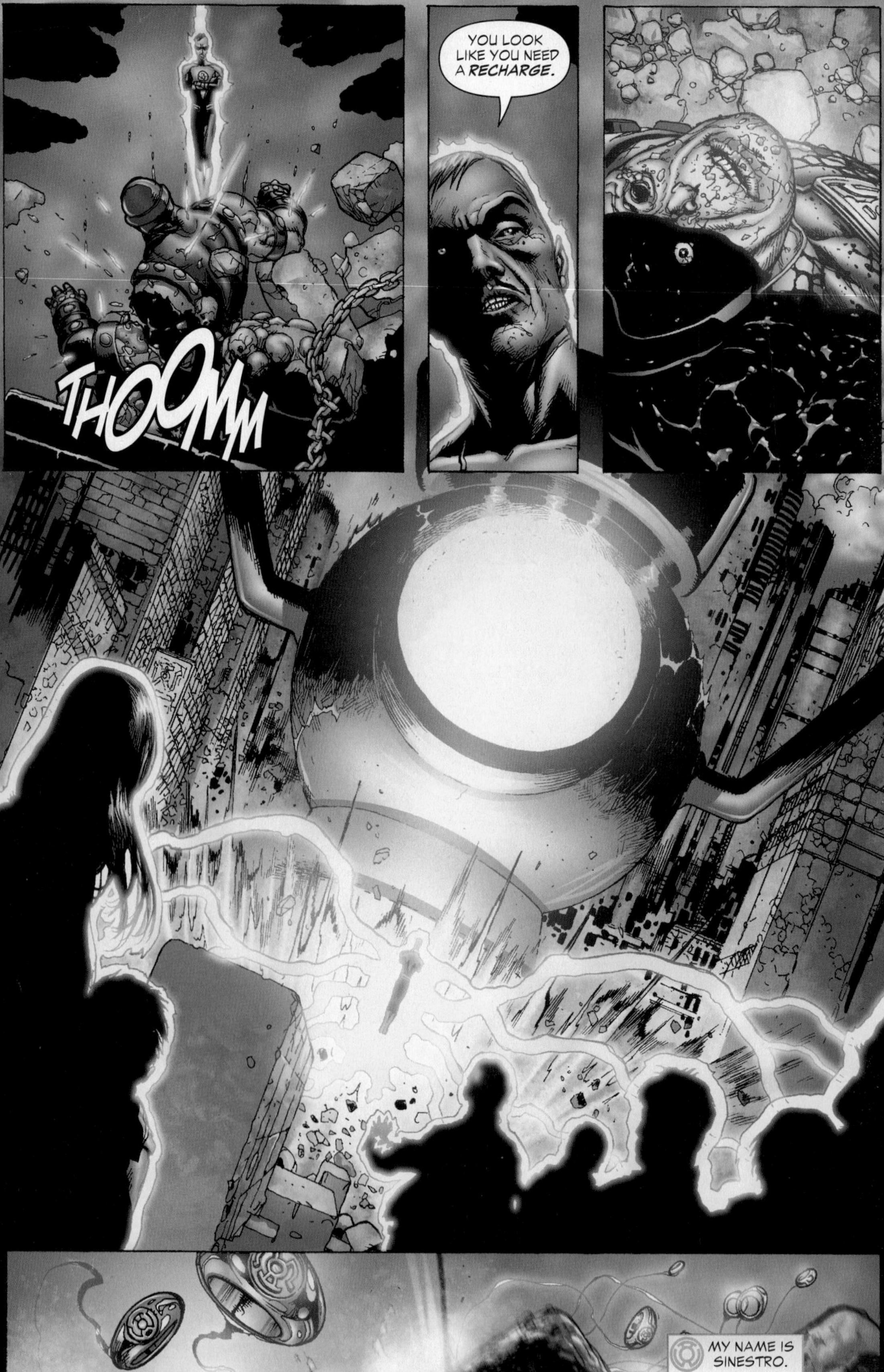
THOOMM
YOU LOOK LIKE YOU NEED A RECHARGE.
MY NAME IS SINESTRO.
I AM THE LEADER OF THE SINESTRO CORPS. SPACE SECTOR 1417.

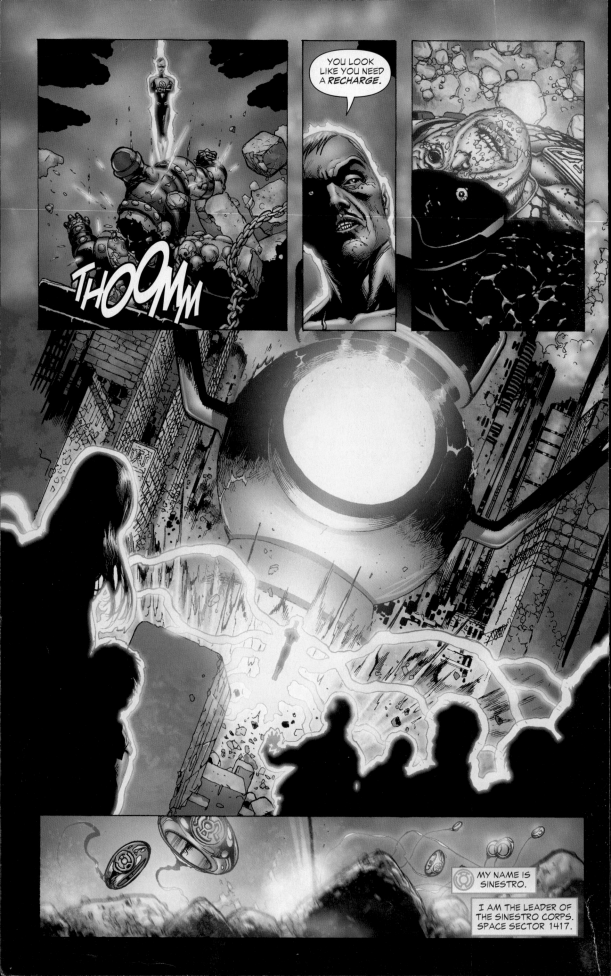

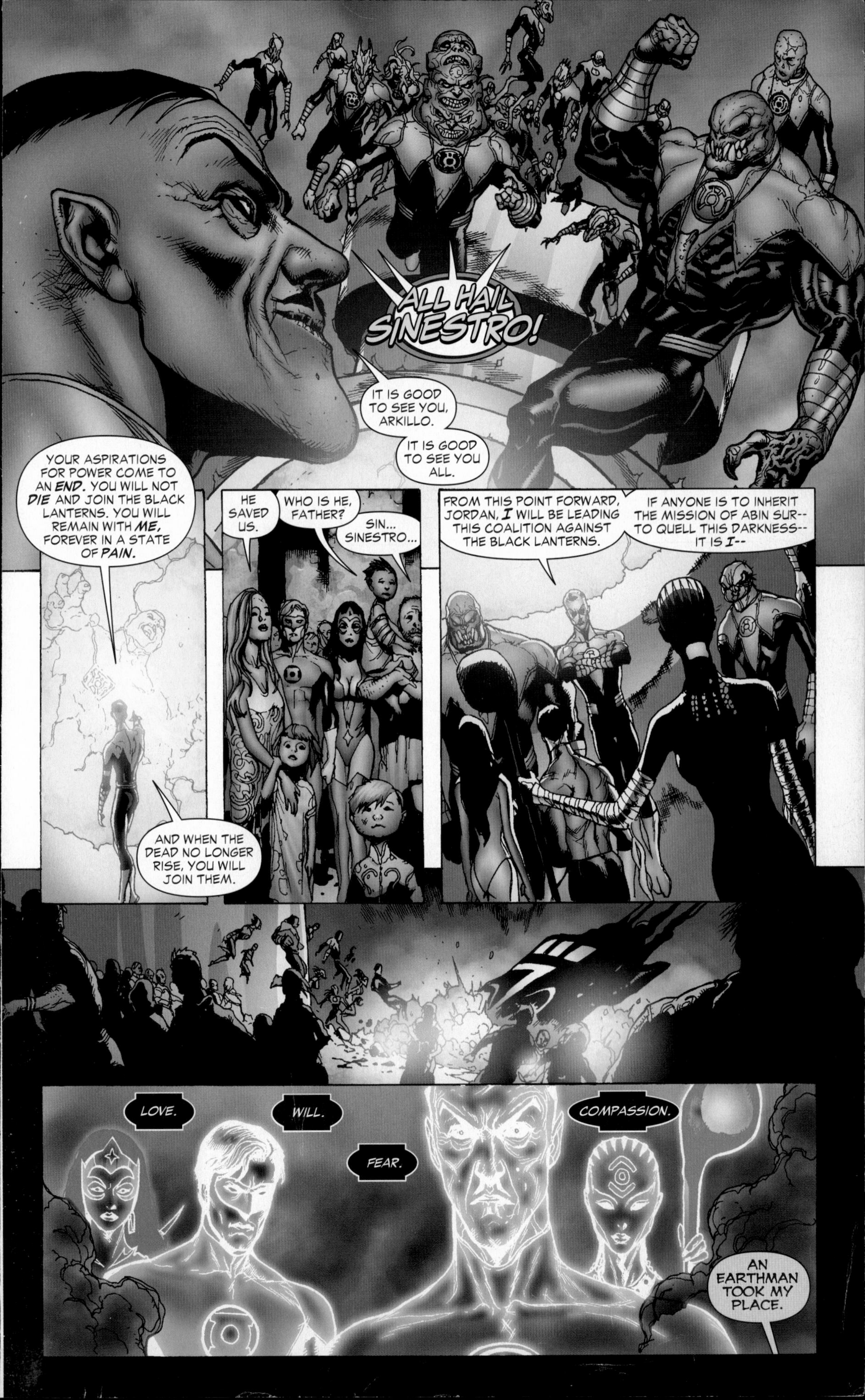
ALL HAIL SINESTRO!
IT IS GOOD TO SEE YOU, ARKILLO.
IT IS GOOD TO SEE YOU ALL.
YOUR ASPIRATIONS FOR POWER COME TO AN END. YOU WILL NOT DIE AND JOIN THE BLACK LANTERNS. YOU WILL REMAIN WITH ME, FOREVER IN A STATE OF PAIN.
AND WHEN THE DEAD NO LONGER RISE, YOU WILL JOIN THEM.
HE SAVED US.
WHO IS HE, FATHER?
SIN... SINESTRO...
FROM THIS POINT FORWARD, JORDAN, I WILL BE LEADING THIS COALITION AGAINST THE BLACK LANTERNS.
IF ANYONE IS TO INHERIT THE MISSION OF ABIN SUR-- TO QUELL THIS DARKNESS-- IT IS I--
LOVE.
WILL.
FEAR.
COMPASSION.
AN EARTHMAN TOOK MY PLACE.

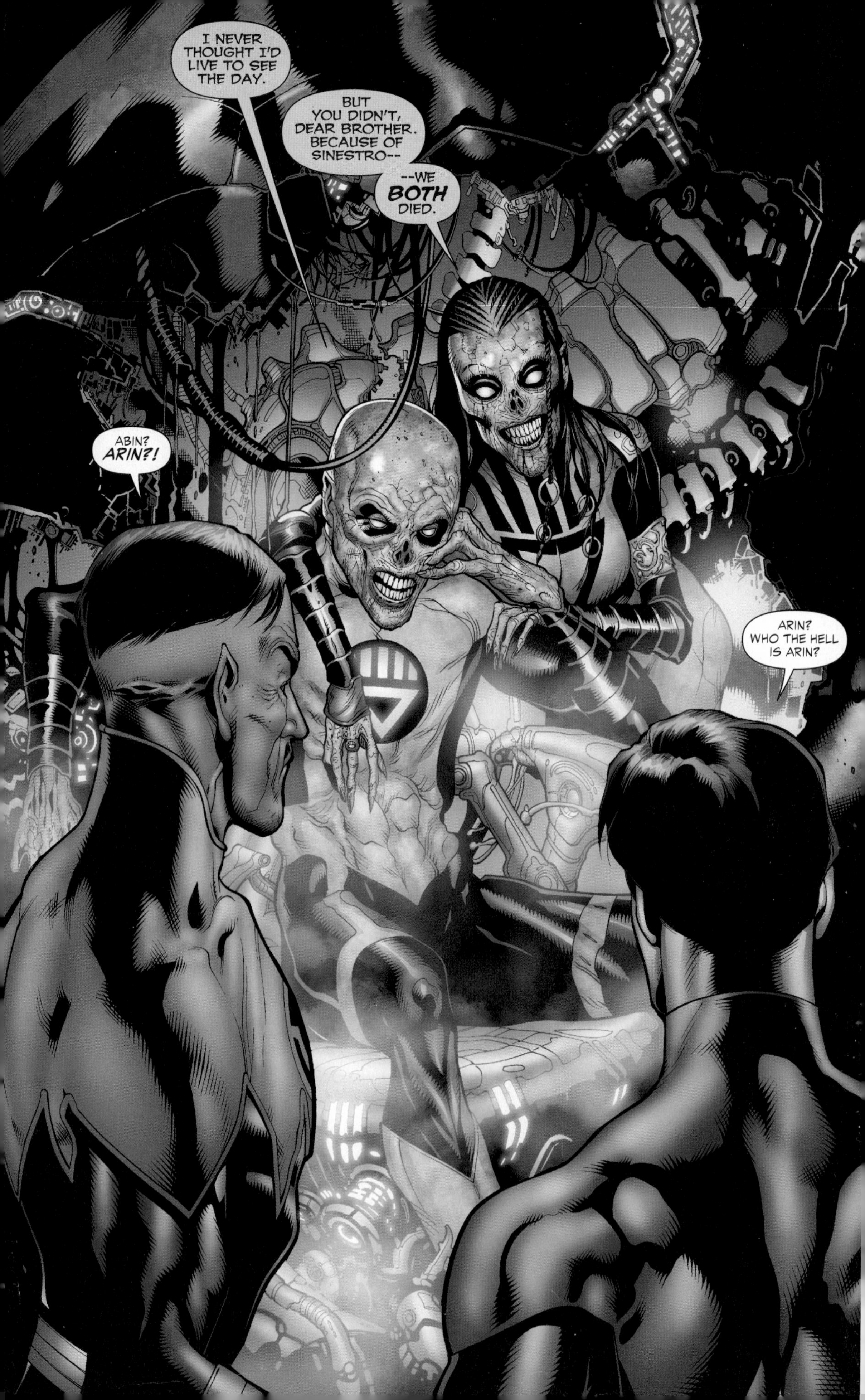
I NEVER THOUGHT I'D LIVE TO SEE THE DAY.
BUT YOU DIDN'T, DEAR BROTHER. BECAUSE OF SINESTRO--
--WE **BOTH** DIED.
ABIN? ***ARIN?!***
ARIN? WHO THE HELL IS ARIN?

GREEN LANTERN 47
Cover by Doug Mahnke and Christian Alamy with Hi-Fi

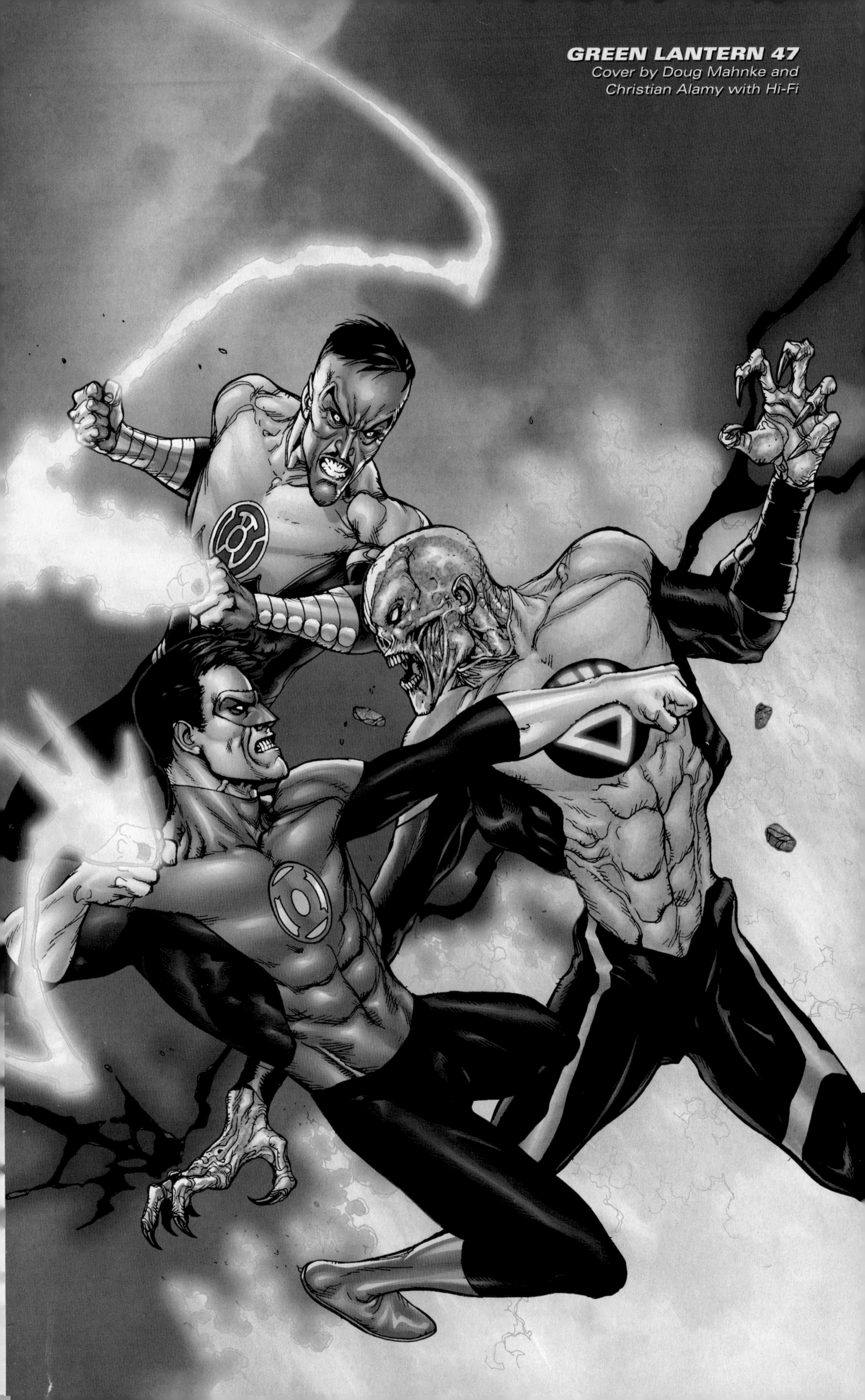

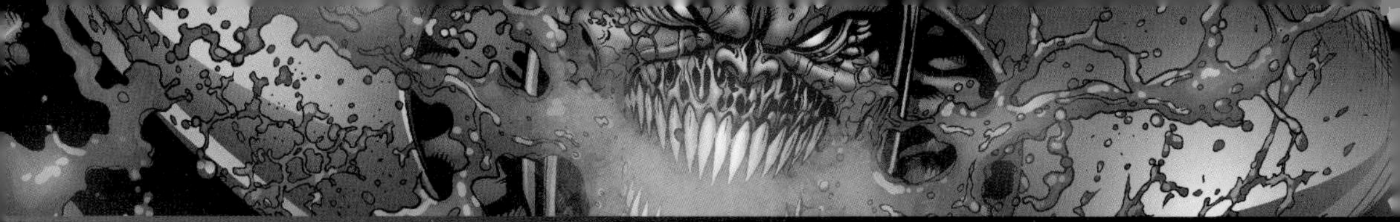

For millennia the planet Ysmault has been home to tragedy. Once the prison to the survivors of the slaughter of Sector 666, where Abin Sur descended into madness, it's also the birthplace of rage and the Red Lantern Corps.

Now the sins of this planet's past are resurrected in horrifying and unspeakable ways...

TO HELL AND BACK

DOUG MAHNKE
PENCILS

CHRISTIAN ALAMY
DOUG MAHNKE
TOM NGUYEN
MARK IRWIN
INKS

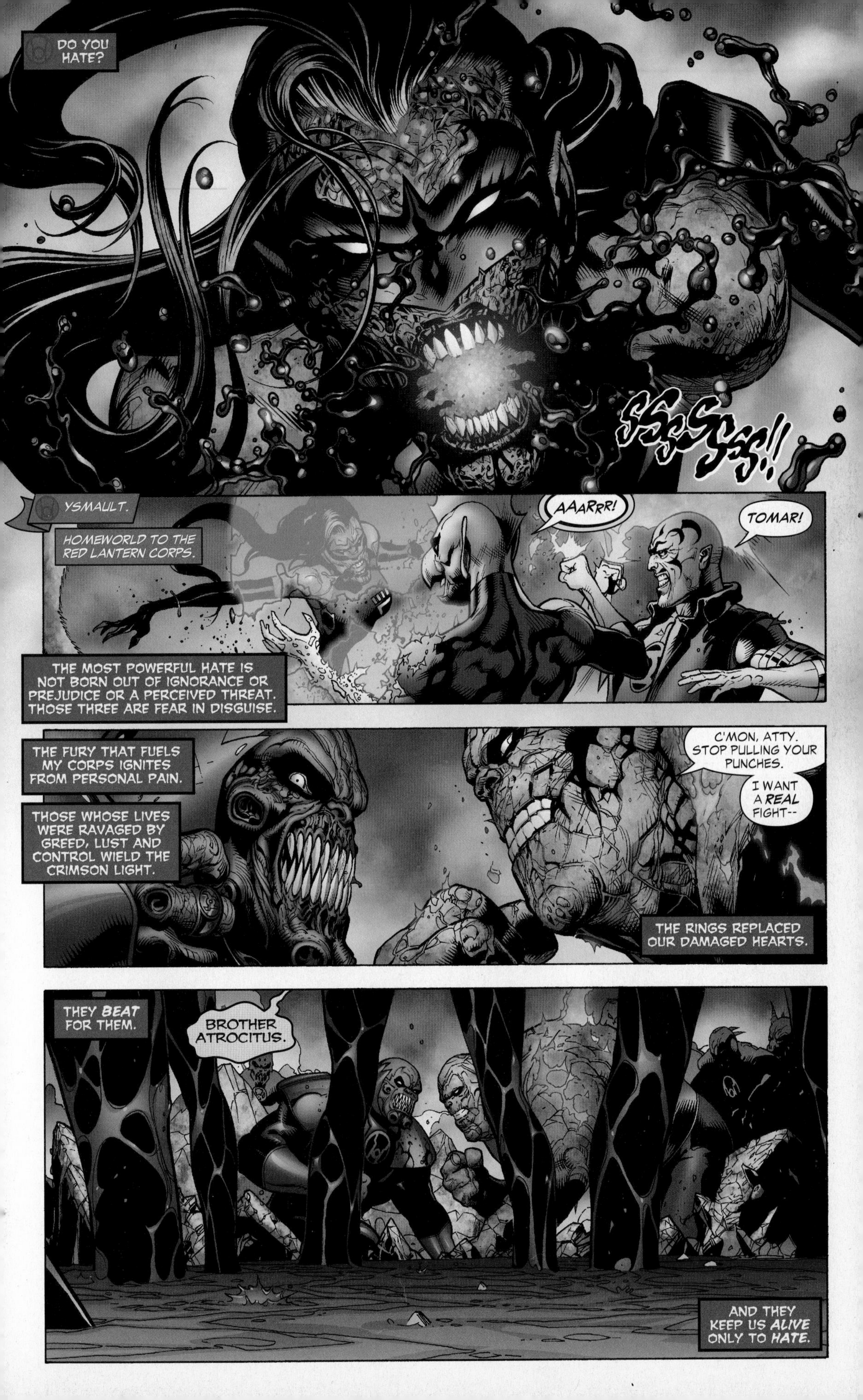
DO YOU HATE?
SSSSSSS!!
YSMAULT.
HOMEWORLD TO THE RED LANTERN CORPS.
AAARRR!
TOMAR!
THE MOST POWERFUL HATE IS NOT BORN OUT OF IGNORANCE OR PREJUDICE OR A PERCEIVED THREAT. THOSE THREE ARE FEAR IN DISGUISE.
THE FURY THAT FUELS MY CORPS IGNITES FROM PERSONAL PAIN.
THOSE WHOSE LIVES WERE RAVAGED BY GREED, LUST AND CONTROL WIELD THE CRIMSON LIGHT.
C'MON, ATTY. STOP PULLING YOUR PUNCHES.
I WANT A REAL FIGHT--
THE RINGS REPLACED OUR DAMAGED HEARTS.
THEY BEAT FOR THEM.
BROTHER ATROCITUS.
AND THEY KEEP US ALIVE ONLY TO HATE.

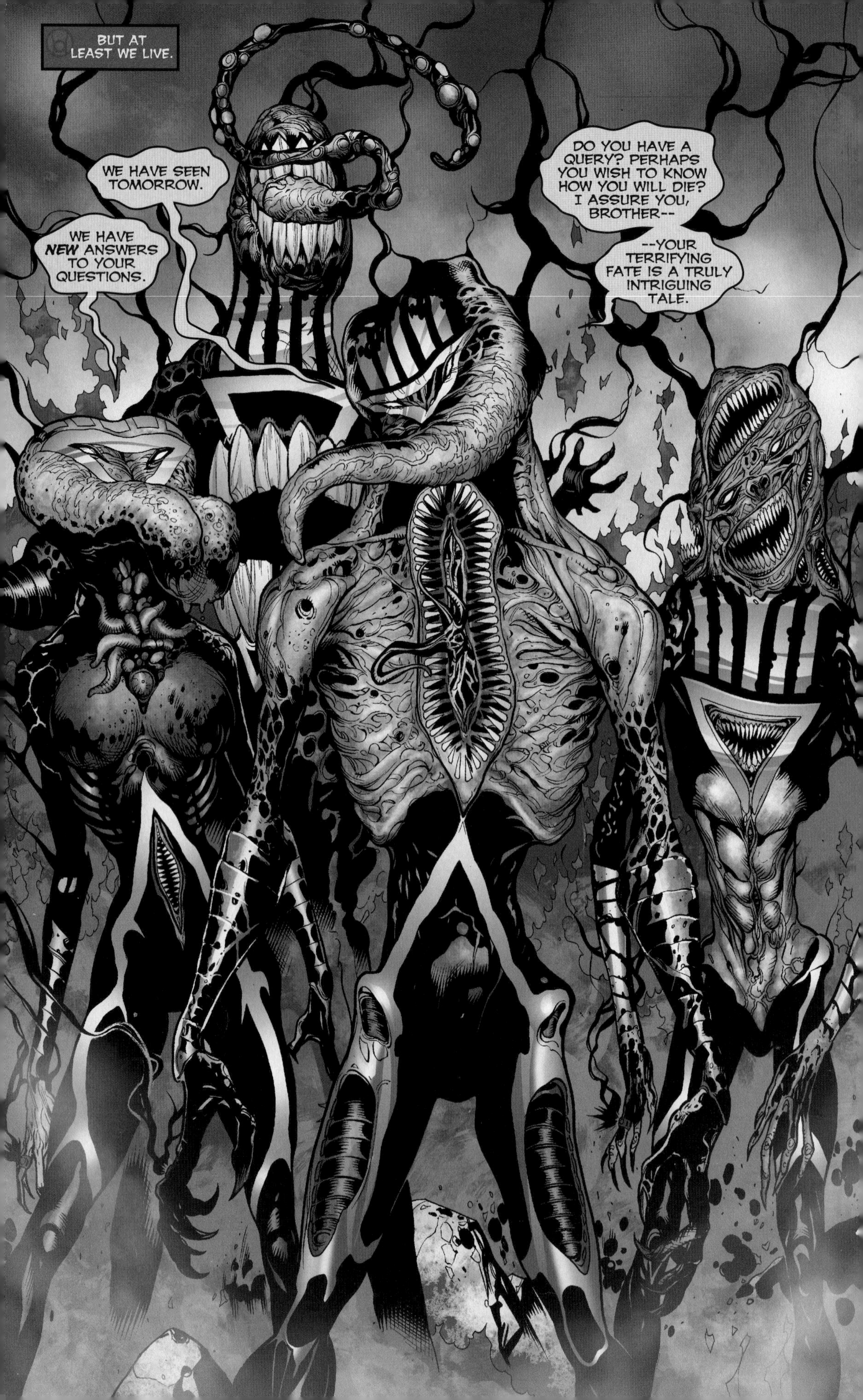
BUT AT LEAST WE LIVE.
WE HAVE SEEN TOMORROW.
WE HAVE NEW ANSWERS TO YOUR QUESTIONS.
DO YOU HAVE A QUERY? PERHAPS YOU WISH TO KNOW HOW YOU WILL DIE? I ASSURE YOU, BROTHER--
--YOUR TERRIFYING FATE IS A TRULY INTRIGUING TALE.

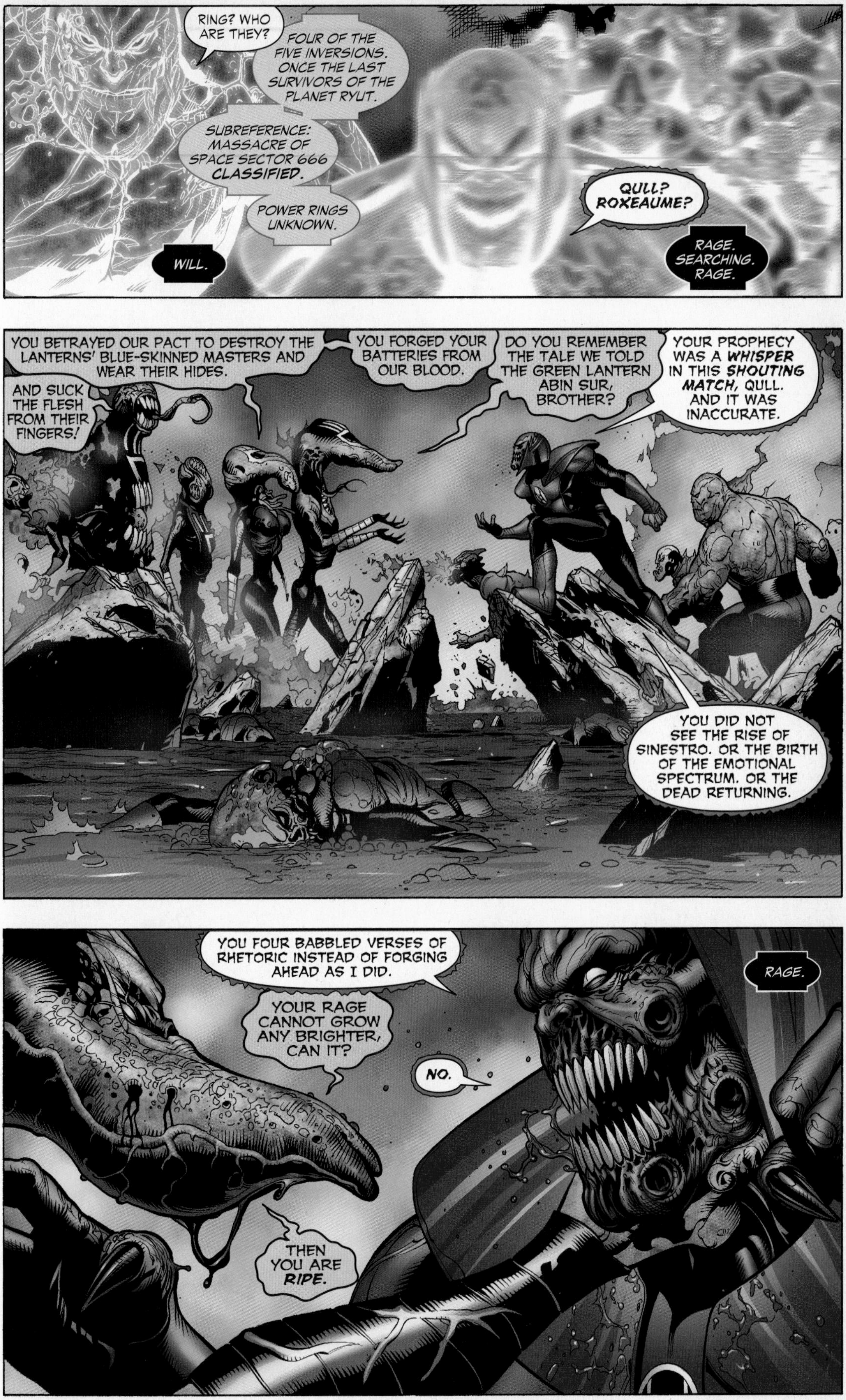
RING? WHO ARE THEY?
FOUR OF THE FIVE INVERSIONS. ONCE THE LAST SURVIVORS OF THE PLANET RYUT.
SUBREFERENCE: MASSACRE OF SPACE SECTOR 666 CLASSIFIED.
POWER RINGS UNKNOWN.
WILL.
QULL? ROXEAUME?
RAGE. SEARCHING. RAGE.
YOU BETRAYED OUR PACT TO DESTROY THE LANTERNS' BLUE-SKINNED MASTERS AND WEAR THEIR HIDES.
AND SUCK THE FLESH FROM THEIR FINGERS!
YOU FORGED YOUR BATTERIES FROM OUR BLOOD.
DO YOU REMEMBER THE TALE WE TOLD THE GREEN LANTERN ABIN SUR, BROTHER?
YOUR PROPHECY WAS A WHISPER IN THIS SHOUTING MATCH, QULL. AND IT WAS INACCURATE.
YOU DID NOT SEE THE RISE OF SINESTRO. OR THE BIRTH OF THE EMOTIONAL SPECTRUM. OR THE DEAD RETURNING.
YOU FOUR BABBLED VERSES OF RHETORIC INSTEAD OF FORGING AHEAD AS I DID.
RAGE.
YOUR RAGE CANNOT GROW ANY BRIGHTER, CAN IT?
NO.
THEN YOU ARE RIPE.

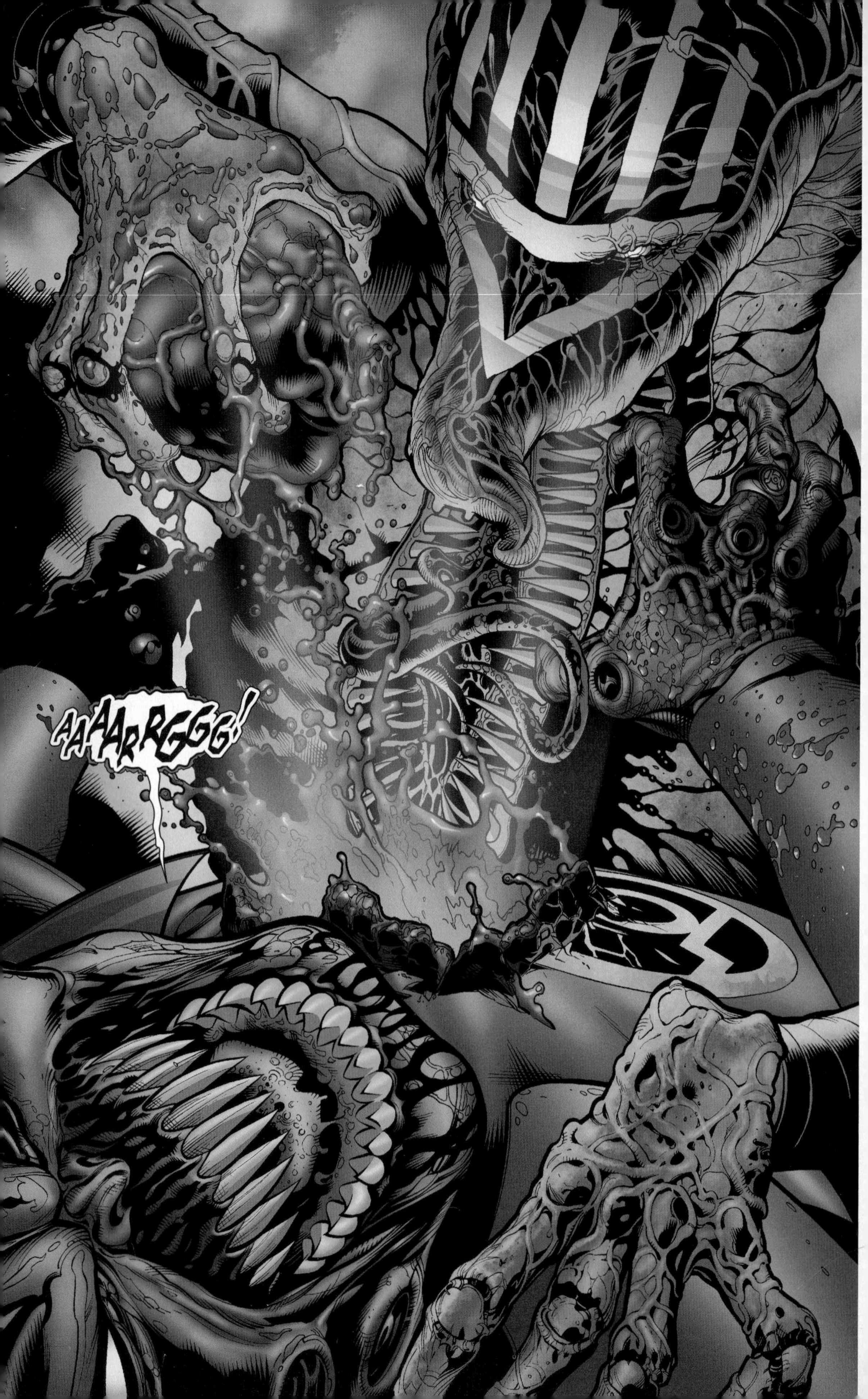
AAAARRGGGG!

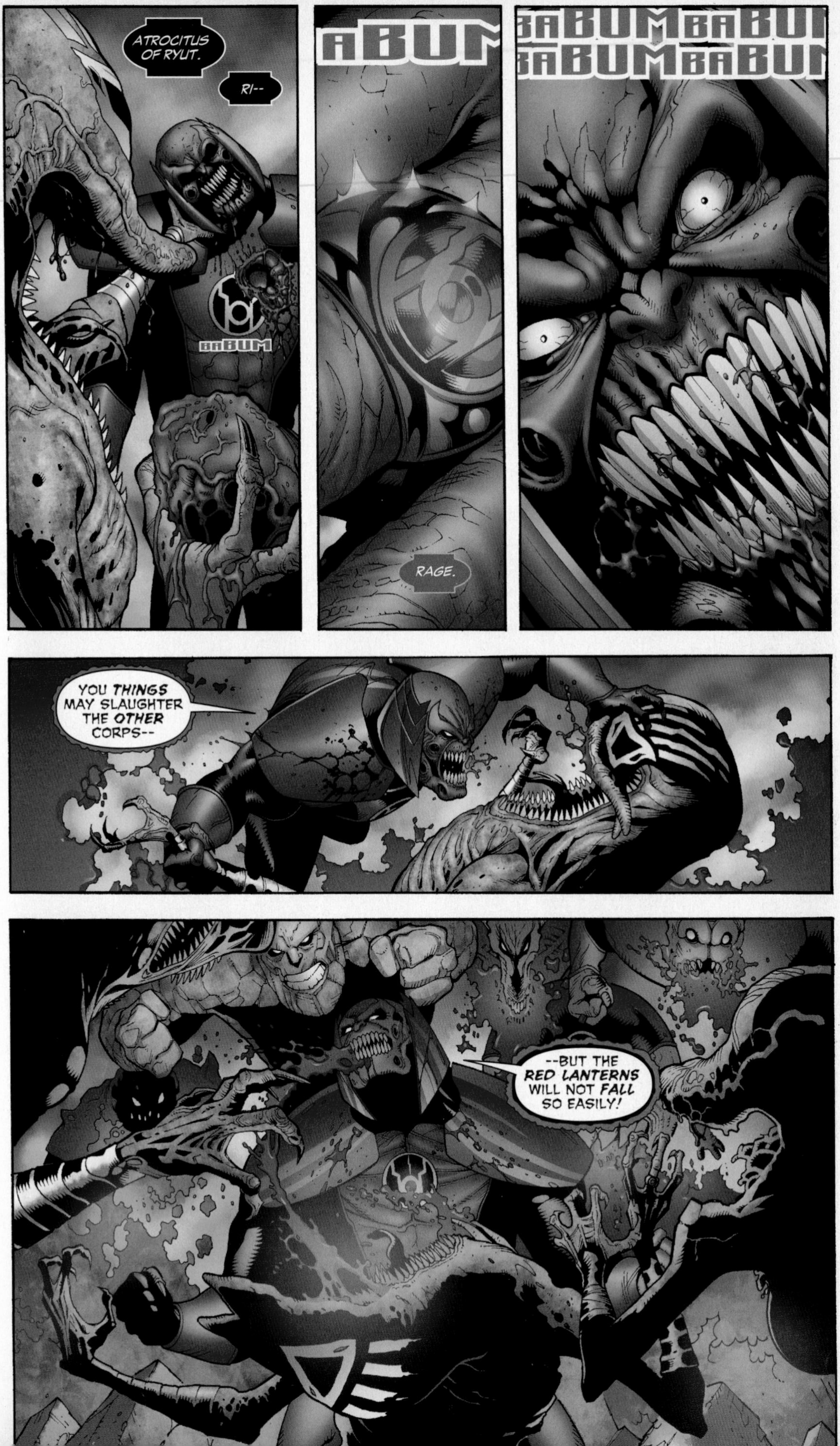
ATROCITUS OF RYUT.
RI--
BABUM
ABUM
BABUMBABU
BABUMBABUI
RAGE.
YOU THINGS MAY SLAUGHTER THE OTHER CORPS--
--BUT THE RED LANTERNS WILL NOT FALL SO EASILY!

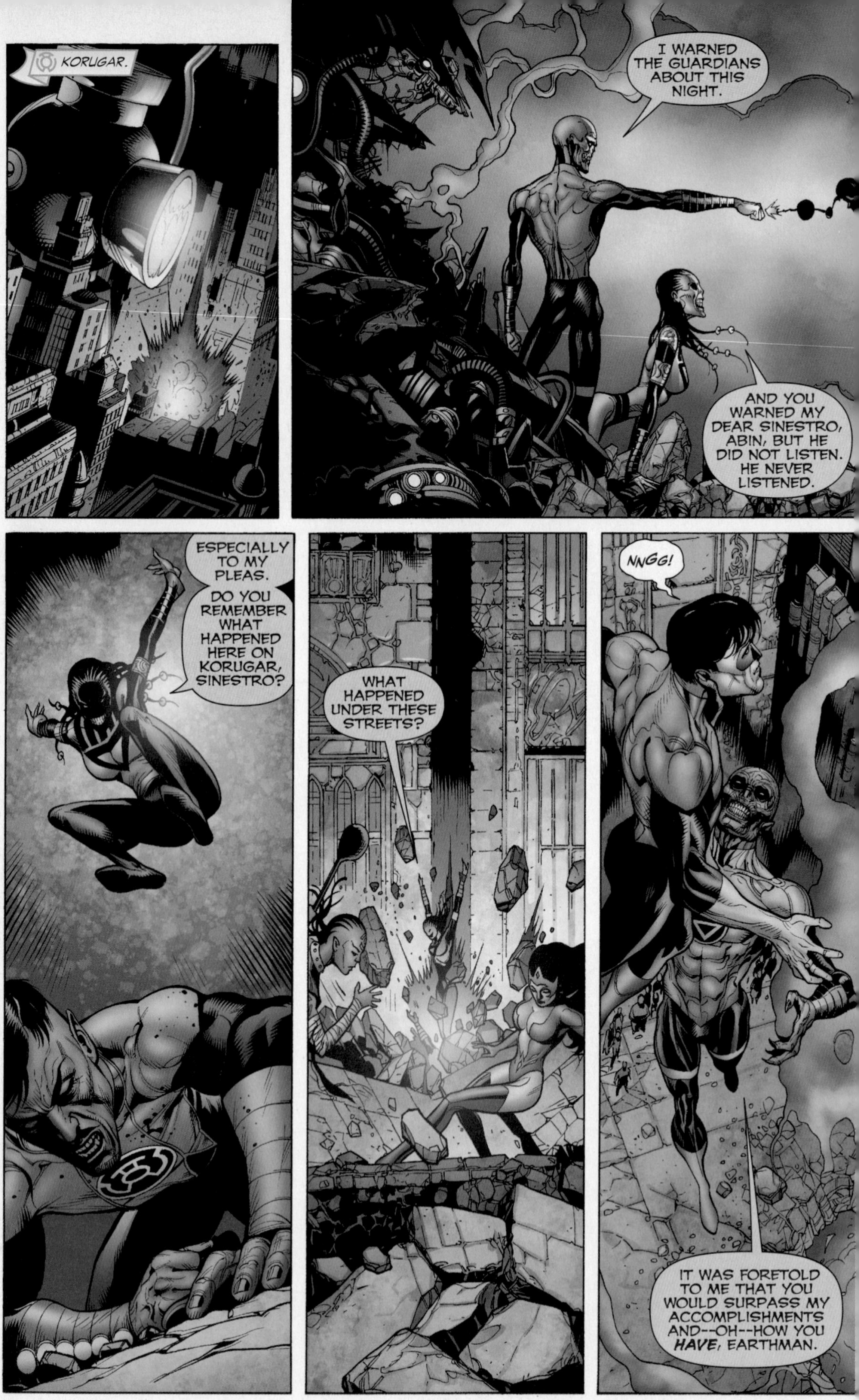
KORUGAR.
I WARNED THE GUARDIANS ABOUT THIS NIGHT.
AND YOU WARNED MY DEAR SINESTRO, ABIN, BUT HE DID NOT LISTEN. HE NEVER LISTENED.
ESPECIALLY TO MY PLEAS.
DO YOU REMEMBER WHAT HAPPENED HERE ON KORUGAR, SINESTRO?
WHAT HAPPENED UNDER THESE STREETS?
NNGG!
IT WAS FORETOLD TO ME THAT YOU WOULD SURPASS MY ACCOMPLISHMENTS AND--OH--HOW YOU HAVE, EARTHMAN.

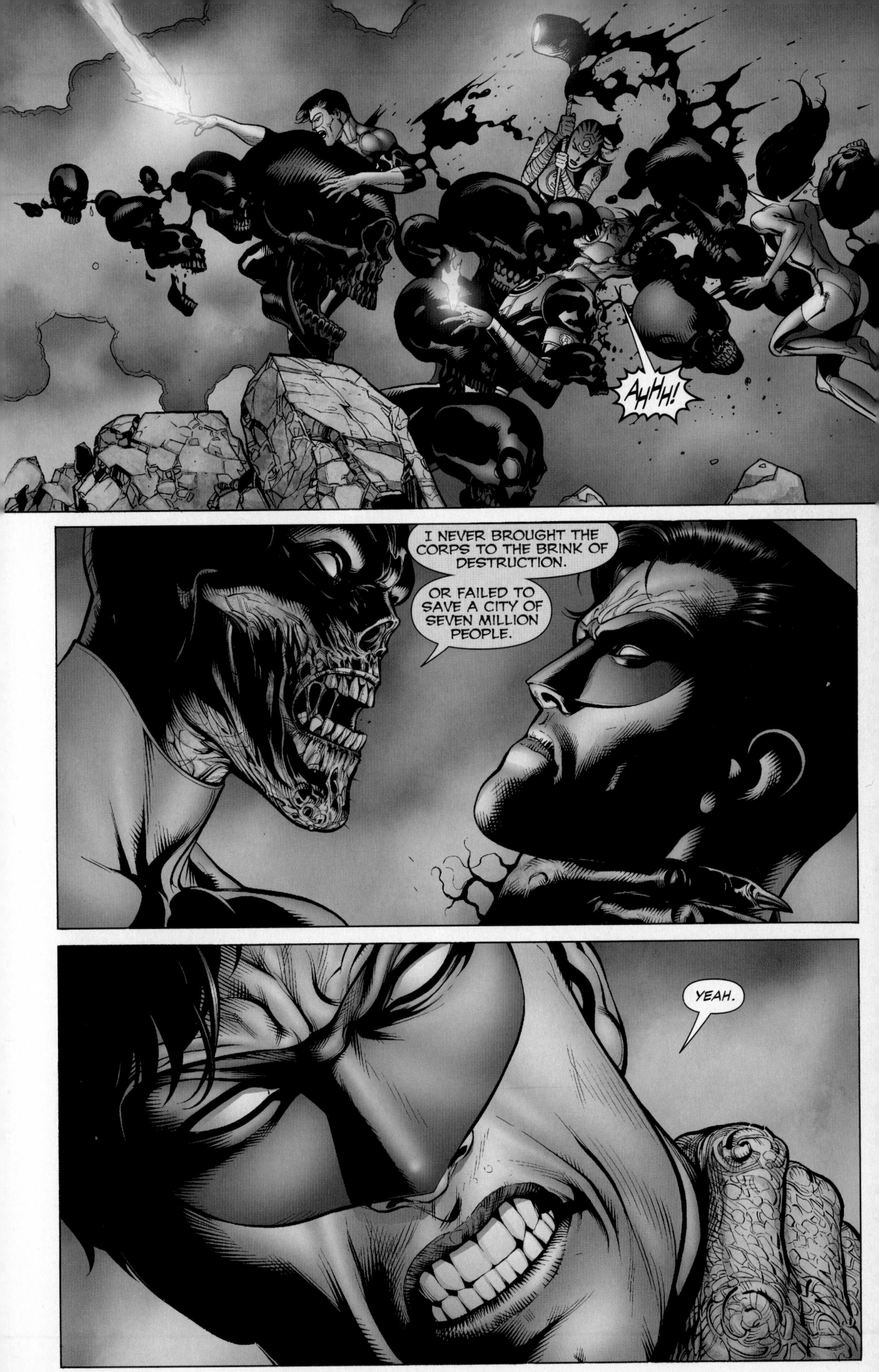
AHHH!
I NEVER BROUGHT THE CORPS TO THE BRINK OF DESTRUCTION.
OR FAILED TO SAVE A CITY OF SEVEN MILLION PEOPLE.
YEAH.

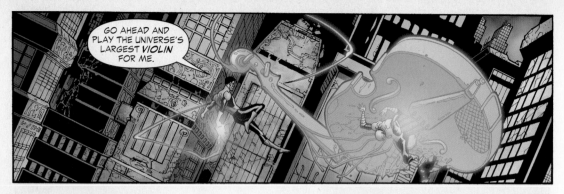

GO AHEAD AND PLAY THE UNIVERSE'S LARGEST *VIOLIN* FOR ME.

IF YOU'RE GOING TO DRAG UP THE #$?%-UPS I'VE MADE OVER THE YEARS AND THROW THEM IN MY FACE, DIG A LITTLE *DEEPER*.

I'VE ALREADY MADE PEACE WITH PARALLAX AND COAST CITY.

NOW LET'S PUT ASIDE THE MASQUERADES, BLACK LANTERN. YOU CAN *ACT* LIKE ABIN SUR, BUT YOU'RE NOT HIM. YOU'RE JUST A PROGRAM THAT'S ABOUT TO GET ERASED.

I WAS OBSESSED WITH THE FUTURE. YOU IGNORE IT. WE COULD NOT BE MORE DIFFERENT, YET THE RING CHOSE YOU. *WHY?*

YOU MAY HAVE FOUND *PURPOSE* IN THE CORPS AS I DID, BUT YOU HAVE NO PATH.

YOU TAKE FLIGHT WITHOUT A DESTINATION.

SO WHAT DOES IT MATTER IF YOU DIE *TOMORROW*--

WILL.

--OR *TODAY?*

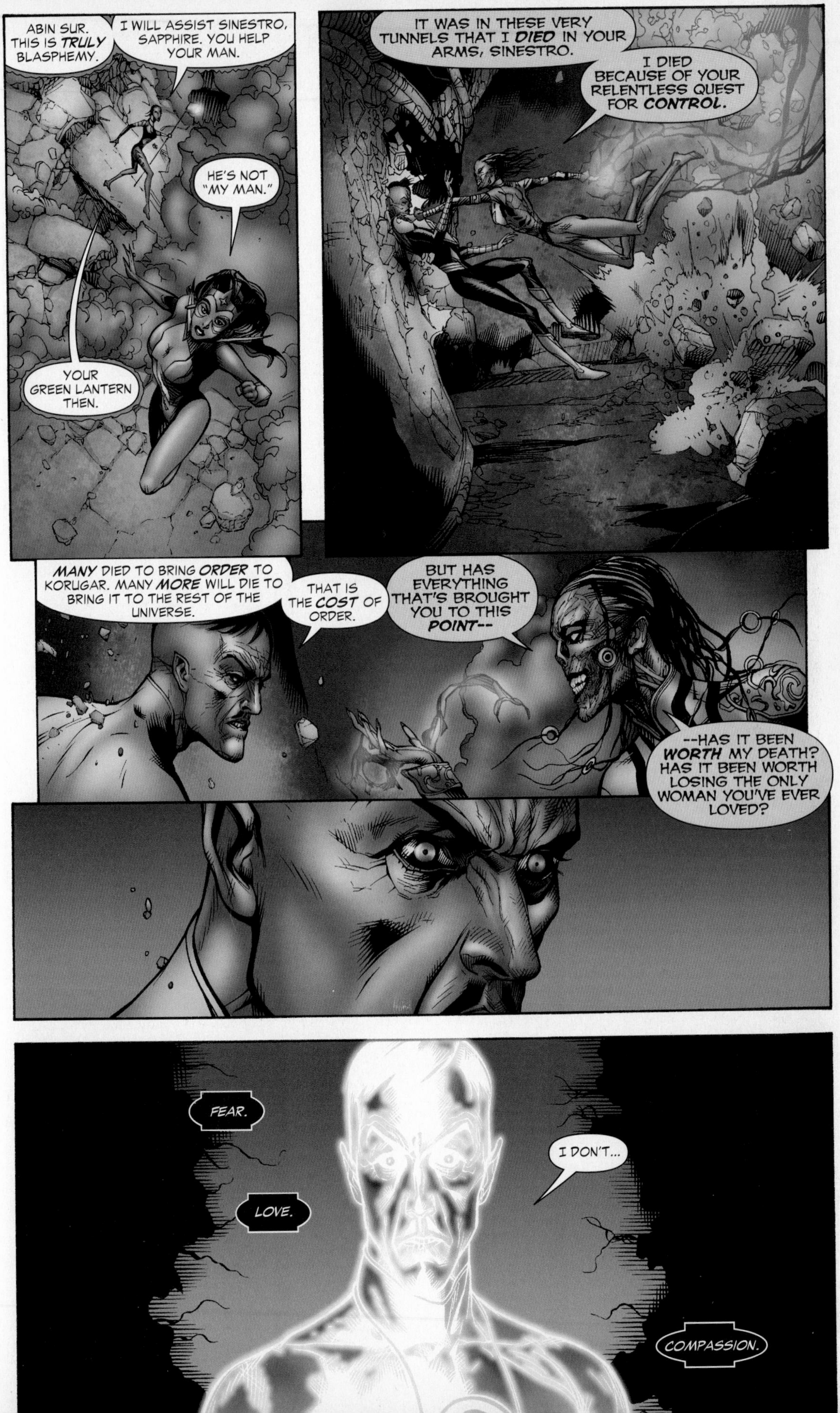
ABIN SUR. THIS IS TRULY BLASPHEMY.
I WILL ASSIST SINESTRO, SAPPHIRE. YOU HELP YOUR MAN.
HE'S NOT "MY MAN."
YOUR GREEN LANTERN THEN.
IT WAS IN THESE VERY TUNNELS THAT I DIED IN YOUR ARMS, SINESTRO.
I DIED BECAUSE OF YOUR RELENTLESS QUEST FOR CONTROL.
MANY DIED TO BRING ORDER TO KORUGAR. MANY MORE WILL DIE TO BRING IT TO THE REST OF THE UNIVERSE.
THAT IS THE COST OF ORDER.
BUT HAS EVERYTHING THAT'S BROUGHT YOU TO THIS POINT--
--HAS IT BEEN WORTH MY DEATH? HAS IT BEEN WORTH LOSING THE ONLY WOMAN YOU'VE EVER LOVED?
FEAR.
I DON'T...
LOVE.
COMPASSION.

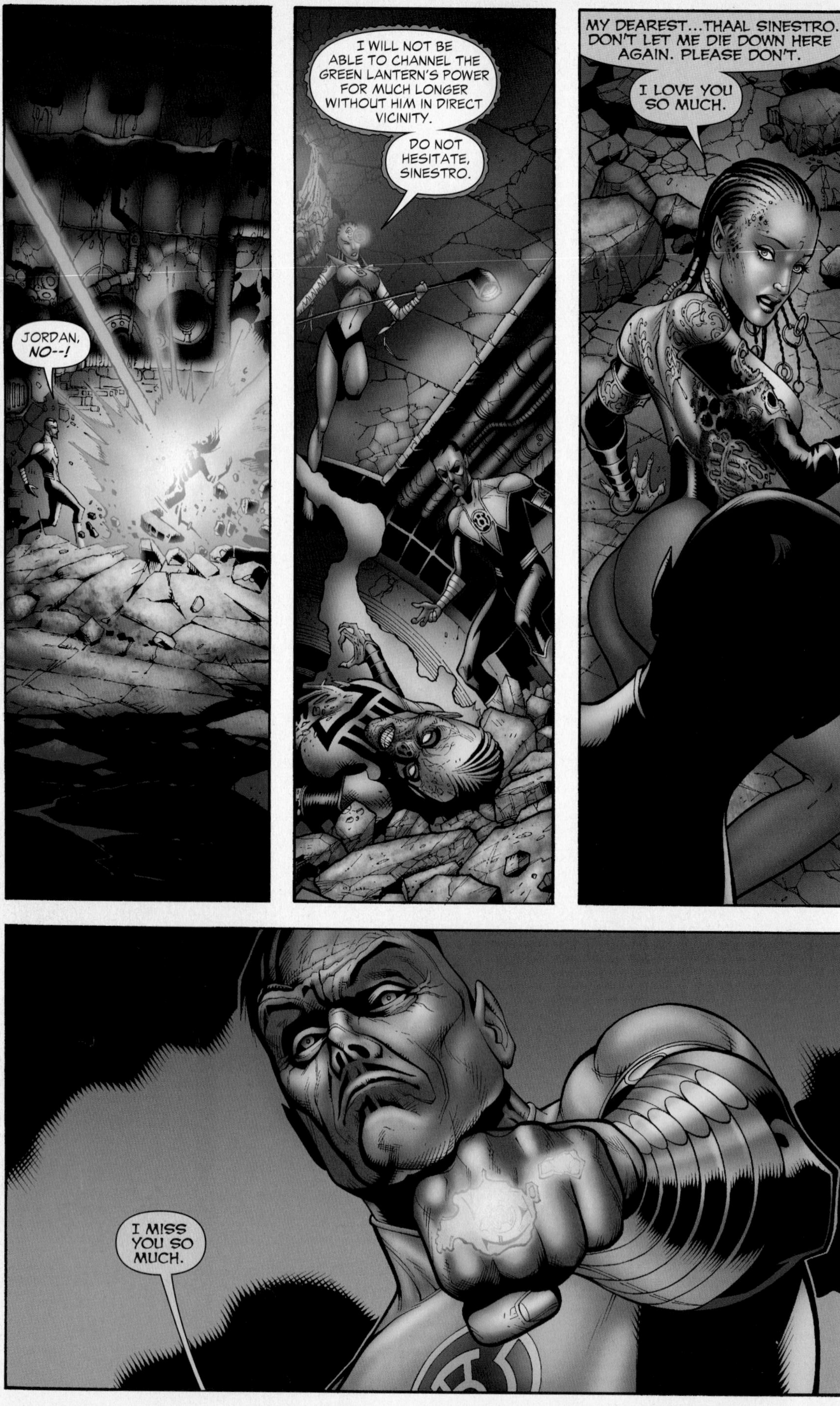
JORDAN, NO--!
I WILL NOT BE ABLE TO CHANNEL THE GREEN LANTERN'S POWER FOR MUCH LONGER WITHOUT HIM IN DIRECT VICINITY.
DO NOT HESITATE, SINESTRO.
MY DEAREST...THAAL SINESTRO. DON'T LET ME DIE DOWN HERE AGAIN. PLEASE DON'T.
I LOVE YOU SO MUCH.
I MISS YOU SO MUCH.

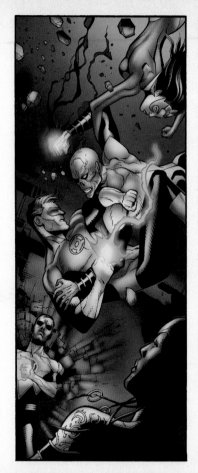

I'M SURE ABIN HAS A *LOT* MORE TO SAY TO *ALL* OF US, BUT YOU'LL FORGIVE ME IF I CUT THE REUNION SHORT.

HAVE SOME *RESPECT* FOR THE DEAD, JORDAN.

THERE'S NO NEED FOR *BANTER*.

INDIGO? I KNOW YOU. I--

CONNECTION SEVERED.

CONNECTION SEVERED.

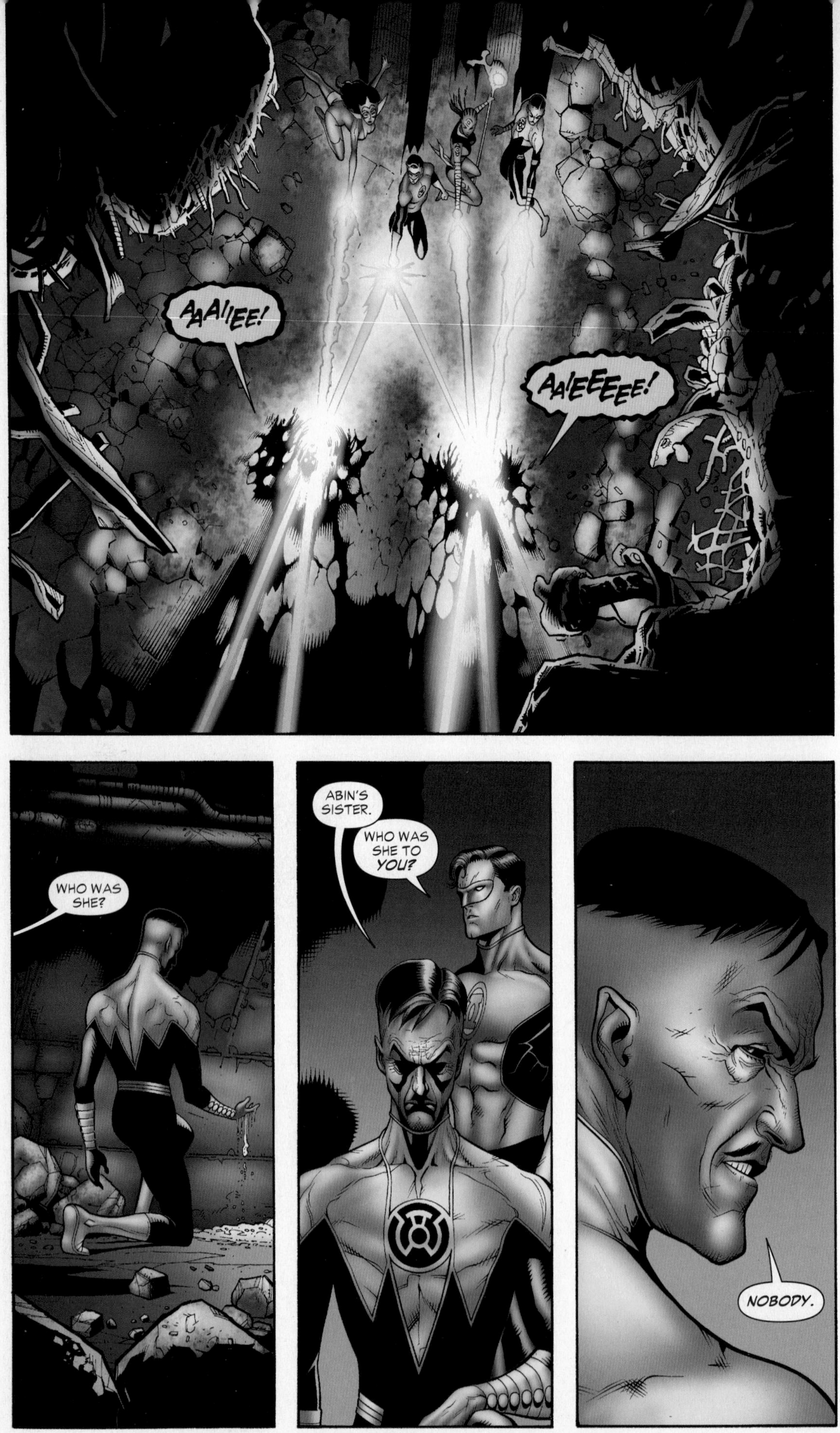
AAAIIEE!
AAIEEEEEE!
WHO WAS SHE?
ABIN'S SISTER.
WHO WAS SHE TO YOU?
NOBODY.

THE DEAD CONTINUE TO RISE. WE NEED TO PULL THIS UNIT TOGETHER QUICKLY, WOMAN. TAKE US TO ATROCITUS--

BEFORE SAINT WALKER?

FROM WHAT WE WITNESSED ON YSMAULT, THE RED LANTERNS' RINGS HAVE REPLACED THEIR HEARTS. THAT MAY GIVE THEM, AND US, AN ADVANTAGE AGAINST THE BLACK LANTERNS.

THE RED LANTERNS ARE UNCONTROLLABLE. THE *BLUE LANTERNS* ARE THE ONLY ONES THAT CAN DOUSE THE FIRE THE REDS SPIT UP.

FRIENDS BEFORE *ENEMIES.*

PRESENT COMPANY *EXCLUDED.*

YOU MIGHT WEAR ABIN'S RING, JORDAN, BUT HIS MISSION IS *MINE.*

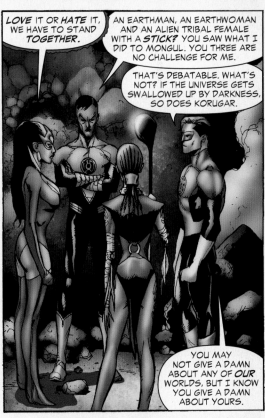

LOVE IT OR *HATE* IT, WE HAVE TO STAND *TOGETHER.*

AN EARTHMAN, AN EARTHWOMAN AND AN ALIEN TRIBAL FEMALE WITH A *STICK?* YOU SAW WHAT I DID TO MONGUL. YOU THREE ARE NO CHALLENGE FOR ME.

THAT'S DEBATABLE. WHAT'S NOT? IF THE UNIVERSE GETS SWALLOWED UP BY DARKNESS, SO DOES KORUGAR.

YOU MAY NOT GIVE A DAMN ABOUT ANY OF *OUR* WORLDS, BUT I KNOW YOU GIVE A DAMN ABOUT YOURS.

I HAVE OVER A HUNDRED MEMBERS OF MY CORPS OVERHEAD WILLING TO GIVE THEIR LIVES TO DEFEND KORUGAR. FROM ANYTHING.

IS THAT A THREAT?

NO.

IT'S A *FACT.*

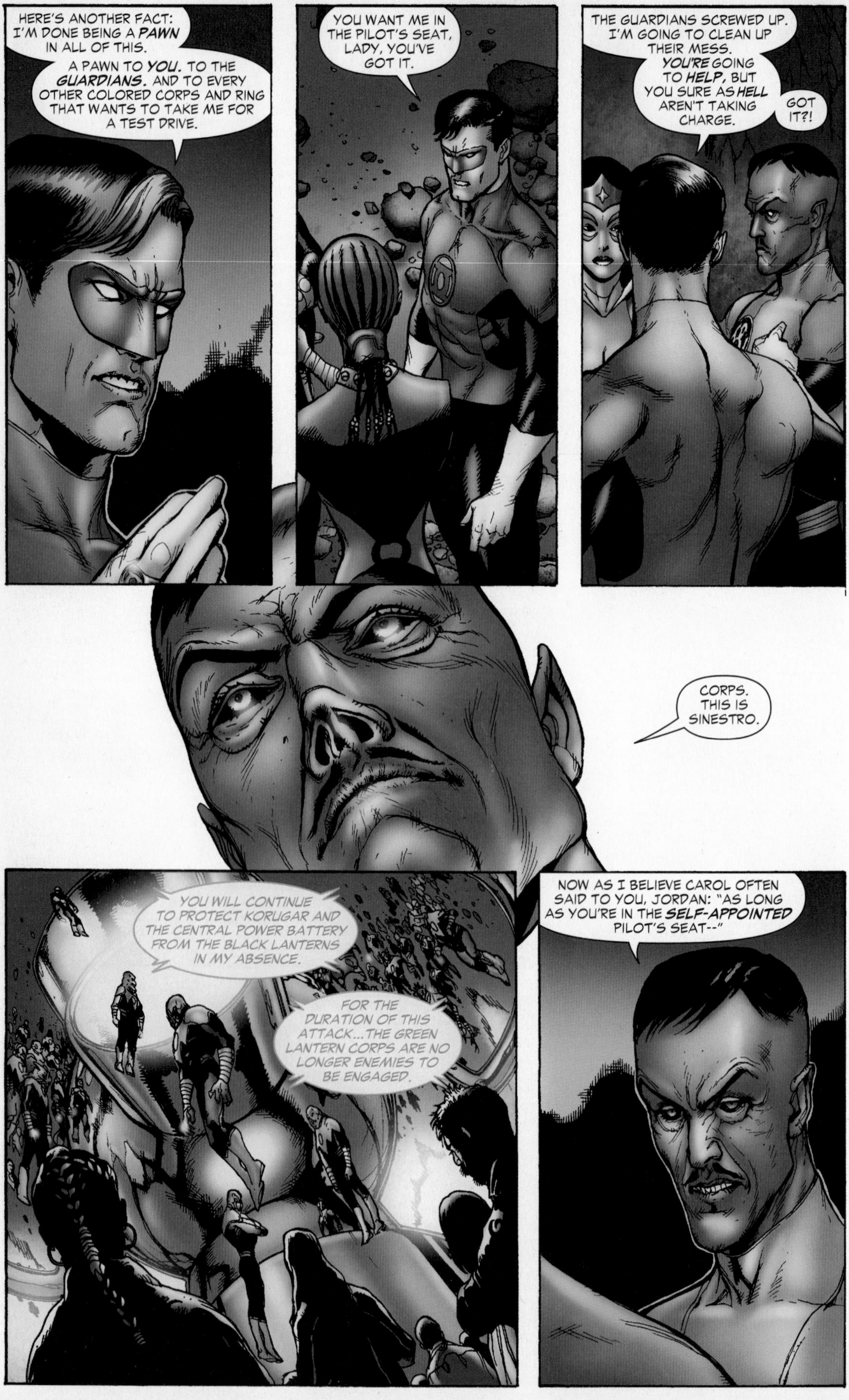
HERE'S ANOTHER FACT: I'M DONE BEING A PAWN IN ALL OF THIS.
A PAWN TO YOU. TO THE GUARDIANS. AND TO EVERY OTHER COLORED CORPS AND RING THAT WANTS TO TAKE ME FOR A TEST DRIVE.
YOU WANT ME IN THE PILOT'S SEAT, LADY, YOU'VE GOT IT.
THE GUARDIANS SCREWED UP. I'M GOING TO CLEAN UP THEIR MESS. YOU'RE GOING TO HELP, BUT YOU SURE AS HELL AREN'T TAKING CHARGE.
GOT IT?!
CORPS. THIS IS SINESTRO.
YOU WILL CONTINUE TO PROTECT KORUGAR AND THE CENTRAL POWER BATTERY FROM THE BLACK LANTERNS IN MY ABSENCE.
FOR THE DURATION OF THIS ATTACK...THE GREEN LANTERN CORPS ARE NO LONGER ENEMIES TO BE ENGAGED.
NOW AS I BELIEVE CAROL OFTEN SAID TO YOU, JORDAN: "AS LONG AS YOU'RE IN THE SELF-APPOINTED PILOT'S SEAT--"

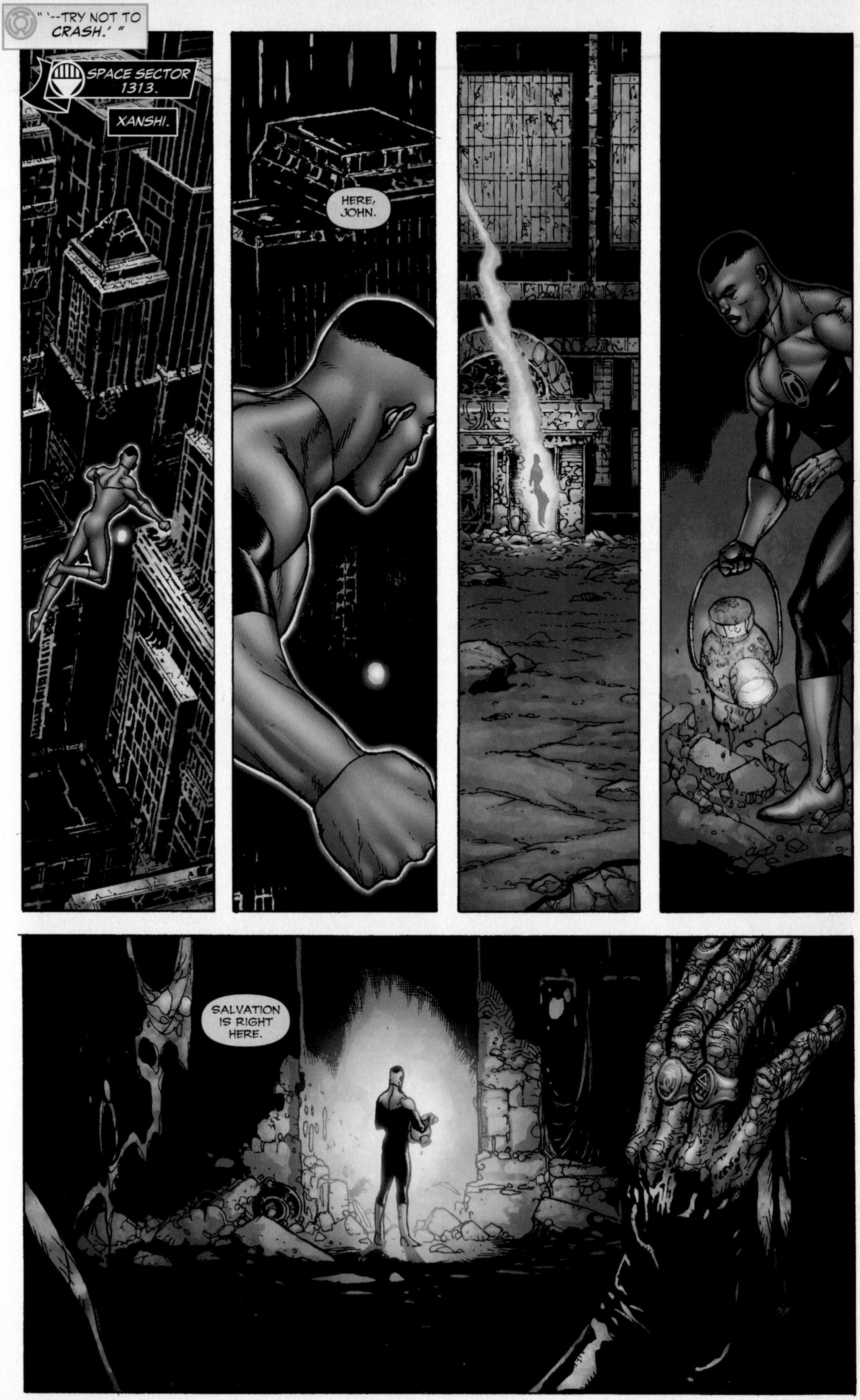
"'--TRY NOT TO CRASH.' "
SPACE SECTOR 1313.
XANSHI.
HERE, JOHN.
SALVATION IS RIGHT HERE.

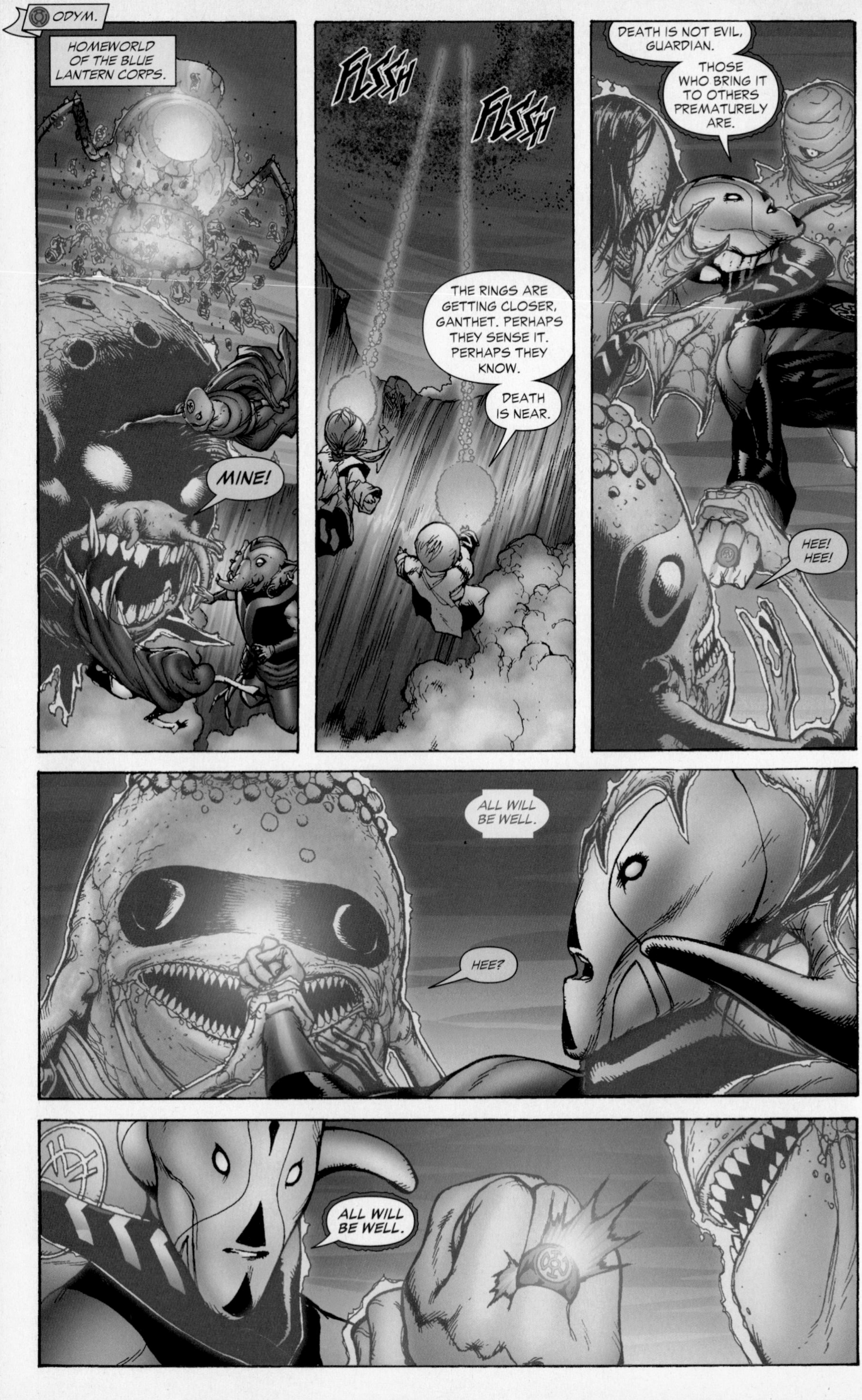
ODYM.
HOMEWORLD OF THE BLUE LANTERN CORPS.
MINE!
FLSSH
FLSSH
THE RINGS ARE GETTING CLOSER, GANTHET. PERHAPS THEY SENSE IT. PERHAPS THEY KNOW.
DEATH IS NEAR.
DEATH IS NOT EVIL, GUARDIAN.
THOSE WHO BRING IT TO OTHERS PREMATURELY ARE.
HEE! HEE!
ALL WILL BE WELL.
HEE?
ALL WILL BE WELL.

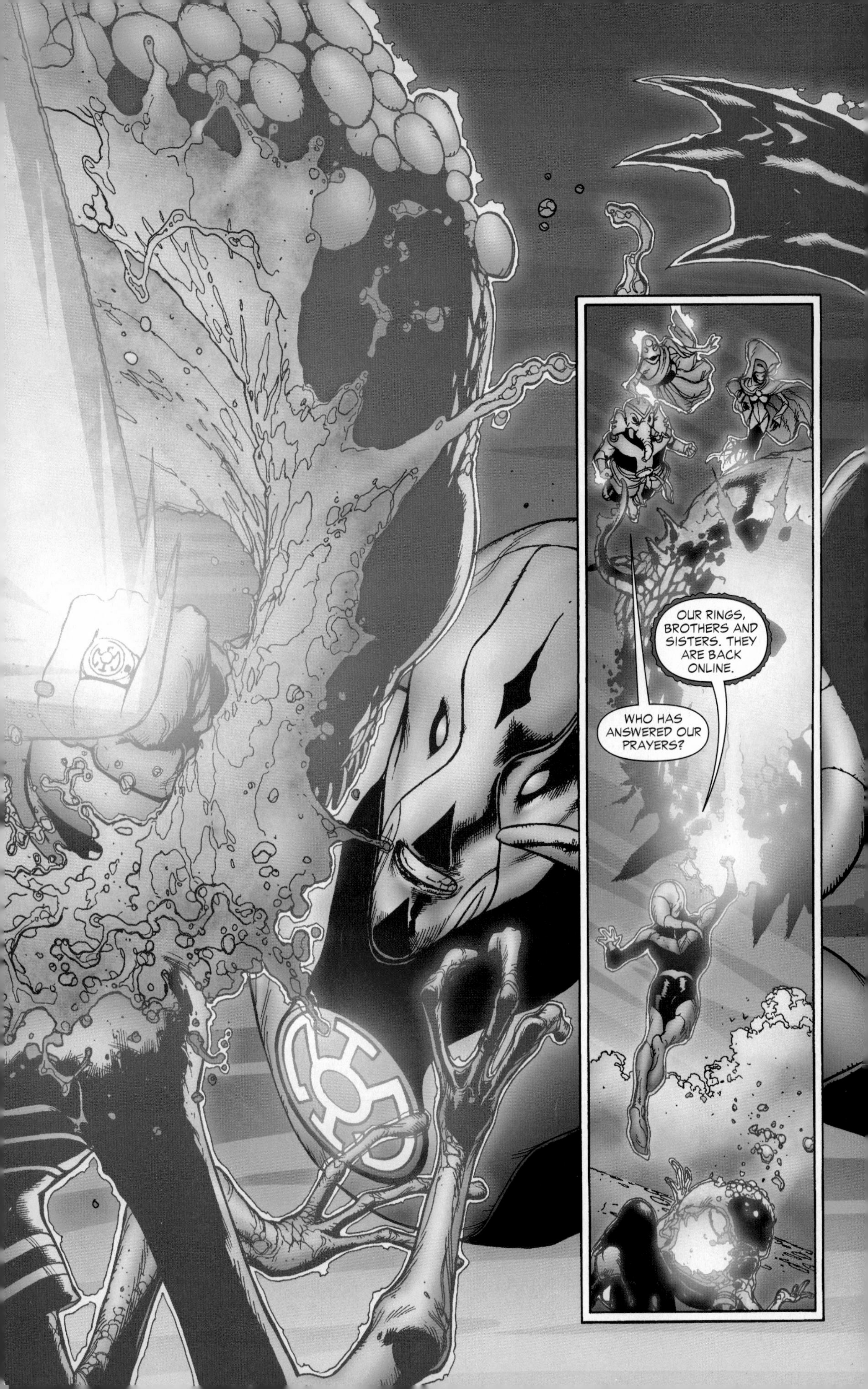
OUR RINGS, BROTHERS AND SISTERS. THEY ARE BACK ONLINE.
WHO HAS ANSWERED OUR PRAYERS?

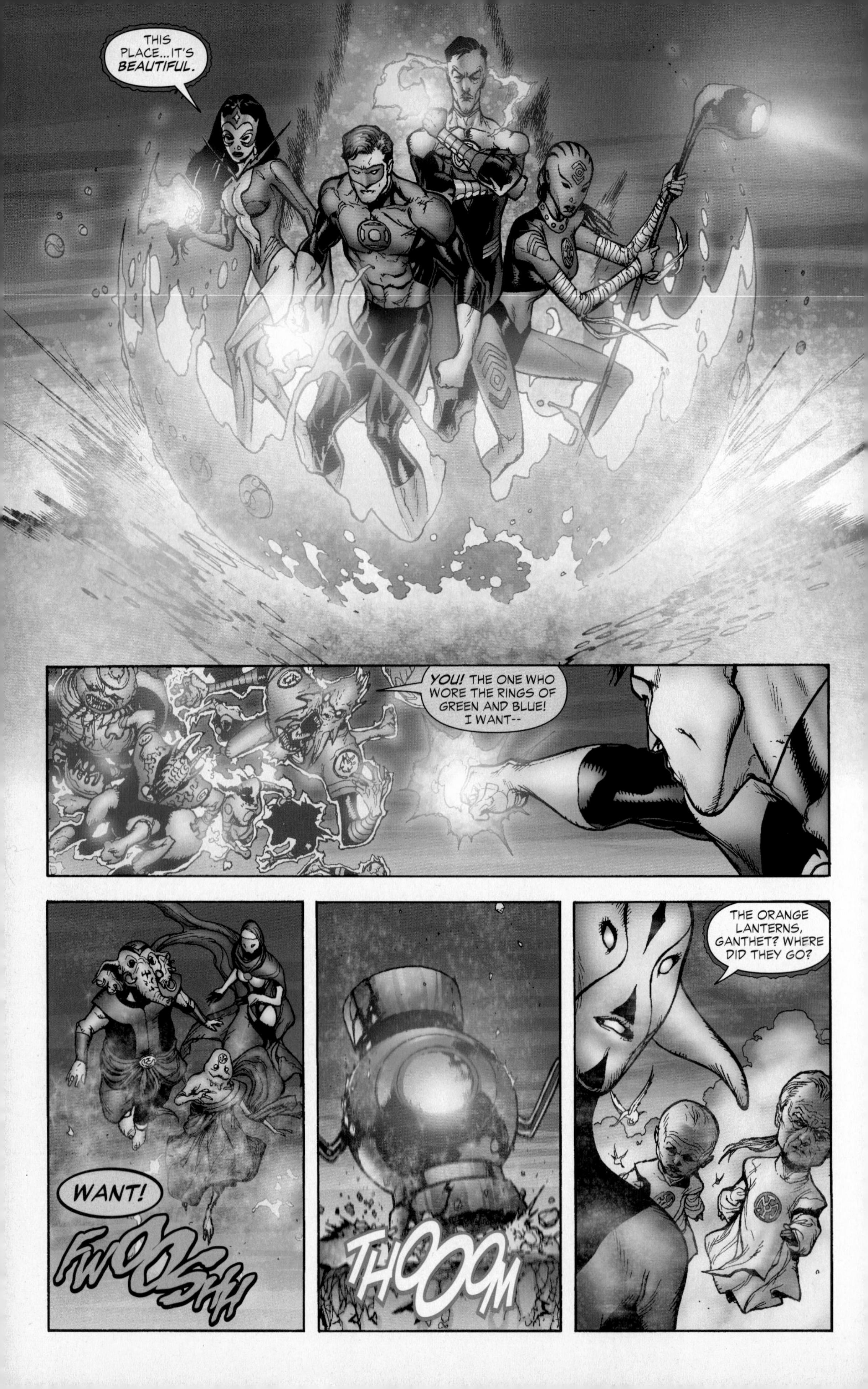
THIS PLACE...IT'S BEAUTIFUL.
YOU! THE ONE WHO WORE THE RINGS OF GREEN AND BLUE! I WANT--
WANT!
FWOOSHH
THOOOM
THE ORANGE LANTERNS, GANTHET? WHERE DID THEY GO?

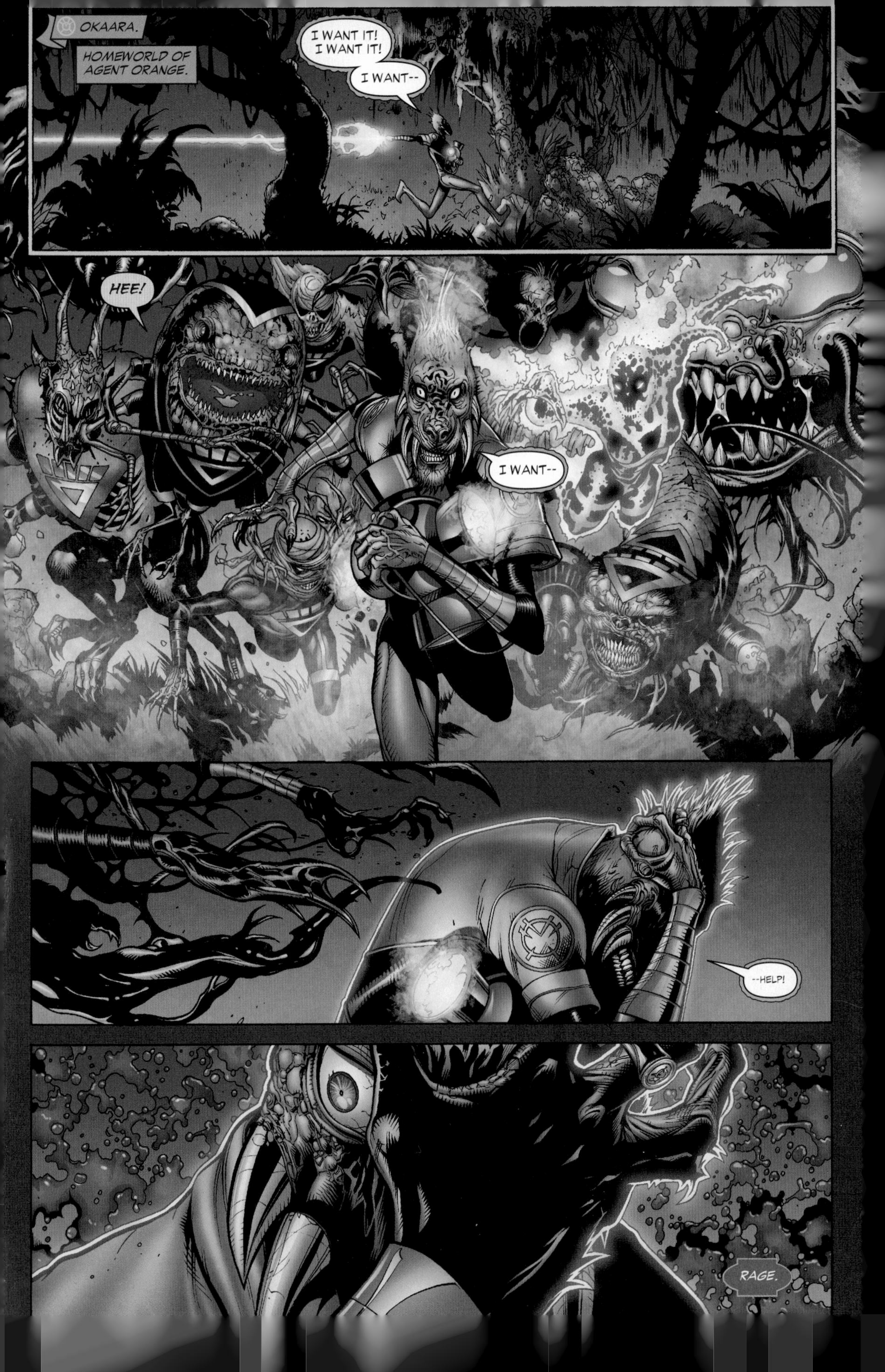
OKAARA.
HOMEWORLD OF AGENT ORANGE.
I WANT IT! I WANT IT!
I WANT--
HEE!
I WANT--
--HELP!
RAGE.

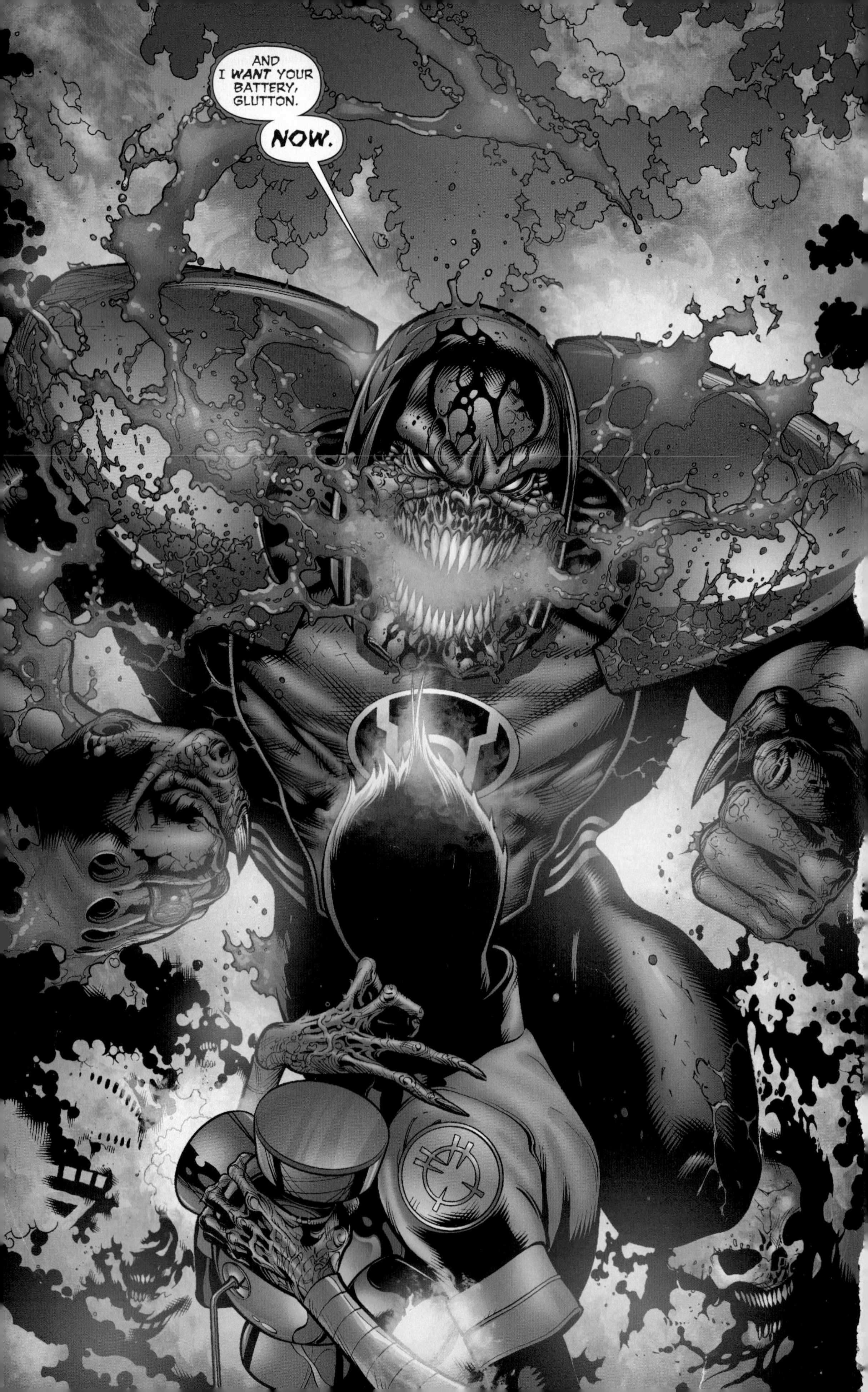
AND I WANT YOUR BATTERY, GLUTTON.
NOW.

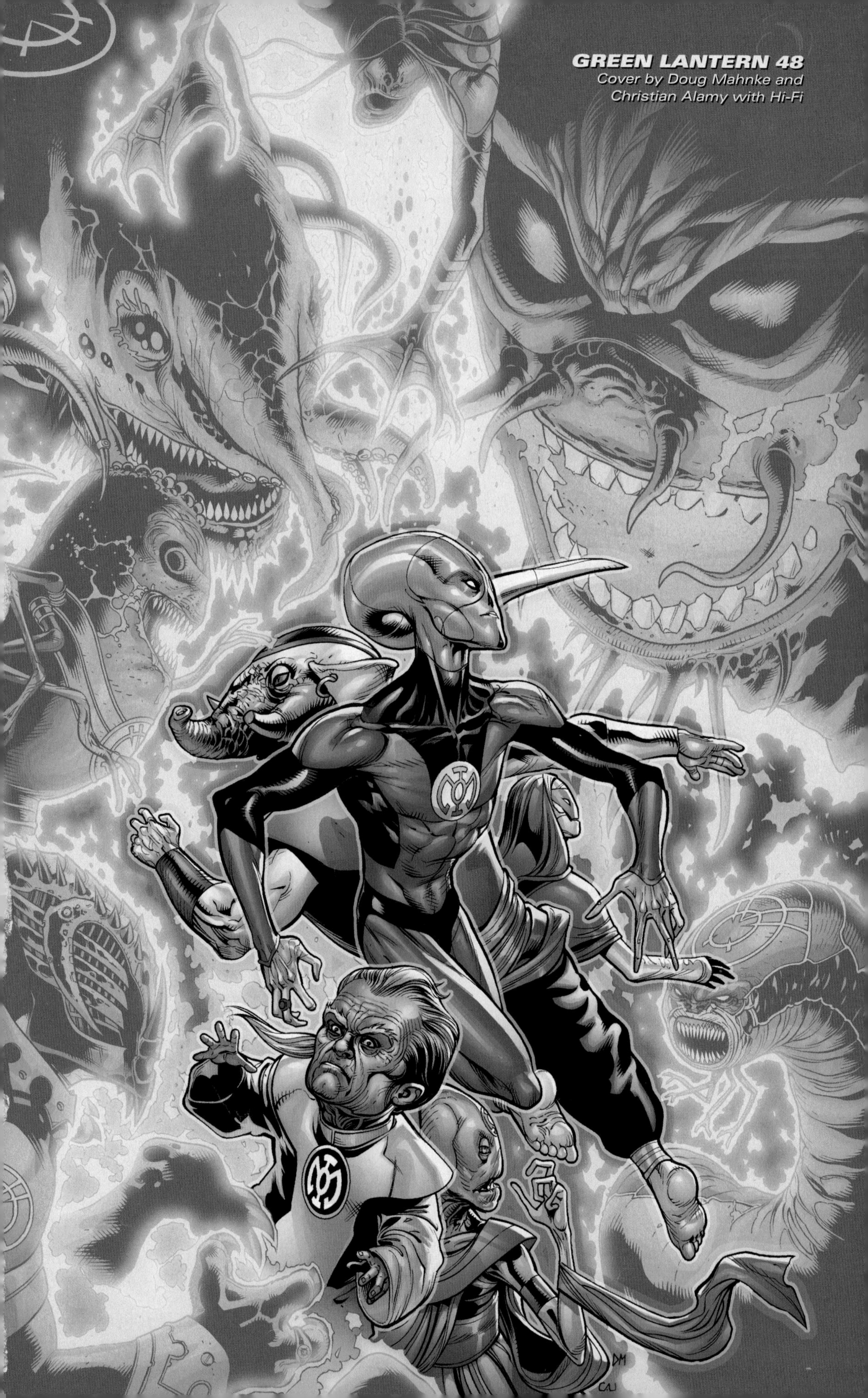

GREEN LANTERN 48
Cover by Doug Mahnke and Christian Alamy with Hi-Fi

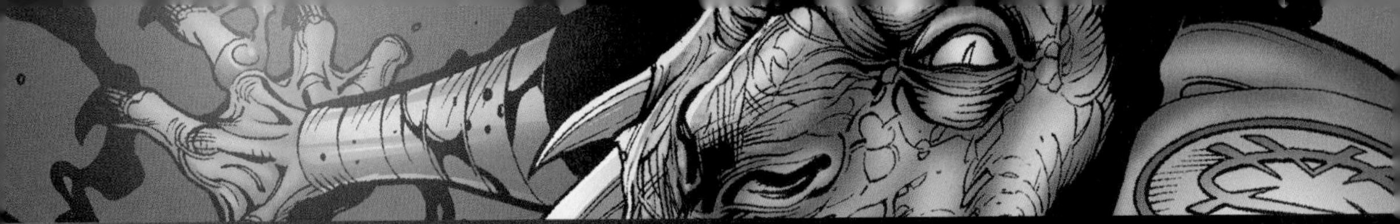

As the heroes' death toll increases, the Black Lanterns' power battery charges. Once full, it's transported to Earth and Black Hand's unseen master reveals himself: Nekron, Lord of the Unliving, rises in Coast City and he is not alone!

Now the universe's last hope lies with Hal Jordan and a band of Lanterns determined to destroy each other...

GIMME A BREAK!

DOUG MAHNKE
PENCILS

CHRISTIAN ALAMY
DOUG MAHNKE
TOM NGUYEN
INKS

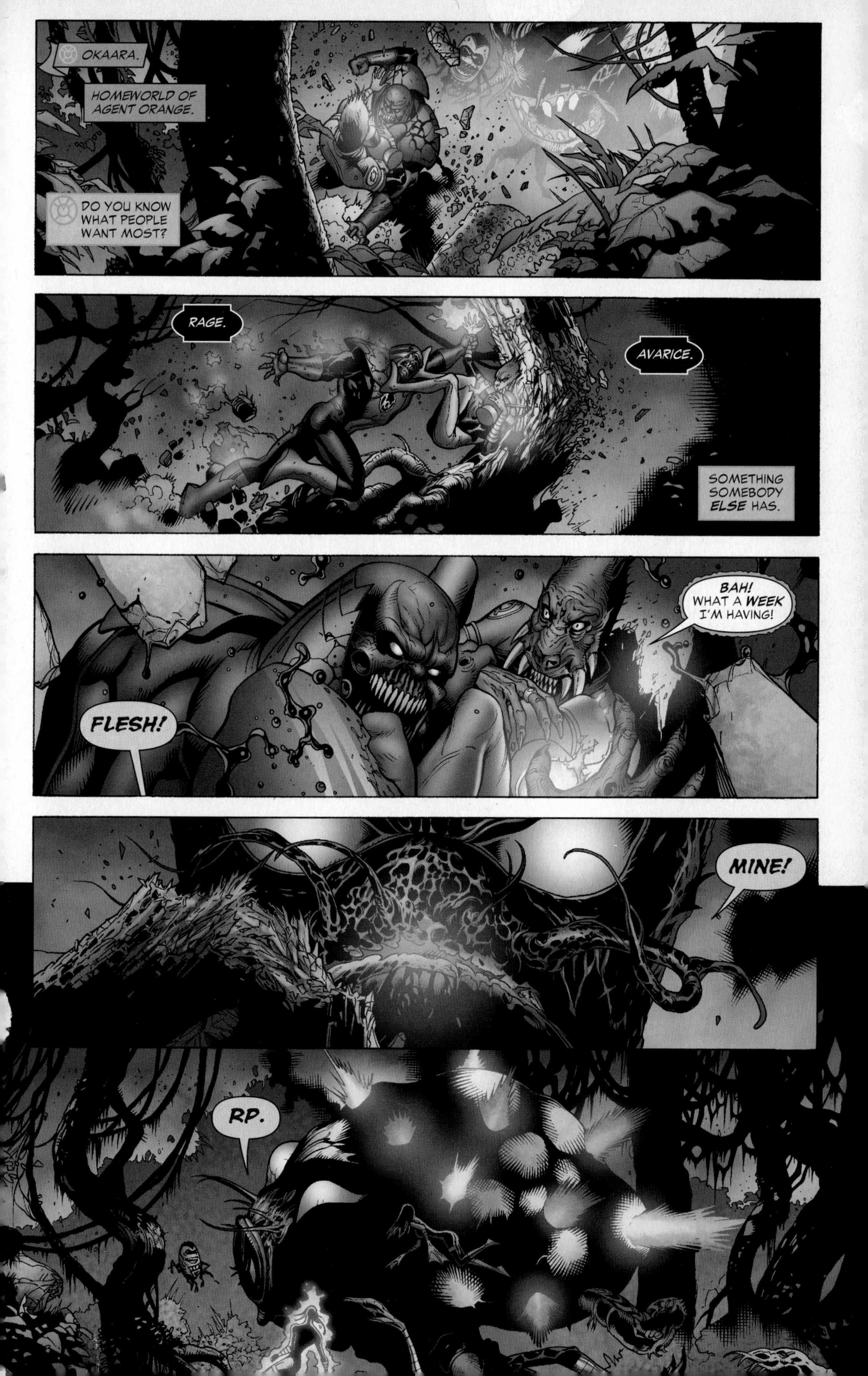
OKAARA.
HOMEWORLD OF AGENT ORANGE.
DO YOU KNOW WHAT PEOPLE WANT MOST?
RAGE.
AVARICE.
SOMETHING SOMEBODY ELSE HAS.
BAH! WHAT A WEEK I'M HAVING!
FLESH!
MINE!
RP.

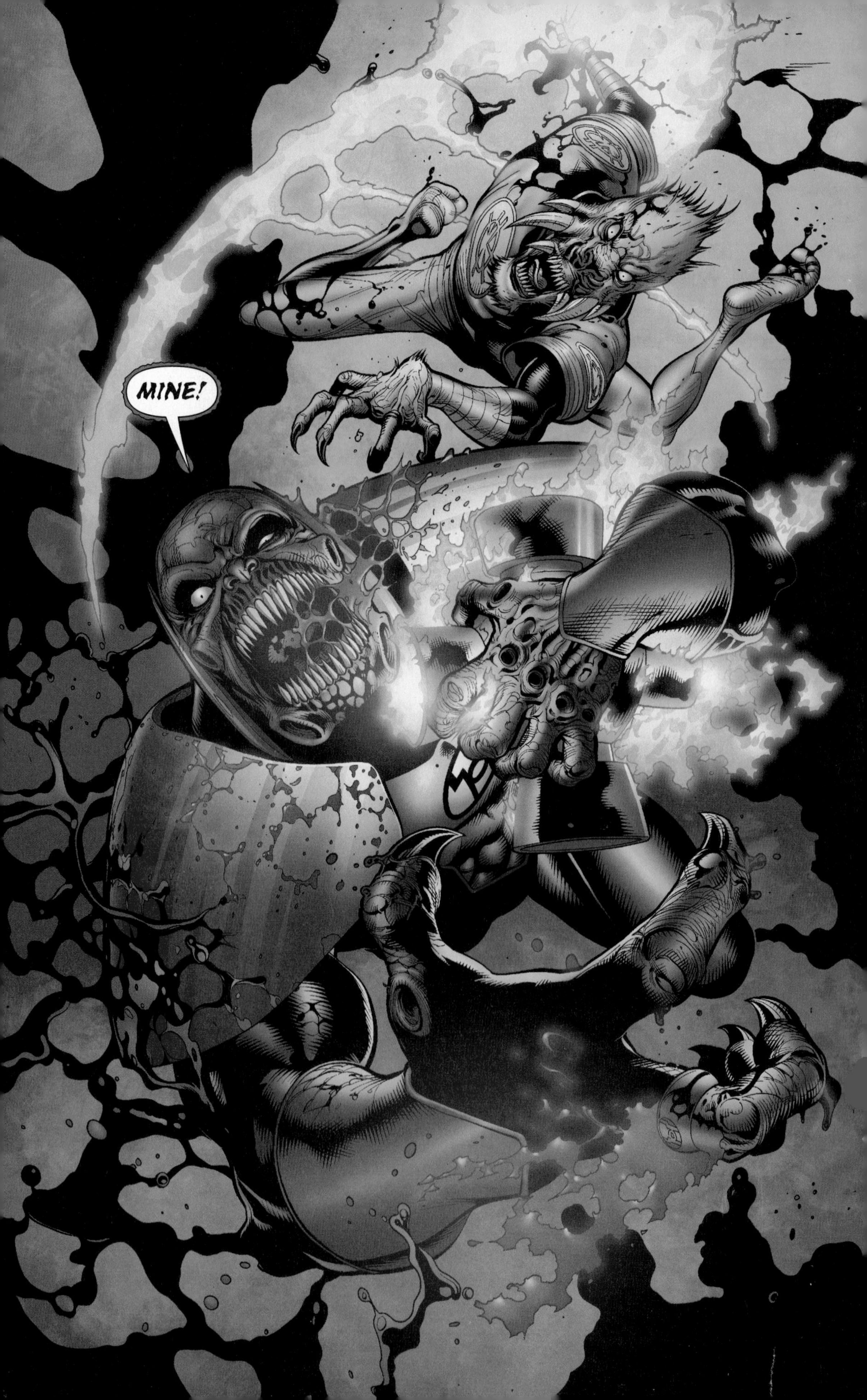
MINE!

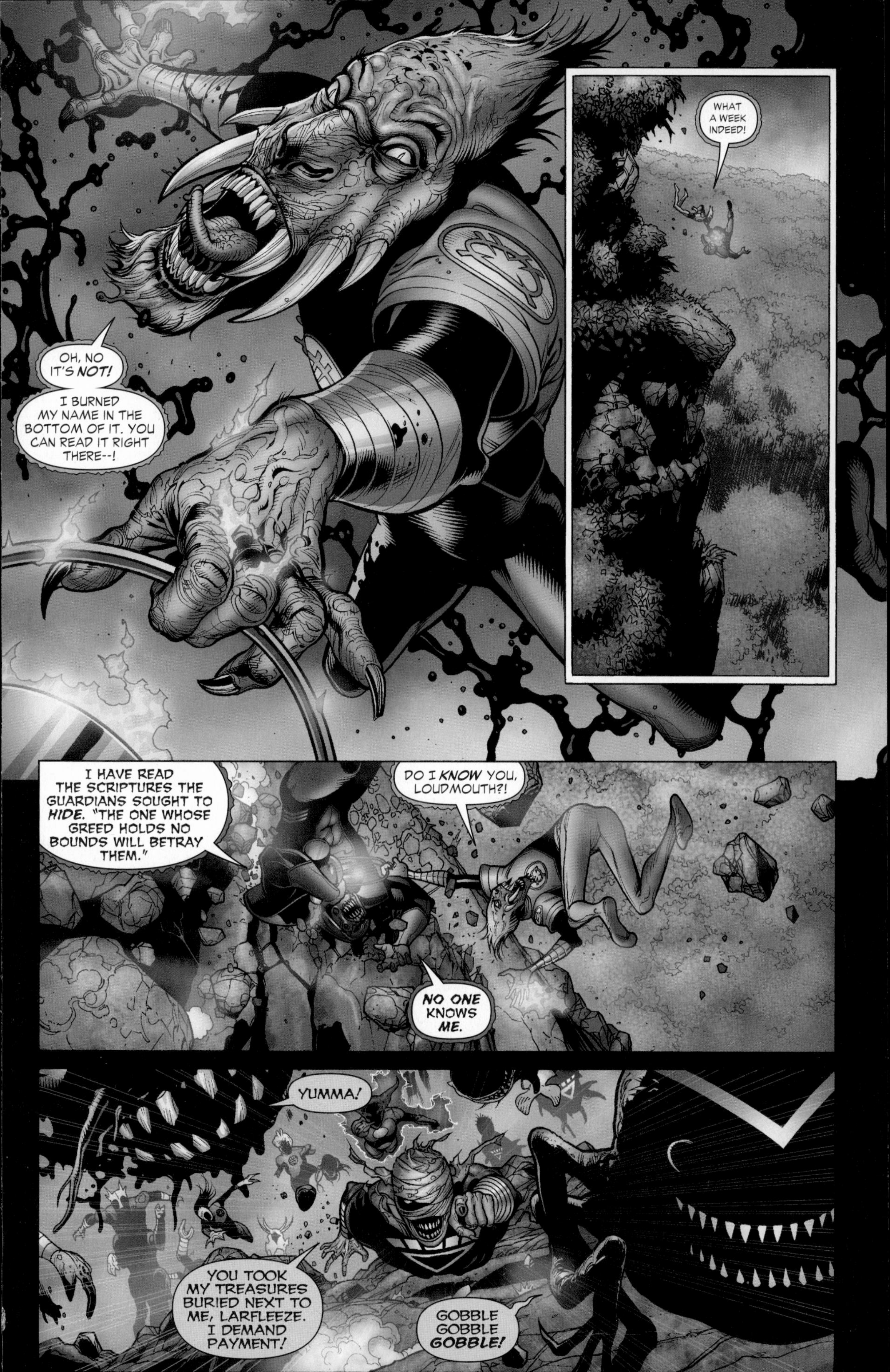
OH, NO IT'S NOT!
I BURNED MY NAME IN THE BOTTOM OF IT. YOU CAN READ IT RIGHT THERE--!
WHAT A WEEK INDEED!
I HAVE READ THE SCRIPTURES THE GUARDIANS SOUGHT TO HIDE. "THE ONE WHOSE GREED HOLDS NO BOUNDS WILL BETRAY THEM."
DO I KNOW YOU, LOUDMOUTH?!
NO ONE KNOWS ME.
YUMMA!
YOU TOOK MY TREASURES BURIED NEXT TO ME, LARFLEEZE. I DEMAND PAYMENT!
GOBBLE GOBBLE GOBBLE!

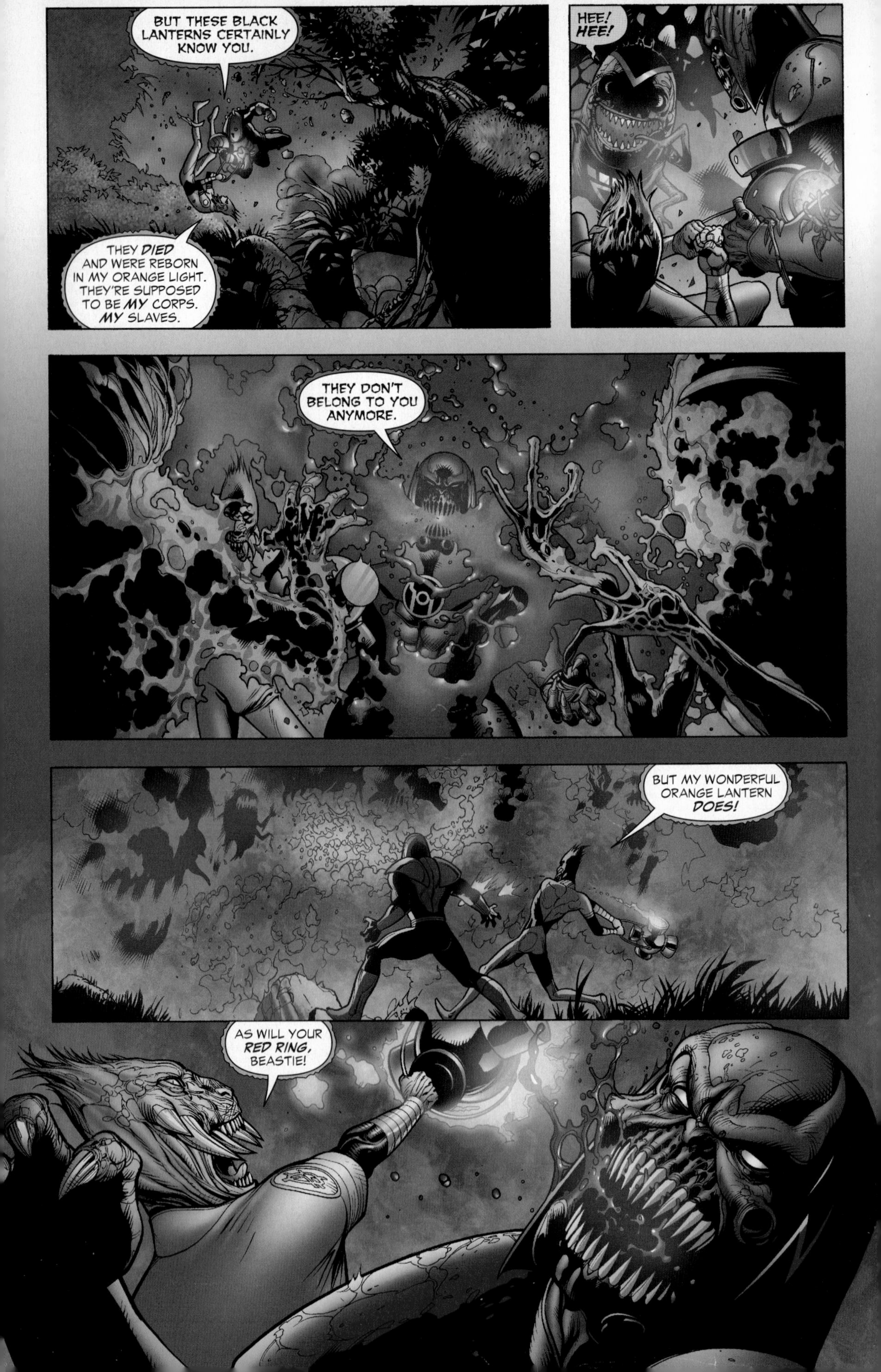
BUT THESE BLACK LANTERNS CERTAINLY KNOW YOU.
THEY *DIED* AND WERE REBORN IN MY ORANGE LIGHT. THEY'RE SUPPOSED TO BE *MY* CORPS. *MY* SLAVES.
HEE! *HEE!*
THEY DON'T BELONG TO YOU ANYMORE.
BUT MY WONDERFUL ORANGE LANTERN *DOES!*
AS WILL YOUR *RED RING,* BEASTIE!

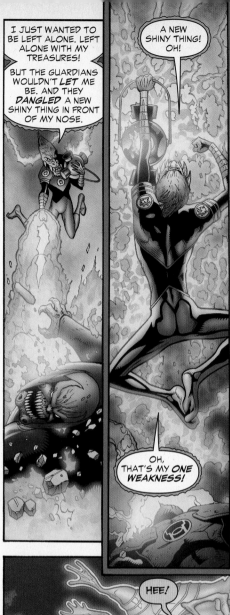

I JUST WANTED TO BE LEFT ALONE. LEFT ALONE WITH MY TREASURES!

BUT THE GUARDIANS WOULDN'T *LET* ME BE. AND THEY *DANGLED* A NEW SHINY THING IN FRONT OF MY NOSE.

A NEW SHINY THING! OH!

OH, THAT'S MY *ONE* WEAKNESS!

HEE!

I GET WHAT I WANT, UNDEAD GOBLINS! AND NOW I *WANT* A BLACK RING!

HEE!

MY ORANGE LANTERNS! *GIVE THEM BACK!*

RED LANTERN! *WAKE UP!*

I THINK WE NEED TO RECONSIDER OUR RELATIONSHIP.

FEAR NOT, LARFLEEZE.

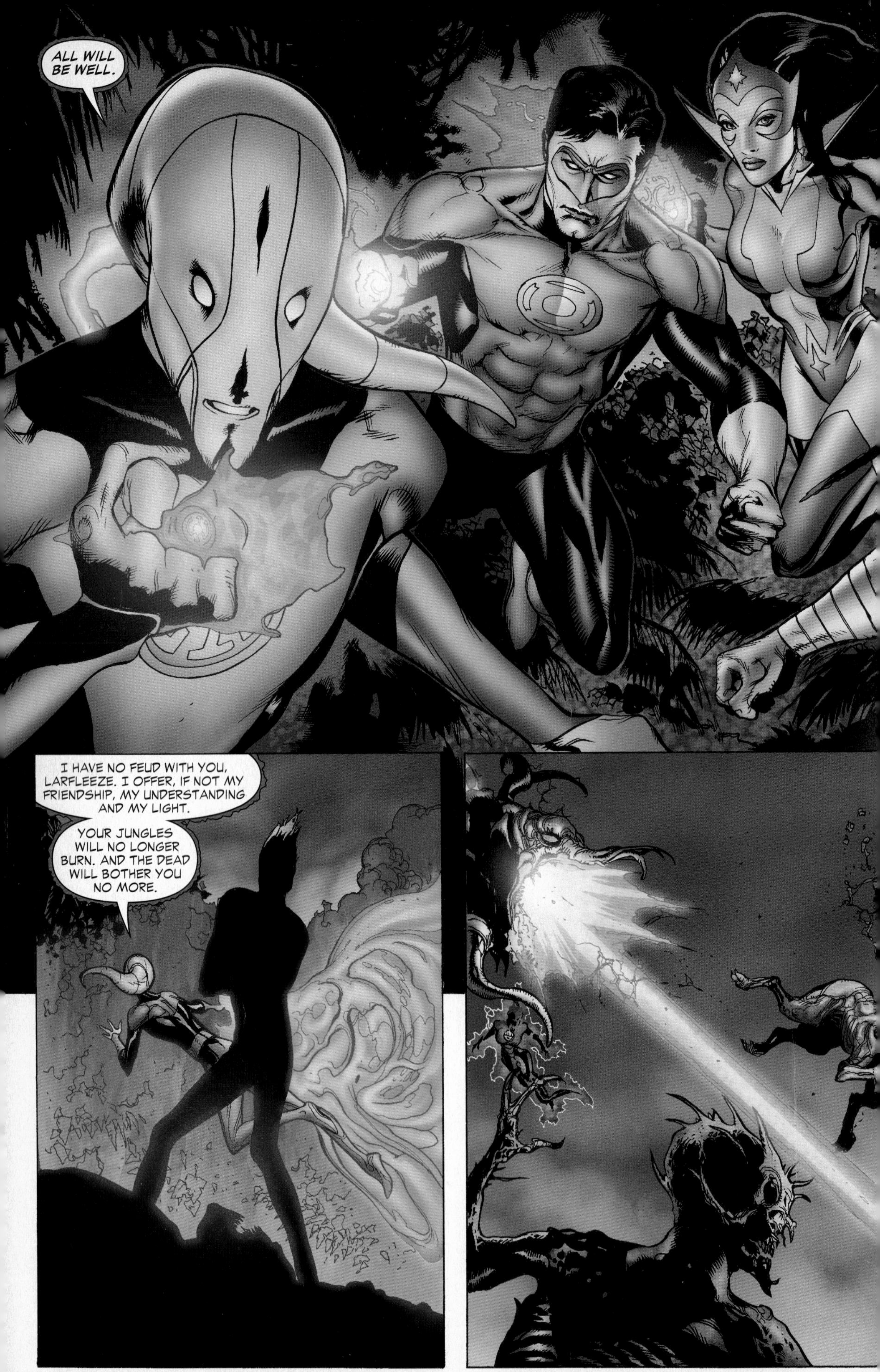
ALL WILL BE WELL.
I HAVE NO FEUD WITH YOU, LARFLEEZE. I OFFER, IF NOT MY FRIENDSHIP, MY UNDERSTANDING AND MY LIGHT.
YOUR JUNGLES WILL NO LONGER BURN. AND THE DEAD WILL BOTHER YOU NO MORE.

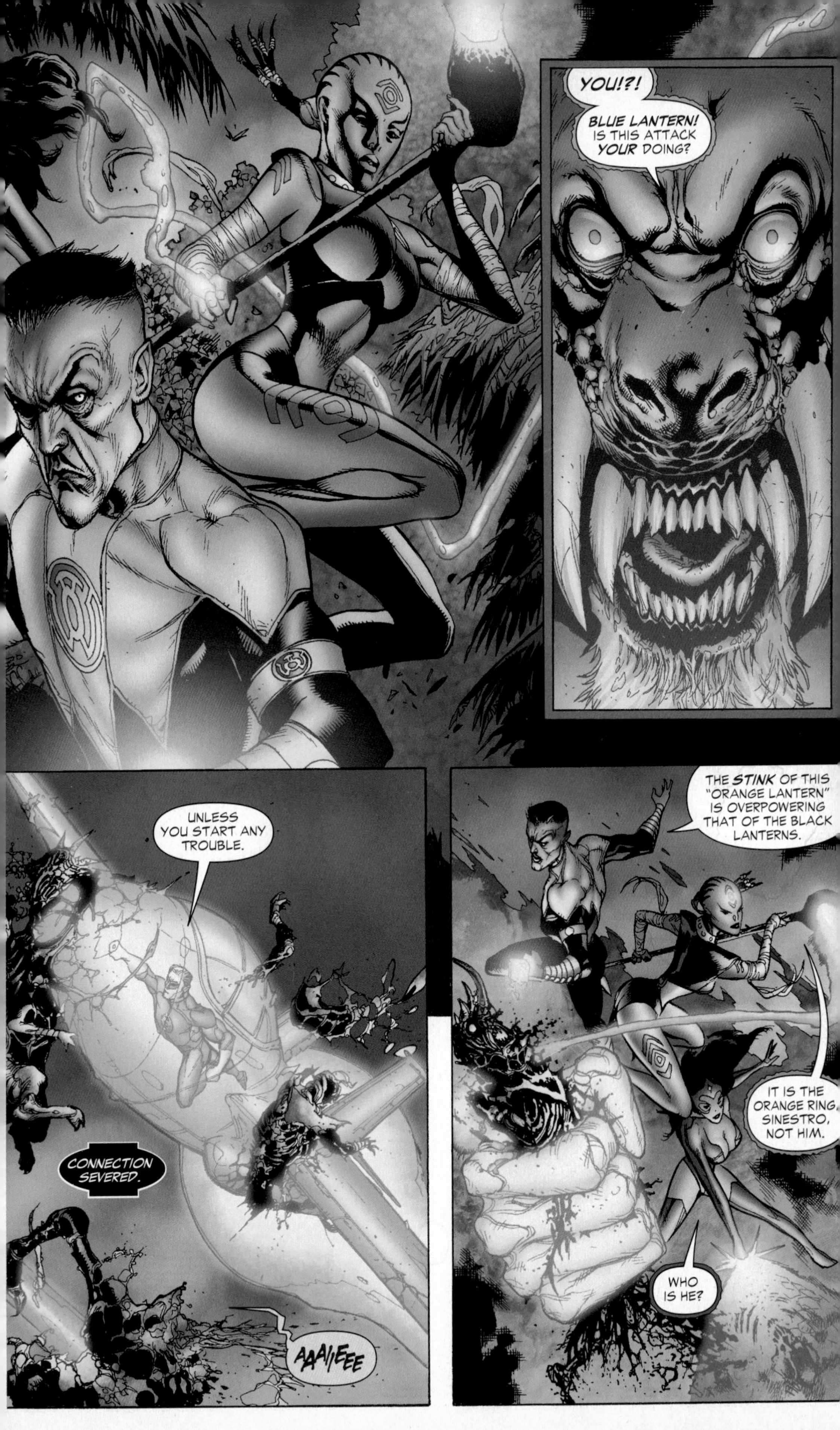
YOU!?!
BLUE LANTERN! IS THIS ATTACK YOUR DOING?
UNLESS YOU START ANY TROUBLE.
CONNECTION SEVERED.
AAAIIEEE
THE STINK OF THIS "ORANGE LANTERN" IS OVERPOWERING THAT OF THE BLACK LANTERNS.
IT IS THE ORANGE RING, SINESTRO, NOT HIM.
WHO IS HE?

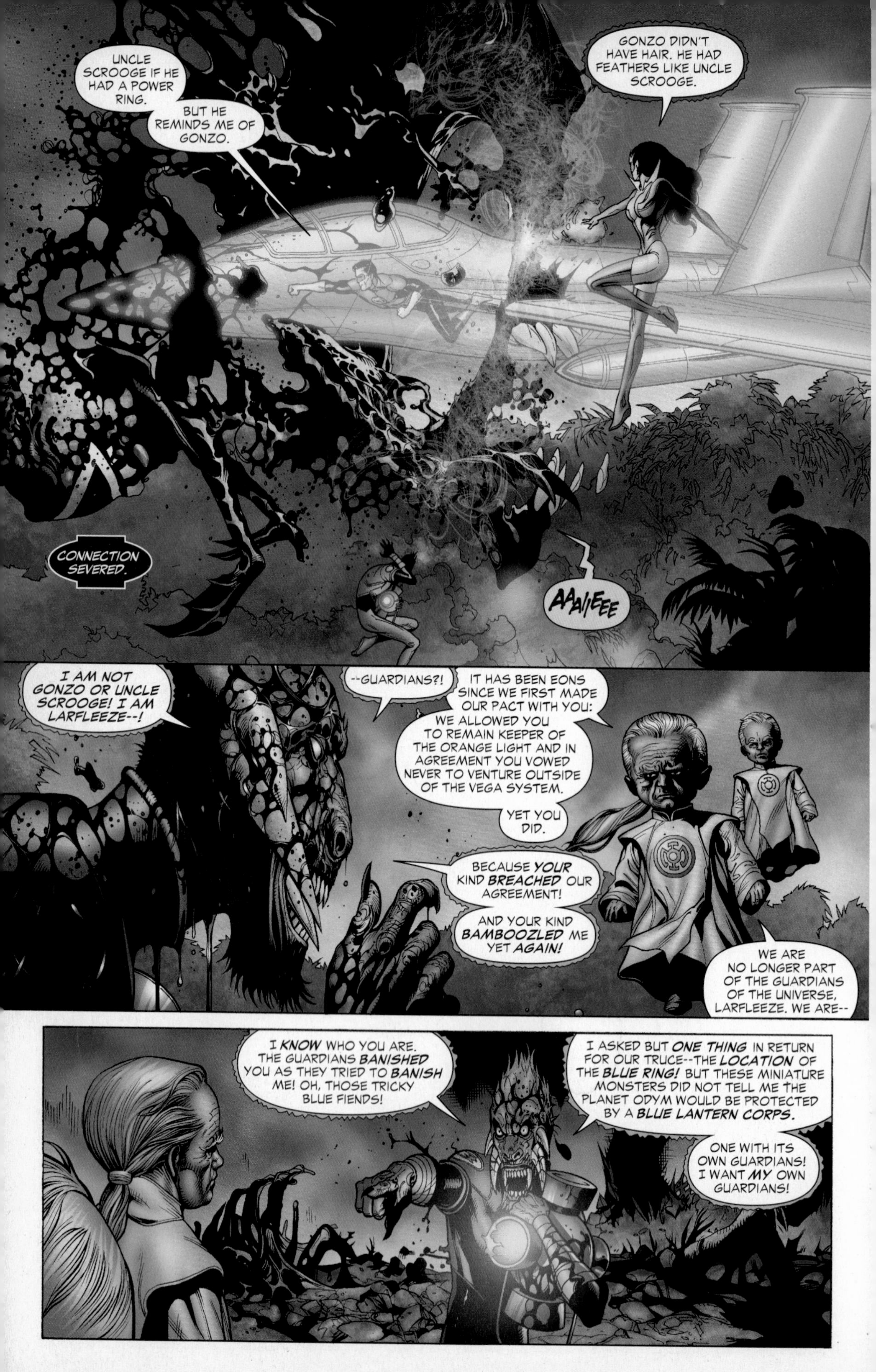
UNCLE SCROOGE IF HE HAD A POWER RING.
BUT HE REMINDS ME OF GONZO.
GONZO DIDN'T HAVE HAIR. HE HAD FEATHERS LIKE UNCLE SCROOGE.
CONNECTION SEVERED.
AAAIIEEE
I AM NOT GONZO OR UNCLE SCROOGE! I AM LARFLEEZE--!
--GUARDIANS?!
IT HAS BEEN EONS SINCE WE FIRST MADE OUR PACT WITH YOU:
WE ALLOWED YOU TO REMAIN KEEPER OF THE ORANGE LIGHT AND IN AGREEMENT YOU VOWED NEVER TO VENTURE OUTSIDE OF THE VEGA SYSTEM.
YET YOU DID.
BECAUSE YOUR KIND BREACHED OUR AGREEMENT!
AND YOUR KIND BAMBOOZLED ME YET AGAIN!
WE ARE NO LONGER PART OF THE GUARDIANS OF THE UNIVERSE, LARFLEEZE. WE ARE--
I KNOW WHO YOU ARE. THE GUARDIANS BANISHED YOU AS THEY TRIED TO BANISH ME! OH, THOSE TRICKY BLUE FIENDS!
I ASKED BUT ONE THING IN RETURN FOR OUR TRUCE--THE LOCATION OF THE BLUE RING! BUT THESE MINIATURE MONSTERS DID NOT TELL ME THE PLANET ODYM WOULD BE PROTECTED BY A BLUE LANTERN CORPS.
ONE WITH ITS OWN GUARDIANS! I WANT MY OWN GUARDIANS!

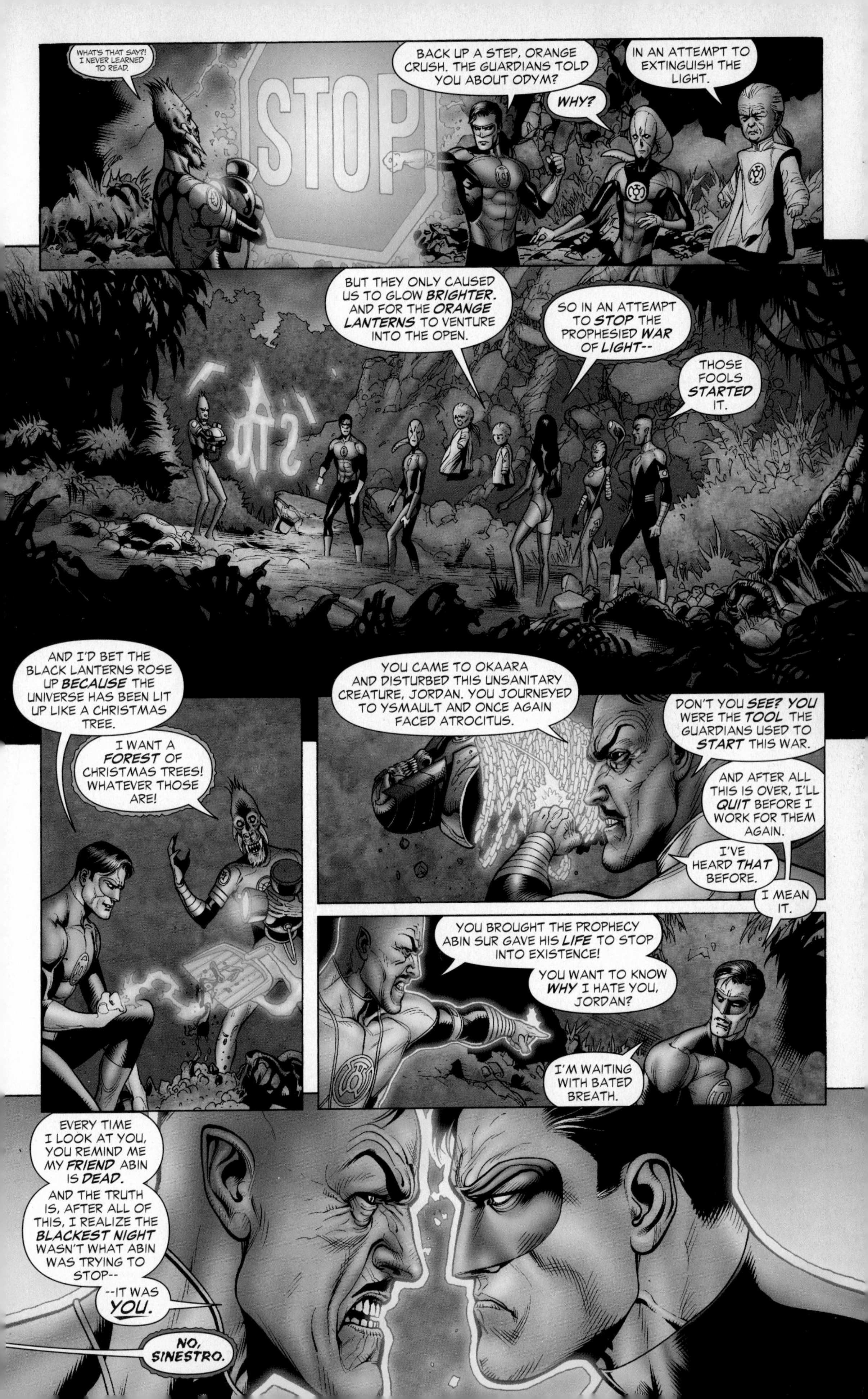
WHAT'S THAT SAY?! I NEVER LEARNED TO READ.
STOP
BACK UP A STEP, ORANGE CRUSH. THE GUARDIANS TOLD YOU ABOUT ODYM?
WHY?
IN AN ATTEMPT TO EXTINGUISH THE LIGHT.
BUT THEY ONLY CAUSED US TO GLOW BRIGHTER. AND FOR THE ORANGE LANTERNS TO VENTURE INTO THE OPEN.
SO IN AN ATTEMPT TO STOP THE PROPHESIED WAR OF LIGHT--
THOSE FOOLS STARTED IT.
AND I'D BET THE BLACK LANTERNS ROSE UP BECAUSE THE UNIVERSE HAS BEEN LIT UP LIKE A CHRISTMAS TREE.
I WANT A FOREST OF CHRISTMAS TREES! WHATEVER THOSE ARE!
YOU CAME TO OKAARA AND DISTURBED THIS UNSANITARY CREATURE, JORDAN. YOU JOURNEYED TO YSMAULT AND ONCE AGAIN FACED ATROCITUS.
DON'T YOU SEE? YOU WERE THE TOOL THE GUARDIANS USED TO START THIS WAR.
AND AFTER ALL THIS IS OVER, I'LL QUIT BEFORE I WORK FOR THEM AGAIN.
I'VE HEARD THAT BEFORE.
I MEAN IT.
YOU BROUGHT THE PROPHECY ABIN SUR GAVE HIS LIFE TO STOP INTO EXISTENCE!
YOU WANT TO KNOW WHY I HATE YOU, JORDAN?
I'M WAITING WITH BATED BREATH.
EVERY TIME I LOOK AT YOU, YOU REMIND ME MY FRIEND ABIN IS DEAD.
AND THE TRUTH IS, AFTER ALL OF THIS, I REALIZE THE BLACKEST NIGHT WASN'T WHAT ABIN WAS TRYING TO STOP--
--IT WAS YOU.
NO, SINESTRO.

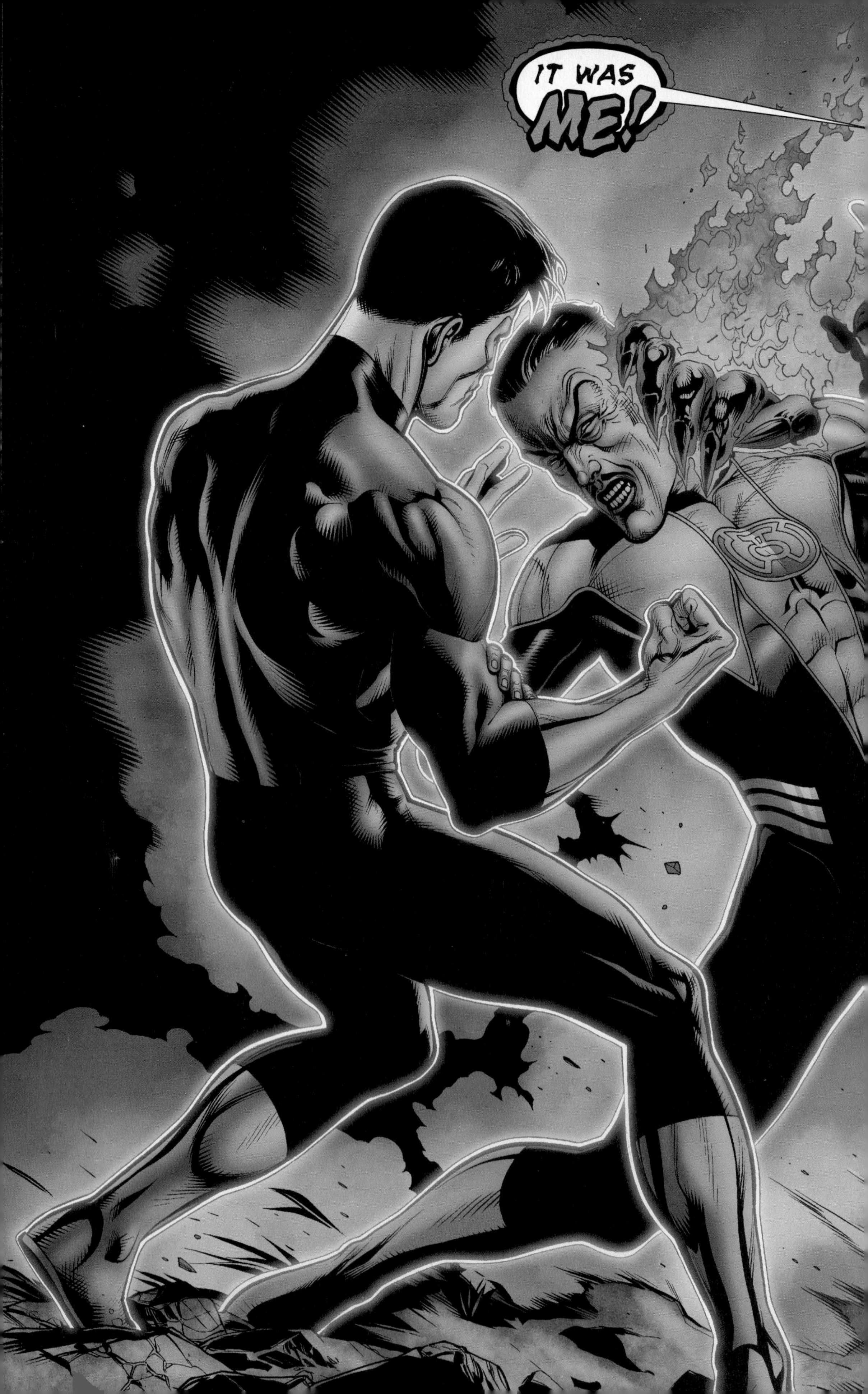
IT WAS ME!

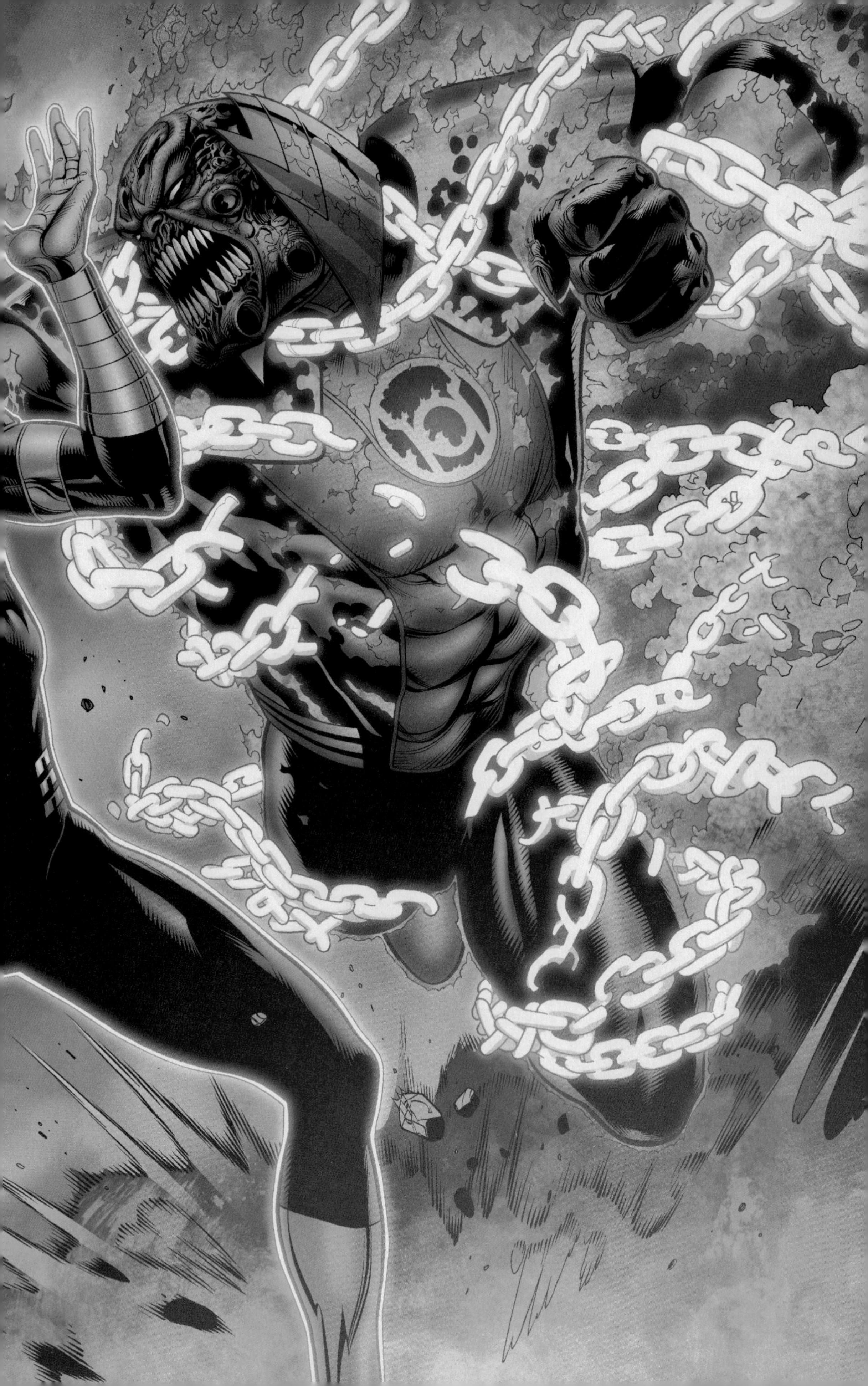

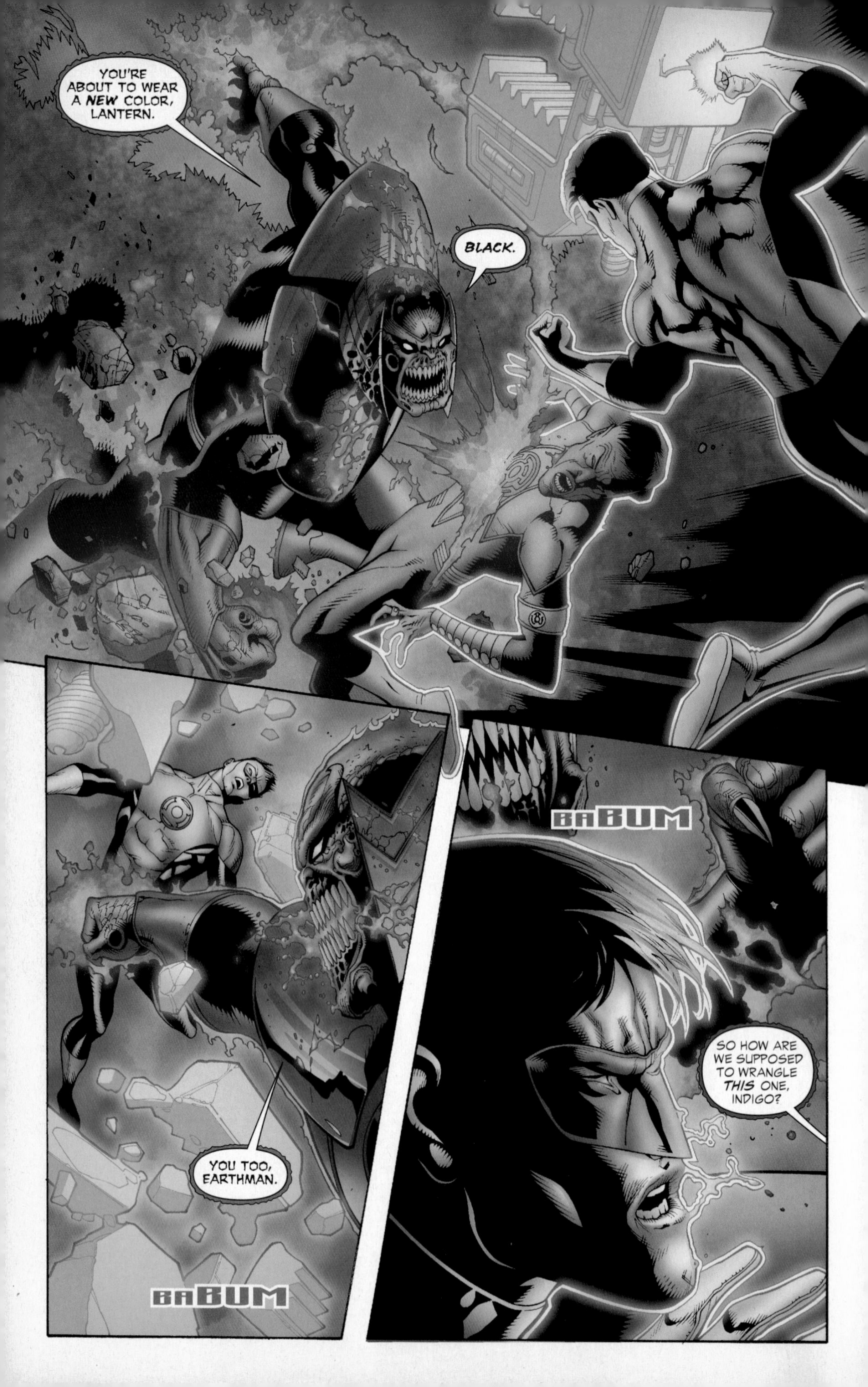

YOU'RE ABOUT TO WEAR A NEW COLOR, LANTERN.
BLACK.
YOU TOO, EARTHMAN.
BABUM
BABUM
SO HOW ARE WE SUPPOSED TO WRANGLE THIS ONE, INDIGO?

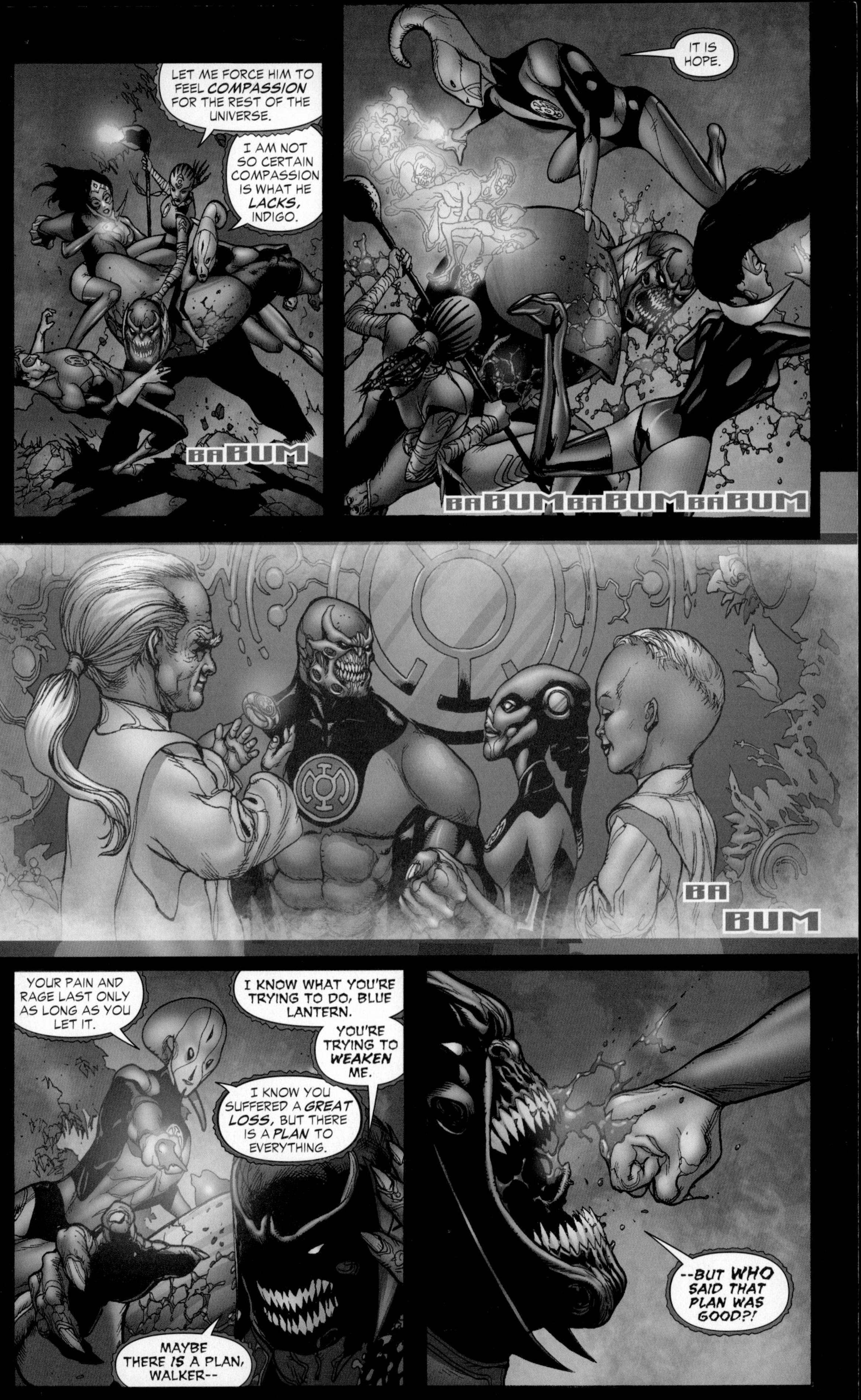
LET ME FORCE HIM TO FEEL COMPASSION FOR THE REST OF THE UNIVERSE.
I AM NOT SO CERTAIN COMPASSION IS WHAT HE LACKS, INDIGO.
BABUM
IT IS HOPE.
BABUMBABUMBABUM
BA BUM
YOUR PAIN AND RAGE LAST ONLY AS LONG AS YOU LET IT.
I KNOW WHAT YOU'RE TRYING TO DO, BLUE LANTERN.
YOU'RE TRYING TO WEAKEN ME.
I KNOW YOU SUFFERED A GREAT LOSS, BUT THERE IS A PLAN TO EVERYTHING.
MAYBE THERE IS A PLAN, WALKER--
--BUT WHO SAID THAT PLAN WAS GOOD?!

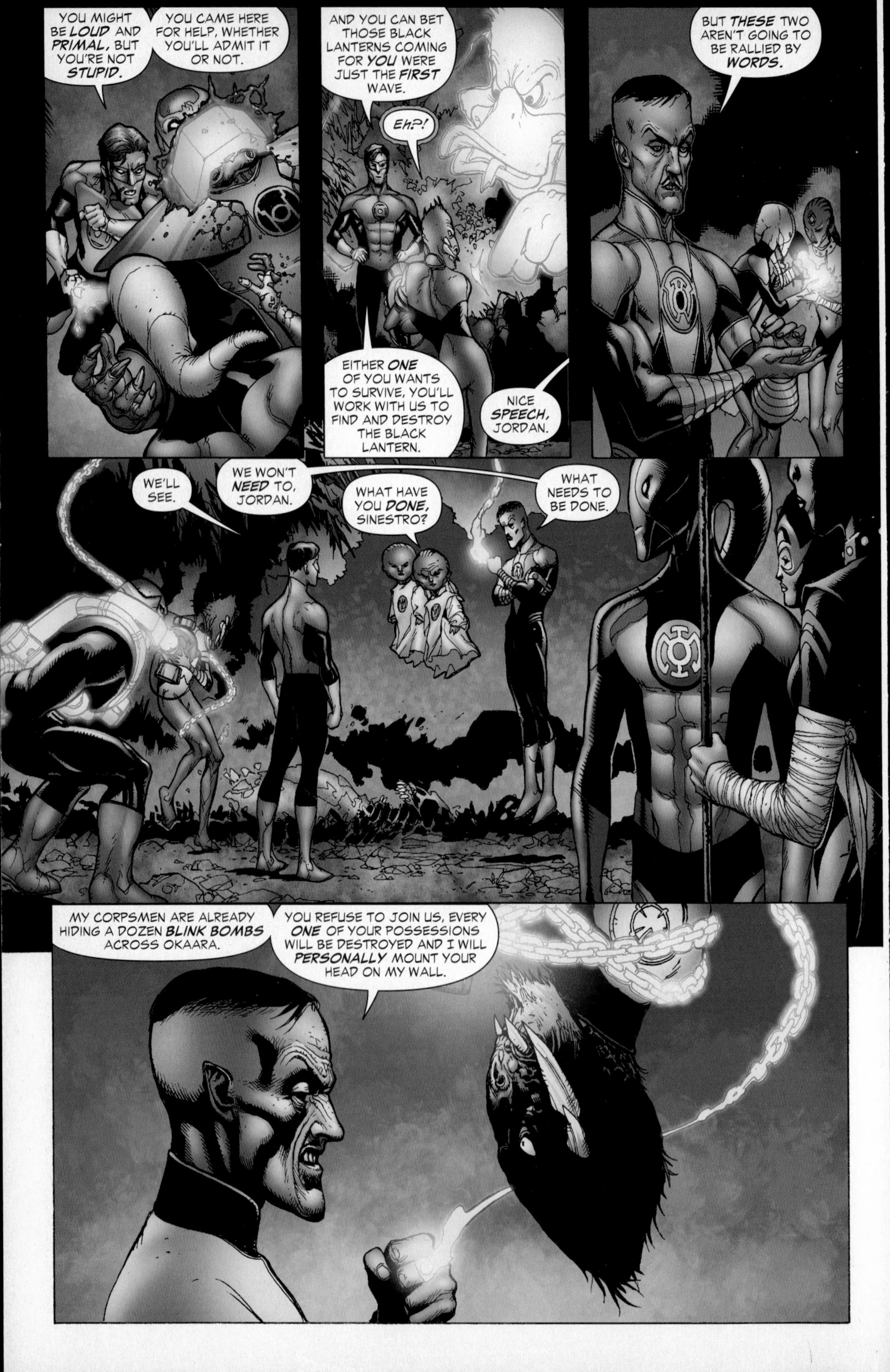
YOU MIGHT BE LOUD AND PRIMAL, BUT YOU'RE NOT STUPID.
YOU CAME HERE FOR HELP, WHETHER YOU'LL ADMIT IT OR NOT.
AND YOU CAN BET THOSE BLACK LANTERNS COMING FOR YOU WERE JUST THE FIRST WAVE.
Eh?!
EITHER ONE OF YOU WANTS TO SURVIVE, YOU'LL WORK WITH US TO FIND AND DESTROY THE BLACK LANTERN.
NICE SPEECH, JORDAN.
BUT THESE TWO AREN'T GOING TO BE RALLIED BY WORDS.
WE'LL SEE.
WE WON'T NEED TO, JORDAN.
WHAT HAVE YOU DONE, SINESTRO?
WHAT NEEDS TO BE DONE.
MY CORPSMEN ARE ALREADY HIDING A DOZEN BLINK BOMBS ACROSS OKAARA.
YOU REFUSE TO JOIN US, EVERY ONE OF YOUR POSSESSIONS WILL BE DESTROYED AND I WILL PERSONALLY MOUNT YOUR HEAD ON MY WALL.

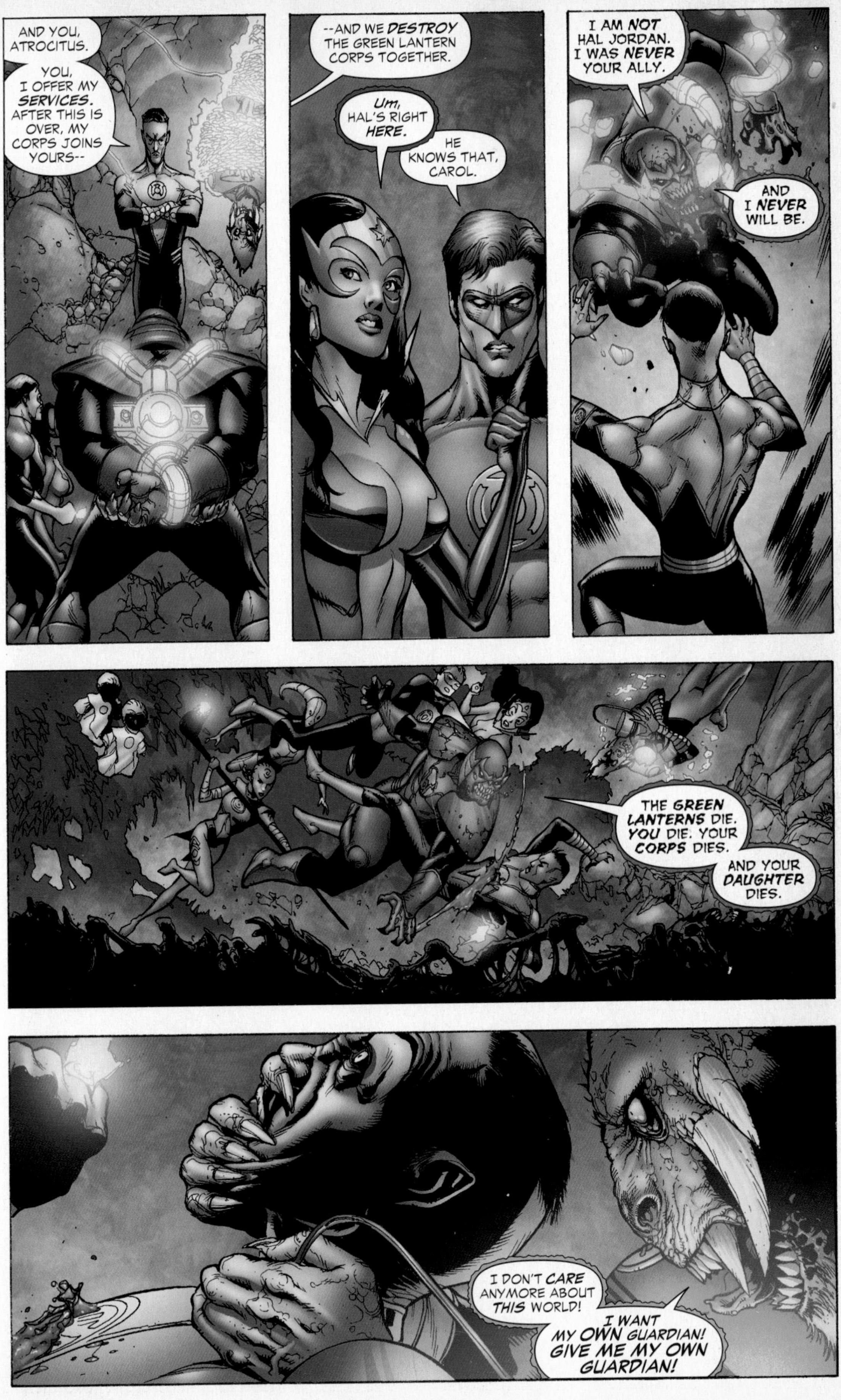
AND YOU, ATROCITUS.
YOU, I OFFER MY SERVICES. AFTER THIS IS OVER, MY CORPS JOINS YOURS--
--AND WE DESTROY THE GREEN LANTERN CORPS TOGETHER.
Um, HAL'S RIGHT HERE.
HE KNOWS THAT, CAROL.
I AM NOT HAL JORDAN. I WAS NEVER YOUR ALLY.
AND I NEVER WILL BE.
THE GREEN LANTERNS DIE. YOU DIE. YOUR CORPS DIES.
AND YOUR DAUGHTER DIES.
I DON'T CARE ANYMORE ABOUT THIS WORLD!
I WANT MY OWN GUARDIAN! GIVE ME MY OWN GUARDIAN!

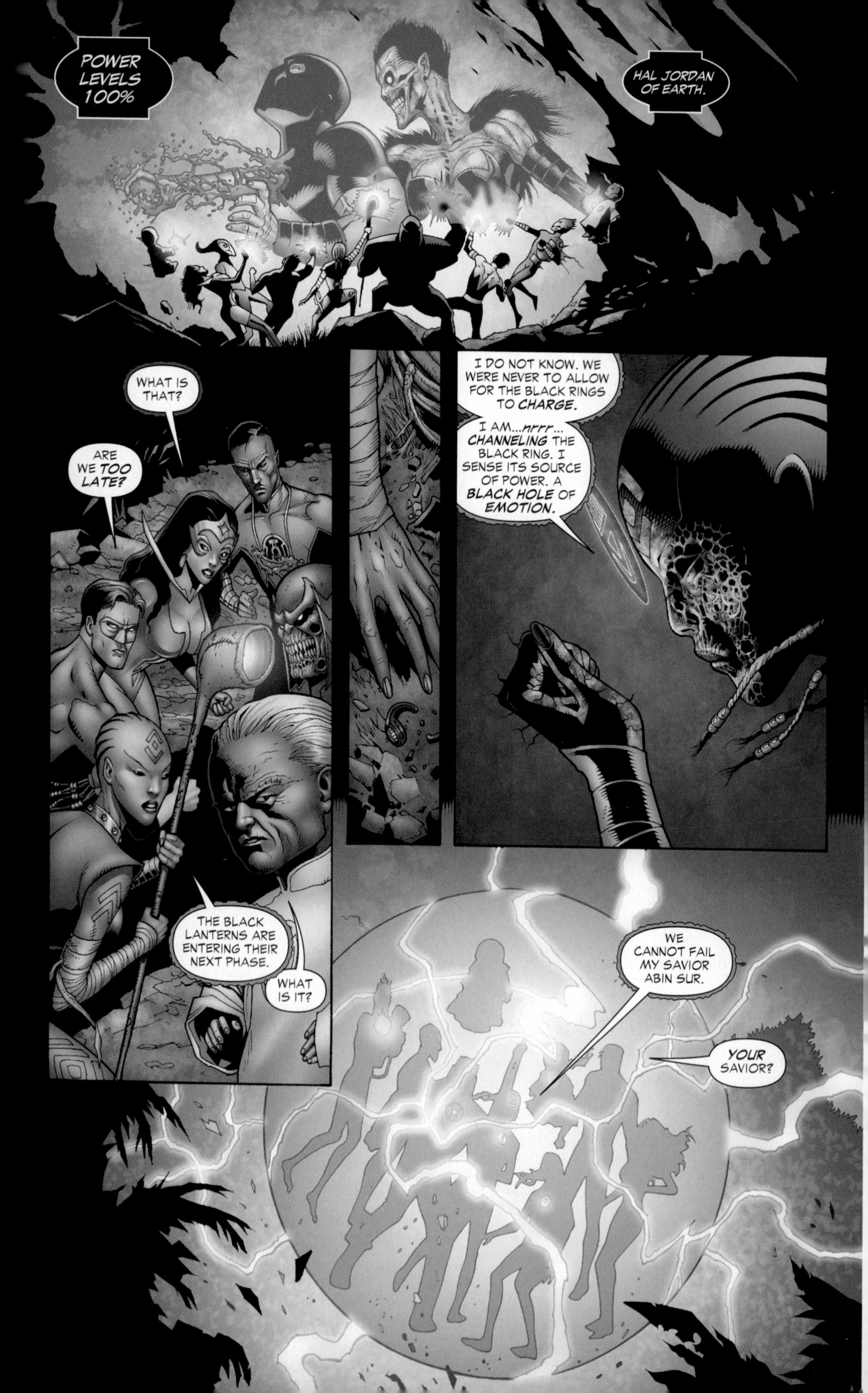
POWER LEVELS 100%
HAL JORDAN OF EARTH.
WHAT IS THAT?
ARE WE TOO LATE?
I DO NOT KNOW. WE WERE NEVER TO ALLOW FOR THE BLACK RINGS TO CHARGE.
I AM...nrrr... CHANNELING THE BLACK RING. I SENSE ITS SOURCE OF POWER. A BLACK HOLE OF EMOTION.
THE BLACK LANTERNS ARE ENTERING THEIR NEXT PHASE.
WHAT IS IT?
WE CANNOT FAIL MY SAVIOR ABIN SUR.
YOUR SAVIOR?

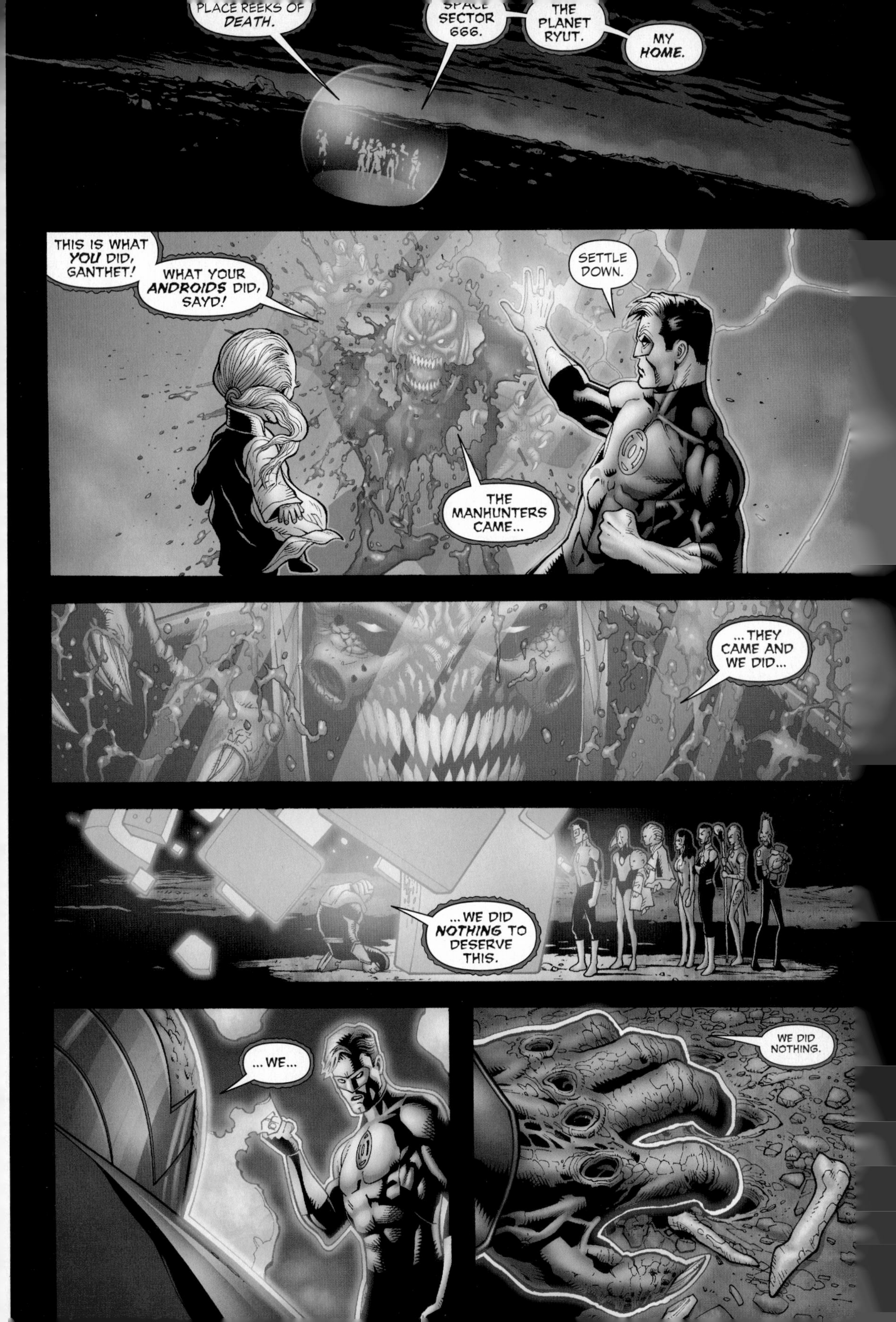
PLACE REEKS OF DEATH.
SPACE SECTOR 666.
THE PLANET RYUT.
MY HOME.
THIS IS WHAT YOU DID, GANTHET!
WHAT YOUR ANDROIDS DID, SAYD!
SETTLE DOWN.
THE MANHUNTERS CAME...
...THEY CAME AND WE DID...
...WE DID NOTHING TO DESERVE THIS.
...WE...
WE DID NOTHING.

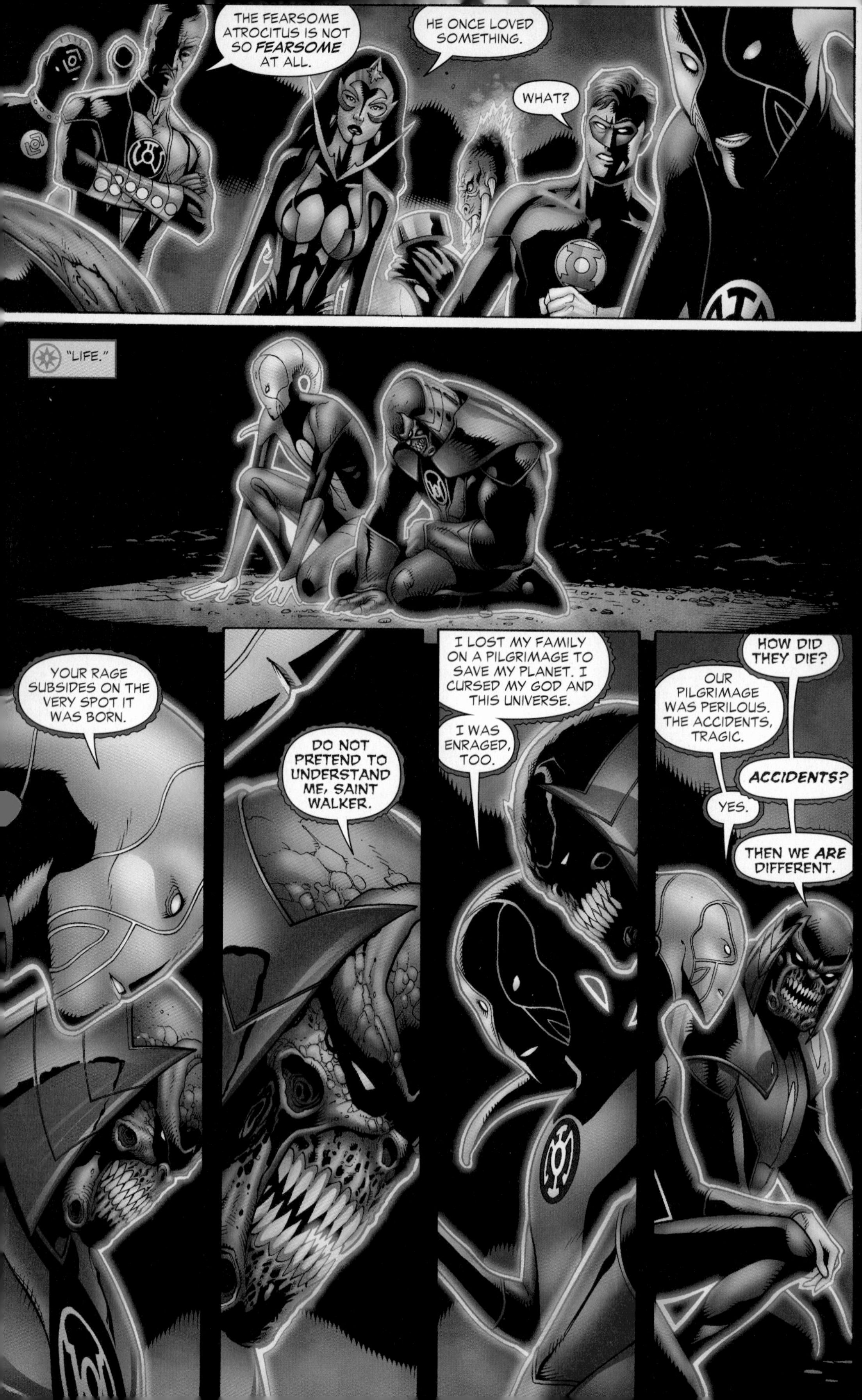
THE FEARSOME ATROCITUS IS NOT SO FEARSOME AT ALL.
HE ONCE LOVED SOMETHING.
WHAT?
"LIFE."
YOUR RAGE SUBSIDES ON THE VERY SPOT IT WAS BORN.
DO NOT PRETEND TO UNDERSTAND ME, SAINT WALKER.
I LOST MY FAMILY ON A PILGRIMAGE TO SAVE MY PLANET. I CURSED MY GOD AND THIS UNIVERSE.
I WAS ENRAGED, TOO.
HOW DID THEY DIE?
OUR PILGRIMAGE WAS PERILOUS. THE ACCIDENTS, TRAGIC.
ACCIDENTS?
YES.
THEN WE ARE DIFFERENT.

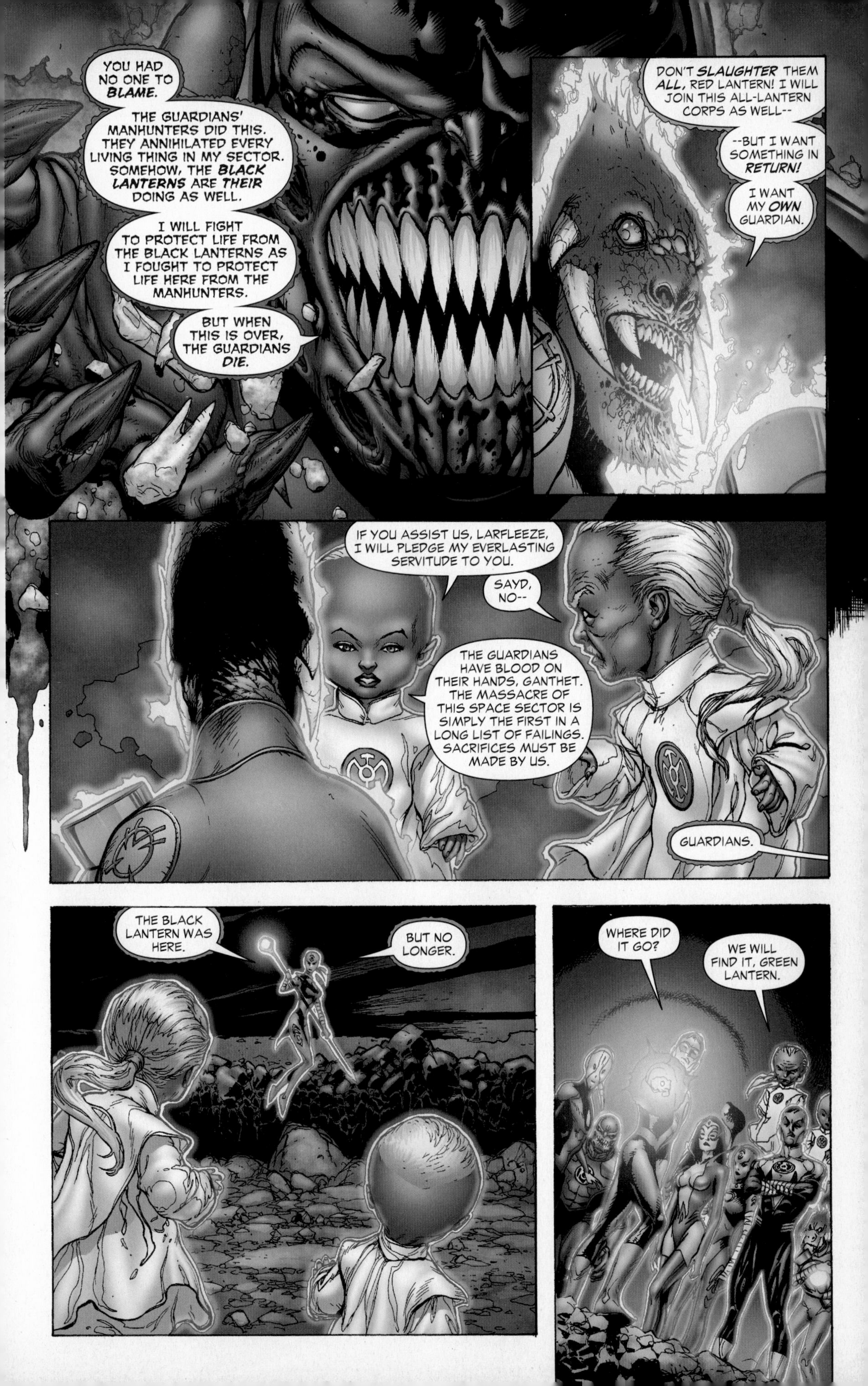

YOU HAD NO ONE TO BLAME.
THE GUARDIANS' MANHUNTERS DID THIS. THEY ANNIHILATED EVERY LIVING THING IN MY SECTOR. SOMEHOW, THE BLACK LANTERNS ARE THEIR DOING AS WELL.
I WILL FIGHT TO PROTECT LIFE FROM THE BLACK LANTERNS AS I FOUGHT TO PROTECT LIFE HERE FROM THE MANHUNTERS.
BUT WHEN THIS IS OVER, THE GUARDIANS DIE.
DON'T SLAUGHTER THEM ALL, RED LANTERN! I WILL JOIN THIS ALL-LANTERN CORPS AS WELL--
--BUT I WANT SOMETHING IN RETURN!
I WANT MY OWN GUARDIAN.
IF YOU ASSIST US, LARFLEEZE, I WILL PLEDGE MY EVERLASTING SERVITUDE TO YOU.
SAYD, NO--
THE GUARDIANS HAVE BLOOD ON THEIR HANDS, GANTHET. THE MASSACRE OF THIS SPACE SECTOR IS SIMPLY THE FIRST IN A LONG LIST OF FAILINGS. SACRIFICES MUST BE MADE BY US.
GUARDIANS.
THE BLACK LANTERN WAS HERE.
BUT NO LONGER.
WHERE DID IT GO?
WE WILL FIND IT, GREEN LANTERN.

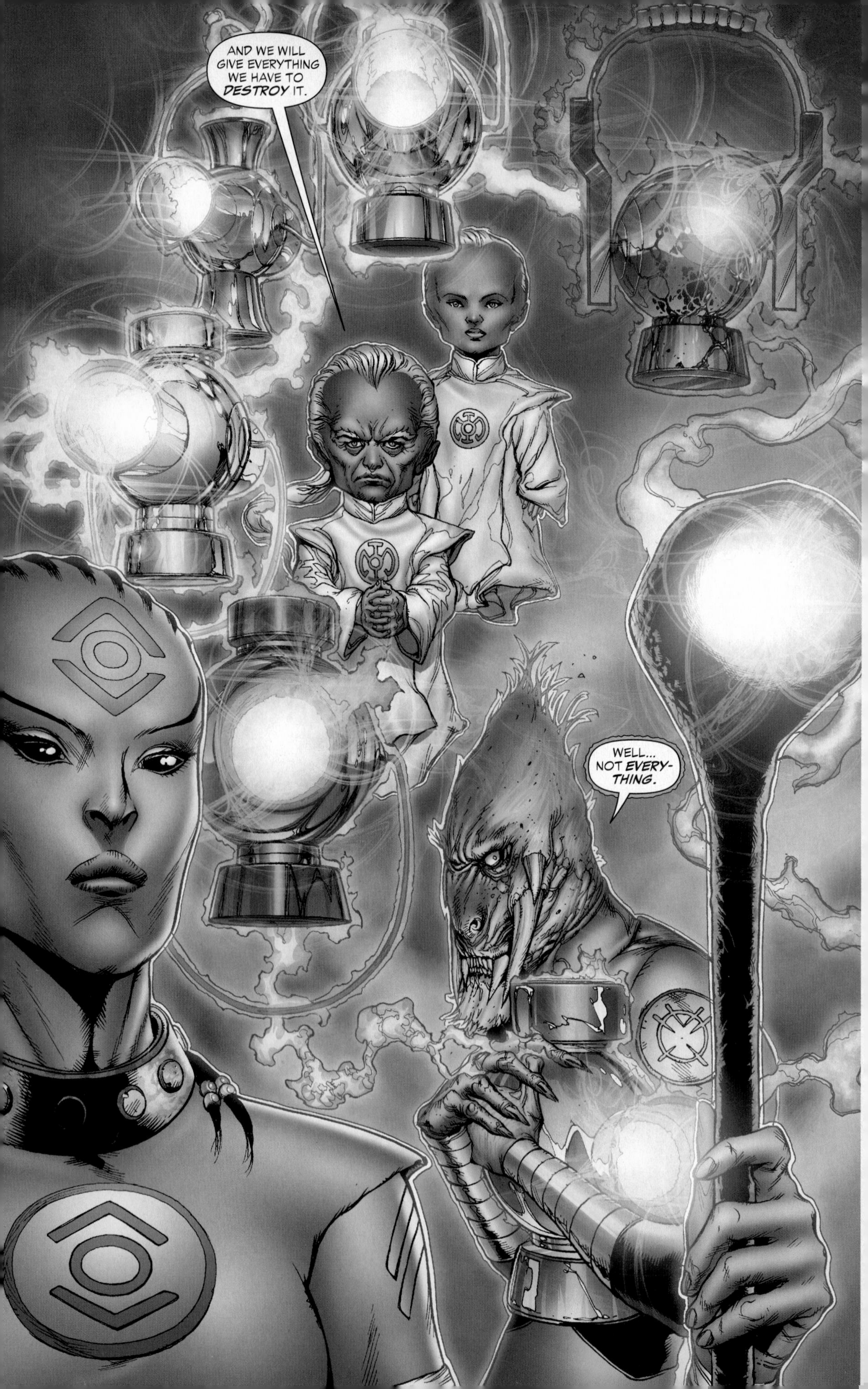
AND WE WILL GIVE EVERYTHING WE HAVE TO DESTROY IT.
WELL... NOT EVERYTHING.

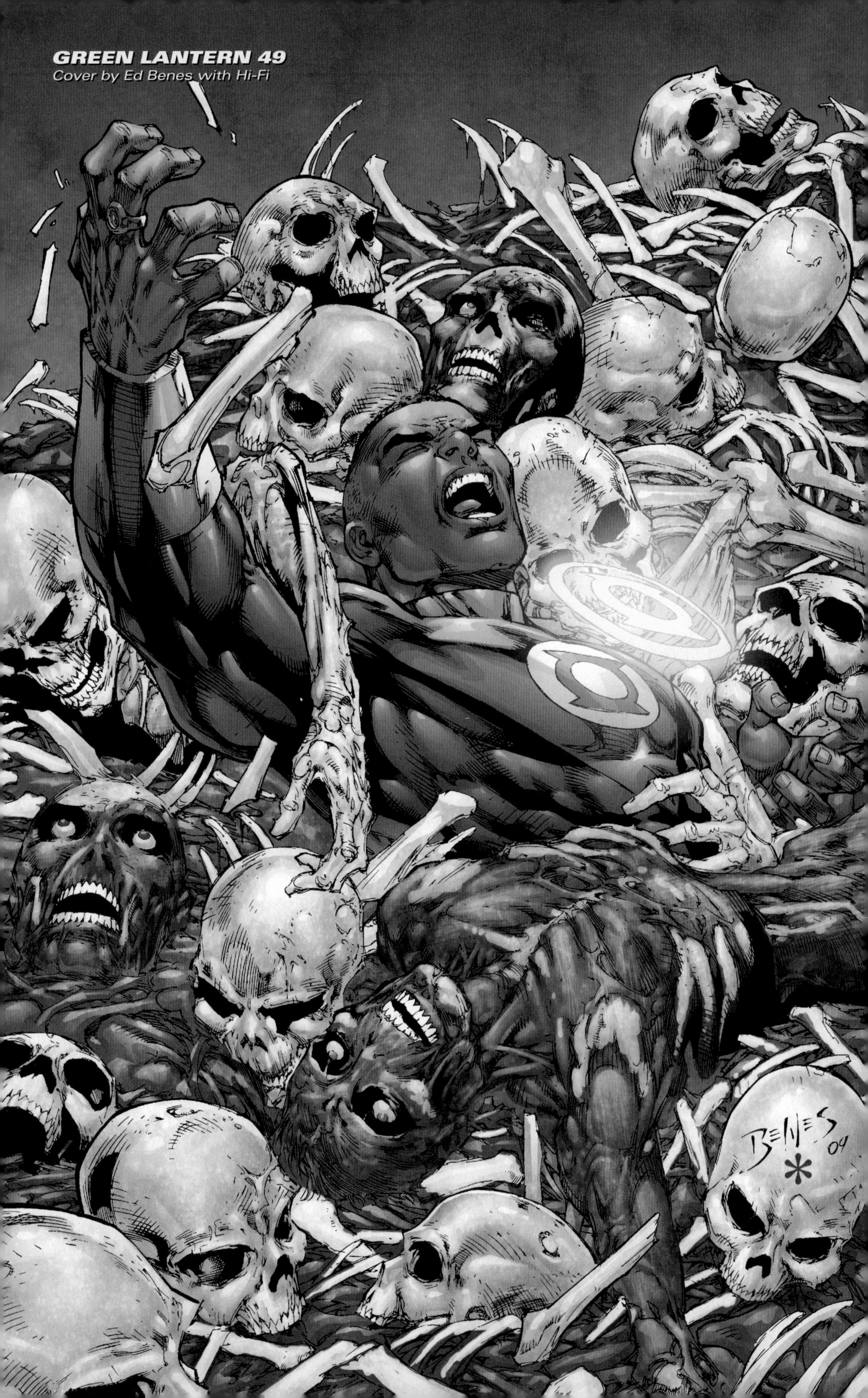
BENES 04

GREEN LANTERN 49
Cover by Ed Benes with Hi-Fi

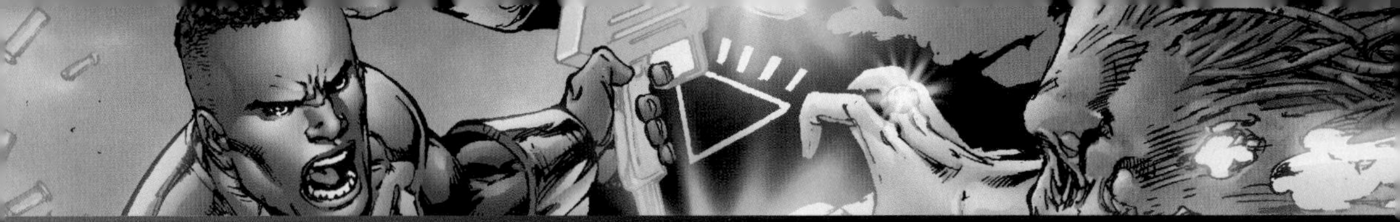

After eradicating the corrupted Guardian "Scar," Hal's team of Carol Ferris, Sinestro, Atrocitus, St. Walker, Indigo-1 and Larfleeze face the might of Nekron's newly empowered Black Lanterns: Superman, Green Arrow, Kid Flash, Superboy, Ice, Donna Troy, Animal Man and Wonder Woman. All heroes who had once died and returned.

However, the Lanterns stand to lose the war if the battle on the resurrected planet Xanshi isn't won first...

SEMPER FI

ED BENES
MARCOS MARZ
PENCILS

ED BENES
LUCIANA DEL NEGRO
INKS

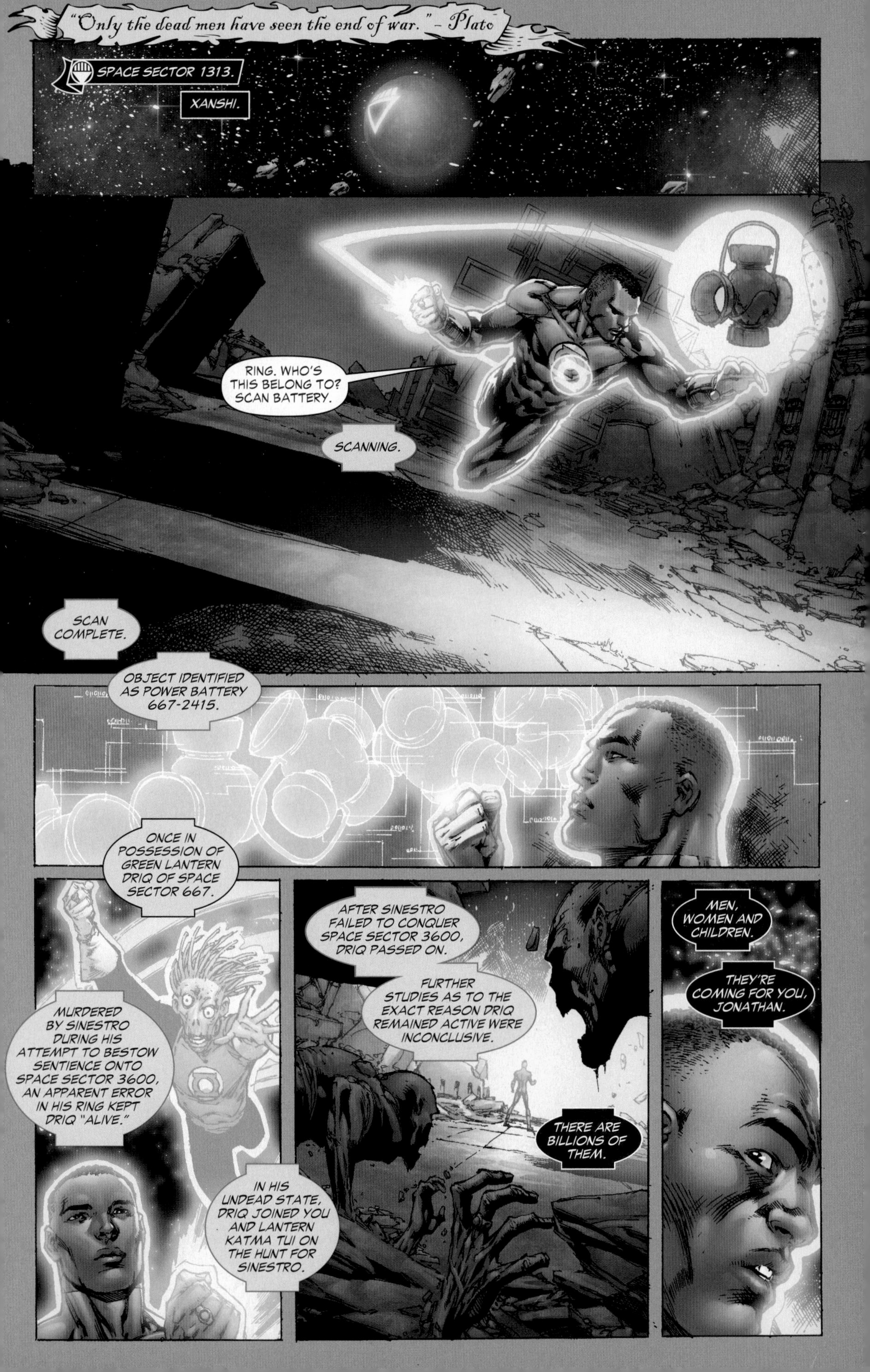

"Only the dead men have seen the end of war." – Plato
SPACE SECTOR 1313.
XANSHI.
RING. WHO'S THIS BELONG TO? SCAN BATTERY.
SCANNING.
SCAN COMPLETE.
OBJECT IDENTIFIED AS POWER BATTERY 667-2415.
ONCE IN POSSESSION OF GREEN LANTERN DRIQ OF SPACE SECTOR 667.
MURDERED BY SINESTRO DURING HIS ATTEMPT TO BESTOW SENTIENCE ONTO SPACE SECTOR 3600, AN APPARENT ERROR IN HIS RING KEPT DRIQ "ALIVE."
IN HIS UNDEAD STATE, DRIQ JOINED YOU AND LANTERN KATMA TUI ON THE HUNT FOR SINESTRO.
AFTER SINESTRO FAILED TO CONQUER SPACE SECTOR 3600, DRIQ PASSED ON.
FURTHER STUDIES AS TO THE EXACT REASON DRIQ REMAINED ACTIVE WERE INCONCLUSIVE.
THERE ARE BILLIONS OF THEM.
MEN, WOMEN AND CHILDREN.
THEY'RE COMING FOR YOU, JONATHAN.

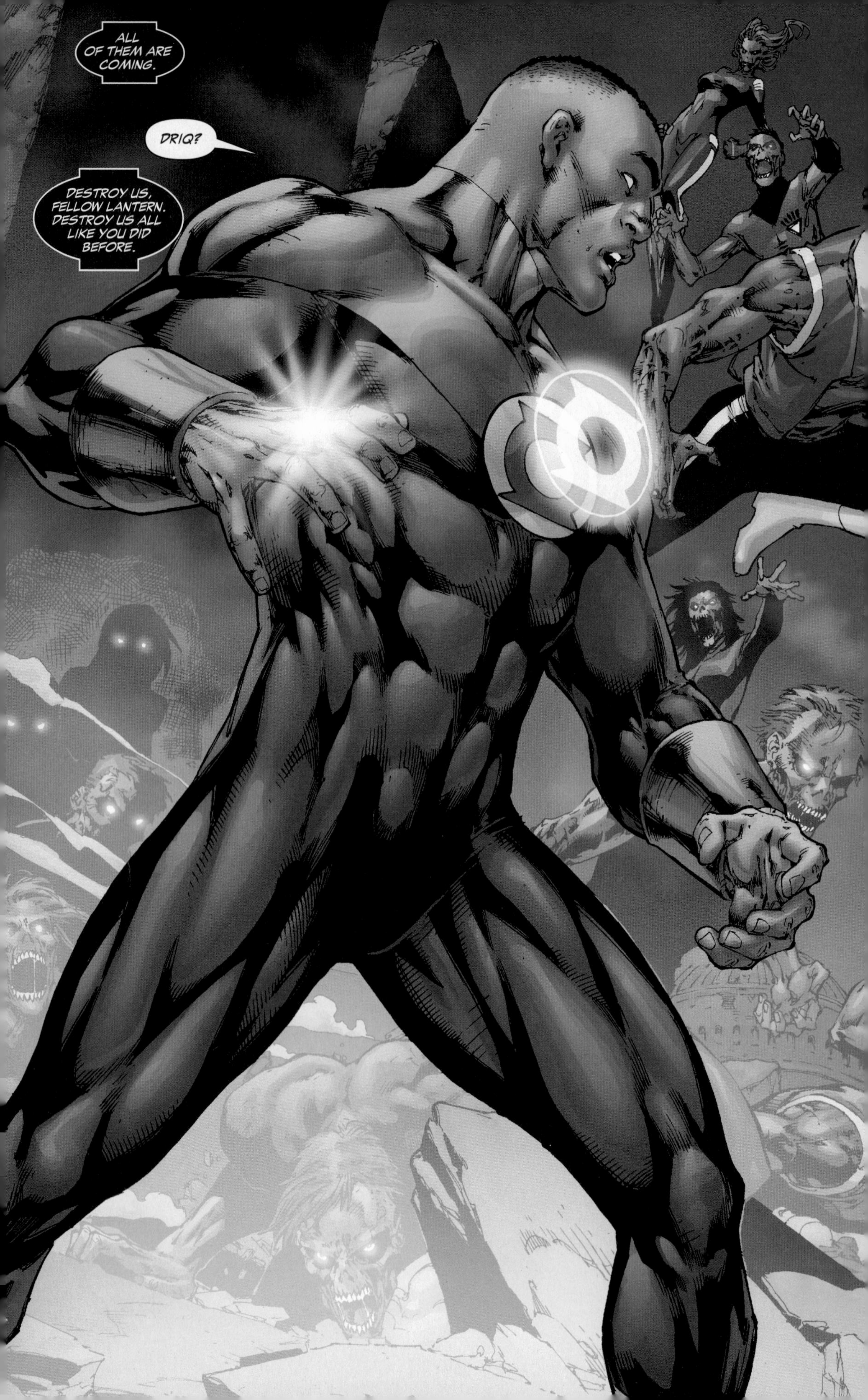
ALL OF THEM ARE COMING.
DRIQ?
DESTROY US, FELLOW LANTERN. DESTROY US ALL LIKE YOU DID BEFORE.

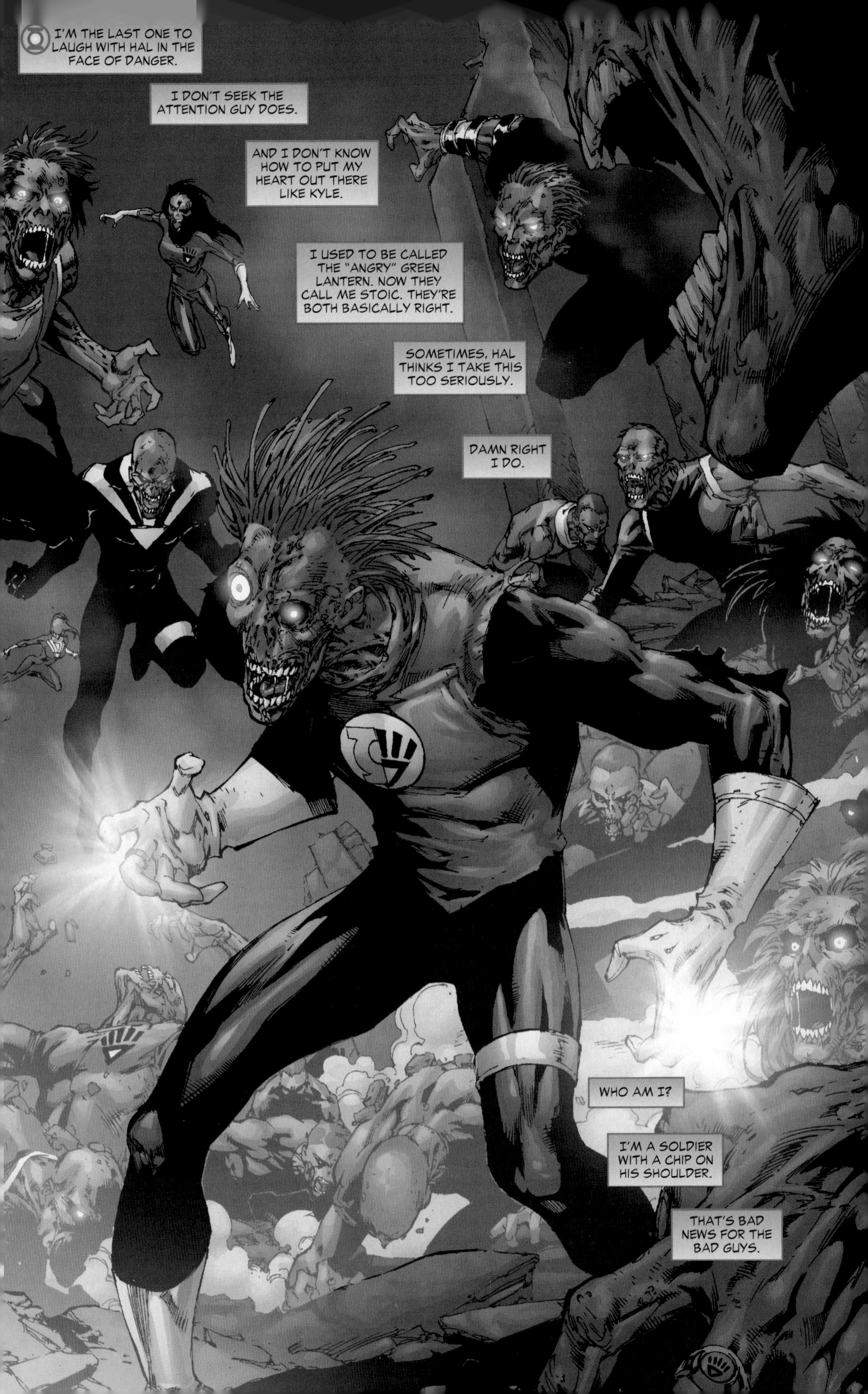
I'M THE LAST ONE TO LAUGH WITH HAL IN THE FACE OF DANGER.
I DON'T SEEK THE ATTENTION GUY DOES.
AND I DON'T KNOW HOW TO PUT MY HEART OUT THERE LIKE KYLE.
I USED TO BE CALLED THE "ANGRY" GREEN LANTERN. NOW THEY CALL ME STOIC. THEY'RE BOTH BASICALLY RIGHT.
SOMETIMES, HAL THINKS I TAKE THIS TOO SERIOUSLY.
DAMN RIGHT I DO.
WHO AM I?
I'M A SOLDIER WITH A CHIP ON HIS SHOULDER.
THAT'S BAD NEWS FOR THE BAD GUYS.

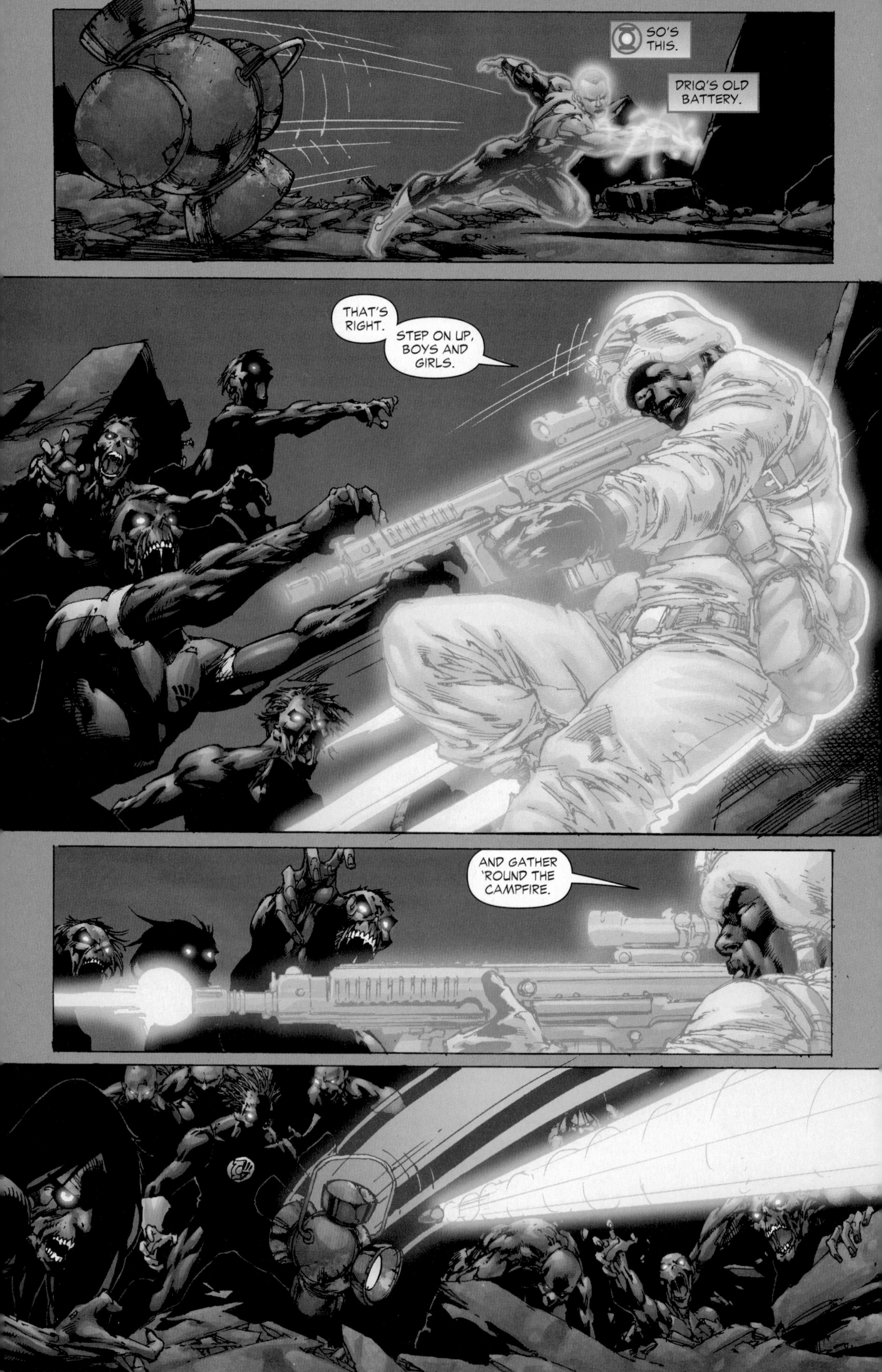
SO'S THIS.
DRIQ'S OLD BATTERY.
THAT'S RIGHT.
STEP ON UP, BOYS AND GIRLS.
AND GATHER 'ROUND THE CAMPFIRE.

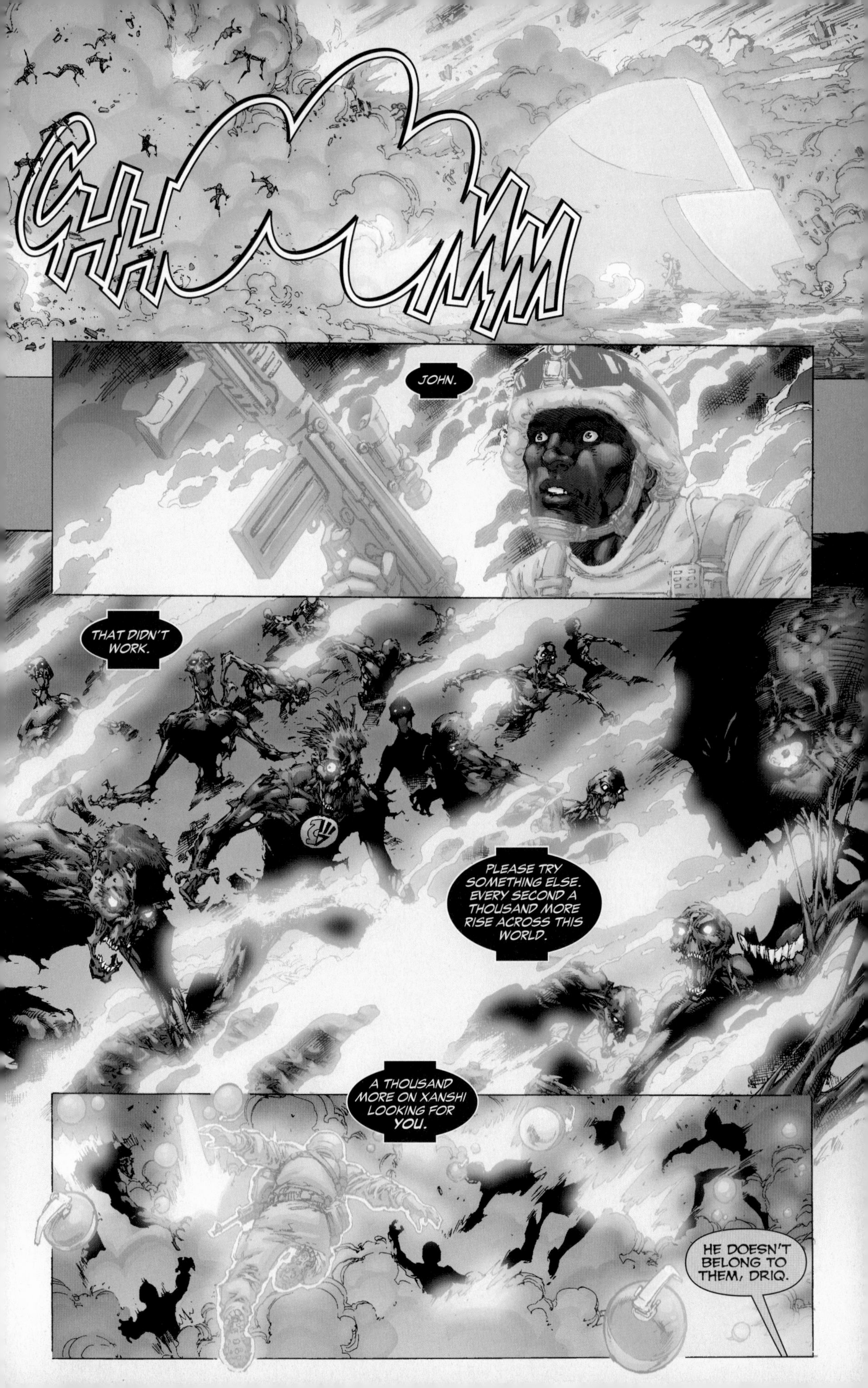
CHHMMM
JOHN.
THAT DIDN'T WORK.
PLEASE TRY SOMETHING ELSE. EVERY SECOND A THOUSAND MORE RISE ACROSS THIS WORLD.
A THOUSAND MORE ON XANSHI LOOKING FOR YOU.
HE DOESN'T BELONG TO THEM, DRIQ.

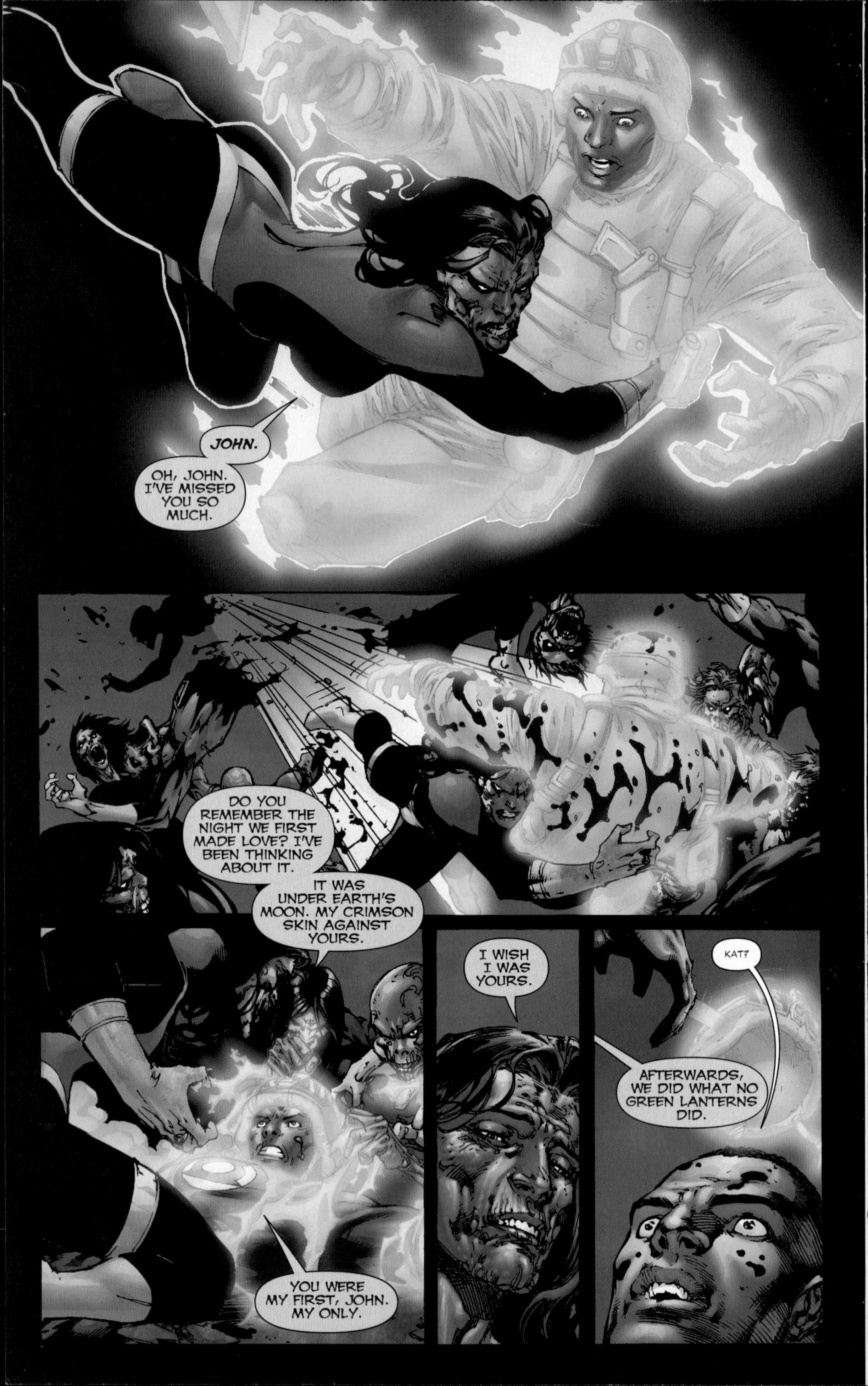
JOHN.
OH, JOHN. I'VE MISSED YOU SO MUCH.
DO YOU REMEMBER THE NIGHT WE FIRST MADE LOVE? I'VE BEEN THINKING ABOUT IT.
IT WAS UNDER EARTH'S MOON. MY CRIMSON SKIN AGAINST YOURS.
YOU WERE MY FIRST, JOHN. MY ONLY.
I WISH I WAS YOURS.
KAT?
AFTERWARDS, WE DID WHAT NO GREEN LANTERNS DID.

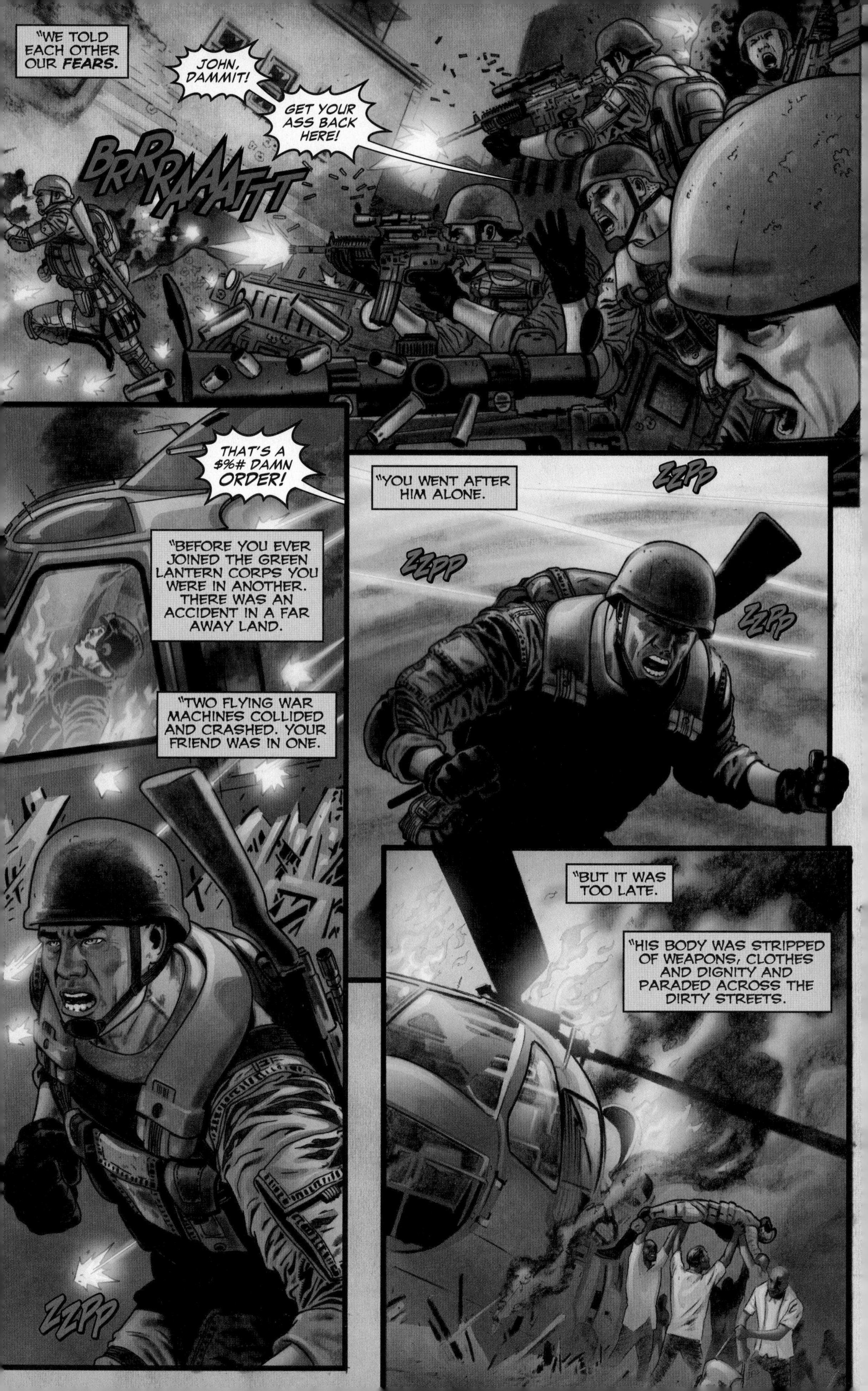
"WE TOLD EACH OTHER OUR FEARS.
JOHN, DAMMIT!
GET YOUR ASS BACK HERE!
BRRRAAATTT
THAT'S A $%# DAMN ORDER!
"BEFORE YOU EVER JOINED THE GREEN LANTERN CORPS YOU WERE IN ANOTHER. THERE WAS AN ACCIDENT IN A FAR AWAY LAND.
"TWO FLYING WAR MACHINES COLLIDED AND CRASHED. YOUR FRIEND WAS IN ONE.
ZZPP
"YOU WENT AFTER HIM ALONE.
ZZPP
ZZPP
ZZPP
"BUT IT WAS TOO LATE.
"HIS BODY WAS STRIPPED OF WEAPONS, CLOTHES AND DIGNITY AND PARADED ACROSS THE DIRTY STREETS.

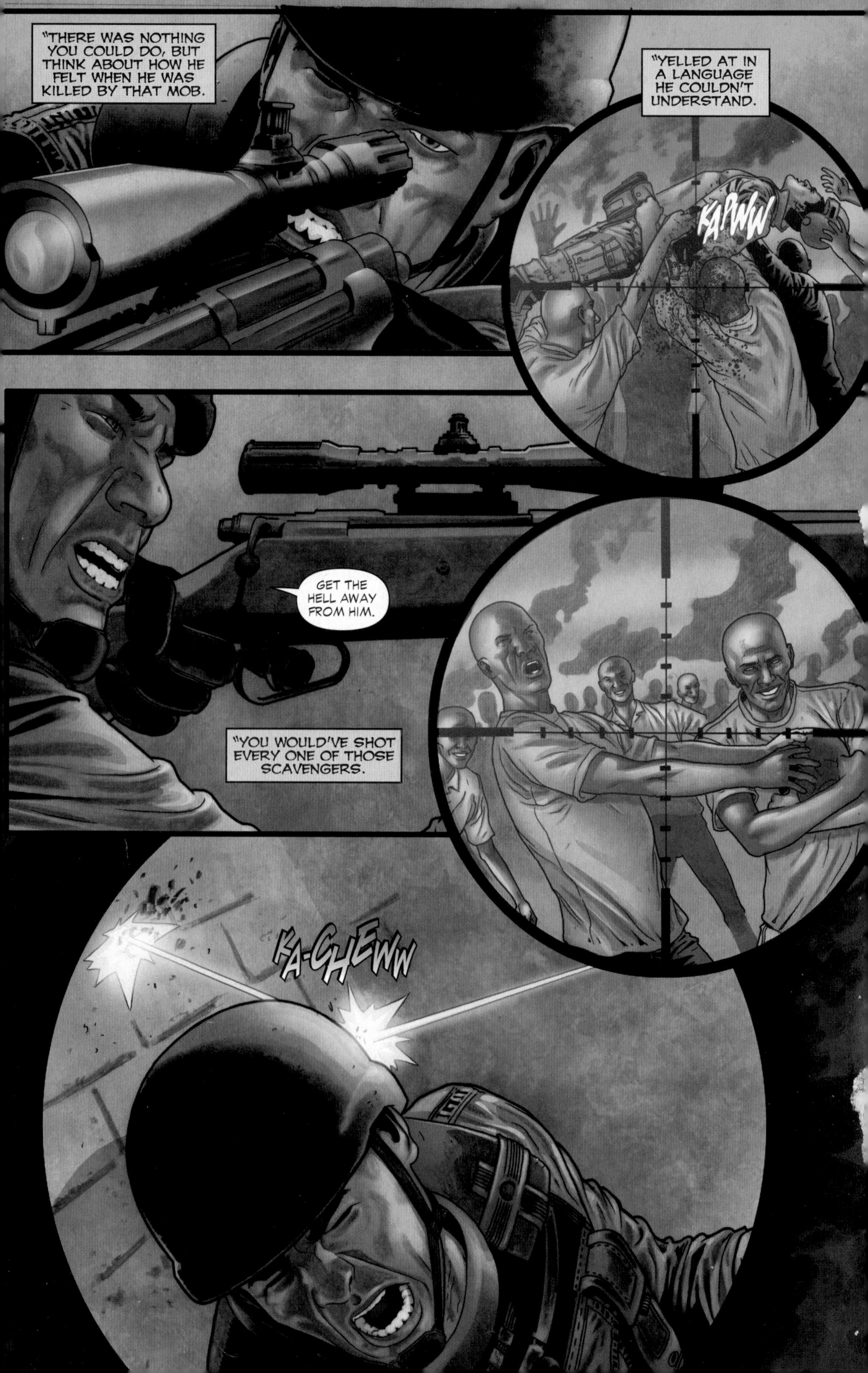

"THERE WAS NOTHING YOU COULD DO, BUT THINK ABOUT HOW HE FELT WHEN HE WAS KILLED BY THAT MOB.
"YELLED AT IN A LANGUAGE HE COULDN'T UNDERSTAND.
KAPWW
GET THE HELL AWAY FROM HIM.
"YOU WOULD'VE SHOT EVERY ONE OF THOSE SCAVENGERS.
KA-CHEWW

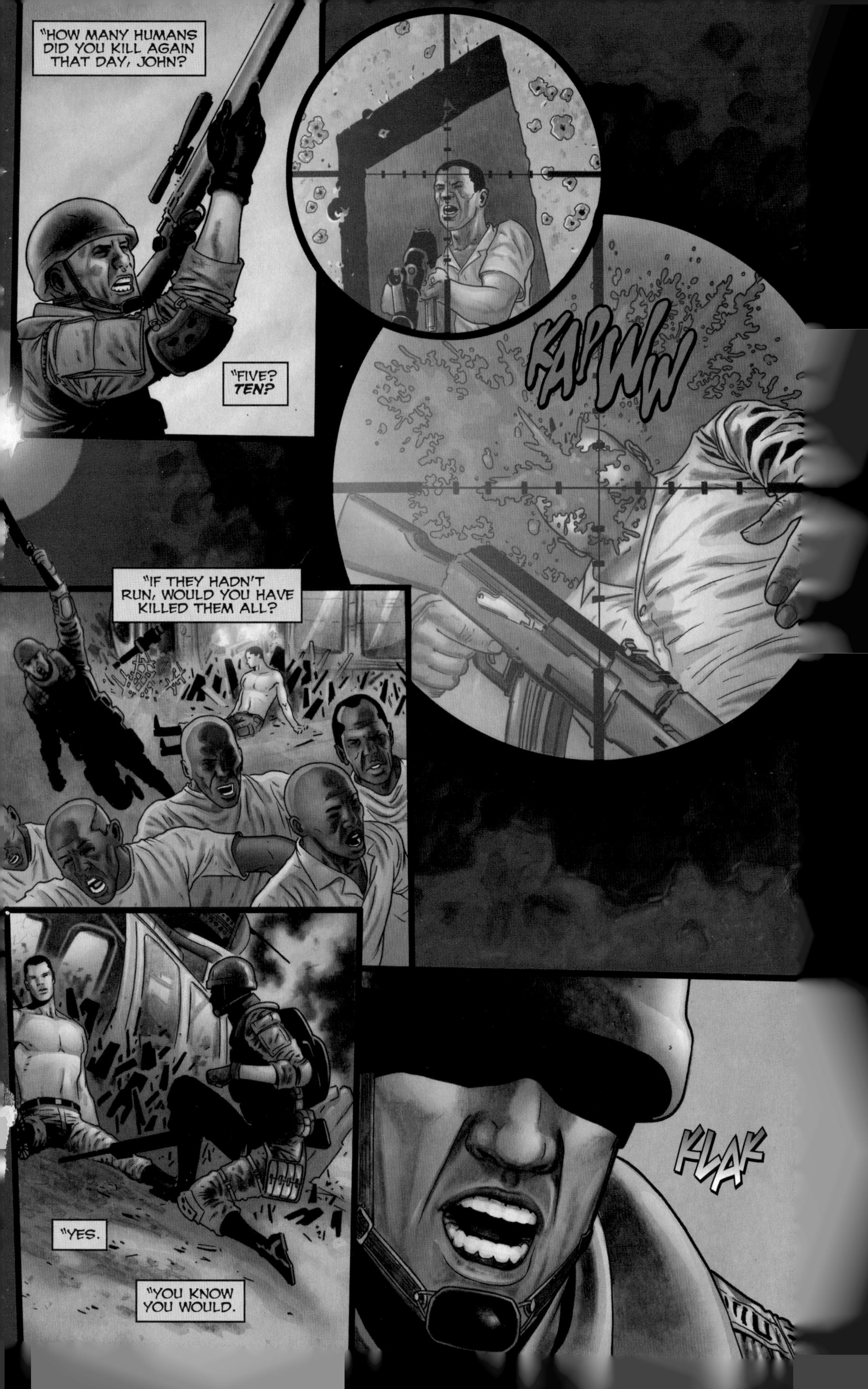
"HOW MANY HUMANS DID YOU KILL AGAIN THAT DAY, JOHN?
"FIVE? TEN?
KAPWW
"IF THEY HADN'T RUN, WOULD YOU HAVE KILLED THEM ALL?
"YES.
"YOU KNOW YOU WOULD.
KLAK

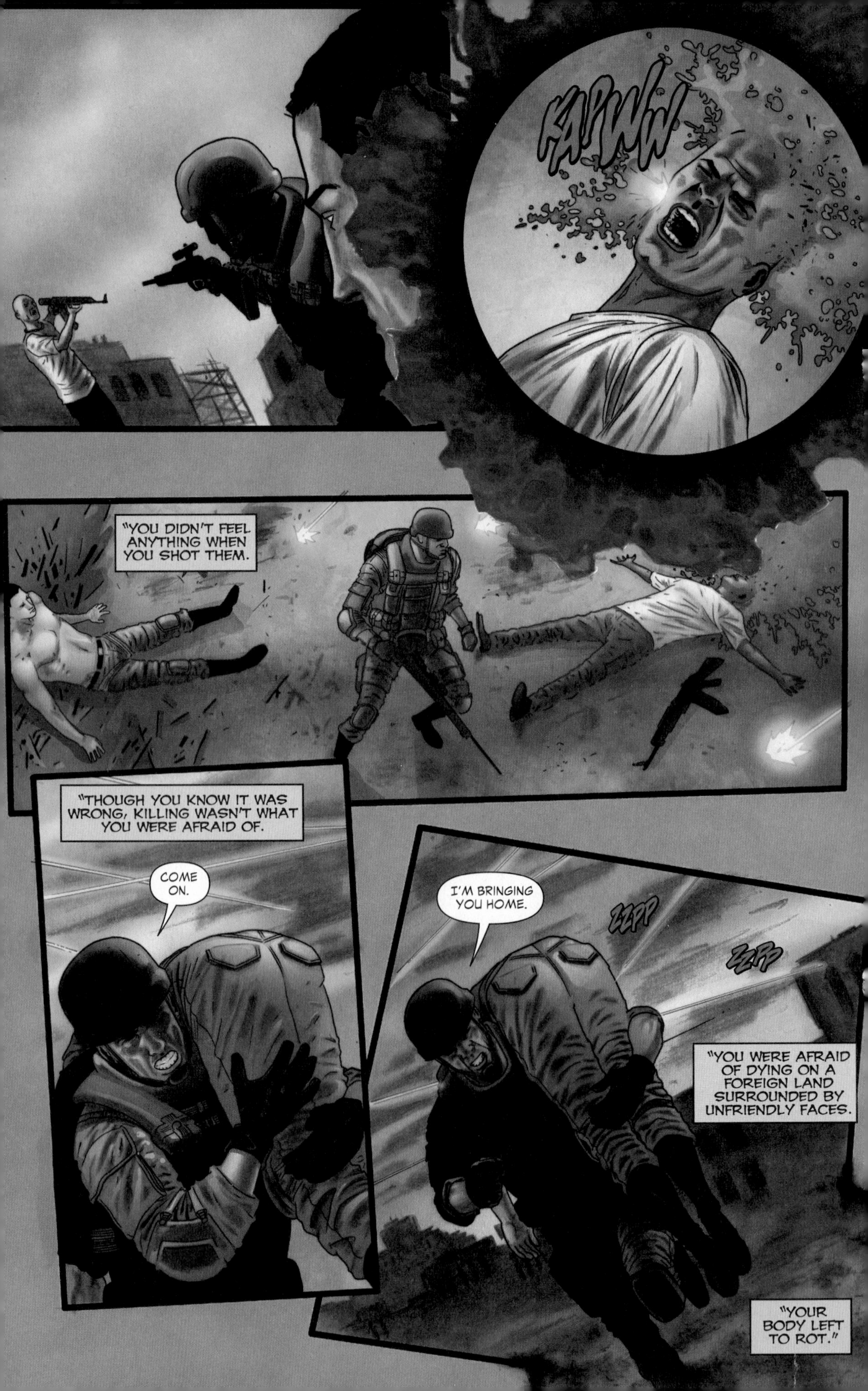
KAPWW
"YOU DIDN'T FEEL ANYTHING WHEN YOU SHOT THEM.
"THOUGH YOU KNOW IT WAS WRONG, KILLING WASN'T WHAT YOU WERE AFRAID OF.
COME ON.
I'M BRINGING YOU HOME.
ZZPP
ZZPP
"YOU WERE AFRAID OF DYING ON A FOREIGN LAND SURROUNDED BY UNFRIENDLY FACES.
"YOUR BODY LEFT TO ROT."

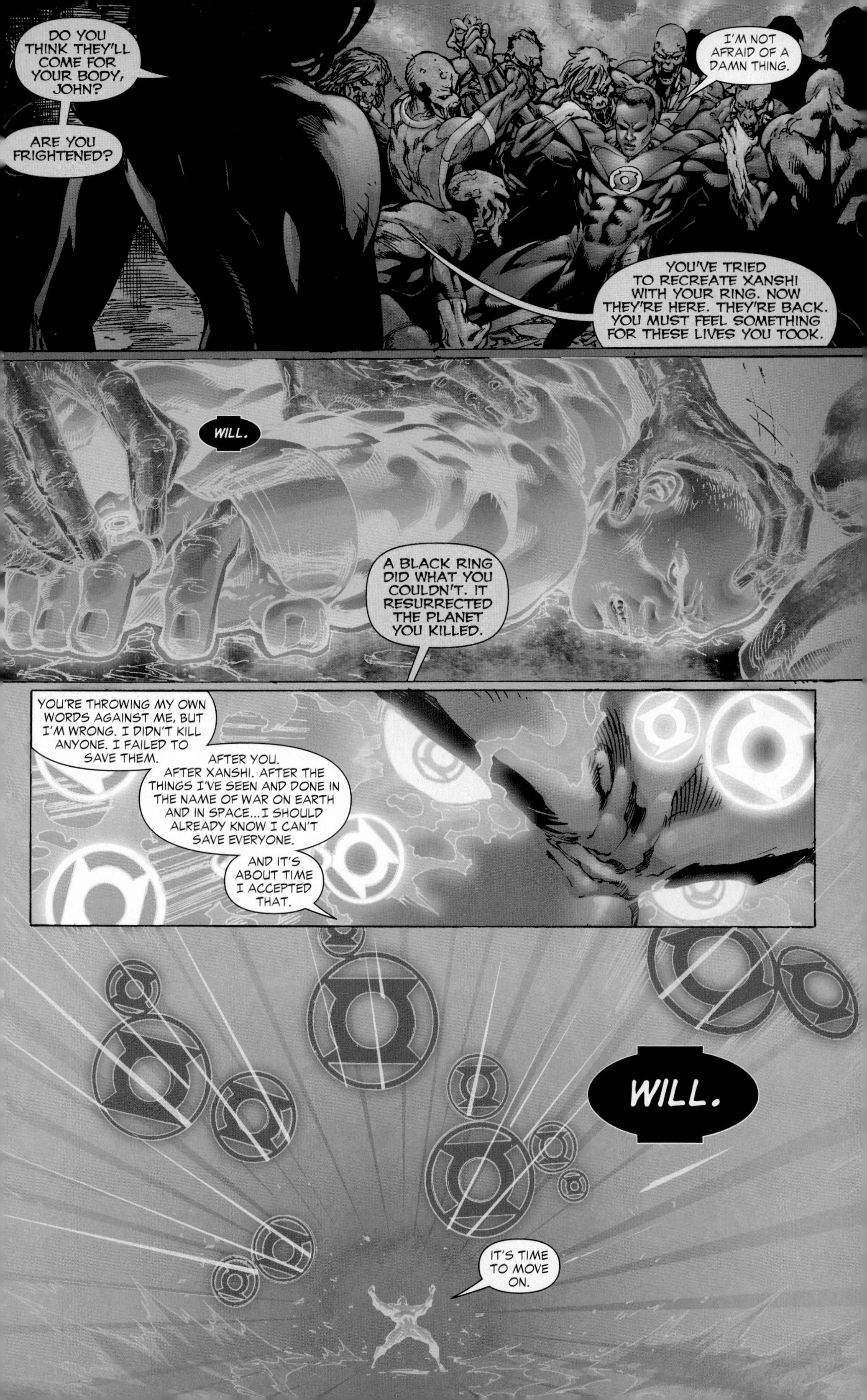
DO YOU THINK THEY'LL COME FOR YOUR BODY, JOHN?
ARE YOU FRIGHTENED?
I'M NOT AFRAID OF A DAMN THING.
YOU'VE TRIED TO RECREATE XANSHI WITH YOUR RING. NOW THEY'RE HERE. THEY'RE BACK. YOU MUST FEEL SOMETHING FOR THESE LIVES YOU TOOK.
WILL.
A BLACK RING DID WHAT YOU COULDN'T. IT RESURRECTED THE PLANET YOU KILLED.
YOU'RE THROWING MY OWN WORDS AGAINST ME, BUT I'M WRONG. I DIDN'T KILL ANYONE. I FAILED TO SAVE THEM.
AFTER YOU. AFTER XANSHI. AFTER THE THINGS I'VE SEEN AND DONE IN THE NAME OF WAR ON EARTH AND IN SPACE...I SHOULD ALREADY KNOW I CAN'T SAVE EVERYONE.
AND IT'S ABOUT TIME I ACCEPTED THAT.
WILL.
IT'S TIME TO MOVE ON.

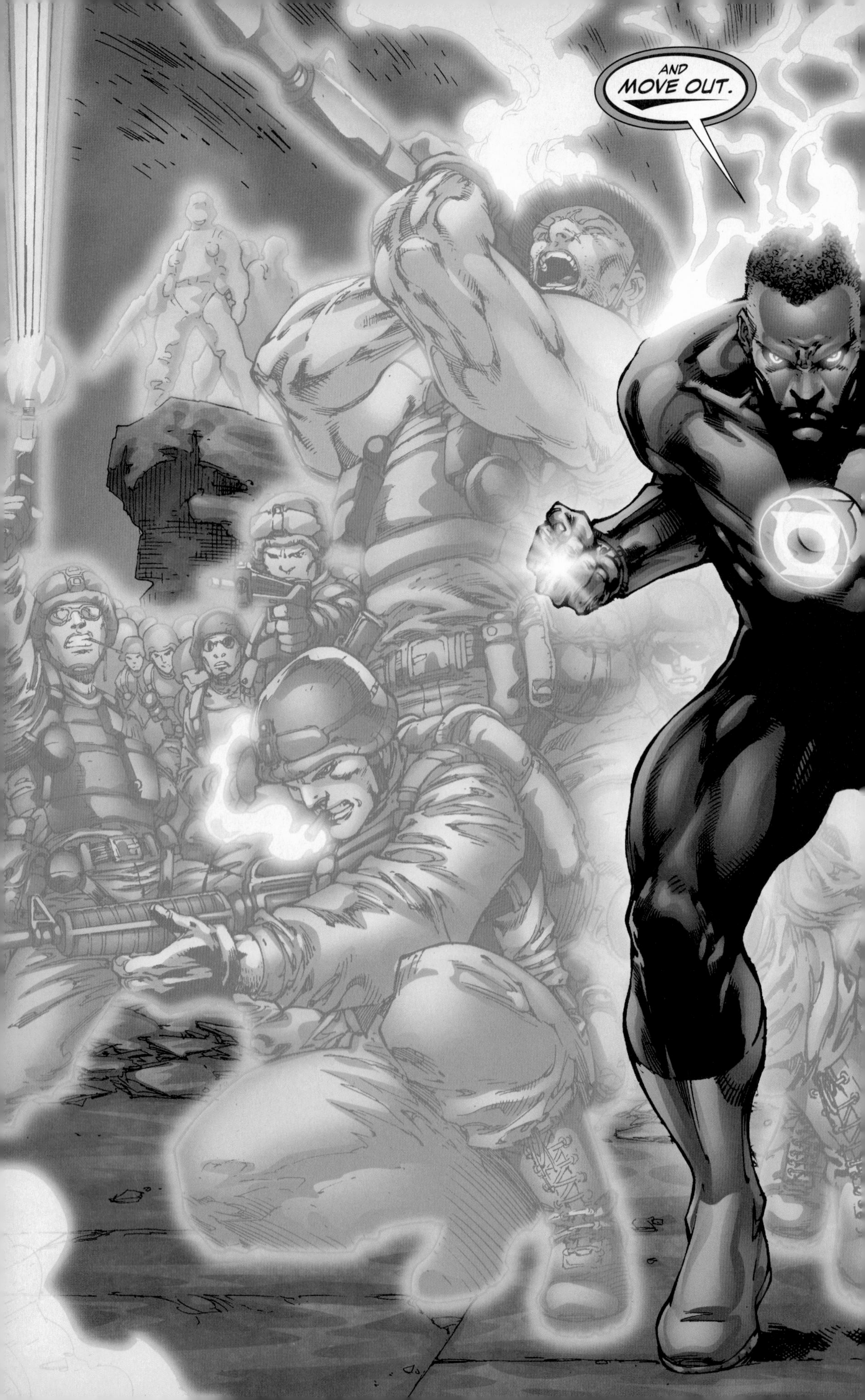
AND MOVE OUT.

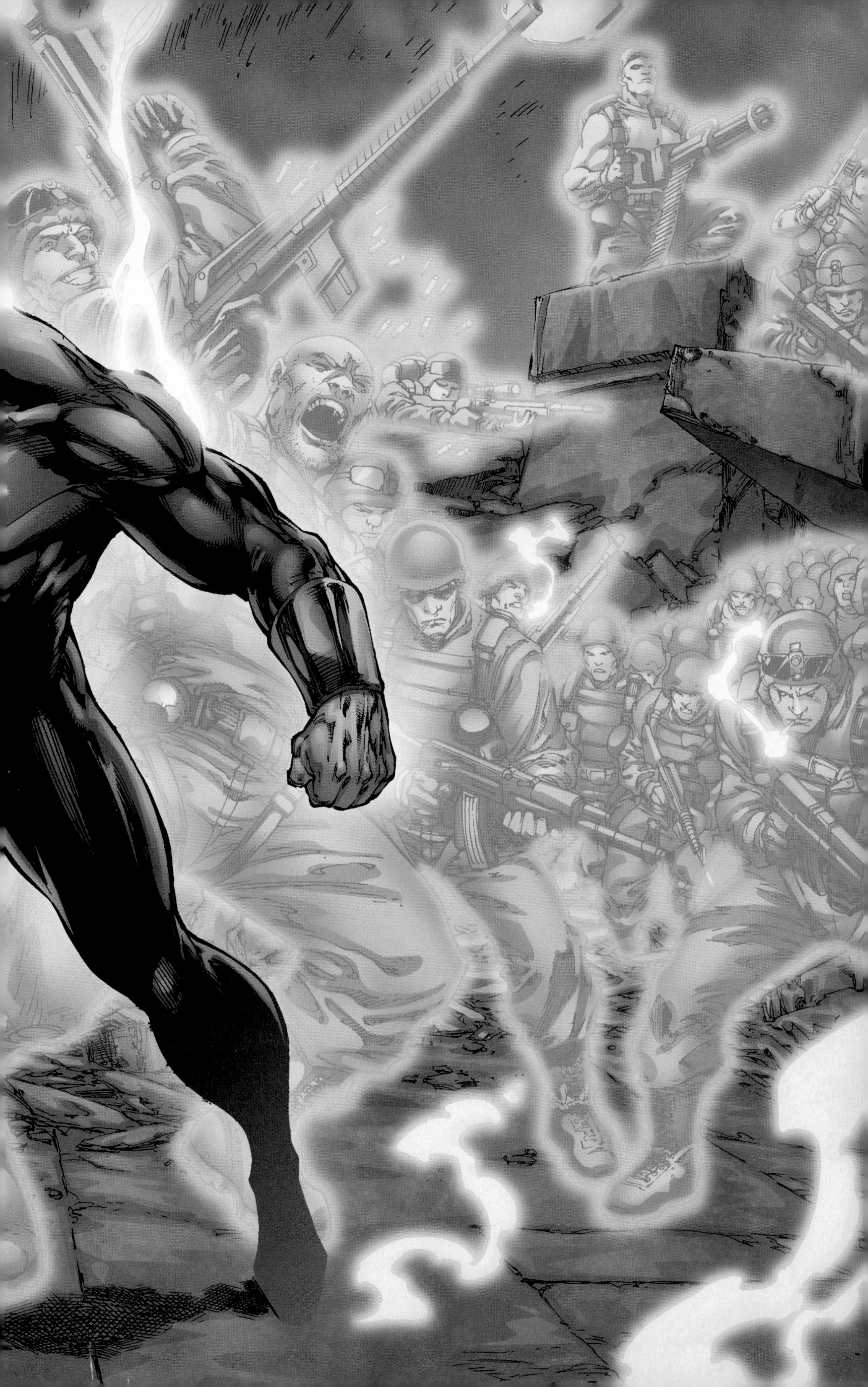

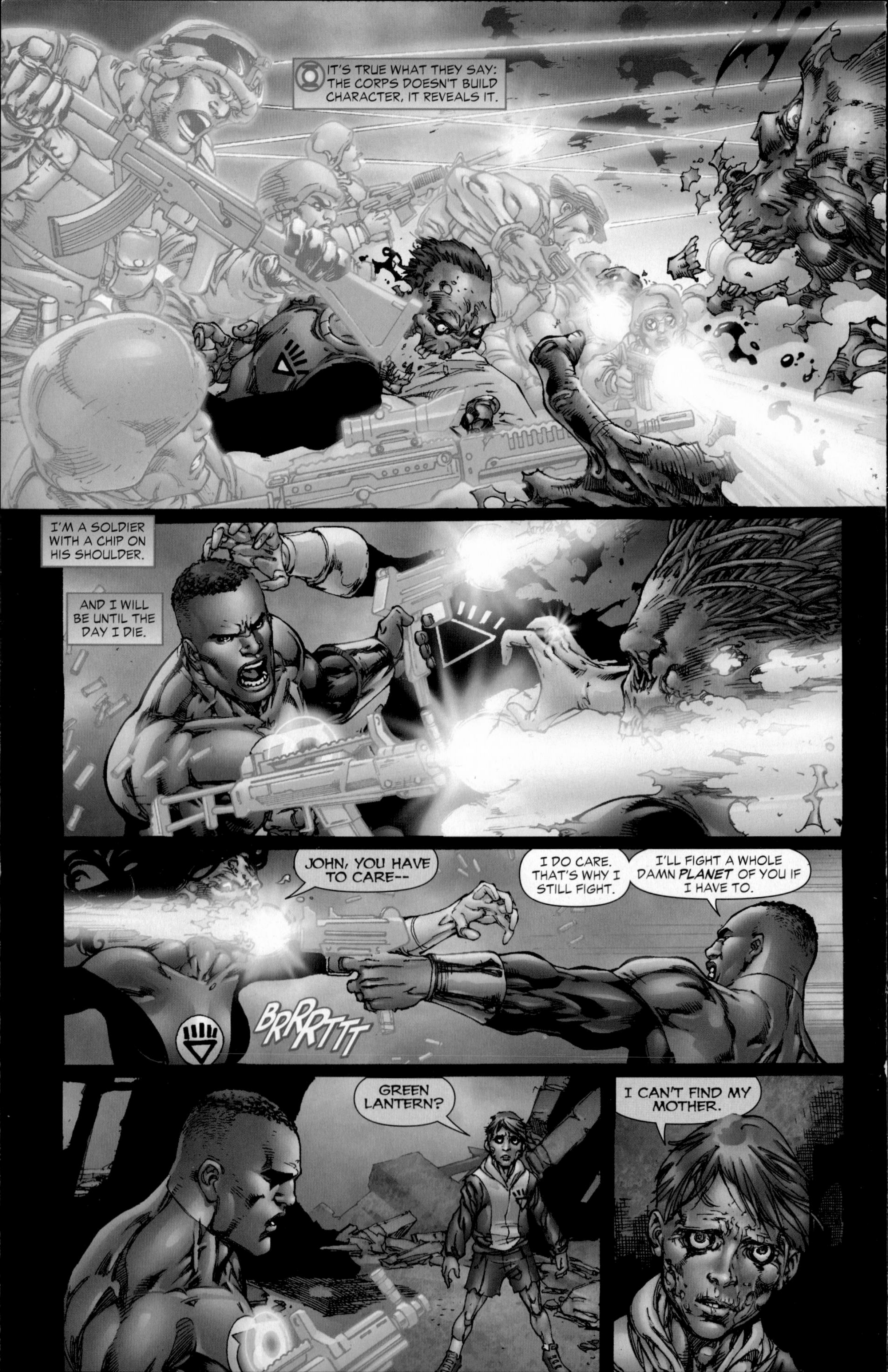
IT'S TRUE WHAT THEY SAY: THE CORPS DOESN'T BUILD CHARACTER, IT REVEALS IT.
I'M A SOLDIER WITH A CHIP ON HIS SHOULDER.
AND I WILL BE UNTIL THE DAY I DIE.
JOHN, YOU HAVE TO CARE--
I DO CARE. THAT'S WHY I STILL FIGHT.
I'LL FIGHT A WHOLE DAMN *PLANET* OF YOU IF I HAVE TO.
BRRRTTT
GREEN LANTERN?
I CAN'T FIND MY MOTHER.

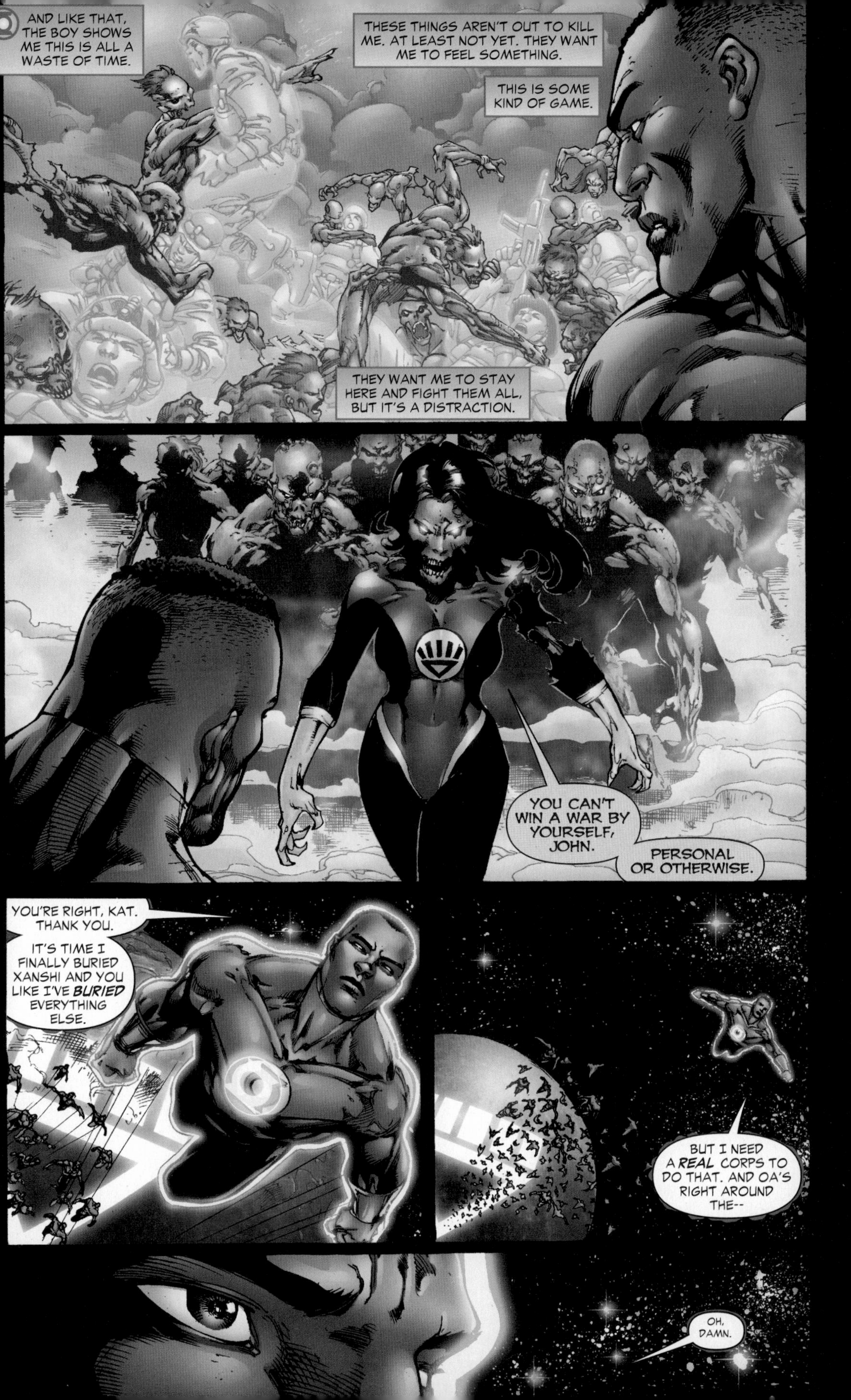
AND LIKE THAT, THE BOY SHOWS ME THIS IS ALL A WASTE OF TIME.
THESE THINGS AREN'T OUT TO KILL ME. AT LEAST NOT YET. THEY WANT ME TO FEEL SOMETHING.
THIS IS SOME KIND OF GAME.
THEY WANT ME TO STAY HERE AND FIGHT THEM ALL, BUT IT'S A DISTRACTION.
YOU CAN'T WIN A WAR BY YOURSELF, JOHN.
PERSONAL OR OTHERWISE.
YOU'RE RIGHT, KAT. THANK YOU.
IT'S TIME I FINALLY BURIED XANSHI AND YOU LIKE I'VE *BURIED* EVERYTHING ELSE.
BUT I NEED A *REAL* CORPS TO DO THAT. AND OA'S RIGHT AROUND THE--
OH, DAMN.

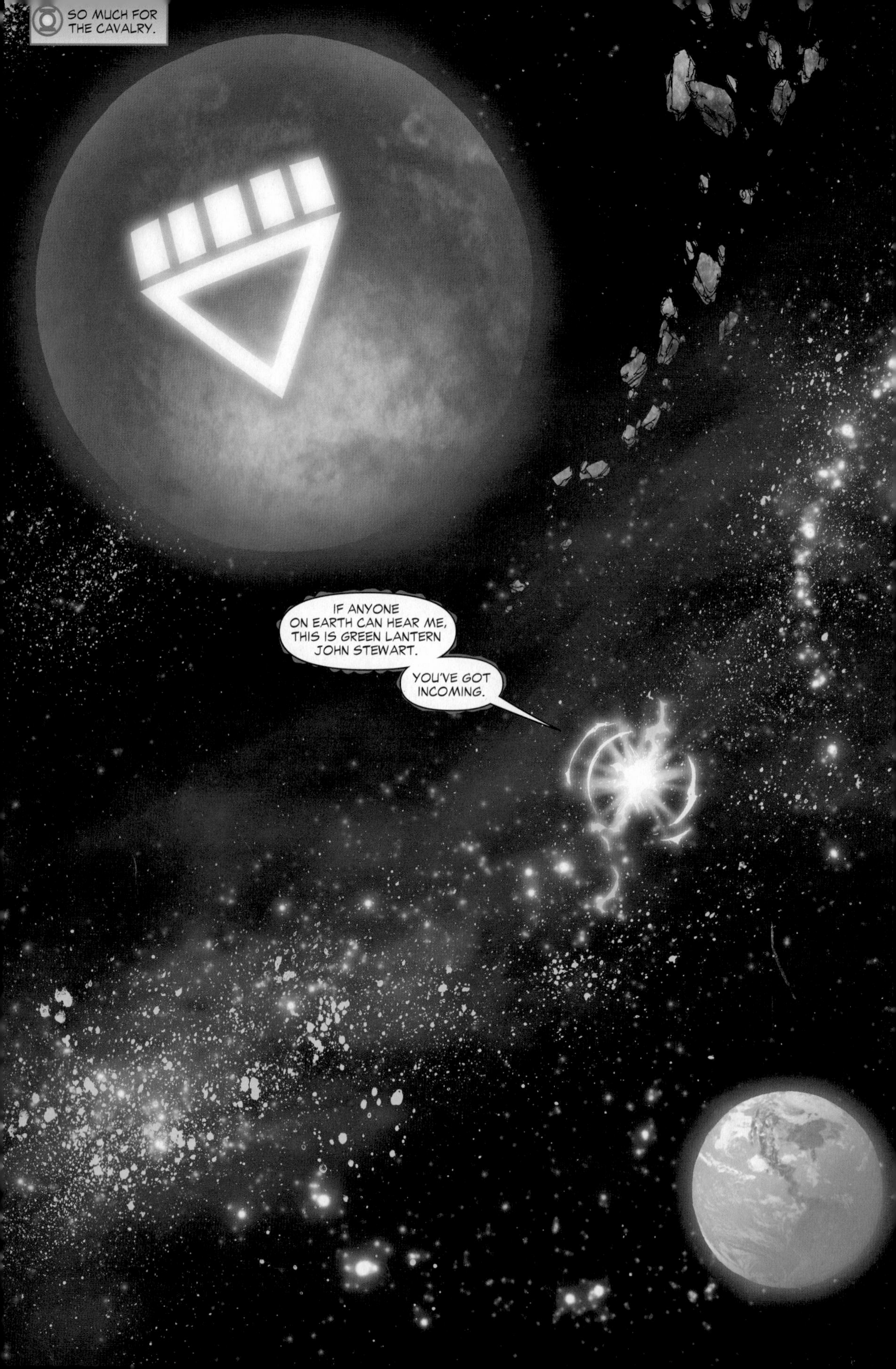
SO MUCH FOR THE CAVALRY.
IF ANYONE ON EARTH CAN HEAR ME, THIS IS GREEN LANTERN JOHN STEWART.
YOU'VE GOT INCOMING.

GREEN LANTERN 50

Cover by Doug Mahnke and Christian Alamy with Pete Pantazis

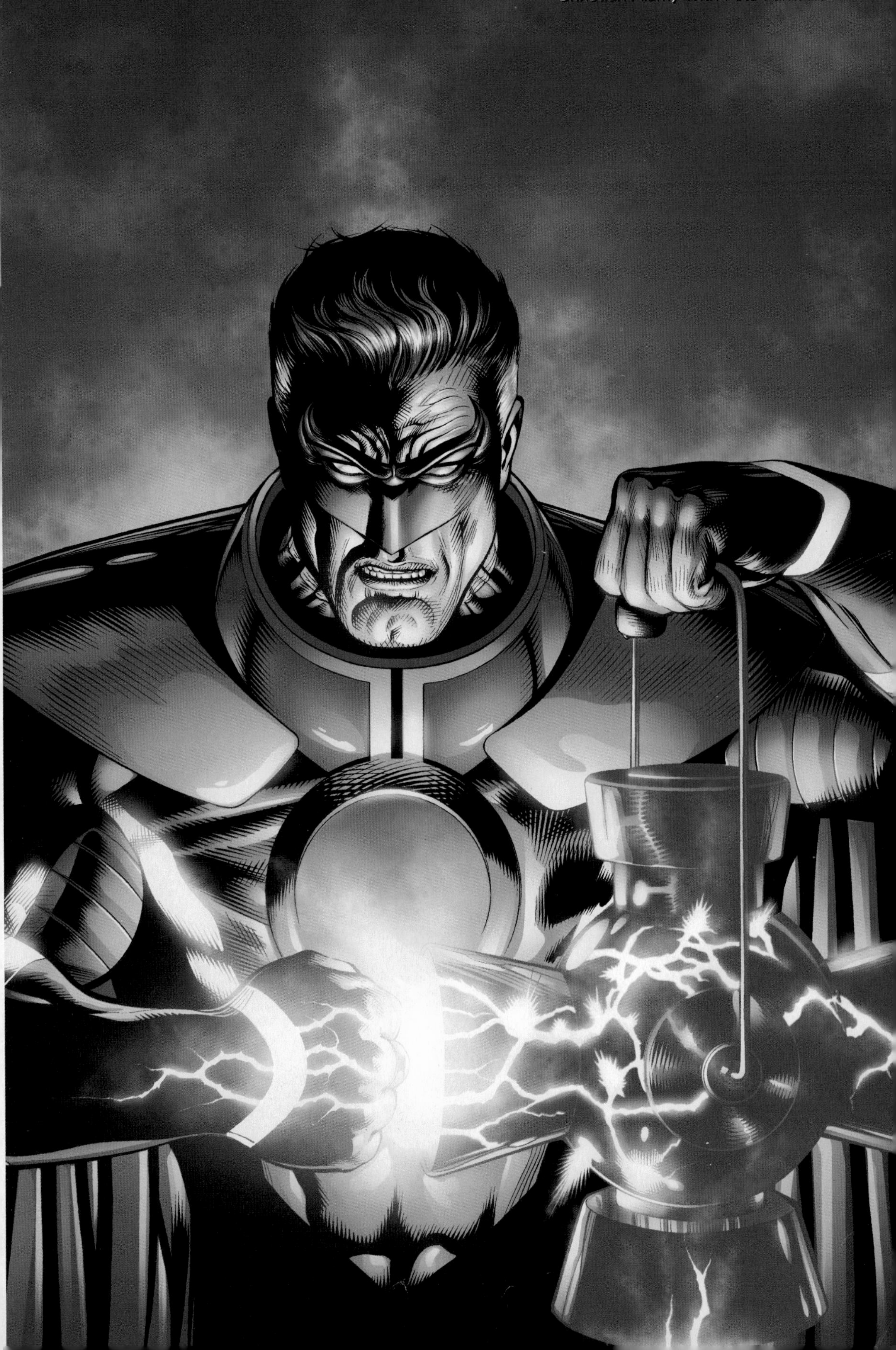

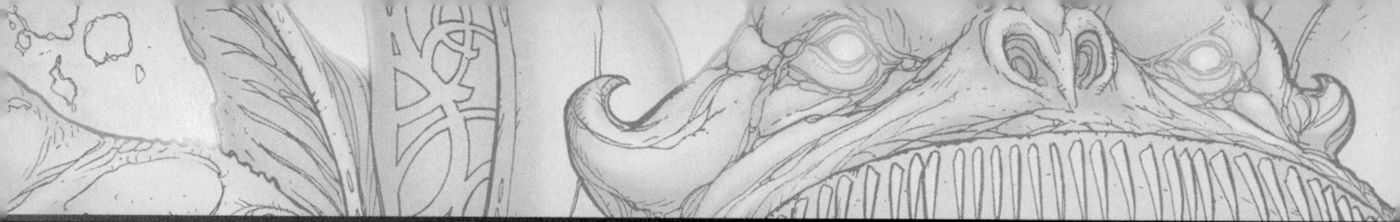

According to the Book of Oa, in the shadow of the Blackest Night the rings of the various colored Corps can deputize an individual for twenty-four hours.

Now the Flash, Mera, Wonder Woman, the Atom, Scarecrow, Lex Luthor and Ganthet have been recruited to fight for the fate of the universe.

But threats from Hal Jordan's past may eclipse them all and dim the Green Lantern light forever...

PARALLAX REBIRTH
PART ONE

DOUG MAHNKE
PENCILS

CHRISTIAN ALAMY
REBECCA BUCHMAN
TOM NGUYEN
MARK IRWIN
DOUG MAHNKE
INKS

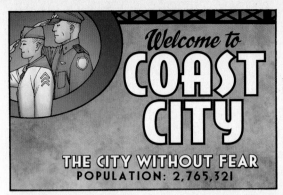

Welcome to
COAST CITY
THE CITY WITHOUT FEAR
POPULATION: 2,765,321
Welcome to
COAST CITY
HE CITY WITHOUT FEAR
OPULATION: 2,765,321

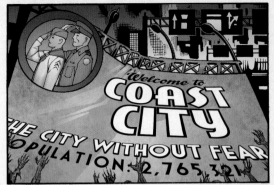

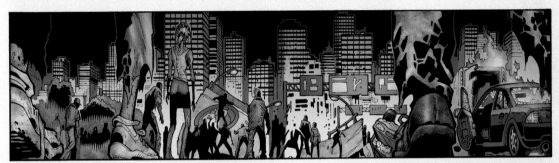

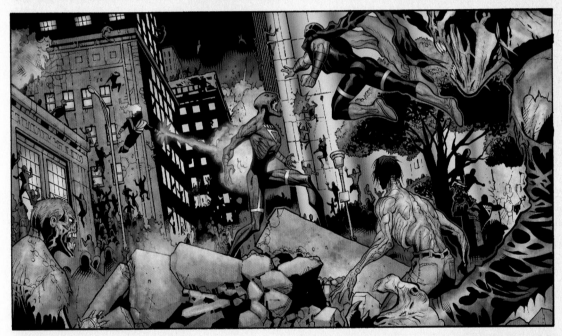

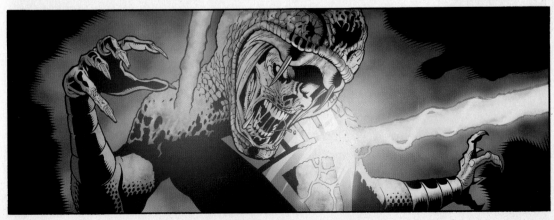

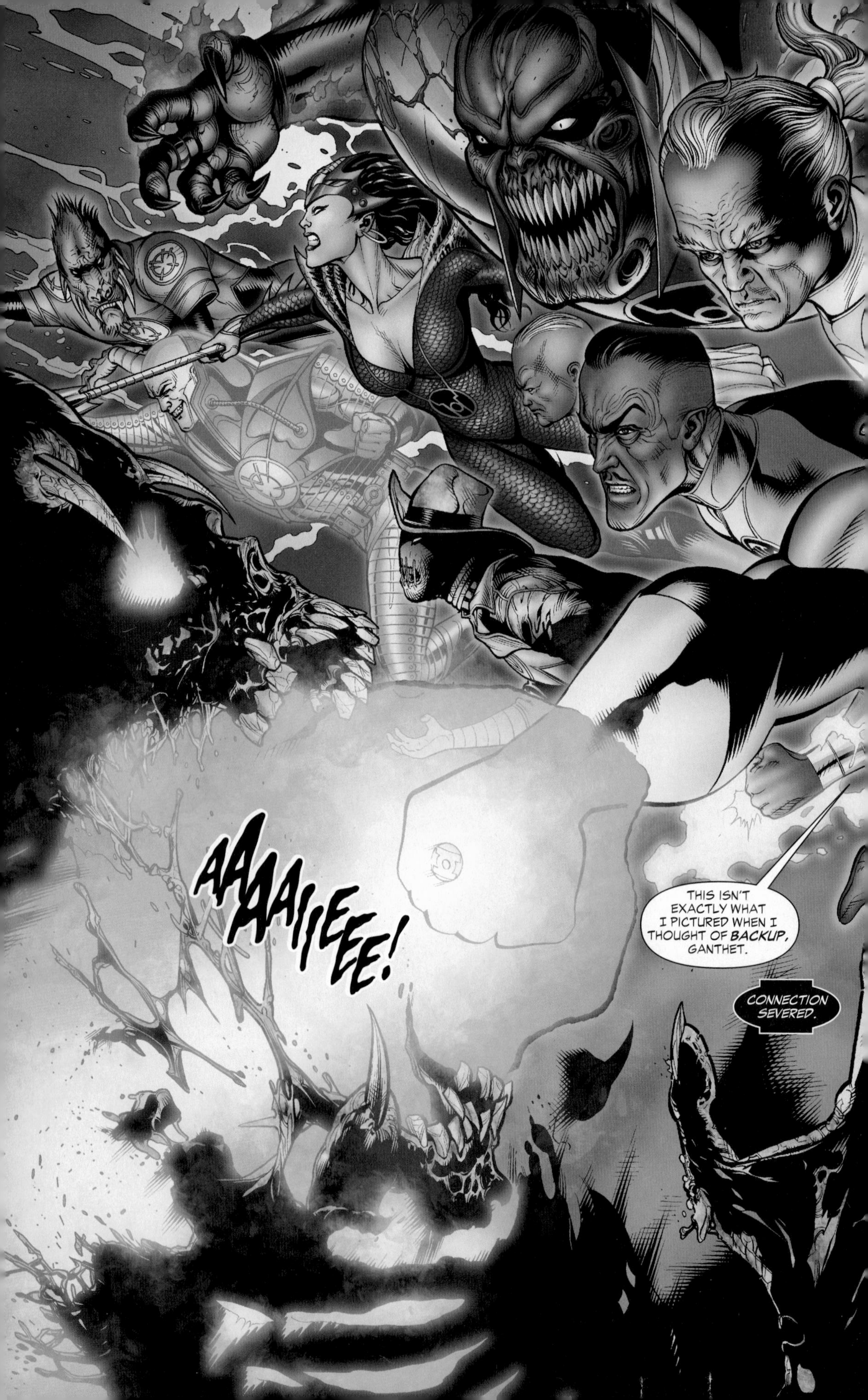
AAAAAIIEEEE!
THIS ISN'T EXACTLY WHAT I PICTURED WHEN I THOUGHT OF BACKUP, GANTHET.
CONNECTION SEVERED.

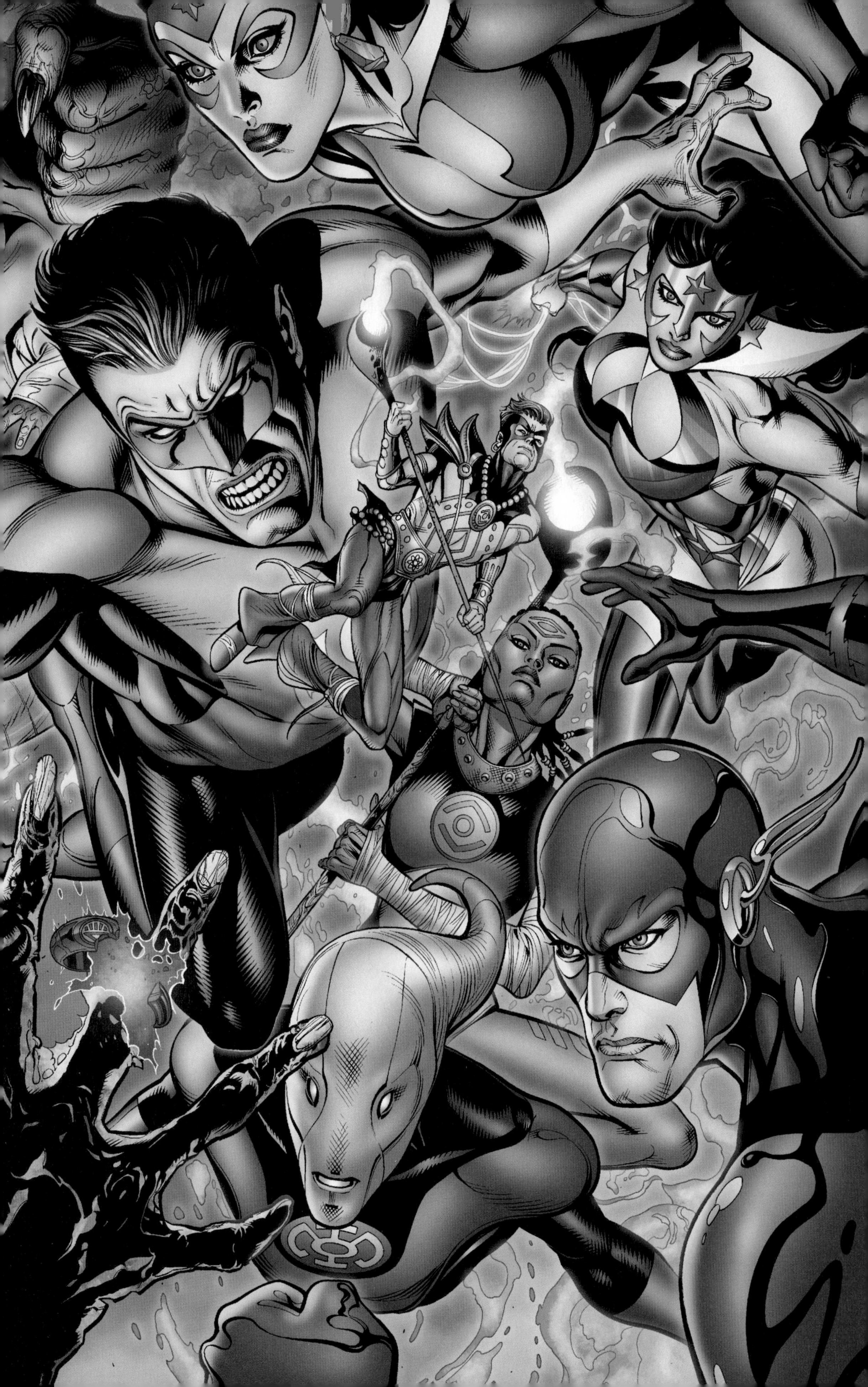

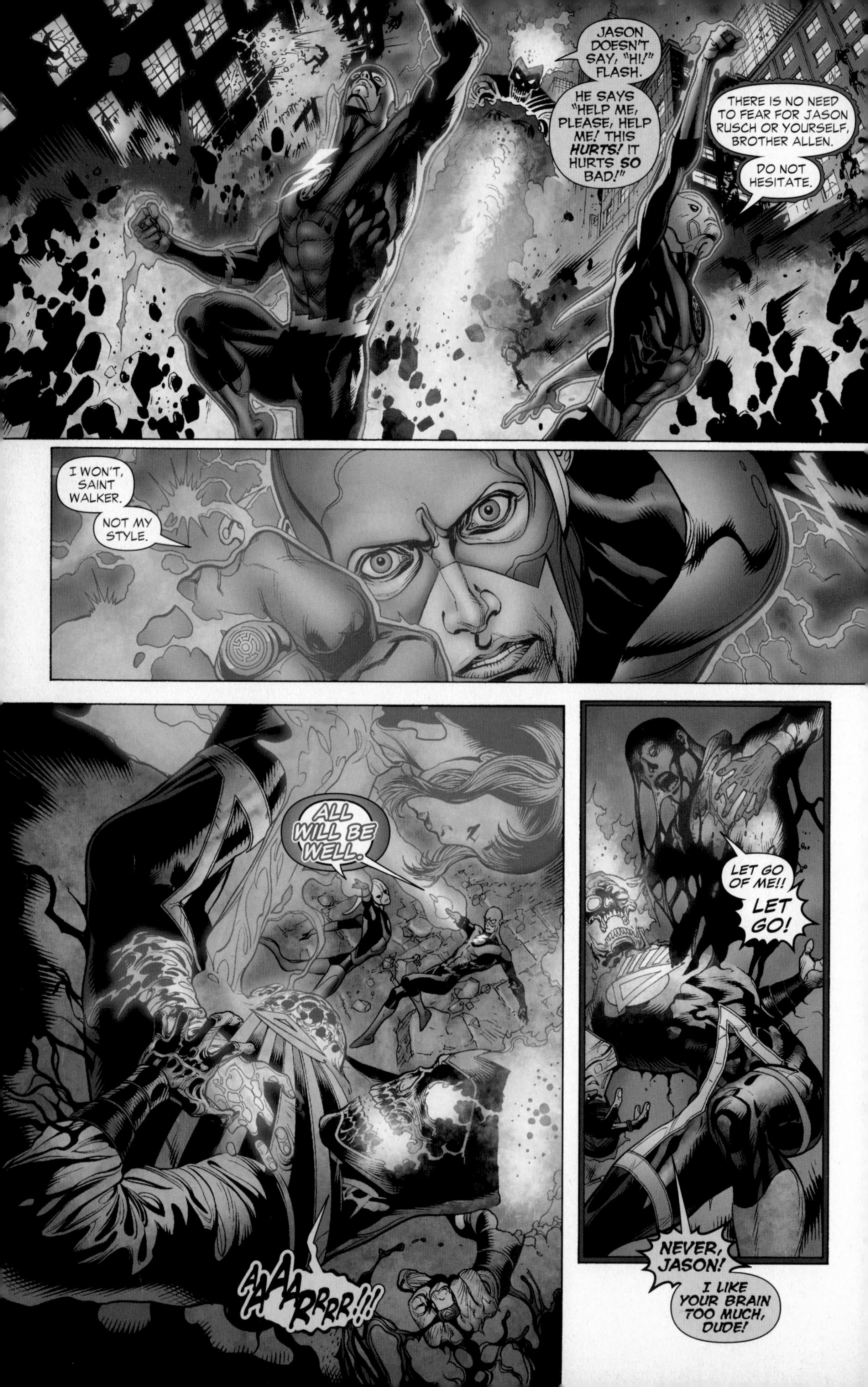
JASON DOESN'T SAY, "HI!" FLASH.
HE SAYS "HELP ME, PLEASE, HELP ME! THIS HURTS! IT HURTS SO BAD!"
THERE IS NO NEED TO FEAR FOR JASON RUSCH OR YOURSELF, BROTHER ALLEN.
DO NOT HESITATE.
I WON'T, SAINT WALKER.
NOT MY STYLE.
ALL WILL BE WELL.
AAAARRRR!!!
LET GO OF ME!! LET GO!
NEVER, JASON!
I LIKE YOUR BRAIN TOO MUCH, DUDE!

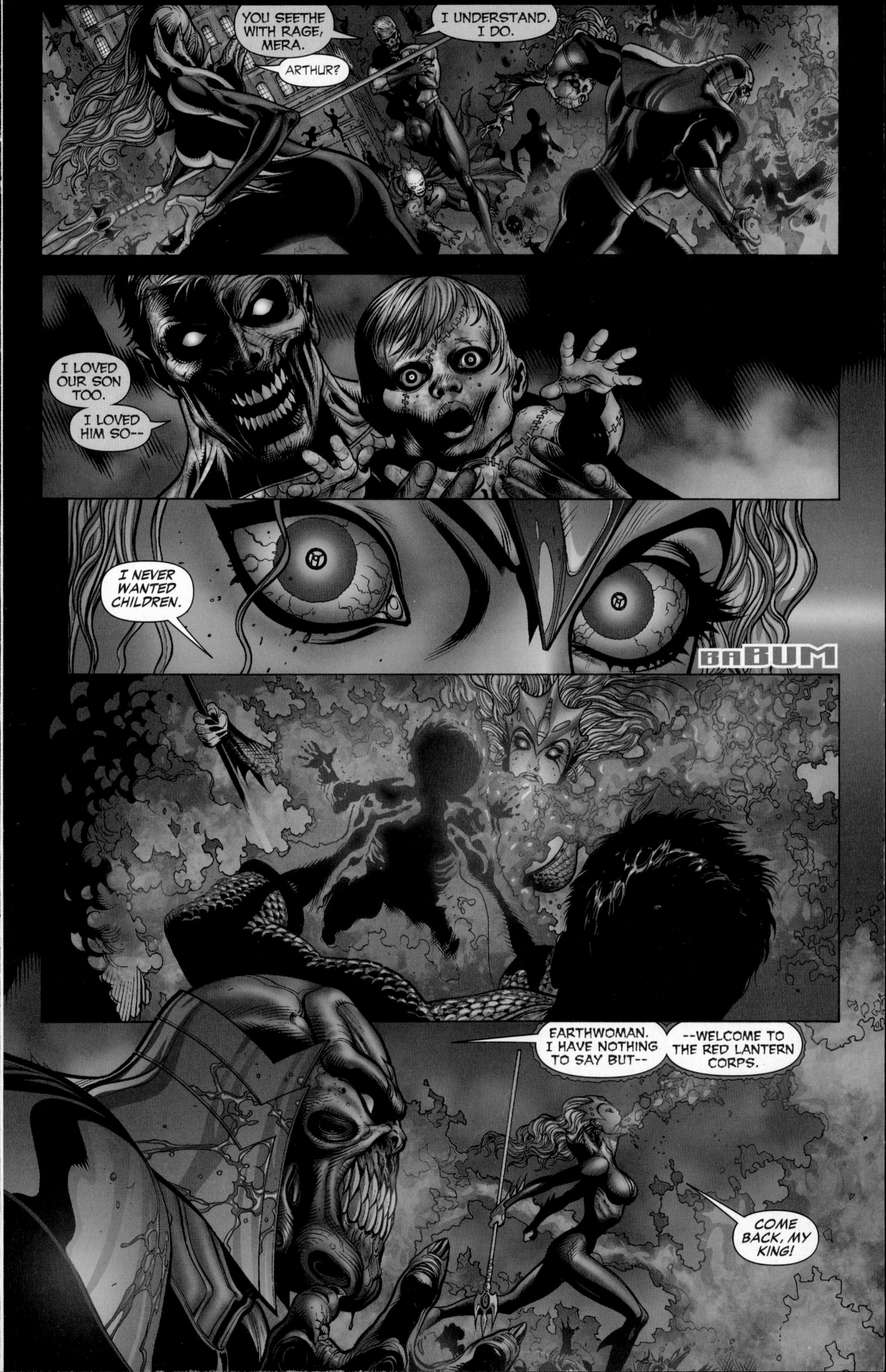
YOU SEETHE WITH RAGE, MERA.
ARTHUR?
I UNDERSTAND. I DO.
I LOVED OUR SON TOO.
I LOVED HIM SO--
I NEVER WANTED CHILDREN.
BABUM
EARTHWOMAN. I HAVE NOTHING TO SAY BUT--
--WELCOME TO THE RED LANTERN CORPS.
COME BACK, MY KING!

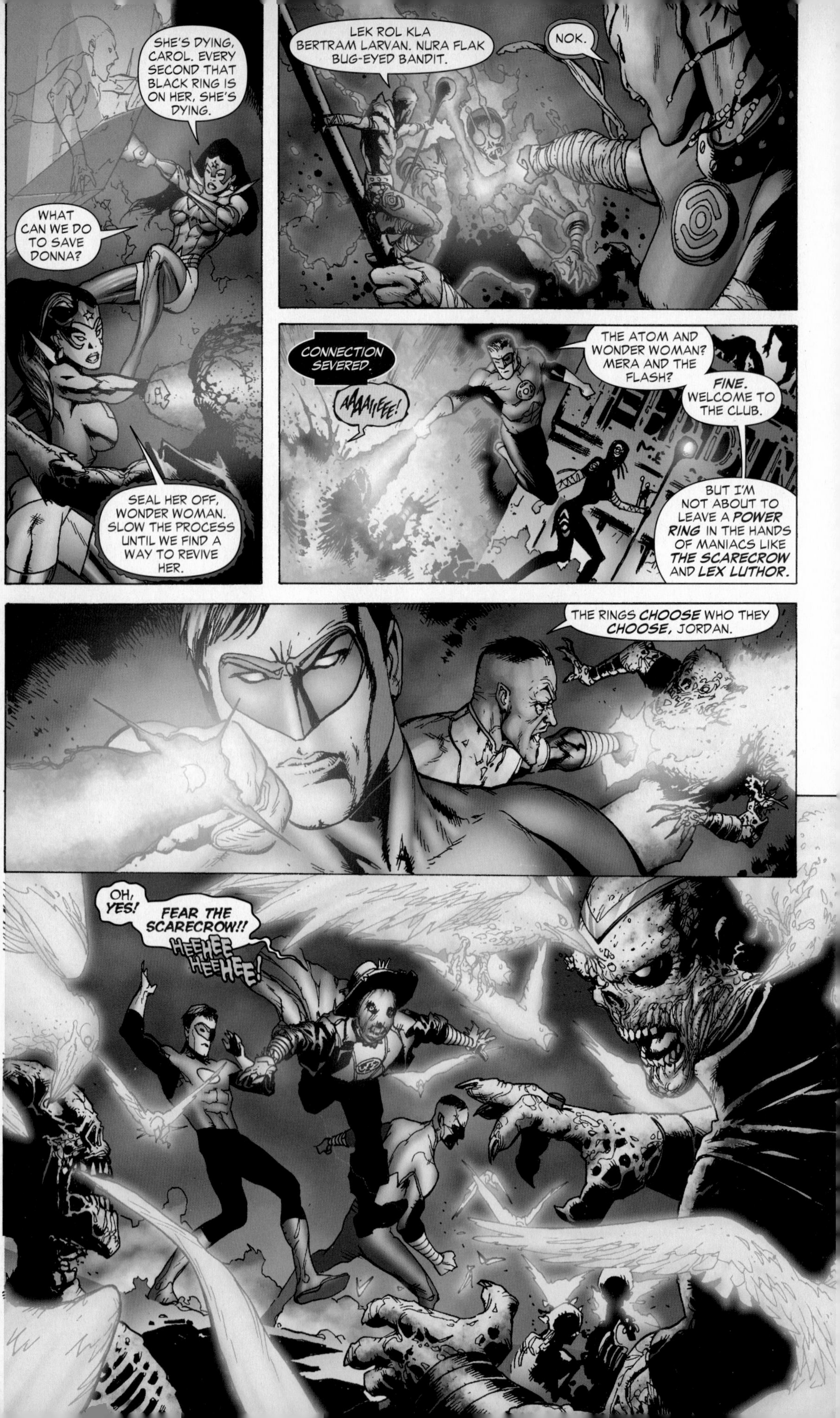
SHE'S DYING, CAROL. EVERY SECOND THAT BLACK RING IS ON HER, SHE'S DYING.
WHAT CAN WE DO TO SAVE DONNA?
SEAL HER OFF, WONDER WOMAN. SLOW THE PROCESS UNTIL WE FIND A WAY TO REVIVE HER.
LEK ROL KLA BERTRAM LARVAN. NURA FLAK BUG-EYED BANDIT.
NOK.
CONNECTION SEVERED.
AAAAIIEEE!
THE ATOM AND WONDER WOMAN? MERA AND THE FLASH?
FINE. WELCOME TO THE CLUB.
BUT I'M NOT ABOUT TO LEAVE A POWER RING IN THE HANDS OF MANIACS LIKE THE SCARECROW AND LEX LUTHOR.
THE RINGS CHOOSE WHO THEY CHOOSE, JORDAN.
OH, YES!
FEAR THE SCARECROW!!
HEEHEE HEEHEE!

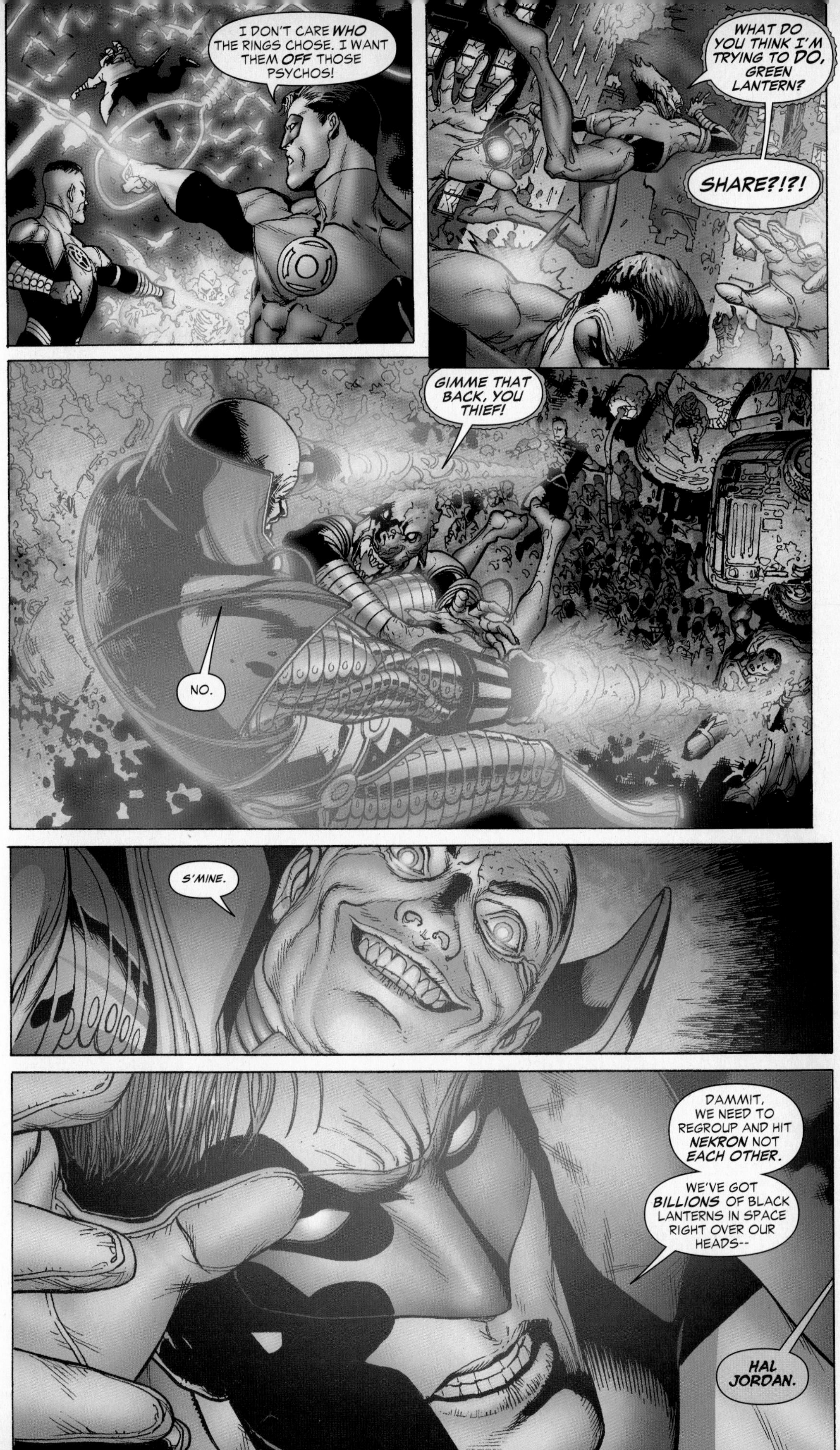
I DON'T CARE WHO THE RINGS CHOSE. I WANT THEM OFF THOSE PSYCHOS!
WHAT DO YOU THINK I'M TRYING TO DO, GREEN LANTERN?
SHARE?!?!
GIMME THAT BACK, YOU THIEF!
NO.
S'MINE.
DAMMIT, WE NEED TO REGROUP AND HIT NEKRON NOT EACH OTHER.
WE'VE GOT BILLIONS OF BLACK LANTERNS IN SPACE RIGHT OVER OUR HEADS--
HAL JORDAN.

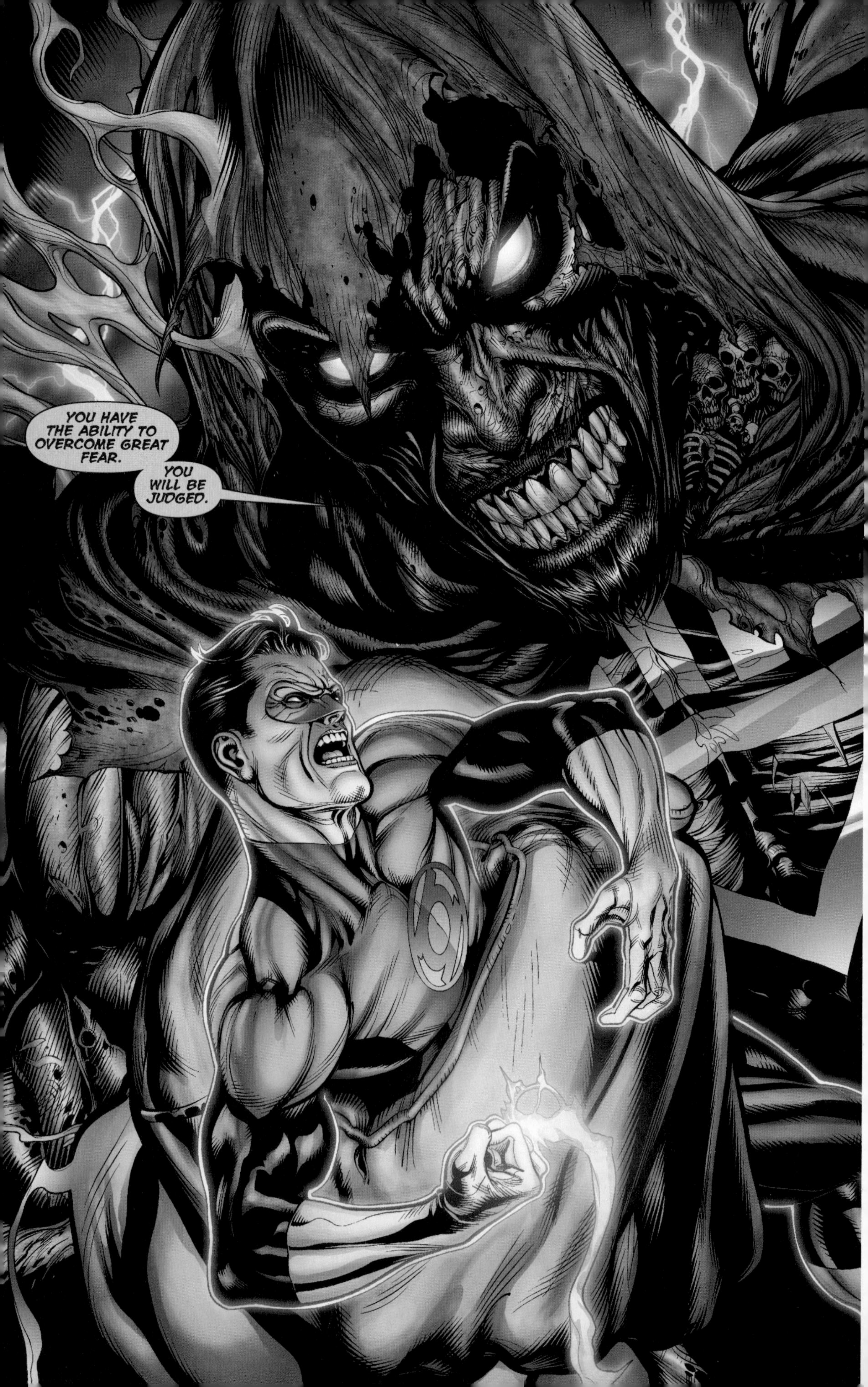
YOU HAVE THE ABILITY TO OVERCOME GREAT FEAR.
YOU WILL BE JUDGED.

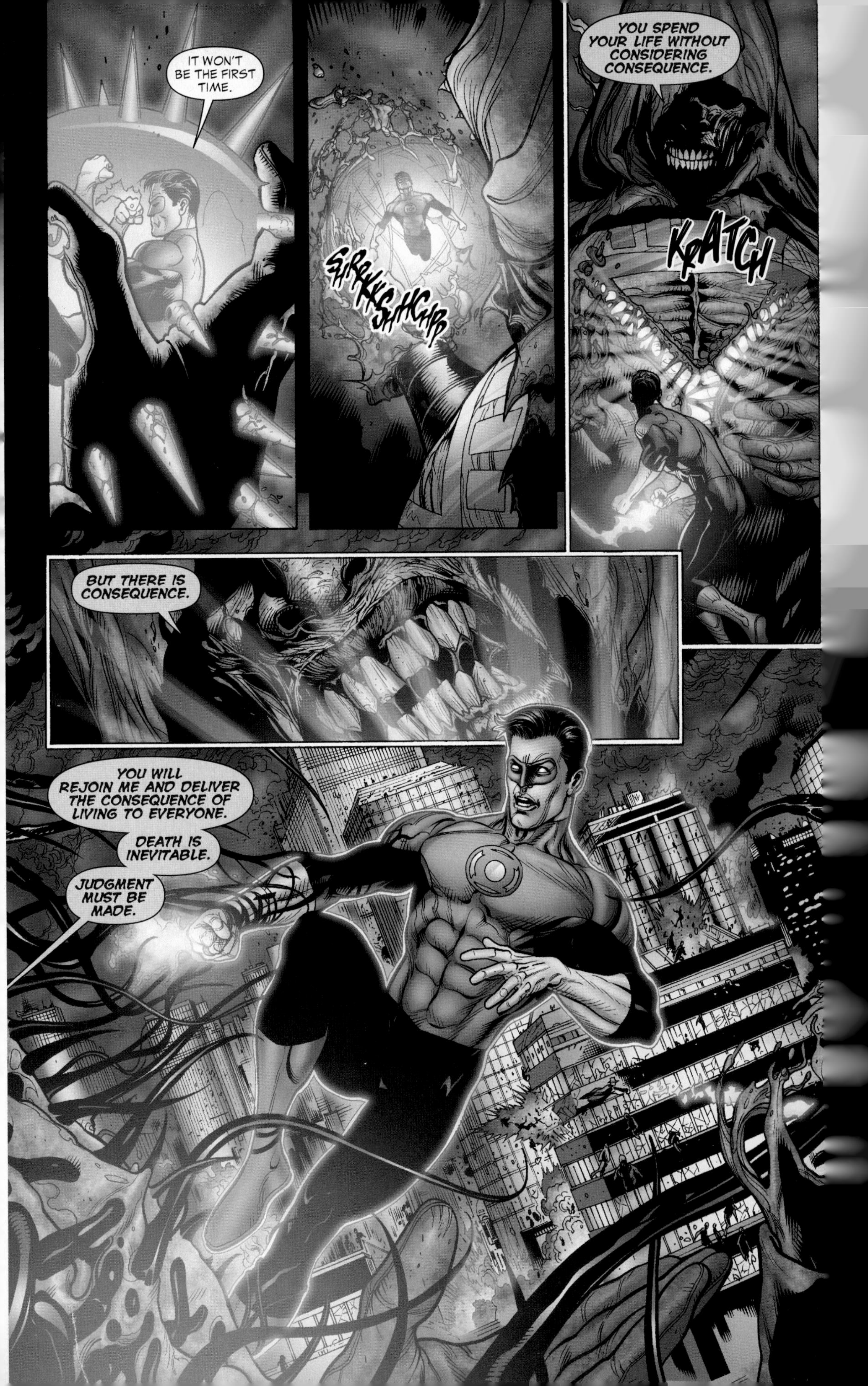
IT WON'T BE THE FIRST TIME.
SHRKKSHCHP
YOU SPEND YOUR LIFE WITHOUT CONSIDERING CONSEQUENCE.
KRATCH
BUT THERE IS CONSEQUENCE.
YOU WILL REJOIN ME AND DELIVER THE CONSEQUENCE OF LIVING TO EVERYONE.
DEATH IS INEVITABLE.
JUDGMENT MUST BE MADE.

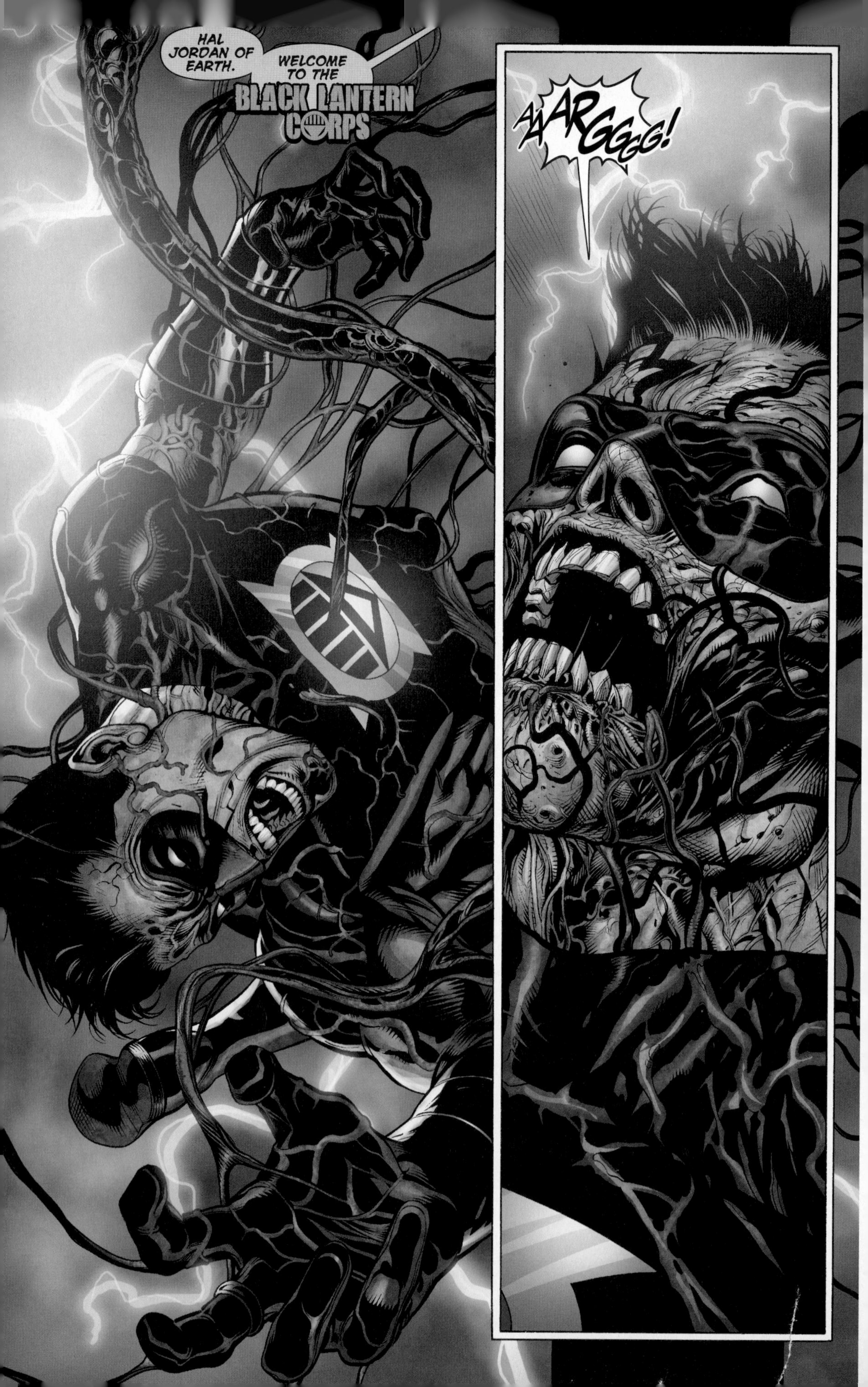
HAL JORDAN OF EARTH.
WELCOME TO THE
BLACK LANTERN CORPS
AAARGGGGG!

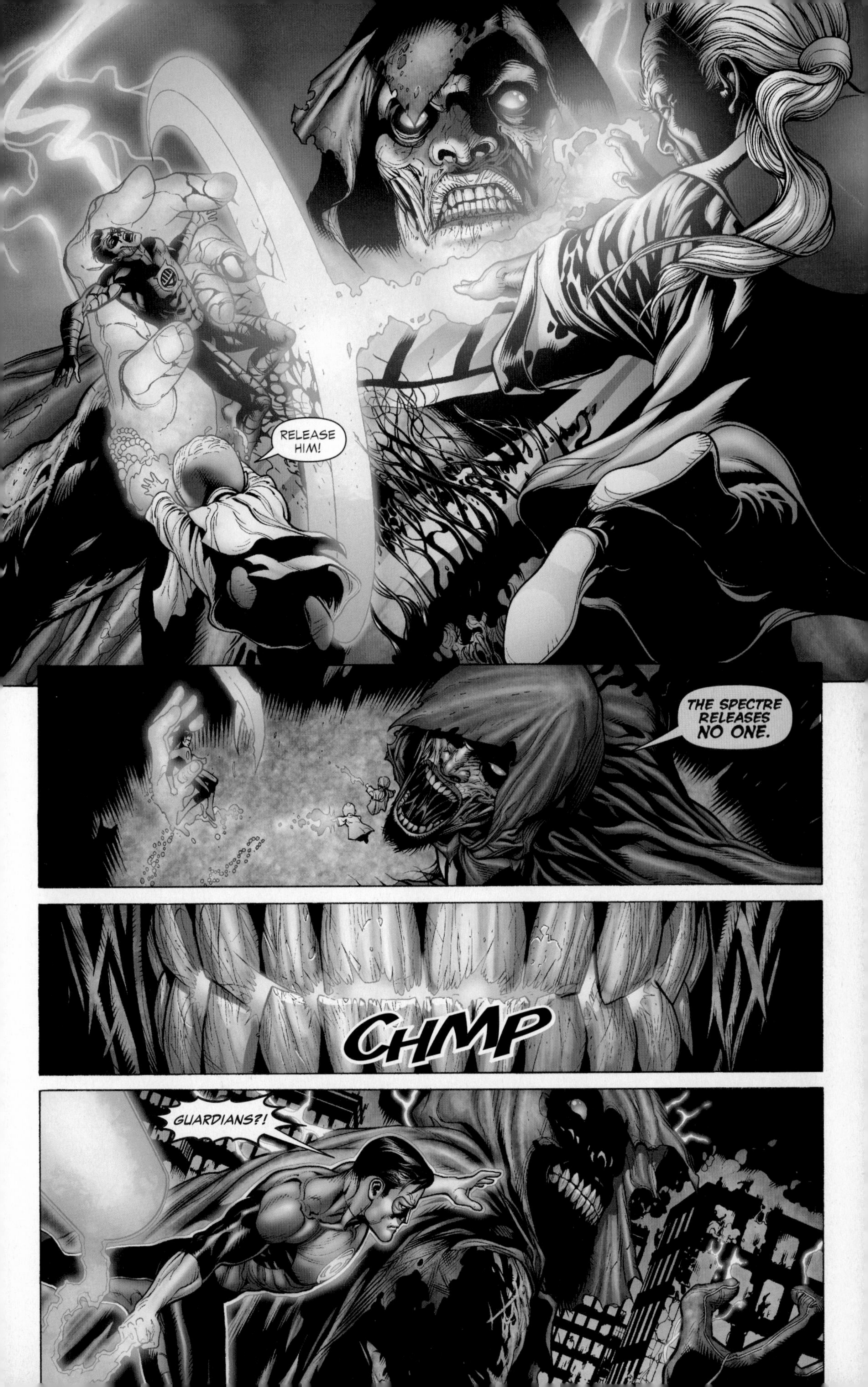
RELEASE HIM!
THE SPECTRE RELEASES NO ONE.
CHMP
GUARDIANS?!

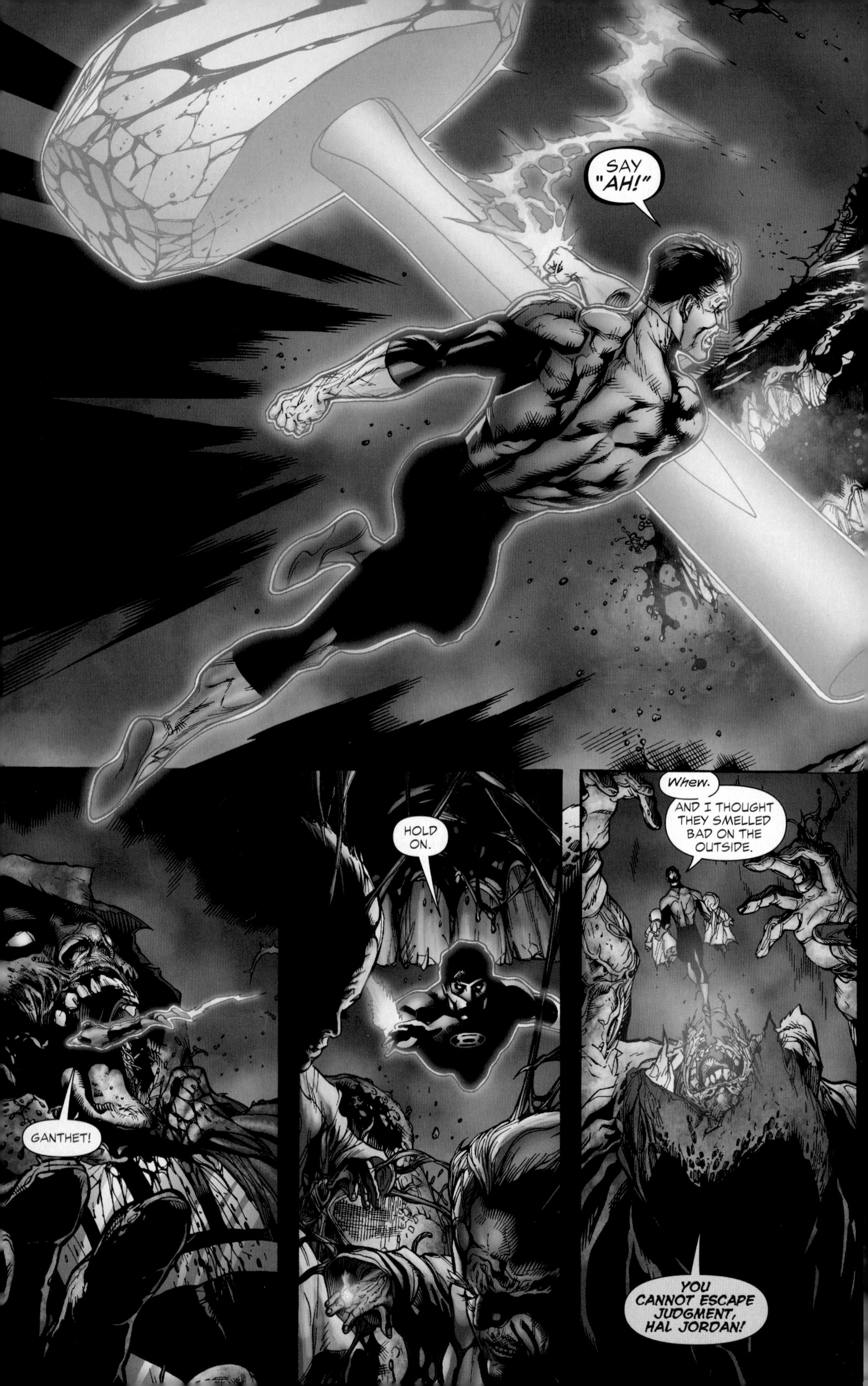
SAY "AH!"
GANTHET!
HOLD ON.
Whew.
AND I THOUGHT THEY SMELLED BAD ON THE OUTSIDE.
YOU CANNOT ESCAPE JUDGMENT, HAL JORDAN!

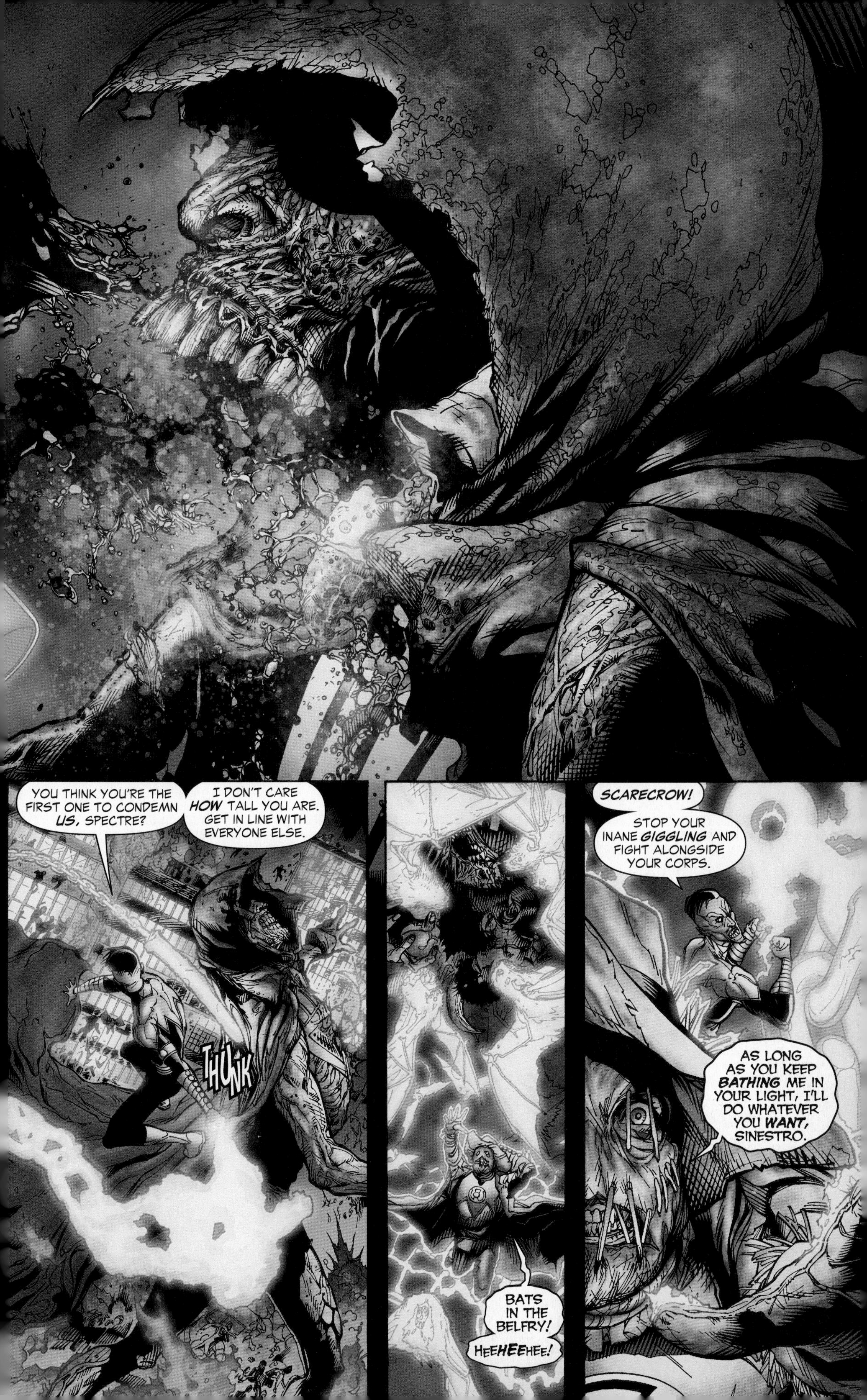

YOU THINK YOU'RE THE FIRST ONE TO CONDEMN US, SPECTRE?
I DON'T CARE HOW TALL YOU ARE. GET IN LINE WITH EVERYONE ELSE.
THUNK
BATS IN THE BELFRY!
HEEHEEHEE!
SCARECROW!
STOP YOUR INANE GIGGLING AND FIGHT ALONGSIDE YOUR CORPS.
AS LONG AS YOU KEEP BATHING ME IN YOUR LIGHT, I'LL DO WHATEVER YOU WANT, SINESTRO.

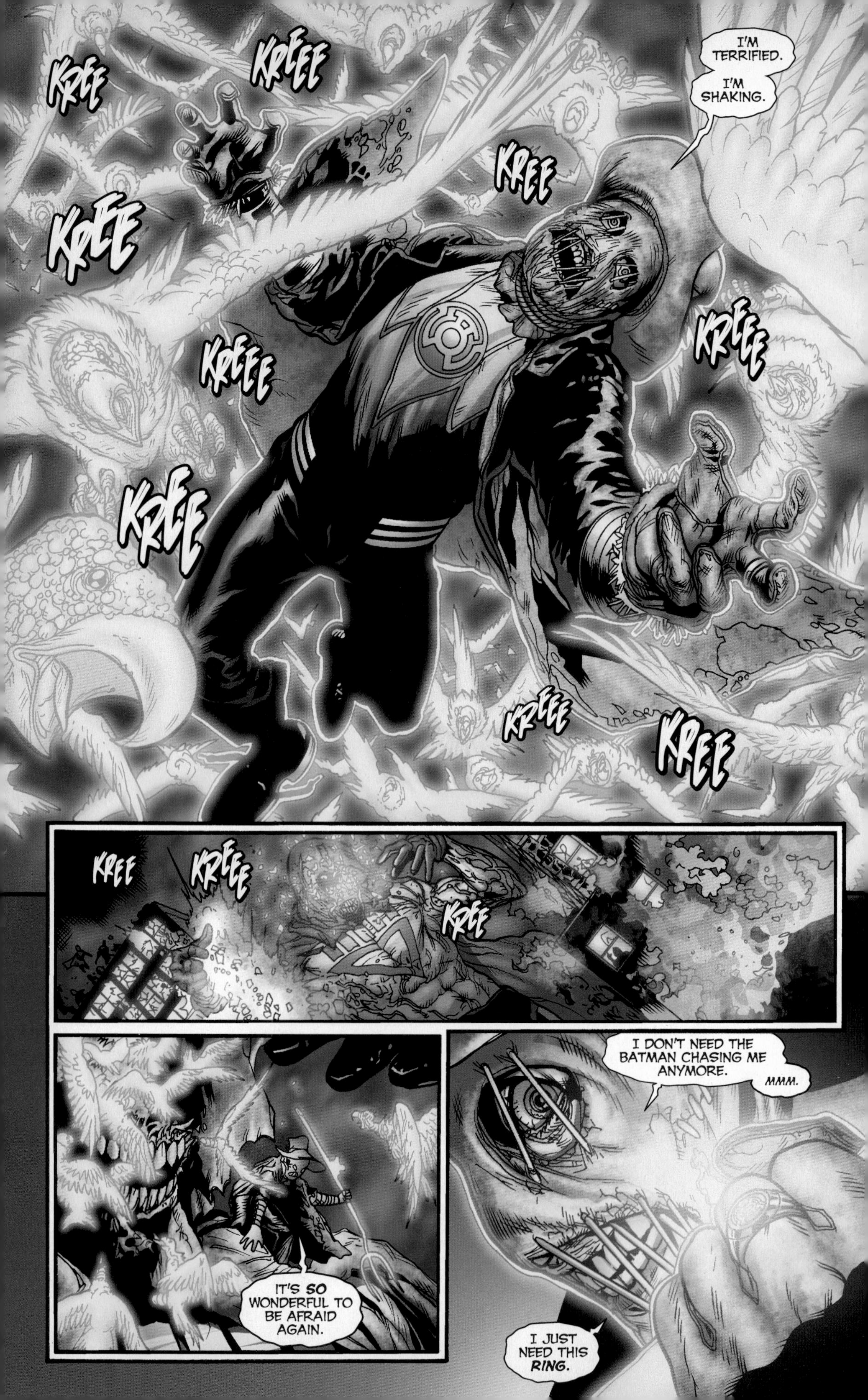
KREE
KREEE
I'M TERRIFIED.
I'M SHAKING.
KREE
KREE
KREEE
KREEE
KREE
KREEE
KREE
KREE
KREEE
KREE
IT'S SO WONDERFUL TO BE AFRAID AGAIN.
I DON'T NEED THE BATMAN CHASING ME ANYMORE.
MMM.
I JUST NEED THIS RING.

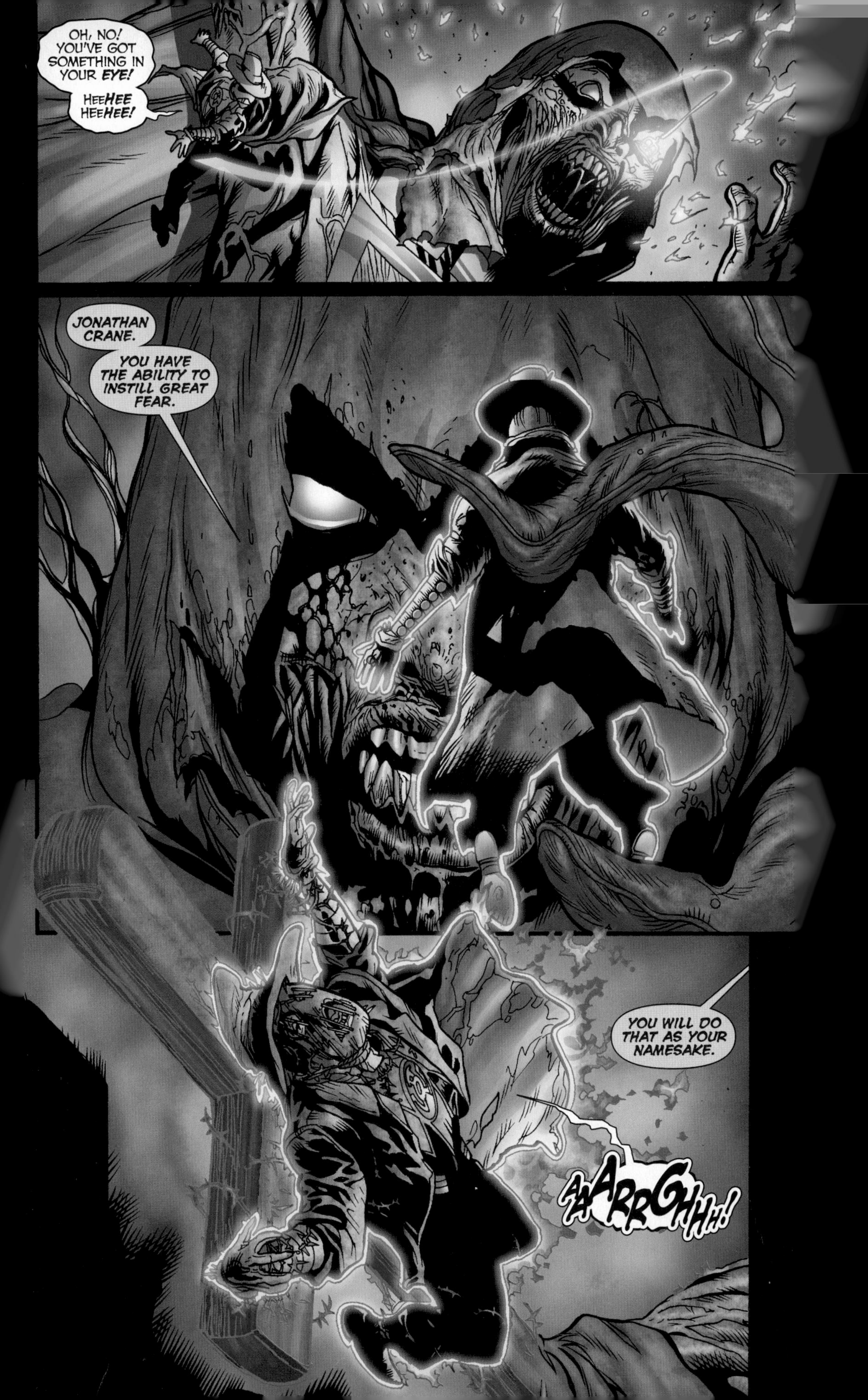
OH, NO! YOU'VE GOT SOMETHING IN YOUR EYE!
HEEHEE HEEHEE!
JONATHAN CRANE.
YOU HAVE THE ABILITY TO INSTILL GREAT FEAR.
YOU WILL DO THAT AS YOUR NAMESAKE.
AAARRGHHH!

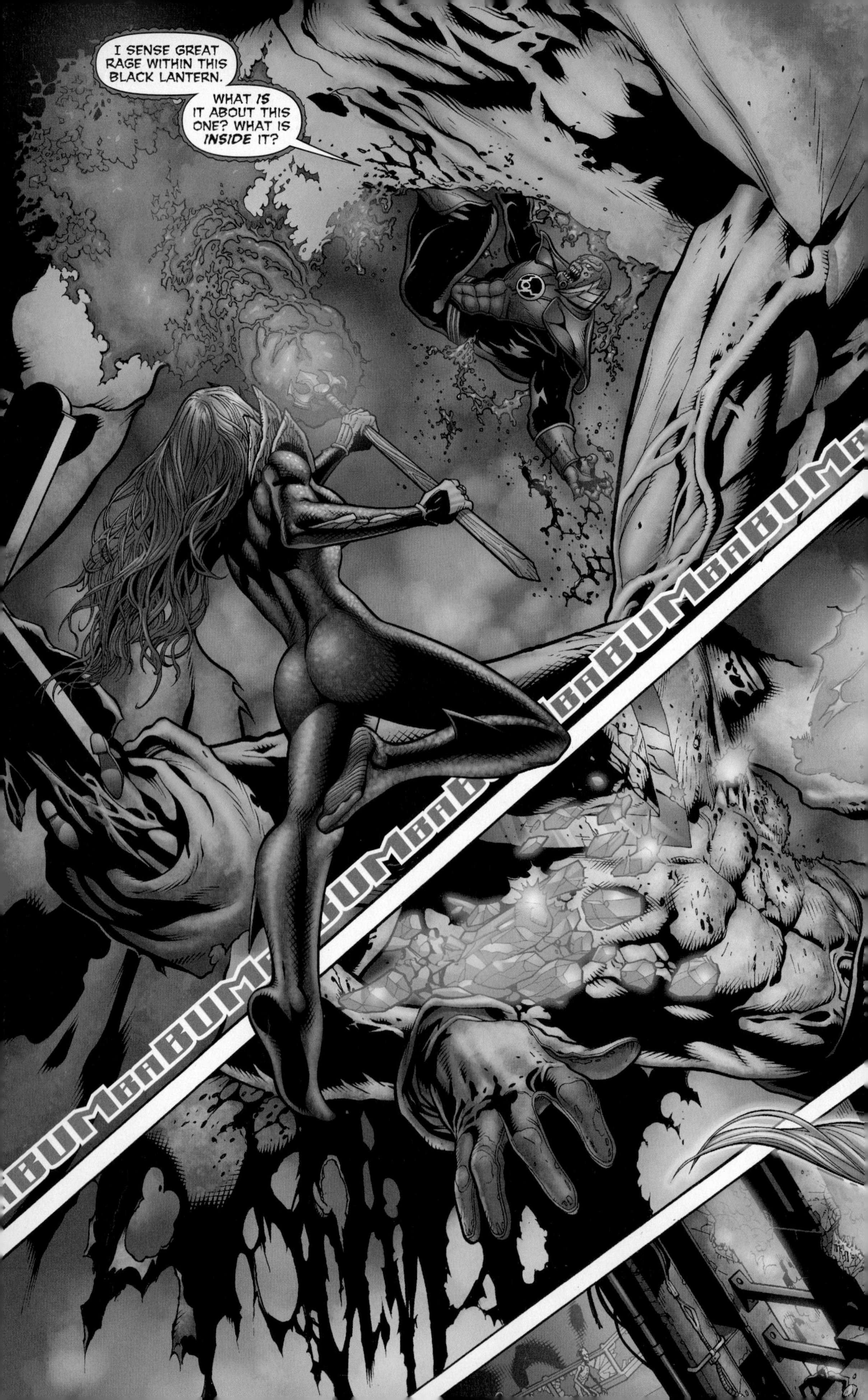
I SENSE GREAT RAGE WITHIN THIS BLACK LANTERN.
WHAT *IS* IT ABOUT THIS ONE? WHAT IS *INSIDE* IT?
BUMbaBUMbaBUMbaBUMbaBUMbaBUMbaBUMba

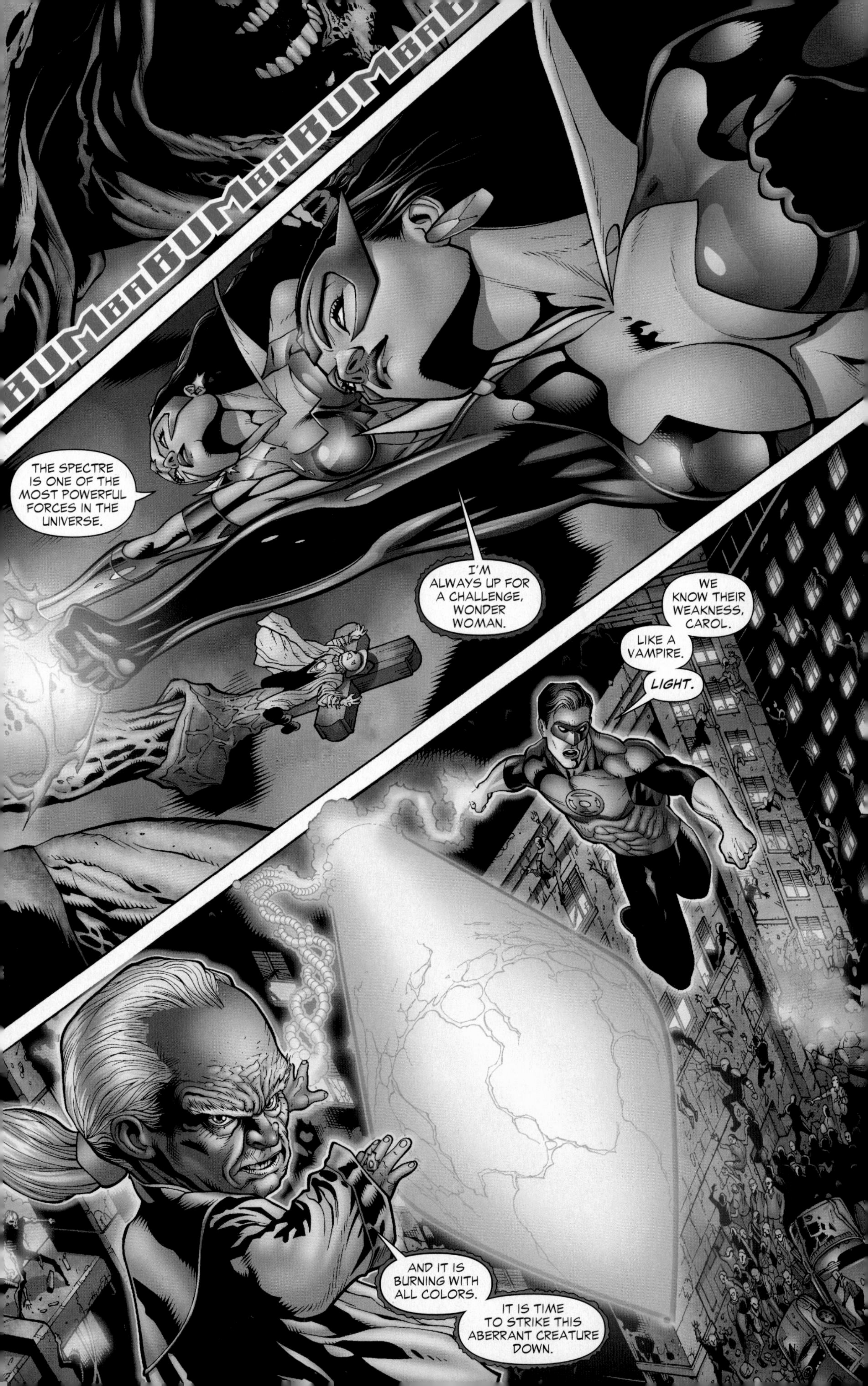
BUMBABUMBABUMBABUMBAB
THE SPECTRE IS ONE OF THE MOST POWERFUL FORCES IN THE UNIVERSE.
I'M ALWAYS UP FOR A CHALLENGE, WONDER WOMAN.
WE KNOW THEIR WEAKNESS, CAROL.
LIKE A VAMPIRE.
LIGHT.
AND IT IS BURNING WITH ALL COLORS.
IT IS TIME TO STRIKE THIS ABERRANT CREATURE DOWN.

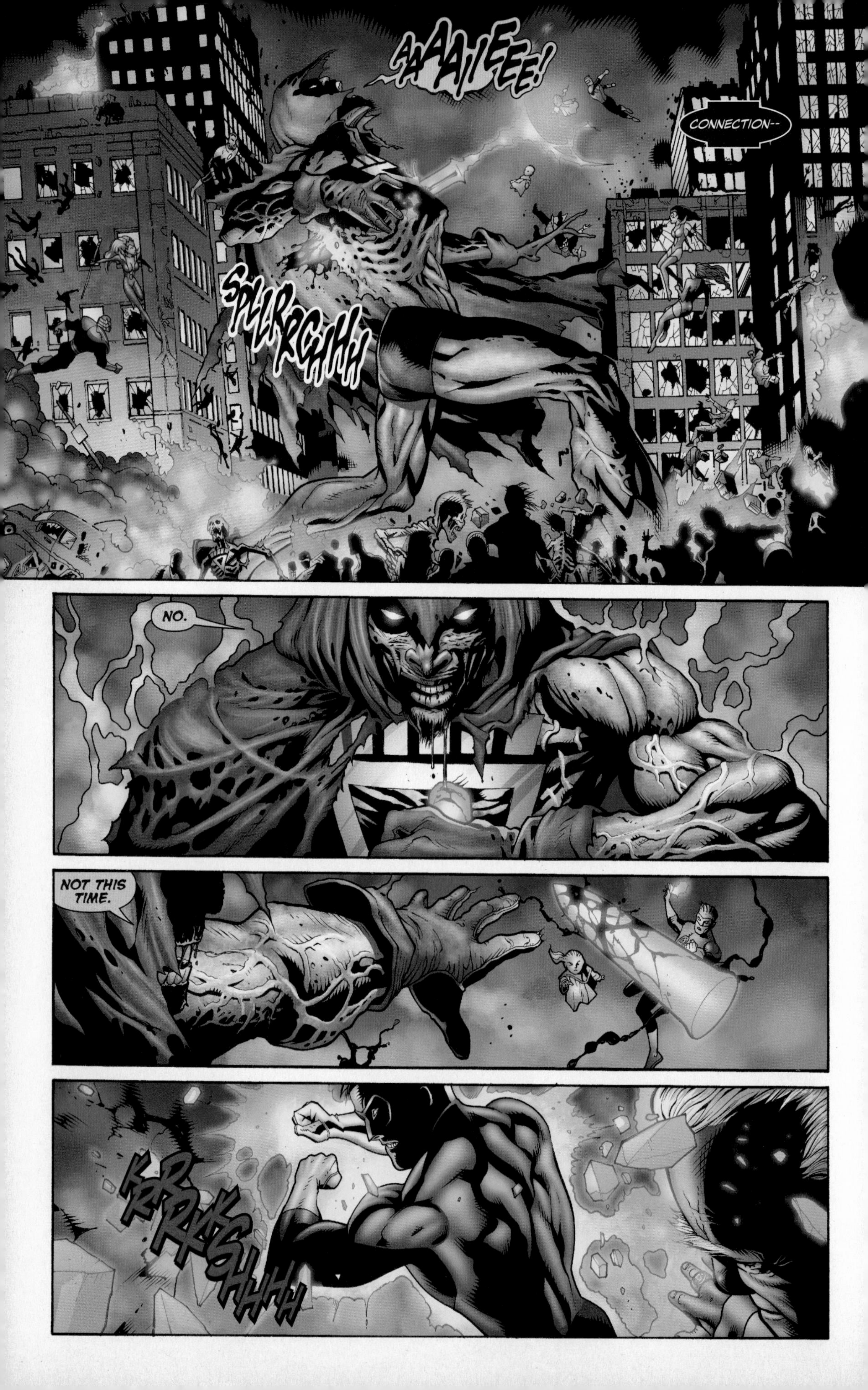
AAAAAIIEEE!
CONNECTION--
SPLLRRGHHH
NO.
NOT THIS TIME.
KRRAKSHHHH

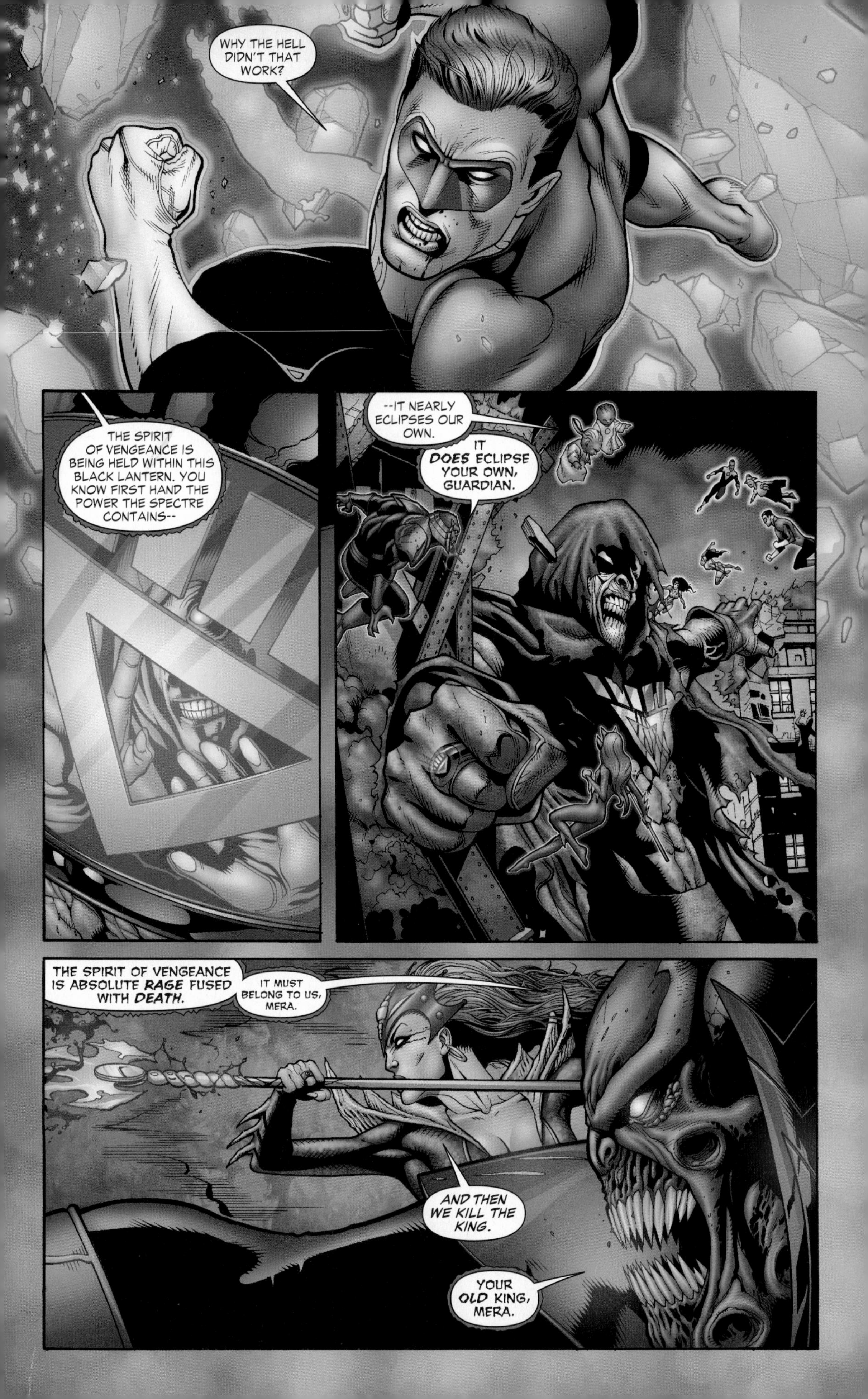
WHY THE HELL DIDN'T THAT WORK?
THE SPIRIT OF VENGEANCE IS BEING HELD WITHIN THIS BLACK LANTERN. YOU KNOW FIRST HAND THE POWER THE SPECTRE CONTAINS--
--IT NEARLY ECLIPSES OUR OWN.
IT DOES ECLIPSE YOUR OWN, GUARDIAN.
THE SPIRIT OF VENGEANCE IS ABSOLUTE RAGE FUSED WITH DEATH.
IT MUST BELONG TO US, MERA.
AND THEN WE KILL THE KING.
YOUR OLD KING, MERA.

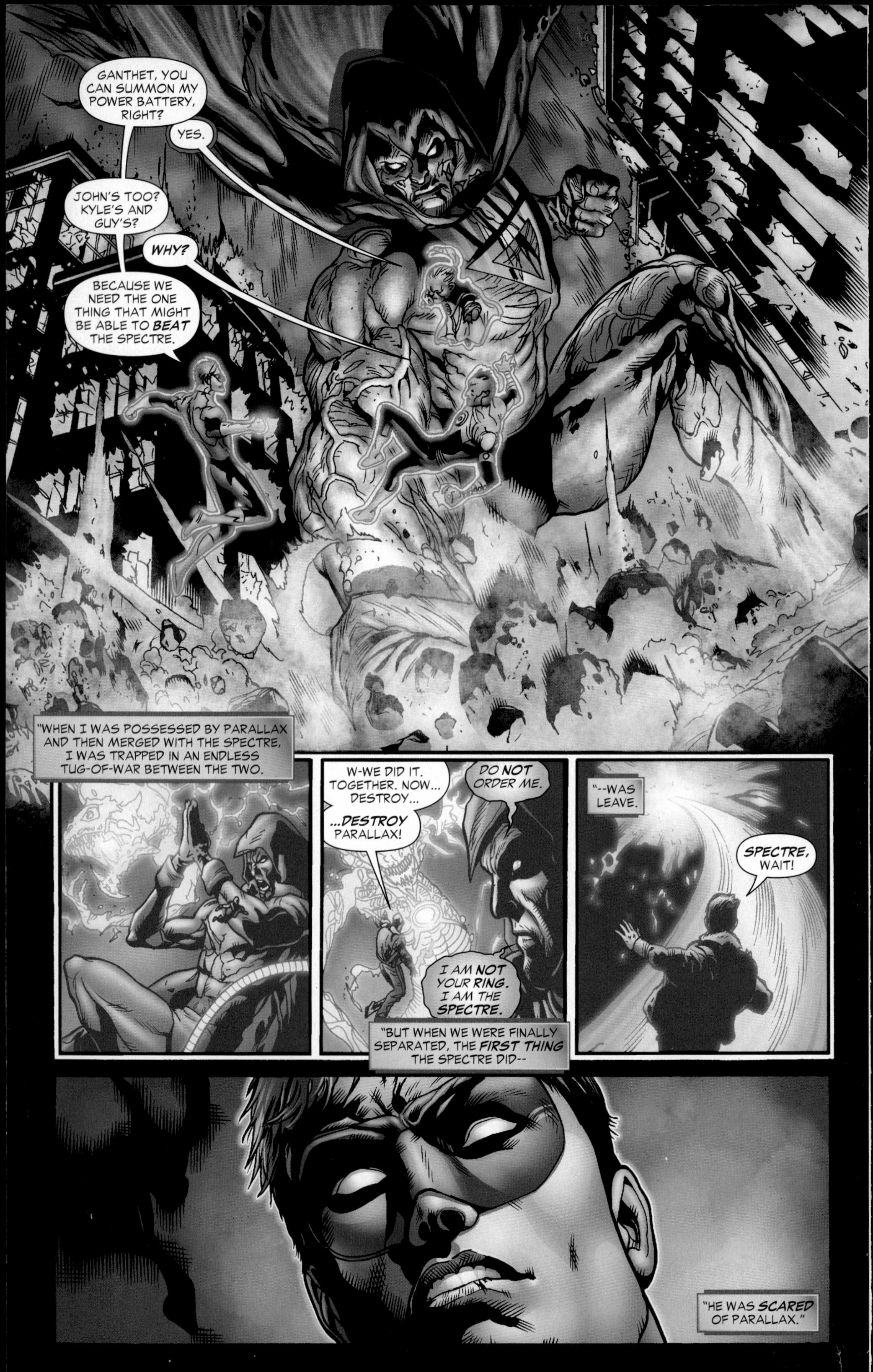
GANTHET, YOU CAN SUMMON MY POWER BATTERY, RIGHT?
YES.
JOHN'S TOO? KYLE'S AND GUY'S?
WHY?
BECAUSE WE NEED THE ONE THING THAT MIGHT BE ABLE TO BEAT THE SPECTRE.
"WHEN I WAS POSSESSED BY PARALLAX AND THEN MERGED WITH THE SPECTRE, I WAS TRAPPED IN AN ENDLESS TUG-OF-WAR BETWEEN THE TWO.
W-WE DID IT. TOGETHER. NOW... DESTROY...
...DESTROY PARALLAX!
DO NOT ORDER ME.
I AM NOT YOUR RING. I AM THE SPECTRE.
"BUT WHEN WE WERE FINALLY SEPARATED, THE FIRST THING THE SPECTRE DID--
"--WAS LEAVE.
SPECTRE, WAIT!
"HE WAS SCARED OF PARALLAX."

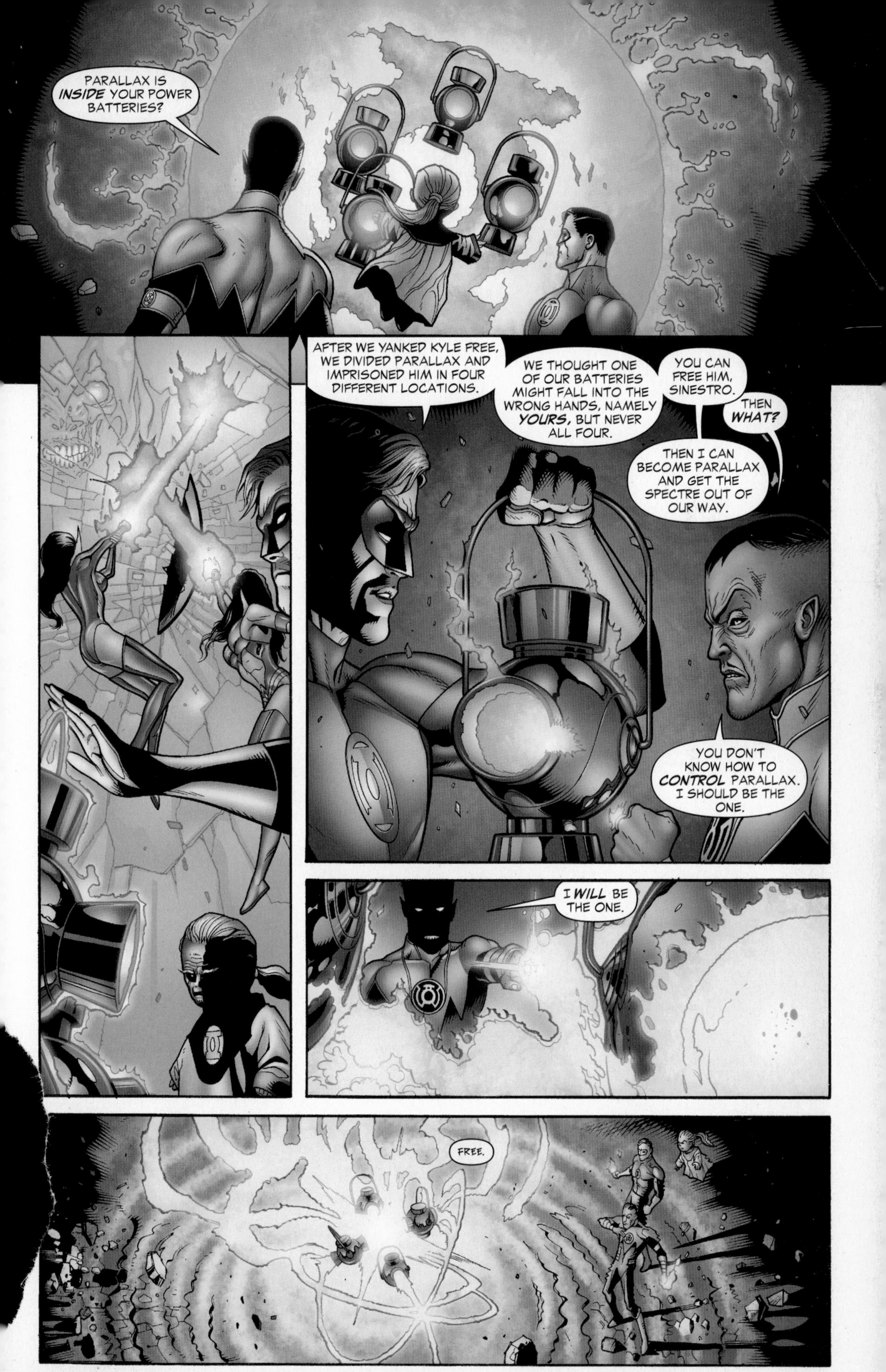
PARALLAX IS INSIDE YOUR POWER BATTERIES?
AFTER WE YANKED KYLE FREE, WE DIVIDED PARALLAX AND IMPRISONED HIM IN FOUR DIFFERENT LOCATIONS.
WE THOUGHT ONE OF OUR BATTERIES MIGHT FALL INTO THE WRONG HANDS, NAMELY YOURS, BUT NEVER ALL FOUR.
YOU CAN FREE HIM, SINESTRO.
THEN WHAT?
THEN I CAN BECOME PARALLAX AND GET THE SPECTRE OUT OF OUR WAY.
YOU DON'T KNOW HOW TO CONTROL PARALLAX. I SHOULD BE THE ONE.
I WILL BE THE ONE.
FREE.

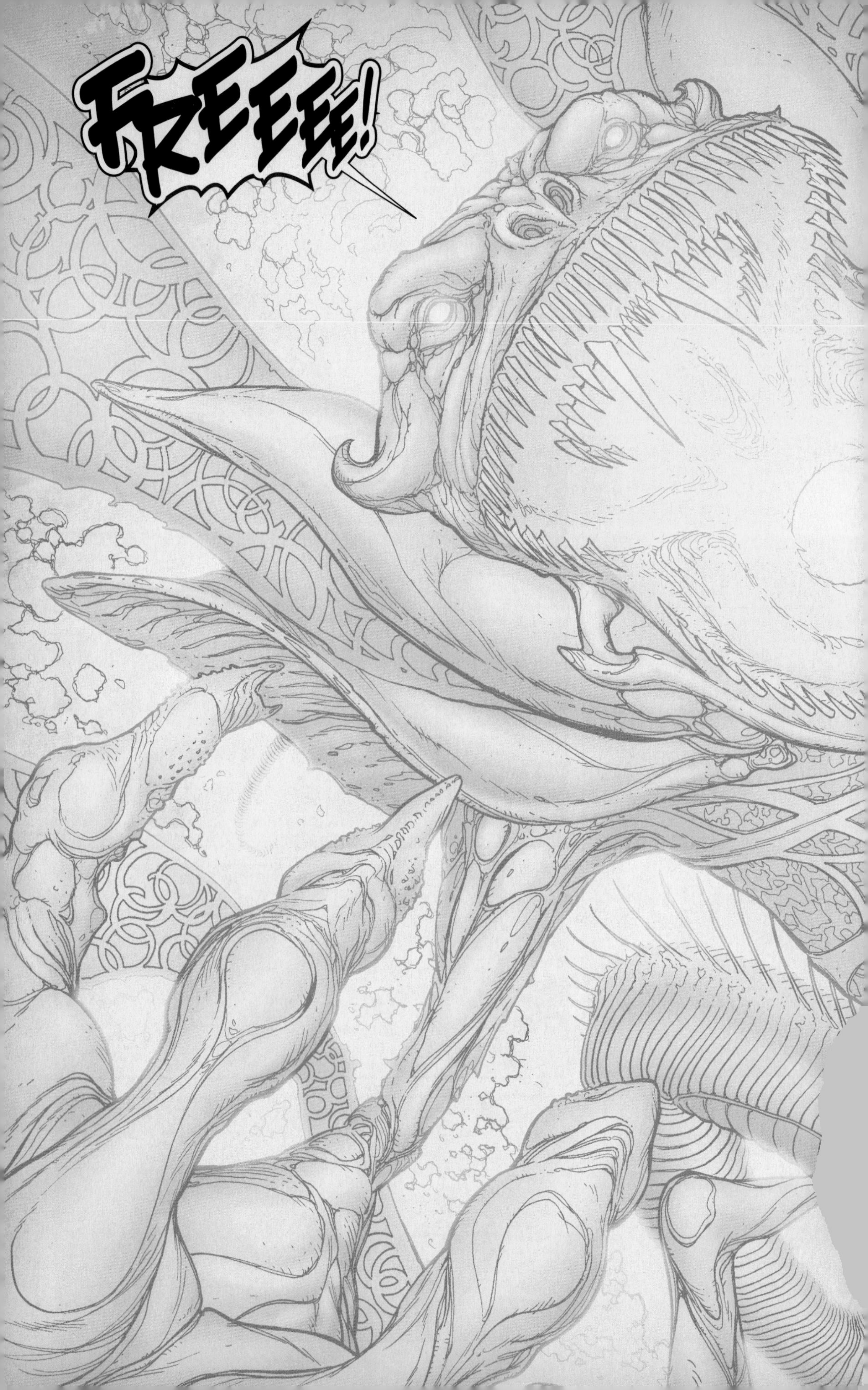
FREEEE!

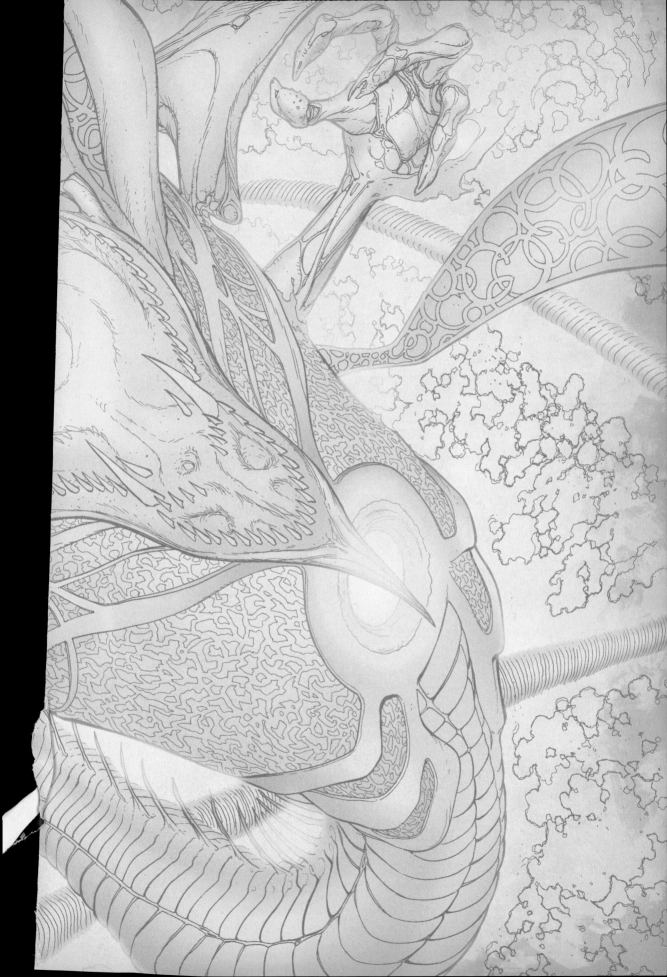

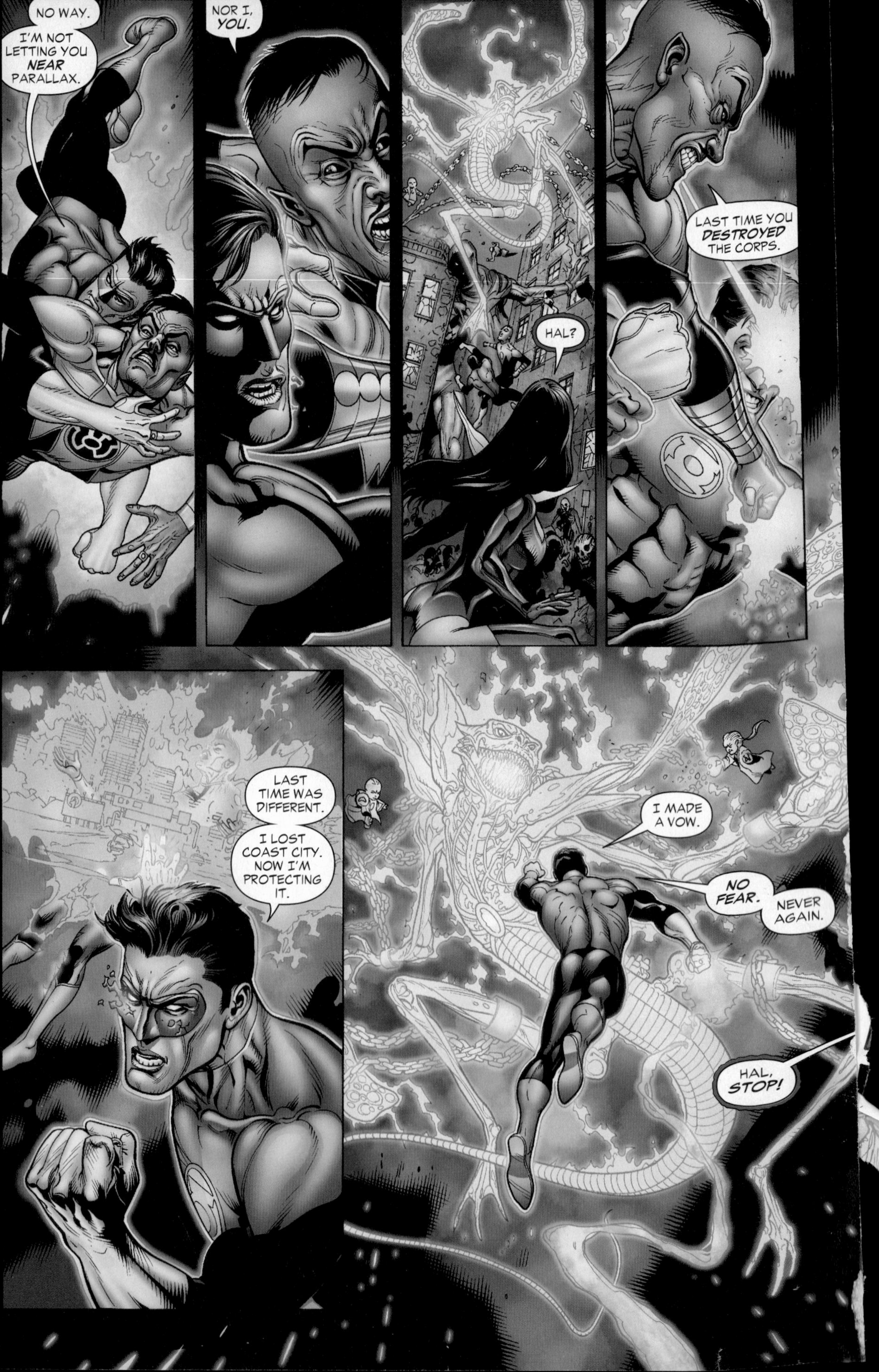
NO WAY.
I'M NOT LETTING YOU NEAR PARALLAX.
NOR I, YOU.
HAL?
LAST TIME YOU DESTROYED THE CORPS.
LAST TIME WAS DIFFERENT.
I LOST COAST CITY. NOW I'M PROTECTING IT.
I MADE A VOW.
NO FEAR.
NEVER AGAIN.
HAL, STOP!

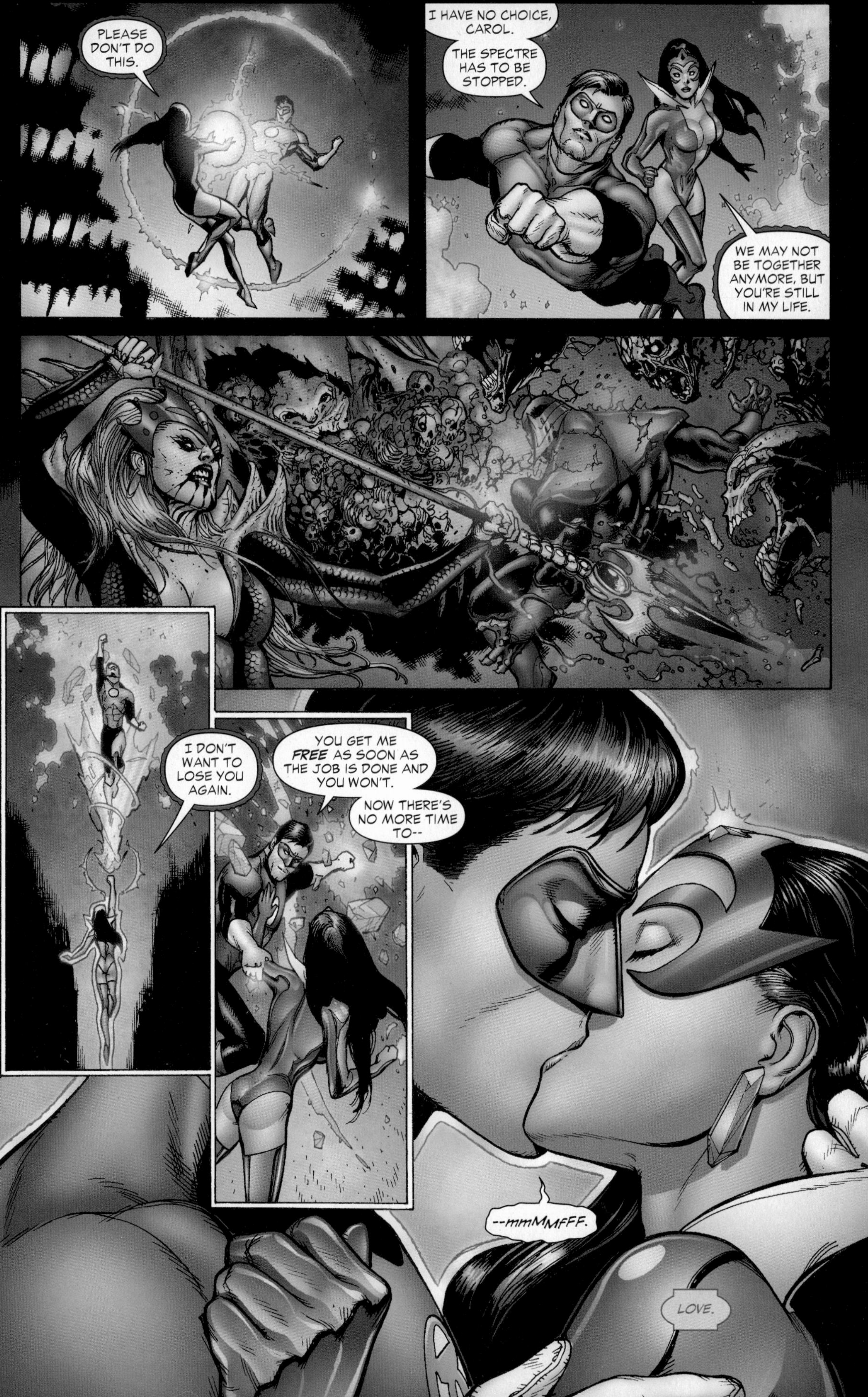
PLEASE DON'T DO THIS.
I HAVE NO CHOICE, CAROL.
THE SPECTRE HAS TO BE STOPPED.
WE MAY NOT BE TOGETHER ANYMORE, BUT YOU'RE STILL IN MY LIFE.
I DON'T WANT TO LOSE YOU AGAIN.
YOU GET ME FREE AS SOON AS THE JOB IS DONE AND YOU WON'T.
NOW THERE'S NO MORE TIME TO--
--mmMMfFF.
LOVE.

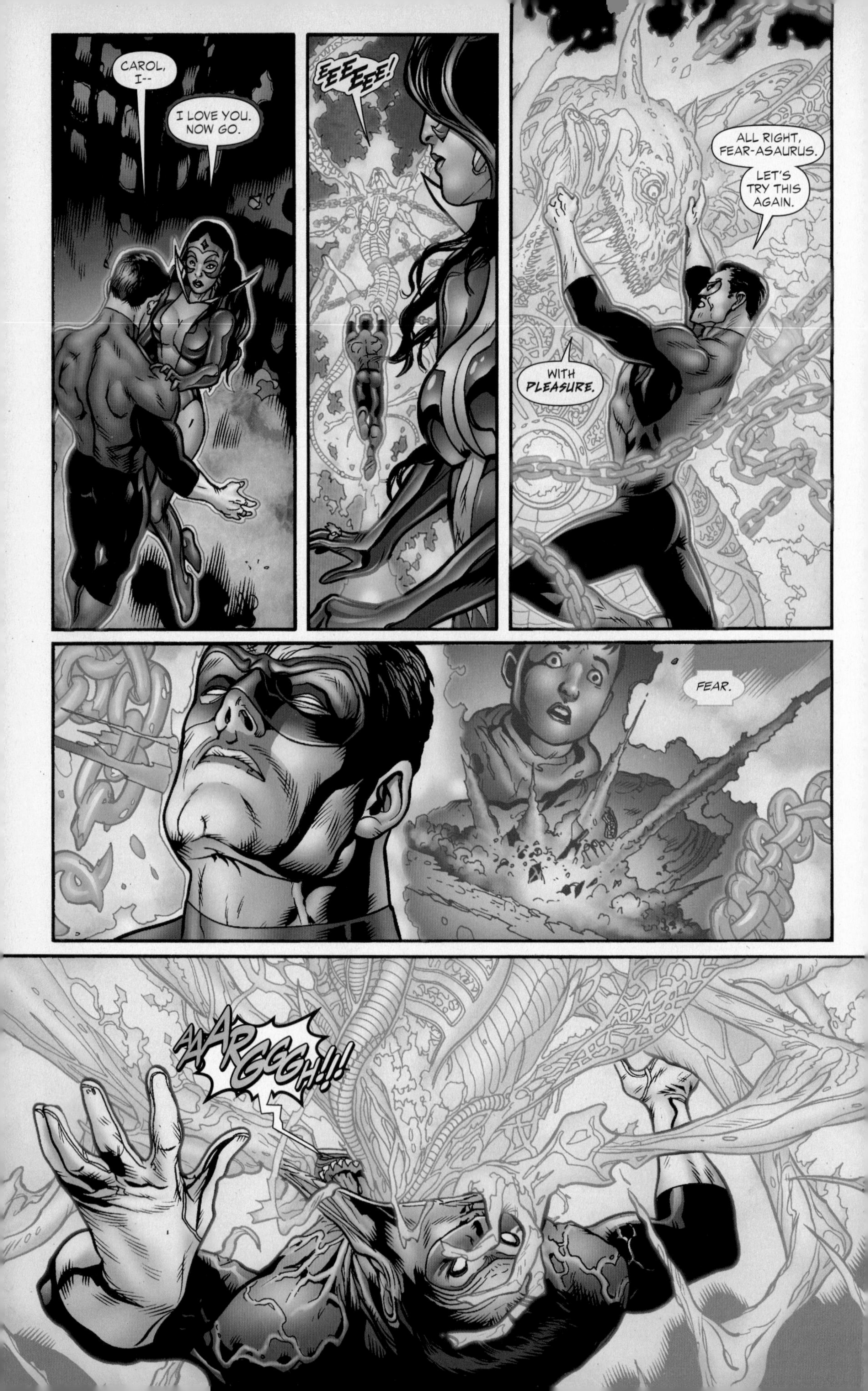
CAROL, I--
I LOVE YOU. NOW GO.
EEEEEE!
ALL RIGHT, FEAR-ASAURUS.
LET'S TRY THIS AGAIN.
WITH PLEASURE.
FEAR.
AAARGGGH!!!

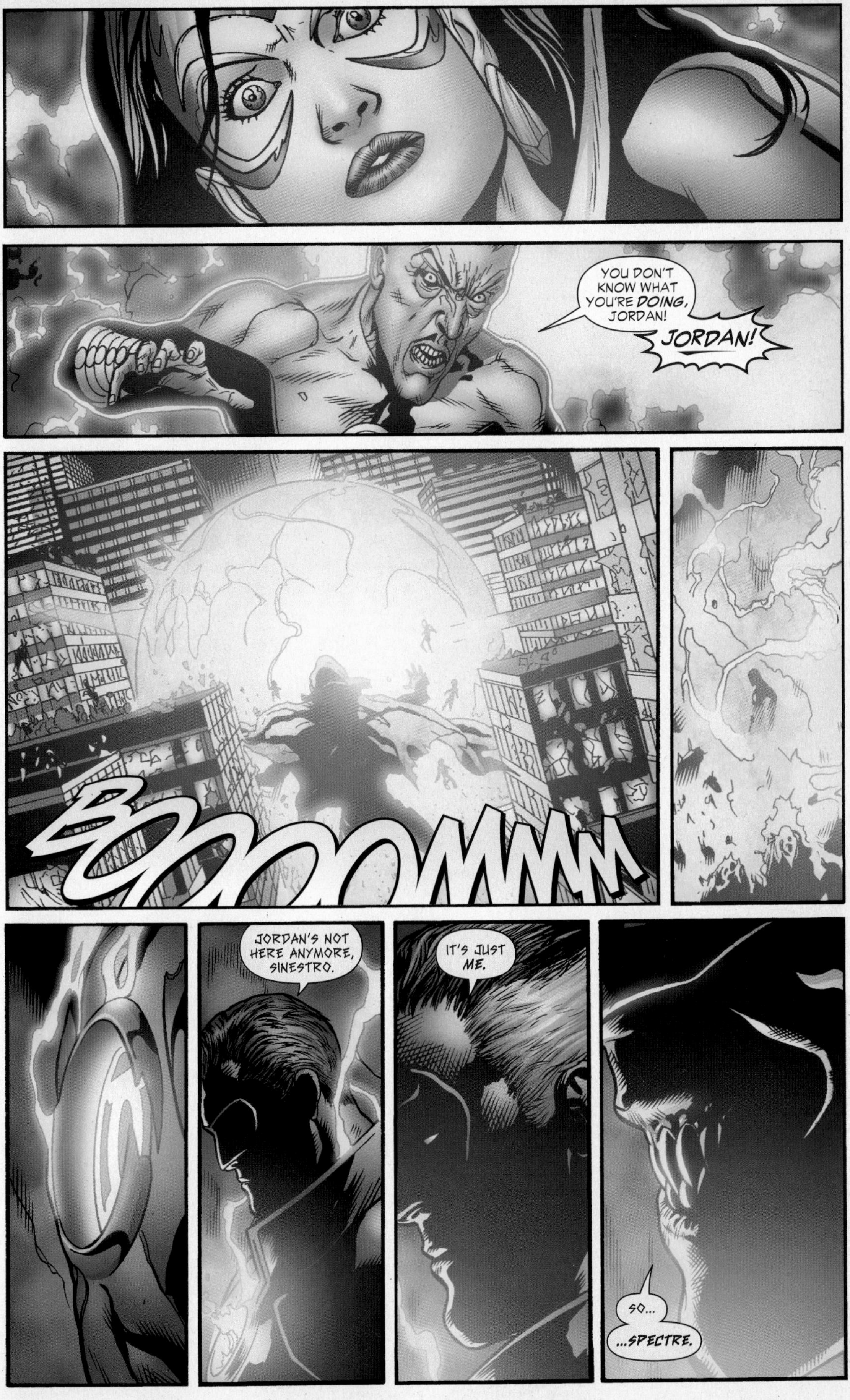
YOU DON'T KNOW WHAT YOU'RE DOING, JORDAN!
JORDAN!
BOOOMMM
JORDAN'S NOT HERE ANYMORE, SINESTRO.
IT'S JUST ME.
SO...
...SPECTRE.

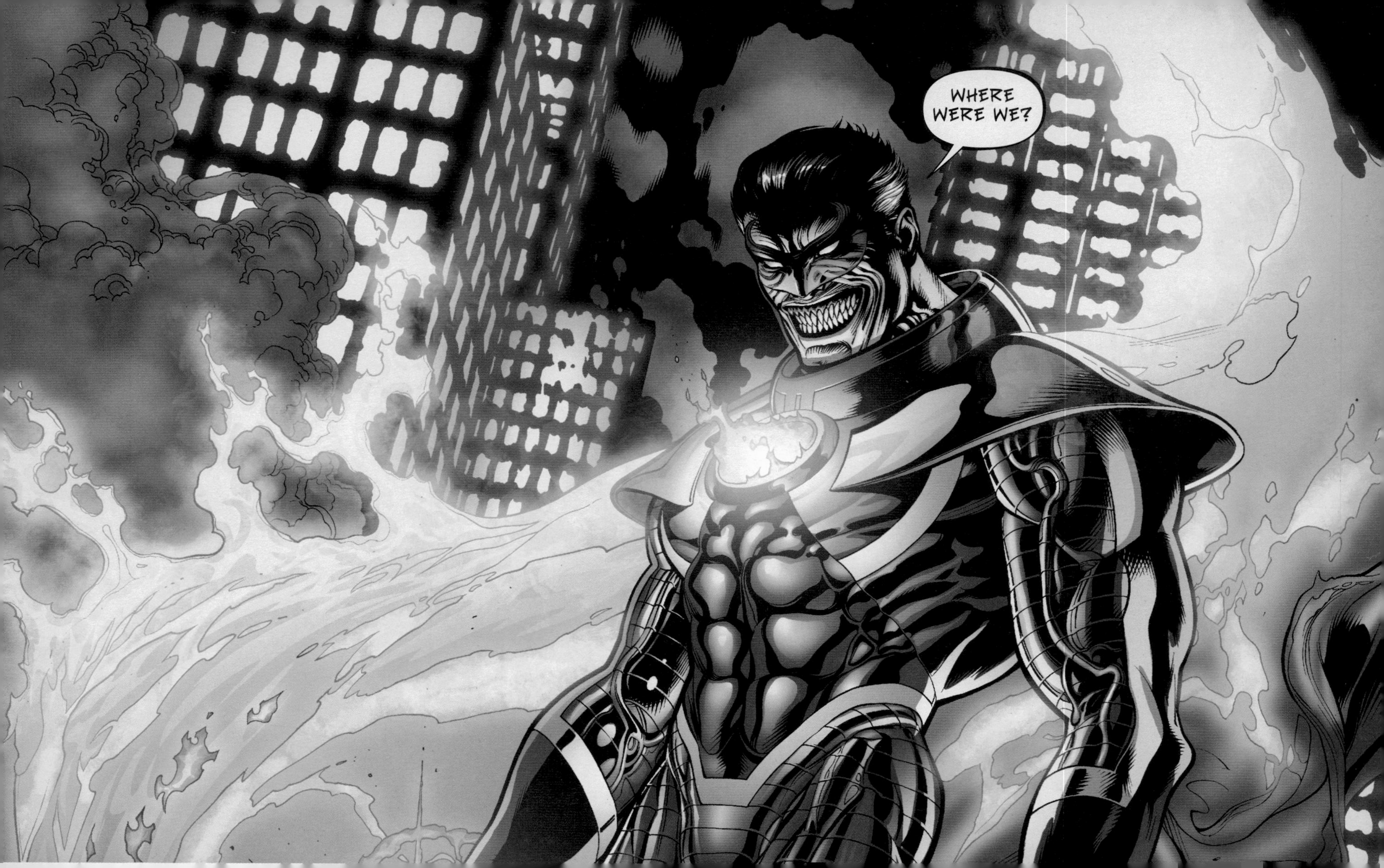
WHERE WERE WE?

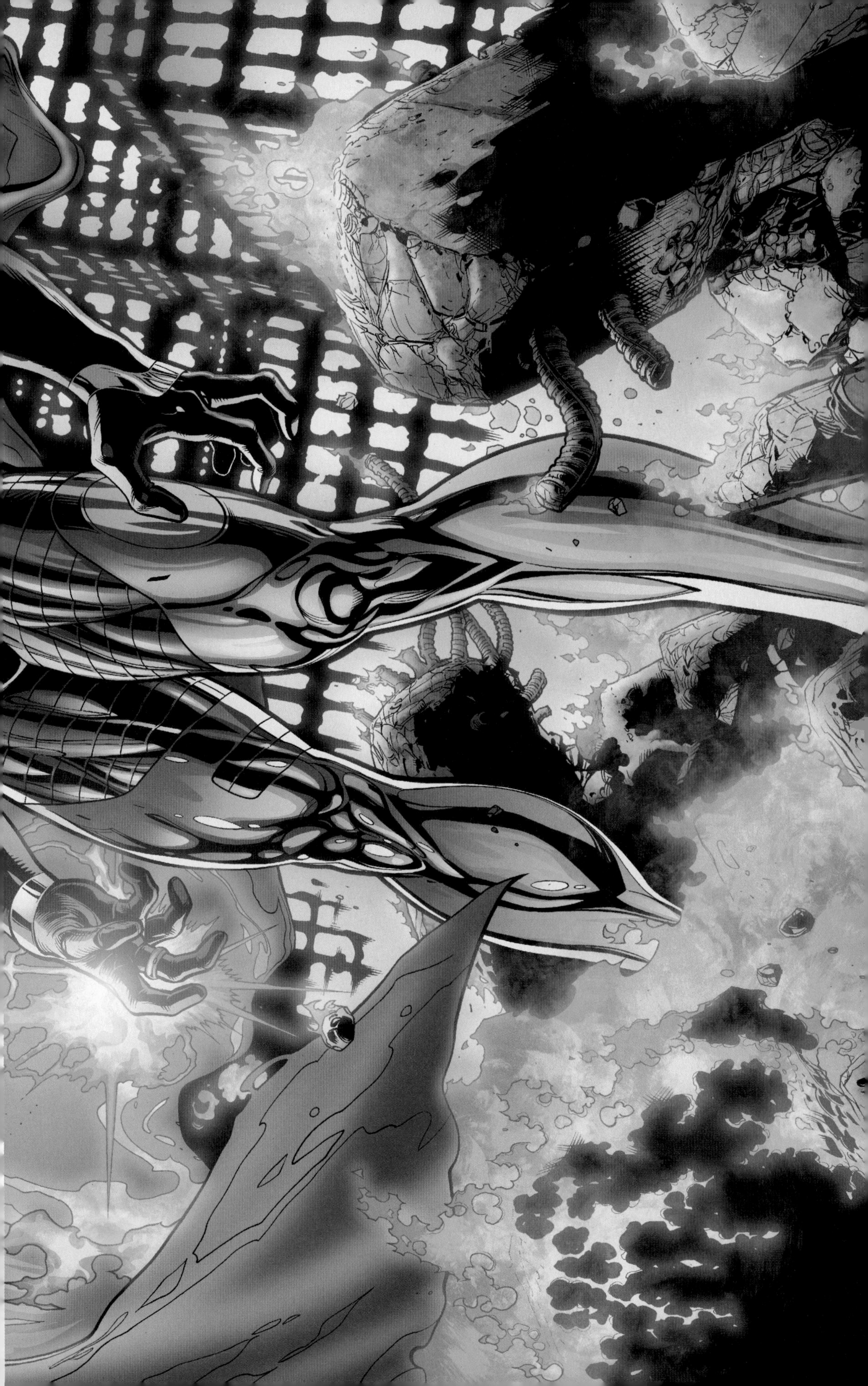

GREEN LANTERN 51
Cover by Doug Mahnke and Christian Alamy with Hi-Fi

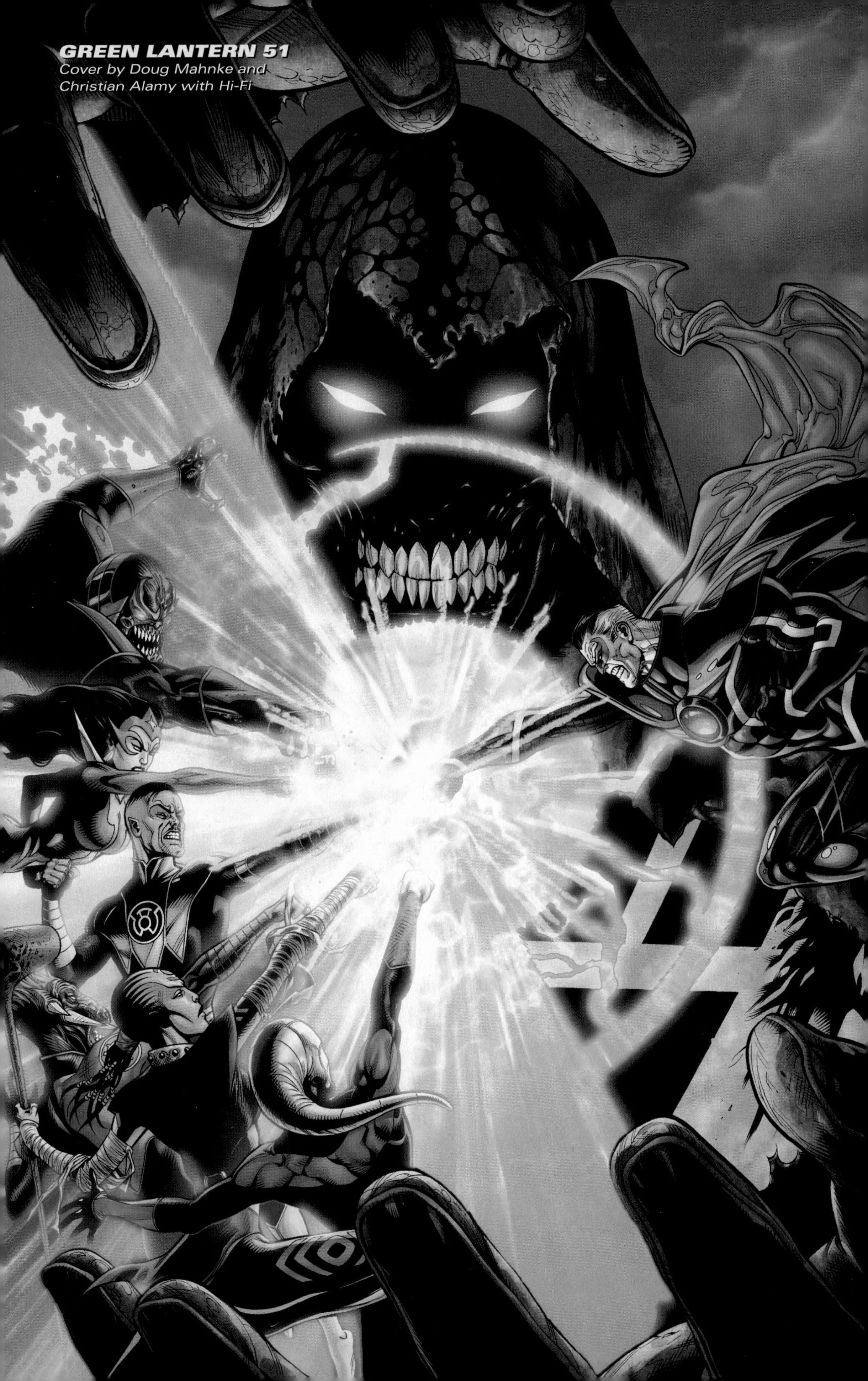

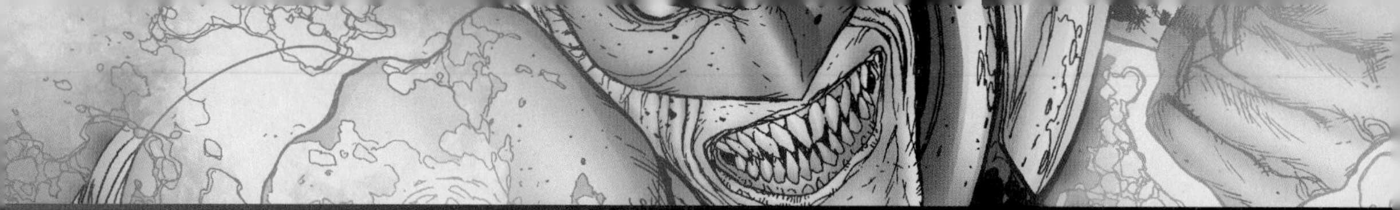

The battle rages on as all the colored Lanterns converge on Earth to battle the Black Lanterns.

But it still may not be enough without a sacrifice...

PARALLAX REBIRTH
PART TWO

DOUG MAHNKE
ART

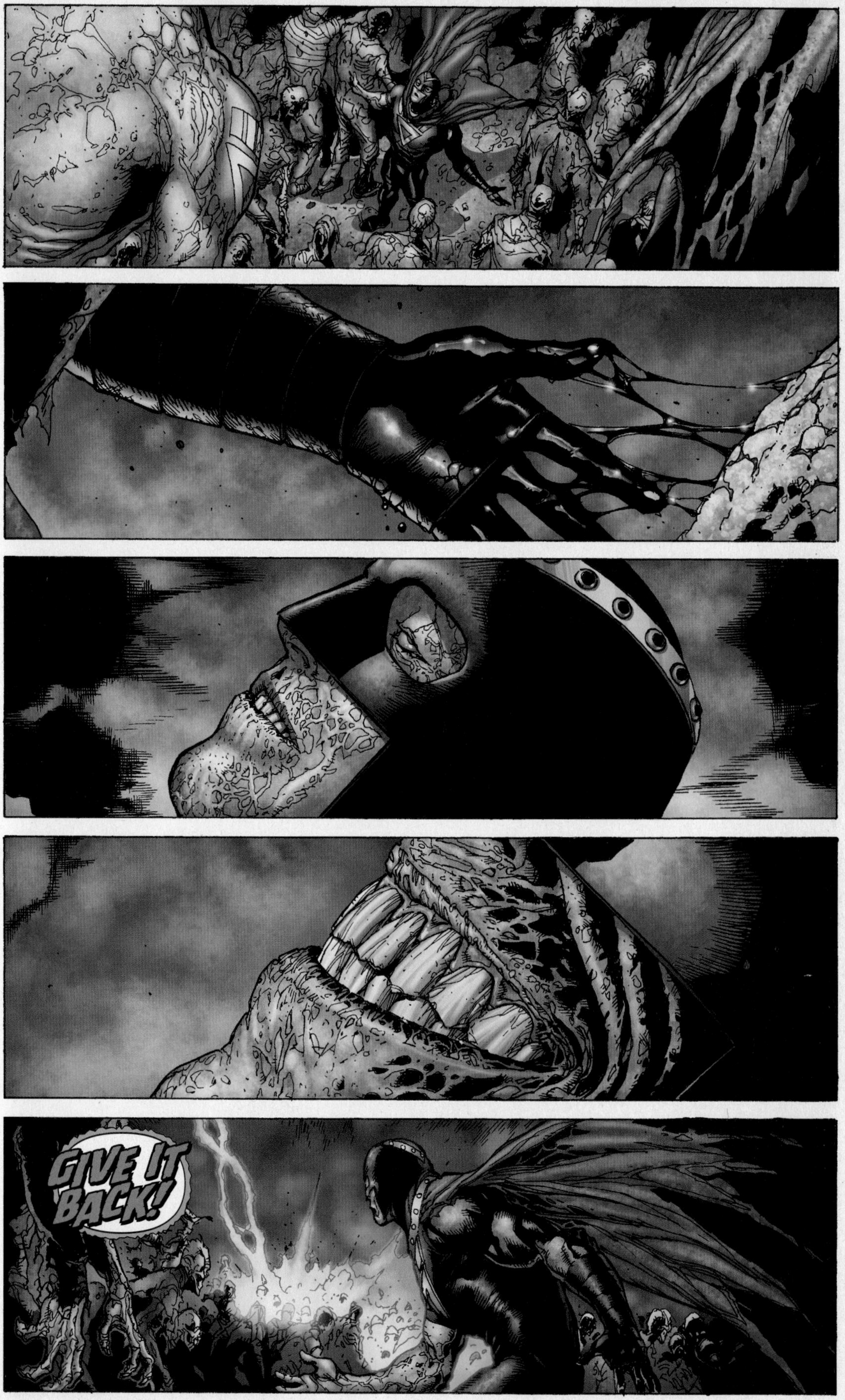
GIVE IT BACK!

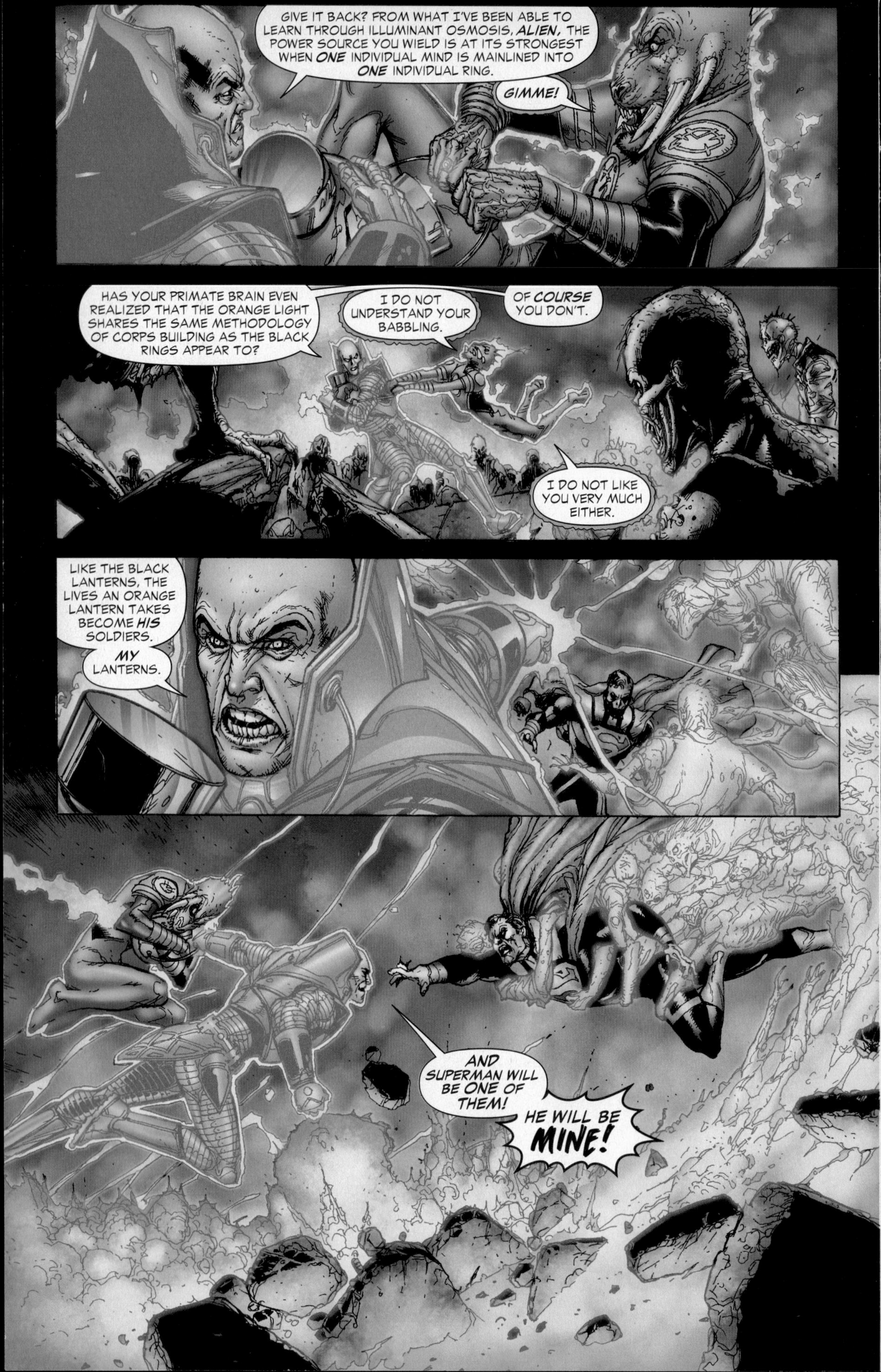
GIVE IT BACK? FROM WHAT I'VE BEEN ABLE TO LEARN THROUGH ILLUMINANT OSMOSIS, *ALIEN*, THE POWER SOURCE YOU WIELD IS AT ITS STRONGEST WHEN *ONE* INDIVIDUAL MIND IS MAINLINED INTO *ONE* INDIVIDUAL RING.
GIMME!
HAS YOUR PRIMATE BRAIN EVEN REALIZED THAT THE ORANGE LIGHT SHARES THE SAME METHODOLOGY OF CORPS BUILDING AS THE BLACK RINGS APPEAR TO?
I DO NOT UNDERSTAND YOUR BABBLING.
OF *COURSE* YOU DON'T.
I DO NOT LIKE YOU VERY MUCH EITHER.
LIKE THE BLACK LANTERNS, THE LIVES AN ORANGE LANTERN TAKES BECOME *HIS* SOLDIERS.
MY LANTERNS.
AND SUPERMAN WILL BE ONE OF THEM!
HE WILL BE **MINE!**

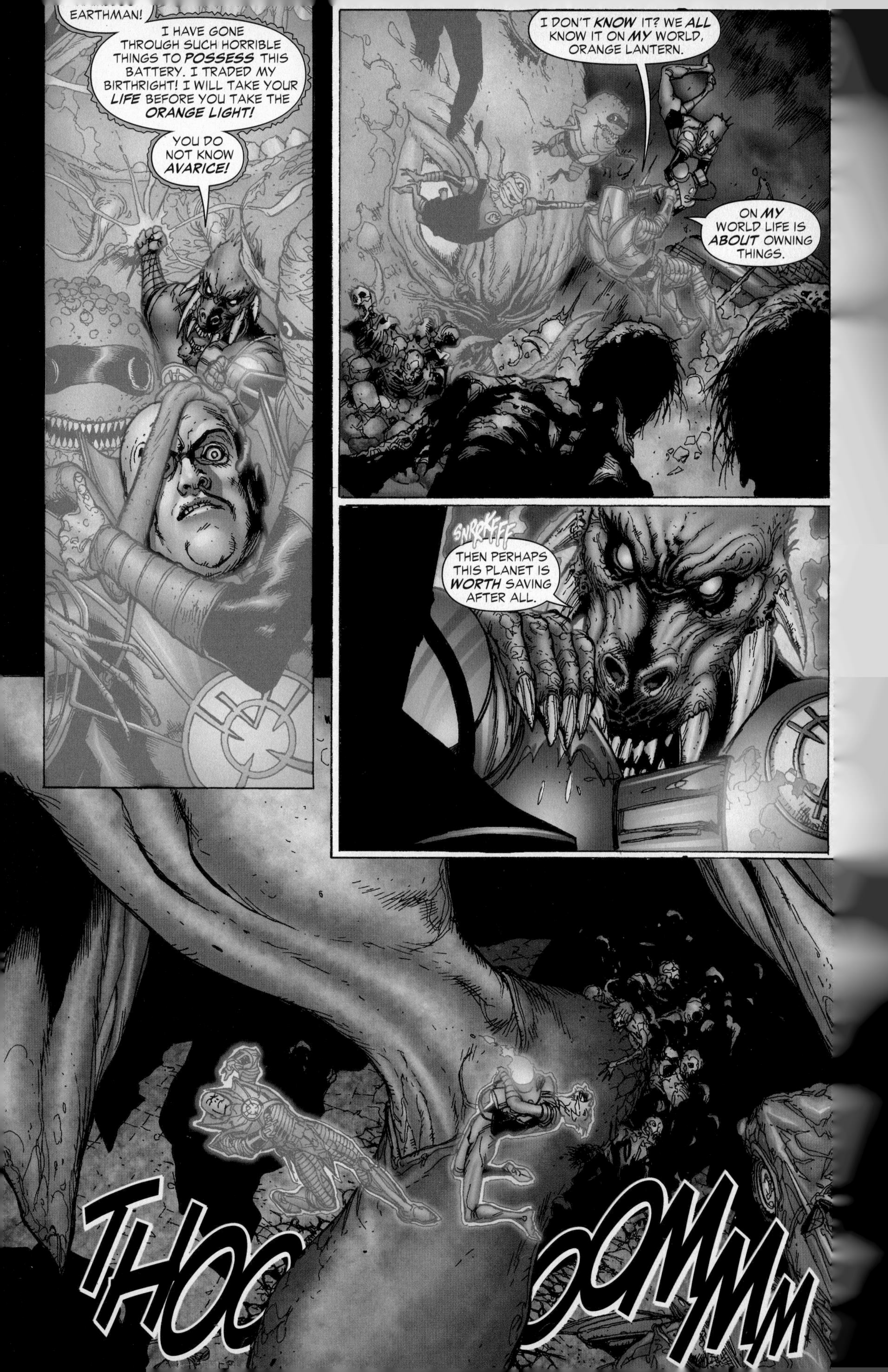

EARTHMAN!
I HAVE GONE THROUGH SUCH HORRIBLE THINGS TO POSSESS THIS BATTERY. I TRADED MY BIRTHRIGHT! I WILL TAKE YOUR LIFE BEFORE YOU TAKE THE ORANGE LIGHT!
YOU DO NOT KNOW AVARICE!
I DON'T KNOW IT? WE ALL KNOW IT ON MY WORLD, ORANGE LANTERN.
ON MY WORLD LIFE IS ABOUT OWNING THINGS.
SNRRKFFF
THEN PERHAPS THIS PLANET IS WORTH SAVING AFTER ALL.
THOO OOMMM

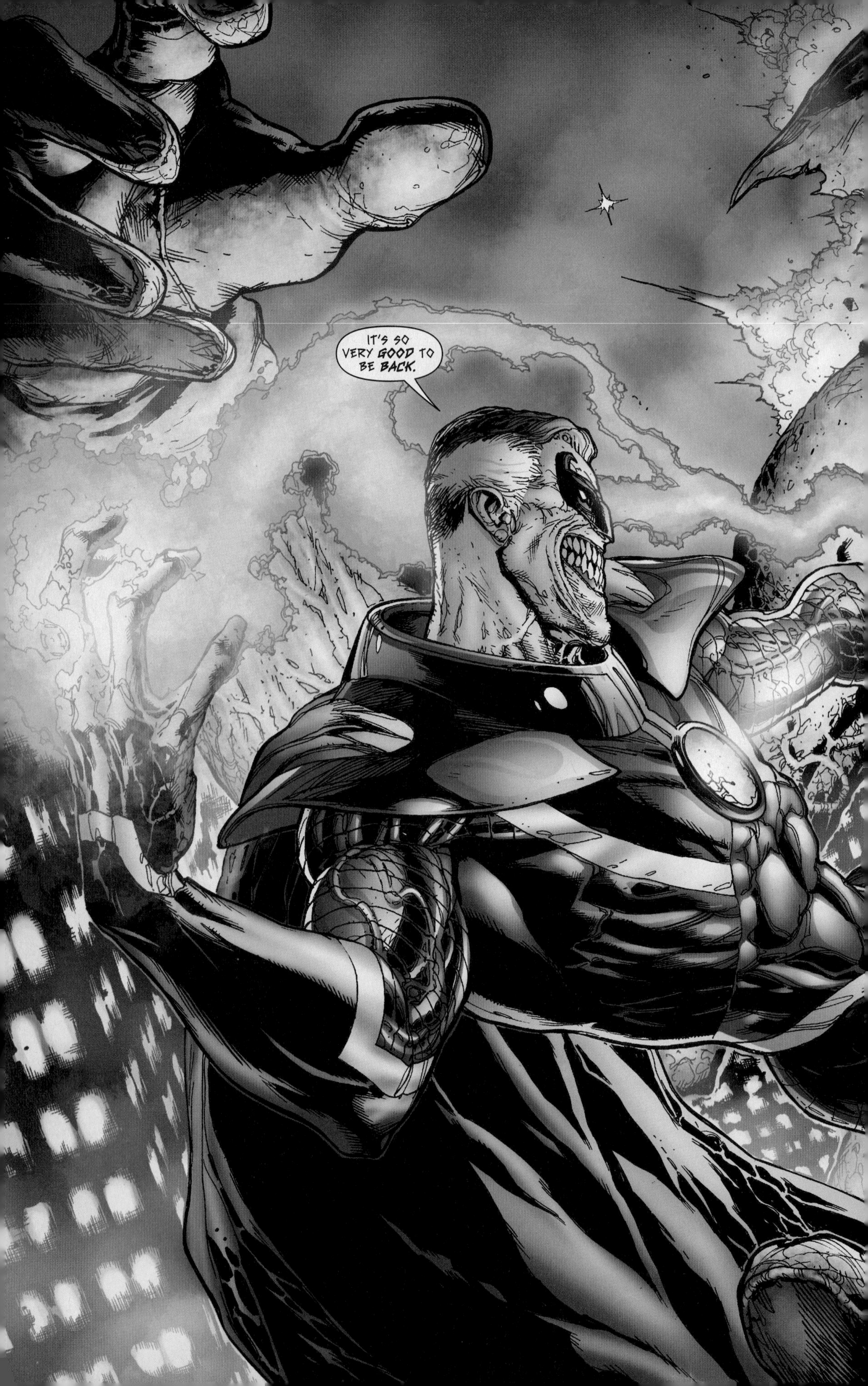
IT'S SO VERY GOOD TO BE BACK.

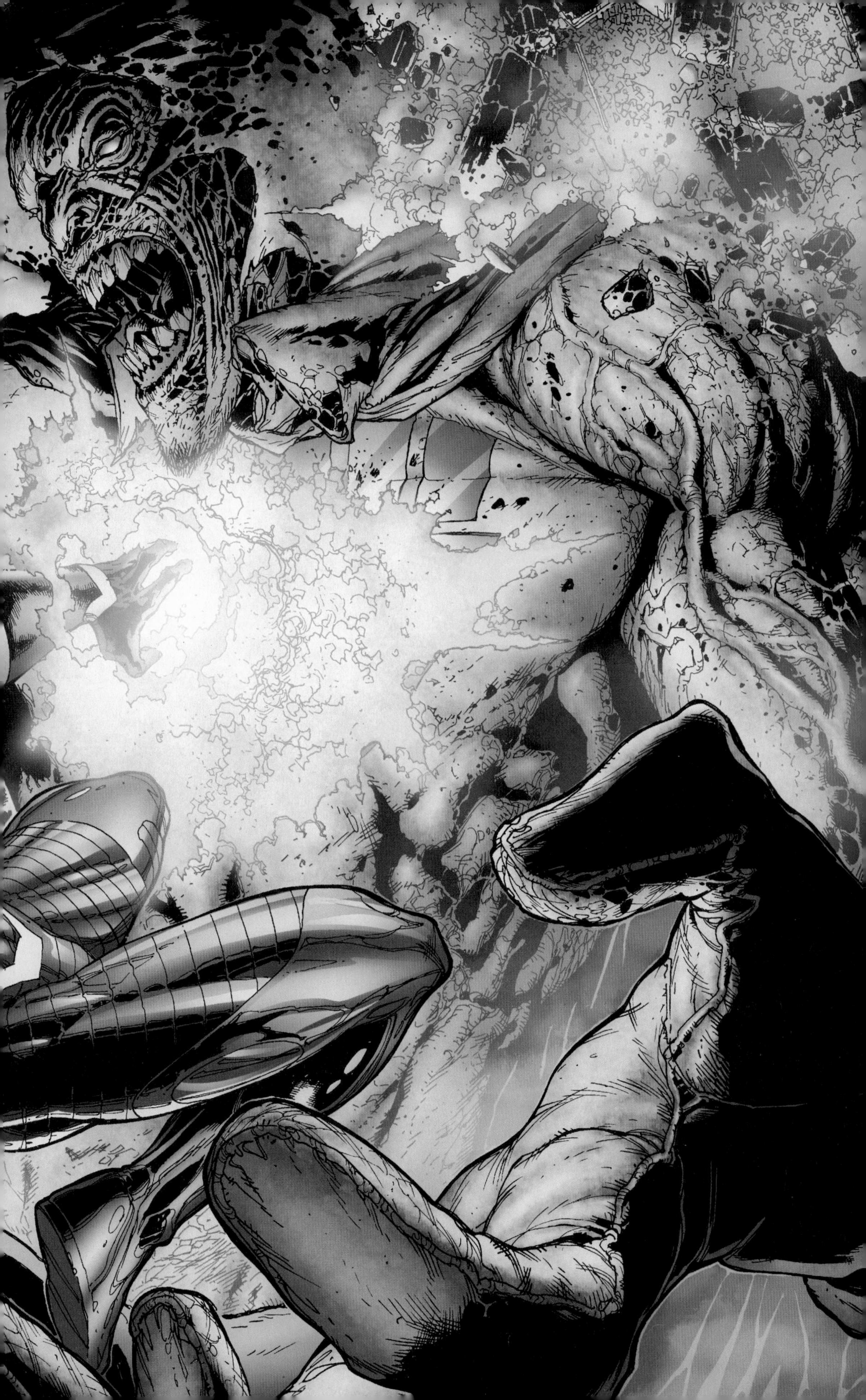

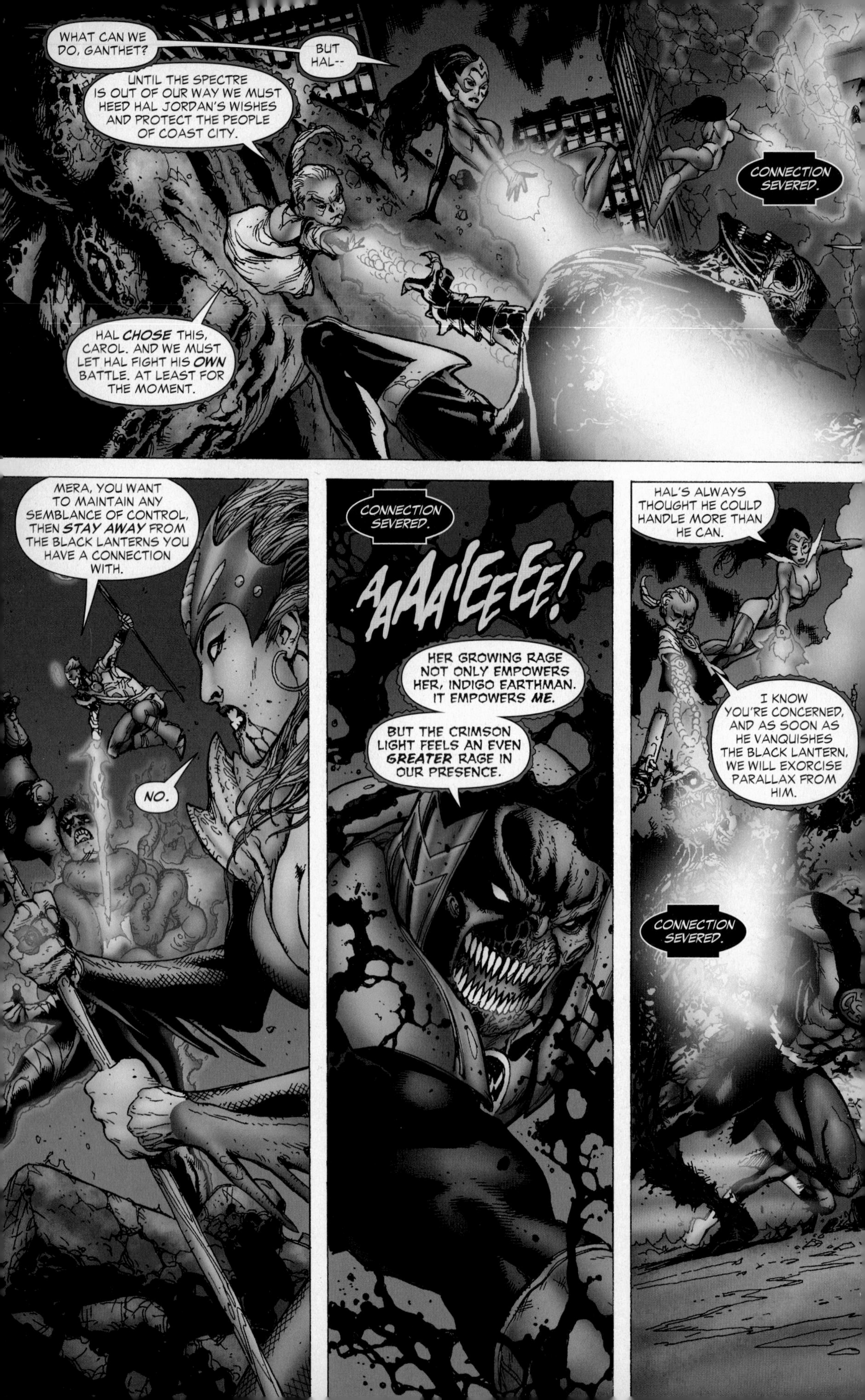
WHAT CAN WE DO, GANTHET?
BUT HAL--
UNTIL THE SPECTRE IS OUT OF OUR WAY WE MUST HEED HAL JORDAN'S WISHES AND PROTECT THE PEOPLE OF COAST CITY.
CONNECTION SEVERED.
HAL CHOSE THIS, CAROL. AND WE MUST LET HAL FIGHT HIS OWN BATTLE. AT LEAST FOR THE MOMENT.
MERA, YOU WANT TO MAINTAIN ANY SEMBLANCE OF CONTROL, THEN STAY AWAY FROM THE BLACK LANTERNS YOU HAVE A CONNECTION WITH.
NO.
CONNECTION SEVERED.
AAAAIEEEEE!
HER GROWING RAGE NOT ONLY EMPOWERS HER, INDIGO EARTHMAN. IT EMPOWERS ME.
BUT THE CRIMSON LIGHT FEELS AN EVEN GREATER RAGE IN OUR PRESENCE.
HAL'S ALWAYS THOUGHT HE COULD HANDLE MORE THAN HE CAN.
I KNOW YOU'RE CONCERNED, AND AS SOON AS HE VANQUISHES THE BLACK LANTERN, WE WILL EXORCISE PARALLAX FROM HIM.
CONNECTION SEVERED.

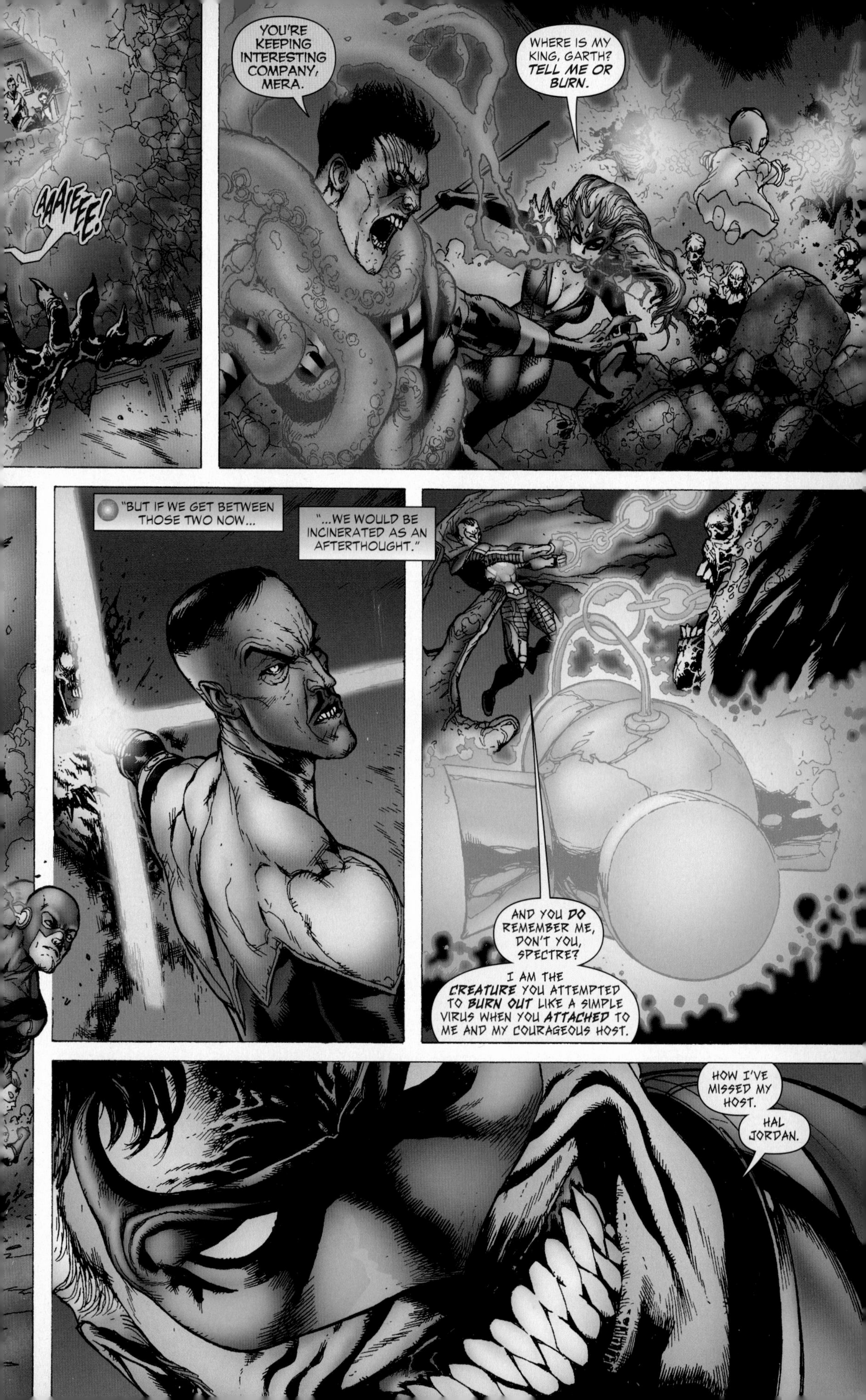
AAAIEEE!
YOU'RE KEEPING INTERESTING COMPANY, MERA.
WHERE IS MY KING, GARTH? TELL ME OR BURN.
"BUT IF WE GET BETWEEN THOSE TWO NOW...
"...WE WOULD BE INCINERATED AS AN AFTERTHOUGHT."
AND YOU DO REMEMBER ME, DON'T YOU, SPECTRE?
I AM THE CREATURE YOU ATTEMPTED TO BURN OUT LIKE A SIMPLE VIRUS WHEN YOU ATTACHED TO ME AND MY COURAGEOUS HOST.
HOW I'VE MISSED MY HOST.
HAL JORDAN.

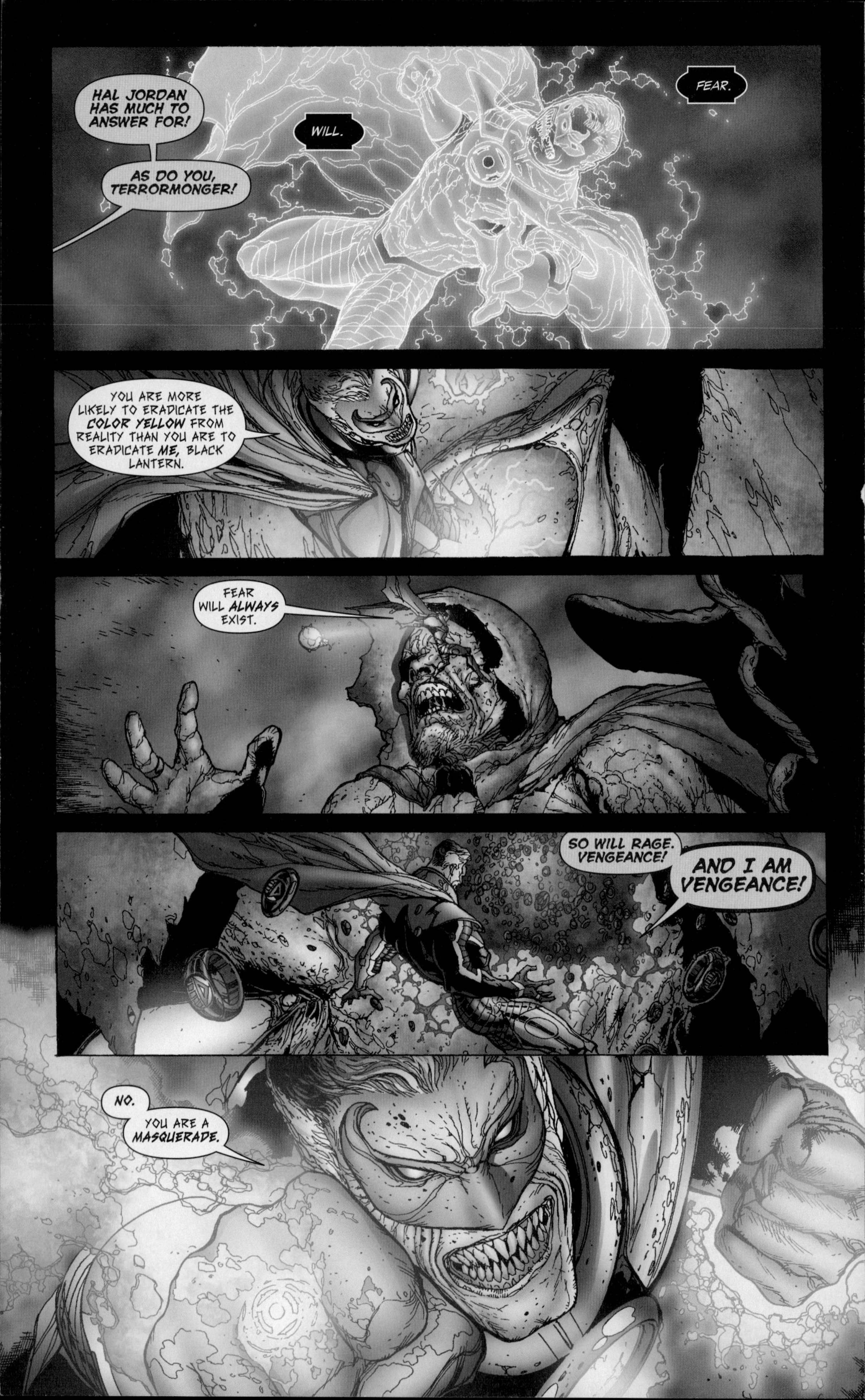

HAL JORDAN HAS MUCH TO ANSWER FOR!
AS DO YOU, TERRORMONGER!
WILL.
FEAR.
YOU ARE MORE LIKELY TO ERADICATE THE COLOR YELLOW FROM REALITY THAN YOU ARE TO ERADICATE ME, BLACK LANTERN.
FEAR WILL ALWAYS EXIST.
SO WILL RAGE. VENGEANCE!
AND I AM VENGEANCE!
NO.
YOU ARE A MASQUERADE.

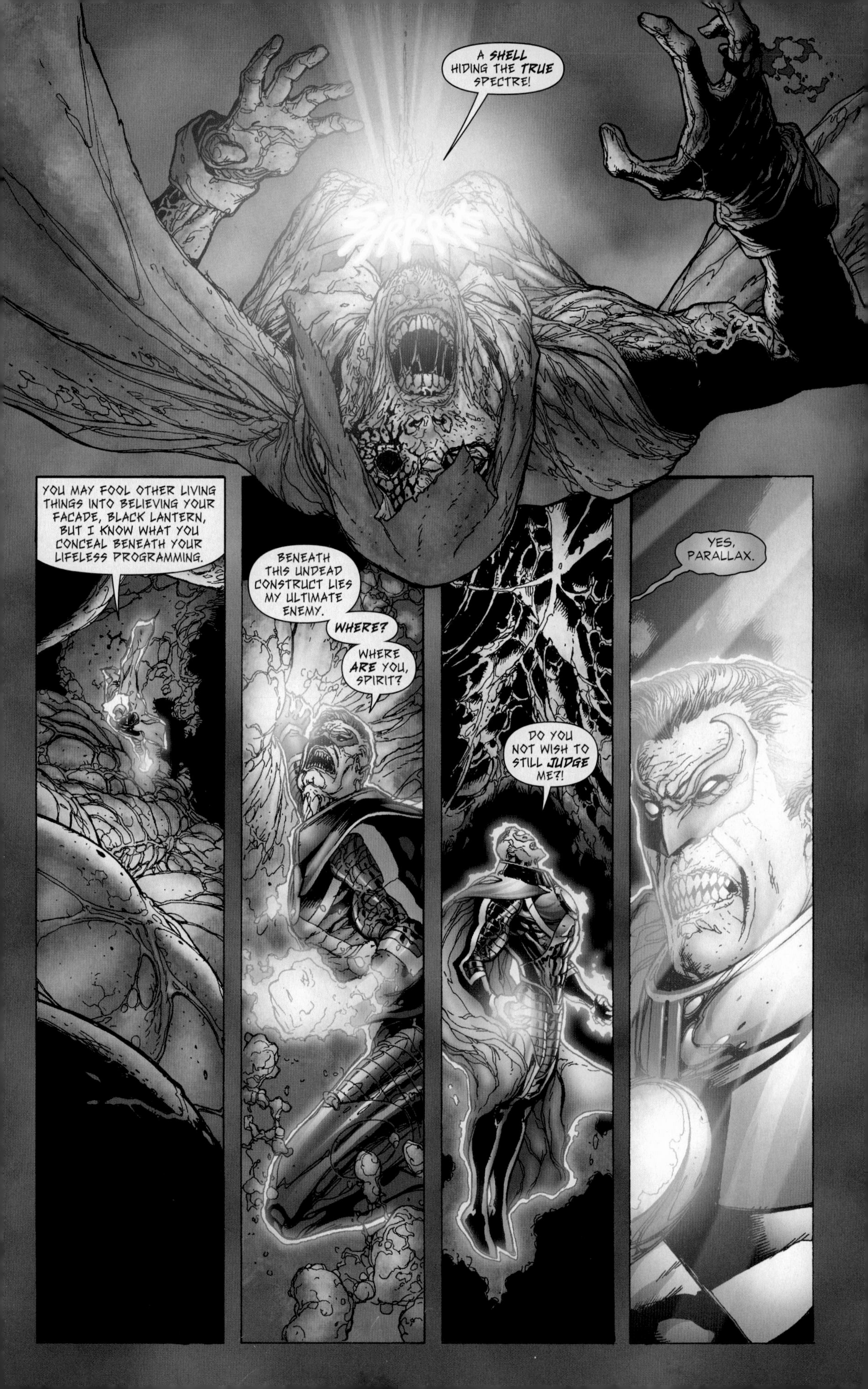
A SHELL HIDING THE TRUE SPECTRE!
YOU MAY FOOL OTHER LIVING THINGS INTO BELIEVING YOUR FACADE, BLACK LANTERN, BUT I KNOW WHAT YOU CONCEAL BENEATH YOUR LIFELESS PROGRAMMING.
BENEATH THIS UNDEAD CONSTRUCT LIES MY ULTIMATE ENEMY.
WHERE?
WHERE ARE YOU, SPIRIT?
DO YOU NOT WISH TO STILL JUDGE ME?!
YES, PARALLAX.

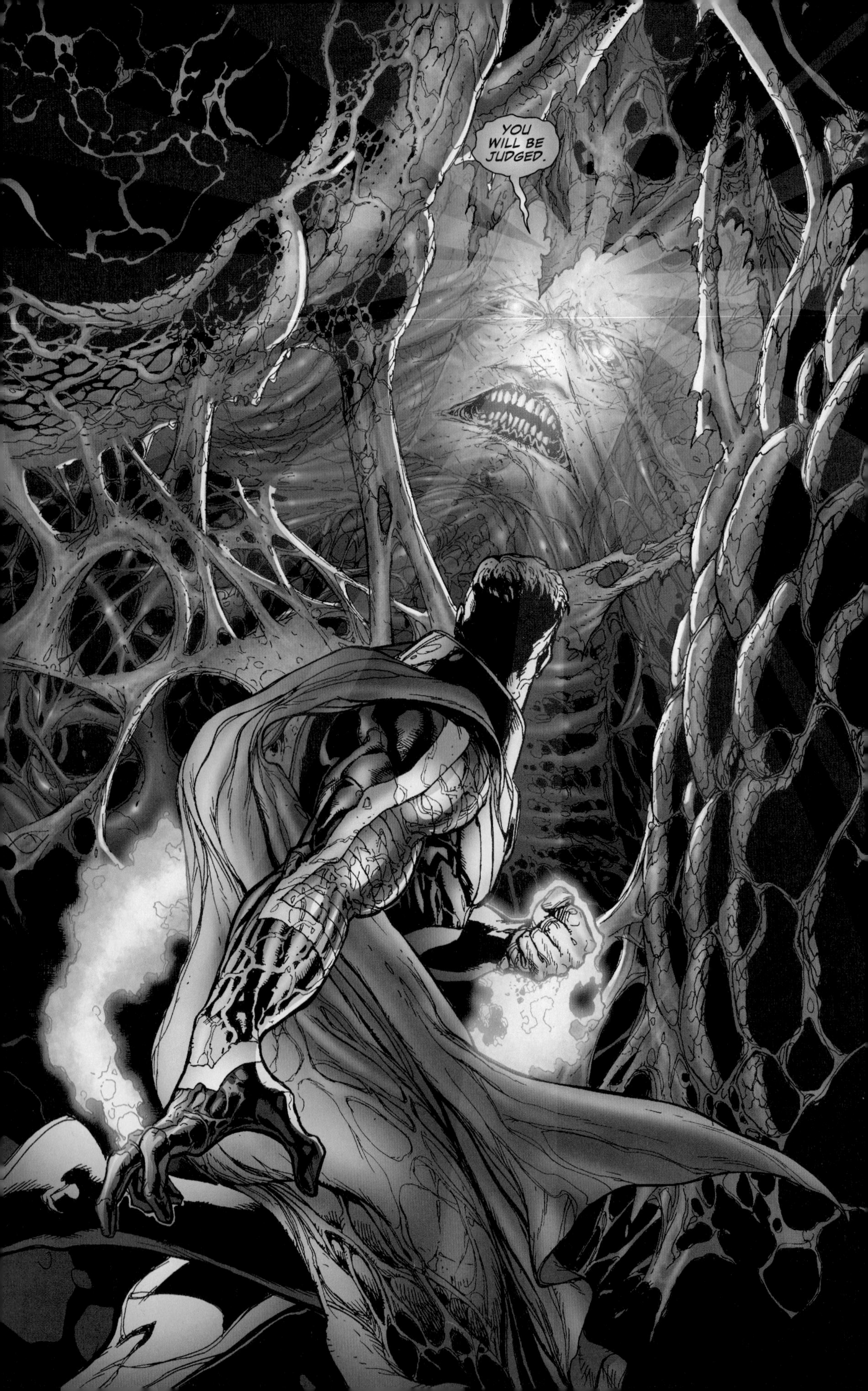
YOU WILL BE JUDGED.

LOOK AT YOU.

GOD'S WEAPON OF BLOODY JUSTICE, CHAINED AND IMPRISONED BY THE *MUTATED* AND *MALIGNED* CARCASS OF YOUR HUMAN SHELTER.

YES.

WE BOTH KNOW WHAT IT'S LIKE TO FIND THAT *SPECIAL SOMEBODY*, DON'T WE? HAL JORDAN. CRISPUS ALLEN.

AND CRISPUS ALLEN IS THE CAUSE OF THIS ALL. HIS BODY WAS TAKEN BY...

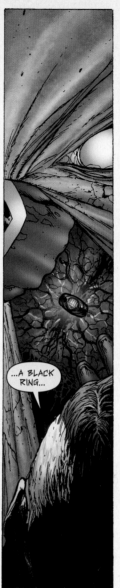

...A BLACK RING...

...THE *REAL* RING. JUST AS YOU ARE THE TRUE SPECTRE UNDERNEATH THIS CORPSE, SO THIS BLACK RING IS THE TRUE SOURCE OF YOUR IMPRISONMENT.

AARRGHH!

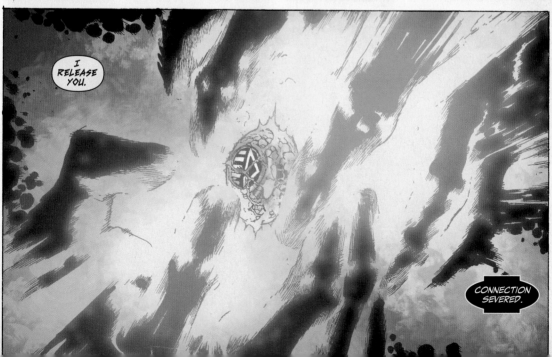

I RELEASE YOU.

CONNECTION SEVERED.

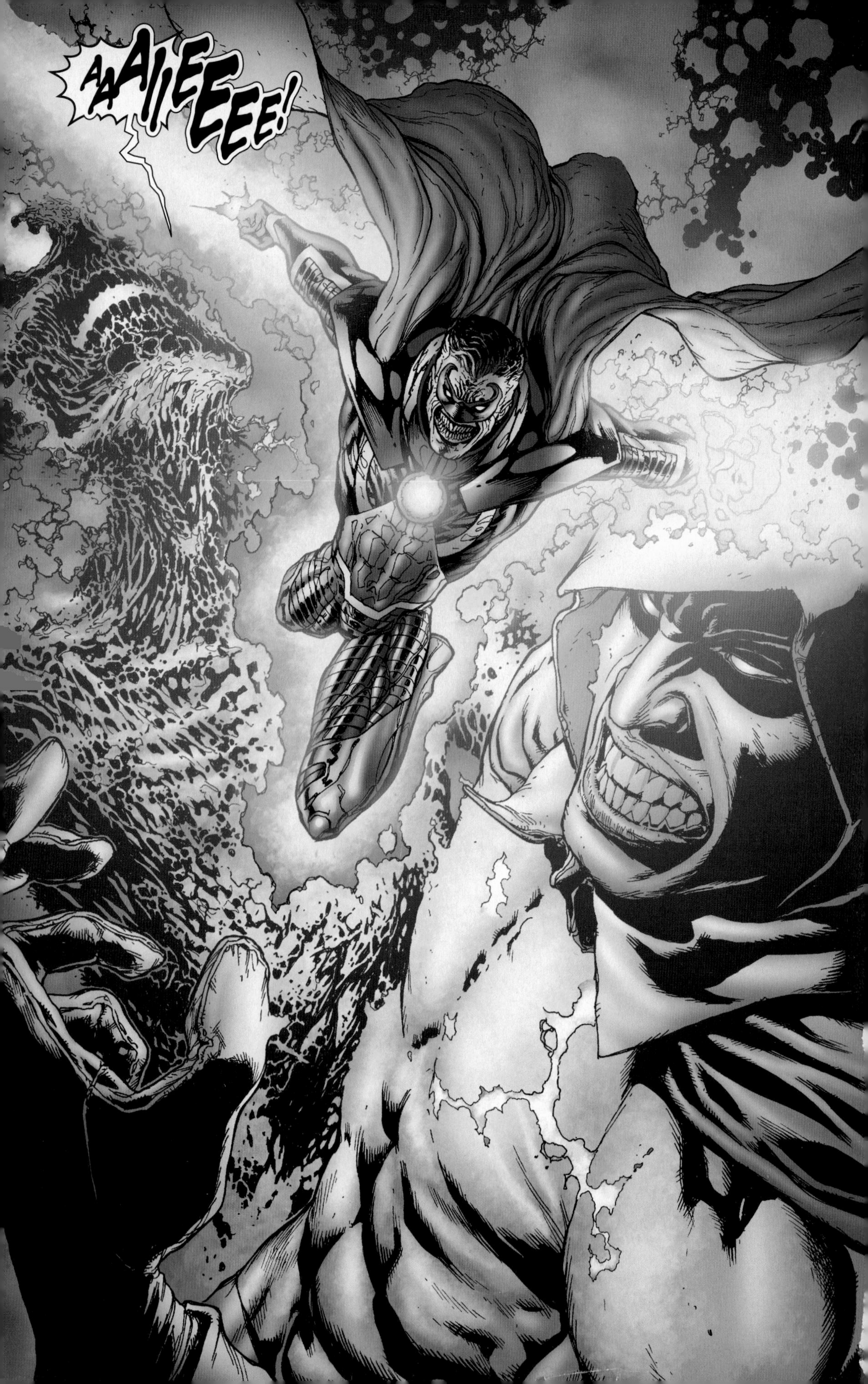
AAAAIIEEEEE!

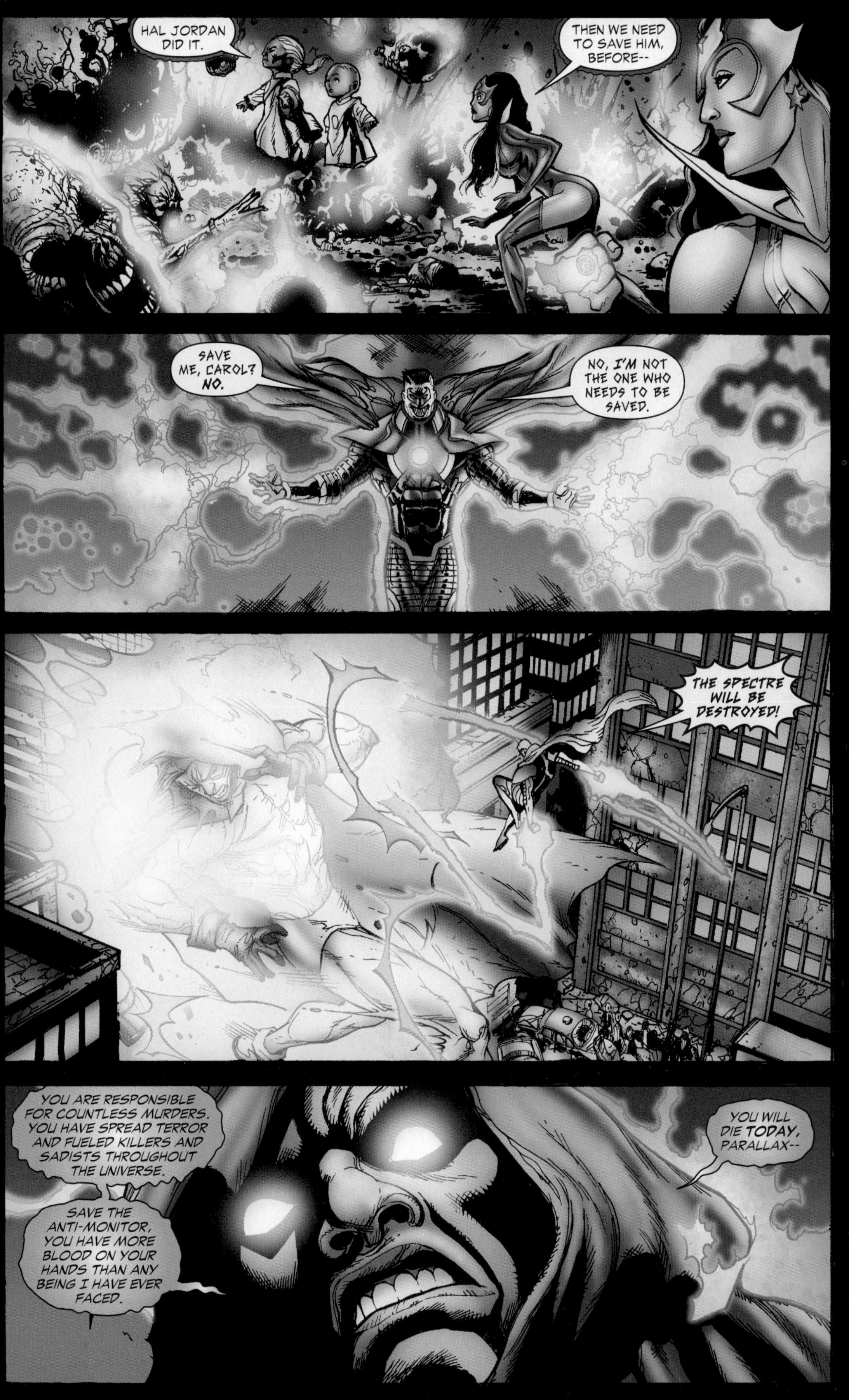
HAL JORDAN DID IT.
THEN WE NEED TO SAVE HIM, BEFORE--
SAVE ME, CAROL? NO.
NO, I'M NOT THE ONE WHO NEEDS TO BE SAVED.
THE SPECTRE WILL BE DESTROYED!
YOU ARE RESPONSIBLE FOR COUNTLESS MURDERS. YOU HAVE SPREAD TERROR AND FUELED KILLERS AND SADISTS THROUGHOUT THE UNIVERSE.
SAVE THE ANTI-MONITOR, YOU HAVE MORE BLOOD ON YOUR HANDS THAN ANY BEING I HAVE EVER FACED.
YOU WILL DIE TODAY, PARALLAX--

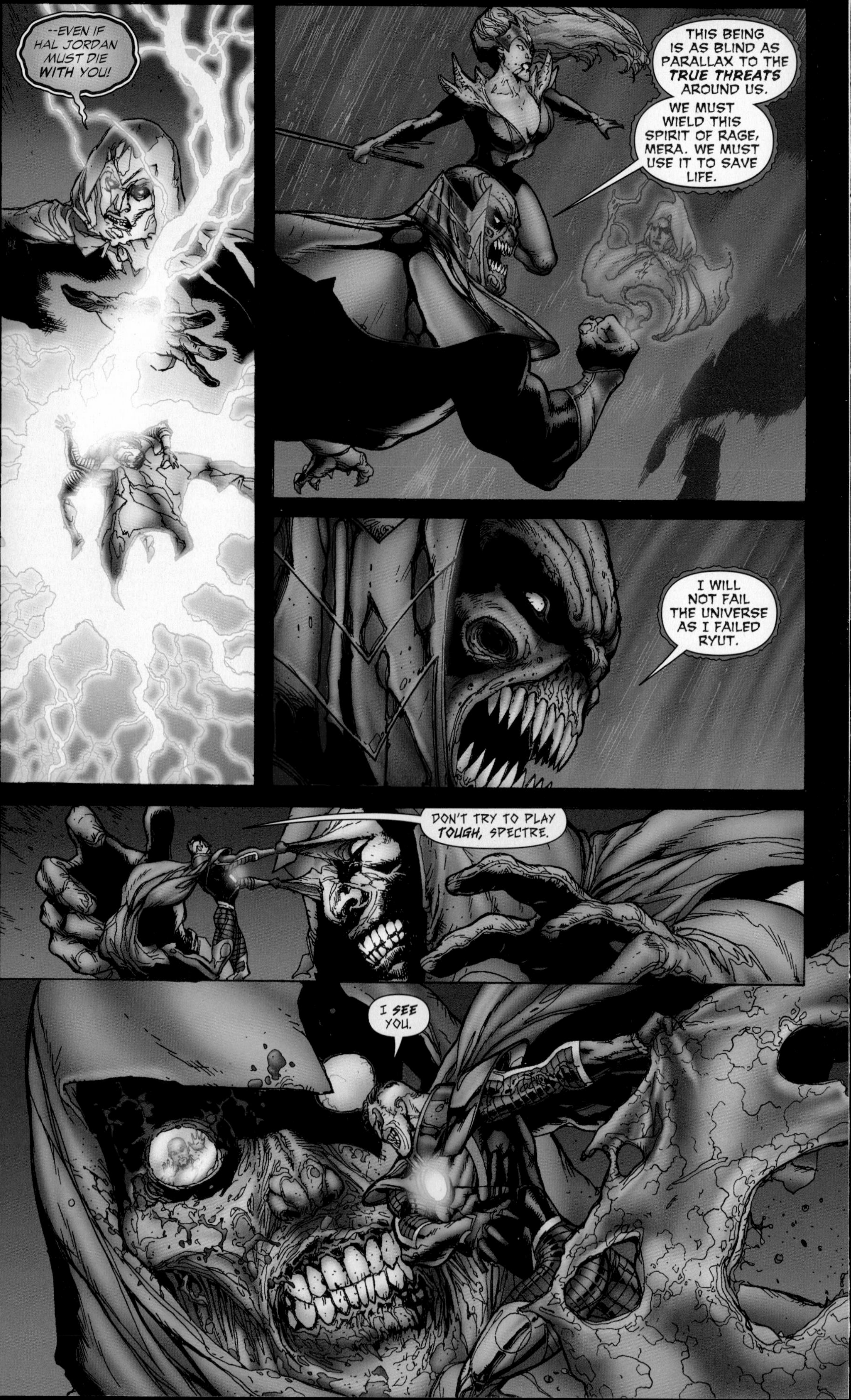
--EVEN IF HAL JORDAN MUST DIE WITH YOU!
THIS BEING IS AS BLIND AS PARALLAX TO THE TRUE THREATS AROUND US.
WE MUST WIELD THIS SPIRIT OF RAGE, MERA. WE MUST USE IT TO SAVE LIFE.
I WILL NOT FAIL THE UNIVERSE AS I FAILED RYUT.
DON'T TRY TO PLAY TOUGH, SPECTRE.
I SEE YOU.

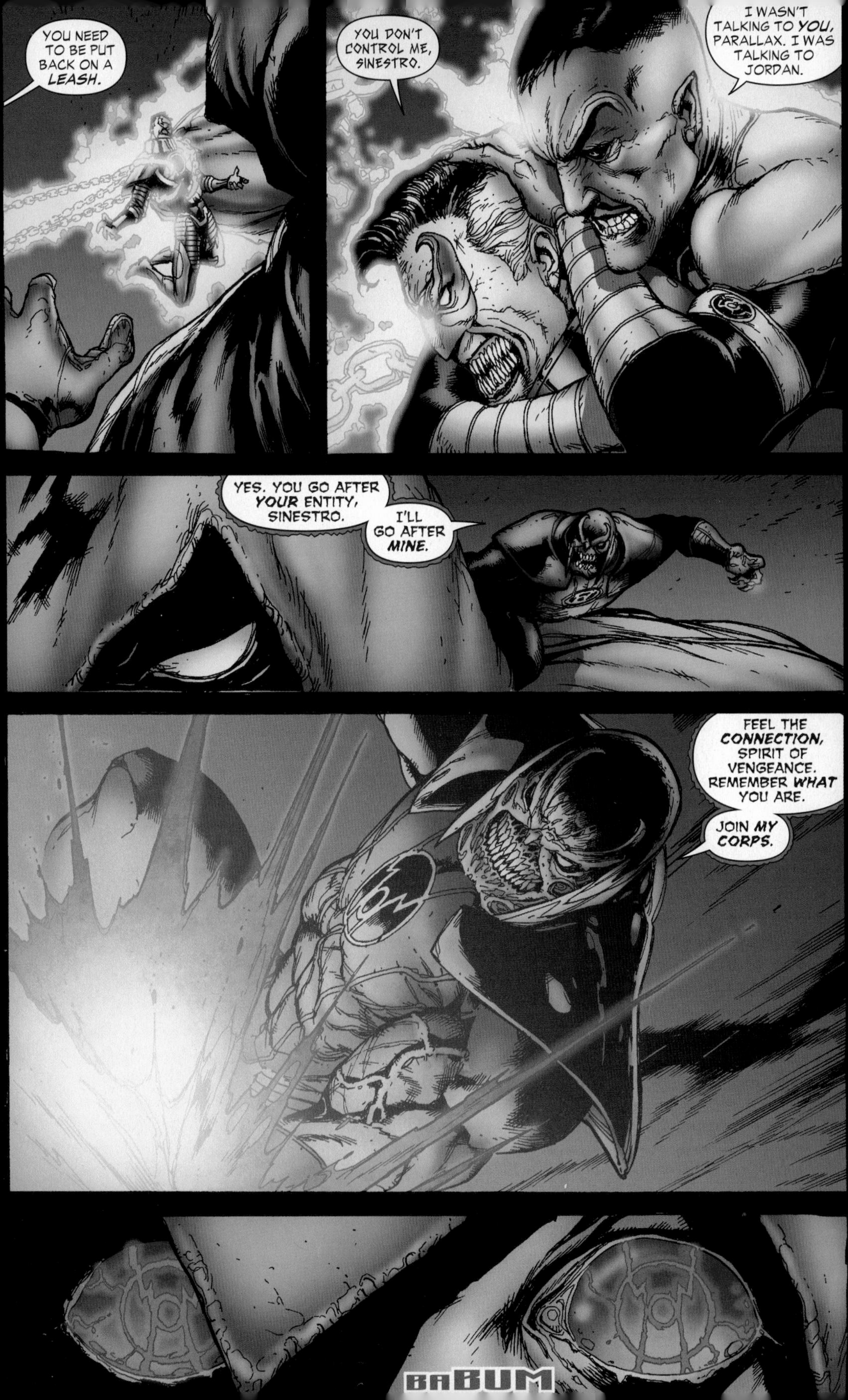
YOU NEED TO BE PUT BACK ON A LEASH.
YOU DON'T CONTROL ME, SINESTRO.
I WASN'T TALKING TO YOU, PARALLAX. I WAS TALKING TO JORDAN.
YES. YOU GO AFTER YOUR ENTITY, SINESTRO.
I'LL GO AFTER MINE.
FEEL THE CONNECTION, SPIRIT OF VENGEANCE. REMEMBER WHAT YOU ARE.
JOIN MY CORPS.
BABUM

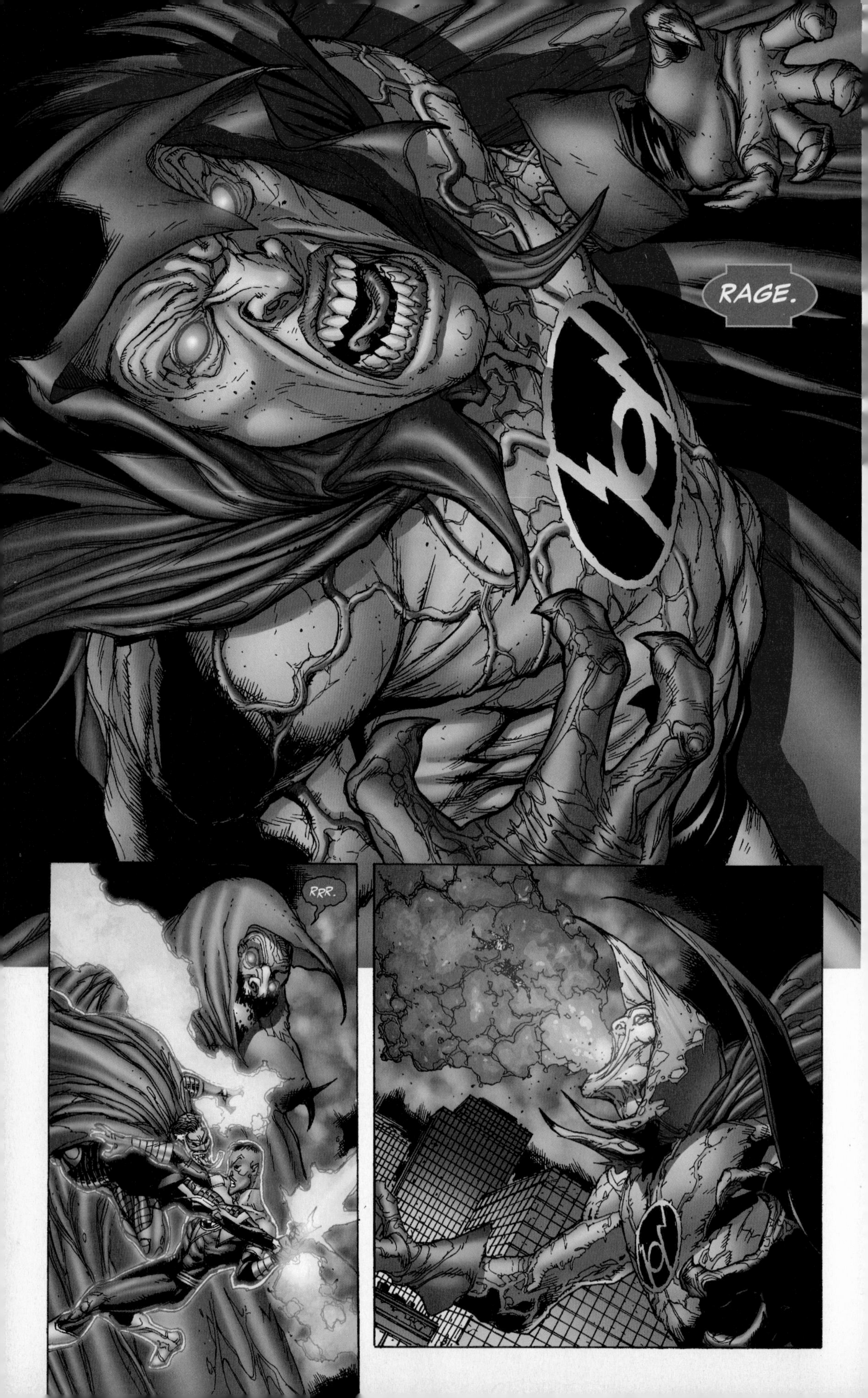
RAGE.
RRR.

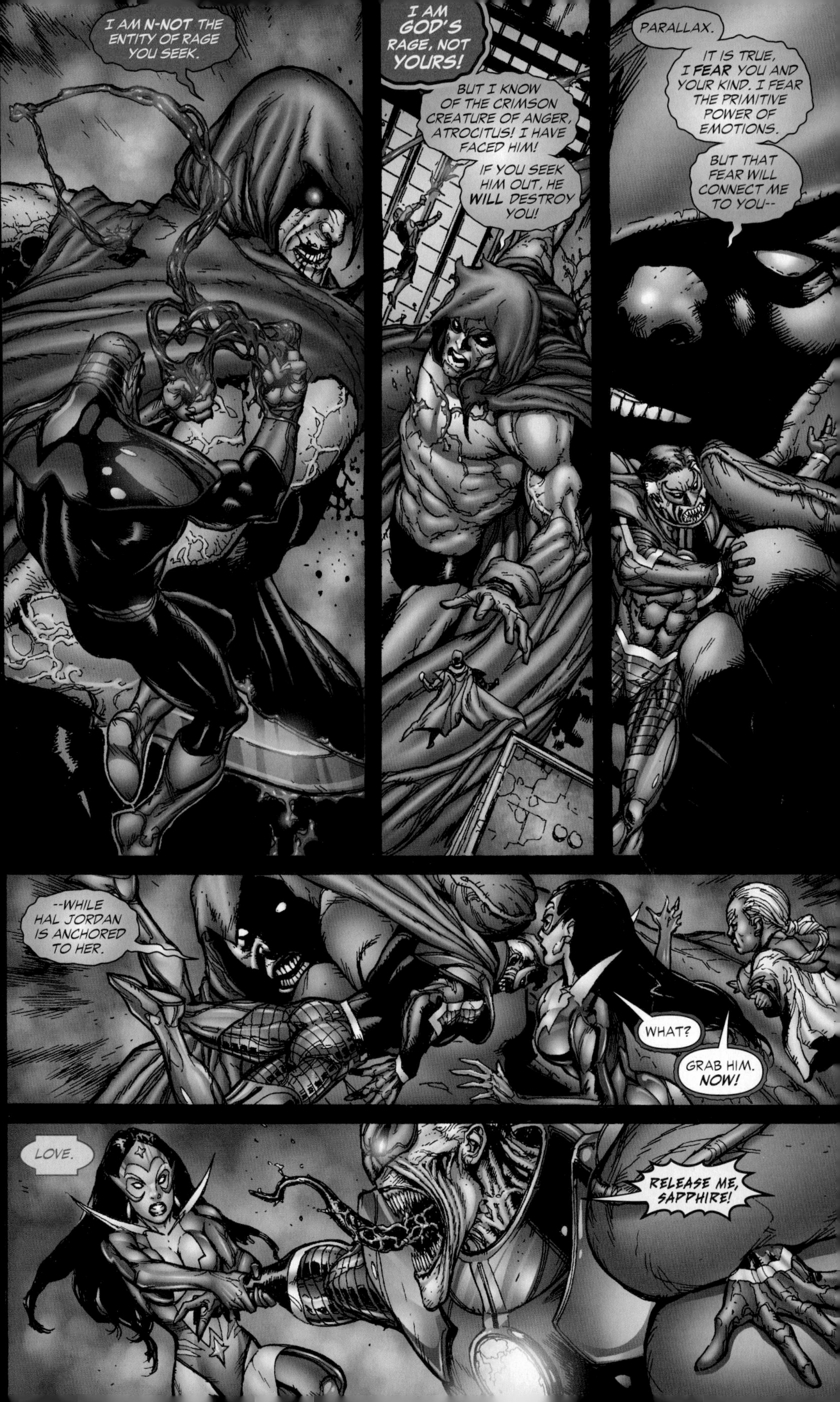
I AM N-NOT THE ENTITY OF RAGE YOU SEEK.
I AM GOD'S RAGE, NOT YOURS!
BUT I KNOW OF THE CRIMSON CREATURE OF ANGER, ATROCITUS! I HAVE FACED HIM!
IF YOU SEEK HIM OUT, HE WILL DESTROY YOU!
PARALLAX.
IT IS TRUE, I FEAR YOU AND YOUR KIND. I FEAR THE PRIMITIVE POWER OF EMOTIONS.
BUT THAT FEAR WILL CONNECT ME TO YOU--
--WHILE HAL JORDAN IS ANCHORED TO HER.
WHAT?
GRAB HIM. NOW!
LOVE.
RELEASE ME, SAPPHIRE!

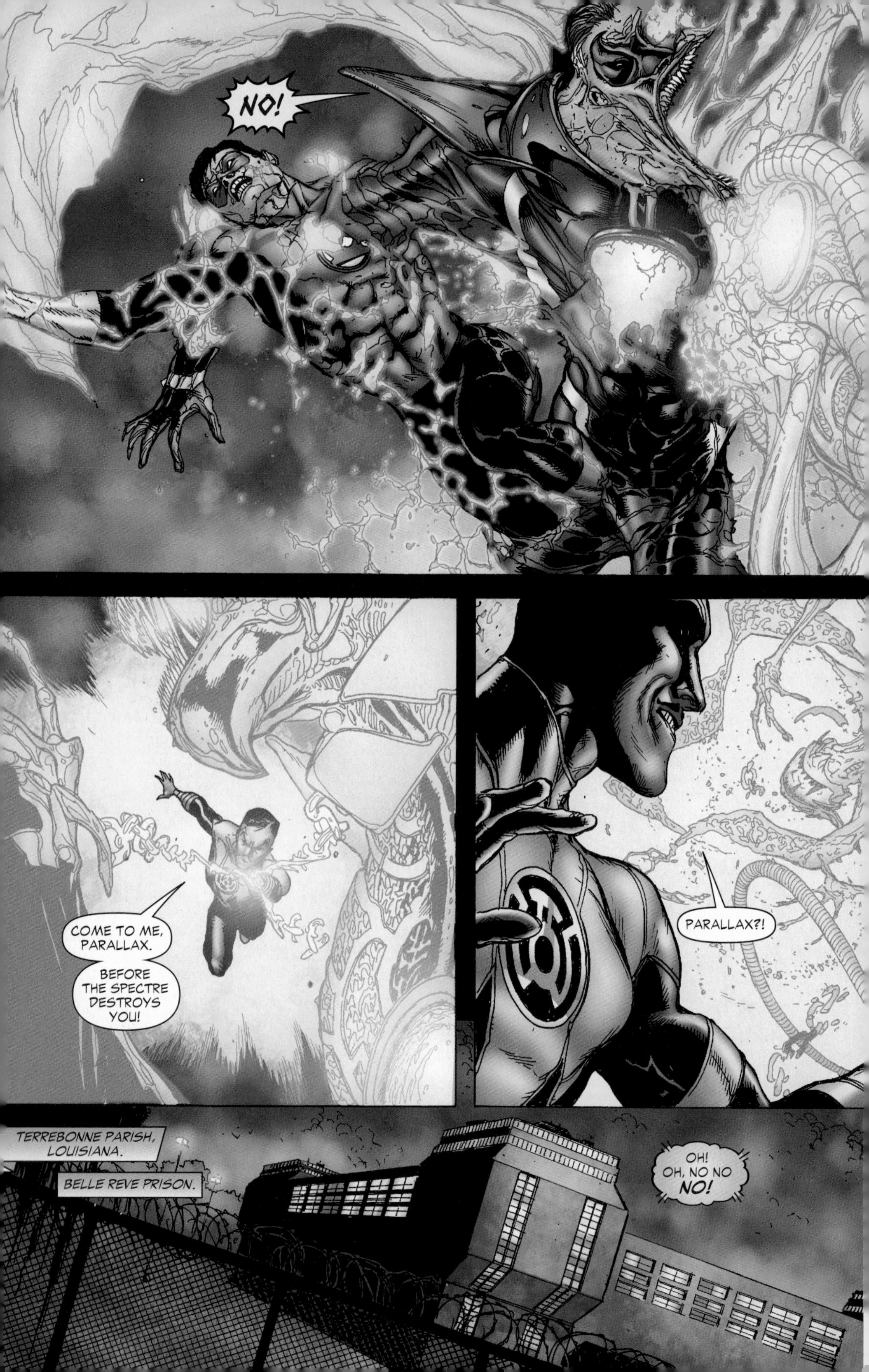
NO!
COME TO ME, PARALLAX.
BEFORE THE SPECTRE DESTROYS YOU!
PARALLAX?!
TERREBONNE PARISH, LOUISIANA.
BELLE REVE PRISON.
OH! OH, NO NO NO!

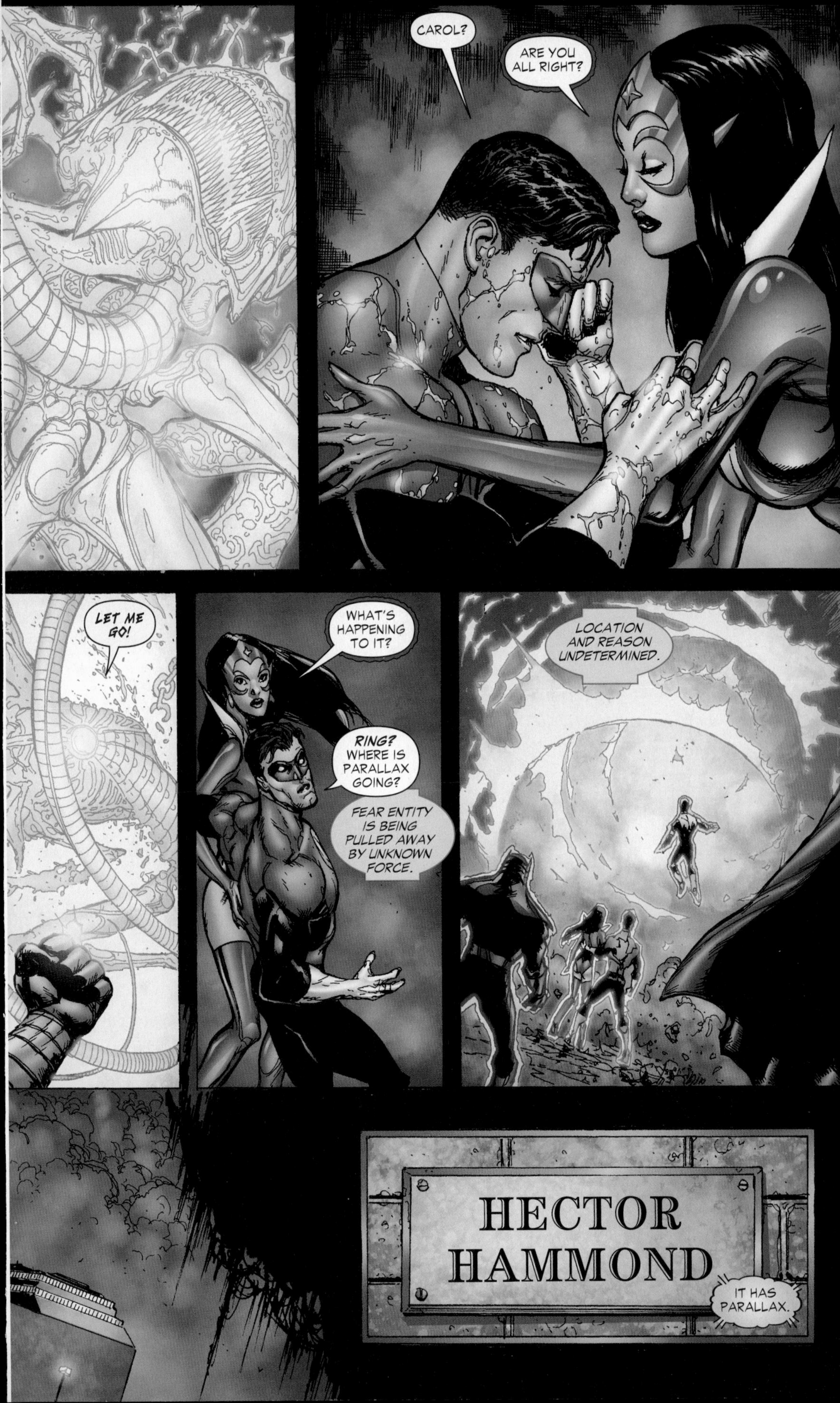
CAROL?
ARE YOU ALL RIGHT?
LET ME GO!
WHAT'S HAPPENING TO IT?
RING? WHERE IS PARALLAX GOING?
FEAR ENTITY IS BEING PULLED AWAY BY UNKNOWN FORCE.
LOCATION AND REASON UNDETERMINED.
HECTOR HAMMOND
IT HAS PARALLAX.

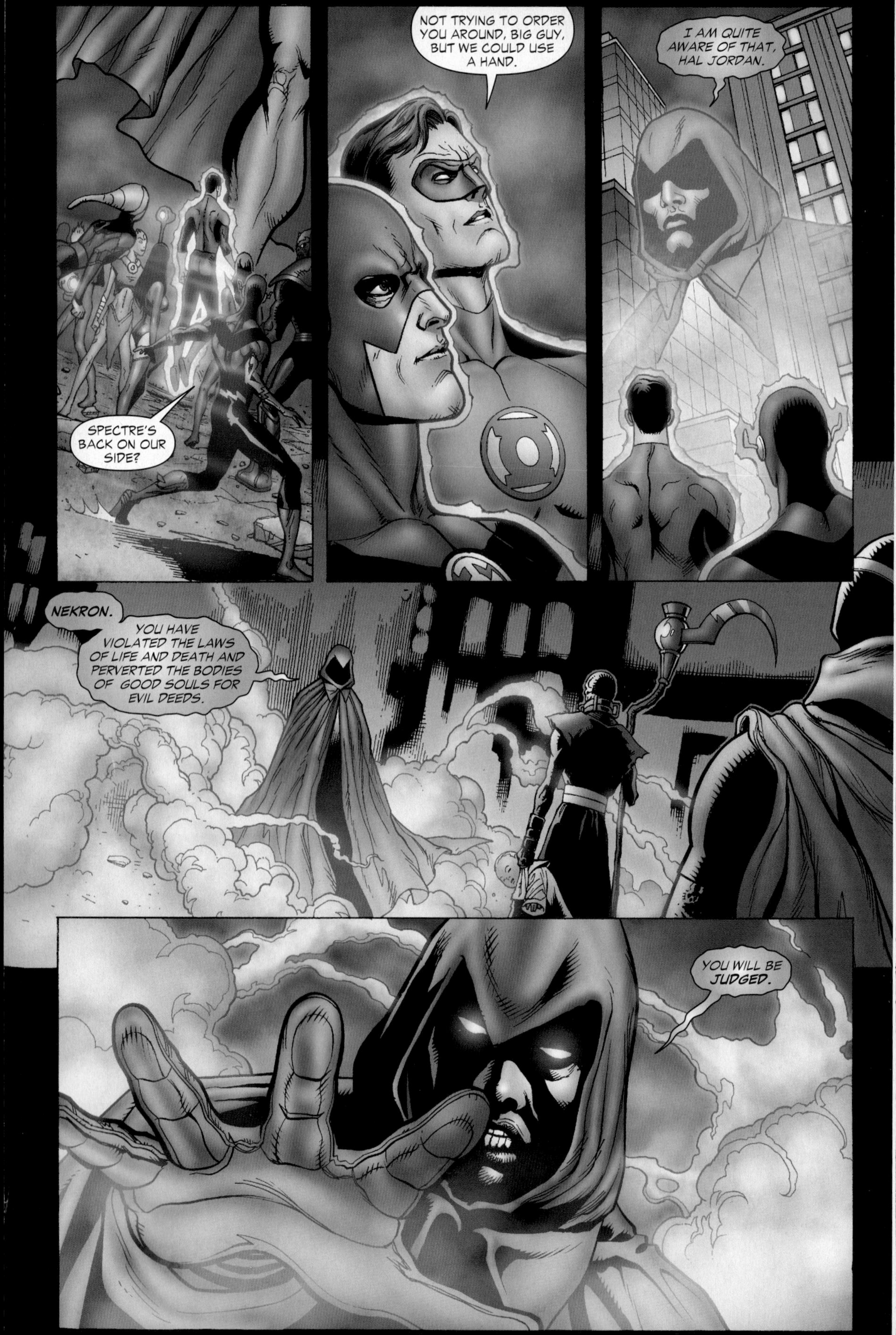
SPECTRE'S BACK ON OUR SIDE?
NOT TRYING TO ORDER YOU AROUND, BIG GUY, BUT WE COULD USE A HAND.
I AM QUITE AWARE OF THAT, HAL JORDAN.
NEKRON.
YOU HAVE VIOLATED THE LAWS OF LIFE AND DEATH AND PERVERTED THE BODIES OF GOOD SOULS FOR EVIL DEEDS.
YOU WILL BE JUDGED.

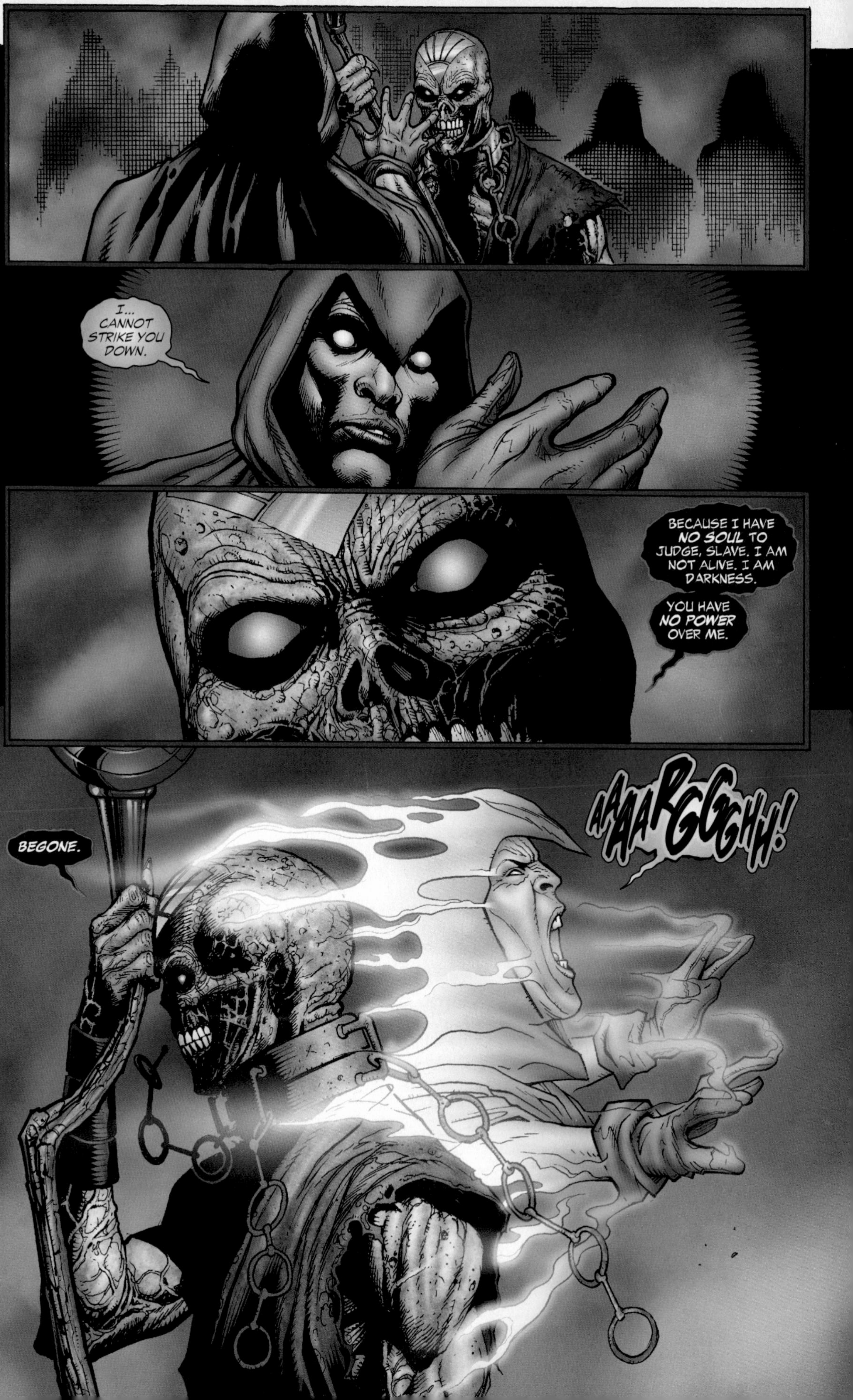
I... CANNOT STRIKE YOU DOWN.
BECAUSE I HAVE NO SOUL TO JUDGE, SLAVE. I AM NOT ALIVE. I AM DARKNESS.
YOU HAVE NO POWER OVER ME.
BEGONE.
AAAARGGGHH!

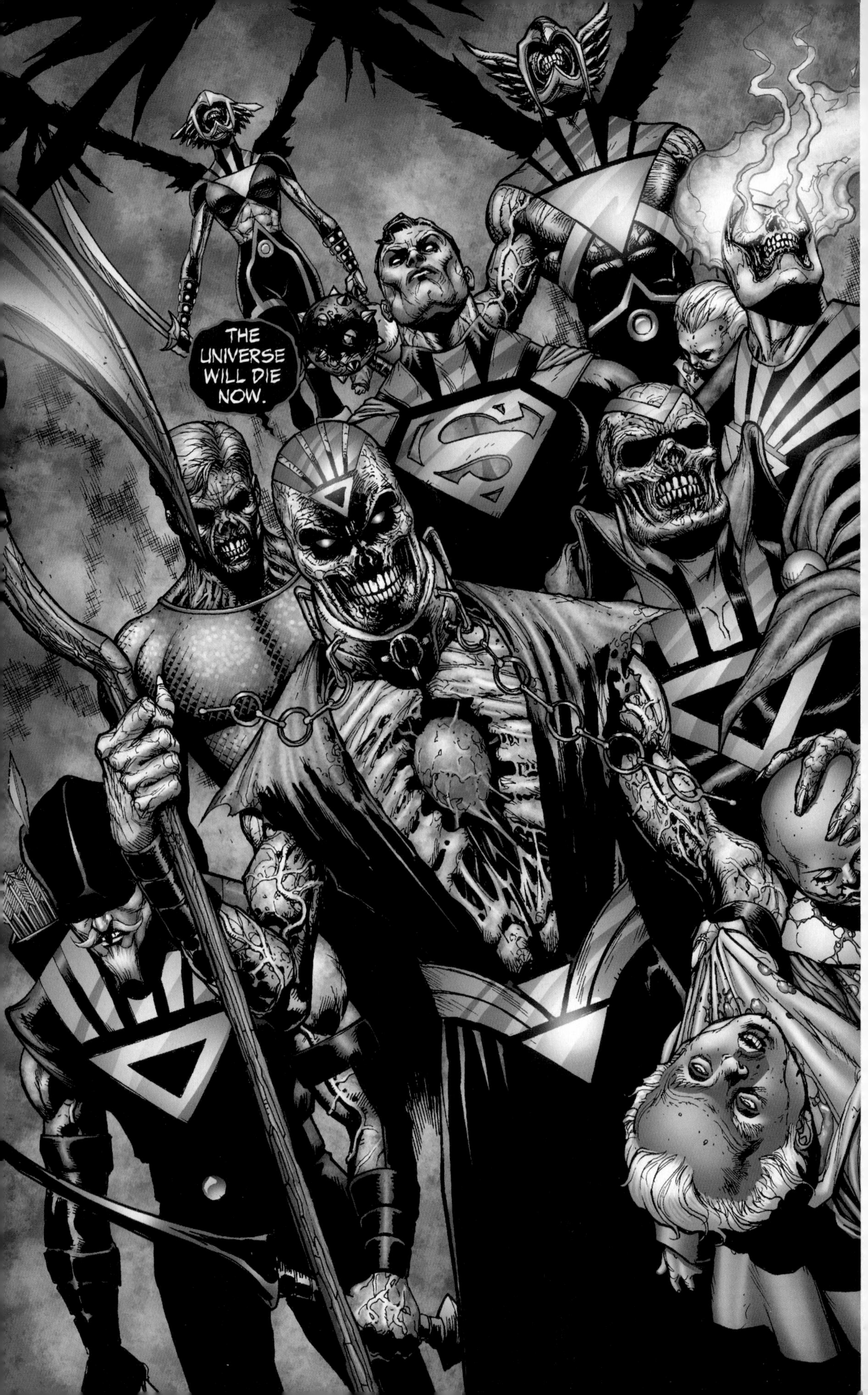
THE UNIVERSE WILL DIE NOW.

GREEN LANTERN 52
Cover by Doug Mahnke and Christian Alamy with Randy Mayor

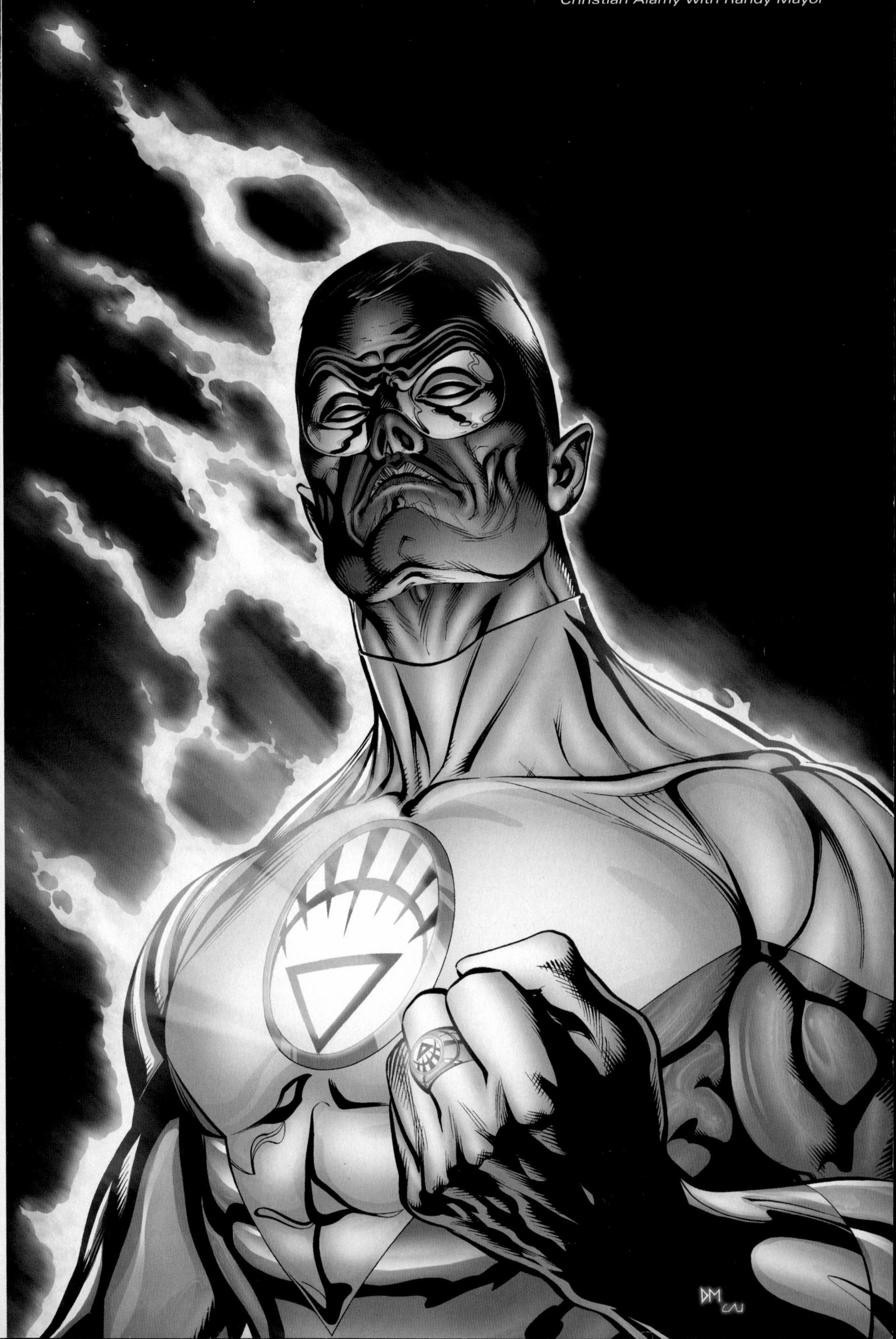

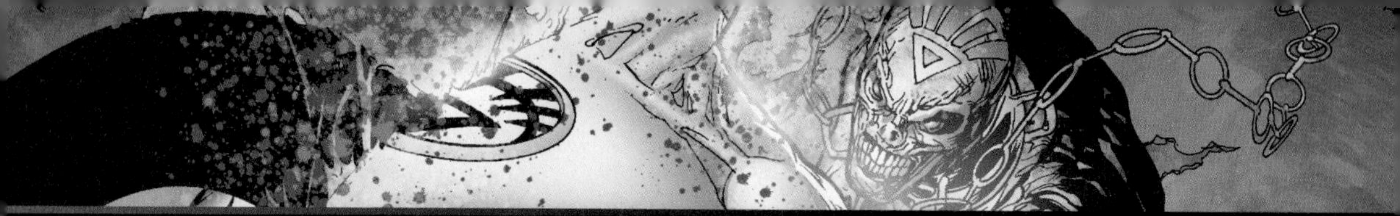

Spilling the blood of one of the Guardians allows Nekron to reveal Earth's oldest and greatest secret.

Buried within our planet is the Entity, the living light that triggered our universe into existence.

Enraged by the lies perpetuated by the self-proclaimed Guardians of the Universe, Sinestro takes matters into his own hands, claiming the white light for himself. May the universe beware his power...

LIFE BLOOD

DOUG MAHNKE
PENCILS

CHRISTIAN ALAMY
DOUG MAHNKE
REBECCA BUCHMAN
KEITH CHAMPAGNE
INKS

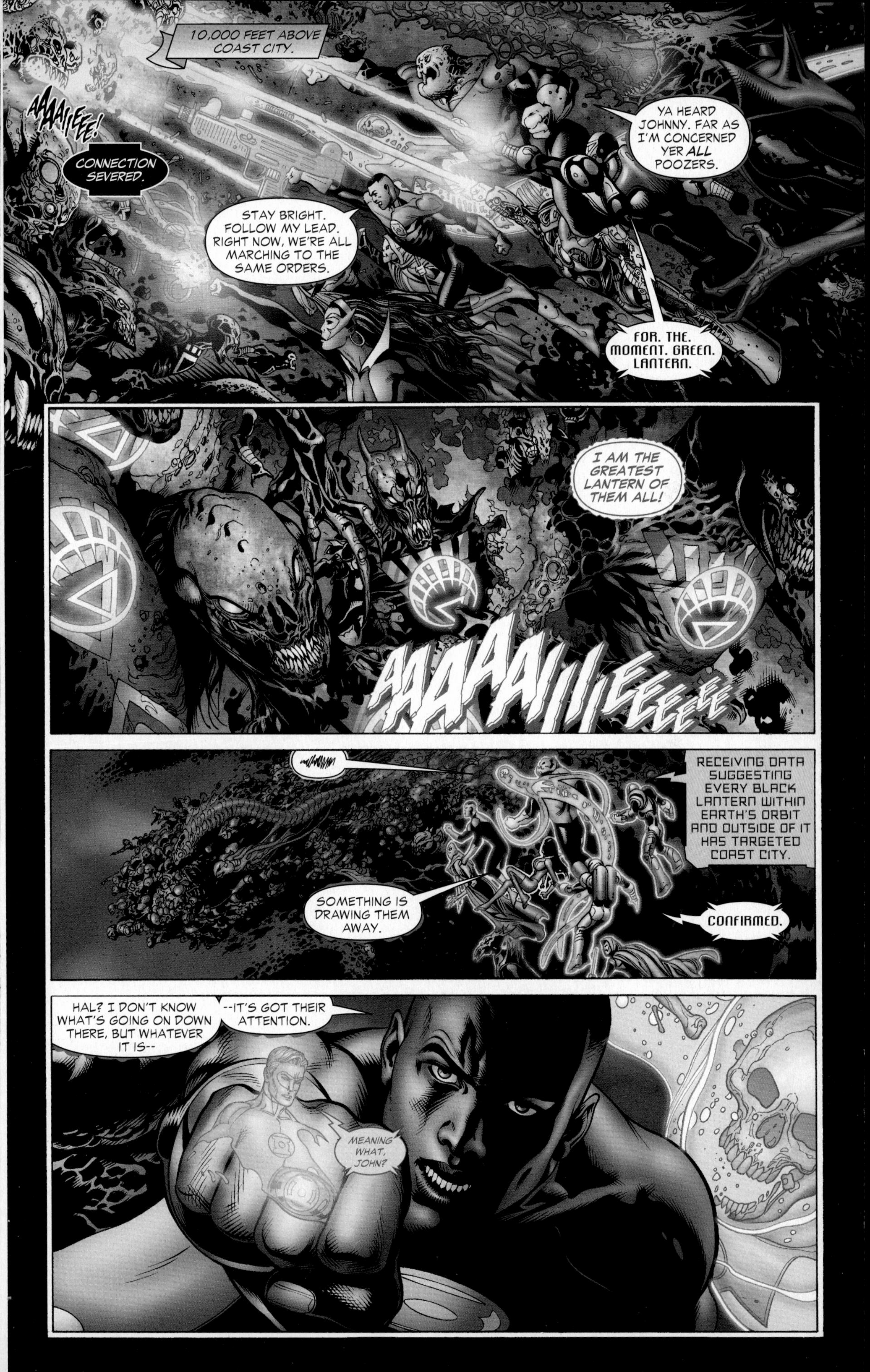
10,000 FEET ABOVE COAST CITY.
AAAAIIEEE!
CONNECTION SEVERED.
YA HEARD JOHNNY. FAR AS I'M CONCERNED YER ALL POOZERS.
STAY BRIGHT. FOLLOW MY LEAD. RIGHT NOW, WE'RE ALL MARCHING TO THE SAME ORDERS.
FOR. THE. MOMENT. GREEN. LANTERN.
I AM THE GREATEST LANTERN OF THEM ALL!
AAAAAIIIIEEEEEE
RECEIVING DATA SUGGESTING EVERY BLACK LANTERN WITHIN EARTH'S ORBIT AND OUTSIDE OF IT HAS TARGETED COAST CITY.
SOMETHING IS DRAWING THEM AWAY.
CONFIRMED.
HAL? I DON'T KNOW WHAT'S GOING ON DOWN THERE, BUT WHATEVER IT IS--
--IT'S GOT THEIR ATTENTION.
MEANING WHAT, JOHN?

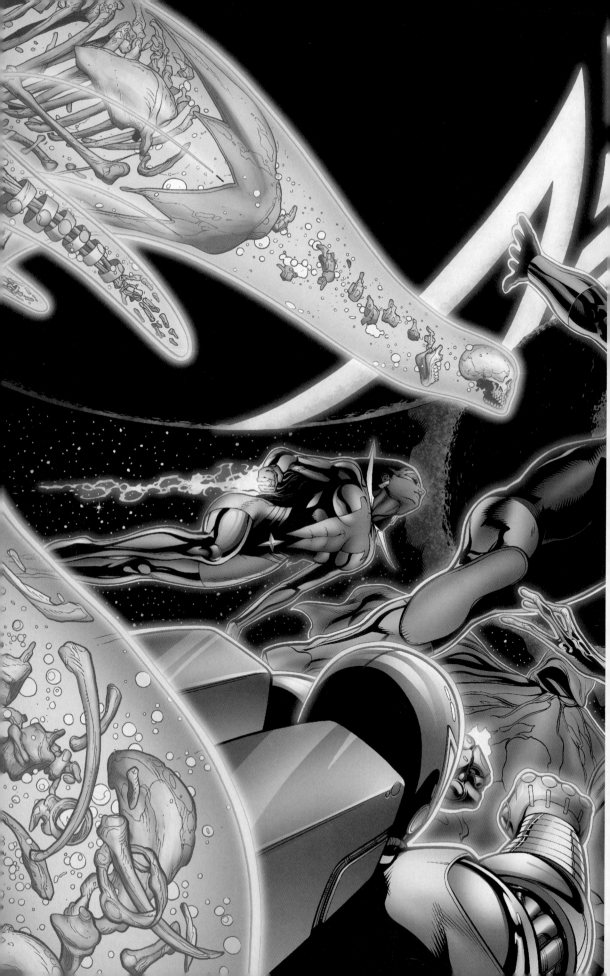

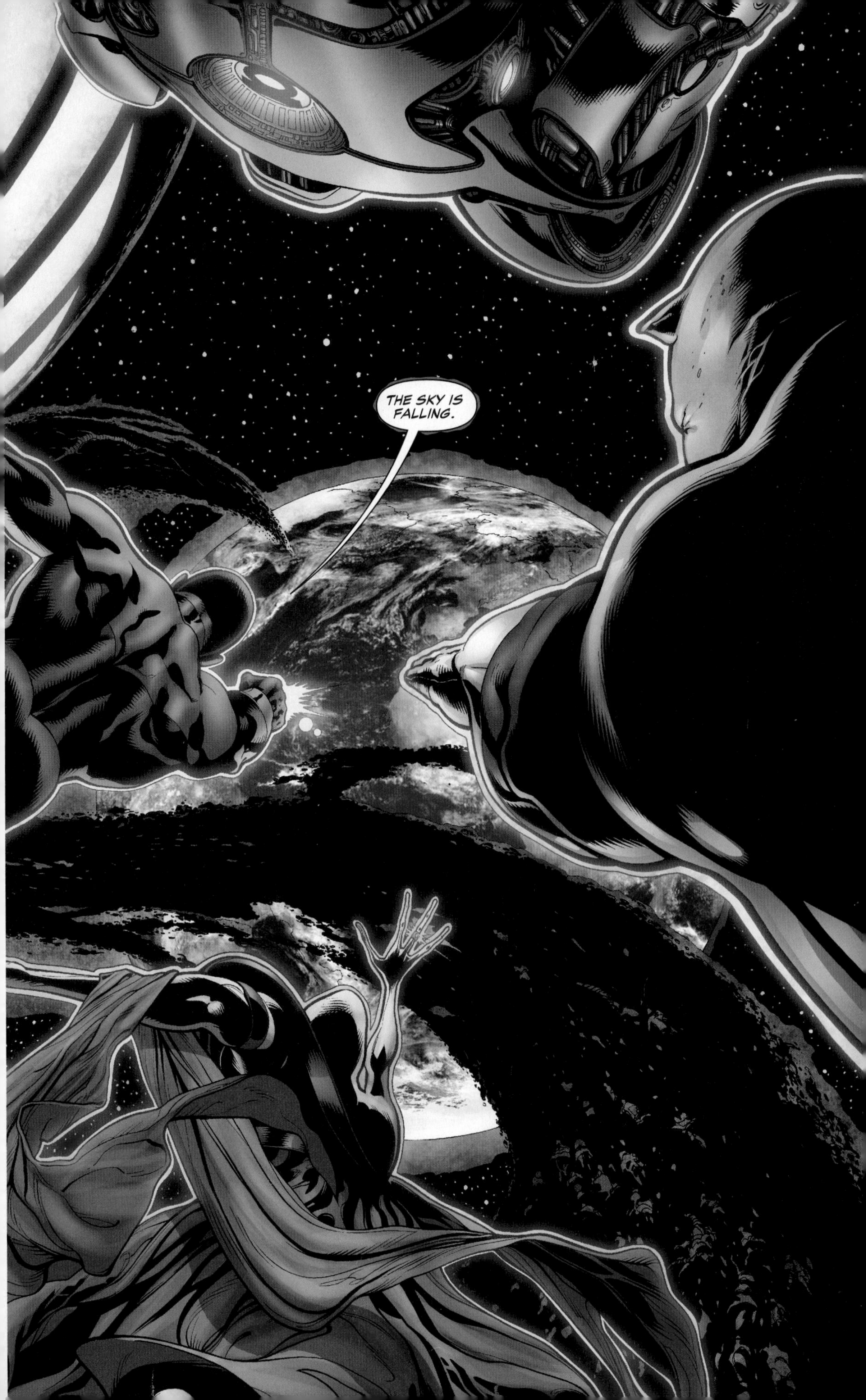
THE SKY IS FALLING.

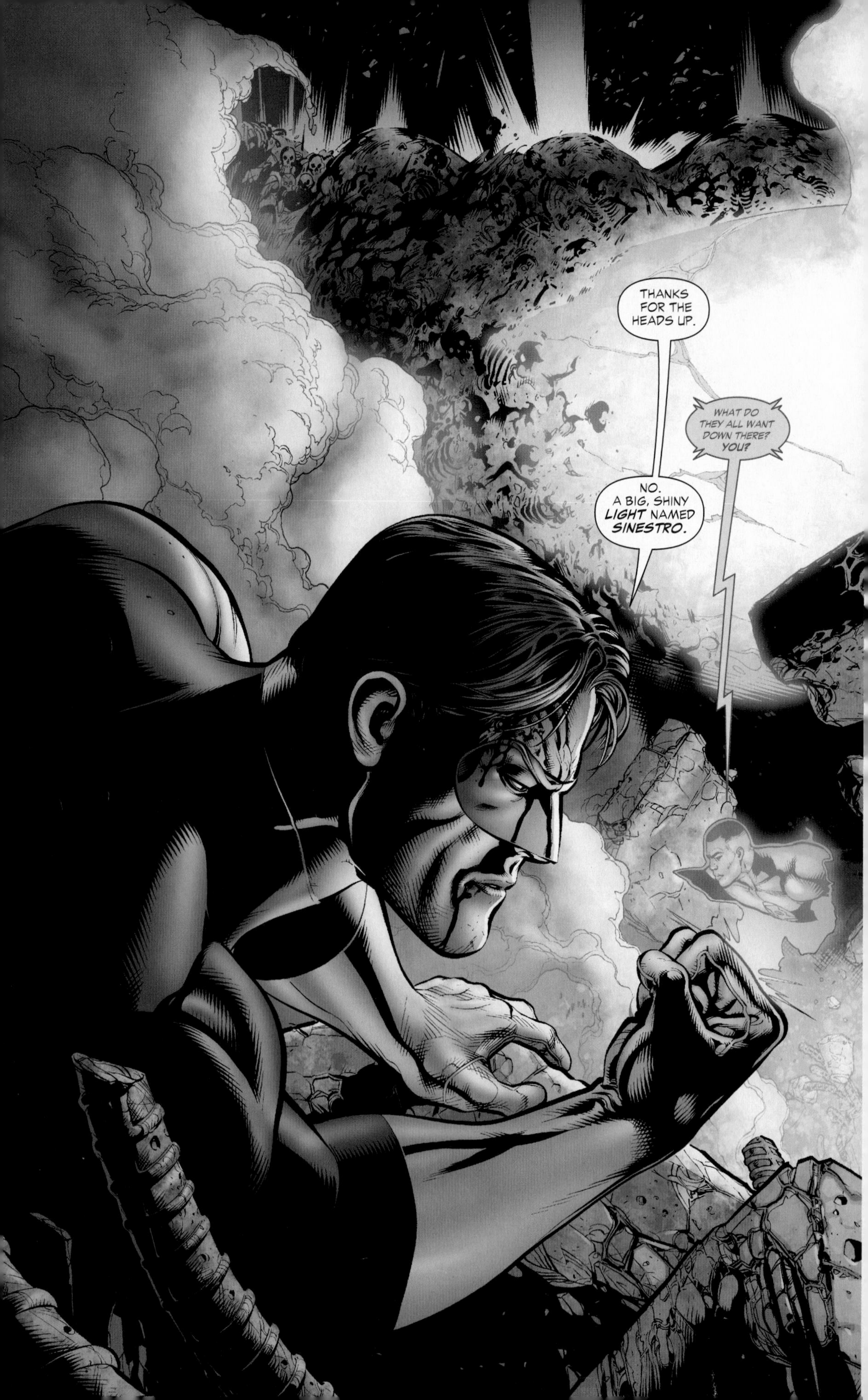
THANKS FOR THE HEADS UP.
WHAT DO THEY ALL WANT DOWN THERE? YOU?
NO. A BIG, SHINY LIGHT NAMED SINESTRO.

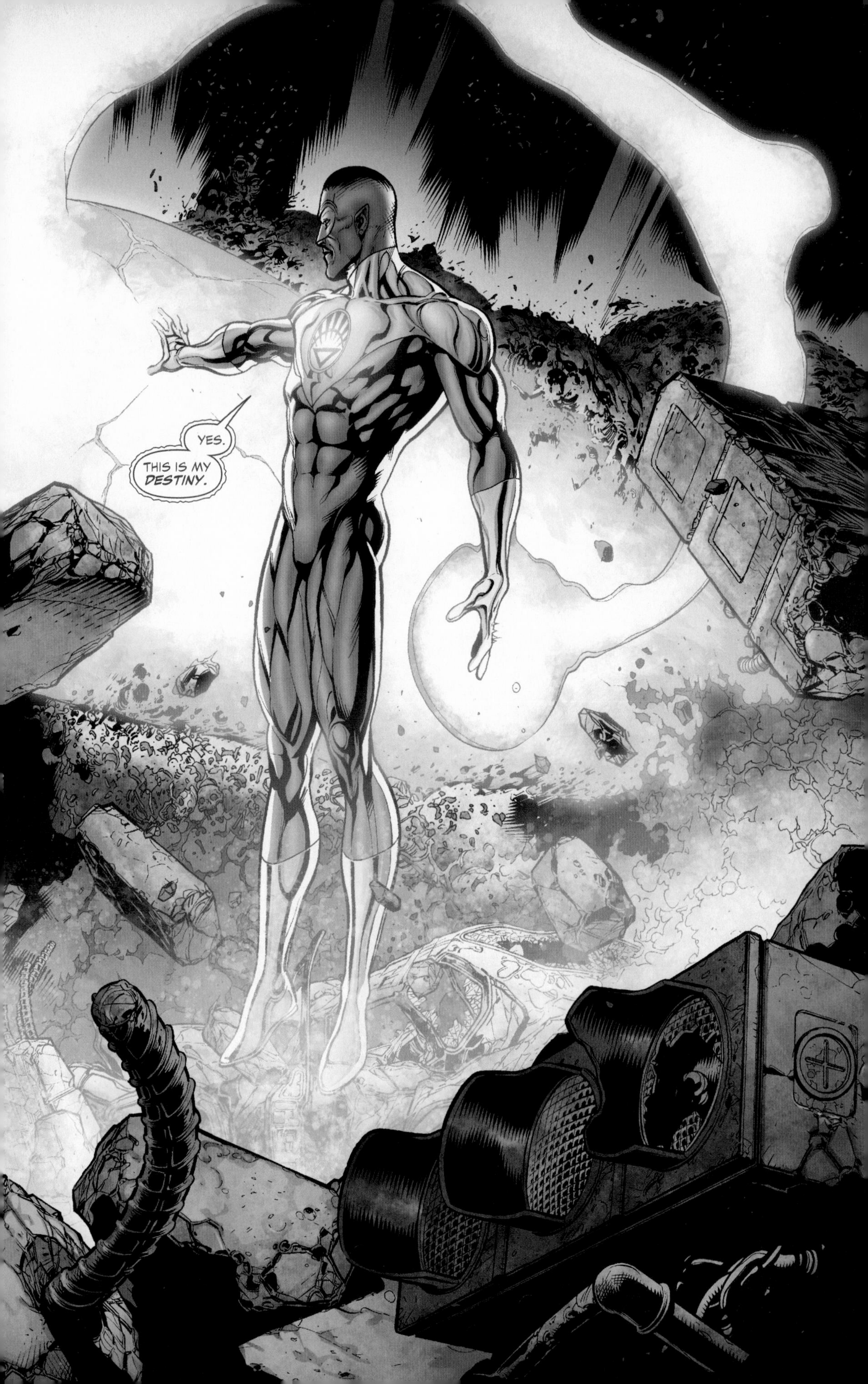
YES.
THIS IS MY *DESTINY*.

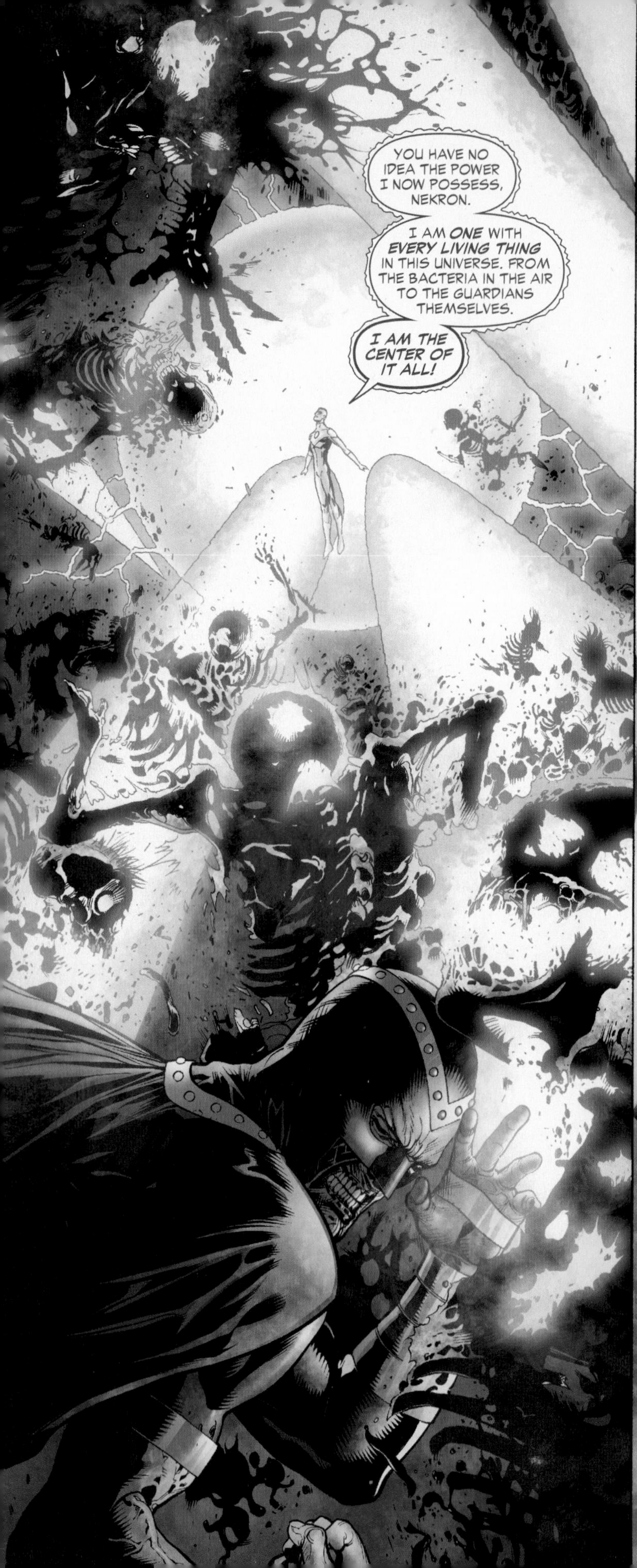
YOU HAVE NO IDEA THE POWER I NOW POSSESS, NEKRON.
I AM *ONE* WITH *EVERY LIVING THING* IN THIS UNIVERSE. FROM THE BACTERIA IN THE AIR TO THE GUARDIANS THEMSELVES.
I AM THE CENTER OF IT ALL!

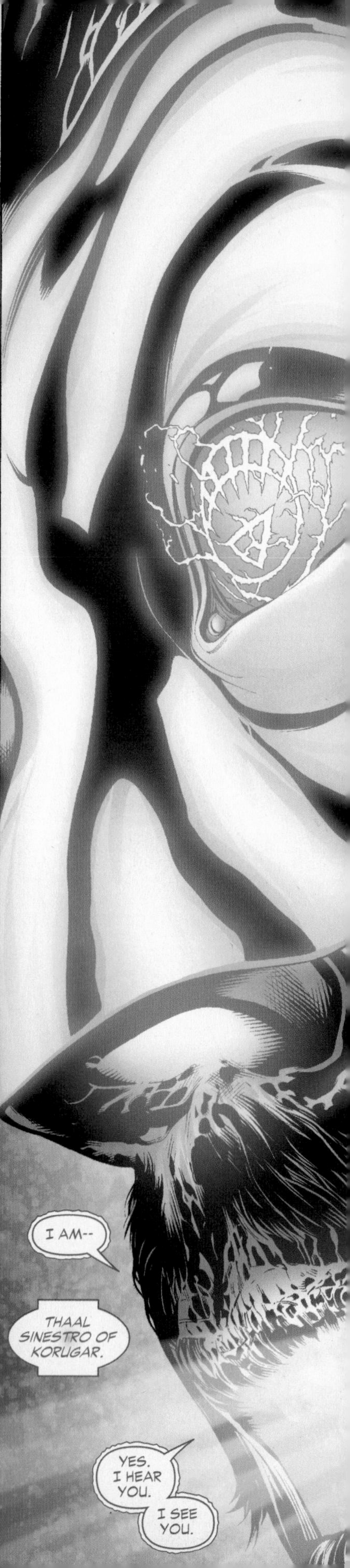
I AM--
THAAL SINESTRO OF KORUGAR.
YES. I HEAR YOU.
I SEE YOU.

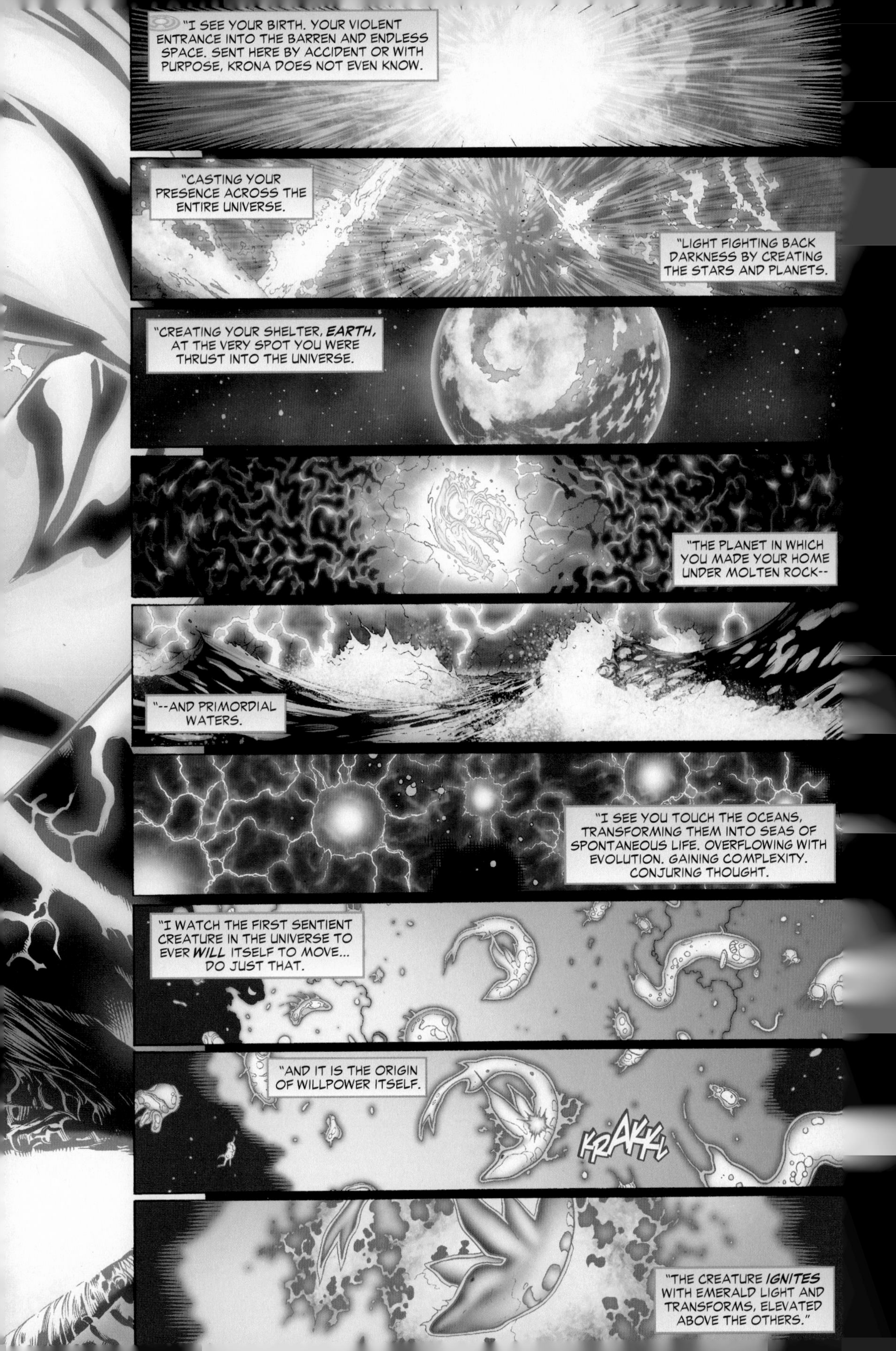
"I SEE YOUR BIRTH. YOUR VIOLENT ENTRANCE INTO THE BARREN AND ENDLESS SPACE. SENT HERE BY ACCIDENT OR WITH PURPOSE, KRONA DOES NOT EVEN KNOW.
"CASTING YOUR PRESENCE ACROSS THE ENTIRE UNIVERSE.
"LIGHT FIGHTING BACK DARKNESS BY CREATING THE STARS AND PLANETS.
"CREATING YOUR SHELTER, EARTH, AT THE VERY SPOT YOU WERE THRUST INTO THE UNIVERSE.
"THE PLANET IN WHICH YOU MADE YOUR HOME UNDER MOLTEN ROCK--
"--AND PRIMORDIAL WATERS.
"I SEE YOU TOUCH THE OCEANS, TRANSFORMING THEM INTO SEAS OF SPONTANEOUS LIFE. OVERFLOWING WITH EVOLUTION. GAINING COMPLEXITY. CONJURING THOUGHT.
"I WATCH THE FIRST SENTIENT CREATURE IN THE UNIVERSE TO EVER WILL ITSELF TO MOVE... DO JUST THAT.
"AND IT IS THE ORIGIN OF WILLPOWER ITSELF.
KRAKKL
"THE CREATURE IGNITES WITH EMERALD LIGHT AND TRANSFORMS, ELEVATED ABOVE THE OTHERS."

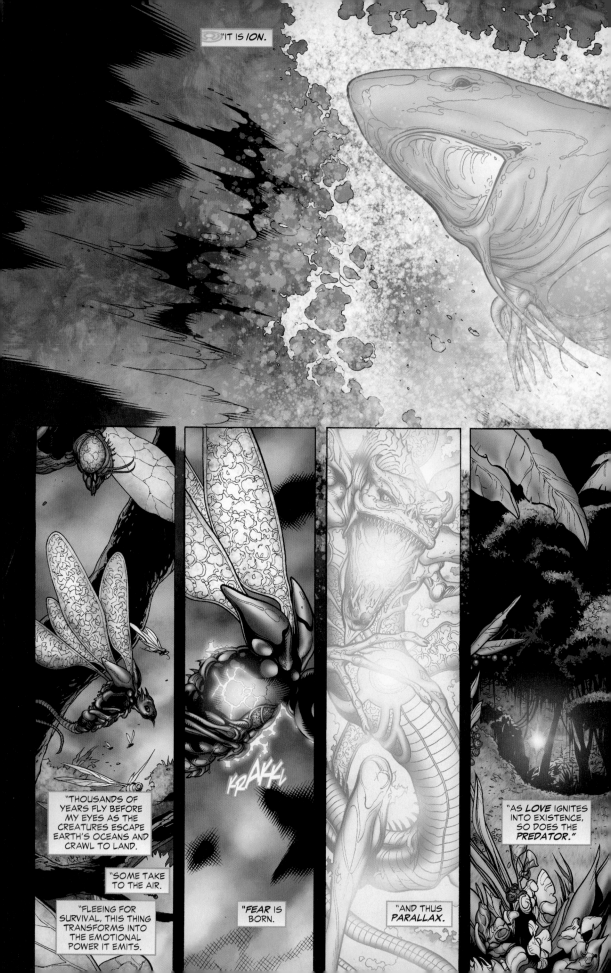

"IT IS *ION*.

"THOUSANDS OF YEARS FLY BEFORE MY EYES AS THE CREATURES ESCAPE EARTH'S OCEANS AND CRAWL TO LAND.

"SOME TAKE TO THE AIR.

"FLEEING FOR SURVIVAL, THIS THING TRANSFORMS INTO THE EMOTIONAL POWER IT EMITS.

KRAKK

"*FEAR* IS BORN.

"AND THUS *PARALLAX*.

"AS *LOVE* IGNITES INTO EXISTENCE, SO DOES THE *PREDATOR*."

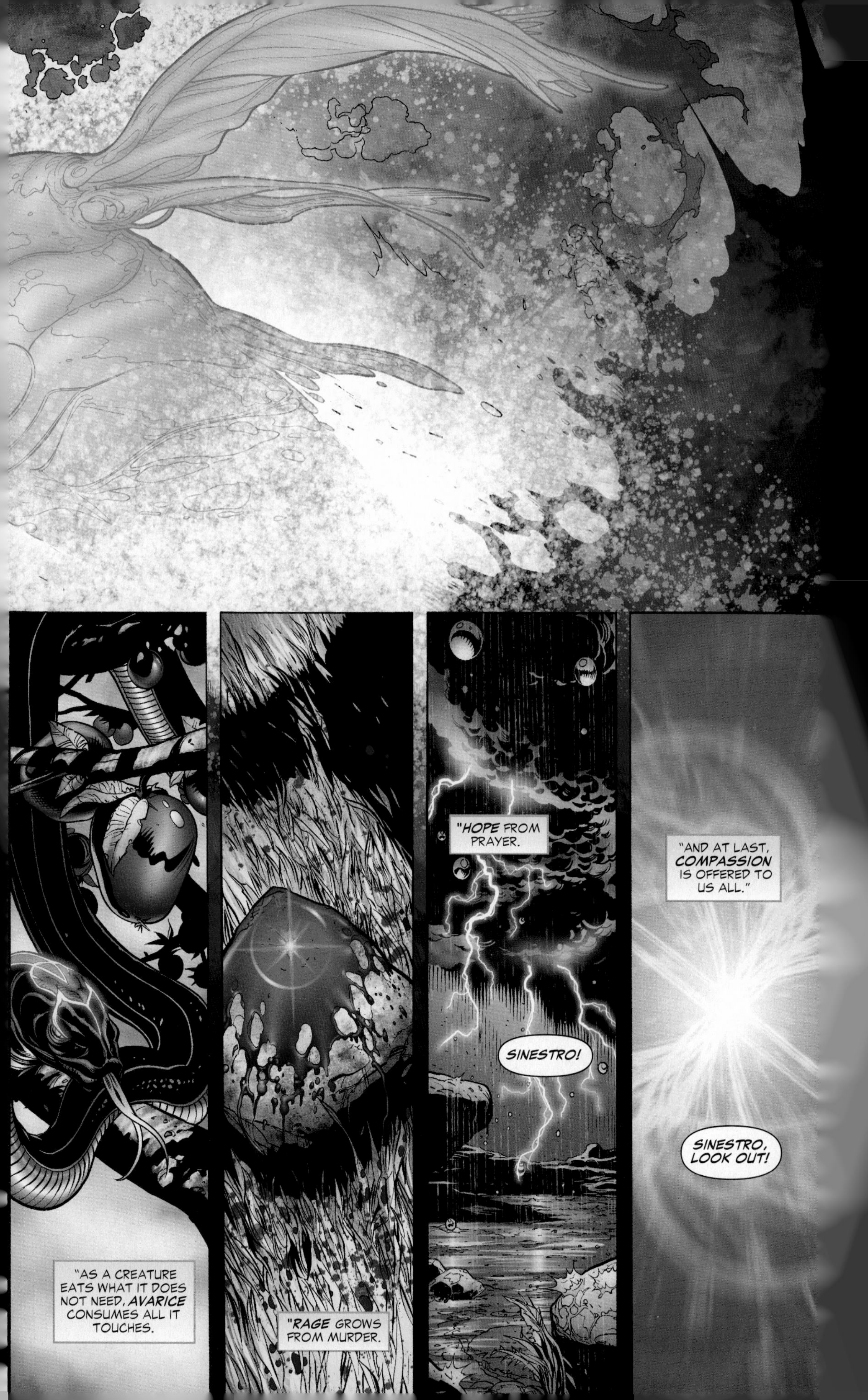
"AS A CREATURE EATS WHAT IT DOES NOT NEED, AVARICE CONSUMES ALL IT TOUCHES.
"RAGE GROWS FROM MURDER.
"HOPE FROM PRAYER.
SINESTRO!
"AND AT LAST, COMPASSION IS OFFERED TO US ALL."
SINESTRO, LOOK OUT!

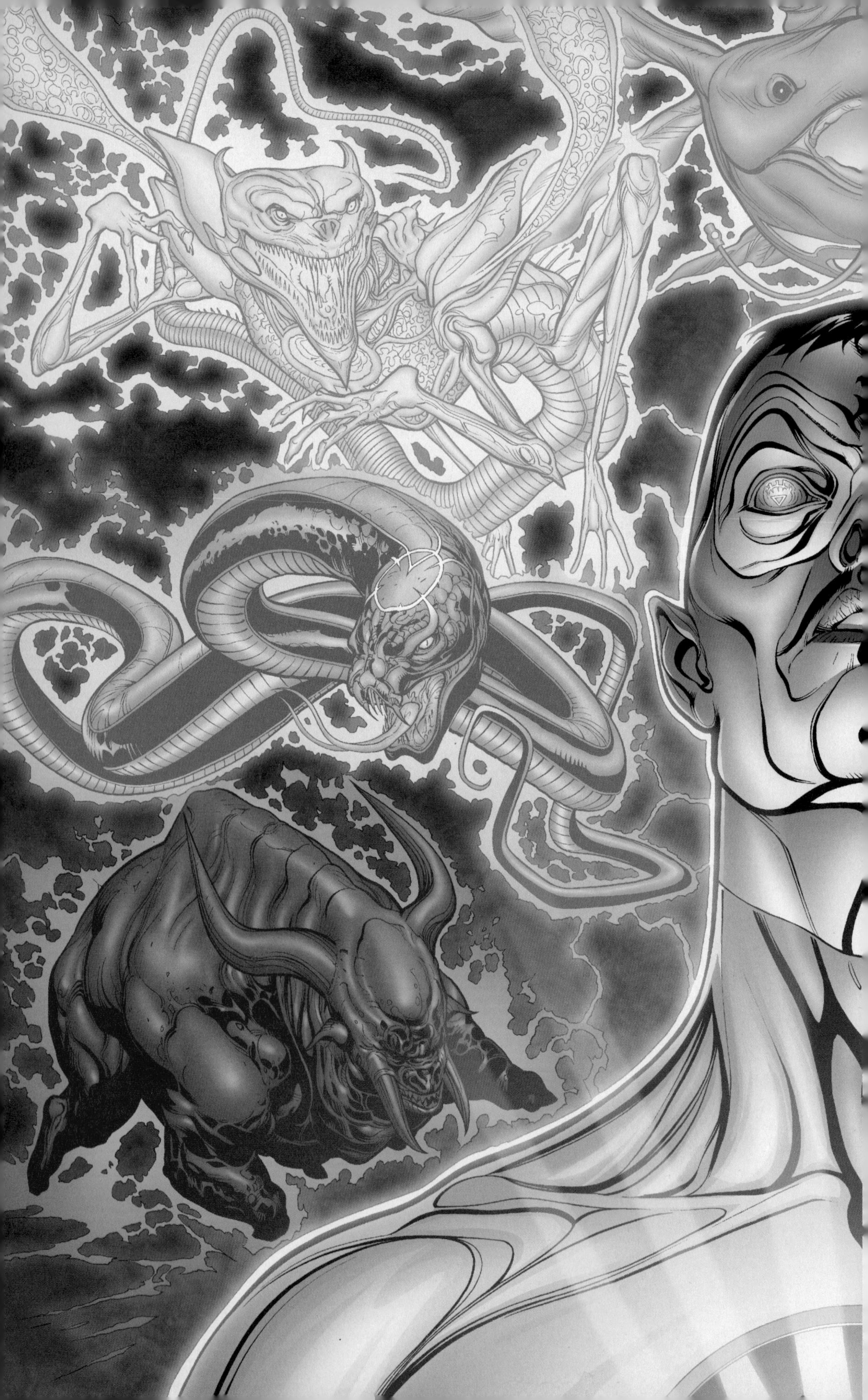

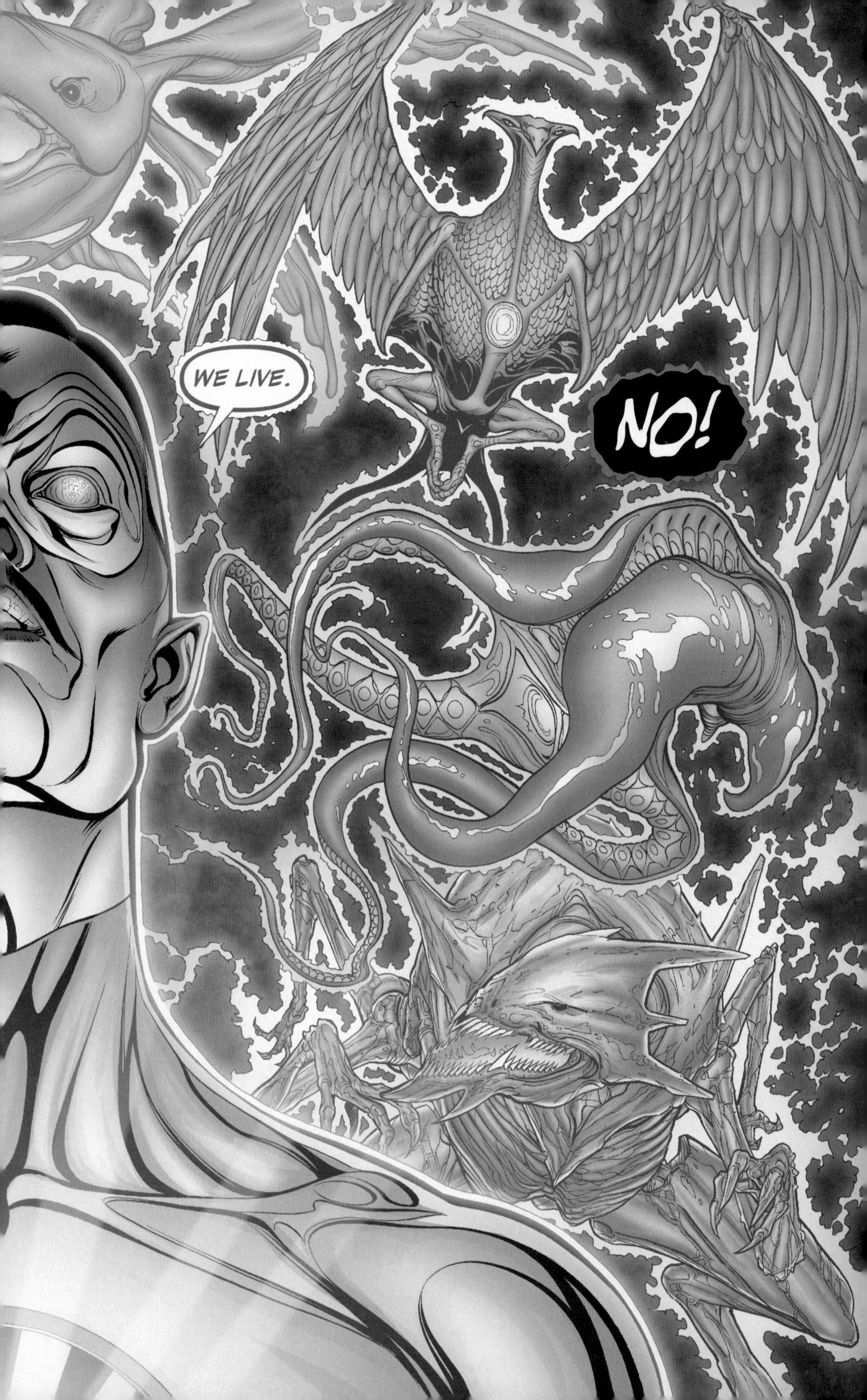
WE LIVE.
NO!

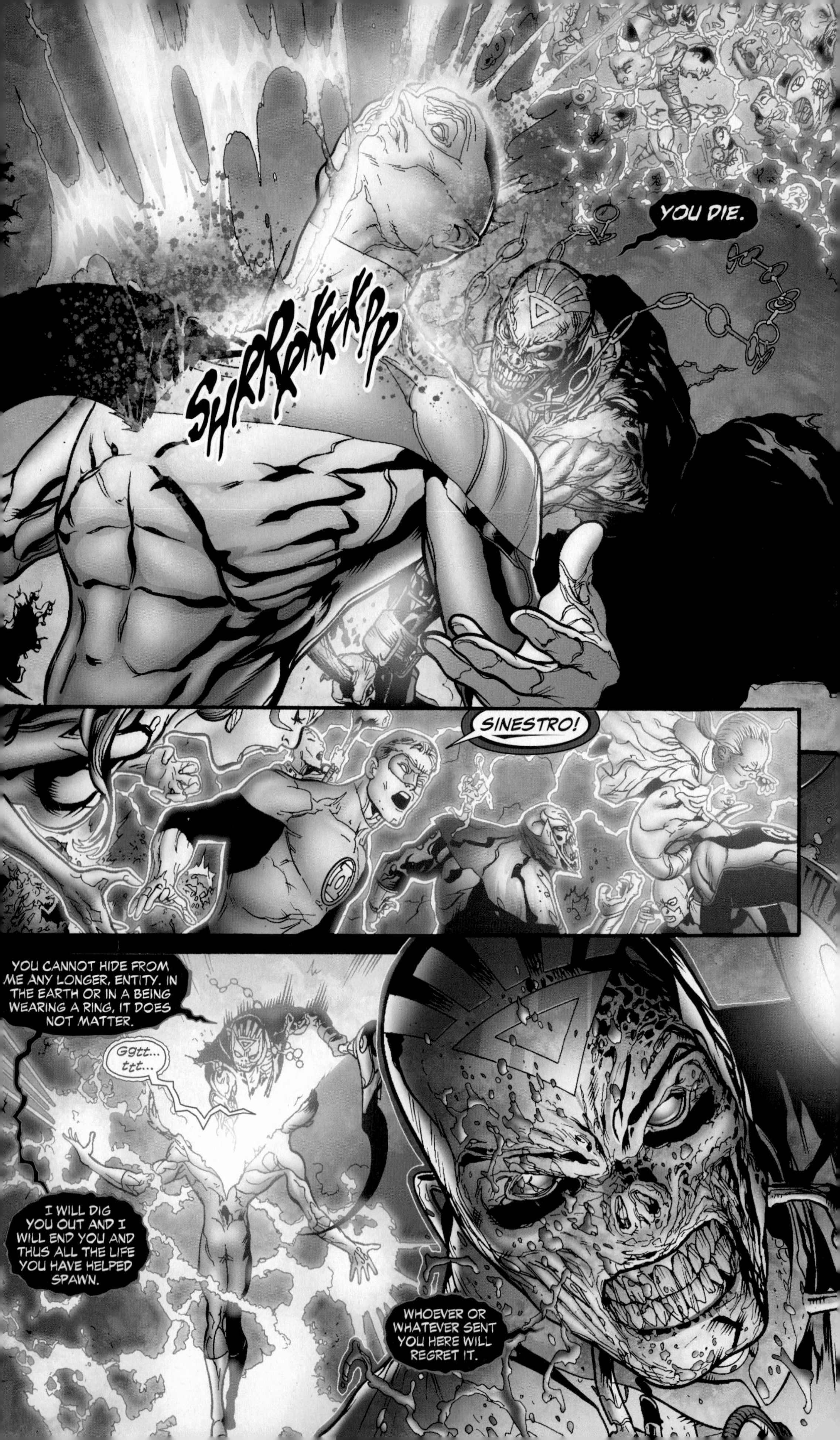
YOU DIE.
SHRRKKKPP
SINESTRO!
YOU CANNOT HIDE FROM ME ANY LONGER, ENTITY. IN THE EARTH OR IN A BEING WEARING A RING, IT DOES NOT MATTER.
Ggtt... ttt...
I WILL DIG YOU OUT AND I WILL END YOU AND THUS ALL THE LIFE YOU HAVE HELPED SPAWN.
WHOEVER OR WHATEVER SENT YOU HERE WILL REGRET IT.

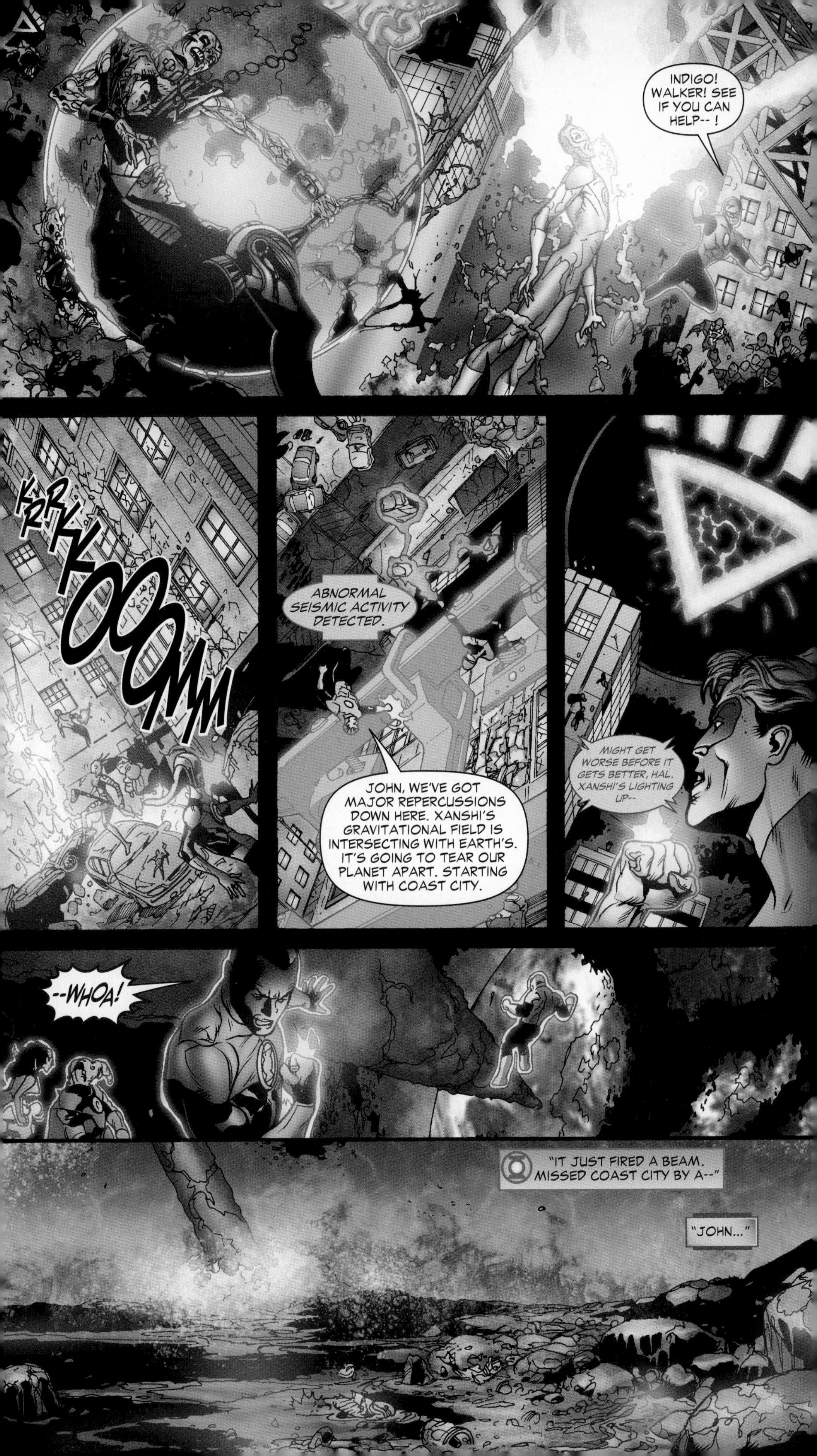

INDIGO! WALKER! SEE IF YOU CAN HELP-- !
KRRKKOOOMM
ABNORMAL SEISMIC ACTIVITY DETECTED.
JOHN, WE'VE GOT MAJOR REPERCUSSIONS DOWN HERE. XANSHI'S GRAVITATIONAL FIELD IS INTERSECTING WITH EARTH'S. IT'S GOING TO TEAR OUR PLANET APART. STARTING WITH COAST CITY.
MIGHT GET WORSE BEFORE IT GETS BETTER, HAL. XANSHI'S LIGHTING UP--
--WHOA!
"IT JUST FIRED A BEAM. MISSED COAST CITY BY A--"
"JOHN..."

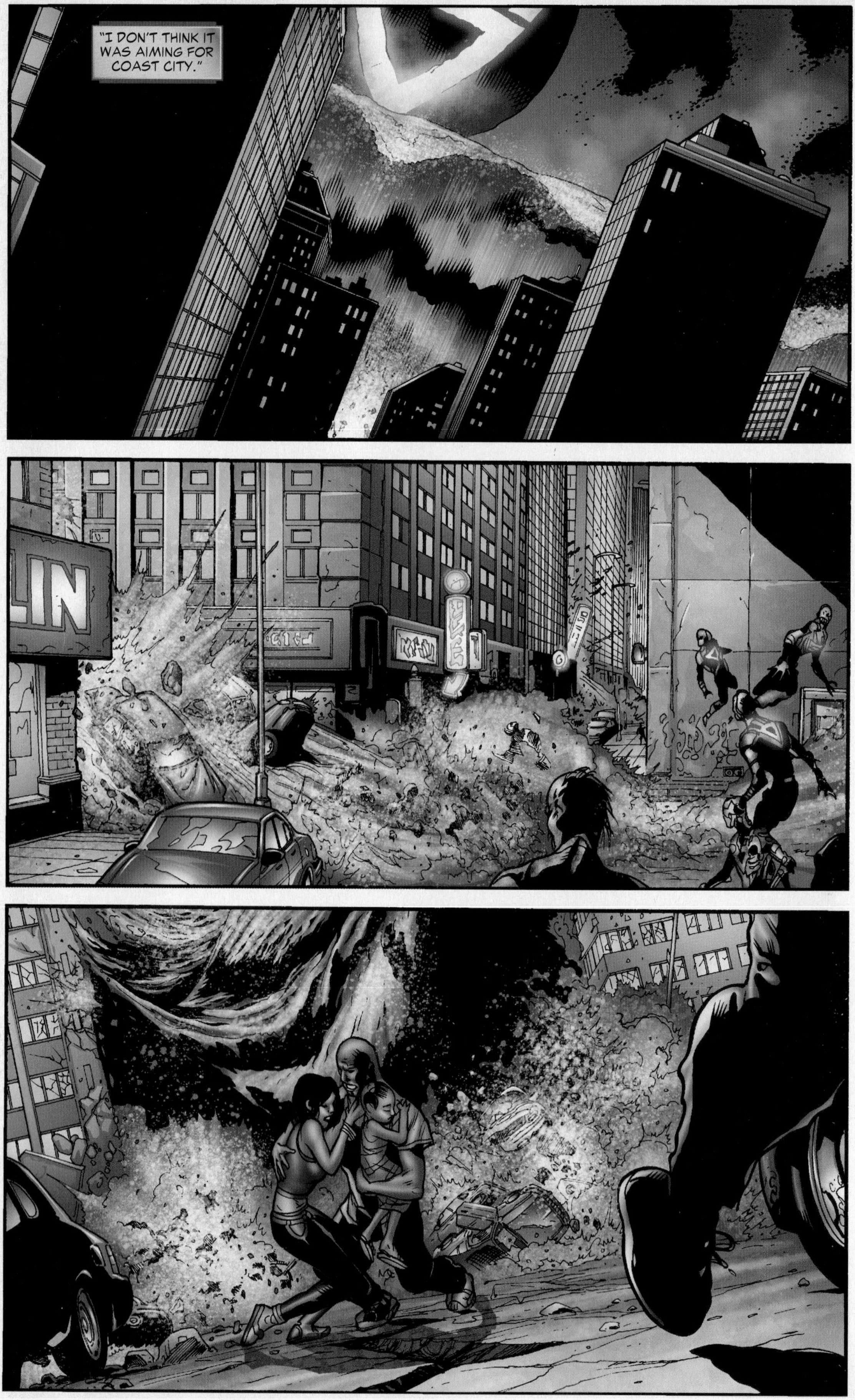
"I DON'T THINK IT WAS AIMING FOR COAST CITY."

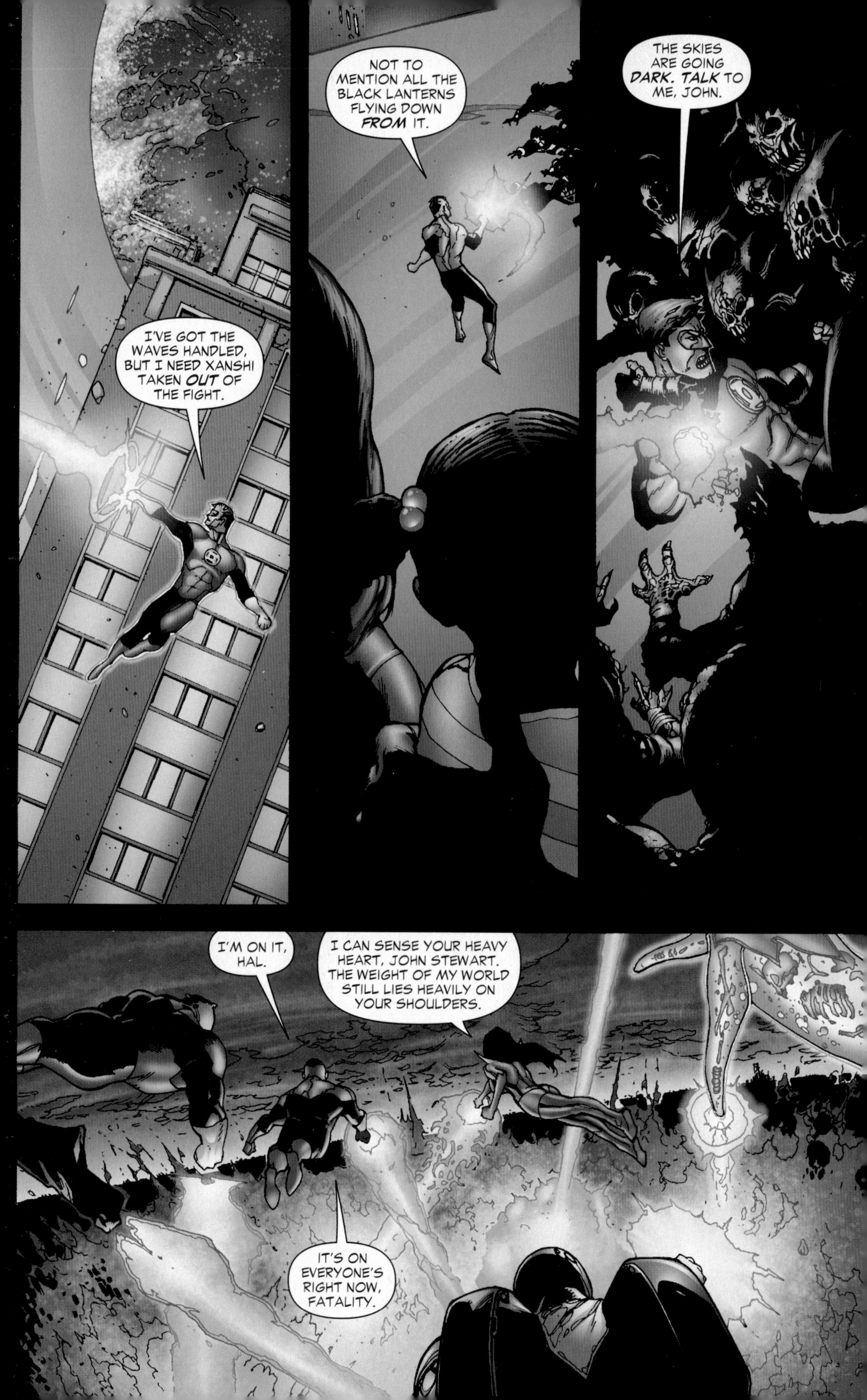
I'VE GOT THE WAVES HANDLED, BUT I NEED XANSHI TAKEN OUT OF THE FIGHT.
NOT TO MENTION ALL THE BLACK LANTERNS FLYING DOWN FROM IT.
THE SKIES ARE GOING DARK. TALK TO ME, JOHN.
I'M ON IT, HAL.
I CAN SENSE YOUR HEAVY HEART, JOHN STEWART. THE WEIGHT OF MY WORLD STILL LIES HEAVILY ON YOUR SHOULDERS.
IT'S ON EVERYONE'S RIGHT NOW, FATALITY.

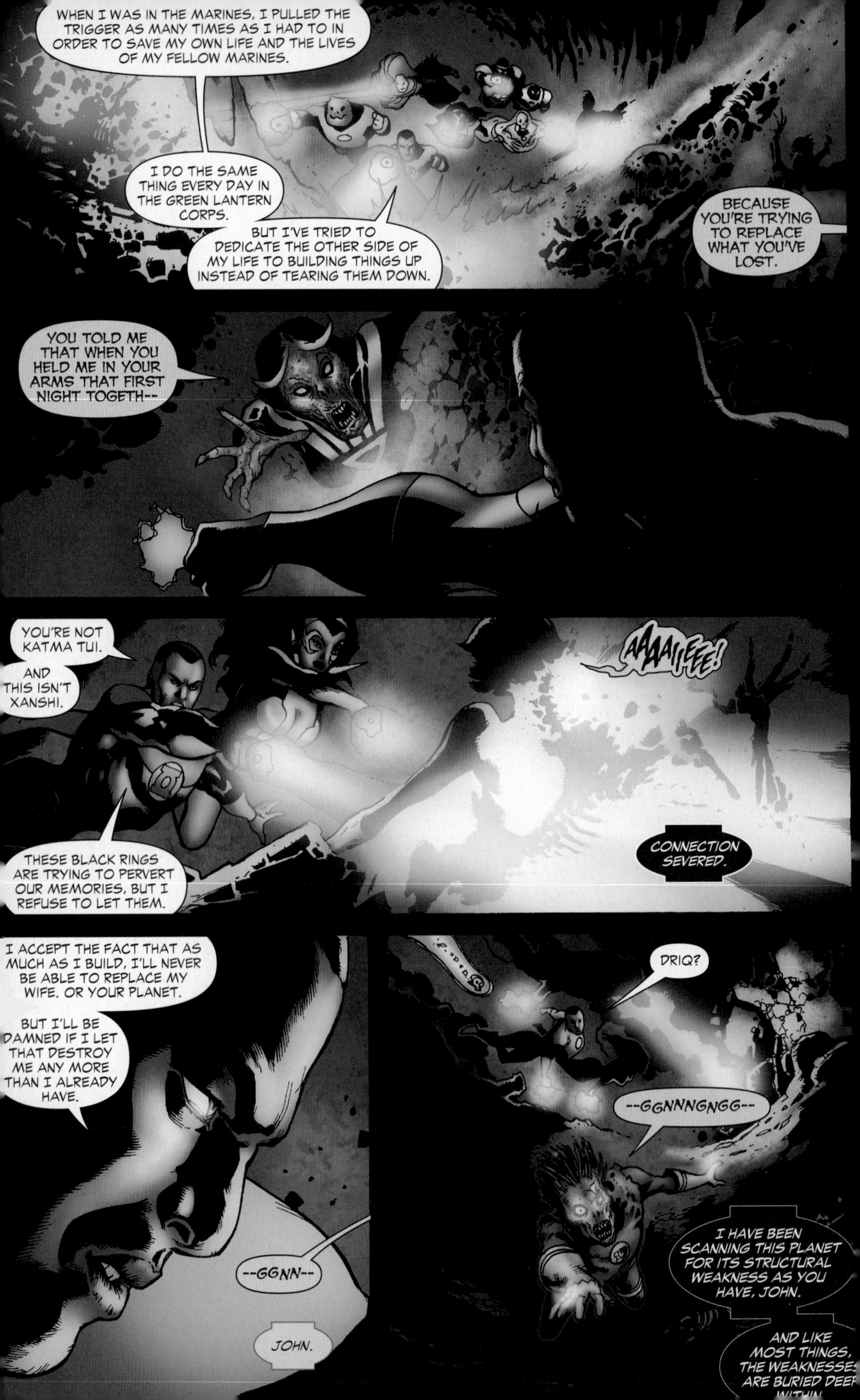
WHEN I WAS IN THE MARINES, I PULLED THE TRIGGER AS MANY TIMES AS I HAD TO IN ORDER TO SAVE MY OWN LIFE AND THE LIVES OF MY FELLOW MARINES.
I DO THE SAME THING EVERY DAY IN THE GREEN LANTERN CORPS.
BUT I'VE TRIED TO DEDICATE THE OTHER SIDE OF MY LIFE TO BUILDING THINGS UP INSTEAD OF TEARING THEM DOWN.
BECAUSE YOU'RE TRYING TO REPLACE WHAT YOU'VE LOST.
YOU TOLD ME THAT WHEN YOU HELD ME IN YOUR ARMS THAT FIRST NIGHT TOGETH--
YOU'RE NOT KATMA TUI.
AND THIS ISN'T XANSHI.
AAAAIIEEE!
THESE BLACK RINGS ARE TRYING TO PERVERT OUR MEMORIES, BUT I REFUSE TO LET THEM.
CONNECTION SEVERED.
I ACCEPT THE FACT THAT AS MUCH AS I BUILD, I'LL NEVER BE ABLE TO REPLACE MY WIFE. OR YOUR PLANET.
BUT I'LL BE DAMNED IF I LET THAT DESTROY ME ANY MORE THAN I ALREADY HAVE.
--GGNN--
JOHN.
DRIQ?
--GGNNNGNGG--
I HAVE BEEN SCANNING THIS PLANET FOR ITS STRUCTURAL WEAKNESS AS YOU HAVE, JOHN.
AND LIKE MOST THINGS, THE WEAKNESSES ARE BURIED DEEP

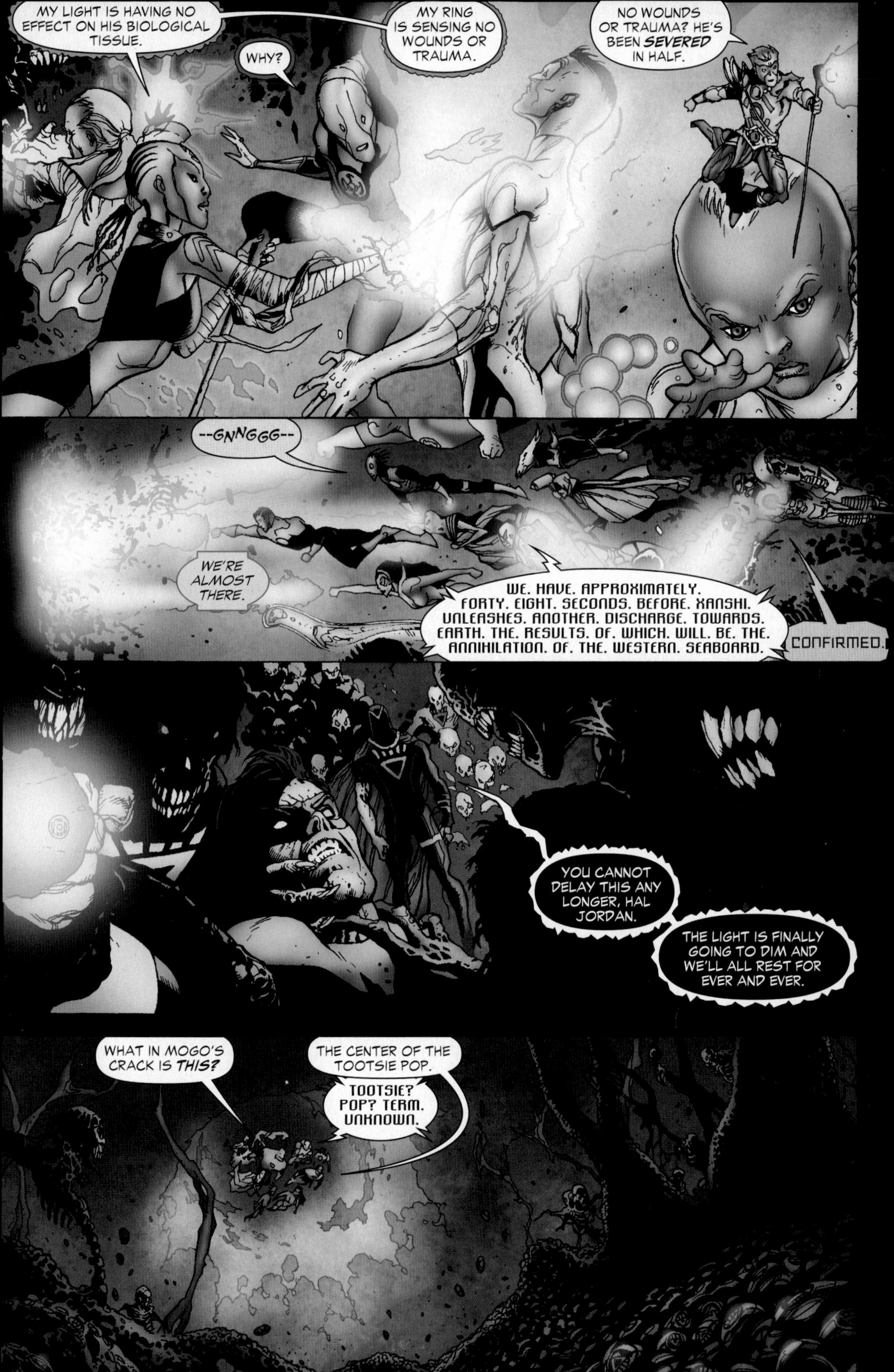

MY LIGHT IS HAVING NO EFFECT ON HIS BIOLOGICAL TISSUE.
WHY?
MY RING IS SENSING NO WOUNDS OR TRAUMA.
NO WOUNDS OR TRAUMA? HE'S BEEN SEVERED IN HALF.
--GNNGGG--
WE'RE ALMOST THERE.
WE. HAVE. APPROXIMATELY. FORTY. EIGHT. SECONDS. BEFORE. XANSHI. UNLEASHES. ANOTHER. DISCHARGE. TOWARDS. EARTH. THE. RESULTS. OF. WHICH. WILL. BE. THE. ANNIHILATION. OF. THE. WESTERN. SEABOARD.
CONFIRMED.
YOU CANNOT DELAY THIS ANY LONGER, HAL JORDAN.
THE LIGHT IS FINALLY GOING TO DIM AND WE'LL ALL REST FOR EVER AND EVER.
WHAT IN MOGO'S CRACK IS THIS?
THE CENTER OF THE TOOTSIE POP.
TOOTSIE? POP? TERM. UNKNOWN.

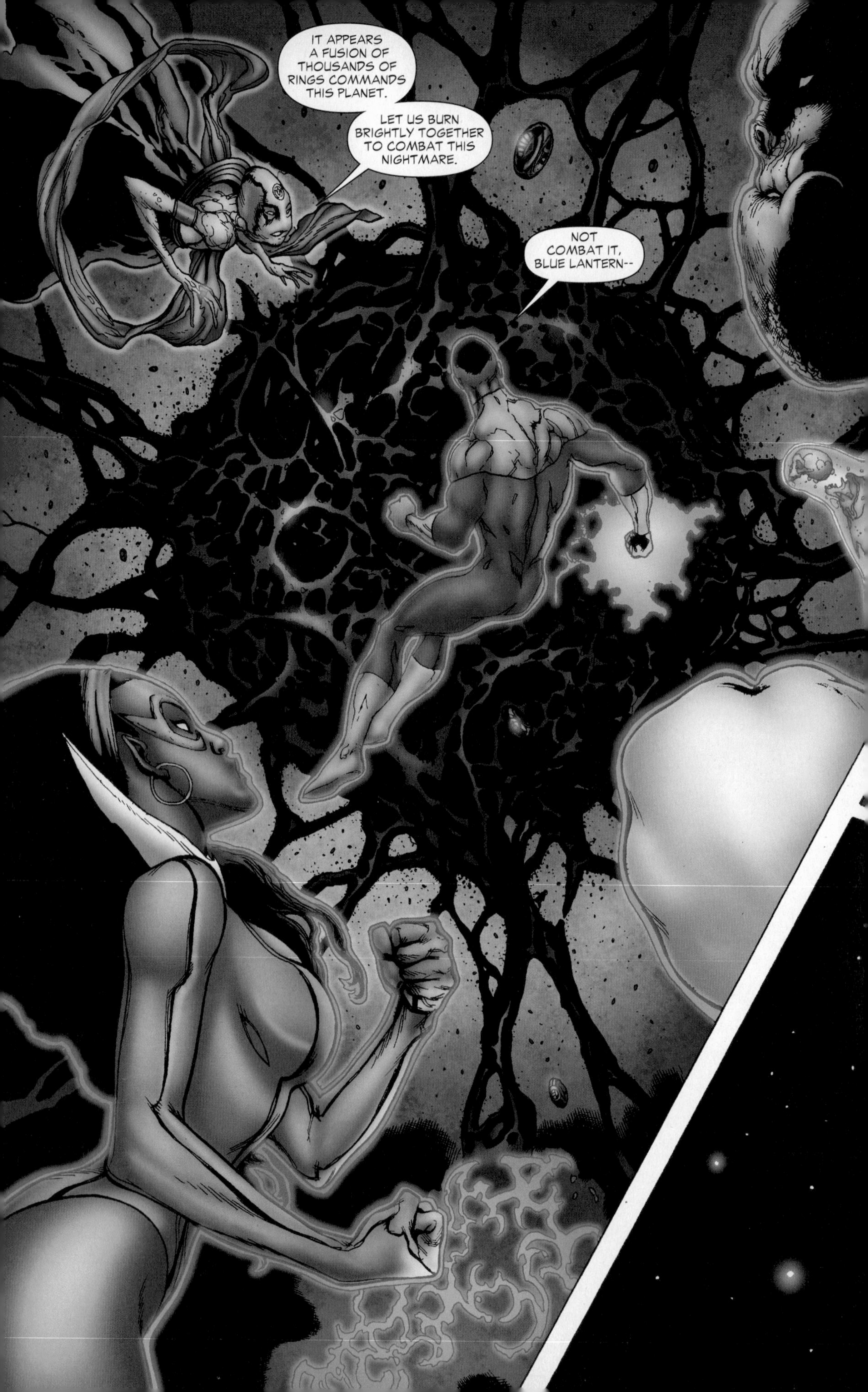
IT APPEARS A FUSION OF THOUSANDS OF RINGS COMMANDS THIS PLANET.
LET US BURN BRIGHTLY TOGETHER TO COMBAT THIS NIGHTMARE.
NOT COMBAT IT, BLUE LANTERN--

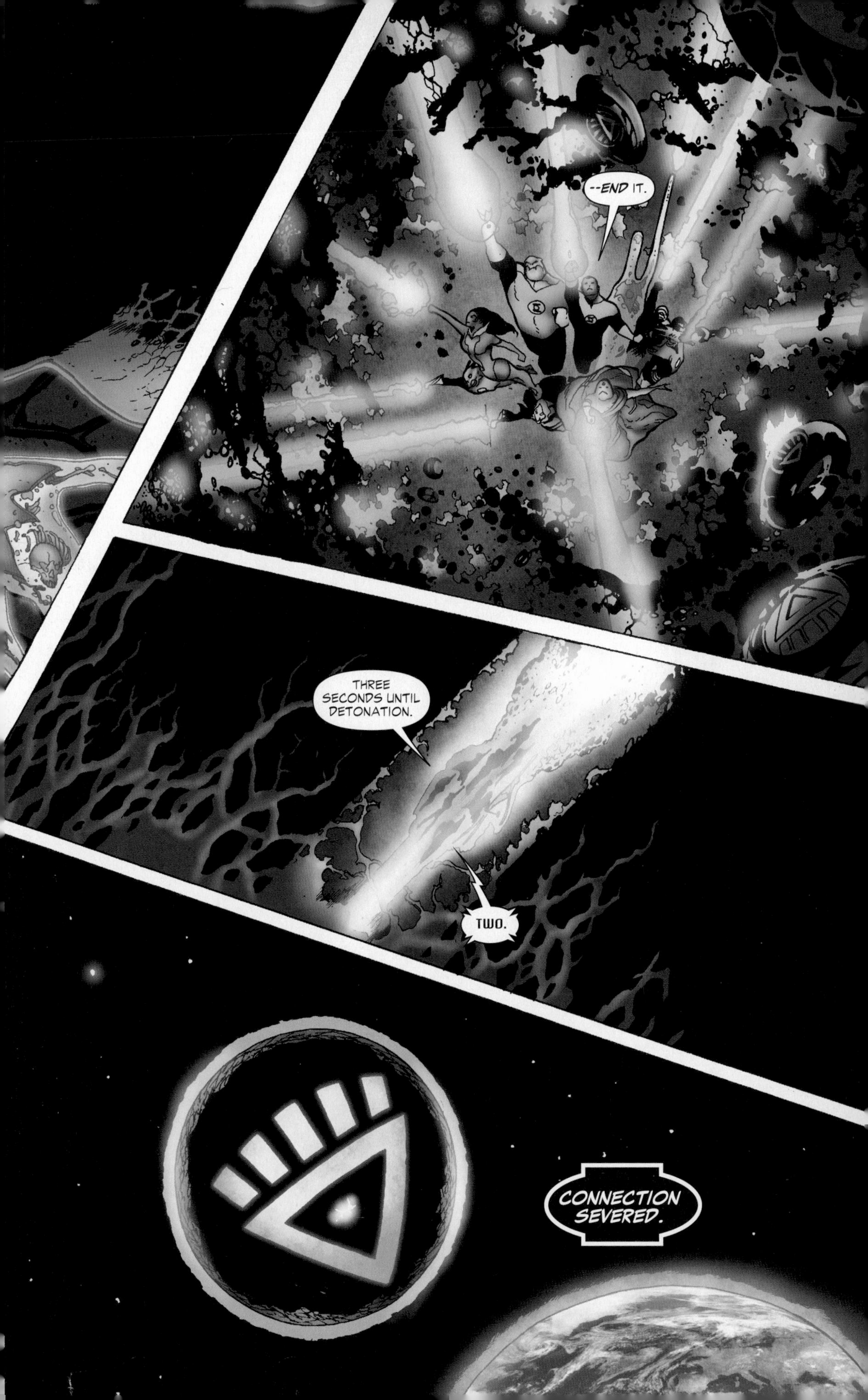
--END IT.
THREE SECONDS UNTIL DETONATION.
TWO.
CONNECTION SEVERED.

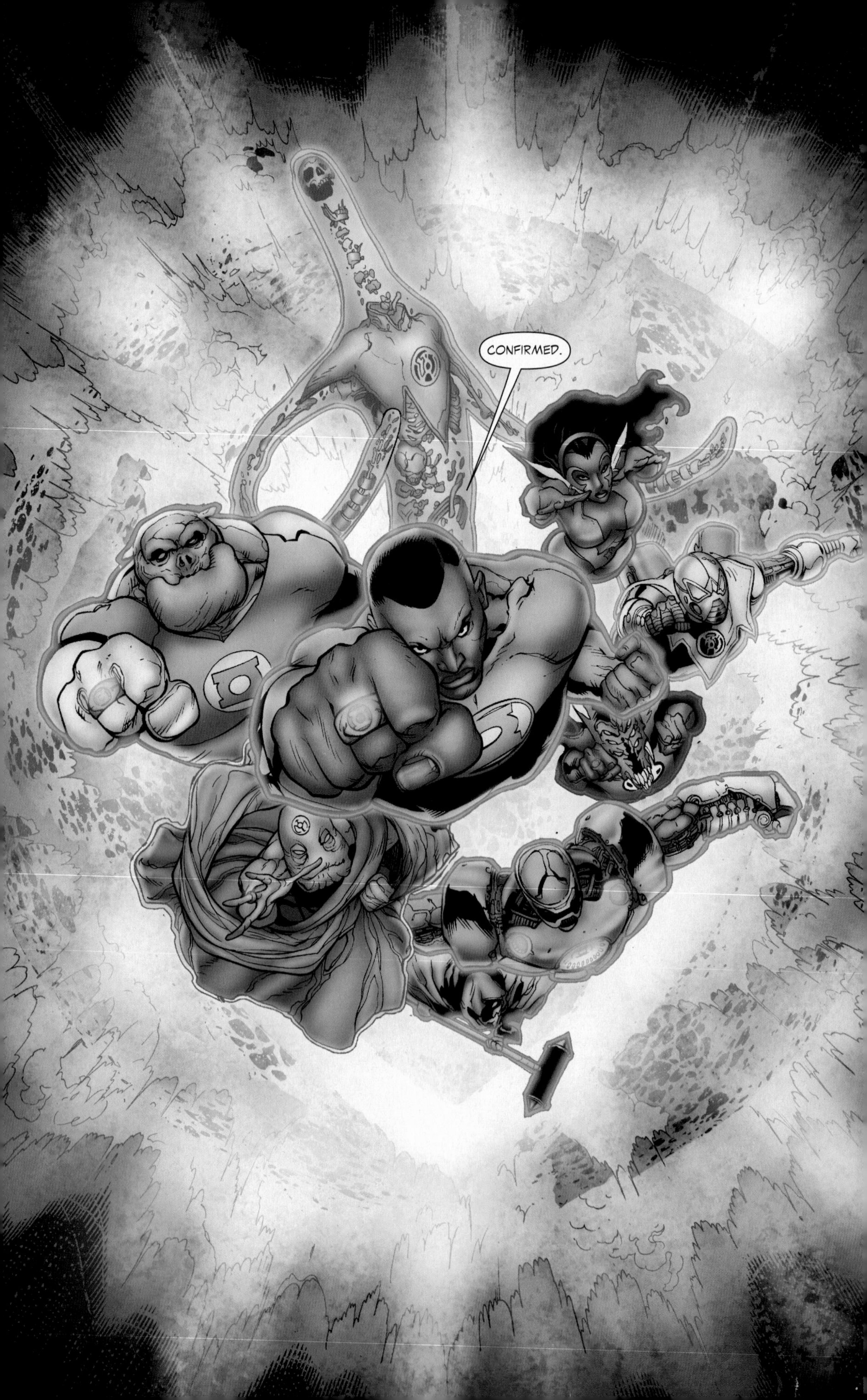
CONFIRMED.

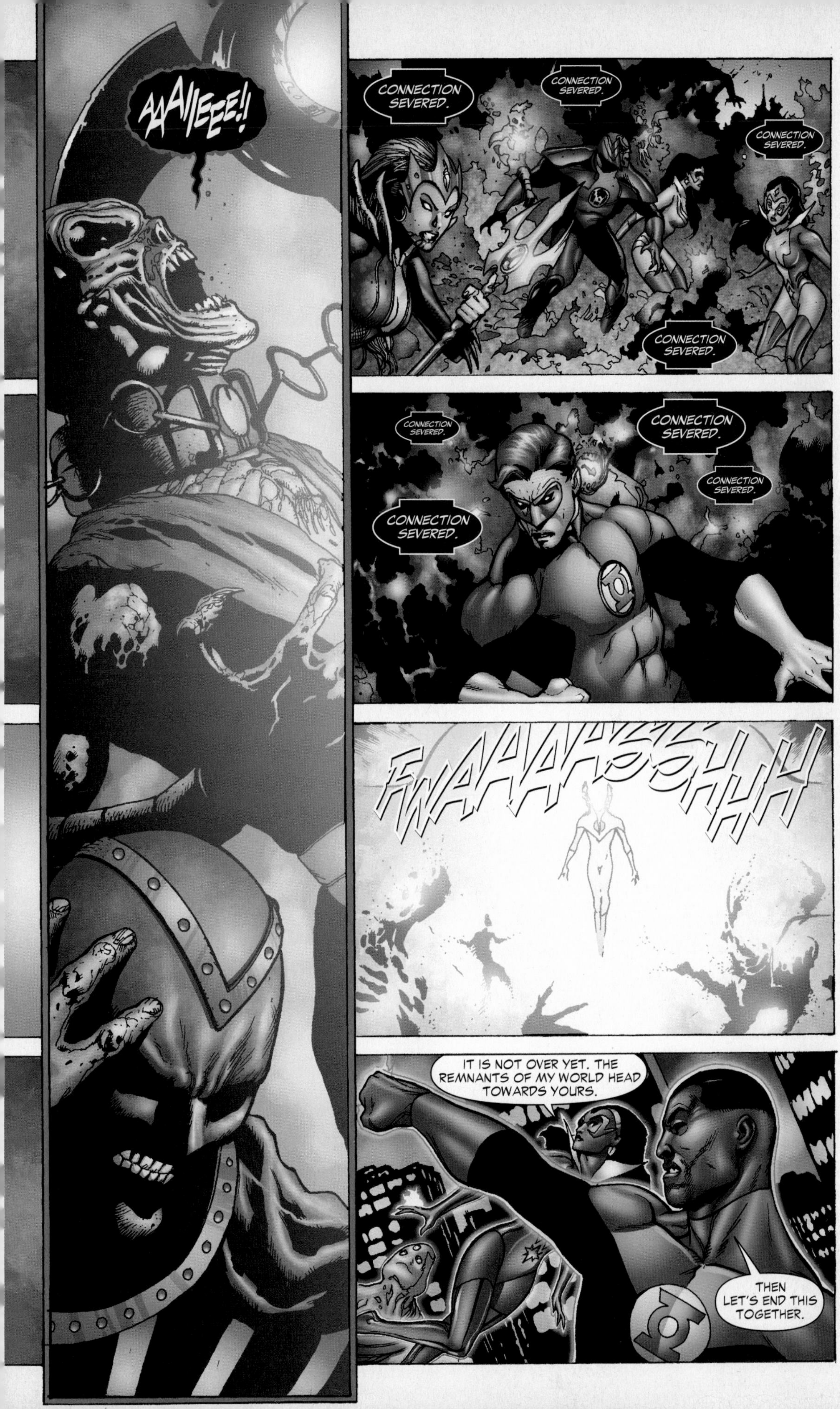
AAAIIEEE!!
CONNECTION SEVERED.
CONNECTION SEVERED.
CONNECTION SEVERED.
CONNECTION SEVERED.
CONNECTION SEVERED.
CONNECTION SEVERED.
CONNECTION SEVERED.
CONNECTION SEVERED.
FWAAAASSHHH
IT IS NOT OVER YET. THE REMNANTS OF MY WORLD HEAD TOWARDS YOURS.
THEN LET'S END THIS TOGETHER.

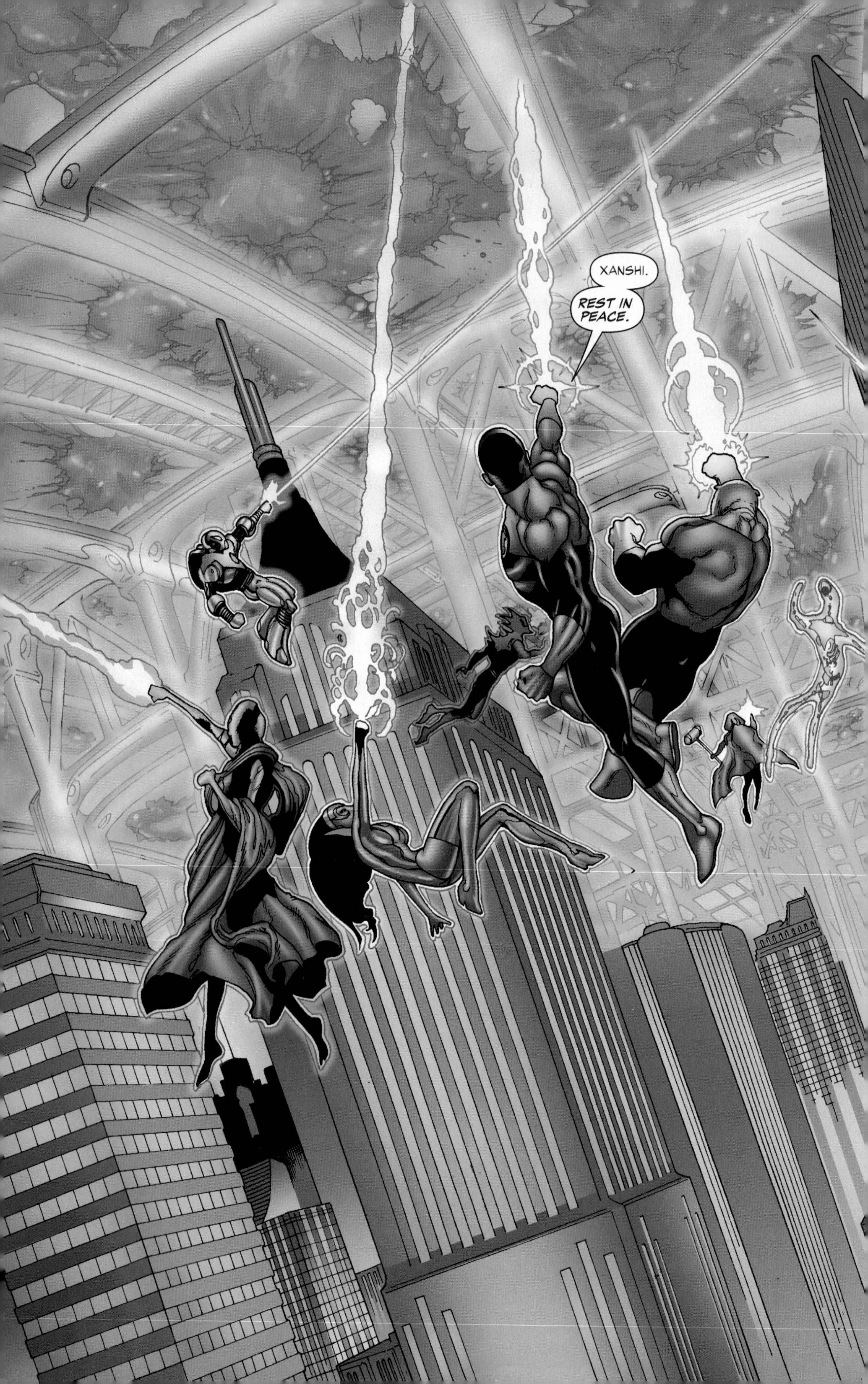
XANSHI.
REST IN PEACE.

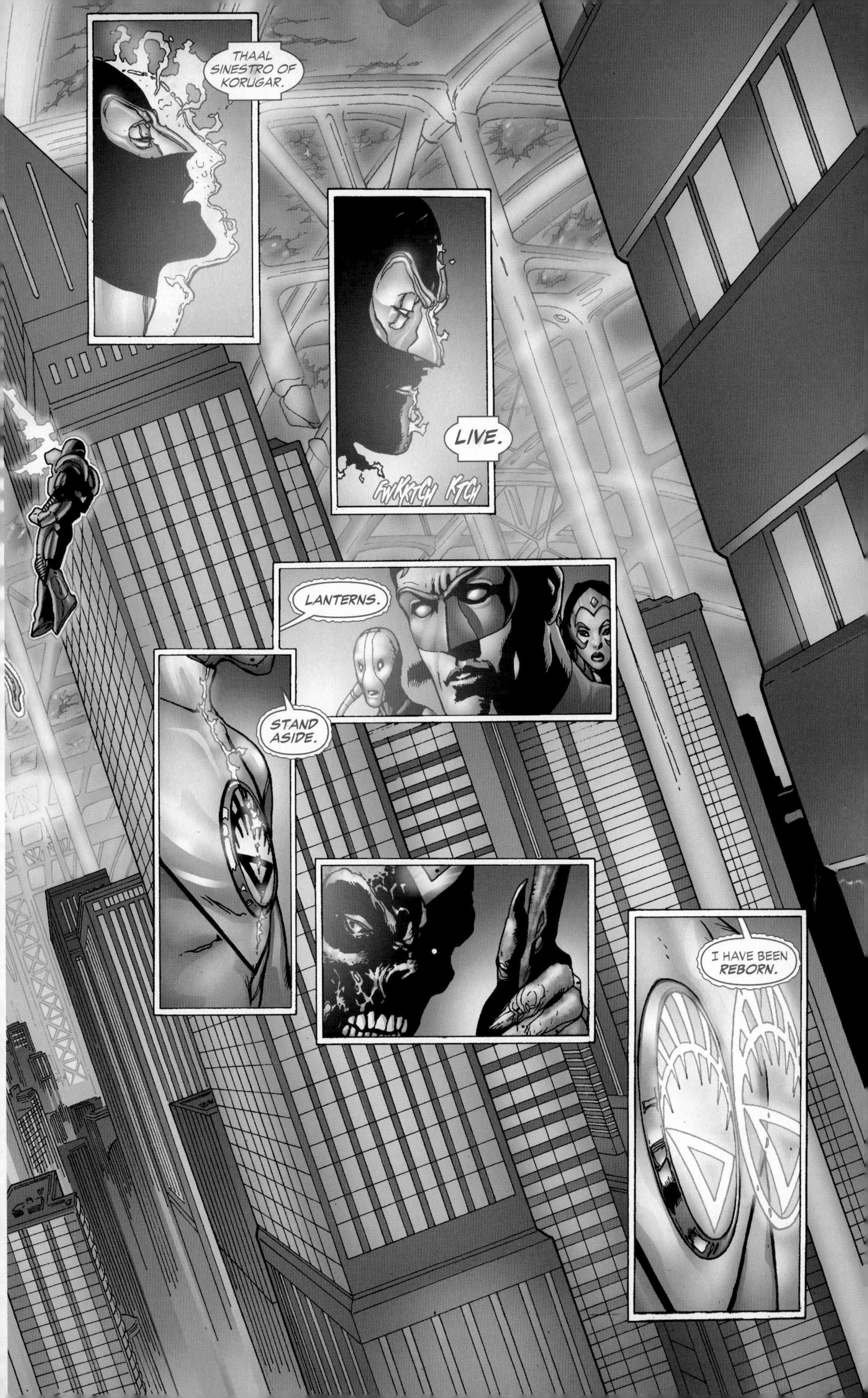
THAAL SINESTRO OF KORUGAR.
LIVE.
FWKKTCH KTCH
LANTERNS.
STAND ASIDE.
I HAVE BEEN REBORN.

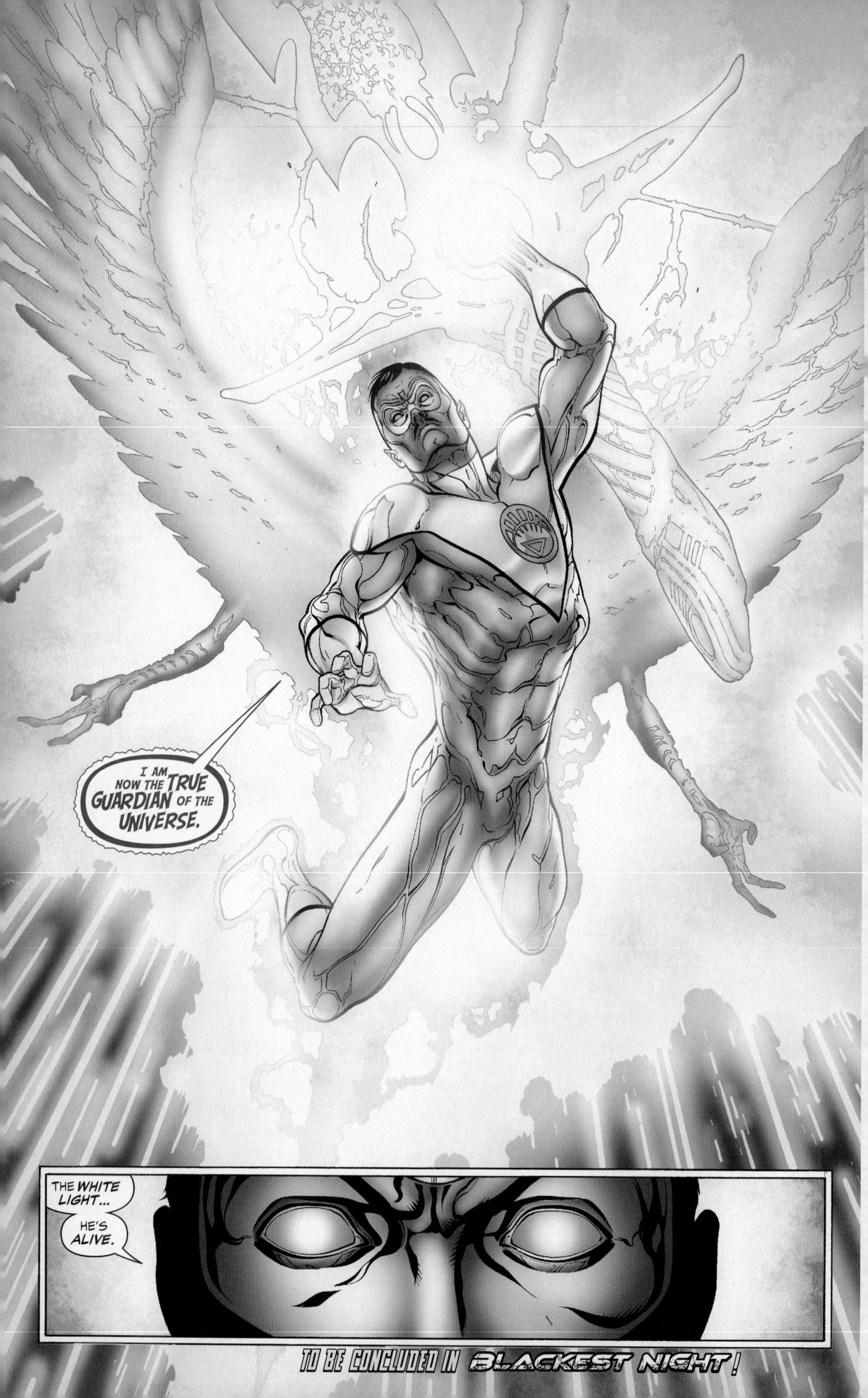
I AM NOW THE TRUE GUARDIAN OF THE UNIVERSE.
THE WHITE LIGHT...
HE'S ALIVE.
TO BE CONCLUDED IN BLACKEST NIGHT!

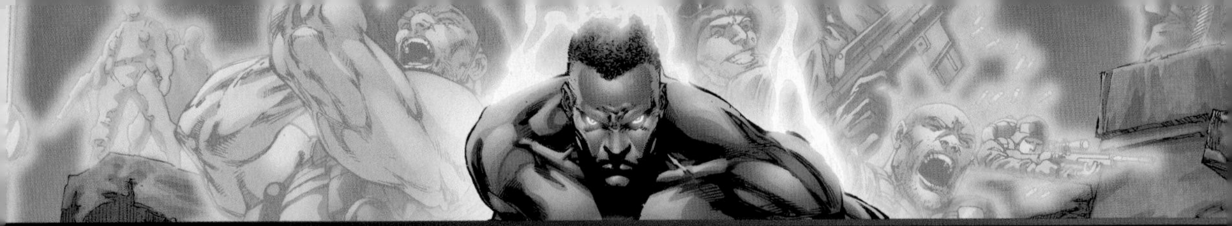

BLACKEST NIGHT GREEN LANTERN VARIANT COVER GALLERY

GREEN LANTERN 43
Cover by Eddy Barrows with Nei Ruffino

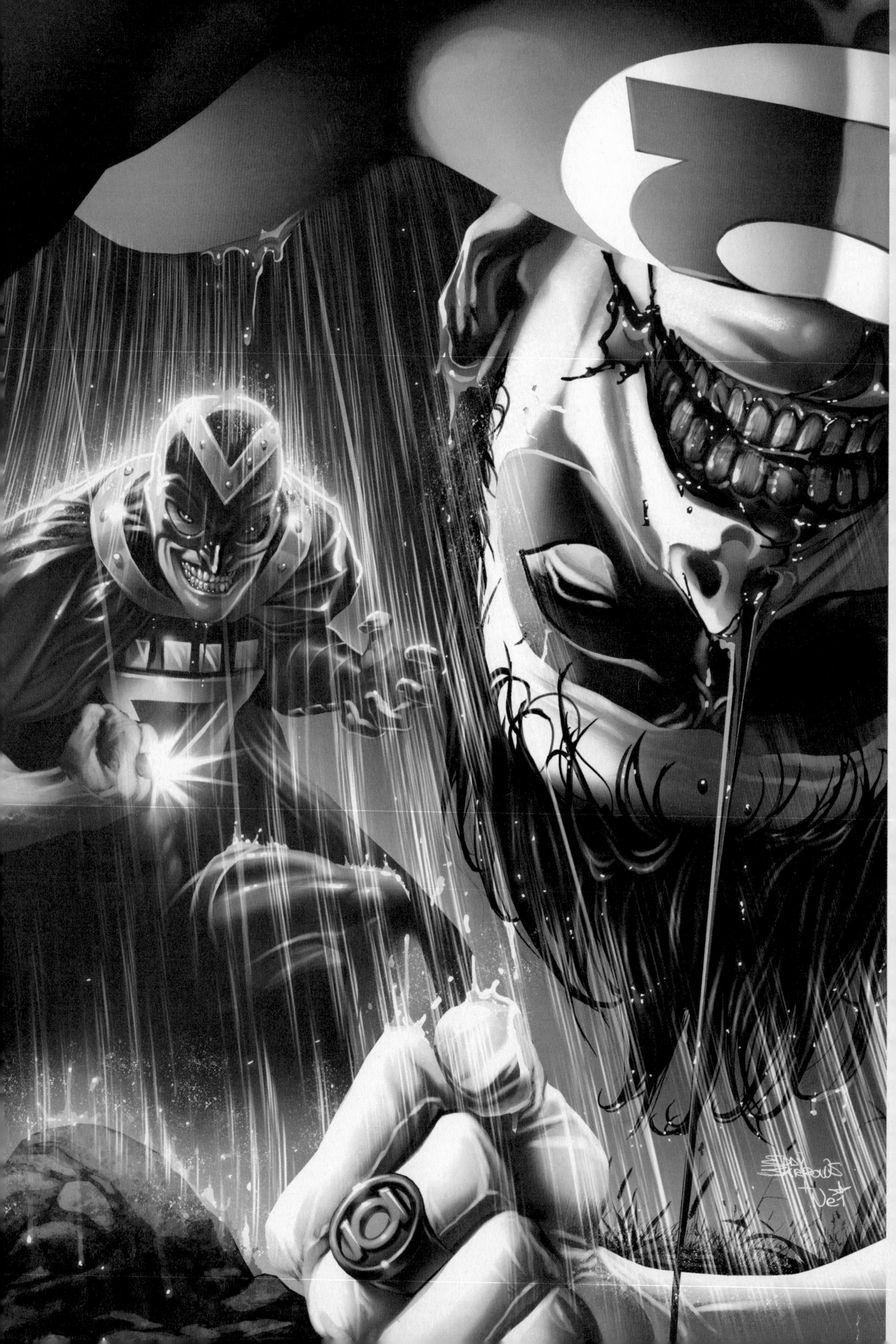

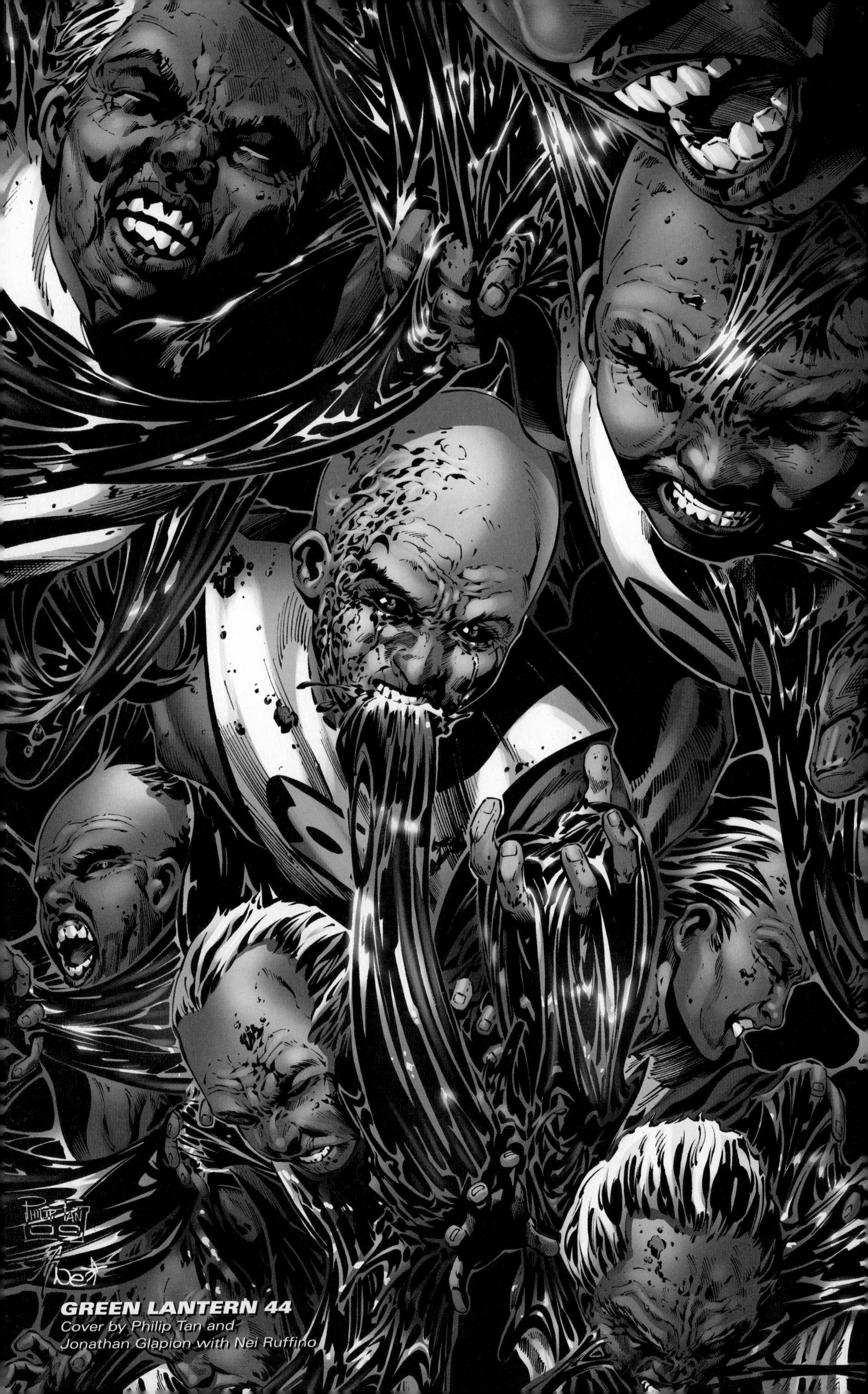

GREEN LANTERN 44
Cover by Philip Tan and Jonathan Glapion with Nei Ruffino

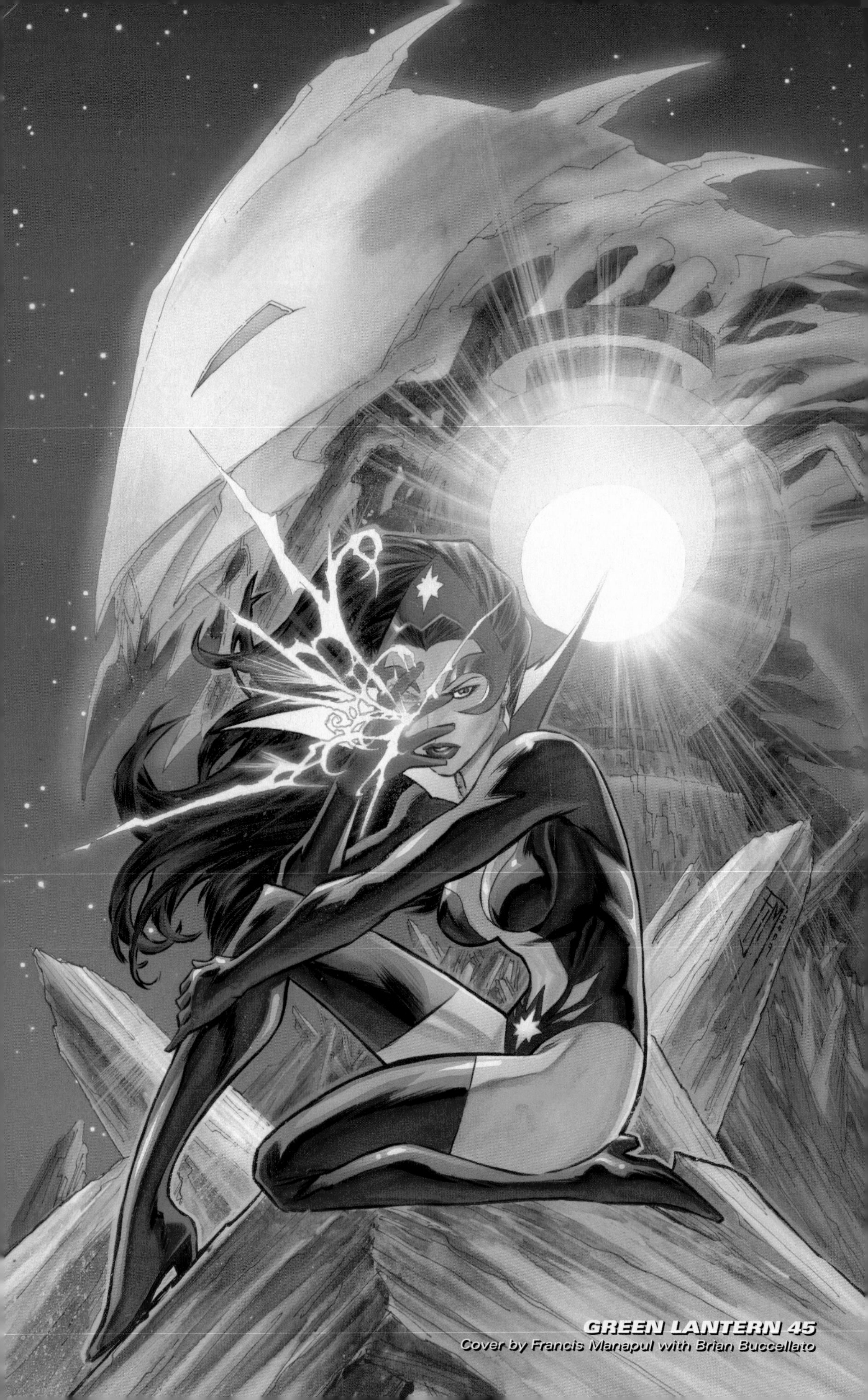

GREEN LANTERN 45
Cover by Francis Manapul with Brian Buccellato

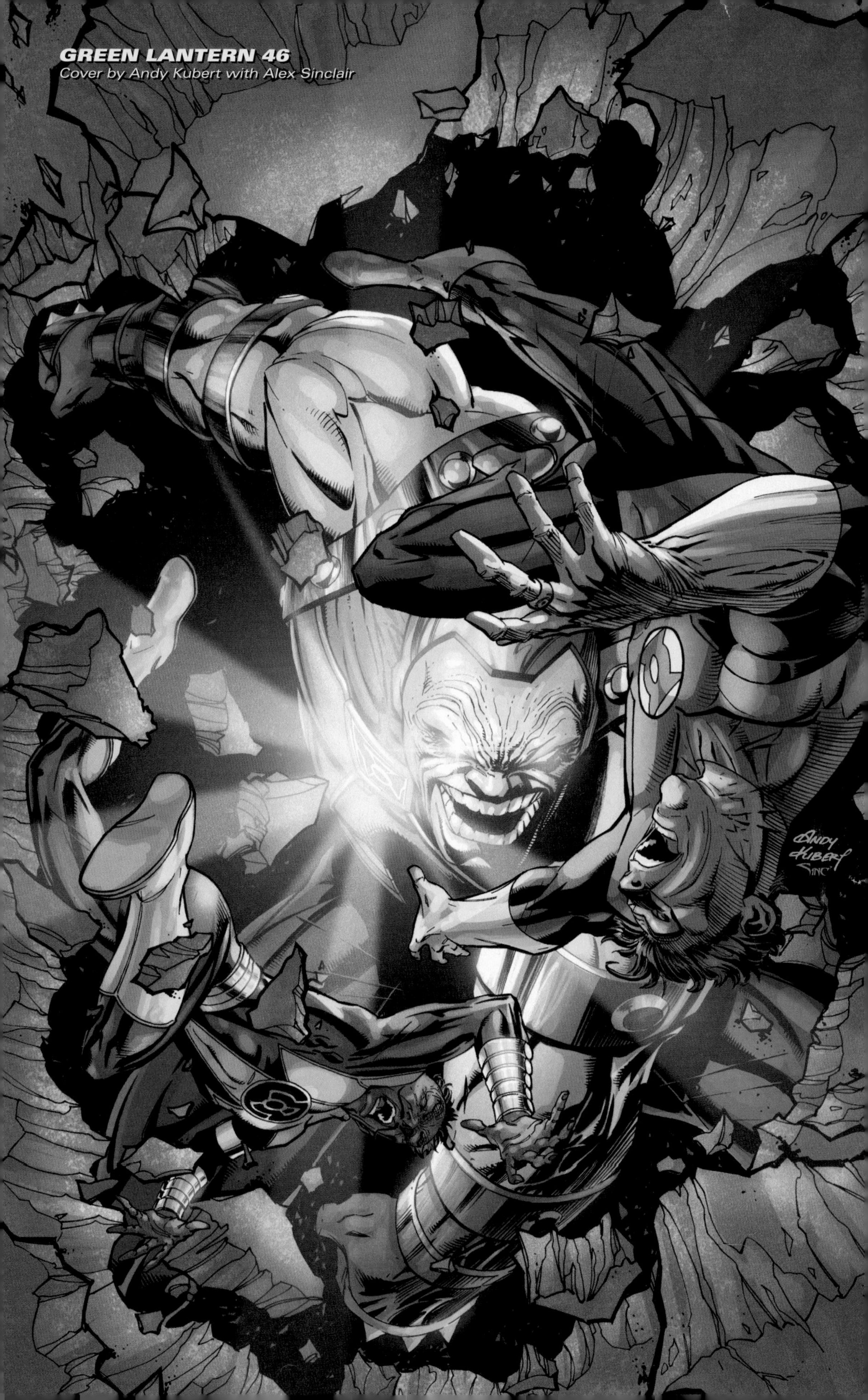

GREEN LANTERN 46

Cover by Andy Kubert with Alex Sinclair

GREEN LANTERN 47

Cover by Ed Benes with Nei Ruffino

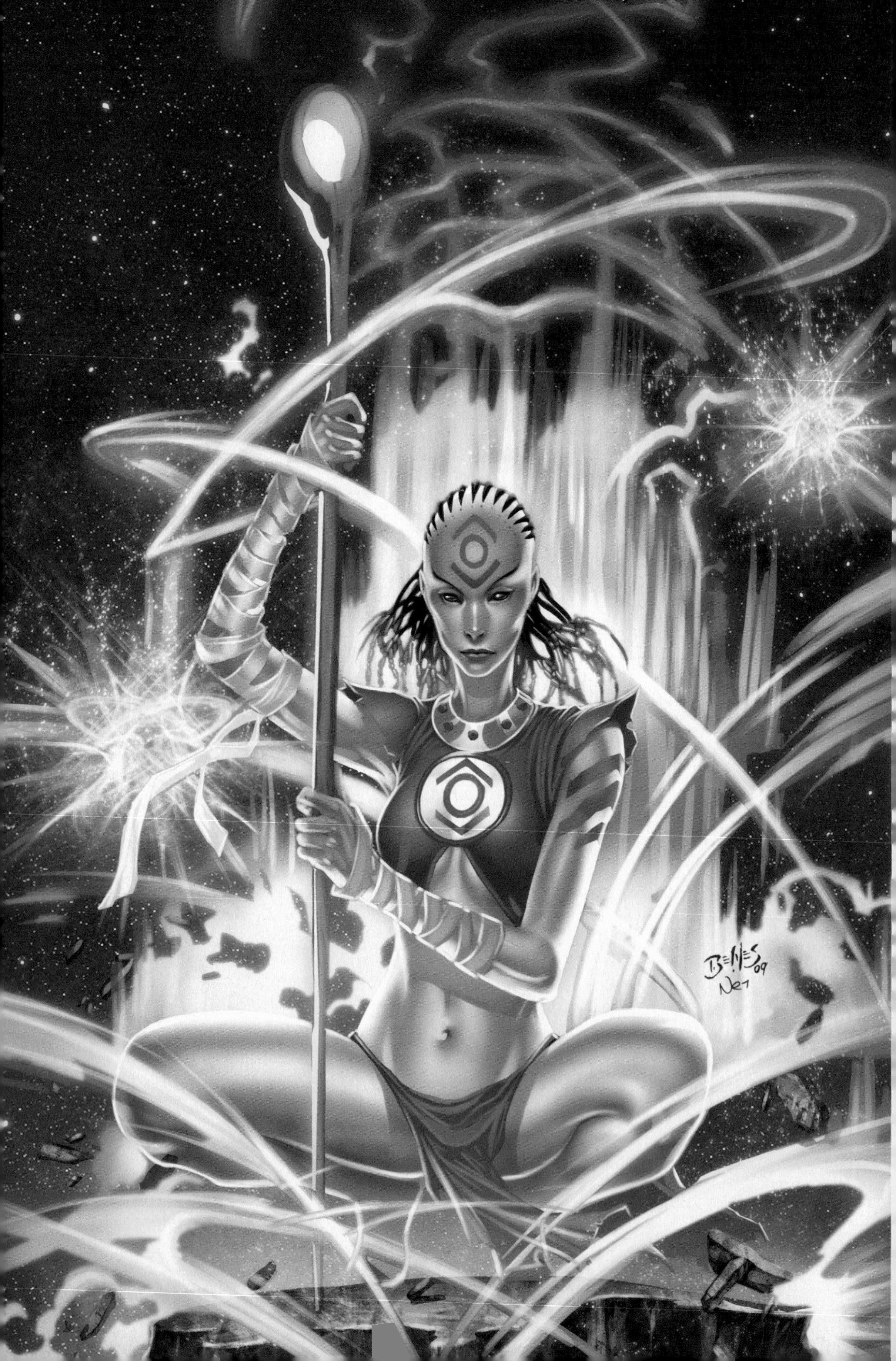
BENES '09
NEI

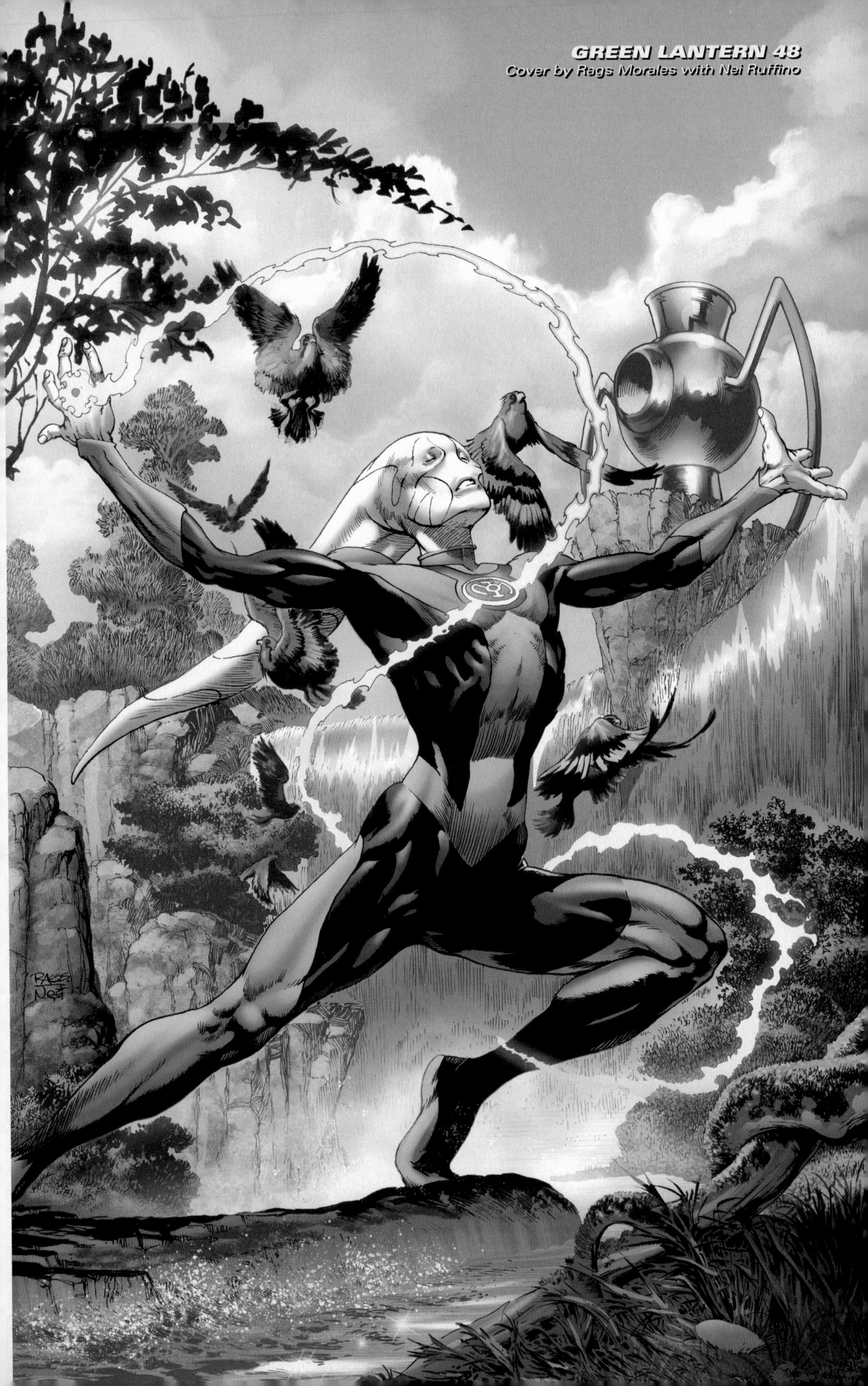

GREEN LANTERN 48
Cover by Rags Morales with Nei Ruffino

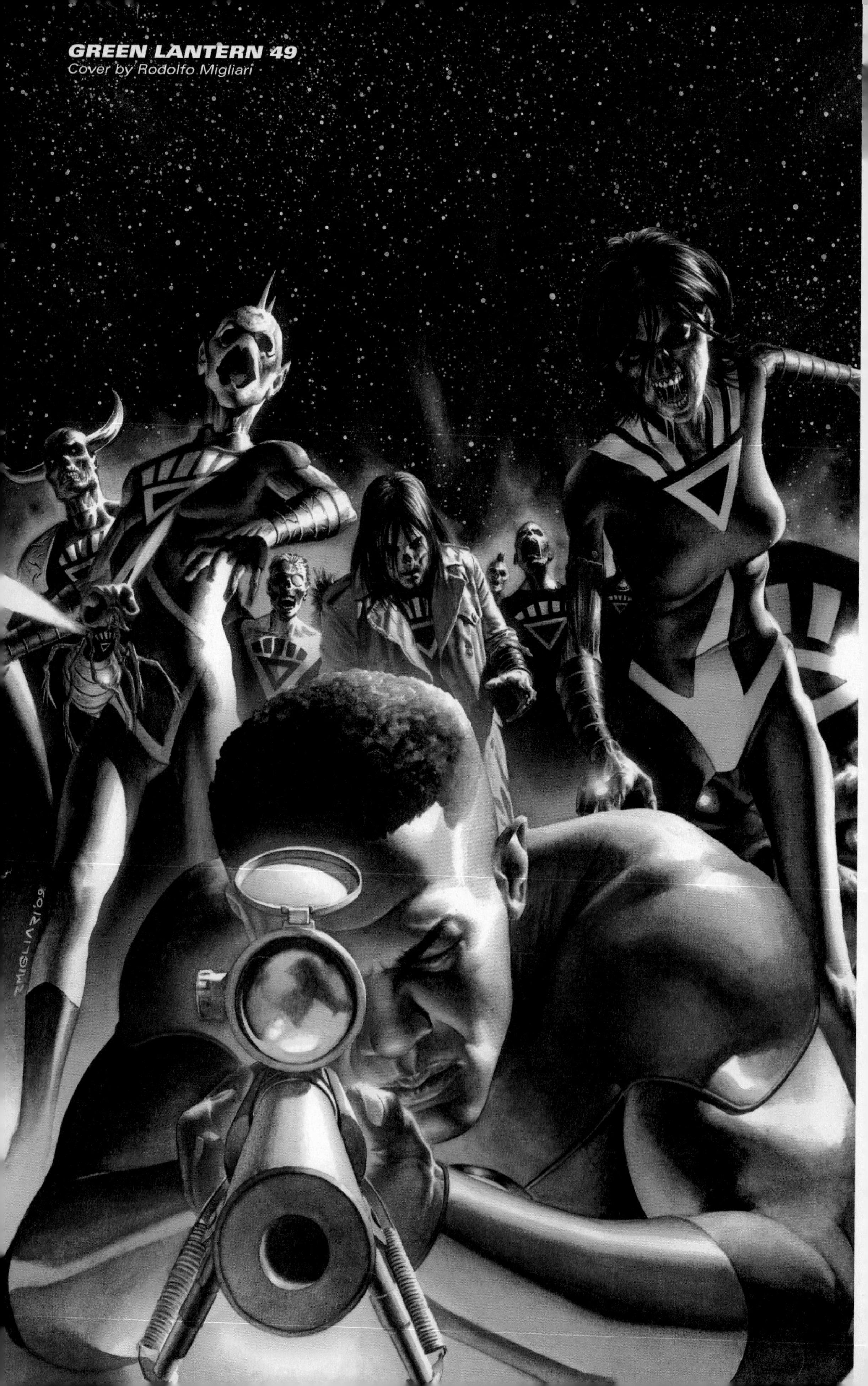

GREEN LANTERN 49
Cover by Rodolfo Migliari

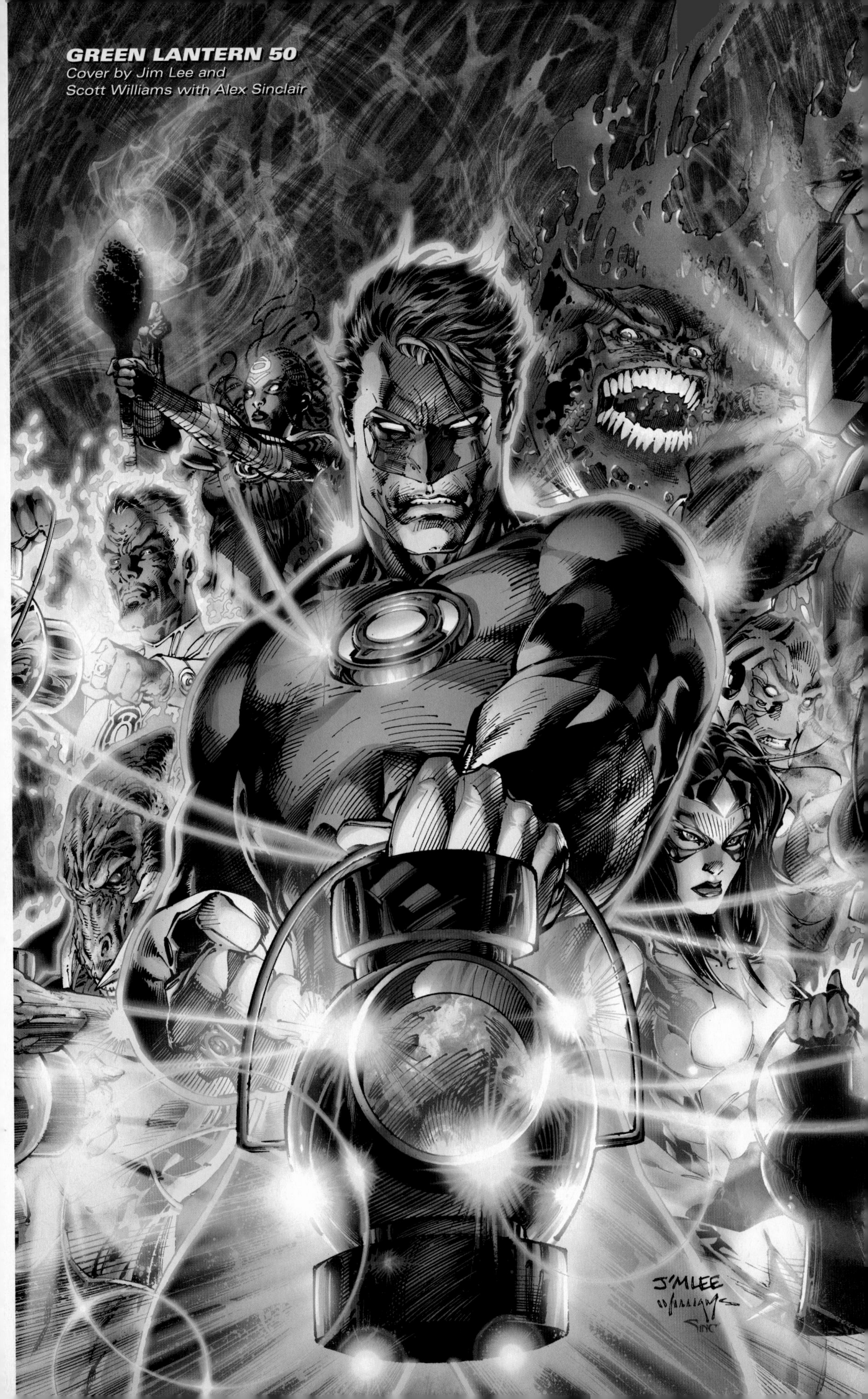

GREEN LANTERN 50
Cover by Jim Lee and Scott Williams with Alex Sinclair

GREEN LANTERN 51
Cover by Greg Horn

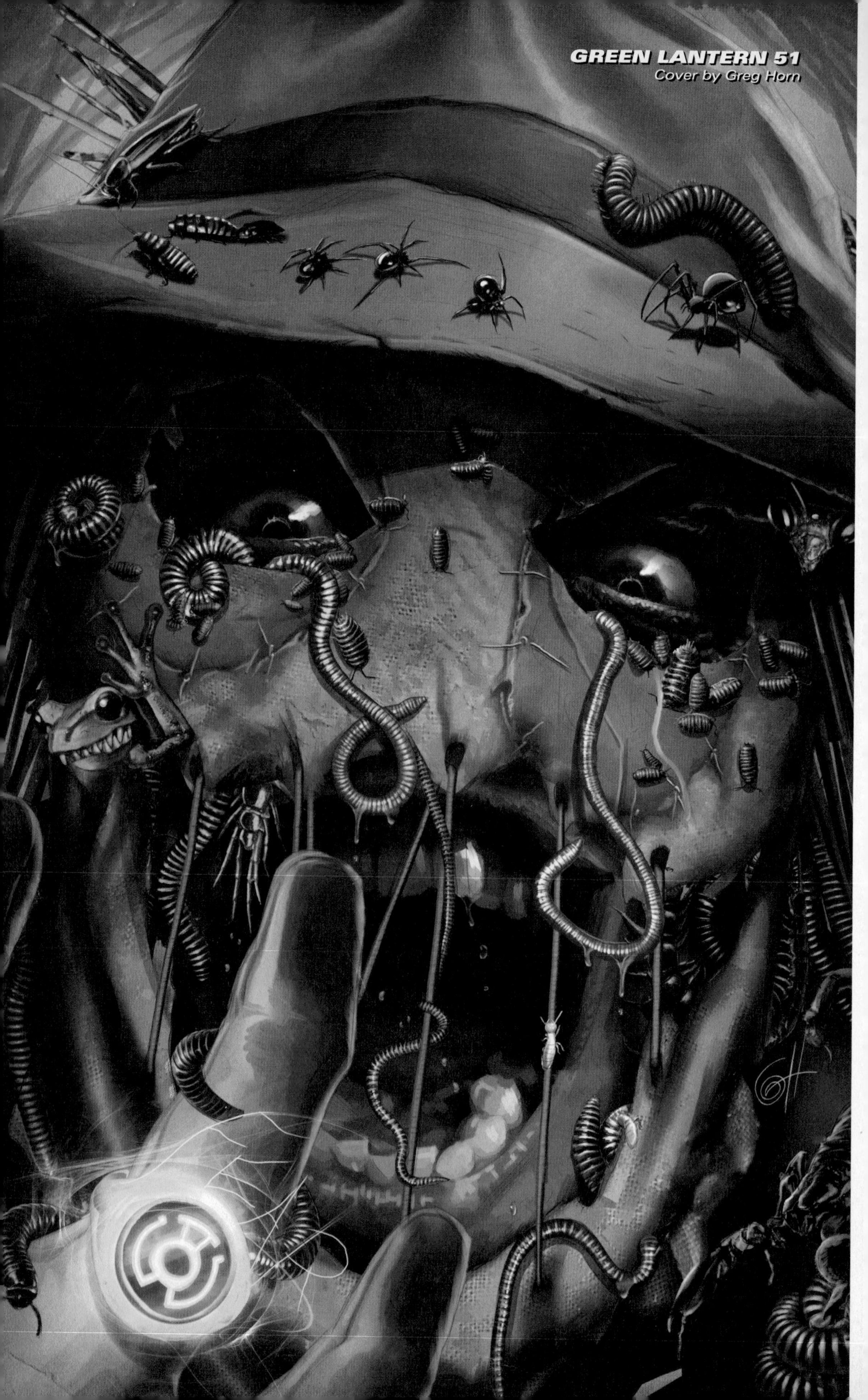

GREEN LANTERN 52

Cover by Shane Davis and Sandra Hope with Barbara Ciardo

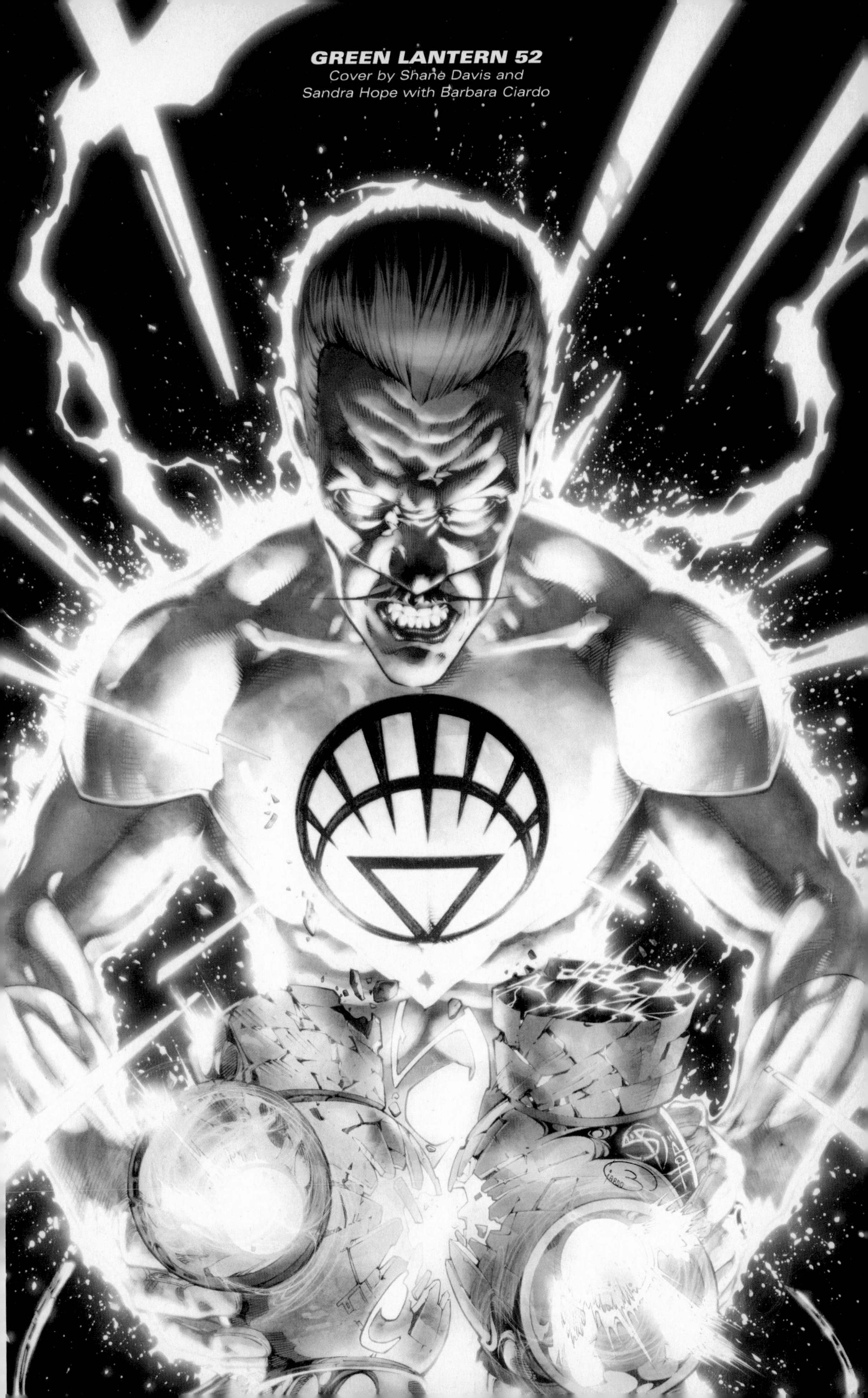

DEPUTY LANTERNS

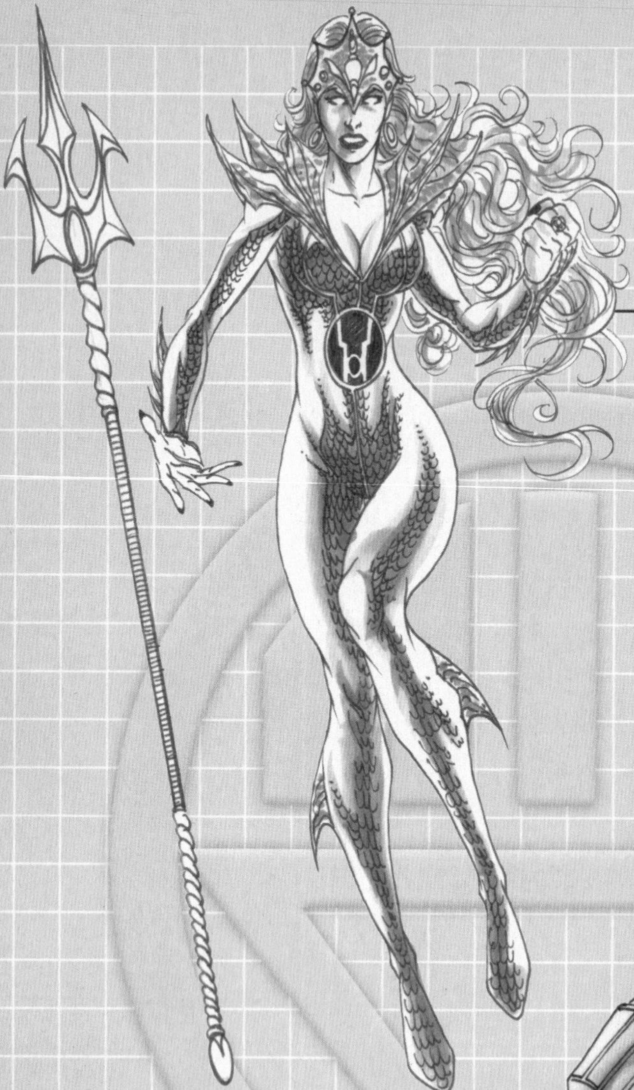

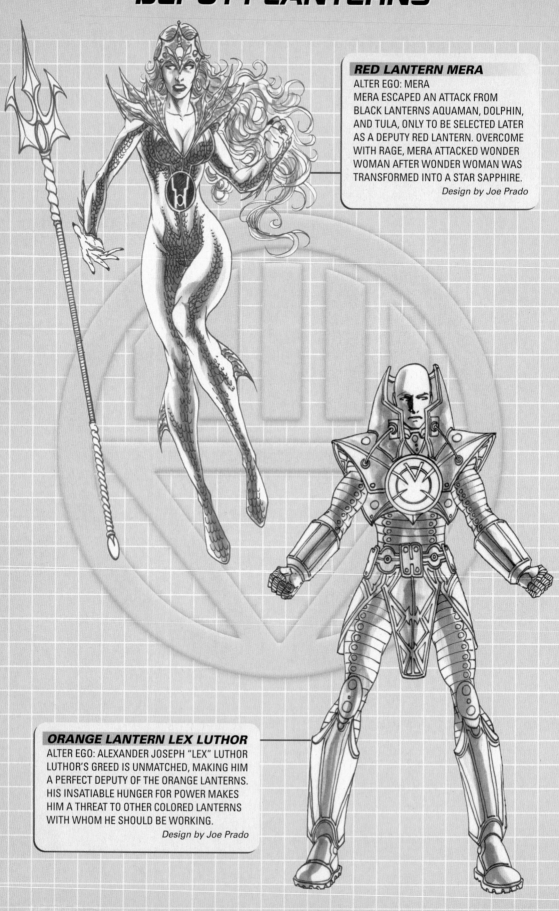

RED LANTERN MERA

ALTER EGO: MERA

MERA ESCAPED AN ATTACK FROM BLACK LANTERNS AQUAMAN, DOLPHIN, AND TULA, ONLY TO BE SELECTED LATER AS A DEPUTY RED LANTERN. OVERCOME WITH RAGE, MERA ATTACKED WONDER WOMAN AFTER WONDER WOMAN WAS TRANSFORMED INTO A STAR SAPPHIRE.

Design by Joe Prado

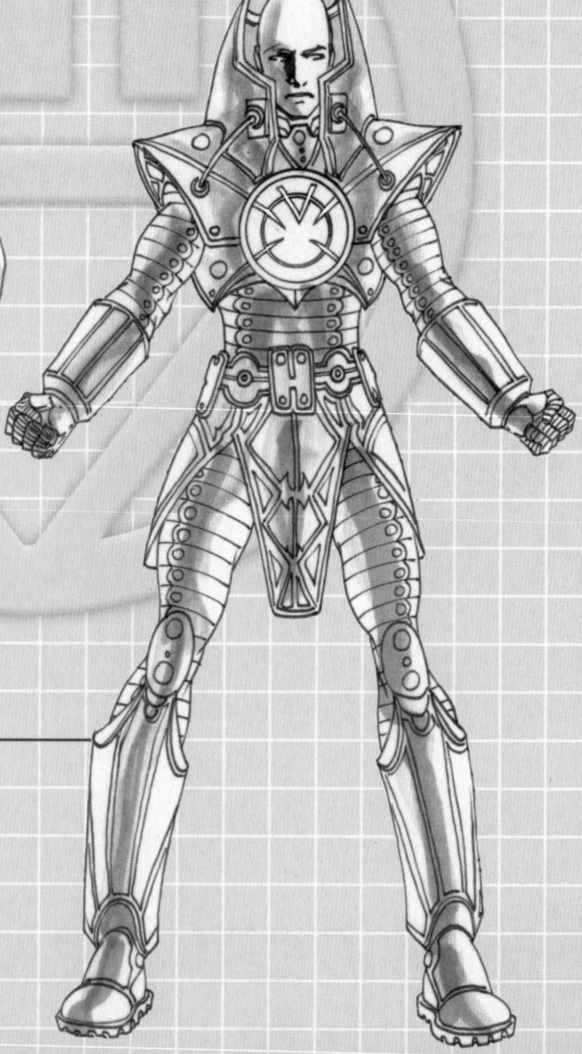

ORANGE LANTERN LEX LUTHOR

ALTER EGO: ALEXANDER JOSEPH "LEX" LUTHOR

LUTHOR'S GREED IS UNMATCHED, MAKING HIM A PERFECT DEPUTY OF THE ORANGE LANTERNS. HIS INSATIABLE HUNGER FOR POWER MAKES HIM A THREAT TO OTHER COLORED LANTERNS WITH WHOM HE SHOULD BE WORKING.

Design by Joe Prado

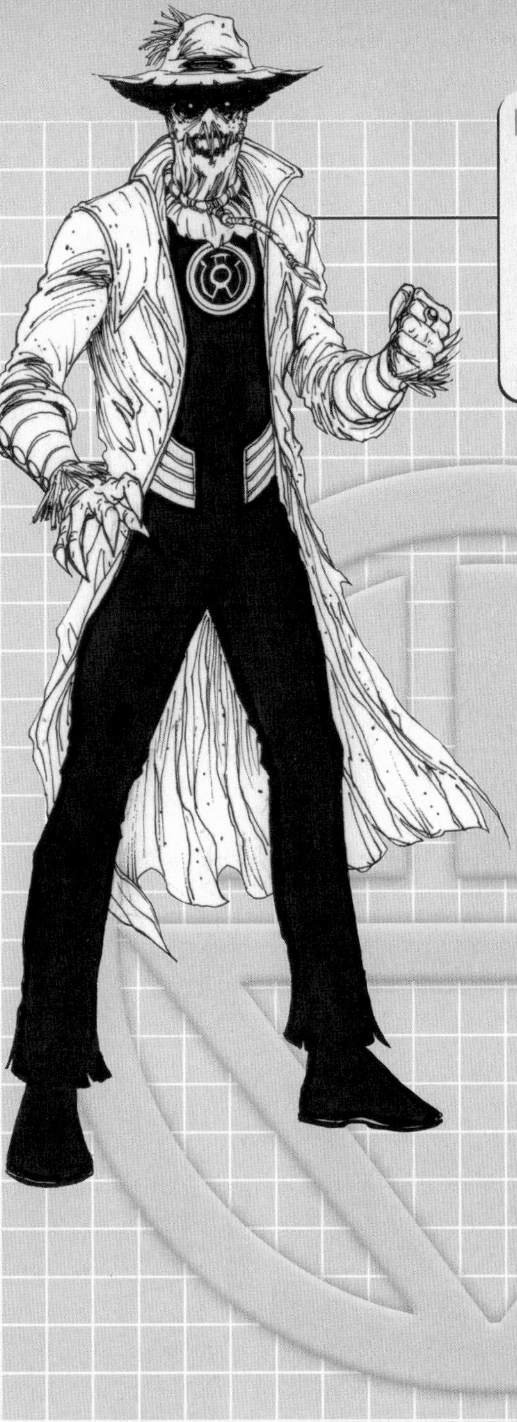

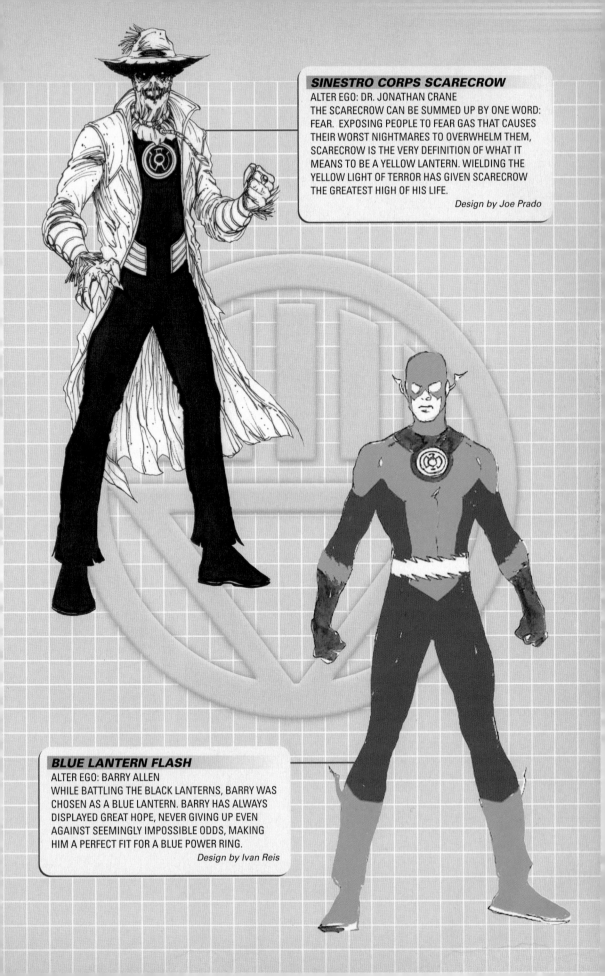

SINESTRO CORPS SCARECROW

ALTER EGO: DR. JONATHAN CRANE

THE SCARECROW CAN BE SUMMED UP BY ONE WORD: FEAR. EXPOSING PEOPLE TO FEAR GAS THAT CAUSES THEIR WORST NIGHTMARES TO OVERWHELM THEM, SCARECROW IS THE VERY DEFINITION OF WHAT IT MEANS TO BE A YELLOW LANTERN. WIELDING THE YELLOW LIGHT OF TERROR HAS GIVEN SCARECROW THE GREATEST HIGH OF HIS LIFE.

Design by Joe Prado

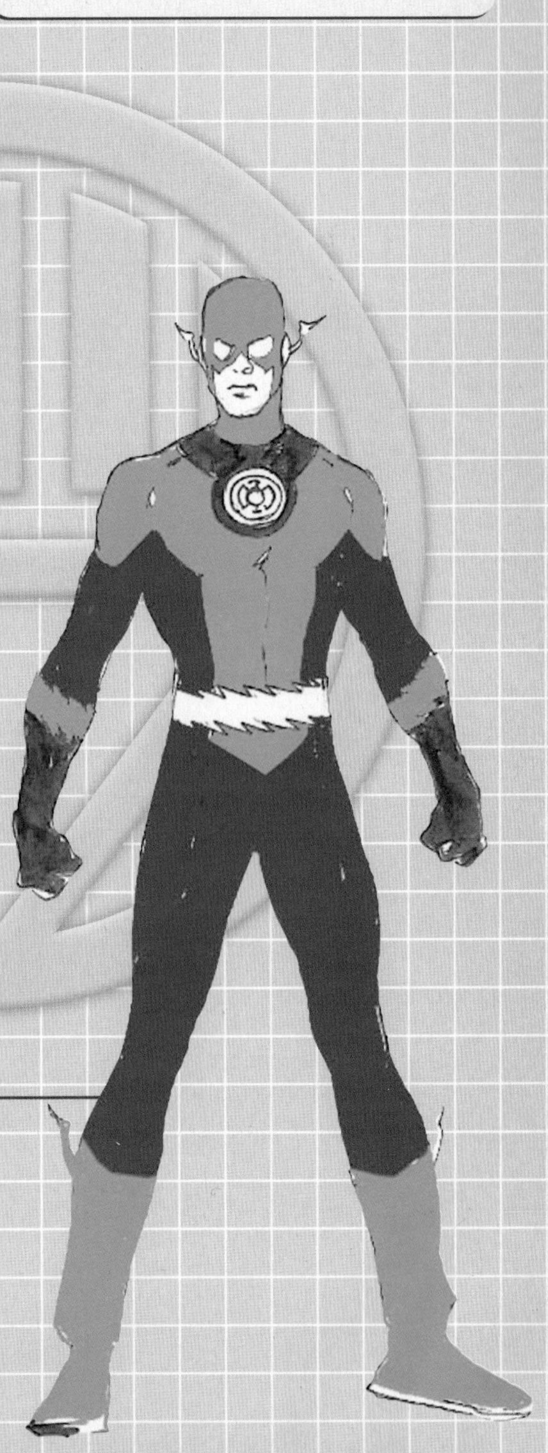

BLUE LANTERN FLASH

ALTER EGO: BARRY ALLEN

WHILE BATTLING THE BLACK LANTERNS, BARRY WAS CHOSEN AS A BLUE LANTERN. BARRY HAS ALWAYS DISPLAYED GREAT HOPE, NEVER GIVING UP EVEN AGAINST SEEMINGLY IMPOSSIBLE ODDS, MAKING HIM A PERFECT FIT FOR A BLUE POWER RING.

Design by Ivan Reis

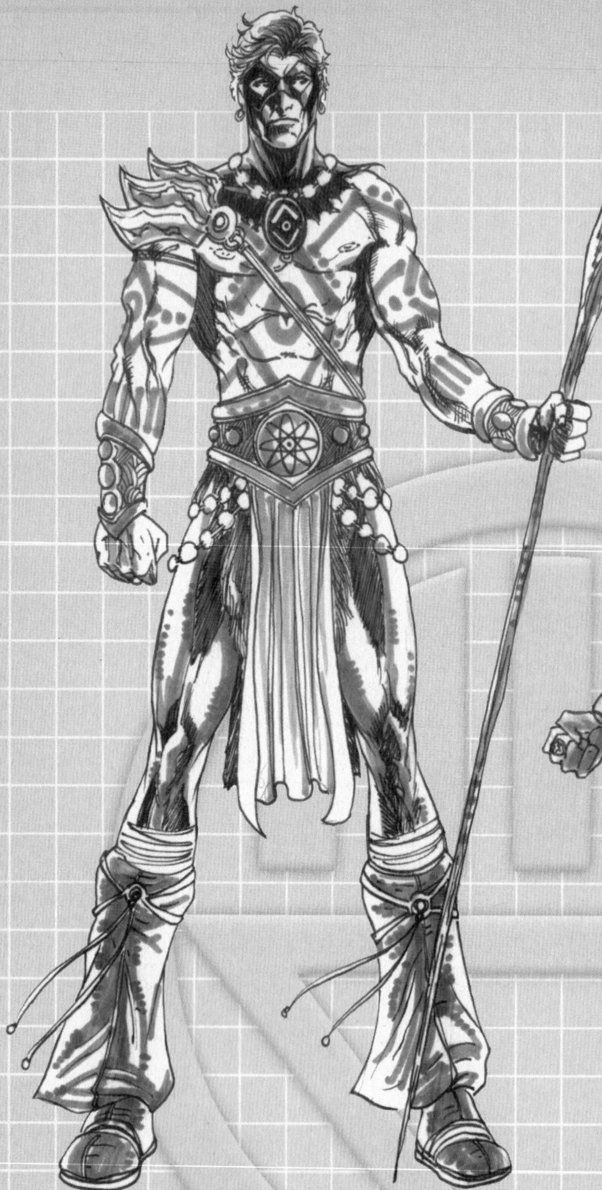

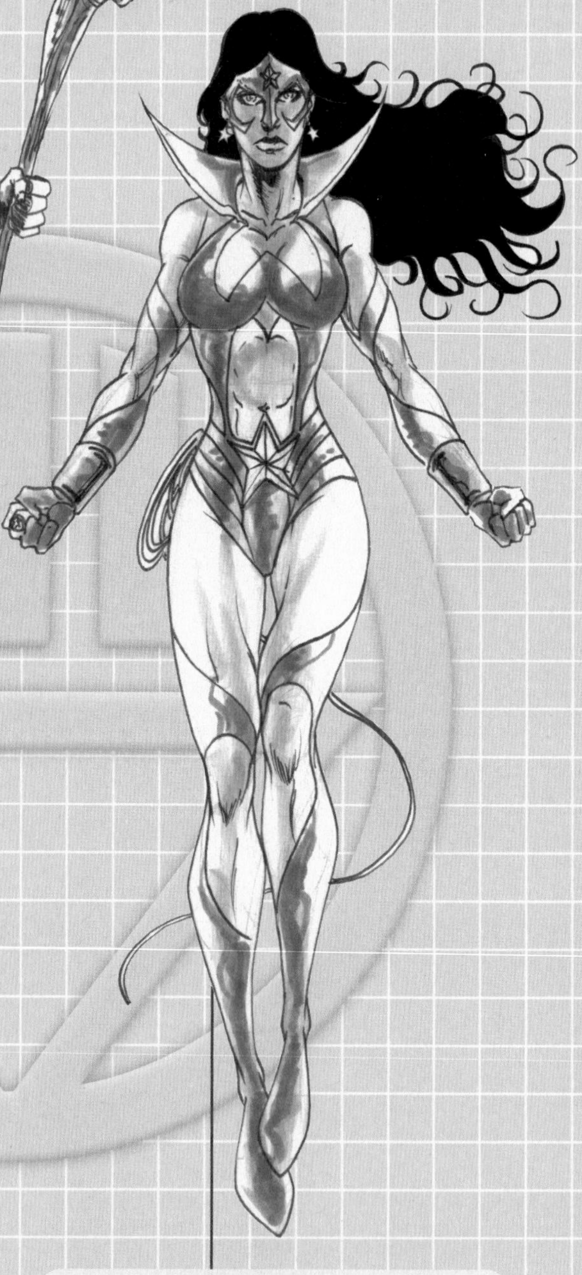

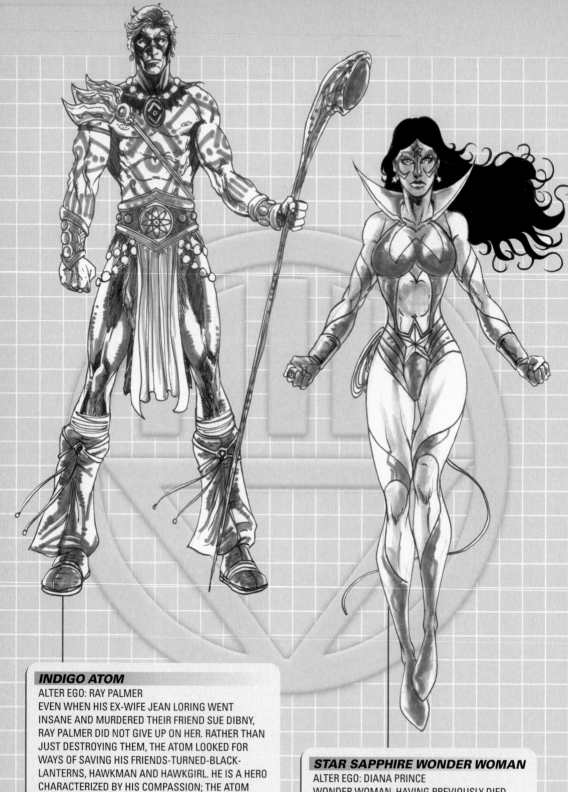

INDIGO ATOM

ALTER EGO: RAY PALMER

EVEN WHEN HIS EX-WIFE JEAN LORING WENT INSANE AND MURDERED THEIR FRIEND SUE DIBNY, RAY PALMER DID NOT GIVE UP ON HER. RATHER THAN JUST DESTROYING THEM, THE ATOM LOOKED FOR WAYS OF SAVING HIS FRIENDS-TURNED-BLACK-LANTERNS, HAWKMAN AND HAWKGIRL. HE IS A HERO CHARACTERIZED BY HIS COMPASSION; THE ATOM MAKES A WORTHY ADDITION TO THE INDIGO TRIBE.

Design by Joe Prado

STAR SAPPHIRE WONDER WOMAN

ALTER EGO: DIANA PRINCE

WONDER WOMAN, HAVING PREVIOUSLY DIED AND THEN BEEN RESURRECTED, IS TURNED BY NEKRON INTO A BLACK LANTERN. BUT HER ALL-EMBRACING LOVE ALLOWS A VIOLET RING TO FIND HER AND SHATTER HER BLACK LANTERN RING, TRANSFORMING HER INTO A STAR SAPPHIRE AND RETURNING HER TO LIFE.

Design by Joe Prado

BLACK LANTERN AQUAMAN

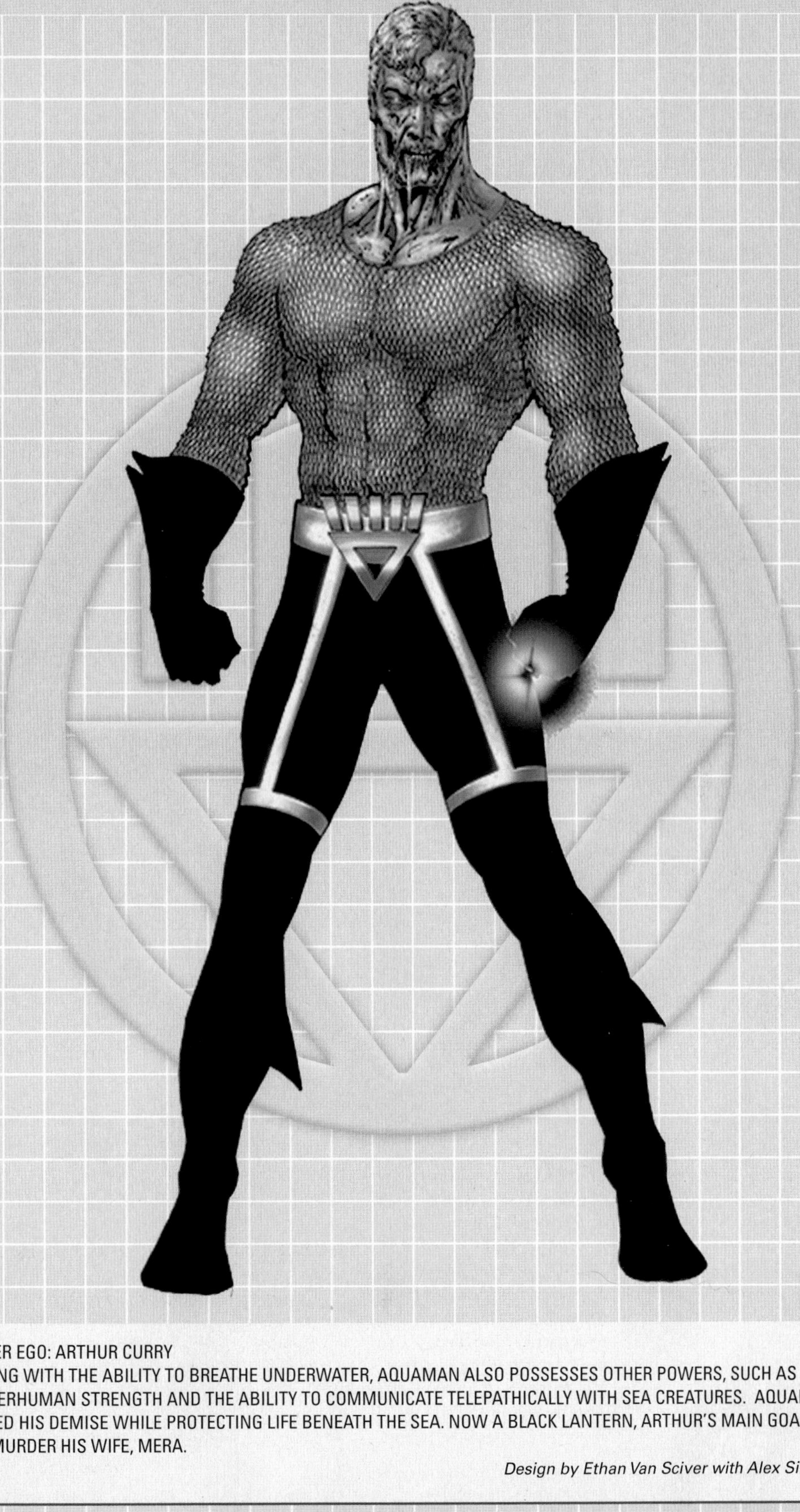

ALTER EGO: ARTHUR CURRY

ALONG WITH THE ABILITY TO BREATHE UNDERWATER, AQUAMAN ALSO POSSESSES OTHER POWERS, SUCH AS SUPERHUMAN STRENGTH AND THE ABILITY TO COMMUNICATE TELEPATHICALLY WITH SEA CREATURES. AQUAMAN FACED HIS DEMISE WHILE PROTECTING LIFE BENEATH THE SEA. NOW A BLACK LANTERN, ARTHUR'S MAIN GOAL IS TO MURDER HIS WIFE, MERA.

Design by Ethan Van Sciver with Alex Sinclair

BLACK LANTERN BATMAN

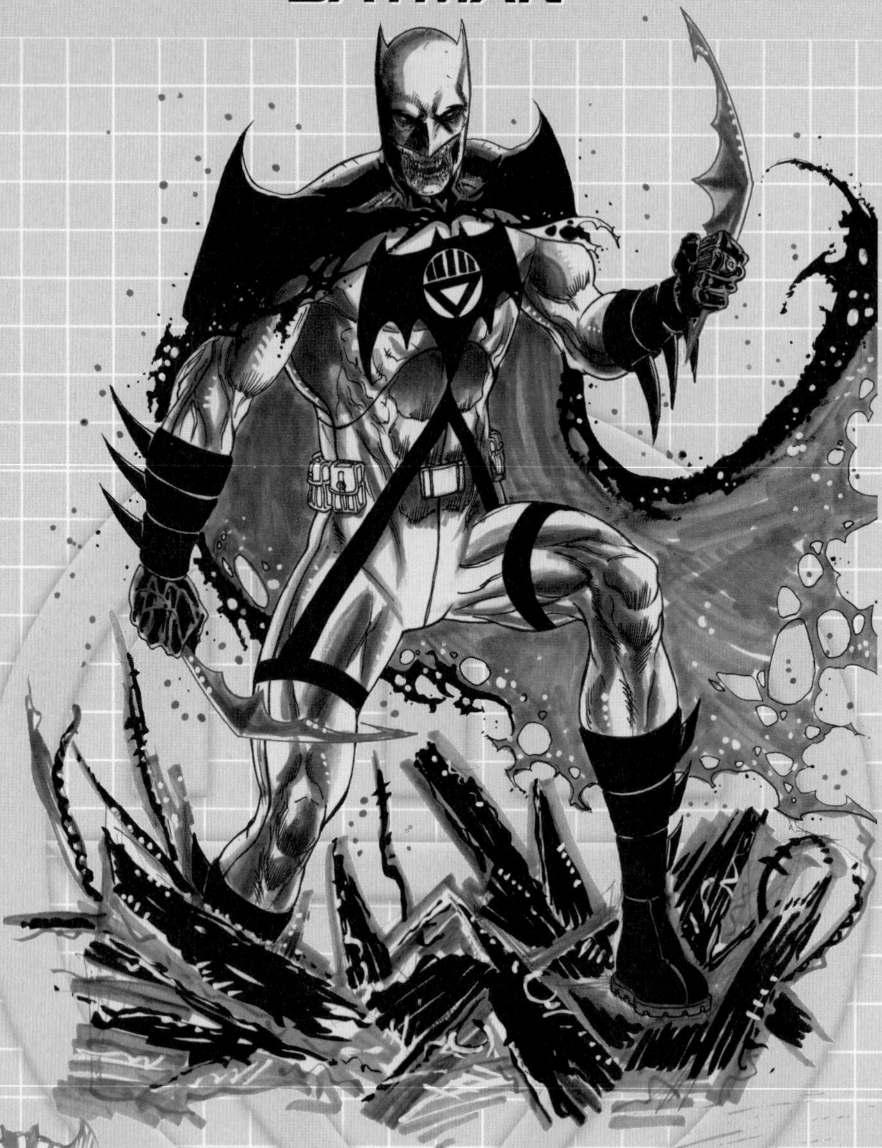

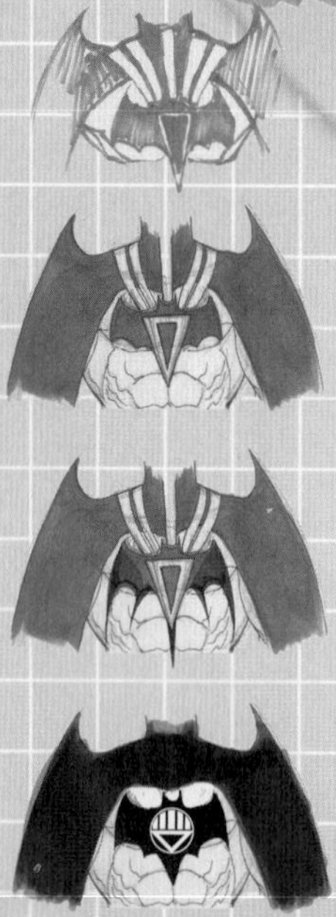

ALTER EGO: "BRUCE WAYNE"
AFTER SHOOTING DARKSEID WITH A RADION BULLET, BATMAN WAS SEEMINGLY KILLED BY DARKSEID'S OMEGA BEAMS. NEKRON USED WHAT HE BELIEVED TO BE BATMAN'S SKULL TO CREATE AN EMOTIONAL TETHER WITHIN OUR HEROES WHO HAD DIED AND BEEN RESURRECTED, CONVERTING THEM INTO POWERFUL BLACK LANTERNS. THE ORIGIN OF THIS BATMAN IS AS YET UNKNOWN.

Design by Joe Prado

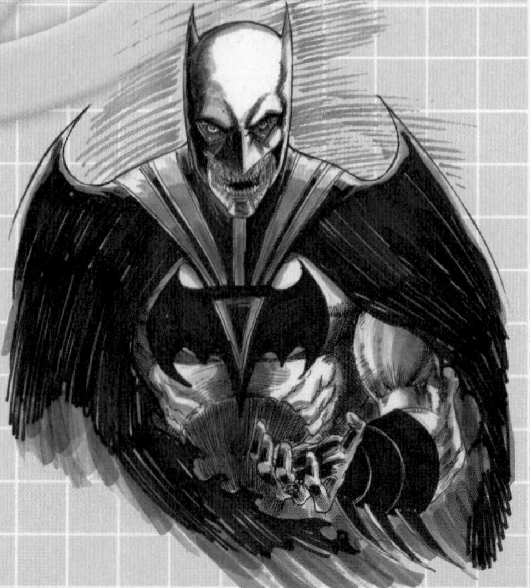

BLACK LANTERN FIRESTORM

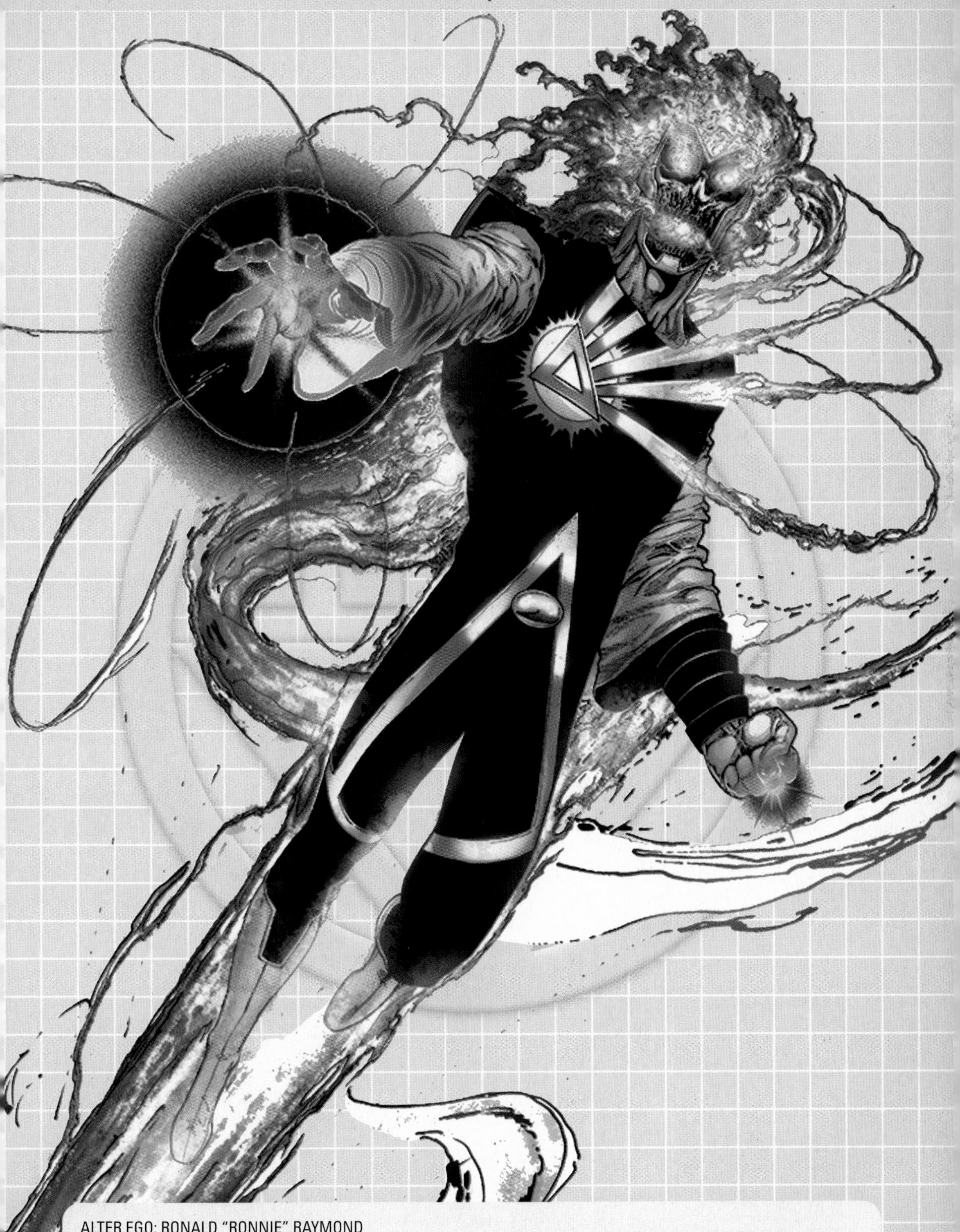

ALTER EGO: RONALD "RONNIE" RAYMOND
AFTER FIRESTORM THE NUCLEAR MAN WAS STABBED BY THE SHADOW THIEF, HE FLEW INTO THE SKY SO NO OTHERS WOULD DIE WHEN HE EXPLODED. SINCE BEING TURNED INTO A BLACK LANTERN BY NEKRON, FIRESTORM HAS GONE AFTER HIS SUCCESSOR, JASON RUSCH.

Design by Ethan Van Sciver with Alex Sinclair

BLACK LANTERN
HAL JORDAN

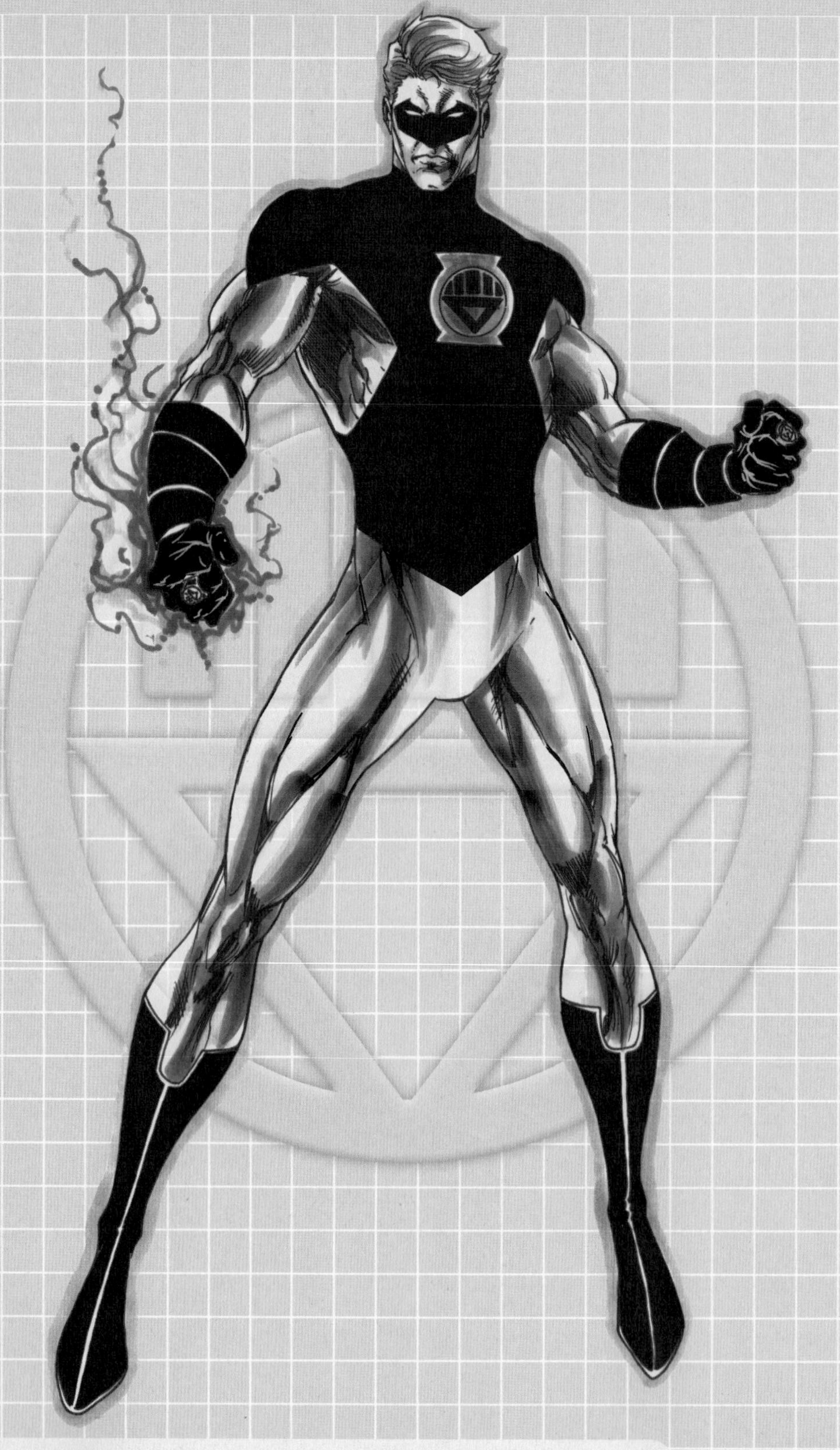

ALTER EGO: GREEN LANTERN
NEKRON WAS UNABLE TO TURN HAL JORDAN INTO A BLACK LANTERN IN HIS FIRST ATTEMPT BUT USED THE SPECTRE TO TURN HIM LATER. FORTUNATELY FOR JORDAN, GANTHET AND SAYD SAVED HIM FROM THAT TERRIBLE FATE.

Design by Joe Prado

BLACK LANTERN MARTIAN MANHUNTER

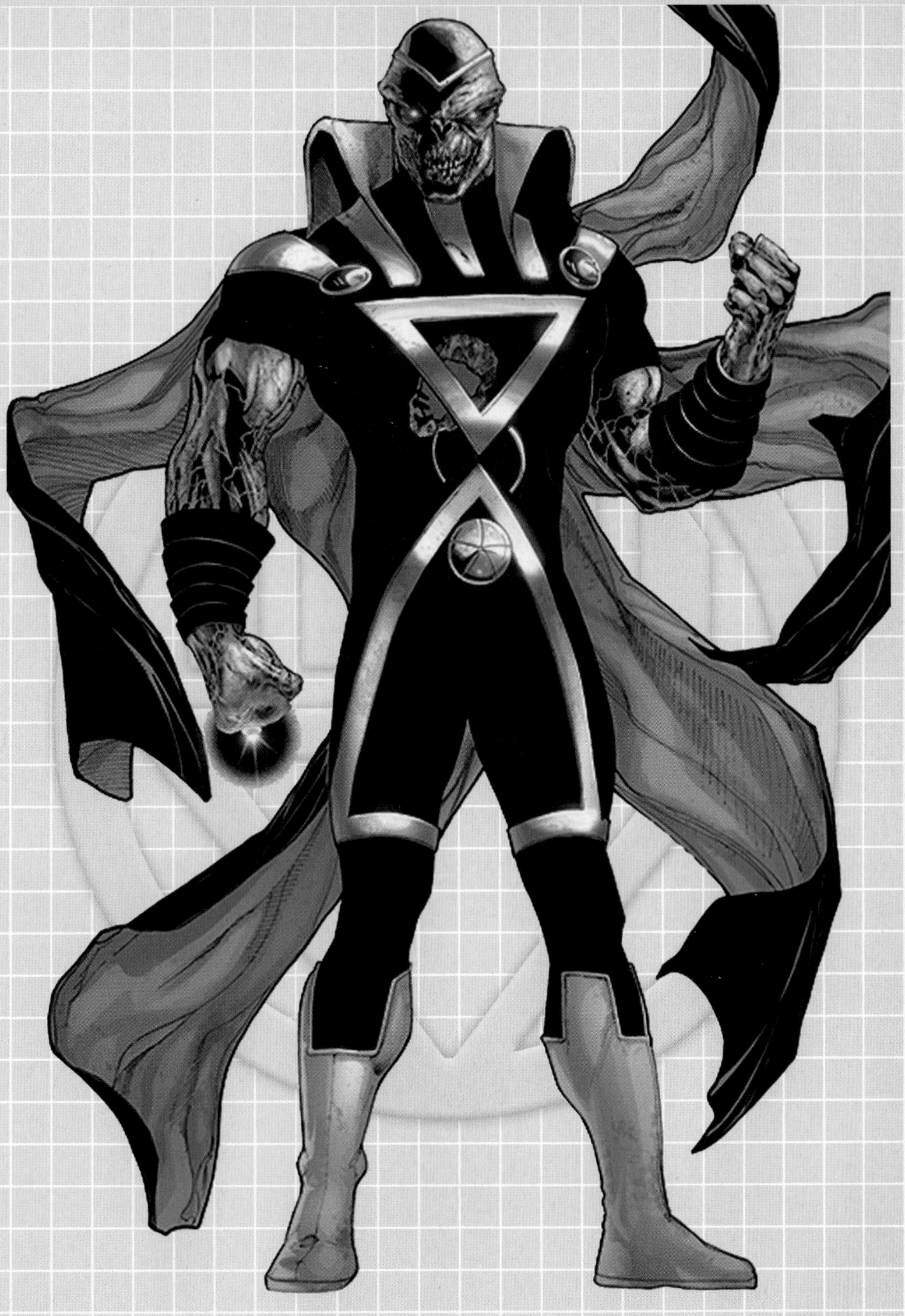

ALTER EGO: J'ONN J'ONZZ
HAILING FROM MARS, MARTIAN MANHUNTER HAS A VAST ARRAY OF SUPERHUMAN ABILITIES INCLUDING TELEPATHY, FLIGHT, INVISIBILITY, INTANGIBILITY AND SHAPE SHIFTING. J'ONN WAS KILLED BY LIBRA BEFORE THE SECRET SOCIETY DURING FINAL CRISIS. AS A BLACK LANTERN, MARTIAN MANHUNTER HAS GONE TO CONFRONT HAL JORDAN AND BARRY ALLEN.

Design by Ethan Van Sciver with Alex Sinclair

BLACK LANTERN SUPERMAN

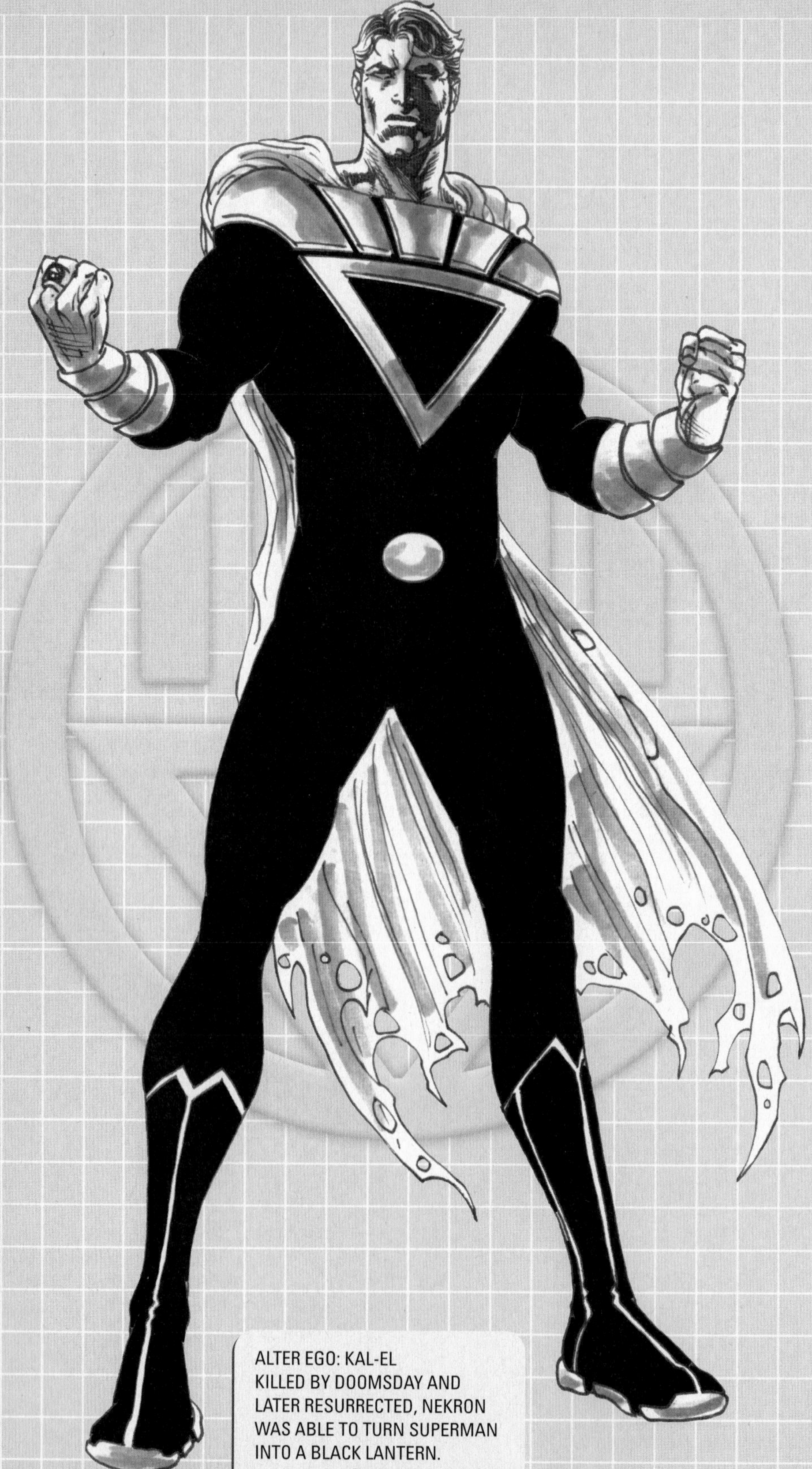

ALTER EGO: KAL-EL
KILLED BY DOOMSDAY AND LATER RESURRECTED, NEKRON WAS ABLE TO TURN SUPERMAN INTO A BLACK LANTERN.

Design by Joe Prado

BIOGRAPHIES

GEOFF JOHNS

Geoff Johns is one of the most prolific and popular contemporary comic book writers. He has written highly acclaimed stories starring Superman, Green Lantern, the Flash, Teen Titans and the Justice Society of America. He is the author of the *New York Times* best-selling graphic novels GREEN LANTERN: RAGE OF THE RED LANTERNS, GREEN LANTERN: SINESTRO CORPS WAR, JUSTICE SOCIETY OF AMERICA: THY KINGDOM COME, and SUPERMAN: BRAINIAC.

Johns was born in Detroit and studied media arts, screenwriting, film production and film theory at Michigan State University. After moving to Los Angeles, he worked as an intern and later an assistant for film director Richard Donner, whose credits include *Superman: The Movie, Lethal Weapon 4* and *Conspiracy Theory.*

Johns began his comics career writing STARS AND S.T.R.I.P.E. and creating Stargirl for DC Comics. Geoff received the Wizard Fan Award for Breakout Talent of 2002 and Writer of the Year for 2005 through 2008 as well as the CBG Writer of the Year 2003 through 2005, 2007 and 2008, and CBG Best Comic Book Series for JSA 2001 through 2005.

After acclaimed runs on THE FLASH, TEEN TITANS and the best-selling INFINITE CRISIS miniseries, Johns co-wrote a run on ACTION COMICS with his mentor, Donner. In 2006, he co-wrote 52, an ambitious weekly comic book series set in real time, with Grant Morrison, Greg Rucka and Mark Waid.

Johns has also written for various other media, including the acclaimed "Legion" episode of SMALLVILLE and the fourth season of ROBOT CHICKEN. He is writing the story of the DC Universe Online massively multiplayer action game from Sony Online Entertainment LLC and has recently joined DC Entertainment as its Chief Creative Officer.

Johns currently resides in Los Angeles, California.

DOUG MAHNKE

Born in 1963 in the Year of the Rabbit, Doug Mahnke embarked on a love affair with comics at the age of five, having received a pile of *Spider-Man* issues from a rugby-playing college student named Mike who lived in his basement. A consistent interest in the medium, coupled with some art skill, landed Doug a job drawing comics for Dark Horse at the age of 24 (the date is known precisely, as it occurred just two weeks before he wed his lovely bride). His first gig was illustrating a moody detective one-shot entitled *Homicide,* written by John Arcudi. The two went on to collaborate on Dark Horse's *The Mask* and their creator-owned series MAJOR BUMMER, originally published by DC.

Since then Doug has worked on a wide variety of titles, including SUPERMAN: THE MAN OF STEEL, JLA, BATMAN, SEVEN SOLDIERS: FRANKENSTEIN, BLACK ADAM: THE DARK AGE and STORMWATCH: P.H.D. After contributing to 2009's FINAL CRISIS, he took over art chores on GREEN LANTERN. He resides in the midwest with his wife and seven kids, one dog, and a bunny named Suzie.

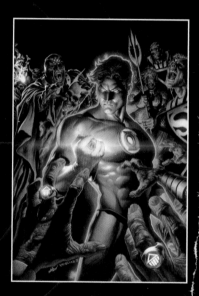

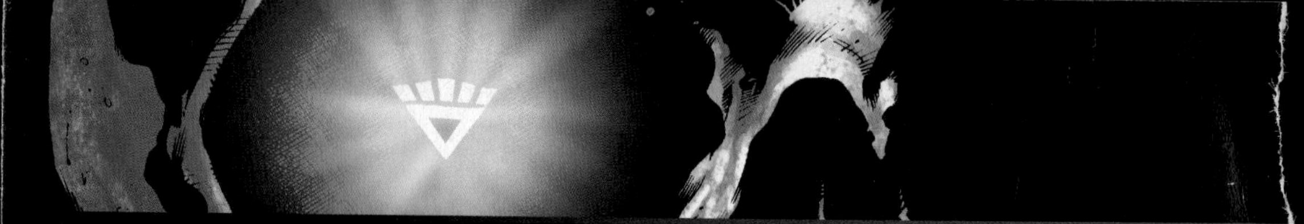